Diversity in US Mass Media

The second edition of *Diversity in US Mass Media* presents a review of the evolution and the many issues surrounding portrayals of social groups in the mass media of the United States. Unfortunately, all too often mass media depictions play a crucial role in shaping our views about individuals and social groups. Filled with instructive insights into the ways social groups are represented through the mass media, *Diversity in US Mass Media* offers a better understanding of groups and individuals different from ourselves.

The revised second edition is filled with recent, illustrative examples from the media. Comprehensive in scope, it addresses a wide range of issues that include representations of race/ethnicity, gender, sexual orientation, disability, class, and religion in films, television, and the press. The authors encourage readers to question what is being presented and explore the extent to which they agree with the perspectives that are described.

Diversity in US Mass Media is an important resource that:

- offers an understanding of how various social groups are being represented in the mass media
- explores how diverse communities inform and intersect with one another
- draws on updated studies on the topic and presents original research and observations
- includes new chapters on media portrayals of mixed race relationships and multiracial/multiethnic people and representations of religion and faith
- is accompanied by a companion website for instructors including many useful pedagogical tools, such as a test bank, viewing list, exercises, and sample syllabi.

Revised and updated, the second edition of *Diversity in US Mass Media* offers a broad perspective on the myriad issues that influence how the media portrays social groups. Throughout the text, the authors show consistencies as well as differences in media representations of minority groups in the United States.

The companion website with additional resources is available at www.wiley.com/go/luther2e

Catherine A. Luther (Ph.D., University of Minnesota) is a professor and the director of the School of Journalism and Electronic Media at the University of Tennessee. Her research focuses on issues involving the intersections of media, gender, and race/ethnicity. She also conducts research in the areas of intercultural and global communication. Her work has appeared in such publications as the *Journal of Communication, Journalism & Mass Communication Quarterly*, and *Journal of Broadcasting & Electronic Media*. She began her professional career working for Japanese television news as a reporter before moving on to *ABC News* to produce stories primarily involving nations and cultures in East Asia.

Carolyn Ringer Lepre (Ph.D., University of Florida) is dean of the School of Communication and the Arts at Marist College. Her research interests are in journalism, particularly magazine writing and news editing. She has published articles in such journals as the *Journal of Magazine & New Media Research* and *Journalism & Mass Communication Educator*. She worked as assistant editor at *Martha Stewart Living* magazine.

Naeemah Clark (Ph.D., University of Florida) is an associate professor in the School of Communications at Elon University. She has edited the book *African Americans in the History of U.S. Media*, published work in *Journalism History* and the *International Journal of Organizational Diversity*, and opinion pieces in various outlets including the *Atlanta Journal Constitution* and *The Huffington Post*. She studies and teaches about economic, programming, and diversity issues related to the media and entertainment industries.

Diversity in US Mass Media

Second Edition

Catherine A. Luther
Carolyn Ringer Lepre
Naeemah Clark

WILEY Blackwell

Registered Office(s)
John Wiley & Sons, Inc., 111 River Street, Hoboken, NJ 07030, USA

Editorial Office
350 Main Street, Malden, MA 02148-5020, USA

For details of our global editorial offices, customer services, and more information about Wiley products visit us at www.wiley.com.

Wiley also publishes its books in a variety of electronic formats and by print-on-demand. Some content that appears in standard print versions of this book may not be available in other formats.

Library of Congress Cataloging-in-Publication Data

Names: Luther, Catherine A., 1962- author. | Lepre, Carolyn Ringer, author. | Clark, Naeemah, author.
Title: Diversity in US mass media / Catherine A. Luther, Carlyn Lepre, Naeemah Clark.
Other titles: Diversity in United States mass media | Diversity in US mass media
Description: Second edition. | Hoboken, NJ : Wiley, 2018. | Includes bibliographical references and index.
Identifiers: LCCN 2017030047 (print) | LCCN 2017013712 (ebook) | ISBN 9781119234012 (pbk.) |
    ISBN 9781119234029 (pdf) | ISBN 9781119234050 (epub)
Subjects: LCSH: Minorities in mass media—United States. | Cultural pluralism
    in mass media—United States. | Mass media and minorities—United States.
Classification: LCC P94.5.M552 U6515 2018 (ebook) | LCC P94.5.M552 (print) | DDC 305.0973—dc23

Paperback ISBN: 9781119234012

Cover image: © Vimvertigo/Gettyimages
Cover design by Wiley

Set in 10/12pt Warnock Pro by Aptara

SKY10035107_070822

Contents

Figures

Tables

Boxes

Preface

Diversity in US Mass Media was conceived by one of its authors during the first semester in which she was teaching a course on "Media and Diversity" at her university. She perceived a need for a book that attempted to comprehensively cover the various areas associated with representations of diversity within the mass media. Many outstanding books exist that cover issues related to media, gender, ethnicity, and class. For the most part, however, they are edited books that cover a wide array of areas but do not necessarily flow in and out of each other. This book has endeavored to show consistencies as well as differences in media representations of minority groups in the United States.

The number of research studies addressing diversity within the mass media has grown over the years with the increasing awareness that inequities in portrayals and coverage of various groups still remain an important issue. This book refers to many of the well-known studies on this topic and also presents some original research and observations that have been provided by the book's authors. Although the authors have made strenuous efforts to be uniform in the writing across the chapters in terms of themes and topics covered, some variations do exist, of course, because of the differing subject matter and the extent to which the phenomenon being discussed has been researched within scholarly circles and among practitioners. For example, in the African American and Hispanic chapters, we present discussions of how these groups have been represented in music and have used music and radio as a channel of communication. The amount of research conducted on this topic with regard to these two groups is quite large, and not to include it would have been negligent. Similar research pertaining to American Indians, Arab Americans, and Asian Americans, does not exist, however, and so this topic was not discussed in these chapters. Another example in terms of the variation in presentation is with regard to gender. The fact that years of research pertaining to mass media and gender have produced large quantities of studies and insight in this area prompted the decision by the authors to provide two separate, but related chapters on gender. In sum, decisions regarding which areas to cover in the chapters were driven by the importance of the topics as they related to the specified social groups and the amount of pertinent existing research.

In this second edition, the book's authors offer updated references and studies. Some of the updates reveal that the media landscape has changed quite a bit since the first edition was published in 2012. In some cases, media content better reflects the identities discussed in the book. In other cases, there has been little or no movement in the way these groups are represented. The second edition also introduces a chapter discussing media portrayals of mixed race relationships and multiracial/multiethnic people, and a chapter on representations of religion and faith. These chapters were added because the authors recognized that there has been a burgeoning body of research and media discussion surrounding these identity-related areas.

We hope that the readers of this book will approach it with a critical eye. While introducing the material, the authors encourage readers also to question what is being presented and explore the extent to which they agree with the perspectives that are described. The book includes many examples to help illustrate the concepts and perspectives discussed; however, readers should consider alternative examples from their own media use that support or contradict those included. We hope that the book will enlighten but also evoke further important questions that need to be considered at the personal and broader social level.

Several people need to be thanked for their individual input into the fruition of the book's first edition and this second edition. For the first edition, our continued thanks go to editors Deirdre Ilkson and Elizabeth Swayze as well as editorial assistant Margot Morse and project manager Alec McAulay. For this edition, many thanks go to project manager Hazel Bird, project editor Dhanashree Damodar Phadate, commissioning editor Haze Humbert, and assistant editor Mark Graney. Also, much gratitude goes to copyeditor Caroline Richards for her keen editorial eye and Arlene Naranjo as well as Justin West for their Spanish-language translations.

The first author of this book, Catherine Luther, would also like to express her heartfelt thanks to her husband, Yosh, and her two boys, Gennick and Jovan. Their patience and understanding were unsurpassed while she worked countless hours on the book. She would also like to dedicate her effort in this book to her mom, Sadayo. With each passing year, she has come to better understand the huge amount of courage it took for her mom to come to the United States as a young bride of an American serviceman with little knowledge of English but a strong determination to learn the language and everything there was to know about her new home.

Carolyn Ringer Lepre, this book's second author, would like to express her eternal gratitude to her husband, Todd, her father, Jim, and her mother, Jackie, who passed away during the writing of this second edition. She would especially like to thank her twin daughters, Sarah and Ainsley, for their endless supply of hugs, kisses, and giggles, and for putting up with all the long evenings and weekends that she spent working instead of playing with them.

The book's third author, Naeemah Clark, would like to thank her family – Kacie, Kam, Betty, and Ken – for their unending suggestions of song lyrics, movie clips, and magazine titles. She is grateful for the opportunity to discuss these important topics at a time when understanding one another's humanity is needed more than ever.

1

Introduction

Within the past few years, each of you has participated in at least one common activity: completing college applications. Besides writing your essays, acquiring your transcripts, and securing your letters of recommendation, you likely had to complete a personal information form, which, along with asking your name, address, and social security number, requested you to check the boxes that indicated your gender and your race or ethnicity. Did your pen pause over those boxes before you marked a particular one? Did you consider leaving the boxes empty? Did you wonder why the questions were relevant?

Universities and colleges collect the information as a way of measuring the extent of "diversity" within their institution. Over the last decade, for various political, social, and even economic reasons, a huge push to promote diversity not only in classrooms but also in workplaces has been evident. But what exactly is meant by the word "diversity"? Diversity is commonly defined as being "composed of differing elements or qualities" (Merriam-Webster 2011) and, more specifically, in the context of social groups, the concept of diversity embraces the ideals of acceptance and respect, and an understanding that groups are made up of unique individuals.

When regarding diversity within the context of mass media, it is important to consider the extent to which an array of representations of individuals or social groups are being presented and the degree to which a multiplicity of voices are being heard or reflected. One must question how individuals and social groups are being portrayed and the underlying reasons for certain patterns of portrayals. Research (e.g., Bandura 2002; Bissell and Zhou 2004; Grogan 2008) has shown that the mass media have played an important role in contouring how individuals perceive and feel about themselves and about others. Every day, individuals make quick judgments about others based on race or ethnicity, gender, disabilities, sexual orientation, class, and age. These judgments, whether fair or unfair, accurate or inaccurate, are based on information gathered not only over years of experience and interactions with family, friends, and other social networks, but also from the constant bombardment of media images and messages that most humans encounter from an early age. This bombardment is almost unavoidable. For instance, though an individual may choose not to own a television in his or her own home, televisions are commonplace in doctors' offices, at airports, and at restaurants.

Exploring and discussing media representations of social groups can be quite complicated. Clear-cut social groups actually do not exist. They run across each other, with each individual a composite of various social groups. For example, you might be a Hispanic lesbian female college student whose family

Diversity in US Mass Media, Second Edition. Catherine A. Luther, Carolyn Ringer Lepre, and Naeemah Clark.
© 2018 John Wiley & Sons Inc. Published 2018 by John Wiley & Sons Inc.

background is upper middle class. Which part of your identity is most important in defining you is really your decision. Nevertheless, as a society, we tend to identify individuals with a main social group. So, although you might believe that your identity of being a female college student is most important to you, another person may consider that your main identity is that of a Hispanic individual.

Thus, one of the challenges in writing this book was to decide which social groups to focus on and how to avoid the tendency to oversimplify these social groups and disregard how they relate to each other. We decided to address the following major social group categories: race or ethnicity, gender, sexual orientation, age, disability, and class. For race/ethnicity, the book covers American Indians, African Americans, Hispanics, Arab Americans, and Asian Americans. The selection includes groups that had the earliest experiences of underrepresentation or distorted portrayals in the US mass media (i.e., American Indians and African Americans) and also includes those groups that are growing in population in the United States and that are increasingly being represented in the mass media (i.e., Asian Americans, Hispanics, and Arab Americans). Within the United States, the number of individuals who identify themselves as being of mixed race has grown. Thus, an additional chapter is devoted to mass media representations of mixed race individuals and couples.

Although the main focus of this book is on social groups that are defined for the most part by uncontrollable characteristics such as physical attributes, a chapter that slightly diverges from that focal point is also included. That chapter is the one on religion. The authors felt it was important to also discuss depictions of religion and faith given the increasing conflation of religion with other social identities. While individuals choose their own religion, how society views their selected religion is fundamentally out of their control and may have major repercussions for their own sense of personal identity.

The authors acknowledge that many other social groups could have potentially been discussed in this book, including such groups as Russian Americans, Italian Americans, lawyers, strippers, or doctors. The list is endless. Think of this book as a starting point for you to go on and explore some of the other social groups in society. As you read through the text, consider issues of intersectionality. It is our combination of identities that makes us individuals. Social groups do not experience things as a monolithic entity, reacting as one mind. One race, gender, age, or class of people will not respond as one mind to a media representation of their group. As you read about the media examples in this book, consider them critically, and make connections for yourself, in addition to considering the connections the authors of this text have tried to make for you between social groups. Think about how one depiction might be viewed positively by some and negatively by others, and how there are varying levels along this continuum. It is important to contextualize issues, placing one social group within the framework of others, and to consider how diverse communities inform and intersect with one another.

To provide you with a basis for understanding why it is important to consider how social groups are being represented in the mass media, in the remaining sections of this introductory chapter we will first introduce you to the concept of social identity and then present you with a preliminary picture of why the social group categories we explore in the book should be examined.

Social Identity

Social identity is a concept that came to the fore in the 1960s and early 1970s, primarily due to increased concerns regarding group conflict. With events such as the Vietnam War, civil and women's rights movements, and the Arab–Israeli conflicts, researchers began to make efforts to understand the roots of the conflicts and how identities might come into play in these group conflicts. Social psychologist Henri Tajfel was one of the more prominent scholars to delve into this question. He was interested in understanding the sources of group conflict and the role of social identity. In his influential work on social identity, Tajfel defines social identity as a self-concept that is based on group membership and the emotional attachments associated with that membership (Tajfel 1974). When an individual identifies him/herself as a group member, his/her beliefs, interests, and actions tend to become aligned with those of the group.

Social identity develops as a social process whereby people categorize not only themselves but the people around them as well (Abrams and Hogg 2004). Humans have a natural drive to categorize or partition the world into units in order to cut down and simplify the amount of information they need to deal with and process. They create schemas or interrelated conceptual units of information that help them encode, remember, and react to incoming information. What often results is the emphasis of differences between the schemas and a de-emphasis of differences within them. In terms of the categorization of people, the same process occurs. Individuals have an inclination to accentuate the shared qualities that they have with members of their own group, while stressing the differences they have with people belonging to other groups. What results is a clear distinction between in-group members and out-group members.

As stated earlier, the groups to which an individual belongs and with which identification takes place can be widespread. An individual's social identity can be considered as being made up of multiple identities. Some of the core identities recognized by researchers (e.g., McCann *et al.* 2004; Wander, Martin, and Nakayama 1999) include gender, age, racial/ethnic, sexual orientation, national, religious, and class, with many of these identities intersecting. Given the understanding that identities are developed through a social process, one can see the potential role of mass communication in influencing the development of each of these identities. Through mass communication, individuals can be exposed to information related to their identities. The information can play a part in creating, reinforcing, modifying, negotiating, or adding to identities.

Racial/Ethnic Identity

When discussing the social inequities that exist within societies and between nations, one of the most often discussed underlying reasons for the inequities is race or ethnicity. In such discussions, the terms "race" and "ethnicity" are often used interchangeably even though in actuality they are distinct.

Race was originally understood as a classification of individual genetics. An assumption was made that if a person was of a particular geographic origin, he or she would have certain physiological characteristics. With a better awareness of the variance that exists across individuals, the categorization of individuals based on biology was recognized as unrealistic. Several scholars from the social scientific community and the humanities called for the entire abandonment of the term "race." Instead, many have called for the use of the term "ethnicity" instead.

Ethnicity encompasses one's own heredity, national origin, and culture (i.e., beliefs, norms, values associated with one's own heritage). The word combinations often found in terms of individual background (e.g., African American, Japanese American, Arab American) are reflective of this. They highlight an acknowledgment of not only the citizenship but also the deeper cultural background of the individual. In other words, the combined term assumes that Arab Americans share cultural norms found in Arab culture and in American homes. Clearly, ethnicity is a much more fluid concept than race.

Table 1.1 Population size by race and ethnicity: 2010 and 2015 comparison in percentage of total population.

Race/Ethnicity	2010 %	2015 %
White	72.4	77.1
Black	12.6	13.3
American Indian and Alaska Native	0.9	1.2
Asian	4.8	5.6
Hispanic or Latino	16.3	17.6
Two or more races	2.9	2.6

Source: "QuickFacts United States." US Census Bureau. https://www.census.gov/quickfacts/table/PST045215/00 (accessed October 6, 2016).

Even with efforts to eradicate the term "race" and replace it permanently with the term "ethnicity," usage of "race" persists. Which term is the proper one to use remains a point of controversy. As such, the term "race" is still used not only by the US government, but also by private and public institutions to identify individuals. The federal government assumes that individuals who are defined as a specific race may come from different ethnic backgrounds (Hobbs and Stoops 2002). By the same token, those who come from a particular ethnic origin may be of any race. Because both "race" and "ethnicity" are used in existing literature, both of these terms will also be used in this book.

Race/ethnicity is an important and frequently sensitive part of our broader social identity. With globalization and the advancement of communication technology, more individuals have the opportunity to encounter individuals from other races or ethnic backgrounds either at first hand or through a mediated source such as the mass media. Thus, it is crucial to nurture a greater understanding and appreciation of the diversity of individuals that make up the world populace.

In terms of the United States, with the increase of immigrants from certain sectors of the world, the racial/ethnic landscape has been dramatically changing over the last few decades. According to the 2010 US Census Bureau report, the populations of Asians and Hispanics are growing at faster rates than any other racial ethnic group (see Table 1.1). In the 2000 Census, 10.24 million individuals reported being Asian; by 2010, that figure had grown to 14.67 million, reflecting a 43.3 percent change. The number of individuals identifying themselves as Hispanic or Latino was 35.31 million in 2000. In 2010, the figure was 50.48 million, representing a 43.0 percent change. The US Census Bureau projects that by the year 2060, 119 million individuals living in the United States will be of Hispanic or Latino origin, representing one third of the total US population; the Asian population is projected to grow to 38.97 million by 2060 (Colby and Ortman 2015).

The percentage of individuals who identify themselves as biracial or multiracial has also been rapidly on the rise. This growth is significant considering that for some time in the history of the United States the mixing of races, especially between Whites and non-Whites, was frowned upon, and children from biracial or multiracial backgrounds often had to endure ridicule. In fact, legislation prohibiting the marriage or even sex between individuals of different races (anti-miscegenation legislation) had been in place in the United States for hundreds of years until the US Supreme Court overturned it in 1967 (Basson 2008). The 2000 US Census was the first to recognize multiracial individuals by providing people with the option of choosing multiple racial backgrounds.

With such fluctuations in the racial/ethnic makeup of the United States, it is important to understand how these groups have been historically, and are currently, represented in the mass media. After all, it is often through the mass media that understandings or misunderstandings are brought about regarding the different racial/ethnic communities.

Gender Identity

Many people view gender as something you are born with. Gender, however, is distinct from biological sex. It is a social construction generated within a particular cultural context. From a very young age, individuals learn the roles and attributes that are associated with males and females (Bem 1993). If resistance surfaces against these accepted roles or attributes, discomfort or even hostility toward the resistance may result. The opposition is looked upon as an affront to the societal or cultural beliefs that exist regarding gender.

Those individuals who represent the opposition might be ridiculed or ostracized as being different. In some cases, a new category might even be created to explain those people who do not quite fit into the established gender categories. For example, when men began to outwardly express interest in designer clothing, and skin and hair products, writer Mark Simpson coined the term "metrosexual" and, thanks to media attention, the term's usage took off. In a 2002 Salon.com article, Simpson described a metrosexual as follows:

> The typical metrosexual is a young man with money to spend, living in or within easy reach of a metropolis – because that's where all the best shops, clubs, gyms and hairdressers are. He might be officially gay, straight, or bisexual, but this is utterly immaterial because he has clearly taken himself as his own love object and pleasure as his sexual preference.

In a recent follow-up, Simpson (2014) claims there has been a generational shift and that for the new metrosexuals it is less about stylish clothes and hairstyles and more about their own muscle-bulging bodies. He writes that their bodies "have become the ultimate accessories, fashioning them at the gym into a hot commodity – one that they share and compare in an online marketplace." To describe this new group of men, he created yet another term – "spornosexuals," so coined as these individuals take cues for their appearance from sport and porn.

It is important to keep in mind, however, that just as societies and cultures evolve, so too do our notions of masculinity and femininity. Though these notions have changed somewhat over time in the United States, traditional views are still quite widely held. For instance, masculine qualities include being strong, ambitious, successful, aggressive, rational, and emotionally controlled. Feminine qualities include being nurturing, sensitive, thin, emotionally expressive, deferential, physically attractive, and concerned with people and relationships. Since gender is learned, not biologically coded, media messages, along with other societal sources, contribute to how individuals define themselves.

Gender scholar Julia T. Wood (2005) notes that just because social meanings of gender are taught, it does not mean individuals passively receive cultural meaning. Choices are made whether to accept or reject messages and whether to reinforce gender norms or to step outside them. When people choose to step outside accepted social boundaries, they tend to provoke change in societal views. For example, years ago, many would have looked down upon women who played basketball on a team in the United States. Now, however, many girls and women are encouraged to be actively involved in the sport, and there are even professional basketball teams under the Women's National Basketball Association (WNBA). Still, female sports are not universally or wholeheartedly accepted. Media coverage of the WNBA is relegated to cable, while NBA coverage is provided on the major broadcast networks. Even in the Olympics, men's basketball is given more airtime than women's basketball. In one study on the 2000 Summer Olympics, only two minutes was given to the US women's team, whereas over two hours of coverage was provided to the men's team (Tuggle, Huffman, and Rosengard 2002). The idea the mass media are, perhaps inadvertently, conveying is that women's basketball is not worth the viewer's (and, as a result, advertiser's) time or money.

Sexual Identity

For a long time in the United States, heterosexuality was considered the only norm, and homosexuality was viewed as abnormal. Homosexuality was deemed a mental illness, even by the medical profession, and the common thought was that individuals could and should be "cured" of the illness. It is against this social backdrop that individuals formed their sexual identity. It goes without saying that for homosexuals it was a time of personal turmoil both externally, at the social level, and internally, at the personal level. The mainstream belief of who they should be was counter to their own sense of self.

Through the social and political efforts of the lesbian, gay, bisexual, and transgender (LGBT) community, understandings regarding sexual orientation have advanced. Although still fighting an uphill battle, the LGBT community has found greater acceptance at the social and political level. For example, due to years of activism, several states in the United States have recently passed legislation recognizing same-sex marriages.

Signs of advancement of understandings regarding sexual orientation have also been noted in the mass media. Whereas any mention of sexuality that veered away from the heterosexual norm was taboo in the early days of mass media, positive depictions and more well-rounded images can now be seen in much of the content. Celebrity culture has certainly helped in this realm. Of note is former Olympic athlete and reality-television star Caitlyn (formerly Bruce) Jenner's transition from male to female. As will be further discussed in Chapter 11, the experiences of a well-known celebrity going through the different stages of the transition process in front of the peering lens of television cameras brought about greater public awareness of the transgender community and some of the formidable obstacles they face in society.

Age Identity

People create schemas based on chronological age, which then become a major part of our own social identity as well. We tend to adopt cultural notions regarding what type of language pattern or behavior is appropriate for certain age groups. Age-based schemas can influence whether a person's talents, contributions, and feelings are acknowledged. Age schemas are internalized at a young age, often as young as 4 years old, long before they are relevant, and are constantly reinforced throughout a lifetime (Dittmann 2003).

Just like the other social identities discussed in this book, age complicates how an individual is perceived. Though no two people are alike, our learned schemas teach us to expect certain things about certain groups of people. For instance, if an individual was watching a man perform complicated stunts on a skateboard, that individual might think, "Wow, that's impressive!" If that individual then approached the man to get a closer look and saw that the man appeared to be in his fifties, the individual's impression of the skateboarder might dramatically change. The individual might encounter a bit of a disjuncture in thought processes. People tend not to expect a 50-year-old man to be doing stunts on a skateboard, simply because of the schemas that have been created for men in that age group.

As baby boomers (i.e., those individuals born during the post-World War II years) age, attempts have been made to revise some of the standard cultural notions associated with old age. For example, the phrase "40 is the new 30" or "50 is the new 40" can be heard. Such phrases really are attempts to change cultural ideas regarding age brackets. As with the other core identities, however, changes in cultural notions regarding age entail a gradual process. The mass media can play a large role in bringing about or resisting the changes. Indications of Hollywood resistance to accepting aging female actresses in leading roles exist, and there are numerous examples of sexist ageism. For example, actress Olivia Wilde was purportedly turned down for the role of the wife of Leonardo DiCaprio's character in Martin Scorsese's *Wolf of Wall Street* because she was viewed as too old for the part; Wilde was only 28 years old at the time (Blay 2016). Due to such discrimination, some actresses (e.g., Jessica Chastain and Rebel Wilson) have chosen to hide their real age for fear of losing parts. The public also has not been kind to aging actresses. As an example, actress Carrie Fisher faced a firestorm of criticism on Twitter for not appearing like her "young" self in reprising her role as Princess Leia in the 2015 *Star Wars: Force Awakens* film.

Disability Identity

Cartoonist John Callahan drew a cartoon showing three people: the first two are shown walking with question marks above their heads; the third person is shown in a wheelchair, also with a question mark above his head, but in the form of the symbol for disability. What Callahan, who became a quadriplegic at the age of 21 as a result of injuries received in a car accident, and who passed away in 2010 at the age of 59, was conveying through this cartoon is that individuals with disabilities are often defined by their disability. In other words, the disability becomes the only social identity for that individual.

Our cultural ideas about disability influence how we view and make judgments about people with disabilities. In certain cultures, disability is perceived as an embarrassment, something that should be hidden from public view. In other cultures, people with disabilities are considered as different, but not inferior, to other individuals. Both cultural notions can be found in the United States.

Class Identity

Every society is divided by certain social stratifications. One form of stratification is socioeconomic class. The socioeconomic class to which individuals belong often shapes how others view them and how they define themselves. People tend to associate certain communication styles, fashion, food, and recreational choices with each class (Devine 2004). For example, you might associate champagne and caviar with upper-class individuals, while linking beer and hot dogs to the lower class. Why are such associations made? They might be loosely based on reality, but many are social constructions often influenced by the mass media.

Studies suggest the mainstream mass media present images or perspectives of the upper class or middle class often but the lower class infrequently (McChesney 2008). When the lower class is portrayed, the depictions are often negative in nature. For example, the poor often are shown as lazy or unmotivated and personally responsible for their own class position (Luther, Kennedy, and Combs-Orme 2006). Such negative portrayals or outright omissions can be problematic. If the images are negative, it is difficult to evoke compassion or understanding from the consumers of those images. If images are absent, viewers might come away with the impression that an insignificant number of individuals actually are poor. The impact of this faulty impression could have a direct impact on social services or legislation designed to help those who are financially underprivileged. If individuals believe the population of low-income families in the United States is lower than it actually is or have negative attitudes toward the poor, then they might be less likely to support services or legislation designed to help that social group.

Organization of the Book

Your professor may reorganize the chapter order of this book to suit the needs of your class, but the authors have laid out a road map designed to help you navigate the complex history and themes inherent in studying media representations of diversity.

Chapter 2 provides a review of the major theoretical frameworks that have bracketed discussion of mass media representations of social groups. Introduced are frameworks not only from the cultural theoretical realms, but also from the social scientific tradition. Chapter 3 focuses on the representations of American Indians, the first group in the United States to have their people portrayed in disparaging ways by those in socially dominant positions. Chapter 4 provides an overview of representations of African Americans, another group that had early experiences of domination and unfair media portrayals. Chapter 5 explores the representations of Hispanics, a growing ethnicity in the United States. Chapter 6 discusses the representations of Arabs and Arab Americans, a group that also is steadily growing in the United States and that has encountered acrimonious mass media depictions because of domestic and international politics dealing with US–Middle East relations. Chapter 7 explores another group that has experienced varying portrayals impacted by domestic and international politics, Asians and Asian Americans. Chapter 8 presents how mixed race individuals and couples have been portrayed in the mass media and how historical notions of race/ethnicity have contoured those portrayals.

Following a focus on race/ethnicity, the book will turn its attention to other demographic categories, beginning with gender. Because of the breadth of research that is available on the subject, two chapters are devoted to gender (Chapters 9 and 10), and explorations of the representations of men and women, as well as notions of masculinity and femininity are discussed. Chapter 11 examines representations of lesbian, gay, bisexual, and transgendered people, a group with an ever-growing political and social voice. This is followed by a chapter discussing age (Chapter 12), and the representations of older people as well as teenagers, and a chapter on disability (Chapter 13), a group with a long history of virtual invisibility in the media.

As you read the book, consider how membership in the social groups discussed in each of the aforementioned chapters influences the social construction of class, the focus of Chapter 14. Given that religion or lack thereof is often viewed as a critical component of one's social identity, Chapter 15 is devoted to representation of religion and faith in the media. Chapter 16 discusses the overall progress the mass media industry has made in addressing issues of diversity. As you will see in reading the chapter, in recent years the mass media industry has taken concrete steps to address some of the concerns regarding representation of social groups and to increase the diversity within their content and their professional organization as well. The final chapter of this book, Chapter 17, provides a general conclusion to the previous chapters and broadens the discussion to what might lie ahead of us in terms of media and diversity. The consequences of media representations are highlighted, including the impact of such representations on individual self-concepts. The chapter also presents information concerning how minority groups have taken steps to create their own mass media in order to promote images that they believe are more representative of their own group. The role of the Internet in either promoting or discouraging diversity is additionally discussed. Also, at the end of the book, look for the Digging Deeper section that is designed to provide research paper topics along with points of synergy throughout the text. These pages are brief but will help to connect the dots and point out where patterns have formed. While this section is helpful after you have read the book, you may also want to dive into this section *before* reading the chapters as it foreshadows key elements found throughout the entire text.

In this book, attempts were made to approach subjects from diverse perspectives. As you move through it, consider the discussion questions and boxes, and evaluate the meaning and impact of the information in each chapter as it relates to your own personal experiences. Only through an understanding of how social groups are represented through the mass media can society become better equipped to evaluate the mediated messages that confront us on a daily basis and work on the task of social acceptance and understanding. Once individuals are able to effectively evaluate these messages and decode messages that contain misinformation or exaggerations, they are in a better position to assess, make judgments, and, ultimately, gain understanding about groups and individuals who are different from them.

Reflection Questions and Thoughts to Consider

1. The social importance placed on certain identities has waxed and waned with the passage of time. Consider US mass media history. Do you believe certain identities (e.g., religious, sexual, gender) were given more notice within the mass media during specific time periods than in other periods?
2. Consider your own identities. Which identity or identities do you believe is most important to you? Why do you think that is the case?
3. How would you think or feel if you saw a little boy playing with a Barbie doll or heard about a young girl attempting to try out for her school's football team? Would you feel awkward or taken aback? Would the behavior come as no surprise? What do you believe are the root causes of your reaction?
4. Think of the area in which you were raised. Have you noticed a change in the racial/ethnic makeup of your area within the past 10 years? If notable changes have taken place, how has the local media addressed or taken advantage of these changes?

References

Abrams, Dominic, and Michael A. Hogg. 2004. "Collective Identity: Group Membership and Self-Perception." In *Self and Social Identity*, edited by Marilynn B. Brewer and Miles Hewstone, 147–181. Oxford: Blackwell.

Bandura, Albert. 2002. "Social Cognitive Theory of Mass Communication." In *Media Effects: Theory and Research*, edited by Jennings Bryant and Dolf Zillman, 121–153. Mahwah, NJ: Lawrence Erlbaum.

Basson, Lauren L. 2008. *White Enough to Be American? Race Mixing, Indigenous People, and the Boundaries of State and Nation*. Chapel Hill, NC: University of North Carolina Press.

Bem, Sandra L. 1993. *The Lenses of Gender: Transforming the Debate on Sexual Inequality*. New Haven, CT: Yale University Press.

Bissell, Kimberly L., and Peiqin Zhou. 2004. "Must-See TV or ESPN: Entertainment and Sports Media Exposure and Body Image Distortion in College Women." *Journal of Communication* 54(1): 5–21. DOI: 10.1111/j.1460 2466.2004.tb02610.x.

Blay, Zeba. 2016. "Basically Decrepit Actress Olivia Wilde was 'Too Old' to Play Leo's Wife." *HuffPost Women*. http://www.huffingtonpost.com/entry/basically-decrepit-actress-olivia-wilde-was-too-old-to-play-leos-wife_us_56e871d3e4b0860f99dac197 (accessed March 31, 2017).

Colby, Sandra L., and Jennifer M. Ortman. 2015. *Projections of the Size and Composition of the U.S. Population: 2014 to 2060*. US Department of Commerce, Economics and Statistics Administration, US Census Bureau. https://www.census.gov/content/dam/Census/library/publications/2015/demo/p25-1143.pdf (accessed March 31, 2017).

Devine, Fiona. 2004. "Middle Class Identities in the United States." In *Rethinking Class: Culture, Identities and Lifestyles*, edited by Fiona Devine, Mike Savage, John Scott, and Rosemary Crompton, 140–162. New York, NY: Palgrave Macmillan.

Dittmann, Melissa. 2003. "Fighting Ageism." *Monitor on Psychology* 5(34): 50.

Grogan, Sarah. 2008. *Body Image: Understanding Body Dissatisfaction in Men, Women, and Children*, 2nd ed. London: Routledge.

Hobbs, Frank, and Nicole Stoops. 2002. *Demographic Trends in the 20th Century: Census 2000 Special Reports*. https://www.census.gov/prod/2002pubs/censr-4.pdf (accessed March 31, 2017).

Luther, Catherine A., Deseriee Kennedy, and Terri Combs-Orme. 2006. "Intertwining of Poverty, Gender, and Race: A Critical Analysis of Welfare News Coverage from 1993–2000." *Race, Gender and Class* 12(2): 10–35.

McCann, Robert M., Kathy Kellermann, Howard Giles, Cynthia Gallois, and M. Angels Viladot. 2004. "Cultural and Gender Influences on Age Identification." *Communication Studies* 55(1): 88–105.

McChesney, Robert. 2008. *The Political Economy of Media: Enduring Issues, Emerging Dilemmas*. New York, NY: Monthly Review Press.

Merriam-Webster. 2011. "Diversity." http://www.merriam-webster.com/dictionary/DIVERSITY (accessed March 31, 2017).

Simpson, Mark. 2002. "Meet the Metrosexual." *Salon.com*, July 22. http://www.salon.com/2002/07/22/metrosexual (accessed March 31, 2017).

Simpson, Mark. 2014. "The Metrosexual is Dead. Long Live the 'Spornosexual.'" *The Telegraph*, June 10. http://www.telegraph.co.uk/men/fashion-and-style/10881682/The-metrosexual-is-dead.-Long-live-the-spornosexual.html (accessed March 31, 2017).

Tajfel, Henri. 1974. "Social Identity and Intergroup Behavior." *Social Science Information* 13: 65–93.

Tuggle, C.A., Suzanne Huffman, and Dana S. Rosengard. 2002. "A Descriptive Analysis of NBC's Coverage of the 2000 Summer Olympics." *Mass Communication and Society* 5(3): 361–375.

Wander, Philip C., Judith N. Martin, and Thomas Nakayama. 1999. "Whiteness and Beyond: Sociohistorical Foundations of Whiteness and Contemporary Challenges." In *Whiteness: The Communication of Social Identity*, edited by Thomas K. Nakayama and Judith N. Martin, 13–26. Thousand Oaks, CA: Sage.

Wood, Julia T. 2005. *Gendered Lives: Communication, Gender, and Culture*. Belmont, CA: Thompson Wadsworth.

2

Theoretical Foundations of Research in Mass Media Representations

Scholars who study mass media representations of social groups tend to adhere to one of two main theoretical perspectives. The first perspective is social psychological and tends to place emphasis on understanding media representations through empirical means, often relying on a systematic content analysis of media material. The second draws from a more critical or cultural perspective with a concentration on how meaning is generated by the mass media. An in-depth, qualitative analysis is often preferred, such as a textual or a discourse analysis. Both perspectives offer a wealth of information regarding how groups of individuals in a society are consistently portrayed and the potential underlying reasons for their portrayals. This chapter will review the major theoretical concepts that fall under each perspective. While other concepts exist, the ones chosen for review here are those that frequently appear in articles and books that seek to understand media images of social groups and their impact on the public.

Mass Media Representations: Social Psychological Perspectives

Researchers adopting a social psychological perspective attempt to understand existing patterns of media representations of social groups by making observations based on agreed methods of systematic inquiry that they believe will ensure objectivity. When describing human thoughts about individuals or groups of individuals, they often speak in terms of the *cognitive schemas* created around the individual or group in question or the stereotypes that evolve from the schemas. As described in Chapter 1, cognitive schemas are interrelated conceptual units of information. They assist individuals in coherently organizing information. Humans naturally want to predict the behaviors of others. Schemas are thought to be one way of allowing such predictions to take place. When these schemas are perceived as useful in grouping and understanding individuals, they are often communicated to other individuals and become stereotypes (Schaller and Latane 1996).

A stereotype can be defined as beliefs about characteristics or attributes of a social group. In his influential book *Public Opinion*, Walter Lippmann asserted that stereotypes were basically "pictures in our head" and that they were necessary in order to take our complex environment and impose some form of order upon it (Lippmann 1922: 3). Since that rudimentary description was first proposed in 1922, several social psychological studies have emerged supporting Lippmann's assertions. Researchers have found that people's ability to process information is limited and that stereotypes

Diversity in US Mass Media, Second Edition. Catherine A. Luther, Carolyn Ringer Lepre, and Naeemah Clark.
© 2018 John Wiley & Sons Inc. Published 2018 by John Wiley & Sons Inc.

act as a heuristic device or a short cut to reduce the amount of information that bombards people on a daily basis (Fiske and Taylor 2013). In other words, stereotypes are a natural part of the categorization process that takes place within the human brain. Regardless of the fact that stereotypes can be viewed as a normal part of cognition, one still has to question why certain stereotypes exist and others do not. Why, for example, is a belief that women have small feet not a stereotype? Of course, women's feet come in all sizes, but people generally think that women have smaller feet in comparison to men. This, however, is not considered to be a stereotype. Is it because it is not socially relevant and the mass media have not zeroed in on this belief?

Communication researchers have long recognized that communication, especially mass communication, is a key player in the formation of stereotypes. Several mass communication theories based on social psychology have been used to understand how stereotypes evolve and how they potentially impact on social knowledge. The following are some of the more frequently used theoretical frameworks that help uncover the types and influences of social categories or stereotypes that are found in mass media.

Framing

Framing is a process in which a perceived reality is organized in such a way that certain aspects of the reality are stressed, while others are de-emphasized, leading to a particular definition or understanding of the social world. One of the founders of the concept of framing, sociologist Erving Goffman, proposed that every individual engages in producing mental schemas or frames that enable them to efficiently identify and interpret information (Goffman 1974). Often these frames are unconsciously created and evolve over time to help people make sense of their environment and whatever changes might occur in that environment. Goffman further proposed that the mass media often promote the development of frames and how individuals use frames. As part of his research, he focused on the types of gender frames frequently found in advertising and asserted that the frames found in advertising often mirror and reinforce dominant societal views. Among his findings was that women in advertisements were often framed as holding subordinate career roles and as emotionally withdrawn.

Goffman also found that in advertisements featuring both men and women, connotations regarding what society deems to be appropriate gender interactions were frequently conveyed through framing. For example, if a woman and man were presented in an advertisement, the woman was usually situated underneath or below the man, while the man towered over her or embraced her in a protective fashion. Such framing suggested men were in the dominant position in society.

Several researchers have since replicated and even expanded on Goffman's frame analysis of gender in advertising. Media researcher Katharina Lindner, for example, analyzed advertisements featured in *Time* and *Vogue* magazines over a 47-year time span from 1955 to 2002 and found that few significant changes had been made in gender framing (Lindner 2004). Women were often shown as subordinate to men and more objectified than men. In other words, the women were found to be secondary in relation to men and were presented with less clothing (Figure 2.1). The author concluded that the images in advertisements, through framing, reinforced the imbalance in social power between men and women.

Journalists have also been found to rely on framing in their work. Within the context of news, communication and political science professor Robert Entman defines framing as "the process of culling a few elements of perceived reality and assembling a narrative that highlights connections among

Figure 2.1 Magazine advertisement for the Matico Aristoflex vinyl plastic tile flooring, April 1956. Reproduced with kind permission of Getty images.

them to promote a particular interpretation," and writes that the end effect of framing is the encouragement of readers or audiences to "think, feel, and decide in a particular way" (Entman 2007: 164).

Journalists are taught to strive for objectivity, but because they are often under pressure to create gripping stories in a time-efficient manner, they too fall back on accessing their mental schemas and engage in the process of framing. When certain frames are consistently presented in the news, they tend to be elevated to widespread themes that are often absorbed by and influence people in all sections of society.

Table 2.1 Race of crime perpetrators as reported by California Department of Justice compared to race of crime perpetrators on television news (1995–1996).

Race	Arrest Rate %	TV Perpetrators %
Black	21	37
White	28	21
Latino	47	29
Other	4	13

Source: Dixon and Linz (2000).

Many researchers who have examined frames in mainstream news stories have found that the frames tend to echo the perspectives of those who hold political and economic power in society (Gitlin 2003; Ryan, Carragee, and Meinhofer 2001). Inequities or discrimination that are found in society can be reflected in the news stories. For example, several studies (e.g., Entman 1994; Entman and Rojecki 2000) have found that crime stories tend to highlight those crimes that are carried out by African American males, despite the fact that the majority of crimes are carried out by Anglo-Americans. Media scholars Travis Dixon and Daniel Linz (2000) analyzed the racial makeup of perpetrators of crime as shown in local television news in the Los Angeles area over a 20-week period and compared those findings with the race of criminal perpetrators as reported by California's Department of Justice. The researchers found that television news did not reflect the figures shown in the crime reports. African Americans were more likely to be portrayed as perpetrators of crime than to actually be arrested (see Table 2.1).

Researchers carrying out studies on the framing of African Americans have argued that by visually and textually associating perpetrators of crime with male African Americans through the framing process, the news sustains the old stereotype of the violent and self-interested African American male. Negative framing of African American females has also been found. One study (Luther, Kennedy, and Combs-Orme 2005) found that in television news stories pertaining to poverty, the stories tended to frame poverty as a female and African American problem. This is despite the fact that governmental data has consistently shown that poverty levels between Anglo-Americans and African Americans do not significantly differ.

The importance of understanding the types of frames that exist in the mass media is underscored by the potential impact these frames have on how individuals view others or themselves. An experimental study (Seate, Harwood, and Blecha 2010) that examined how frames in a news story about the arrest of an athlete might influence the extent to which readers would perceive the athlete as guilty indeed found some form of impact. Those experimental participants who were exposed to a story that framed the athlete in an accusatory manner perceived the athlete as culpable of the accused crime. Another theory that helps to explain how messages might influence perceptions is social comparison theory.

Social Comparison Theory

Social comparison theory states that individuals have a natural drive to compare themselves with others for self-evaluation purposes. It is rooted in a theoretical assertion made in the early 1900s by social scientists, which stipulated that self-concepts are relative and frequently based upon how individuals compare to others in psychological as well as physical characteristics. The concept was formalized and expanded into a theory in the 1950s with social psychologist Leon Festinger's classic work on social comparison. Festinger (1954) proposed that people seek information that allows them to make personal evaluations of themselves. By making such evaluations, individuals are able to better understand themselves and the social standards that exist with regard to how people should appear, think, and act. Festinger found that in order to fulfill this natural drive, individuals actively look for other individuals with whom they can compare themselves.

Since Festinger first presented the theory, several researchers (e.g., Collins 2000; Suls and Wills 1991) through their studies have provided empirical support to the notion that individuals define themselves in relation to others and come to understand social standards through social comparisons. They have also broadened our understanding of the theory and have challenged some of Festinger's earlier propositions. Festinger envisioned the locus of control over the comparison process as residing within the individual and not the environment. He saw individuals as the ones who use the social environment to satiate their information-seeking and evaluation needs. Researchers have since challenged this notion. According to these researchers, the social environment plays much more of an active and often powerful role in social comparison behaviors. They propose that the social environment actually often prompts individuals to make comparisons. For example, simply being confronted by a large billboard featuring an attractive male model might prompt men to start making comparisons with the model without the men consciously making the decision to compare.

Researchers have also challenged Festinger's classic notion regarding whom individuals are most likely to compare themselves with. Festinger proposed that, when presented with a range of individuals with whom to compare oneself, people will select individuals who are perceived to be similar to them. He reasoned that individuals want a sensible estimate of their abilities or values, so they are more likely to compare themselves to people who are similar. Comparing themselves to people who are at a higher or lower level would not provide them with essential information. Contrary to this proposition, however, studies (e.g., Buunk *et al.* 1990; Kruglanski and Mayseless 1990) following Festinger's work have shown that people often choose to compare themselves with dissimilar others. For example, one may evaluate oneself against a lower standard to mitigate the effects of a particular negative attribute, or against a higher standard when making a comparison that promises self-enhancement or assurance of self as an outcome. People may engage in social comparisons with others as a way of resolving discrepancies between their actual self and their ideal self.

With the understanding that individuals often compare themselves with dissimilar others and that the social environment may often provoke comparisons, researchers now recognize the potential role media may play in the comparison process. Thus, research into media images of people and social groups, and the comparisons audience members might make with these images, has gained prominence in recent years. In particular, a large number of studies have focused on the impact of media presentations of idealized images. For example, in one of the earlier US studies on media images and social comparison conducted in the 1990s, mass communication researcher Renee Botta (1999) found that young females who watched television shows featuring "thin" characters and who compared themselves with those characters were more likely to express dissatisfaction with their own bodies and exhibit signs of eating disorders. Another study (Luther 2009) found that young Japanese male and female teenagers who engaged in social comparison behavior with models in Japanese fashion magazines were more likely to believe that good looks and a slender body were important attributes for men and women to possess in order to succeed in careers and to become ideal spouses.

Marketing professor Marsha Richins argues advertising can also foster consumer desires through the process of social comparison. She writes that by "inducing social comparison with idealized images and by raising consumers' expectations about what ought to be in their own lives, particularly with respect to consumer goods," advertising can increase consumerism and, in the end, contribute to personal discontent (Richins 1996: 125). Social comparison theory assumes that comparisons with others begin at a young age and carry through to adulthood. In essence, youngsters are being socialized through the comparison process. Recent research has found that social comparison behaviors also take place via social media. One study (Chou and Edge 2012) found that the more time individuals spent on Facebook, the more they agreed that other people had better lives and were happier than they were. Another study (Verduyn *et al.* 2015) found through experiments that passive use of Facebook (e.g., viewing pictures, reading posts) as opposed to active use (e.g., clicking likes, commenting, etc.) increased feelings of envy and negatively impacted the affective wellbeing of the person.

Socialization

Socialization is the means by which individuals, beginning at an early age and continuing throughout their lives, learn about societal norms, values, and beliefs. In order for any society to survive, it becomes important to sustain degrees of accord and commonality among its members. Socialization can be thought of as ways in which these bonds are ensured. Psychologist Eleanor Maccoby (2007: 13) defines socialization as the "processes whereby naïve individuals are taught the skills, behavior patterns, values, and motivations needed for competent functioning in the culture in which the child is growing up." Although the amount of learning that occurs during childhood is vast and lasting, as individuals enter into new stages of their lives, the old patterns of social behavior are often reinforced while new patterns are also adopted.

Researchers have traditionally focused on such socializing agents as family, peers, and schools. Increasingly, however, many have acknowledged the media as serving as a major socializing agent. With abundant forms of mass media now available to youngsters, including television, the Internet, and video games, the media are thought to either reinforce other agents' socialization influences or undermine such socialization by presenting alternative viewpoints. For example, studies (e.g., Signorielli 2007) suggest television commercials targeted at children tend to reinforce beliefs about gender roles by suggesting which toys girls and boys should select for play and by showing them how they should behave during play. Aggression and action are most often shown for boys, while subdued play is often depicted for girls. Under the socialization thesis, by merely observing such behaviors repeatedly, these boys and girls will learn and practice those behaviors.

In recent years, researchers have incorporated cognitive theories in order to understand the observational learning process. According to cognitive script theory, individuals form cognitive templates or scripts of behaviors that help them to then quickly assess and react to future behaviors. Scripts thus allow individuals to more efficiently process information and guide them in their social assessments and behaviors. The initial acquisition of scripts requires a great deal of cognitive effort, but once they are inputted, they can easily be activated by environmental cues (Hanson 2007).

Of course the extent to which the social behaviors depicted in the media are encoded into the thought processes does depend on that individual's background and the way in which media influences interact with the individual's other socializing agents. The effectiveness of the media to socialize is also determined by the manner in which social behaviors are presented by the media. First of all, the content needs to attract the attention of the individual; then it has to become integrated into the thought processes via script encoding (Huesmann *et al.* 2003). Whether or not the behavior is integrated often depends on whether or not the individual identifies with the character carrying out the behavior. Similarities in age and sex have been found to be factors increasing the likelihood of identification taking place (Harwood 1999; Hoffner 1996).

Another significant factor is if rewards or punishment are associated with the depicted behavior. If rewards are associated, an individual is more likely to learn that behavior; if punishment is tied to the behavior, learning is less likely (Bandura 2002; Dubow, Huesmann, and Greenwood 2007). For example, if a teen-targeted movie shows a male teen character making fun of another character's ethnicity and other characters who witness the incident laugh in support of the male teen who did the taunting, teens viewing the movie might more likely learn that it is acceptable to make fun of someone based on their ethnicity, since affirmation of the behavior was presented.

It must be stressed that media socialization tends to rest on the notion that an individual is being exposed to similar patterns of images from an early age on into adulthood. In other words, the socialization process is long term. This notion is related to yet another theoretical concept that has been widely used to understand the potential influences of media on social perceptions of social groups. That theoretical concept is cultivation theory.

Cultivation Theory

Cultivation theory proposes that mass media contour or cultivate the viewpoints of individuals regarding their surrounding environment. The theory was first proposed by communication scholar George Gerbner in the late 1960s to explain the broader role of television in shaping culture and society. In describing television and the process of cultivation, Gerbner (1998: 181) wrote that "only repetitive, long-range, and consistent exposure to patterns common to most programming, such as casting, social typing, and the 'fate' of different social types, can be expected to cultivate stable and widely-shared images of life and society." Since its establishment, numerous studies based on cultivation theory have been conducted.

Researchers working for the Cultural Indicators Project, first initiated by Gerbner, regularly conduct content analyses of television programs and note the primary portrayals, themes, and values that are conveyed. They then conduct surveys among the general public to gain a sense of their worldviews and compare the responses with what they found in their television content analyses (see Box 2.1).

Through their repeated studies, researchers have found that correlations or associations tend to exist between the messages conveyed in television programming and the levels of television consumption. In other words, those who are high consumers of television programming tend to be more likely to express views that are in line with what is being consistently conveyed in the programs than those who are low consumers of television. For example, Gerbner's team of researchers found that women are often portrayed as helpless victims in television programming as compared to men (Gerbner 1998). They also found that those who are heavy viewers of television are less likely to say they would vote for a female political candidate. From these findings, the researchers have surmised that television's representation of women as powerless is leading heavy viewers of television to be less likely to express support for a female political candidate.

Cultivation research has come in for some criticism. One of the major criticisms is that causality between television exposure and viewer opinion cannot be shown. Only a relationship can be shown

---

Box 2.1 Cultural Indicators Project

The following are questions that were posed in a telephone survey conducted in 1973, as part of the Cultural Indicators Project under the direction of George Gerbner. Respondents were asked to estimate the actual answers to the questions. Gerbner found that those who were heavy viewers of television were more likely to provide answers that were more aligned with television than with reality. As one of the early cultivation studies, the 1973 work marked the beginning of a long-running research initiative.

Questions (and Gerbner's findings)

1. US population as a percentage of world population. (Gerbner's finding: TV overestimates and heavy viewers overestimate.)
2. Population density of US vs. other countries. (Gerbner's finding: TV overestimates and heavy viewers overestimate.)
3. Percentage of white Americans employed as professionals and managers. (Gerbner's finding: TV overestimates and heavy viewers overestimate.)
4. Percentage of people employed as pro athletes, entertainers, artists. (Gerbner's finding: TV overestimates and heavy viewers overestimate.)
5. Percentage of males with law enforcement jobs. (Gerbner's finding: TV overestimates and heavy viewers overestimate.)
6. Percentage of crimes that are violent. (Gerbner's finding: TV overestimates and heavy viewers overestimate.)
7. Percentage of Americans who are victims of violent crime. (Gerbner's finding: TV overestimates and heavy viewers overestimate.)
8. Your chance of encountering violence. (Gerbner's finding: TV overestimates and heavy viewers overestimate.)

Source: Gerbner and Gross (1973).

---

to be present. Nevertheless, the theory remains highly influential in the realm of academic research and the theory continues to evolve. Researchers (e.g., Coenen and Bulck 2016; Kahlor and Eastlin 2011) have strived to differentiate between the types of cultivation effects that might occur. They have made a distinction between a first-order cultivation and second-order cultivation that can take place. First-order cultivation refers to the cultivation of perceptions regarding the prevalence of the phenomenon in question (e.g., the number of violent crimes committed each year). Second-order cultivation is in reference to the beliefs that are nurtured in relation to the phenomenon (e.g., boys are more aggressive than girls).

Recent cultivation studies have incorporated the effects of new forms of media, including social media. For example, communication researchers Jennifer Lewallen, Brandon Miller, and Elizabeth Behm-Morawitz (2016) wanted to explore the cumulative impact consumption of celebrity media would have on materialistic attitudes among young adults. Using cultivation theory as its basis, the researchers found that the greater the exposure to celebrity-focused media (i.e., celebrity blogs, celebrity reality programs, celebrity magazines, celebrity news), the higher the levels of materialism.

In another one of Behm-Morawitz's studies that she conducted together with information and new media researcher David Ta, the researchers found evidence suggesting that virtual racial and ethnic representations in video games could influence the racial/ethnic beliefs of individuals (Behm-Morawitz and Ta 2014). The researchers argue that extensive periods of video game playtime could lead to the cultivation of racial/ethnic stereotyping.

Cultivation theory also veers away from other social science inspired theories in that the researchers who adhere to it dismiss the notion that there is an immediate and measurable mass media effect on audience members. The researchers, instead, assume that the influences of mass media are gradual in nature and can often not be easily detected in the short term. They also assume that the social reality constructed by mass media tends to be aligned with the needs of the societal elites, whose central aim is to maintain the status quo. Given these stances, researchers who work under cultivation theory come closer to the more critical perspective of media impact on social reality.

Media Representations: Critical Perspectives

The critical perspective takes on a long-term view of the impact of mass communication on social notions regarding individuals and groups. In contrast to the social scientific orientation that tends to focus on the short-term influences of media, it takes on a more holistic approach by examining the role of mass media in sustaining or bringing about changes in our understandings of ourselves, of others, and of the societies in which we live.

Although cultural studies is now practiced worldwide, including in the United States, the roots of the critical perspective of media representations can be traced to Europe, especially in the work that emanated from the University of Frankfurt, commonly known as the Frankfurt School, in the 1930s. Some of the prominent scholars associated with this school were Theodor Adorno, Max Horkheimer, and Leo Lowenthal. The scholars took on a neo-Marxist viewpoint that argues elites within society have direct control over the modes of production and productive relations (base) that drive a society's economy (Hardt 1992). By having such control, those elites essentially are also in control of a society's culture (superstructure) including its religion, ideology, and arts. Frankfurt School critical scholars viewed popular culture and mass media as debased forms of culture. Mass media were thought to be art forms turned into simple commodities designed for mass consumption. The scholars argued that the primary motives behind the production of media products for mass dissemination was profit and the maintenance of social power by the elites.

Several of those associated with the Frankfurt School were eventually forced to leave Germany during World War II and several chose the United States as their new home. After settling into US universities such as Columbia University in New York City, the Frankfurt School scholars continued with their writings and heavily influenced mass communication researchers in the United States as well.

Another group of researchers coming from a neo-Marxist critical perspective who have had a significant impact on mass communication research are those associated with British cultural studies. British cultural studies is said to have initially developed in the 1950s and 1960s. The founders, Raymond Williams, E.P. Thompson, and Richard Hoggart, were literary scholars and evening school instructors who taught individuals from a lower social stratum in Britain. Through their interactions with these students, the three scholars came to realize that they wanted to better understand the daily struggles and coping strategies of those they taught. In particular, they were interested in understanding how those in positions of societal power were able to dominate over the lives of their students, or, more specifically, minority groups and individuals from underprivileged backgrounds.

Hoggart established the Centre for Contemporary Cultural Studies at the University of Birmingham in 1964 and by doing so formally launched cultural studies. The fundamental idea that was stressed was that the one way in which elites were able to maintain their social control of the underclass was through their domination of the production and usage of culture. In order to better explain and help others to comprehend this process of elite domination through culture, Williams presented the concept of hegemony as key to the process.

Hegemony

Hegemony refers to the dominance of political and social elites over those with less power. The dominance permeates society in such a manner that those being ruled are often not aware of, or are accepting of, the dominance. It is carried out through cultural, political, and economic means. The concept of hegemony was adopted by Raymond Williams and other cultural studies scholars and was inspired by the works of Antonio Gramsci. Gramsci was a journalist and political activist in Italy during the early 1900s. One of the founding members of Italy's Communist Party, Gramsci was imprisoned for his writings and activism in the 1920s by Italian dictator Benito Mussolini. While in prison, in efforts to understand why individuals would be willing to live under bourgeois values and elite subjugation, he wrote about the process of hegemony as part of his series of essays. Gramsci (1971) suggested that individuals were not only controlled through direct coercion, but also through hegemony. He maintained that by creating a hegemonic culture that became deeply embedded in public consciousness, elites were able to effectively exert their control.

Williams incorporated Gramsci's hegemony into the cultural studies arena. He describes hegemony as follows:

> Hegemony supposes the existence of something which is truly total, which is not merely secondary or superstructural, like the weak sense of ideology, but which is lived at such a depth, which saturates the society to such an extent, and which, as Gramsci put it, even constitutes the substance and limits of common sense for most people under its sway, that it corresponds to the reality of social experience very much more clearly than any notions derived from the formula of base and superstructure. (Williams 1980: 37)

In accordance with this line of thought, Williams and those who espouse the concept of hegemony would argue, for example, that the distribution of American movies, music, clothing brands, and fast-food restaurants in other parts of the world is a way in which the United States is maintaining its power over the people living in those areas of the world.

Williams further expanded the notion of hegemony by acknowledging the possibility of forming an oppositional culture or counter-hegemony as a means to go against the imposition of the elites' cultural hegemony. Unlike the scholars from the Frankfurt School who entirely dismissed popular culture, Williams and his cultural studies cohorts recognized the prospect of popular culture playing a part in counter-hegemonic efforts.

The individual who followed in Williams's footsteps and became well known for his work in cultural studies is Stuart Hall. Hall also responded to the struggles of minorities and the underclass and concentrated on studying how popular culture was part of the hegemonic imposition of elites, but also how it could be used as a form to counter elite hegemony (Turner 1996). In particular, he focused his research efforts on the intersections of media, class, gender, and race. He was interested in deciphering how mass media construct social identities through representation.

The Concept of Representation

Representation is the forms of language that are used to convey ideas that are generated in society for purposes of communication. It is thought to be key to our understanding of the world that surrounds us. As defined by Hall (1997: 17), "Representation is the production of meaning of the concepts in our minds through language. It is the link between concepts and language which enables us to refer to either the 'real' world of objects, people or events, or indeed to imaginary worlds of fictional objects, people and events."

Language as used here does not merely refer to words, both written and verbal, but rather any entity which functions to help people to communicate with each other. Language might be musical notes, visual images, or nonverbal signs. The concept of representation provides insight into the source of meanings and why they exist by connecting language with the concepts that we associate with the language.

There are three theoretical approaches to representation: the reflective, the intentional, and the constructionist approach. The reflective approach assumes that language is simply a reflection of the true meaning that is inherent within an object, person, idea, group, or event. Language is an imitation or mirror of whatever reality exists. Thus, a clear parallel is present between that which is being understood and that which is conveying the understanding. The second approach is the intentional approach. This approach focuses on the creators of the meanings and assumes that meanings that exist are conscious creations of the authors. In other words, pictures or words are conveying what the source of those words or pictures intended to convey. To illustrate the difference between the reflective and intentional approach, let us assume the existence of a picture of the US Capitol building in Washington, DC. The picture is in black and white and shows a dark overcast sky hovering above the Capitol building. An individual coming from a reflective approach would say the picture is a reproduction of the Capitol building. The picture is simply capturing the essence of the Capitol building. On the other hand, a person taking up the intentional approach would say that the photographer wanted to capture the problems members of Congress are dealing with in passing legislation.

Hall dismisses the first two theoretical approaches to representation as being flawed. Instead, he submits the constructionist approach as more accurately capturing the process of representation. The constructionist approach affirms that language does not reproduce things or convey the intentions of the language producer. Rather, it is a part of the systems of knowledge production through which meanings are created. Essentially, what is asserted is that things do not have inherent meaning, and private meanings created by the authors cannot be directly imposed on others. Things take on meaning only through the process of representation, which connects the object or sign with a concept based on social conventions. As such, the constructionist approach recognizes the social nature of language.

Those coming from the cultural studies perspective assert that understanding the notion of societal power is crucial to unveiling the underlying sources of representation. Influenced by French philosopher Michel Foucault's work on the production of knowledge, cultural studies scholars assume that the meanings generated through representation are very much shaped by the historical and cultural context in which they are produced, and that they are intertwined with the relations of power. According to this viewpoint, through representation oppressors at various levels of social life can exert their power over the oppressed.

In terms of the concept of stereotype, then, cultural studies scholars perceive it differently from those coming from a social psychological perspective. In cultural studies, stereotyping is viewed as a set of representational practices. Stuart Hall (1997: 17) characterizes stereotyping as reducing "people to a few, simple, essential characteristics, which are represented as fixed by Nature." Cultural studies scholars recognize that categorizing people is a necessity in order to make sense of things. Placing people in such categories as "nurse," "teacher," "father," "mother," and so forth is needed. They assert that the problem is that stereotyping goes far beyond categorizing or typing by reducing individuals to a few simple characteristics and presenting them as unchangeable because they are determined by nature (see Box 2.2). The end result is that stereotyping symbolically erects fences or boundaries around groups of individuals, thus enabling exclusion to come about. Those who fall outside of the boundary of what is considered normal or mainstream are considered to be the "Others."

Box 2.2 "Ideal" images of males

Idealized male body and facial images are found on countless magazine covers and are found in thousands of magazine advertisements. How would social scientists approach these images using social comparison theory? What would they say about these images and their potential impact? How would researchers coming from a cultural studies perspective interpret these messages? Would they perceive these images as a source of liberation for men or a source of hindrance?

Figure 2.2 Are these the ideal male figures that women and men should admire? Reproduced with kind permission of Shutterstock.

Because popular culture is viewed as being very much a part in the process of representation and the creation of meanings, cultural studies scholars have explored how social boundaries can be created, and even broken, through popular culture in such areas as race, class, sexuality, and gender. Popular culture, including mass media, is viewed as being able to serve as a hegemonic force or a counter-hegemonic force that either imposes restrictions upon or acts as a means of liberation for various social groups. For example, coming from a cultural studies perspective, media scholars Kelly Poniatowski and Erin Whiteside (2012) analyzed television commentary of the hockey games at the 2006 Winter Olympic games to explore how the commentaries were constructing race within the context of the games. Through a qualitative analysis, the researchers found that a privileging of white hockey players could be detected. Among their findings was that white players were represented as being physically large and strong as well as morally good.

Another theoretical perspective that recognizes mass media as being either a source of liberation or a hindrance for social groups is feminism. Many parallels can be found between cultural studies and feminism. In fact, those who practice in both areas acknowledge each perspective's influence on their own area.

Feminist Theory

Many come across the notion of feminism or feminist theory but are not quite sure of its real meaning or significance. The exact theoretical perspective of feminism is actually difficult to pin-point. Part of the reason for this difficulty is because those who practice feminism resist being neatly defined or placed in a category. Another is that several strands of feminism have made their mark. The strands include radical feminism, environmental feminism, and Marxist feminism. Each has developed specific focuses of research and theoretical frameworks.

For example, Marxist feminists have concentrated on understanding class division and how it serves as a factor in the oppression of women. They explore how women perceive themselves and how their perceptions are related to their class position. On the other hand, radical feminists describe the root of women's oppression as being tied to sexuality, reproduction, and mothering. They urge women to separate themselves from men, both at an emotional and sexual level. Only then, they argue, can women realize their full potential.

Regardless of their focus, however, what feminists have in common is their assertion that acknowledgment of the female perspective is needed. They argue that, for decades, the philosophies and theories that have come about in all fields of study, from the hard sciences to the social sciences, were primarily created from a male perspective. Female perspectives were either ignored or silenced. This, they say, must change.

Feminists are not calling for the total disregard of theories that were formulated by men. Those theories are recognized by feminists as having contributed to knowledge and as serving as a foundation for further theories. What they are attempting to do is to further improve social inquiry and encourage a diversity of approaches and perspectives to research. They have also sought to advance the position of females and female institutions by encouraging a specific research focus on these areas.

Three Waves of Feminism

Historians of feminism have identified three phases of this movement. The first, referred to as the first wave, came about in the United Kingdom and then the United States during the mid-1800s in an effort to bring about equal property rights and individualism. The term "feminism" is said to have grown out of an intellectual movement called *feminisme* at around the same period in France, and the term entered the United States in 1906 (Baumgardner and Richards 2000). The movement grew as more women struggled for the right to vote. The culmination of the first wave took place in the 1920s when women both in the United Kingdom and the United States were able to gain the right to vote.

The second wave followed and continued until the 1990s. Heavily influenced by Marxism as well as Freudian psychoanalysis, the feminist movement during this phase focused on reproductive freedom and workplace equality. The radical feminist perspective is said to have emerged alongside the liberal feminist perspective. While the liberal feminists sought to restructure existing power institutions in order for women to play larger societal roles, radical feminists proposed the idea of a need to break down patriarchal systems and urged a separation of men and women. Exemplifying the radical perspective, after the first Women's Liberation convention in the United States, the Redstockings Manifesto doctrine was released by radical feminists. It stated:

> We identify the agents of our oppression as men. Male supremacy is the oldest, most basic form of domination. All other forms of exploitation and oppression (racism, capitalism, imperialism, etc.) are extensions of male supremacy; men dominate women, a few men dominate the rest. (MacNamara 2006: 25)

Beginning in the 1990s, the third wave of feminism has veered away from a call for complete equality between men and women. Instead, it has called for a greater acknowledgment of differences between men and women and a celebration of those differences. Third-wave feminists charge that what is important is that women have choices in what they do with their lives, whether the choice is to take on traditional roles as mother and wife or to push into nontraditional roles. As part of the third wave, a subgroup of feminists has taken a contrary view of traditional sexism and has asserted that women can gain societal power through their femininity and sexuality. Materialism, sexuality, and outward appearances are viewed as positives under this perspective. Some have labeled these feminists as "lipstick feminists" (MacNamara 2006).

In all three phases of feminism, voicing a feminist perspective and conducting research in the area has been a difficult endeavor. For a long time, feminist research was frequently not valued and was, instead, dismissed as insignificant. Those who wrote or conducted studies from a feminist perspective often encountered rejection from traditional academic publications and had no other option but to create their own outlets.

Over the last couple of decades, the situation has dramatically improved, with feminist research appearing in top-tier journals and more academic publications showing an appreciation for the contributions made by feminists. Feminists, in turn, have broadened their fields of study and have more closely examined the intersections between gender and other social identities such as class and ethnicity. They have also increasingly examined the role of communication in gender issues. Studies have been conducted in such areas as how inequities and domination can be revealed in various forms of communication, and how communication, including mass media, can potentially serve to empower women. For example, communications scholars Dunja Antunovic and Marie Hardin (2013) examined how women bloggers were defining their identities and conceptualizing sports through their engagement in blogging. Through their examination of the profiles of women bloggers that were tagged under the label of sports blogs on the popular blog aggregate site *BlogHer*, the researchers found that women bloggers tended to understand sports from a spectatorship perspective and rejected the notion that sports primarily fell under the sphere of maleness. The women bloggers also showed an inclination to offer resources to others regarding sports and physical health and shared their experiences with sports.

Those who engage in men's studies have also used feminist perspectives in order to study male depictions in the media and understand how men can also be oppressed through the various structural constraints and societal expectations placed on men. Feminists stress that scholars coming from their perspective, whether they be men or women, should not limit themselves to creating knowledge for publications but should actively apply their knowledge in the real world. In other words, they encourage action-oriented feminist research and call for researchers to provide a voice to those they research. Similar calls are made by researchers who use queer theory for their studies.

Queer Theory

Queer theory is said to have emerged in the late 1980s and into the 1990s as a way to undo normative beliefs about sexuality and gender. Pulling away from the binary definitions that are often imposed on individuals in terms of their identity, the theory has allowed for a critical reinterpretation of mainstream discourse from a queer perspective. By rejecting "all categorizations as limiting and labeled by dominant power structures" (Kirsch 2000: 33), the theory allows researchers to transcend society's conceptions of identities and power.

Queer theory is viewed as a theory of social action that not only fosters deeper understandings in regard to the construction of gender and sexual identities but also promotes social justice-related activism. For media scholars, queer theory provides a vehicle in which pervasive heteronormative narratives within mass media may be exposed and challenged. Media content (e.g., representations of characters in films and television) may be reassessed through a queer lens. It allows for one to imagine a world that opposes privileged discourses and practices. As an example, communication and social movement scholar Cheryll Ruth Reyes Soriano (2014) did a case study on an LGBT political party, Ladlad, in the Philippines and on how online media facilitated the organization's ability to connect with others and further their initiatives to resist oppressive power structures.

Concluding Remarks

This chapter's overview of theoretical frameworks that have guided research in the area of mass media and diversity is by no means complete. Several other theories exist that inform or can potentially inform this area of study. The frameworks that have been introduced, however, represent those that frequently appear in articles and books that seek to understand media images of social groups and the images' impact on the public. A select number of the individual chapters that follow in this book will complement this chapter by introducing further theories that apply more specifically to the particular chapter's topic.

Reflection Questions and Thoughts to Consider

1. According to cultivation theory, individuals who are heavily exposed to television programming often adopt the views and beliefs expressed in television shows. Given this, think of the reality programs that focus on relationships, such as ABC Television's *The Bachelor* (2002 debut) or CBS Television's *Big Brother* (2000 debut). If a person were to heavily view these programs, what assumptions do you think they might develop about human relationships?

2. Consider the following two passages regarding golfer Tiger Woods, which were published after it was revealed that although he was married, he had numerous affairs with women. The first is from a *New York Times* online article (http://www.nytimes.com/2010/02/20/sports/golf/20woods.html) and the second from an *Us Weekly*'s online article (http://www.usmagazine.com/celebrity-body/news/tiger-woods-didnt-wear-condoms-with-two-flings-2009712). How are the two passages framing Tiger Woods?

New York Times:

In his first public appearance after the November head-on collision of his squeaky clean image and an unsavory secret life, Tiger Woods was somber in expressing remorse, stern in scolding the news media for stalking his family and reporting untruths, and spiritual in saying he had drifted from the Buddhist principles he was taught as a child … While some of the players at the Accenture tournament declined to comment, others offered understanding and support … Ben Crane said: "I thought it was an amazing conference. I thought Tiger was very humble. And, you know what? I think we all love him as a golfer and as a family man."

Us Weekly:

"A lot of times, people who have affairs get this attitude, like, I am larger than life – I'm unstoppable," Harris [relationship expert] tells Us. "Plus, he [Tiger] has no impulse control, clearly." With numerous STD risks, Findling [psychotherapist] says Woods' wife "is the one paying the price" for his unprotected sexual encounters. "This is the mother of his children, and by doing this, he's demonstrating that he's not caring about Elin's [Tiger's wife] physical or mental health," Findling tells Us. "She's raising his children, and he's left her stressed out, humiliated, devastated, destroyed."

3. Think about social comparison theory and your comparison behavior. With whom do you often compare yourself? Do you tend to compare yourself with your friends, with celebrities, with models in advertisements? How do you often feel after making such comparisons? Do you think your usage of social media has heightened your social comparison behaviors?

4. In considering the different perspectives that represent feminist theory, with which perspective do you believe you might be more aligned?

References

Antunovic, Dunja, and Marie Hardin. 2013. "Women Bloggers: Identity and the Conceptualization of Sports." *New Media & Society* 15(8): 1374–1392.

Bandura, Albert. 2002. "Social Cognitive Theory of Mass Communication." In *Media Effects: Advances in Theory and Research*, edited by Jennings Bryant and Dolf Zillman, 121–153. Mahwah, NJ: Lawrence Erlbaum.

Baumgardner, Jennifer, and Amy Richards. 2000. *Manifesta: Young Women, Feminism, and the Future*. New York, NY: Farrar, Straus and Giroux.

Behm-Morawitz, Elizabeth, and David Ta. 2014. "Cultivating Virtual Stereotypes?: The Impact of Video Game Play on Racial/Ethnic Stereotypes." *The Howard Journal of Communication* 25: 1–15.

Botta, Renee A. 1999. "Television Images and Adolescent Girls' Body Image Disturbance." *Journal of Communication* 49(2): 22–41.

Buunk, Bram P., Rebecca L. Collins, Shelley E. Taylor, and Nico W. VanYperen. 1990. "The Affective Consequences of Social Comparison: Either Direction Has Its Ups and Downs." *Journal of Personality and Social Psychology* 59(6): 238–249.

Chou, Hui-Tzu, and Nicholas Edge. 2012. "'They are happier and having better lives than I am': The Impact of Using Facebook on Perceptions of Others' Lives." *Cyberpsychology, Behavior and Social Networking* 15(2): 117–121.

Coenen, Lennert, and Jan Van den Bulck. 2016. "Cultivating the Opinionated: The Need to Evaluate Moderates the Relationship Between Crime Drama Viewing and Scary World Evaluations." *Human Communication Research* 42(3): 421–440.

Collins, Rebecca L. 2000. "Among the Better Ones." In *Handbook of Social Comparison Theory and Research*, edited by Jerry Suls and Ladd Wheeler, 159–171. New York, NY: Kluwer Academic/ Plenum.

Dixon, Travis L., and Daniel Linz. 2000. "Over-representation and Underrepresentation of African Americans and Latinos as Lawbreakers on Television News." *Journal of Communication* 50(2): 131–155.

Dubow, Eric F., L. Rowell Huesmann, and Dara Greenwood. 2007. "Media and Youth Socialization: Underlying Processes and Moderators of Effects." In *Handbook of Socialization: Theory and Research*, edited by Joan E. Grusec and Paul D. Hastings, 404–430. London: Guilford Press.

Entman, Robert. 1994. "African Americans According to TV News." *Media Studies Journal* 8(3): 29–38.

Entman, Robert. 2007. "Framing Bias: Media in the Distribution of Power." *Journal of Communication* 57(1): 163–173.

Entman, Robert, and Andrew Rojecki. 2000. *The Black Image in the White Mind*. Chicago, IL: University of Chicago Press.

Festinger, Leon. 1954. "A Theory of Social Comparison: Women and Health Processes." *Human Relations* 7: 117–140.

Fiske, Susan T., and Shelley E. Taylor, eds. 2013. *Social Cognition: From Brains to Culture*, 2nd ed. New York, NY: McGraw-Hill.

Gerbner, George. 1998. "Cultivation Analysis: An Overview." *Mass Communication and Society* 1(3–4): 175–195.

Gerbner, George, and Larry Gross. 1973. "Cultural Indicators: The Social Reality of Television Drama." ERIC. http://eric.ed.gov/ERICWebPortal/contentdelivery/servlet/ERICServlet?accno=ED079390 (accessed March 31, 2017).

Gitlin, Todd. 2003. *The Whole World Is Watching*, 2nd ed. Berkeley, CA: University of California Press.

Goffman, Erving. 1974. *Frame Analysis: An Essay on the Organization of Experience*. New York, NY: Harper & Row.

Gramsci, Antonio. 1971. *Selections from the Prison Notebooks of Antonio*, edited and translated by Quintin Hoare and Geoffrey Nowell Smith. New York, NY: International Publishers.

Hall, Stuart. 1997. *Representation: Cultural Representations and Signifying Practices*. London: Sage.

Hanson, Katherine. 2007. "Cognitive Script Theory." In *Encyclopedia of Children, Adolescents, and the Media*, edited by Jeffrey J. Arnett, 185–187. Thousand Oaks, CA: Sage.

Hardt, Hanno. 1992. *Critical Communication Studies: Communication, History and Theory in America*. London: Routledge.

Harwood, Jake. 1999. "Age Identification, Social Identity Gratifications, and Television Viewing." *Journal of Broadcasting & Electronic Media* 43: 123–136.

Hoffner, Cynthia. 1996. "Children's Wishful Identification and Parasocial Interaction with Favorite Television Characters." *Journal of Broadcasting & Electronic Media* 40(3): 389–402.

Huesmann, L. Rowell, Jessica Moise-Titus, Cheryl-Lynn Podolski, and Leonard D. Eron. 2003. "Longitudinal Relations between Children's Exposure to TV Violence and Their Aggressive and Violent Behavior in Young Adulthood: 1977–1992." *Developmental Psychology* 39(2): 201–221.

Kahlor, LeeAnn, and Matthew S. Eastlin. 2011. "Television's Role in the Culture of Violence Toward Women: A Study of Television Viewing and the Cultivation of Rape Myth Acceptance in the United States." *Journal of Broadcasting & Electronic Media* 55(2): 215–231.

Kirsch, Max H. 2000. *Queer Theory and Social Change*. New York: Routledge.

Kruglanski, Arie W., and Ofra Mayseless. 1990. "Classic and Current Social Comparison Research: Expanding the Perspective." *Psychological Bulletin* 108(2): 195–208.

Lewallen, Jennifer, Brandon Miller, and Elizabeth Behm-Morawitz. 2016. "Media Diet and the Cultivation of Emerging Adults' Materialism." *Mass Communication and Society* 19: 253–274.

Lindner, Katharina. 2004. "Images of Women in General Interest and Fashion Magazine Advertisements from 1955 to 2002." *Sex Roles* 51: 409–422.

Lippmann, Walter. 1922. *Public Opinion*. New York, NY: Macmillan.

Luther, Catherine A. 2009. "Importance Placed on Physical Attractiveness and Advertisement-Inspired Social Comparison Behavior among Japanese Female and Male Teenagers." *Journal of Communication* 59(2): 279–295.

Luther, Catherine, Deseriee A. Kennedy, and Terri Combs-Orme. 2005. "The Intertwining of Poverty, Gender, and Race: A Critical Analysis of Welfare News Coverage from 1993–2000." *Race, Gender and Class* 12(2): 9–32.

Maccoby, Eleanor E. 2007. "Historical Overview of Socialization Research and Theory." In *Handbook of Socialization: Theory and Research*, edited by Joan E. Grusec and Paul D. Hastings, 13–41. London: Guilford Press.

MacNamara, J.R. 2006. *Media and Male Identity: The Making and Remaking of Men*. New York, NY: Palgrave Macmillan.

Poniatowski, Kelly, and Erin Whiteside. 2012. "'Isn't He a Good Guy?': Constructions of Whiteness in the 2006 Olympic Hockey Tournament." *Howard Journal of Communications* 23(1): 1–16.

Richins, Marsha L. 1996. "Materialism, Desire, and Discontent: Contributions of Idealized Advertising Images and Social Comparison." In *Marketing and Consumer Research in the Public Interest*, edited by Ronald Paul Hill, 109–132. Thousand Oaks, CA: Sage.

Ryan, Charlotte, Kevin M. Carragee, and William Meinhofer. 2001. "Theory into Practice: Framing, the News Media, and Collective Action." *Journal of Broadcasting & Electronic Media* 45(1): 175–182.

Schaller, Mark, and Bibb Latane. 1996. "Dynamic Social Impact and the Evolution of Social Representations: A Natural History of Stereotypes." *Journal of Communication* 46 (Autumn): 64–71.

Seate, Anita Atwell, Jake Harwood, and Erin Blecha. 2010. "'He was Framed!' Framing Criminal Behavior in Sports News." *Communication Research Reports* 27(4): 343–354.

Signorielli, Nanch. 2007. "Television's Gender-role Images and Contribution to Stereotyping: Past, Present and Future." In *Handbook of Children and the Media*, edited by Dorothy G. Singer and Jerome L. Singer, 124–358. Thousand Oaks, CA: Sage.

Soriano, Cheryll Ruth Reyes. 2014. "Constructing Collectivity in Diversity: Online Political Mobilization of a National LGBT Political Party." *Media, Culture & Society* 36(1): 20–36.

Suls, Jerry, and Thomas Ashby Wills. 1991. *Social Comparison: Contemporary Theory and Research*. Hillsdale, NJ: Lawrence Erlbaum.

Turner, Graeme. 1996. *British Cultural Studies*. London: Routledge.

Verduyn, Philippe, David Seungiae Lee, Jiyoung Park, Holly Shablack, Aruaba Ovell, Joseph Bayer, and Ethan Kross. 2015. "Passive Facebook Usage Undermines Affective Well-being: Experimental and Longitudinal Evidence." *Journal of Experimental Psychology: General* 144(2): 480–488.

Williams, Raymond. 1980. *Problems in Materialism and Culture*. New York, NY: Verso.

3

Representations of American Indians

At the end of season 1 (2015) of popular Netflix comedy *Unbreakable Kimmy Schmidt* (2015 debut), the character Jacqueline ("Jackie Lynn") Voorhees (played by white actress Jane Krakowski) reveals that her blonde, blue-eyed wealthy Manhattanite persona is a facade. Removing her contacts to reveal her brown eyes and showing her dark hair roots, Jacqueline shares with the audience that she is simply passing as a white woman and is in fact from the Lakota tribe. In season 2 (2016) Jacqueline's attempts at embracing her Lakota identity becomes a major satirical subplot of the show. Although the subplot provides opportunities for Native actors to appear on a popular mainstream program (Jacqueline's parents are played by Cherokee actress Sheri Foster and Comanche actor Gil Birmingham), the usage of stereotypical jokes to highlight Jacqueline's clumsy rediscovery of her Lakota background triggers criticisms of the show. Scenes such as Jacqueline performing a wacky dance in a cornfield because she believes it is a Lakota ritual for the "corn god" or Jacqueline howling like a wolf after she takes down a high school band "Indian" mascot are seen as examples of how a marginalized group can be further marginalized through humor. The use of a white actress with no American Indian ancestry also comes under criticism (ICTMN 2015). Defenders of the show also voice their opinion, saying that the show is able to raise questions about why offensive beliefs and practices are able to persist. For example, *Huffington Post* writer Claire Fallon (2016) argues, "Part of the value simply comes from portraying Native experiences and struggles – in addition to providing some sharp commentary, like Jackie Lynn's flabbergasted 'The Redskins? How is this still a thing?' – on a popular TV show. This shouldn't be such a significant victory, but to some degree, it is. For now, at least."

The criticisms and praise bestowed on *Unbreakable Kimmy Schmidt*'s American Indian subplot illustrate the complexities involved in the creation and interpretation of media representations of indigenous populations. Although several well-meaning efforts have been made to portray American Indians in a more accurate manner by acknowledging and exploring the differing Native cultures and traditions that exist, many have tended to falter and inadvertently reinforce the blatant stereotypes of Native peoples that have endured over the years.

This chapter will first provide a historical context to the images of American Indians that are often observed in the mass media. It will then explore the prominent depictions that have been found in film, television, and the printed press. The chapter will also discuss the various efforts that have been made to improve those depictions. Please note that disagreement does exist with regard to which terms should be used in reference to this social group. According to the US Department of the Interior Indian Affairs, "American Indian" is used in reference to those belonging to indigenous tribes within the

Diversity in US Mass Media, Second Edition. Catherine A. Luther, Carolyn Ringer Lepre, and Naeemah Clark.
© 2018 John Wiley & Sons Inc. Published 2018 by John Wiley & Sons Inc.

continental United States. "Native American" is more broadly used to refer to all indigenous people, including American Indians, Native Hawaiians, and Alaska natives, living not only in the United States, but also in Mexico, Canada, and Central/South America. Since the focus of this chapter is on how indigenous people within the United States are represented within US mass media, "American Indian" is preferentially used in this chapter. However, Native Americans, Indigenous peoples, Native peoples, and Indians are also used interchangeably, especially to signify their usage within said historical context.

Historical Background to American Indian Representations

American Indians are currently defined as those individuals who are descendants of the earliest inhabitants of the land now known as the United States. If an individual has at least one quarter of tribal blood, he/she is generally considered to be American Indian (Tan, Fujioka, and Lucht 1997). Many Indigenous Nations also keep tribal rolls, which help individuals to determine their American Indian ancestry.

The overarching representations of American Indians found in the mass media can be traced back to the late 1400s when European explorers first encountered the people of the Americas (Riding In 2006). In search of land and gold, European explorers came to the Americas with an attitude of privilege and a sense of sanctity over the indigenous people they met. They came with a stance that Europeans represented civilization and all that was good, while the Indians they encountered represented hedonism and barbarism. Europeans held the view that the Indians needed to be guided toward "civilized progress," and that they needed to be educated in Christianity (Weston and Coward 1997).

The pattern of European colonizers using stereotypes to justify their power over individuals whose land they coveted was manifested in the Americas. Although the cultures and languages of American Indians were diverse, the colonizers viewed the various tribes or nations as a whole. No distinctions were made in terms of the people's values and customs. The colonizers saw the Indians through one lens, and the imageries that were concocted for one indigenous person or group were effortlessly extended to all American Indian people. The two prominent – and opposing – images that emerged were the "noble savage" and the "evil savage" (Jojola 2003: 19). The noble savage signified the childlike, innocent creature who was in touch with nature and did not pose a threat to the colonizers. The evil savage represented the subhuman and vicious figure who was opposed to civilization.

From their very first encounters with the American Indians, the colonizers used the two dichotomous images in accordance with their needs. When gaining knowledge from the American Indians regarding the cultivation of food and the lay of the land, the Europeans labeled Indians as people who were gentle and who could be easily swayed toward Christianity. When American Indians resisted the Europeans' encroachment onto their lands, however, they were quickly branded as hostile and barbaric. As historian James Riding In (2006: 18) describes it, "Colonial ambitions for territory to settle, resources to exploit, people to enslave, and souls to proselytize ensured that people characterized one day as kind, noble, and trustworthy would be denigrated and warred against the next day." The use of "evil savage" imagery facilitated the violence that was used against the American Indians (Engels 2005: 356).

Inhumane and racist attitudes and behaviors toward the Native peoples continued even during the time in which independence from England was being sought by the North American colonizers. Although a certain amount of sympathy for the Indians was evident, a sense of superiority still overwhelmingly permeated the writings that were disseminated during that period. For example, Benjamin Franklin, in a 1764 pamphlet he wrote concerning the revenge-spurred massacre of 20 Indian children, women, and men in Pennsylvania, shows compassion for the American Indians who were killed. Franklin notes, "The only Crime of these poor Wretches seems to have been, that some had a reddish brown Skin and black Hair" (Steffens 1978: 31). As conveyed by the quote, although Franklin does show compassion toward the Indians, in characterizing the Indians as "wretches" he demonstrates that he is unable to entirely pull himself away from the condescending attitude toward American Indians that prevailed.

As the European Americans moved further west in the 1800s and continued to systematically usurp the lands of the Native Nations, sentiments of sympathy became a rarity. The majority of the writings presented the extermination of American Indians as either justified or needed in the name of progress. Even when the "noble savage" image was emphasized, underlying self-serving purposes often existed. For example, in 1887, a bill designed to sanction the breakup of tribal lands into parcels to allow individual Indians to farm or ranch their own land was passed as the Dawes Act. Purportedly created to encourage Indians to assimilate into the European American culture, the "noble savage" image was used to summon support for the act. The Dawes Act actually had a long-lasting detrimental impact. It paved the way for swindlers and speculators to grab precious land that had belonged to the Indian tribes, and left many American Indians landless and in poverty (Riding In 2006). The act remained in effect until 1934.

Into the twentieth century, even with the dwindling lands and population of American Indians, the "noble savage" and "evil savage" representations continued to take hold of popular imagination and further shaped Euro-American attitudes and actions toward Indigenous Nations. In fact, with the growth of communication technology, the dichotomous images became even more entrenched through mass media. Motion pictures, in particular, familiarized and vividly brought to life these images to a broader realm of society.

American Indians in Film

Beginning with the silent motion picture era, the American film industry perpetuated the contrasting stereotypes of the noble and evil savage through its portraits of Native peoples. More often than not these films opted to portray American Indians as evil savages (Kilpatrick 1999). Whether savage or noble, however, the Indian characters were frequently played by white actors, especially if the roles were substantial in nature.

Silent films introduced and ingrained into the minds of the public the generic Indian. In describing the generic male Indians found in the films, literature scholar Jacquelyn Kilpatrick writes, "Most male Hollywood Indians of the silent screen and the following era stood flat-footed with their arms folded high on their chests, said very little but could be seen grunting, and had an almost perpetual scowl on their faces" (1999: 34). In contrast, female Indian characters were often shown as non-threatening, submissive, and sexually enticing to the white male gaze.

In the many Western silent films, the hostile and barbaric male Indian character served as a basis for storylines in which the white hero would save the day by vanquishing the villainous Indians. One of the classics to portray American Indians in such a negative light is D.W. Griffith's 1913 silent film *The Battle of Elderbrush Gulch* (see Figure 3.1).

The film follows the experiences of two young girls who are sent off to the Western frontier community of Elderbrush Gulch to live with their uncles. The climax of the film occurs when members of the local Indian tribe attack the homestead on which the girls and their uncles live. In the attack, the Indians are portrayed as vicious. Referred to on-screen as "savages," they are shown killing the fleeing settlers, and in one scene are shown scalping one of them. Despite the Indians' ruthlessness, however, the white settlers are shown in the film as prevailing.

Figure 3.1 Screenshot of *The Battle of Elderbrush Gulch* (1913).

Griffith's film conveys the notion that American Indians are bloodthirsty and subhuman. In contrast, it depicts the white settlers as innocent victims, or heroes who are justified in killing Indians. In fact, at the very beginning of the film, the following words appear to set up this idea: "A tale of the sturdy Americans whose lifework was the conquest of the Great West."

When sound was adopted in the film industry, similar images of American Indians appeared. Even with the added sound, the Indian characters in the films were seldom given the chance to speak for themselves. In fact, silence among the Indian characters was so prevalent that the voice of a narrator was often inserted to speak on behalf of the Indians (Churchill 1998).

When Indians were given an opportunity to talk, the script called for them to speak in a clipped manner, such as in the 1939 film *Scouts to the Rescue.* In her analysis of the fictional American Indian speech that is found often in films, linguist Barbra Meek (2006: 103) describes such speech as "Hollywood Injun English," that borrows from "baby talk" as well as "foreigner talk." Among the few examples of attempts to provide a more sensitive approach to Native portrayals were *Broken Arrow* (1950), starring James Stewart as Tom Jeffords, a former Union Army officer who persuades Apache Indian leader Chief Cochise (played by non-American Indian actor Jeff Chandler) to sign a peace treaty with the US government, and *Apache* (1954), starring Burt Lancaster (a non-American Indian actor) as an Apache warrior waging a one-man war against the US cavalry. Unfortunately, in many of these films, the final message is that Euro-Americans were correct in possessing the American lands and that Native Nations were ill equipped to handle progress. In his critique of *Broken Arrow*, film scholar Frank Manchel (2003: 101) writes:

> It portrayed Indian/white relations in the old West not as they were, but as Euro-Americans wanted them to be. The film's treatment of the Chiricahua Apache culture minimizes the importance of land to their lives; ignores the diseases, devastation, and disruption brought by Euro-Americans to Native American society; and legitimizes the treaty signed between Cochise and the U.S. government.

The coming of the Vietnam War and the social movements of the late 1960s brought a change to Hollywood, in that greater efforts were made to show the inequities committed against American Indians (see Box 3.1). The film *Tell Them Willie Boy Is Here* (1969) is one example of such an attempt.

Box 3.1 Taking a stand against the film industry

Figure 3.2 Sacheen Littlefeather speaks on behalf of Marlon Brando at the 1973 Academy Awards ceremony. Screenshot.

In 1973, actor Marlon Brando was awarded the Oscar® for his performance in the box office hit *The Godfather*. At the Oscar ceremony, instead of Brando appearing to accept the award, American Indian woman Sacheen Littlefeather, dressed in traditional American Indian clothing, walked up to the podium and made a speech informing the viewing audience that because of the film and television industries' mistreatment of Native peoples, Brando would not accept the award. She also tied the Oscar refusal to the protests that were then occurring at Wounded Knee (see discussion of this event later in this chapter). The audience was stunned and news of this action quickly spread across the world. The following is a transcript of her speech:

> Hello. My name is Sacheen Littlefeather. I'm Apache and I'm president of the National Native American Affirmative Image Committee, and I am representing Marlon Brando this evening and he has asked me to tell you in a very long speech, which I cannot share with you presently because of time but I will be glad to share with the press afterwards, that he very regretfully cannot accept this very generous award. And the reasons for this being are the treatment of American Indians today by the film industry, and on television and movie reruns and also with recent happenings at Wounded Knee. I beg at this time that I have not intruded upon this evening and that we will in the future our hearts and our understandings will meet with love and generosity. Thank you on behalf of Marlon Brando.

The event can be viewed via a link provided on the Academy Awards Acceptance Speech Database: http://aaspeechesdb.oscars.org/link/045-1.

The film, based on Harry Wilson Lawton's book *Willie Boy: A Desert Manhunt*, recounts the experiences of a Paiute-Chemehuevi American Indian, Willie Boy (played by Robert Blake), who flees into the southern California desert with his American Indian lover, Lola (played by Katharine Ross), after killing her father in self-defense. The film follows the tortuous escape of the couple as they are hunted down by white vigilantes. Lola ultimately dies from a gunshot wound to the chest, and it is uncertain whether she has committed suicide or whether Willie Boy has killed her to save her from the posse. Willie Boy's life comes to an end by the hands of deputy sheriff Cooper (played by Robert Redford) who has chosen to believe that Willie Boy has killed Lola, and charges ahead of the mob. Cooper returns the body of Willie Boy to the young man's tribe. When the sheriff complains to the deputy sheriff that the vigilantes will be disappointed in not being able to see the dead body, Cooper replies, "Tell them we're all out of souvenirs."

Tell Them Willie Boy Is Here is said to have been not only a statement against the deep-rooted prejudices toward American Indians and the atrocities committed against them but also a commentary on the United States' bloody engagement in the war with Vietnam. In discussing the film, writer Angela Aleiss (2005: 123) quotes the director of the film, Abraham Polonsky, as stating in regard to the story told in the film, "It's fundamental to human history – this terrible thing [genocide] that we do ... Not just because they're Indians, but because this is a general human situation."

Even with efforts to show more multidimensional American Indian characters and storylines, several films that followed *Tell Them Willie Boy Is Here* faltered by still catering to Euro-American perspectives or audience needs. The continued casting of non-American Indians in critical Native roles is one sign of such faltering. Examples of this are the films *The Legend of Walks Far Woman* (1984), starring non-American Indian actress Raquel Welch as a Sioux tribeswoman, and *Dark Wind* (1992), starring non-American Indian actor Lou Diamond Phillips as a Navajo police officer.

Even in the recent blockbuster *Twilight* films, non-Natives were used to play American Indians in the films. Based on the *Twilight* book series, the films follow the romance between a young woman, Bella Swan (played by Kristen Stewart), and a dashing vampire, Edward Cullen (played by Robert Pattinson). Set in Forks, Washington, near the lands of the Quileute Nation, the films do feature American Indian characters. Not all of the Native characters, however, are played by American Indians. The old Hollywood standby of "If they look Native American, that is good enough," appears to have been followed to a certain extent. For example, one of the leading characters, Jacob Black, is a young man from the Quileute community who also vies for the affection of Bella. Having an American Indian play the part of Jacob would have been a perfect opportunity to give an American Indian a leading presence in the film series. The creators of the films opted for Taylor Lautner, however, an actor who is of German, French, and Dutch descent, and who, only after being cast, claimed to have some American Indian ancestry on his mother's side.

The characterization of Jacob and his close tribal friends and family is also of some concern. In the second film installment of the *Twilight* saga, *New Moon* (2009), Bella finds out that Jacob can shape-shift into a werewolf, as can all of his fellow Quileute members. When this shape-shifting occurs, the characters become violent and lose control of their senses. If they are not in werewolf form, Jacob and American Indian friends often are shown walking around shirtless, even when they are sitting at the table for breakfast. Some have criticized these depictions. First, they say that the werewolf transformations and the shirtless appearances reinforce the old "uncivilized," "one with nature," and "savage" stereotypes tied to Native peoples. While the director of *New Moon* perhaps went overboard by continuously showing the young American Indian men as shirtless, and the lack of self-control the men exhibit when they shape-shift into werewolves does revive the stereotype that American Indian men are inherently violent, it should be pointed out that the link between wolves and the Quileute people is nothing new. In its cultural history section (https://quileutenation.org/history), the official Quileute Nation website states that ancient legend has it that the Quileute people were transformed from wolves into people.

Some have even applauded the portrayals of the American Indians in the *Twilight* movies, including the actors and actresses who fill the roles of the Quileute tribe. In his Reuters article, reporter Alex Dobuzinskis (2010) notes that what *Twilight* was able to do that many films failed to do before was basically to treat American Indian teenagers like normal kids, kids who wear jeans, order pizza, and go to school, with "no leather loincloths, no hair feathers, no dancing around campfires, no tales of woe on reservations." American Indian actor Chaske Spencer, who plays pack leader Sam Uley, is quoted in Dobuzinskis's article as saying he believes *Twilight* squashes stereotypes, and allows American Indian actors to play characters who are three-dimensional and possess quick wits and generous spirits. He notes that many times indigenous people are forced into "leathered and feathered" roles, which are stereotypical "cowboy and Indian" parts in movies about the Old West.

In a move to give some depth to the stereotypical "cowboy and Indian" dynamic, Johnny Depp jumped at the chance to play Tonto in *The Lone Ranger* (2013). In the film Depp plays the sidekick to John Reid/The Lone Ranger (played by Armie Hammer). Prior to shooting the film, Depp said he wanted to reimagine the role of Tonto, which had been criticized as being racist for decades. In the film, he wears white and black war paint and a fierce ebony eagle as a part of his headdress. Even though the story is told through Tonto's eyes with him as the hero in many scenes, allegations of racism persisted. For example, Tonto still spoke in broken English and his garb was not traditional to any particular tribe, especially the Comanche that he was supposed to represent (Rothman 2013).

One film that succeeds in presenting more accurate American Indian depictions and offers sympathetic portrayals is the Academy Award-winning 1990 film *Dances With Wolves*. The film is about an army lieutenant, John J. Dunbar (played by Kevin Costner), who is assigned to a deserted military outpost in the West. Dunbar lives there alone, but is harassed by members of a Sioux tribe. Eventually Dunbar decides to confront the neighboring tribe members. As he is walking to their location, he happens upon a white woman (played by Mary McDonnell) who is dressed in Sioux Indian dress and is close to dying after having slit her wrists and legs. Dunbar carries her to the tribe and finds out that the woman, named Stands With A Fist, had just lost her Indian husband and was in mourning. He further discovers that the Sioux tribe raised the woman after Pawnee Indians killed her parents.

Through Stands With A Fist, Dunbar befriends the Sioux tribe and adopts many of its cultural ways. After saving the tribe's women and children from a Pawnee attack, Dunbar, who by now is called Dances With Wolves, is accepted into the tribe and given permission to marry Stands With A Fist. After his marriage, through a series of events, Dunbar is captured by army troops but is eventually rescued by members of the Sioux tribe. He then leaves with the tribe to move further north. After the tribe reaches its new settlement location, however, he announces that he and Stands With A Fist must move on so that that his presence does not put the tribe at further risk. In one of the more poignant scenes of the film, as Dunbar and Stands With A Fist ride off on their horse, a young member of the Sioux tribe, Wind In His Hair (played by American Indian actor Rodney A. Grant), who had become close to Dunbar after initially being his foe, cries out in the Lakota language that Dances With Wolves will always be his friend.

Deemed as a film of historical and cultural importance, *Dances With Wolves* was heralded and has been named as a film that should be included in the Library of Congress's National Film Registry. It is true that the producers of the film took efforts to portray the Sioux tribe's customs, clothing, and language in an accurate manner. Nevertheless, critics have charged that the film reinforces the demarcation between good and bad American Indians by showing the Sioux Indians as good and the Pawnee Indians as bad (Jojola 2003: 17).

Critics have also charged that films such as *Dances With Wolves* and *Tell Them Willie Boy Is Here*, although valiantly attempting to portray Native peoples in a more authentic and complex manner, still were told from a Euro-American perspective. They reflected the efforts of white Americans trying to come to terms with their own historical actions against American Indians. The same can be said of the 1995 Disney animated film, *Pocahontas*.

Pocahontas is based on an historical American Indian woman and follows her developing relationship with English explorer John Smith. The film begins by introducing Pocahontas as the daughter of the Chief of the Powhatan tribe who is supposed to marry, against her wishes, one of her father's strongest warriors. It then moves to tell the story of her encounter with John Smith and their ensuing love for each other. Pocahontas teaches Smith the language and traditions of her people, and her appreciation for nature. When Smith is mistakenly sentenced to death for the murder of the warrior whom Pocahontas was to marry, she comes to his rescue by throwing herself upon his body as the executioner is about to approach him with a hatchet.

In her critique of *Pocahontas*, anthropology professor Pauline Turner Strong (2003) points out that the filmmakers of *Pocahontas* did consult with Native peoples and American Indian scholars in making the film, but ultimately they relied more heavily on their own views and their own beliefs of what should be reflected in the film. While trying to construct a more compassionate picture of American Indians and their encounters with European explorers, the film still relies on the ever-persistent "noble savage" imagery. The character of Pocahontas conveys this imagery by serving as an intermediary between her people and the English explorers, and even by being willing to sacrifice her life to save the life of her love, John Smith. Furthermore, the filmmakers rely on Disney's formula of creating a Barbie-doll type of princess figure for the Pocahontas character. With a light complexion, hourglass figure, and large breasts, the Pocahontas that is presented to moviegoers is a sexualized and seductive character. Her sexuality is creatively heightened in scenes during which Pocahontas and Smith are frolicking together in nature and embracing each other in a passionate kiss. In essence, the filmmakers provided Pocahontas with traits that a mainstream, mainly Euro-American, audience would find palatable, or even enticing.

As demonstrated by *Pocahontas*, *Dances With Wolves*, and *Tell Them Willie Boy Is Here*, what was needed in these films was the incorporation of a larger degree of Native perspectives. Filmmakers need to pay more attention to creative voices from the Native communities. In 1998, that need was filled to a certain extent by the movie *Smoke Signals*. The film was the first to be directed, written, and co-produced by American Indians (Cobb 2003). Director Chris Eyre, from the Cheyenne community, and writer Sherman Alexie, from the Coeur d'Alene community, took great pains to create a film that would break down American Indian stereotypes by calling attention to those stereotypes through humor, while also telling a poignant story from a Native perspective.

Smoke Signals follows the journey of two American Indian friends, Thomas Builds-the-Fire (played by American Indian actor Evan Adams) and Victor Joseph (played by American Indian actor Adam Beach). The friends travel from their home on the Coeur d'Alene reservation in Idaho to Phoenix, Arizona, to pick up the ashes of Victor's recently deceased alcoholic and abusive father who had abandoned Victor at an early age. During their travel, Victor learns more about his father through Thomas and through a female friend of Victor's father whom they meet in Phoenix. In the end, Victor is able to deal with the hatred he had felt toward his father and make peace.

Although *Smoke Signals* was a small budget film without star billing, it was endorsed by the Sundance Institute and was able to secure a distribution deal with Miramax. As the first American Indian feature-length film to be made that presented Native peoples in leading roles, it led the way for other American Indian directors and actors to find success, or at least hope for success, in the commercial film industry. More recently, filmmakers such as transgender and Native filmmaker Sydney Freeland and her film *Drunktown's Finest* (2016) are finding their way to screens via showcases such as Sundance's Native and Indigenous program and the American Indian Film Festival. Still, these examples of American Indians creating commercial content for widespread distribution are rare in film and even rarer in the entertainment television industry.

American Indians in Entertainment Television

As with the film industry's success in producing films with an American Western theme, with the introduction of television one of the more popular genres to hit the airwaves was also Westerns. Among the first shows to present an American Indian character was the popular show *The Lone Ranger* (1949–1957). The series began with Clayton Moore starring as the masked Texas Ranger and Jay Silverheels (a Canadian Mohawk Indian) playing the Lone Ranger's Native sidekick, Tonto. Throughout the various adventures that the Lone Ranger and Tonto experienced, Tonto was always depicted as a faithful follower. Although in several episodes Tonto does rescue the Lone Ranger, for the most part he was shown in the program as being not quite as skilled or intelligent as his heroic mentor and he spoke in broken English.

Following *The Lone Ranger*, Native peoples appearing as sidekicks and in stereotypic ways continued to be the norm in television. In other Western television, shows such as *Gunsmoke*, which ran from 1955 to 1975, and *Bonanza*, which aired from 1959 to 1973, American Indians were only shown as secondary characters and were normally cast in enemy roles, as marauding Indians threatening the white main characters (Larson 2006).

During the 1960s and 1970s, two television programs did feature major characters of Native Nations heritage. The first program, *Hawk* (1966), starred Burt Reynolds (an actor of Cherokee ancestry) as a half-Iroquois New York City police officer, and the second, *Nakia* (1974), starred Robert Forster (a non-American Indian actor) as a Navajo deputy sheriff. Both shows were short-lived due to poor ratings. Following the two programs' failure, it would not be until the 1990s that the networks would take another chance on presenting American Indian characters in leading roles.

In 1993, actor Chuck Norris, who is part Cherokee, played Cordell Walker, a Texas Ranger, in the television action drama show, *Walker, Texas Ranger* (1993–2001). The character of Walker was also part American Indian. The show essentially followed Walker's efforts to carry out criminal investigations with his partner, Jimmy Trivette (played by Clarence Gilyard). Straight-laced, smart, and skilled in the martial arts, Walker's character could be considered as quite positive. *Walker, Texas Ranger* is, so far, the only long-running successful series to have featured a Native character in the leading role, although the character was not full American Indian. Native characters are far more likely to appear in supporting roles.

The Alaska-set comedy drama *Northern Exposure* (1990–1995) was one program that presented a number of American Indian characters. The show followed the experiences of a fresh-out-of-medical-school New York City doctor, Dr. Joel Fleischman (played by Rob Morrow), who is forced to take up practice in a small Alaskan town for financial reasons. Several prominent Native characters were featured in the show, all played by actors of American Indian descent, including Fleishman's receptionist, Marilyn Whirlwind (played by Elaine Miles); the local medicine man, Leonard

Quinhagak (played by Graham Greene); and the creative moviemaker, Ed Chigliak (played by Darren E. Burrows). These characters, presented as representing the Tlingit culture, were provided with nonstereotypical, varied traits. Nevertheless, certain criticisms of the show did arise. For example, although the character of Marilyn was intelligent and perceptive, some charged that her never-changing stoic expression reinforced the stereotype of Native peoples as unemotional. Furthermore, although producers of the show did attempt to represent the American Indian Tlingit culture in a fairly accurate manner, several episodes were made in which tribal traditions and clothing were misrepresented (Taylor 1996). In one episode in particular, Marilyn performs a Native dance not characteristic of the Tlingit culture while wearing a traditional dress and accessories from the Cayuse-Nez Perce culture, the culture from which the actress playing Marilyn actually originated.

The criticism that *Northern Exposure* came under was minimal in comparison to the criticism launched against *Dr. Quinn, Medicine Woman* (1993–1998). The show was about a white female doctor of prominent upbringing, Dr. Michaela Quinn (played by Jane Seymour), who sets up practice in a small town in Colorado during the 1860s, and ends up falling in love with a rugged mountaineer, Byron Sully (played by Joe Lando). While the show explored many social issues involving gender, the show was criticized for not examining the plight of American Indians during that time period. Although the producers attempted to show the Cheyenne people that were presented in the program in an accurate manner in terms of clothing and language, critics charged that they were essentially represented in a highly docile manner. The running message in the show was that American Indians were resigned to their fate and that the course of history involving the Native peoples was inevitable. In describing the show, anthropology professor S. Elizabeth Bird (1996: 248) writes,

> The show frequently opens with a scene in the idyllic Cheyenne village, where the inhabitants wander to and fro wearing benign expressions of content. A few have names but no real personalities, and no story lines focus on them directly. Rather, they function as plot devices to allow Michaela and Sully to make a point. Indeed, Dr. Quinn illustrates perfectly the point that the Indian of popular culture is a White creation that meets White needs.

Taking a similarly critical stance on the show, Ted Jojola has characterized *Dr. Quinn, Medicine Woman* as "an awful, awful apologist's series done in a historical revisionist tradition" (2003: 19).

Since the airing of *Dr. Quinn, Medicine Woman*, for the most part the number of American Indian characters represented in television programs has been negligible. Moreover, when they have been presented in bit parts, they have been portrayed either as dysfunctional (e.g., poor, lazy, alcoholics) or as superstitious and mystical (Stroman and Dates 2008). The "Other" or "outsider" image associated with indigenous people has been strengthened in these portrayals. It is as if the strides in portrayals that were made in the 1990s have been sliding backward.

The short-lived television series *Men in Trees* (2006–2008) had an opportunity to highlight American Indians and present them in a more diverse and well-rounded fashion. The series, however, failed to do so. *Men in Trees* followed the exploits of relationship coach and radio host Marin Frist (played by Anne Heche) who leaves her exciting life in New York City for a simpler one in the fictional small town of Elmo, Alaska. Although set in Alaska, the show failed, in contrast to the efforts of *Northern Exposure*, to substantively feature American Indians. One of the main characters, Sara Jackson, was supposedly an American Indian single mother working at the town bar that Marin frequented. The character, however, was not key in comparison to the other characters, and was played by Suleka Mathew, who is of Asian Indian lineage.

Hell on Wheels (2011–2016), an A&E Western drama series about the construction of the Transcontinental Railroad in the mid-1800s, had as one of its subplots a story that featured Joseph Black Moon (played by Eddie Spears, a member of the Lower Brulé Sioux Tribe), the son of a Cheyenne chief who converts to Christianity. The subplot involved Black Moon helping the man who converted him, the Reverend Nathaniel Cole (played by Tom Noonan), set up a church tent in a town-like encampment called Hell on Wheels. As part of the subplot, Black Moon becomes romantically involved with the preacher's daughter, but the romance is short-lived, as is the character of Black Moon. By the end of season 2, Black Moon is rejected by his love interest, who says that people would never accept their interracial relationship, and then kills Reverend Cole. Black Moon steps into the woods to rediscover his Cheyenne roots, never to be seen again in the series.

Another program set in contemporary times is the crime drama series *Longmire*. The series began on A&E in 2012 until it was canceled in 2014 and then picked up by Netflix in 2015. The program revolves around Sheriff Longmire (white actor Robert Taylor) fighting crime in a small county in Wyoming. In its premiere episode, it becomes clear that tensions exist between the predominantly white county residents and the American Indians living in a neighboring Cheyenne reservation. In that episode, Sheriff Longmire is investigating a murder and, suspecting the murderers might be living on the reservation, heads to the reservation with his deputy Victoria "Vic" Moretti (Katie Sackhoff). Longmire tells Moretti who he intends to interview and the following exchange between the two ensues:

MORETTI: And you think the tribal police are going to help us do that.

LONGMIRE: I'd like to think that if there's a murder involved they'll put aside petty personal differences and help us find a killer.

MORETTI: They may not think that you throwing their police chief in prison is exactly petty.

LONGMIRE: He is the one to decide to run the extortion racket, not me.

Longmire then pulls his Sheriff's truck up to the entrance of the reservation only to be blocked by the Cheyenne police. As Longmire exits his vehicle, one of the tribal police, Mathias, steps up to Longmire and punches him.

LONGMIRE: You said you would try to knock me out the next time you saw me. You really keep your word did [*sic*] you Mathias.

MATHIAS: What do you want?

LONGMIRE: I want to speak to some people here who live on the res.

MATHIAS: You don't get it. You don't have authority here. Those are the treaty rules. And I know how important treaties are to you whites.

LONGMIRE: I know you're pissed at me. There's been a murder.

The series shows the still existing race-based conflicts involving the community and does attempt to show the challenges that the American Indian community faces. Through characters such as Longmire's long-time friend and confidante Henry Sanding Bear (played by American Indian Lou Diamond Phillips), the audience is exposed to American Indians who break away from stereotypes associated with Native people. Standing Bear is a businessman who lives a progressive lifestyle, while also taking pride in his Cheyenne heritage. At the same time, however, certain reinforcements of long-running representations of American Indians persist. The American Indians featured in the

Figure 3.3 Longmire and Henry Standing Bear together from the Netflix series *Longmire* (2012–). Screenshot.

program tend to be associated in some way with the reservation and several of the episodes implicate them in crime, either as perpetrators or as victims. Moreover, the star character of the program, Longmire, is a powerful white man. Although Henry Standing Bear's character is charming, he is essentially Longmire's crime-fighting sidekick (Figure 3.3). Here is a thought to consider: If American Indian actor Lou Diamond Phillips instead of white actor Robert Taylor had played Longmire, would the series have survived this long?

In commercial television, as demonstrated by *Longmire*, it is a consistent pattern that if American Indians are represented, they are secondary to white characters. The television realm where we find exceptions to this is on public television. An example is the 2009 documentary television series entitled *We Shall Remain*. The five-part series covered the major historical events involving Native Nations that took place from the 1600s to the 1900s and told the stories from American Indian perspectives. The project included Native and non-Native filmmakers, actors, as well as scholars, and was hailed as comprehensive and fair. As part of Public Broadcasting System's American Experience initiative, the efforts and care put into presenting more accurate depictions of American Indians and their experiences through this documentary perhaps comes as no surprise. Unfortunately, commercial television, as earlier discussed, has not shown similar efforts.

This privileging of Whites over American Indians is not unique to television entertainment programming but is also reflected in television advertisements. For example, in one study (Li-Vollmer 2002) examining commercials that aired during children's television shows, the researcher found that a majority of the characters in the commercials were white, and they were often in the position of important roles (i.e., main speaker, initiator of action). American Indians were dramatically under-represented and were often lost in the background among a group of other children. In another study (Mastro and Stern 2003) that examined minority representation in advertisements appearing during prime-time broadcast network television programming, the researchers found that of the 2,290 speaking characters they analyzed, only a mere 0.4 percent of the characters were Native people, and these characters most often were seen in advertisements for large retail stores such as Wal-Mart.

Exacerbating this lack of substantive representation of American Indians in television advertisements are the still existing stereotypical images of Native people that are used to advertise products in general. From the Indian maiden image on Land O-Lakes products to the knife-wielding Indian warrior of Ken Jo markets, the images that draw on longstanding stereotypes have the effect of promoting a "symbolic annihilation" of real American Indians (Sanchez 2012). In essence, the stereotypes become the reality.

The trend of severe lack of representation of American Indians in entertainment television and advertising is apparent in the news media as well. Native people tend to appear in the news only during times of conflict, and are virtually absent at other times.

Representations of American Indians in the News

With the introduction of the printing press in the 1400s, the images that European colonizers had of North American Indians were widely disseminated in Europe (Riding In 2006). Early Spanish explorers associated cannibalism, promiscuity, immorality, and child-like naivety with the Indians. Although the notion of cannibalism was eventually abandoned, the English settlers who followed the Spanish picked up many of the same imageries and reflected them in their publications.

Benjamin Harris, the editor of the first newspaper to be established in the American colonies, is said to have used the dichotomous "good" versus "bad" Indian categories in his Boston publication *Publick Occurrences, Both Forreign and Domestick* (Weston and Coward 1997). In writing about American Indians in 1690, Harris refers to those Indians who were open to the colonists' ideas and Christian ways as the "good" Indians, while those who resisted colonist influences as the "bad" Indians. The editor warned colonists to be wary of the "bad" Indians and not fall victim to their depraved behaviors. Harris went as far as to blame, without proof, the disappearance of two children from the Boston area on the local American Indians.

From the days of Harris's publication up until the twentieth century, the "captivity narrative" became prevalent in the popular press (Bird 1999: 61). Although often unsubstantiated, tales of women and children being captured and despoiled by crazed Indians often filled the pages of newspapers. Such stories frequently accompanied descriptions of the battles between the American Indian tribes and the Euro-American settlers. Newspaper articles, in reporting the battles, favored the settlers and portrayed the Indians in highly negative and stereotypical terms. In an 1859 news item, the editor of the *New York Tribune*, Horace Greeley, described American Indians as "slave[s] of appetite and sloth, never emancipated from the tyranny of one animal passion save by the more ravenous demands of another" (Weston and Coward 1997: 28). Battle victories by the US Army were hailed, while battles won by the Native peoples were disparaged. When cavalries were defeated, the press would frequently exaggerate the number of American Indians who fought in the battle and would characterize the loss as a "massacre" (Harjo 2003). Such rhetoric was emblematic of newspaper writings during that period in US history. As media researcher Charles Lewis (2011: 50) writes, "newspapers – written by whites for whites – were key promoters of manifest destiny, a nationalistic and racial ideological process that primarily emerged in the United States of the 1840s and 1850s" (see Box 3.2).

Toward the end of the 1800s, as military defeats forced American Indians to relocate to reservations or assimilate, the number of Native Nations began to dwindle. If any stories were provided about American Indians during this time period, the focus was on the dying Native peoples and cultures. The coverage tended to be superficial, with no in-depth analysis of why the people and traditions were vanishing (Harjo 2003). It was not until World War I that more positive stories regarding American Indians began to surface. The valuable service provided by Native peoples in the war effort was the impetus for such coverage. Ironically, both the noble savage image and the evil savage image were used in the press stories. Descriptions of Indians as brave, loyal, and patriotic ran alongside descriptions of Indians as cunning and deadly in war battles. With such articles being published, calls to provide American Indians with US citizenship grew and in 1924 the US Congress granted citizenship to all Native peoples born within the United States.

Box 3.2 An opposing voice: *Cherokee Phoenix*

In 1828, the first American Indian newspaper, *Cherokee Phoenix*, was introduced in the United States. It was printed in both English and in the Cherokee language. Its purpose was to inform the Cherokee people of the US government's decisions that were impacting on them, especially the decisions to move Native tribes further west. It was a vehicle by which Cherokee communities could communicate and unite. Its founding editor, Elias Boudinot, is said to have chosen the name *Cherokee Phoenix* after the mythical bird that emerged from the ashes of a burning fire into new life.

Cherokee Phoenix later changed its name to *Cherokee Phoenix and Indians' Advocate* and broadened its scope of coverage to include challenges and issues facing all American Indians. After internal conflicts in the editorial positions being taken in the paper, Boudinot resigned as editor in 1832 and was replaced by Elija Hicks. Under Hicks's direction, the paper became more vocal against the actions of the US federal government and gave American Indians a voice in opposing their forced removal and assimilation.

Because of financial difficulties and pressures from the federal government, *Cherokee Phoenix and Indians' Advocate* was closed in 1834. The paper, however, was later revived and is now called by its original name, *Cherokee Phoenix*. It and other Native papers, such as the *Navajo Times*, *The Seminole Tribune*, and the *Tribal Observer*, all have an online presence. The *Cherokee Phoenix* (www .cherokeephoenix.org) covers the happenings of the Cherokee Nation, including how well their sports teams are performing and the outreach programs that exist for the Cherokee people. It also includes links to hard-hitting stories dealing with such important issues as poverty and health.

———————————

Source: Brannon (2005).

Heroic stories of American Indians engaged in battle on behalf of the United States became even more prevalent during World War II. Again, however, the stories tended to be couched in familiar stereotypical terms. For example, in an *Arizona Republic* article, the story begins, "Hang onto your scalps, Hitler, Hirohito, and Mussolini, for twenty-nine red-blooded young Americans are on the warpath" (Weston 1996: 88). Rather than simply presenting these soldiers as brave American men, the article chose to frame the men in Hollywood-inspired stereotypes of Native peoples by the usage of the terms "scalps," "red-blooded," and "warpath."

One of the more popular war-related topics to be touched upon in the World War II news stories pertained to the "code talkers" or the American Indian servicemen who effectively used their native language to communicate secret messages for the military. While the stories praised the American Indians for the contributions, journalism professor Mary Ann Weston has pointed out that these stories also inadvertently placed a distance between American Indians and other Americans. She writes:

> On the one hand, Indians such as the Navajo code talkers were portrayed positively as making unique contributions to the Allied victory. But a more subtle point made by the stories was that these Indians were a people apart, so removed from mainstream civilization that few outside their group even recognized their language. Thus, Indians were portrayed as both a part of mainstream America (aiding the war effort) and a separate, alien group (speaking an unknown language) simultaneously. (Weston 1996: 94)

Following World War II and the brief period of positive news coverage of American Indians, the press turned toward stories regarding efforts to terminate federal funding and services to Native peoples. Calls for termination were made under the guise of providing emancipation to American Indians and showed a complete disregard for the treaties that had been made between the US government and Native peoples (Weston 1996). In hopes of encouraging termination and the eventual closure of reservations, the Bureau of Indian Affairs paid American Indians to move out of their reservations and into cities. Those who chose to move were assisted in finding jobs and housing. Those journalists who supported the relocation program often relied on government officials as sources and painted the program as successful. Those who did not support the program criticized the plan while depicting American Indians as hopeless victims left to fend for themselves. Whether or not they were written in support of the program, the news stories tended to provide little agency to the indigenous peoples that were being affected. They were portrayed as lost, child-like souls who needed some form of guidance.

In the late 1960s, the press became more sensitive to racial issues and its failure to provide them with adequate coverage. Inspired by the Kerner Commission report that urged fairer coverage of matters involving African Americans, which will be discussed in Chapter 4, news media personnel endeavored to use the Commission's recommendations in their coverage of American Indians as well (Weston 1996). Regardless of these efforts, reliance on old stereotypes of American Indians still remained. In particular, in the 1960s and 1970s, as environmental concerns grew, the "noble savage" image steadily found its way into news stories to discuss how the environment should be protected and maintained.

As activism among Native Nations grew in the late 1960s with the establishment of the American Indian Movement (AIM) in 1968, the "savage Indian" imagery also showed a presence in the news stories. One such case was in the coverage of the 1969–1971 takeover of Alcatraz Island in San Francisco Bay by 89 American Indians. The activists took over the island, claiming that the land had originally belonged to American Indians, and offered to buy the land back with glass beads and red cloth (Larson 2006). From the beginning, the event was actually planned as a way to gain publicity for the rights of American Indians. Although it was a major event, the majority of the coverage was local, with scant coverage by the national press. Initially, the coverage was sympathetic in tone, with the novelty of American Indian activism emphasized (Smith and Warrior 1996). As the months passed and as the activists became more aggressive in their tactics, the press turned against them and utilized the "savage" American Indian imagery. Such coverage continued until federal marshals moved in on June 11, 1971, to remove the last remaining activists.

Another incident that illustrates the use of the "savage Native" imagery by the press with regard to American Indian activists is the 1973 Wounded Knee takeover. Members of AIM took over a number of buildings at the Wounded Knee settlement on the Pine Ridge Sioux reservation. The group wanted to call attention to the dismal living conditions at the reservation and to seek the dismissal of the leader of the tribal government who they claimed was corrupt. In addition to the tribal police, federal marshals and FBI agents surrounded the buildings. In the ensuing clashes between the federal agents and activists, two Wounded Knee Indians were killed and one federal marshal was seriously injured. The takeover lasted for a few months before the activists stood down after lengthy negotiations.

The coverage of Wounded Knee was at first sympathetic with the "heroic noble Indian" imagery often used. As time went on, however, the imagery became negative. In her analysis of the news coverage of Wounded Knee, journalism professor Mary Ann Weston found, for example, that the

Chicago Tribune referred to the activists as "militant Indians," "outlaws," and "gun-toting and gun-firing criminals" (Weston 1996: 145). Such representations were also reflected in the local press. In summarizing press coverage of the incident, Weston writes that the stories "left a cumulative image of AIM as outsiders, armed interlopers who had descended on a peaceful village and dispossessed the residents, upsetting the tranquility and economy of the region. They were depicted, in the parlance of Western movies, as 'renegade' or 'hostile' Indians who had attacked the 'pacified' village" (Weston 1996: 147).

Since the 1970s, stories regarding American Indians have appeared in the press infrequently. When they do appear, reminiscent of the coverage of the 1960s and 1970s, the stories tend to be about conflict situations between non-Native and Native government or corporate officials. Studies that have examined how these conflicts have been covered have found that they tend to lend credence to the stances of the non-Natives, rather than the Indigenous Americans. For example, one study analyzed how the mainstream newspapers in Minnesota and Wisconsin covered the Wisconsin government's challenge of the spearfishing rights of the Anishinabe people during 1996 (Perkins and Starosta 2001). In their examination, the researchers found that the news articles often belittled the significance of the Anishinabe people by presenting or highlighting accounts from the viewpoints of Wisconsin state officials and those in the tourism industry. Furthermore, while the names of state officials appeared in the headlines of the news articles, the names of the major Anishinabe tribal leaders did not appear. In fact, when the tribal leaders were mentioned within the news stories, the reporters failed to provide them with their official titles, thus denying them a certain form of credibility.

Similar coverage was found in another study that examined Minnesota's local mainstream press coverage of its state's attempt to expand government involvement in the casino gaming industry in direct competition with the American Indian gaming operations. In his critical analysis of articles appearing in two major newspapers in Minnesota, *Minneapolis Star Tribune* and the *St. Paul Pioneer Press*, professor of cultural and rhetorical studies Martin Lang found that the papers focused on the legislative proceedings and failed to illuminate the negative impact, both economically and socially, that the state-gaming expansion would have on Minnesota's Native communities. He concludes that the journalistic norms of objectivity and sourcing actually led to the generation of news stories that "rendered American Indian interests invisible and effectively silenced the people themselves" (Lang 2015: 96).

Thus, in considering press coverage of Native people, it can be seen that they have tended to be entirely dismissed or have been covered in such ways that make them the "Other." In the portrayals that are presented to the public, they are either the noble savage or child of earth who serve as reminders of the care that must be taken in protecting the earth, or the "savage" Indian who is willing to break the law to attain certain goals. The Native American Journalists Association has closely monitored the visuals and wording used in mainstream news media when covering events and issues related to American Indians and has criticized those that hark back to stereotypical notions. The association has also provided advice on how the press can avoid writings and images that might evoke stereotypes. Indigenous Nations have also actively engaged in countering the negative images and messages on new media platforms.

American Indians and New Media

The Internet offers a place for American Indians to educate and inform the general public, and a place to gather and share as a group. Many Native Nations have set up websites to provide a more diverse selection of images and cultural information about their people. What is key in these efforts is their endeavor to tell their stories through their own perspectives. By doing so, they have achieved a form of empowerment.

Some well-regarded sites include the following:

- *Native Village* – http://www.nativevillage.org: An award-winning website created for youth, families, educators, and others interested in learning more about the diverse cultures of Native people. Each month a four-volume publication is posted, filled with articles of relevance to American Indians. The site also offers a separate youth forum, run by the International Council of Thirteen Indigenous Grandmothers, who have as their mission to nurture, educate, and train their children, and links to resources for American Indians or those interested in learning more about Indigenous peoples.
- *NativeWeb* – http://www.nativeweb.org: An international, nonprofit, educational organization that provides online resources about Indigenous Nations, peoples, and organizations around the world. The site offers news stories, links to hosted websites, and information about jobs, Native law and legal issues, and events. Its founder David Cole passed away in 2015, but the site still remains as an important resource center.
- *Oneida Indian Nation* – http://oneidaindiannation.com: The Oneida Indian Nation, located in central New York, hosts this site, which includes information on cultural events, tribal history, and community stories. The site also offers career links, financial advice, and health outreach, as the Oneida Indian Nation is also a major community employer.
- *Kumeyaay.com* – http://kumeyaay.com: Kumeyaay.com is an interesting example of a tribal news blog produced by tribal members for the tribal community. The Kumeyaay Nation is a branch of the Native Yuman Indians of North America, who primarily reside in southern California and Baja. The site posts articles from local and national news media that is of relevance to the tribal community.
- *Indianz.com* – http://www.indianz.com: Provides news, information, and entertainment from American Indian perspectives. It offers a mix of original content, on topics including legislation, health, and politics, and a daily summary of reporting by other news media on topics of interest to a Native audience. Indianz.com is based on the Winnebago Reservation in Nebraska.

Besides websites, American Indian organizations have increasingly used social media to reach out to their communities, especially the younger generation who have shown a preference for using smartphones to access information and for entertainment. For example, the American Indian Relief Council that was set up to help American Indians living in the Northern Plains has not only a website, but a Facebook page and Twitter account. American Radio Network, dedicated to giving Native voices an opportunity to reach out to tribal communities and the general public through its affiliated reservation-based stations and top urban market stations, also has a Facebook page and a Twitter account. It also distributes a podcast called Native America Calling that covers a variety of subject matters including hard-hitting political issues and entertainment through its call-in program format. Impromptu media have also been formed when tribal nations have found a need to do so. As an example, when the residents of the Standing Rock Sioux reservation organized protests against the nearby construction of the Dakota Access oil pipeline in 2016, organizers formed a radio broadcast station on 87.9 FM called Spirit Resistance Radio. Protesters also took to social media to voice their opposition by using such hashtags as #NODAPL, #NoDakotaAccess, and #ReZpectOurWater.

Concluding Remarks

In her book on hate crimes against American Indians, criminology and justice professor Barbara Perry asserts that the verbal insults and threats that Native peoples must endure are widespread and are often not reflected in federal hate crime statistics (Perry 2008). Through her interviews with American Indians from varying backgrounds, she found that many had similar stories to share in terms of the discrimination they have faced. For example, several working in the service industry reported that sometimes clients make it clear to them that they do not want to deal with an American Indian, often choosing to wait for another attendant. One Arizona female that Perry interviewed even spoke of an experience where she heard the client state, "I really don't want to be served by the Indian" (Perry 2008: 2–3).

It is an assumption that media images of American Indians have played a part in cases of discrimination. This possibility is strong, given the existing evidence that exposure to stereotypical mass media images of American Indians do correlate with negative beliefs regarding Native peoples. In one study, for example, individual perceptions of television representations of American Indians were found to be predictors of engagement in stereotyping (Tan, Fujioka, and Lucht 1997). Thus, a serious need exists to address media-disseminated stereotypes of American Indians.

As indicated in this chapter, certain efforts have already been made to improve mass media representations of American Indians. Much of this has been thanks to various American Indian associations. Many have not only sought to change mass media images, but also to eradicate other forms of representation. One of these efforts has been to eliminate some of the sports team and mascot names that Native peoples have found to be offensive. Such teams as the "Washington Redskins," the "Kansas City Chiefs," and the "Atlanta Braves" still exist, and many fans who attend the teams' games still don stereotypical "American Indian outfits" and perform the "tomahawk chop." In discussing what Indigenous people find offensive about these appropriations, communication researcher Jackson Miller writes, "'It's not so much the fact that a team is named after a race of people or the color of that people's skin'; instead, what protesters find offensive are 'the sham rituals and ridiculous impersonations that become a part of those rituals'" (Miller 1999: 189). Because of the greater ethnic sensitivity that American Indian associations have been able to nurture among the mainstream press and the public, however, many college and high schools have changed the names of their teams and mascots to less offensive ones. For instance, Miami University in Oxford, Ohio, changed its mascot from the Redskins to the RedHawks in 1997 (Steinberg 2009).

Tribal communities have also been able to counter some of the negative imagery through their own media creations. Several radio stations, most licensed to tribal governments, have been successful in producing programs not only in English but also in Native languages. Established in 2002, *SAY* magazine, a Native owned and operated business, currently is the largest lifestyle magazine for Native peoples, and in 2008 was honored with the award for General Excellence by the Native American Journalists Association. *Native Peoples* magazine, founded in 1987, is devoted to providing compelling stories on Native culture and art. Red Nation Film Festival showcases the works of American Indian filmmakers and actors/actresses in its annual film festival that is held every year during the month of November as part of American Indian Heritage Month. Red Nation Television Network provides original programming featuring American Indian actors, producers, musicians, and on-air personalities through its online platform. They characterize themselves as "The Authentic Voice of American Indian & Indigenous Media" (http://rednationtv.com).

Reflection Questions and Thoughts to Consider

1. As discussed in this chapter, several American Indian groups have attempted to convince sports teams to discontinue the use of the names of Indigenous peoples as names of their teams or mascots (e.g., Redskins, Braves, etc.). What is your stance on this? Do you also believe such names should be changed?

2. Think of the films and television shows you have viewed over this last year. How many American Indian characters do you recall that were featured in them? What does this tell you about the current state of affairs?

3. American Indians have also been featured as superheroes in comic book-inspired feature films. For example, the 2014 *X-Men: Days of Future Past* included the superhero Warpath (played by Booboo Stewart, who has Blackfoot ancestry). If you were asked to write a brief one-page essay on the meanings that the character's depiction in the film might be conveying to audiences regarding American Indians, what would you write?

4. American Indian activist groups have taken different measures to have their needs known to the US federal and state governments, such as holding marches and protest gatherings. They have been increasingly utilizing the Internet to tie activists together and spread their word to non-Indigenous peoples. Take a look at the website of the International Indian Treaty Council (www.iitc.org), a nongovernmental organization whose goal is to support grassroots Indigenous peoples in their fight against injustices committed against them. Founded in 1974, the organization is recognized by the United Nations Economic and Social Council. How effective do you think their website is in terms of drawing people together and building awareness of issues impacting on Indigenous peoples?

References

Aleiss, Angela. 2005. *Making the White Man's Indian: Native Americans and Hollywood Movies.* Westport, CT: Praeger.

Bird, S. Elizabeth. 1996. "Not My Fantasy: The Persistence of the Indian Imagery in Dr. Quinn Medicine Woman." In *Dressing in Feathers: The Construction of the Indian in American Popular Culture*, edited by S. Elizabeth Bird, 245–262. Boulder, CO: Westview Press.

Bird, Elizabeth. 1999. "Gendered Construction of the American Indian in Popular Media." *Journal of Communication* 49(3): 61–83.

Brannon, Frank. 2005. *Cherokee Phoenix, Advent of a Newspaper: The Print Shop of the Cherokee Nation, 1828–1834.* Tuscaloosa, AL: SpeakEasy Press.

Churchill, Ward. 1998. *Fantasies of the Master Race: Literature, Cinema and the Colonization of American Indians.* San Francisco, CA: City Lights Publisher.

Cobb, Amanda J. 2003. "This Is What It Means to Say Smoke Signals: Native American Cultural Sovereignty." In *Hollywood's Indian*, edited by Peter C. Rollins and John E. O'Connor, 206–228. Lexington, KY: University Press of Kentucky.

Dobuzinskis, Alex. 2010. "Native American Actors See New Image in 'Twilight.'" *Reuters*, June 28. http://www.reuters.com/article/film-us-twilight-idUKTRE65J2U320100629 (accessed April 9, 2017).

Engels, Jeremy. 2005. "Equipped for Murder: The Paxton Boys and the 'Spirit of Killing All Indians' in Pennsylvania, 1763–1764." *Rhetoric and Public Affairs* 8(3): 355–382.

Fallon, Claire. 2016. "The Native Plot on 'Kimmy Schmidt' Makes Us Cringe, But is it All Bad?" *Huffington Post*, April 29. http://www.huffingtonpost.com/entry/unbreakable-kimmy-schmidt-native-americans_us_5722747fe4b01a5ebde515be (accessed April 3, 2017).

Harjo, Suzan Shown. 2003. "Redskins, Savages, and Other Indian Enemies: A Historical Overview of American Media Coverage of Native Peoples." In *Hollywood's Indian: The Portrayal of the Native American in Film*, edited by Peter C. Rollins and John E. O'Connor, 62–77. Lexington, KY: University Press of Kentucky.

ICTMN Staff. 2015. "'Unbreakable Kimmy Schmidt' Has Two Native American Actors. It Needed Three." *Indian Country Today Media Network*, March 11. http://indiancountrytodaymedianetwork.com/2015/03/11/unbreakable-kimmy-schmidt-has-two-native-american-actors-it-needed-three-159559 (accessed April 3, 2017).

Jojola, Ted. 2003. "Absurd Reality II: Hollywood Goes to the Indians." In *Hollywood's Indian: The Portrayal of the Native American in Film*, edited by Peter C. Rollins and John E. O'Connor, 12–26. Lexington, KY: University Press of Kentucky.

Kilpatrick, Jacquelyn. 1999. *Celluloid Indians: Native Americans and Film*. Lincoln, NE: University of Nebraska Press.

Lang, Martin. 2015. "Written Out of Their Own Story: The Rhetorical Colonialism of Journalistic Practice." *Communication Studies* 66(1): 85–102.

Larson, Stephanie Greco. 2006. *Media and Minorities: The Politics of Race in News and Entertainment*. Lanham, MD: Rowman & Littlefield.

Lewis, Charles. 2011. "Wise Decisions: A Frontier Newspaper's Coverage of the Dakota Conflict." *American Journalism* 28(2): 48–80.

Li-Vollmer, Meredith. 2002. "Race Representation in Child-Targeted Cartoons." *Mass Communication and Society* 5(2): 207–228.

Manchel, Frank. 2003. "Cultural Confusion: *Broken Arrow*." In *Hollywood's Indian: The Portrayal of the Native American in Film*, edited by Peter C. Rollins and John E. O'Connor, 91–106. Lexington, KY: University Press of Kentucky.

Mastro, Dana E., and Susannah R. Stern. 2003. "Representations of Race in Television Commercials: A Content Analysis of Prime-Time Advertising." *Journal of Broadcasting & Electronic Media* 47(4): 638–647.

Meek, Barbra A. 2006. "And the Injun Goes 'How!': Representations of American Indian English in White Public Space." *Language in Society* 35(1): 93–129.

Miller, Jackson B. 1999. "A Performative Struggle for Control of an Image." *Quarterly Journal of Speech* 86: 188–202.

Perkins, Daniel J., and William J. Starosta. 2001. "Representing Co-culturals: On Form and News Portrayals of Native Americans." *The Howard Journal of Communication* 12: 73–84.

Perry, Barbara. 2008. *Silent Victims: Hate Crimes Against Native Americans*. Tucson, AZ: University of Arizona Press.

Riding In, James. 2006. "American Indians in Popular Culture: A Pawnee's Experiences and Views." In *Images of Color, Images of Crime*, 3rd ed., edited by Coramae Richey Mann, Marjorie S. Zatz, and Nancy Rodriguez, 16–30. Los Angeles, CA: Roxbury Publishing.

Rothman, Lily. 2013. "Johnny Depp as Tonto: Is *The Lone Ranger* Racist?" *Time*, July 3. http://entertainment.time.com/2013/07/03/johnny-depp-as-tonto-is-the-lone-ranger-racist (accessed April 3, 2017).

Sanchez, Victoria. 2012. "Buying into Racism: American Indian Product Icons in the American Marketplace." In *American Indians and the Mass Media*, edited by Meta G. Carstarphen and John P. Sanchez, 153–168. Norman, OK: University of Oklahoma Press.

Smith, Paul Chaat, and Robert Allen Warrior. 1996. *Like a Hurricane: The Indian Movement from Alcatraz to Wounded Knee*. New York, NY: New Press.

Steffens, Pete. 1978. "Franklin's Early Attack on Racism: An Essay Against a Massacre of Indians." *Journalism History* 5(1): 8–12, 31.

Steinberg, Dan. 2009. "When the Redskins Became the RedHawks." *The Washington Post*, April 1. http://voices.washingtonpost.com/dcsportsbog/2009/04/when_the_redskins_became_the_r.html (accessed April 3, 2017).

Stroman, Carolyn A., and Jannette L. Dates. 2008. "African Americans, Latinos, Asians, and Native Americans in the Media: Implications for Adolescents." In *The Changing Portrayal of Adolescents in the Media Since 1950*, edited by Patrick E. Jamieson and Daniel Romer, 198–220. New York, NY: Oxford University Press.

Strong, Pauline Turner. 2003. "Playing Indian in the 1990s: Pocahontas and The Indian in the Cupboard." In *Hollywood's Indian: The Portrayal of the Native American in Film*, edited by Peter C. Rollins and John E. O'Connor, 187–205. Lexington, KY: University Press of Kentucky.

Tan, Alexis, Yuki Fujioka, and Nancy Lucht. 1997. "Native American Stereotypes, TV Portrayals, and Personal Contact." *Journalism and Mass Communication Quarterly* 74: 265–284.

Taylor, Annette M. 1996. "Cultural Heritage in Northern Exposure." In *Dressing in Feathers: The Construction of the Indian in American Popular Culture*, edited by S. Elizabeth Bird, 229–244. Boulder, CO: Westview Press.

Weston, Mary Ann. 1996. *Native Americans in the News: Images of Indians in the Twentieth Century Press*. Westport, CT: Greenwood Press.

Weston, Mary Ann, and John M. Coward. 1997. "The Native Americans." In *U.S. News Coverage of Racial Minorities*, edited by Beverly Ann Deepe Keever, Carolyn Martindale, and Mary Ann Weston, 23–62. Westport, CT: Greenwood Press.

4

Representations of African Americans

On September 20, 2015, Viola Davis, star of the ABC series *How to Get Away with Murder* (2014 debut) won the Emmy Award for Best Actress in a Drama Series. In part, Davis won the award for a scene where she stares into a mirror, takes off her wig and makeup before confronting her husband for having an affair. Davis's image of a black woman wearing her natural hair and stark face was a captivating and brave choice rarely seen on television. Davis's win made television history – she was the first African American to win in the category in the 67 years of the Emmy Awards.

In her acceptance speech, Davis credited several African American actors including Taraji P. Henson and Gabrielle Union for helping to pave the way for women of color to have lead roles in episodic television. She quoted Harriet Tubman when she reminded Hollywood that when race and gender intersect, there are significant obstacles to the roles available: "The only thing that separates women of color from anybody else is opportunity. You cannot win an Emmy for roles that are simply not there." While most of the viewing audience cheered for Davis, there was some public backlash. The most publicized was from *General Hospital* (1963 premiere) actor Nancy Lee Grahn. Grahn, a white actress, tweeted a series of messages disagreeing with Davis's speech that included:

> I wish I loved #ViolaDavis Speech, but I thought she should have let @shondarhimes write it. #Emmys

> Viola Davis winning lead actress Emmy's historic. My upset is acting awards dont fix racial injustice. As an actor I see how irrelevant we r

> I never mean to diminish her accomplishment. I wish I could get her roles. She is a goddess. I want equality 4 ALL women, not just actors. (Grahn 2015; TheWrap.com 2015)

The social media reaction was swift and furious. Responses ranged from educative to angry. Some tweets directed at Grahn insisted that she was just jealous of Davis's success, while others accused her of being a racist. Grahn tried to defend her point then ultimately apologized for her offending tweets, saying she had been "schooled" by many of the sentiments expressed via Twitter. She also said that she had long been a defender of women's rights, but lamented that she had not fully grasped the privilege she had as a white woman in the media industry and the world. Grahn's Twitter controversy illustrates that race is still a divisive topic in the world of entertainment even though

Diversity in US Mass Media, Second Edition. Catherine A. Luther, Carolyn Ringer Lepre, and Naeemah Clark.
© 2018 John Wiley & Sons Inc. Published 2018 by John Wiley & Sons Inc.

programs such as *How to Get Away with Murder, Empire* (2015 debut), and Donald Glover's *Atlanta* (2016 debut) feature Blacks in front of and behind the camera.

Through the pictures they choose and the narratives they construct, the mass media relay, sometimes indirectly or unconsciously, discriminatory ideas about Blacks to the public. At the same time, the mass media have undoubtedly also played a positive role in bringing to light the injustices that have been inflicted on African Americans. For example, during the civil rights movement, television helped to awaken the general public to the unfair oppression that Blacks were encountering on a daily basis. Seeing images of peaceful civil rights protesters being attacked by angry mobs and herded by water surging from fire hoses convinced many viewers sitting in the comfort of their homes that changes needed to be made. In effect, television helped to galvanize the public toward supporting civil rights legislation.

This chapter discusses the dynamic relationship between African Americans and the mass media. It will first examine the historical roots of African American images, then go on to explore current media portrayals and how media ownership impacts these images.

Historical Background to African American Representations

Any discussion of African Americans and the media is closely tied to the history of this population in America. Millions of Africans were taken from their families and homes thousands of miles away to work without wages on the sugar, cotton, and other farms in the American colonies. Those who did not perish on the dangerous trip, shackled in the bowels of a lethally overcrowded ship, landed in an America where the enslavement of humans was legal and an accepted part of the country's economic structure.

Once on the plantations, the slaves lived in ramshackle dwellings, frequently ate what their masters discarded, and were often physically and sexually brutalized by their owners. Slaves were bought and sold as if they were livestock. Rarely did the traders consider the husbands and wives, brothers and sisters, and mothers and children being separated on the auction block. This systemic disregard for the feelings, emotions, sensibilities, and, ultimately, lives of these human beings dictated how this group was seen in society for years to come. Even though slavery across the country was ended in 1865 with the passage of the 13th Amendment, a majority of Blacks faced institutional and social discrimination that resulted in second-class citizenry. Between the years of 1876 and 1965, states supported so-called Jim Crow laws ("Jim Crow" is a derogatory term referring to a buffoonish black man), which were instituted as a means of placating Southern Whites who feared the encroachment of free Blacks into their communities. The laws negated Blacks' civil rights by relegating them to "separate but equal" accommodations, with the effect of creating inferior conditions for Blacks in public places such as schools, movie theaters, and restaurants. For example, Blacks and Whites could both go to movies, but Blacks were forced to sit or stand in a separate section that was farther away, often with obstructed views of the screen.

Individuals such as Martin Luther King, Jr., Rosa Parks, Malcolm X, and Jesse Jackson gained prominence because of their ability to captivate the minds of young people and motivate their parents of all colors to take action. Public demonstrations, including bus boycotts, lunch counter sit-ins, and marches across bridges, in towns, and on Washington, DC, along with some violent rioting, shone a light on the sadness and anger that permeated the black community. Such actions culminated in the important 1954 Supreme Court decision, *Brown v. Board of Education of Topeka, Kansas*, which marked a significant change in the treatment of Blacks across the country. The Supreme Court unanimously ruled that forcing Linda Brown and other black students to attend segregated schools was not only unfair, but also unconstitutional. In effect, the Court ruling proclaimed that separate was not equal and racial integration was the law. The change in the law coupled with vigorous civil rights activities helped to change the status of African Americans in the United States.

Of course, laws cannot change what is in people's hearts and minds. Bigotry against African Americans still exists; nearly every week there is a story in the news dealing with claims of racially motivated violence, workplace discrimination, or a public person making a race-related faux pas. Still, the country is healing from the scars left by slavery, condoned prejudice, and unfair treatment. As the status of African Americans has evolved in the United States, films, radio and television outlets, newspapers, and magazines have offered content more reflective and relevant to the lives of this group.

African Americans in Film

In his classic book on Blacks in American film, film historian Donald Bogle identified six prevalent representations of African Americans (Bogle 2013: 3–34). The first he classified as the "Tom." This character is a kind-hearted and submissive black man. He is well liked and willing to endure white domination. The second is the "Coon." This character is selfish, ignorant, and has no drive in life. He is the minstrel type that enjoys entertaining others. The third type is the "Bad Buck." The Bad Buck is characterized as violent and having pent-up rage. He is physically strong and threatening, especially to Whites.

Bogle's fourth classification is that of a loud, argumentative, usually large, black woman – the "Mammy." She is often devoted more to her white boss's family than her own. The fifth classification, also of a woman, is the "Tragic Mullato." She is a mixed race woman who is viewed as exotic and sexually attractive, especially to white men. Because of her mixed race, however, she is doomed to some form of tragedy in the end. The final classification by Bogle is the "Buddy/Sidekick." This character is basically present to support the main white character, often put in positions of saving his white buddy. As this section explores the differing films that have featured African Americans and the images that have been associated with them, it will become apparent that together with a few new types of African American characters, the character classifications that Bogle pinpointed are, indeed, present in many of the films, from those produced during the silent film era until the present time.

In the early days of film, distorted film representations of African Americans inflamed racist sentiment. For example, films such as 1915's *Birth of a Nation*, featuring aggressive black men – the "bad buck" type – being lynched by the Ku Klux Klan, only inflamed racist sentiment present in some white communities. *Birth of a Nation*, which was initially entitled *The Clansman*, was the highest grossing movie in the era of silent film and was lauded for its then cutting-edge camera techniques. The film's plot focuses on the Stoneman and Cameron families who are friends until the Civil War begins. The Stoneman boys, raised by an abolitionist father, become Union soldiers; the Camerons from South Carolina join the Confederate army. Like many films about the Civil War, it is a tale of star-crossed romance, friend versus friend, and tragic death. What makes the film problematic is that the Ku Klux Klan, the white supremacy organization, is portrayed as being the heroic victor against lascivious black men. The film's African American and mulatto characters (played by white actors, including George Siegmann and Walter Long) were portrayed as ignorant, and as thieves, interlopers, and potential rapists.

The silent film, directed by the pioneering filmmaker D.W. Griffith, who also directed *The Battle of Elderbrush Gulch*, which was discussed in Chapter 3, was heralded by critics as the greatest film ever made. Conversely, the negative content led the activist group National Association for the Advancement of Colored People (NAACP) to demand, unsuccessfully, that the film be banned. Similar complaints were made of the *Tarzan* series of films, the first produced in 1932, where the black Africans, also played by Whites in blackface (greasepaint intended to make them look like Blacks), were inarticulate savages. The harmful depiction of Blacks was problematic because these films were successful and often provided a segregated society the only glimpses into black life available to white Americans. Moreover, casting Whites in the roles of people of color symbolically removed race from the films altogether. Not only were the stories incomplete and injurious, but also audiences were not given the chance to see *real live* African American professional actors.

Some African American filmmakers were creating positive images of Blacks on film, but the work of these independent producers and directors did not reach the national, crossover prominence of that produced by the big studios. In the early 1900s, brothers George and Nobel Johnson began to make films through their Lincoln Motion Picture Company that were designed to celebrate racial uplift and life in middle-class African American society. One such film, *The Realization of a Negro's Ambition* (1916), depicted the main character, James, a recent Tuskegee graduate, as he strikes out on his own, feeling unfulfilled in his life of work on the family farm. He is confronted with racist obstacles, and is unable to find a job, until he risks his life to stop a runaway horse and buggy, saving the life of a white oil magnate's daughter. The oil man gives James a job, which subsequently leads to James discovering oil on his father's farm, leading to great wealth for him and his father. His dreams were now realized, despite the prejudice he found around him, and he chooses to stays on the farm, with his family. Another African American producer and director, Oscar Devereaux Micheaux, produced silent and talking films (e.g., *The Homesteader* [1919] and *When Men Betray* [1928]) between 1918 and 1948. One of Micheaux's lauded films, *Murder in Harlem* (1935), starred African American actor Clarence Brooks as a night watchman who is unjustly accused of murder when he finds the body of a white woman while doing his rounds. Brooks is illustrative of the plight of actors of color in the first decades of film. He had a few roles of prominence including playing a doctor in 1931's *Arrowsmith*, but he also was cast as an unnamed porter, butler, and valet in other films. Clearly he was talented and charismatic enough to play more complex roles, but taking parts as servants allowed him to work much more frequently.

Talking pictures of the 1930s and 1940s saw the big studios producing musicals again featuring white actors in blackface. Well-known actors Al Jolson, Mickey Rooney, and Fred Astaire all wore blackface while satirizing black dialect, music, or dance, presenting the "coon" type of image (see Figure 4.1).

At the same time, movies called "race films" starred actors of color who had adventures, worked, and fell in love in circles of other Blacks. Lighter skinned actresses such as Nina Mae McKinney and Lena Horne, who starred in several race films (*Hallelujah!* [1929] and *Stormy Weather* [1943]), became international beauties. Actor Bill "Bojangles" Robinson's dancing talents were featured alongside white actresses such as Shirley Temple in the 1920s and 1930s. Paul Robeson, an imposing figure, often portrayed a strong black man who resisted white oppression.

Although many African Americans appeared in the race films, several rose to national prominence playing the more negative roles provided in the big studio films. Hattie McDaniel was awarded the Best Supporting Actress Academy Award, the first Oscar awarded to any African American, for her performance in *Gone with the Wind* (1939). McDaniel played the now iconic "Mammy" who raised

Figure 4.1 Mickey Rooney and Judy Garland wearing black face paint for a scene in the musical *Babes in Arms*, directed by Busby Berkeley for MGM (1939). Reproduced with kind permission of Getty Images.

the film's lead Scarlett O'Hara (portrayed by Vivien Leigh). *Gone with the Wind* is the love story of Scarlett and Rhett Butler (played by Clark Gable), set against the background of the Civil War. There is no doubt that Leigh's Scarlett is the star of the film; she is gorgeous and cunning as she charms and uses men to save her family's Southern plantation. Still, McDaniel's Mammy provides the heart in the film. Even when Scarlett is unlovable, Mammy is there to guide her. In one scene, Scarlett is tempted to run across a field to embrace Ashley Wilkes, another woman's husband, when he returns from war. Mammy reminds Scarlett that Ashley belongs to another and Scarlett must respect that fact. As the controversial role of Mammy is unpacked, it is clear that she is more than just a household servant who fixes dinner and tightens Scarlett's corset. She is a substitute mother for her impetuous charge.

McDaniel's stellar performance could not overcome the plague of racism. She could not attend the film's premiere in Atlanta, Georgia, because the venue, in accordance with Jim Crow practices, had a "no Blacks" rule, and her husband could not sit with her at the segregated Academy Awards ceremony. Many African Americans and other critics were frustrated with McDaniel's stereotypical black servant roles, and felt that it was wrong for these roles to continually be cast. On the flip side, McDaniel noted that she accepted all roles that were offered to her, and that she would rather *play* a maid than *be* one. The characters she played often were strong-willed women who commanded respect in their households, even if they did still clean the house.

The 1950s, 1960s, and 1970s saw black actors in a wide variety of film roles. Perhaps the most celebrated African American actor at this time was Sidney Poitier. Poitier's films were successful with audiences of all races. Films such as *Lilies of the Field* (for which he won the 1963 Best Actor Academy Award) and *To Sir, with Love* (1967) had Poitier helping white characters in a nonthreatening way as a handyman and teacher, respectively. Conversely, Poitier's turn as Virgil Tibbs in *In the Heat of the Night* (1967) ruffled a few feathers when he slapped a white man across the face after the man slapped him. Seemingly, the slap was just a case of "if someone hits you, you can hit them back," but in the 1960s, Tibbs's retaliatory action was considered to be unacceptable behavior for a black man.

Similar to the race films of the 1940s, many African American actors found prominence by starring in "blaxploitation" films where they were the stars acting alongside other African American actors. Communication scholar Celeste A. Fisher defines the blaxploitation film genre as one that made individuals on the fringes of society important by depicting a "Super Black," or lone hero, who could be a man or a woman, who challenged dominant culture and won (Fisher 2002). Films such as *Sweet Sweetback's Baadasssss Song* (1971) and the *Shaft* trilogy (1971, 1972, 1973) featured black men successfully doing battle with white and black authority figures and winning women of different races. The heroes and heroines of these films (e.g., Richard Roundtree as John Shaft, Tamara Dobson as Cleopatra Jones [1973]) were champions for African Americans who wanted to see some triumph over the Whites they felt were oppressing them. In other words, the films provided some catharsis for black viewers who wanted to reclaim a part of their individuality and power over those who were discriminating against them.

With this character type, just as with many of the stereotypical role types that have been discussed in this chapter and in other chapters in this book, other exceptions may spring to mind. Analyzing media is never simple, as there is more than one way to interpret the way a character is presented and certainly more than one way of looking at the portrayal of a minority group.

Another representation that has surfaced throughout film history is that of the "magical Negro." Communication researchers Cerise L. Glenn and Landra J. Cunningham argue that media-produced racial images require discussing the unsettled condition of race relations in the United States. They assert that Whites have not completely accepted Blacks as equals and hold attitudes of white superiority; as a result, as Blacks move closer into the realm of "acceptability" among Whites, the images in movies can be critical of this acceptance (Glenn and Cunningham 2009). Communication and public affairs researchers Robert Entman and Andrew Rojecki (2001b: 53) call this position between acceptance and rejection "liminality," which is defined as the "unsettled status of Blacks in the eyes of those who produce the dominant culture and of those who consume it." Glenn and Cunningham suggest that because of Blacks' liminal status, new stereotypes emerge to take the place of old ones. In this case, instead of having life histories, love affairs, or families, black characters have magical powers. Folk wisdom is often used by the black character and noted as being more important than intelligence.

In films such as *The Green Mile* (1999) and *The Legend of Bagger Vance* (2000), the white characters are in desperate need of help and must turn to the lone black character in the film for salvation. In *The Green Mile*, Michael Clarke Duncan plays John Coffey, a larger-than-life African American man who is accused of murder and put on death row. John is far from a murderer and holds supernatural healing powers to cure sickness and eternal life. In the end, John is executed for someone else's crime, but he transfers immortality to the prison guard who was kind to him. These characters of color possess a magical power that they are more than willing to use – often to the detriment of their own lives – to better the life of these white characters. In the *Matrix* trilogy – *The Matrix* (1999), *The Matrix Reloaded* (2003), and *The Matrix Revolutions* (2003) – Morpheus, the African American leader of the group of rebels, and The Oracle, a female African American guide, both spend all their time and energy working to help Neo, the white male lead, in his quest to save humankind. Neither African American character seems to have any sense of identity other than to use his or her magical power to help save Neo, and make clear that without him, all hope is lost. The "magical Negro" is a stereotype that has supplanted the characterization of the mammy with the gift of song or the butler who can solve a family crisis with a tap dance (Glenn and Cunningham 2009). The figure is a non-threatening presence to the white characters and serves as little more than a lucky rabbit's foot.

The most recent decades also introduced audiences to black filmmakers. Producers and directors such as Spike Lee (*Do the Right Thing* [1989]; *Crooklyn* [1994]), John Singleton (*Boyz n the Hood* [1991]; *Baby Boy* [2001]), Tyler Perry (*Diary of a Mad Black Woman* [2005]; *Madea's Witness*

Figure 4.2 Powerful poster for the 2016 film *Birth of a Nation*, which tells the story of a slave revolt. Here, Nate Parker (as Turner) wears the American flag as a noose. This film received the buzz of the 2016 Sundance Film Festival.

Protection [2012]), Ava DuVernay (*Selma* [2014]), Effie Brown (*Dear White People* [2014]), and Nate Parker (with a new version of *Birth of a Nation* [2016]) made movies about the different aspects of the African American experience, including stories about history and family, that appealed to moviegoers of varying ethnicities and races because they were funny or poignant (Figure 4.2). Here, as is the case with Hispanic filmmakers (see Chapter 5), African American producers, directors, and writers strive to make films that will appeal to audiences across racial lines while employing relatively large numbers of actors who struggle to find quality parts in Hollywood (see Box 4.1).

African Americans in Entertainment Television

Media studies professor Catherine Squires (2009) draws five conclusions that surfaced in her analysis of television programs featuring African Americans:

1. Mainstream media only show extremes in the black community, not a continuum of actions and identities.
2. Whites believe stereotypical depictions of Blacks, thus perpetuating harmful racial stereotypes.

Box 4.1 *Precious* **and African American reliance on others**

The story of a poor, overweight, troubled African American teen captivated movie audiences in 2009. *Precious: Based on the Novel "Push" by Sapphire* challenged audiences of all walks of life to deal with topics such as poverty, physical abuse, teen motherhood, and incest. Although the film received critical acclaim and elevated two of its stars (Mo'Nique and Gabourey Sidibe) into movie stardom, some members of the African American community were disappointed in the stark portrayal of black life in the film.

One critic was Ishmael Reed, an author who writes about issues related to race and culture. Reed challenges that the film only shows the harshest extremes in black family life. The black mother is angry and violent. The black father is sexually abusive. The black teen is pregnant (because of the father) and illiterate. Conversely, the white characters in the film are generally helpful and caring. Reed suggests that *Precious* only furthers an oft-repeated theme in films: Blacks need altruistic Whites to save them. Reed cites 1996's *Dangerous Minds*, a film where a white teacher encourages Hispanic and African American students to embrace literature. The 2007 Hilary Swank film, *Freedom Writers*, has a similar pattern, as does the 2009 blockbuster *The Blind Side*, for which Sandra Bullock won a Best Actress Academy Award. Even films based on American history have been found to give Whites the spotlight in saving Blacks. More concerning, President Lyndon Johnson is incorrectly painted as being a fervent supporter of the civil rights movement in the 2015 Martin Luther King biopic *Selma*. Reed explains this phenomenon by saying that these types of stories flatter white audiences, drawing them to theaters to see films with black characters (Reed 2010: 25).

These storytelling devices also are cringeworthy because the aforementioned films were heavily marketed to white audiences. The images may create a picture of the African American community that is vastly different than the norm for these audiences. Strengthening Reed's objection to *Precious* are the film's high-profile supporters, producer Tyler Perry and Oprah Winfrey, who both have large white fan bases. Perry and Winfrey's visible lauding of the film only serves to legitimize these hurtful stereotypes of the African American family.

Have you seen *Precious*, *Selma*, or *The Blind Side*? Do you agree with Reed's thoughts about the portrayals in these films?'

---

3. Differences between Blacks and other ethnic groups are blown out of proportion to incite conflicts and controversy.
4. Media producers must be held accountable for racist texts.
5. Blacks need to create and use their own media to distribute better information and less racial bias in coverage of black life.

To understand this list, it is important to acknowledge that Blacks have appeared on television in a variety of ways, but as the following list demonstrates, many of the appearances conjure negative images of black life or ignore the nuances that make up life in neighborhoods, homes, and families no matter what the race.

In 1951, *Amos 'n' Andy* (a program that originated on the radio with white actors voicing the lines of African American characters) featured an all-black neighborhood. The program was popular until it ended in 1953, but some considered its humorous – yet stereotypical – depiction of the African American community offensive. One example of this funny, yet problematic, dialogue occurred in an episode where George "Kingfish" Stevens (played by Tim Moore) is telling Andy (played by Spencer Williams) that he can learn to fly an airplane:

KINGFISH:	You see, Andy, the first thing you need to fly is excellent eyesight. Now how much is 10 plus 10?
ANDY:	20
KINGFISH:	OK. Now what's ten times two?
ANDY:	20
KINGFISH:	Oh, you see Andy, you has 20/20 vision.

Amos 'n' Andy presented a new dynamic. The characters were upwardly mobile, living in a community of self-sufficient Blacks. Yet, the program also painted these relatively successful people as being ignorant and inarticulate. Viewers were given the impression that African Americans were capable of achieving decent standards of living, but were not bright enough to be taken seriously.

Between the late 1950s and the 1980s, African Americans appeared on television in numbers and ways not seen in the first two decades of television. Particularly groundbreaking, although short-lived, *The Nat King Cole Show* (1956–1957) was a variety show where Nat King Cole would welcome guests of all colors to his stage to perform and chat. Although he was an international singing star, the National Broadcasting Company (NBC) had difficulty finding sponsors for this program and opted to foot the bill for the year it aired. The network, aware of racial sensitivities in the South, cautioned Cole against touching any of his white female guests – a far cry from the kiss-hug-kiss ritual found on today's talk show couches. There was virtually no other sole African American lead in a program until the premier of Diahann Carroll's situation comedy *Julia* (1968–1971). Carroll played Julia, a widowed nurse with a son, Corey. The program touched ever so lightly on racial issues, but really was focused on a middle-class woman living a happy racially integrated life.

Counter to the sanitized racial discussions in *Julia*, Norman Lear, acclaimed producer of *All in the Family* (1971–1979), introduced audiences to two socially relevant programs. *Good Times* (1974–1979) was an often harsh look at the day-to-day life of a poor family, the Evanses, living in a Chicago government housing project. The family was constantly under the gun to pay their rent or purchase groceries for their family of five. Their downtrodden depiction was highlighted by the exploits of the older Evans son, James Junior, known as J.J. He frequently got into jams with his girlfriends, gangs, and loan sharks. After his crisis was solved at the end of each episode, he would clap his hands together, leap into the air, and, with a big toothy grin, say that everything was "dy-no-mite." This gesture, which became a popular culture icon, is reminiscent of the jumping, dancing buffoonery of Jim Crow.

Another relevant Lear program, *The Jeffersons* (1975–1983), was about a hardworking African American family who moved out of their lower-middle-class Queens, New York, neighborhood to a luxury apartment in Manhattan. The Jeffersons owned a chain of dry cleaning stores throughout New York City, which is how they could afford their large apartment, expensive vacations, and nice clothes. Still, the lead character George (played by Sherman Hemsley) was particularly bigoted against Whites. In nearly every episode, he referred to his white upstairs neighbor using racial slurs such as "honkey" or "whitey." Another *Jeffersons* character, their maid Florence (played by Marla Gibbs), was also reminiscent of the stereotypical roles historically reserved for Blacks. While she was witty, she had the brashness of a mammy figure and, in the early years of the show, was inarticulate.

These representations of African Americans were limiting and stereotypic. However, they all told a truth about fears of race mixing, the contributions of strong black women in America, systemic poverty, and a growing black middle class in America.

Much of the discussion of African Americans on television centers on the 1980s juggernaut *The Cosby Show*, for several reasons. First, *The Cosby Show* (1984–1992) was a wildly successful sitcom for NBC that established the network's ratings dominance throughout the late 1980s and 1990s. The power of this show was significant because this series, centering on an upper-middle-class African American family, consistently appealed to audiences of all races because of its funny scripts and charming actors.

When the program debuted in September of 1984, the unconventional and loving childrearing of Dr. Heathcliff Huxtable (portrayed by Bill Cosby) and his attorney wife Claire (portrayed by Phylicia Rashad) was praised for its positive storytelling. The Huxtables taught their five children valuable life lessons about self-reliance, honesty, and hard work in their three-story brownstone in Brooklyn Heights, New York. The program was also praised for introducing prime-time audiences to black artists, dancers, and musicians, although there was some criticism that the Huxtables were not accurate representatives of the average African American family. The economic disparity between black and white families was invisible on the program. The family was fully assimilated into upper-middle-class white society; therefore, the persistent segregation in the United States also was not addressed. Racism was virtually nonexistent.

Critics claimed that ignoring these all-too-true facets of African American life was disingenuous and unrealistic. Although the purpose of the program was to depict a positive, loving, nuclear family, it also created an impression that everyday race-based issues disappeared in middle-class society. Ironically, the final episode of *The Cosby Show* aired the same day as the racially motivated Los Angeles riots, which were fueled after white police officers were acquitted of beating an African American man (Tucker 1997). The juxtaposition of the burning city and the ideal Huxtables only served to emphasize that the groundbreaking sitcom was a bit of a utopia.

Post-*Cosby*, the African American family has been depicted in a variety of ways – some more positively than others. For example, the UPN and WB networks created a prime-time ghetto that in effect segregated shows featuring African Americans to certain days of the week. One family-focused show that aired on these nights was the comedy *The Wayans Brothers* (1995–1999), which was criticized for showing stereotypic images of black males as ne'er-do-well jokesters. Also on the schedule was the family program *Moesha* (1996–2001), starring singer Brandy. This became the first television program to feature the daily life of an African American teenage girl. Reality television also provided some glimpses of the African American family. Rappers Rev. Run and Snoop Dog had cameras follow their real families. Although the reality aspects of the programs were contrived, they did show black families with both parents involved in the rearing of their children.

Generally, African Americans are represented on television series in multiethnic/multiracial casts. Programs such as the *CSI* series (2000–2015) and associated spin-offs, *NCIS: Los Angeles* (2009 debut), *NCIS: New Orleans* (2014 debut), and *Scandal* (2010 debut), are just a handful of the hour-long dramas that feature characters of color sharing screen time and solving fictional problems. The Blacks who appear on programs of this type are woven into the shows as doctors, lawyers, and police officers. In most of these procedural programs, where solving a crime is paramount, the personal lives of the characters are secondary. As a result, race is not much discussed.

Another hour-long program worthy of elaboration is *Grey's Anatomy* (2005 debut). This medical drama spotlights the joys and sorrows of the multiracial doctors who staff Seattle Grace Hospital.

The program is helmed by an African American woman, Shonda Rhimes, who spent the beginning of her career writing films such as the Britney Spears flop *Crossroads* (2002) and Disney's *The Princess Diaries 2* (2004). Rhimes, who is the show's creator and executive producer, as well as one of the many writers, says it was important to her to have actors of every color for every role. She wrote the original script as "cast color blind," originally leaving out last names for certain characters, including the competitive Christina Wang (played by Asian American Sandra Oh) and "The Nazi" Miranda Bailey (played by African American Chandra Wilson). The character of "The Nazi" was first conceived as a petite blonde. In an interview published in *Broadcasting & Cable*, Rhimes intimates that she creates television worlds that look like her world – diverse in many ways (Albiniak 2005). When asked about how the minority characters seem more heroic on *Grey's* than on other programs in prime time, she responded that, like all the characters, she tried to make them three-dimensional, not purposely heroic: "They are at times petty, heroic, tired, angry, not interested in their jobs, interested in their jobs ... when you only have one character of color in a show, [three-dimensionality] doesn't necessarily get to happen" (Robichaux 2006: 28).

Rhimes's leadership at ABC has grown. She is the executive producer of three shows aired on Thursday nights; *Grey's Anatomy*, *Scandal*, and *How to Get Away with Murder* make up "Thank God It's Thursday" (TGIT). Others are joining her ranks. For example, Courtney Kemp Agboh is the showrunner of the Stars hit *Power* (2014 debut). Still, these women are a rarity in the world of broadcast network television; there are very few female showrunners and even fewer African Americans.

Another program with an African American executive producer is *Empire*. In January 2015, Lee Daniels and his producing partner Danny Strong created a sensation with this show, which airs on FOX. The fun, funky drama looks at the dazzlingly turbulent life of music industry mogul Lucious Lyon (Terrence Howard), and his search for a worthy successor in his bloodline. Since the beginning, audiences have been buzzing about Taraji P. Henson's scene-stealing turn as the ex-con matriarch of the family, Cookie Lyon. Although Lucious's swag and sway are more than the typical TV patriarch (he calls President Obama by his *first* name!), he is a modern black father that wants to provide a solid foundation for his family. The program tackles issues that are known to be taboo in the black community, such as mental illness and homosexuality.

Another type of black family is also under the spotlight on ABC's *Black-ish* (2014 debut). According to the premise of the show, Andre Johnson (Anthony Anderson) is raising his kids in an upper-middle-class neighborhood, with white friends, and in a society that is different from the one where he grew up. He becomes bothered when his children and wife seem to be taking on too many characteristics he sees as white, such as his son letting his friends call him Andy instead of his actual name, Andre. At one point, the two exchange words:

ANDRE (the father): Andy? That's not even close to Andre.
ANDRE (the son): I think it says I'm edgy but approachable.
ANDRE (the father): I think it says I hate my father and I play field hockey.

Over time, Andre begins to feel that he needs to teach his family how to be Black, not "Black-ish." Andre's rebuke of the influence of "white" culture in his kids' lives is so over the top that it's almost a farce. He has an African coming-of-age ceremony when his teenaged son asks for a bar mitzvah. In its 2015 premiere, Andre instructs his younger son that he can decide whether or not to use the "N" word, but he should never use it in mixed company. The Johnsons are different in many ways from the Lyons, but both series make it clear that there is no one way to represent the black family because there is no monolithic Black culture.

In terms of television programming targeted at young children, a 1993 examination of animated programs on the ABC, CBS, and NBC networks found that three of 20 programs featured minority characters (Greenberg and Brand 1993). Upon closer examination, the researchers found that the regular characters in these three programs were African American. The Public Broadcasting Service (PBS), on the other hand, showed a world in which a broad spectrum of minority characters was integral to its programs' actions. The adult characters were employed in a variety of occupations, both white collar and blue collar. The same content analysis revealed that commercial stations had tapped into diversity to peddle products; however, public television programming promoted an inclusive culture in its presentation of life lessons. A 2007 study of children's programming found that the content, indeed, featured a wide variety of minority groups. In fact, there were a few programs with African American characters in the lead. These programs, *The Proud Family* (2001–2005) and *That's So Raven* (2003–2007), focused on smart girls who were leaders among their groups of friends (Clark and Perkins 2007).

These images in television programming need to be carefully considered alongside the possible impact they might have on young viewers. The television screen serves as an early window on to a society that can be very different from what they have seen inside of their homes. As discussed in Chapter 2, the media have been shown to be an agent in *socialization* in two ways. First, the media reinforce existing values. Second, the media offer norms and values through content. As a result, viewers learn to operate in life using these established norms (Gerson 1966).

Some children's programs can make youngsters more tolerant of different races. More specifically, *Sesame Street* (1969 debut; HBO bought rights to show from PBS in 2016) has been shown to inspire acceptance of other races in white children (Gorn, Goldberg, and Kanungo 1976). Although children are only exposed to *Sesame Street* for a finite time, the years they spend with the program are full of diverse content. African American children have been the focus of several studies about media-related socialization. Health communication scholar Carolyn Stroman, in her analysis of literature dealing with television's socialization of black children, found that television gave the impression that Blacks were invisible or unvalued in America. These findings lent credence to black parents' concerns that "television might influence black children's attitudes toward their own racial group; facilitate black children's development of low self-concepts through its nonrecognition of negative, stereotyped treatment of Blacks; and compete with black family socialization by teaching attitudes and behavior that are not taught in the home" (Stroman 1984: 79–100). Stroman found more positive results six years later. This investigation revealed that African Americans were portrayed in a positive light, with good jobs and stable families (Stroman 1991).

African American Music

Music has had close ties with African Americans throughout history. In the 1800s, slaves sang songs to lift their spirits and communicate their plight (Barnes 2005). Workers who earned their livings in mines, factories, and on farms in the early to mid-1900s had songs that spoke of the hazards of their working conditions (le Roux 2005). The Jazz Age of the 1920s saw Blacks and Whites turning to African American culture (music, dance, and slang) as a form of social rebellion. The mass marketing or commodification of the culture led to simplification and some exploitation of the true fabric of the culture (Enzensberger 1974). Still, artists such as Bessie Smith, James Reese Europe, and Ferdinand "Jelly Roll" Morton gained widespread fame among white and black audiences during this time.

The civil rights movement of the 1960s and 1970s featured black musicians soulfully detailing the disappointments of racism and the struggle for equality. Nina Simone's upbeat "Young, Gifted, and Black" and her lament to race relations "Mississippi Goddam," and The Chi-Lites' somewhat militant "Power to the People," linked artists and their words with a movement that was designed to change the country. Black music could be politicized during this period for several reasons (Watson 2001). First, record executives recognized the financial benefits that came with connections to large-scale activism. Second, grassroots leaders turned to musicians as a way to support their causes. Finally, as protests became hip, so did the artists (including James Brown and Jimi Hendrix) who participated in them.

More recently, rap and hip-hop music has been credited, and sometimes blamed, as the voice of many young African Americans. Research has found that the presence of rap and hip-hop music in the black community has been both vilified and celebrated. While images of misogyny, homophobia, and violence appear in some of the lyrics, other songs offer positive storytelling options for African American youth. In her study of the key audiences for rap and hip-hop music, sociologist Rachel Sullivan found that teen girls listen to the music because of the beat rather than the lyrics (Sullivan 2003). Sullivan also found that there is very little difference between how teens of different races perceive rap. The genre was popular among the respondents of all races, but African Americans were able to name more rap artists than any other group. In sum, she found there was universal acceptance of the notion that rap is a truthful reflection of society.

In early 2016, music icon Beyoncé Knowles released the song "Formation" to awaken America to issues relevant to Knowles and all black lives through frank imagery. The lyrics celebrate the beauty and pride of black women that are rarely celebrated in American culture:

> My daddy Alabama, Momma Louisiana
> You mix that Negro with that Creole, make a Texas Bamma
> I like my baby heir with baby hair and afros
> I like my Negro nose with Jackson Five nostrils
> Earned all this money, but they never take the country out me
> I got a hot sauce in my bag, swag.

In a powerful image in the song's video, set in New Orleans, Knowles is languishing on top of a police squad car that sinks in a large body of water. The image harkens back to the stories of police brutality told during the aftermath of 2005's Hurricane Katrina and the spate of deaths of African Americans in police custody in the years between 2014 and 2016.

Representations of African Americans in the News

In the 1960s, years of racial injustice and the assassination of civil rights leader Martin Luther King, Jr. combined to create a primal scream in black America. Following three years of riot-filled summers, President Lyndon B. Johnson appointed Senator Otto Kerner to lead the National Advisory Commission on Civil Disorders (the Kerner Commission) in July of 1967. The Commission reported that the news media were partially to blame for the rash of violence because, "The communications media, ironically, have failed to communicate." In its final report (National Advisory Commission on Civil Disorders 1968), the Commission pointed to broadcast news as the source of information African Americans most often used, and that the news media did not properly analyze and report on the race problems in the country. Because there was little acknowledgment of a problem, no solutions could be offered. Furthermore, the "white press" controlled much of the media and there was conscious or unconscious bias found in the news coverage. The Commission argued that these elements only served to strengthen the distrust African Americans had of the white power structure.

Since the time of the Kerner Commission report, research shows that there have been problematic images of Blacks on television news. Communication and public affairs professor Robert Entman found that local television news paints a picture of African Americans being defendants in need of physical restraint. Furthermore, his 1992 study found that African Americans tend to appear as criminals on television news more than other racial/ethnic groups, whereas Whites are shown as the victims. Entman argues that such representation of African Americans is not due to racism, but to journalists' dependence on the same sources to tell their stories and on their emphasis on stories dealing with crime and victimization (Entman 1992).

This depiction of African Americans as perpetrators can create presuppositions of the group for viewers. In other words, the images can prime or prompt viewers to make judgments about African Americans using information that comes easily to mind. *Priming* is defined as "the process by which activated mental constructs can influence how individuals evaluate other concepts and ideas" (Domke, Shah, and Wackman 1998). The role of priming is salient for African Americans (or any group, for that matter) because it creates and reinforces stereotypes. In another study, political communication experts Franklin Gilliam and Shanto Iyengar investigated how the local news can prime viewers, and determined that images of race in the local news can be powerful in shaping attitudes (Gilliam and Iyengar 2000). When a newscast contained five seconds of African American or Hispanic offenders, the viewers expressed an increased level of fear and support for stronger crime policies than subjects who were not exposed to these perpetrators. Although Gilliam and Iyengar noted that the fear levels were increased in viewers of all races, Whites and Asian Americans thought stiffer penalties were in order; the same images conjured thoughts of injustice and prejudice for African Americans and Hispanics. Seven years later, communication scholar Travis Dixon conducted a more in-depth investigation of race in the news, finding that study participants were able to remember darker skinned perpetrators more than their lighter skinned counterparts (Dixon 2005). A follow-up on the aforementioned study, conducted a year later, found that heavy news viewers were more likely to find a televised suspect guilty if the suspect had light-brown, medium-brown, or dark skin than if the suspect was white (Dixon and Maddox 2006).

Readers also are primed to construct social reality for African Americans. For example, media researchers Linus Abraham and Osei Appiah examined the impact of placing images of Blacks with stories regarding the three-strikes law and school vouchers. The three-strikes law mandates that if someone is convicted of a felony three times, judges are statutorily required to set a life sentence – no matter the severity of the third crime. School vouchers are government-subsidized coupons that allow parents who normally could not afford it to send their children to private schools. When stories about these two items were coupled with pictures of Blacks, stereotypes such as Blacks being uneducated, poor, and violent were primed (Abraham and Appiah 2006). Conversely, when audiences were exposed to stories that contained counter-stereotypical content, the readers experienced reduced stereotypical views (Ramasubramanian 2007).

The devaluing of African Americans persists in television news. African Americans are rarely used as authoritative leaders or sources on local or national news stories (Entman and Rojecki 2001a). African American victims of crimes do not receive as much coverage as white victims, nor are African Americans celebrated when they are triumphant. Stories such as the kidnapping of JonBenet Ramsey, a young white child, and the rescue of Jessica Lynch, a white soldier who was rescued in Iraq, receive the lion's share of television time. Similar stories featuring Shoshana Johnson, an African American soldier who was a prisoner of war in Iraq, and the dozens of children of color who go missing each year do not receive the same attention (Chaney 2008).

Research on the way newspapers deal with African Americans produces similar findings to the studies of TV news. Much of the research dealing with newspapers and African Americans centers on the *agenda setting* function of the medium. Communication scholars Maxwell McCombs and Donald Shaw determined the media's emphasis on a story gives the story a place of importance in the minds of its readers (McCombs and Shaw 1972). For example, social science researchers Kathryn Pickle, Sandra C. Quinn, and Jane D. Brown investigated coverage of HIV/AIDS in five African American newspapers during the height of the crisis in African American communities (Pickle, Quinn, and Brown 2002). They found that these newspapers covered HIV/AIDS as a health issue, criticized the government for not mitigating the problem, credited advocates, and delved into the conspiracy theories that claimed that Blacks were targets for the disease as a plot against the community. An analysis of mainstream newspaper coverage of inequities in the healthcare of African Americans illustrates that there has been an increase in these stories, with little discussion of the causes for the disparities in the healthcare system (Taylor-Clark *et al.* 2007).

Framing, discussed in Chapter 2 as a device used to tell a story, also determines how an audience thinks about a story. Entman's studies relating to criminal representations of African Americans, discussed earlier in this chapter, were actually conducted under the theoretical framework of framing. Numerous other studies that have explored the relationship between news media and representations of African Americans have also relied upon framing (see Box 4.2). The following list provides examples of such studies and gives a general idea of the main findings:

- Studies dealing with coverage of the civil rights movement frequently show that Southern papers did not fully tell the story of the movement (Friedman and Richardson 2008; Spratt *et al.* 2007).
- Joao H. Costa Vargas researched coverage in the *Los Angeles Times* of the riots that followed the acquittal of four police officers who were videotaped beating Rodney King. The newspaper was found to have incorrectly blamed Blacks for most of the violence and hosted a debate, based on false premises, about race and retribution (Costa Vargas 2004).
- The reaction to Hurricane Katrina, which devastated large swaths of New Orleans' African American community, has been studied through the lens of race. For example, race played a role in shaping attitudes about the government response to the storm. African Americans were more likely than non-African Americans to blame President Bush as opposed to local and state government for the failures of the relief effort (Haider-Markel, Delehanty, and Beverlin 2007).
- Social media, especially Twitter, have become places where stories about the victimization of black males and police brutality can be told through words and images. More than traditional media sources, social media have become advocacy outlets for those interested in justice for black males (Bonilla and Rosa 2015). The Black Lives Matter movement is one such hashtag that has gotten the attention of the public and high-profile political figures.

Box 4.2 President Obama and political depictions

The election of Barack Obama, a man with a white American mother and black Kenyan father, signified a turning point in American history. Some say the election demonstrated that racism was dissipating in favor of a more ethnically tolerant populace. A few pundits questioned if the Obama win signaled that the United States was now a postracial society. In a postracial society, the color of one's skin would no longer be a factor in how people perceived others; therefore, it would not impact how people decided to vote. While these sentiments have some validity, several incidents during the 2008 campaign illustrated that there were some citizens who, at the very least were racially and culturally insensitive and, at the most, overt bigots. Images with racist undertones appeared on signs held at rallies, on T-shirts, and on websites. These images portraying Obama as a monkey or Muslim terrorist sparked much debate and scorn from liberal and conservative commentators. The media publicized a handful of firings that stemmed from people distributing these messages via email.

Of course, images poking fun at some aspect of a political figure is not rare. For example, derisive images of 2016 Republican presidential nominee Donald Trump were persistently distributed via social media and displayed on television during his time on the campaign trail. Many of these images portrayed Trump as a baboon, an orangutan, or a shark. Still, there was not as much public outrage about these images. Certainly, there was no widespread media coverage of people being fired for sharing a joke about Trump at the workplace.

What accounts for the difference in the way these images are perceived? Should there be a difference in how the public reacts to these images? Is race the only element off limits when it comes to political satire?

The presence of African Americans in newsrooms can influence newspaper coverage. In one study of local news story assignments at the *Milwaukee Journal Sentinel*, minority reporters wrote a majority of the stories dealing with minority issues; white reporters wrote most of the stories about business and government. The researchers posit that there are several possible explanations for the pattern found, with two particularly plausible ones. They argue that it is possible that the power status of Whites who controlled the newspaper were segregating minorities to the pages of the newspaper that were less "powerful" and lacked a wide appeal. Another explanation is that minority journalists prefer to cover minority issues, just as a reporter with an interest in entertainment might prefer to cover entertainment issues. One African American reporter who was quoted in the study echoes this sentiment, stating: "With black reporters, I think the reason most end up writing about 'black' issues is because African Americans in general are preoccupied with social and racial issues and thus gravitate toward those kinds of stories more" (Pritchard and Stonbely 2007: 239).

Where newspaper reporters have somewhat limited column space and time to cover most of their daily stories, a magazine reporter has more time and space to delve deeper into stories. Because magazines can be niched to specific interests, the longer, more detailed, feature-type articles appearing in magazines and their accompanying images create a profound story for the readers. The representation of African Americans in magazines is particularly relevant when considering the media's impact on beauty, politics, and popular culture.

In February 1996, *Sports Illustrated* was lauded for featuring its first African American model, Tyra Banks, on the cover of their much-perused swimsuit edition. A bikini-clad Banks shared the cover with Argentine model Valerie Mazza (Delaney 1996) (Figure 4.3). This history-making turn was covered in *Newsweek* and *Time* magazines, though not everyone celebrated the appearance. First, the picture of

Figure 4.3 Valeria Mazza and Tyra Banks on the *Sports Illustrated* swimsuit cover.

Banks and Mazza appeared with the cover story, "South African Adventure." Was the magazine only saying that Banks was worthy of the cover shot in an issue about the "exotic" dark continent? Also, by pairing Banks with a similarly styled white-looking model hinted that the magazine was not convinced that Banks could sell the swimsuit issue herself. Interestingly, Banks had been used as the sole cover model on several publications for men, including *GQ*, three months before the *Sports Illustrated* cover.

Much of the hubbub surrounding Banks's cover revolved around that idea that images found in the print media have been shown to shape and reflect contemporary beauty standards for white individuals and people of color. By placing Banks on the cover of the much anticipated and purchased swimsuit issue, *Sports Illustrated* was acknowledging the mass appeal of an African American woman. The appearance of African American figures on magazine covers is significant because this is the image designed to capture the buyer. *Sports Illustrated* had indeed increased the number of African Americans on its cover between 1954 and 2004; however, this increase was not in proportion to the increase of African Americans in sports (Primm, DuBois, and Regoli 2007).

Studies about African American readership focus on adult and adolescent readers. In a study comparing the presence of women of color in magazines in 1999 and 2004, researchers Travis Dixon and Juanita Covert, using US Census data, found that African American women were underrepresented in both years (Dixon and Covert 2008). However, the presence of women of color did increase between these years. Because girls tend to seek guidance and identity from nonfamilial influences during their teen years, media influences are particularly profound during this time (Gilliam and Iyengar 1998). As such, teen magazines with their glossy pictures and heart-rending features are magnets for this group. Adolescent girls are voracious readers of these periodicals, which aid in shaping their attitudes and behaviors. In focus groups with adolescent African American, Hispanic, and white girls who read *Seventeen*, the girls said that they used both the magazine and parental guidance to understand their feelings about boys and their own femininity. In a particularly telling comment, one African American girl said, "They [the magazines] make the [Black] girls look less feminine than white girls," after observing white models in feminine poses and a black model holding a baseball (Bell Kaplan and Cole 2003: 146). In the case of this study, only African American girls noticed that they were underrepresented in the pages of *Seventeen* – Hispanic girls made no mention of the deficiency.

The ways in which African Americans are presented in magazines, as well as in other forms of media, are very much tied to advertising.

African Americans and Advertisements

By 2007, industry publication *Advertising Age* estimated that the burgeoning African American middle class had a collective buying power of near $900 billion (Frazier 2008). To capitalize on this audience, Procter & Gamble joined forces with agencies that specialize in targeting African Americans to sell paper towels and laundry soap. Carol H. Williams, the President, Chief Executive, and Chief Creative Officer of Carol H. Williams Advertising, said her company's teaming with P&G "is not just a feel-good situation, the right thing to do. It is smart marketing that could increase your bottom line significantly" (Elliot 2003).

In some cases, attempts to grab a share of this $900 billion have led to less than desirable outcomes. For example, the overemphasis of African Americans in malt liquor ads led 22 interest groups to criticize the brewers of this inexpensive beverage, which has a greater potency than beer (Rothenberg 1989). Critics were concerned that people in the African American community might identify with the people in the ads, increasing drinking in the population.

Advertisements featuring women of color have been found to maintain and create stereotypes. For example, advertisements featuring white women as beautiful and black women as oversexed persist (Sengupta 2006). Media researcher Cynthia Frisby, using social comparison theory, which, as discussed in Chapter 2, addresses how people compare themselves to others, found that African American women who have existing negative feelings about their bodies tend to have lower satisfaction with their bodies when exposed to African American models in advertisements (Frisby 2004). Social comparison is amplified when the consumer makes an upward (idealized) comparison.

Because the aim of advertising is to entice large segments of the public to purchase goods and services, advertisers are charged with presenting their wares in an appealing manner. For this reason, advertising is often a slice of reality. Sociologist John Grady measured how advertising mirrored racial integration between 1936 and 2000. Grady, using advertisements found in *Life* (a magazine synonymous with Americana), found that there was limited white/black integration even though sociological studies found Whites having a strong commitment to integration (Grady 2007).

With the growing buying power of African Americans, not only advertisers but also those within the African American community have endeavored to establish their own media outlets. Those successful in their media businesses have gone beyond the African American target to attract general audiences and readers as well.

African Americans in the Media Business

It could be argued that, more than any other minority group, African Americans have a tradition of establishing their own press as a way to tell their own stories to their own communities. African Americans who feel disenfranchised by the mainstream media turn to alternative media to find sources they trust (Vercolliti and Brewer 2006). The spirit of African American entrepreneurship is found in the history of many publications geared toward Blacks. The *Chicago Defender* is considered one of the most significant black weekly newspapers in history. A glance at its "About Us" page tells readers it was founded by Robert S. Abbott in 1905. The *Defender* has been credited with influencing elections and helping to integrate the Chicago police and fire departments. During the Harlem Renaissance in the 1920s and 1930s, black writers, journalists, artists, and musicians challenged racism and stereotypes and through cultural and intellectual creation promoted racial and social integration, and worked to shed light on continued injustices. For instance, noted African American journalist Marvel Cooke, who began her writing career as W.E.B. DeBois's editorial assistant at *The Crisis*, the magazine of the NAACP, spent most of the 1920s and 1930s writing exposés about such subjects as segregation and discrimination in New York for local newspapers. One of her most recognized and heralded pieces (co-authored by Ella Baker) was a five-part series entitled "The Bronx Slave Market," published in 1950, in which Cooke went undercover as a domestic worker to tell of the unfair, exploitative, and demeaning practices that continued 100 years after the abolishment of slavery (Jones-Webb, Baranowski, and Wagenaar 1997).

The largest African American-owned publishing company, Johnson Publishing Company (JPC), was home to the African American lifestyle magazine *Ebony*, until the magazine was sold to African American-owned Clear View Group in 2016, due to financial struggles. In a comment regarding the sale of the magazine, Linda Johnson Rice, the daughter of the founder of Johnson Publishing, stated: "This is the next chapter in retaining the legacy that my father, John H. Johnson, built to ensure the celebration of African-Americans" (Chanick 2016). The company also sold its online-only *Jet* magazine.

According to its website, Essence Communication, Inc. founded *Essence*, a magazine for African American women, in 1969. Although its target demographic is women, former editor-in-chief Susan L. Taylor invited men to a yearly edition titled, "Say Brother." *Essence* features style, entertainment, and advice, packaged in a glossy, fashionable publication. The advertising spaces are full of images of fragrances, cosmetics, and clothes signaling that African American women are viable and valuable consumers. African American-owned magazines are significant because the trade association, Magazine Publishers of America, estimates that the 86 percent of African Americans who read magazines read more issues per month than any other ethnic group ("Drawing on Diversity for Successful Marketing" 2011).

The media empire of the first black female billionaire Oprah Winfrey cannot be ignored when discussing successful African American-owned media businesses. Winfrey's $345 million company, Harpo, employs more than 400 people. Winfrey used her wildly successful syndicated daily talk show to create a brand that a racially mixed public turns to for lifestyle education and spiritual enrichment. From this foundation, Winfrey has produced several motion pictures for TV and the big screen, and owns all or a part of a cable network (OWN), the Rachel Ray talk show, the Dr. Phil Show, and the Dr. Oz show. Winfrey's massive success is unprecedented and remarkable given that there is a general paucity of African American ownership in the broadcasting industry. Chiefly, the lack of capital is to blame (Hoovers n.d.).

The Internet has also provided a platform for African Americans to take part in the media business. Some of the Internet companies created to provide content targeted at African Americans are owned by large conglomerates, yet they do employ African Americans who play substantive roles in these companies. Examples of such companies are:

- *The Root* is an online magazine that was launched in 2008 through the efforts of Dr. Henry Louis Gates, Jr. The magazine's site describes it as "the premier news, opinion and culture site for African-American influencers." http://www.theroot.com. The magazine can be followed via its Facebook page and Twitter site (@theroot).
- BlackRefer.com, a Google-type search engine, provides users with links to African American-related news and commercial websites.
- The most popular website related to African Americans, Black Planet, offers a dating service, news, and entertainment updates.

Concluding Remarks

The history and representation of African Americans in the mass media is a varied one. The majority of the literature about media representations of African Americans indicates that there has been some disparity in the way the race was portrayed in the past and present. Changes in training, employment, and ownership have encouraged more accurate and balanced representations in the black press and in mainstream media. The constantly evolving face of the media and color of the country ensures that there is social and financial incentive in doing complete reporting and characterizations.

The Internet has helped in this regard through the creation of several sites that serve as unique sources for African Americans. A 2014 Pew study found that Internet use is increasing – 87 percent of Whites and 80 percent of Blacks are Internet users. The widespread availability of broadband technology helps close the divide with regard to Internet access, with 74 percent of Whites and 62 percent of Blacks having broadband connection in their homes. Moreover young, college-educated, and higher income African Americans are just as likely as young, college-educated, higher income Whites to be Internet and broadband users: 86 percent of African Americans aged 18–29 have broadband in their homes; 88 percent of black college graduates and 91 percent of African Americans with an annual household income of $75,000 or more per year also have broadband in their homes. Hashtags such as #BlackLivesMatter and #BlackTwitter contribute to an increase in young Blacks using the short messaging service (see Table 4.1).

Table 4.1 Comparative Twitter usage based on age and race.

	Whites	African Americans
18–29	29%	40%
30–49	21%	21%
50–64	10%	9%

Source: Pew Research Center (2014).

Reflection Questions and Thoughts to Consider

1. The history of African Americans in the United States has seen some sorrows and some joys. How has the music of the country been impacted by these highs and lows? Can you make a list of genres and/or songs that reflect the moods of the African American experience?
2. Have you ever flipped through the pages of a magazine targeted at African American women? Pick up an *Essence* magazine. Compare it to *Cosmopolitan.* Is there much difference between how the women are photographed in these publications? Are the stories similar? How are non-African American women portrayed in *Essence?* How are African American women portrayed in *Cosmopolitan?*
3. Who are the most influential African Americans in media today? What makes them important? Who are some up and coming leaders? What will this group add to our media landscape?
4. Do a comparison of the political/news websites. Start with the left-leaning *Huffington Post,* and then turn to Breitbart.com, which has a more conservative bent. Then look at the African American-focused TheRoot.com. How are these sites using words, images, and multimedia technologies to speak to their respective audiences? Where are the sites similar? How are they different?

References

Abraham, Linus, and Osei Appiah. 2006. "Framing News Stories: The Role of Visual Imagery in Priming Racial Stereotypes." *The Howard Journal of Communications* 17: 183–203.

Albiniak, Paige. 2005. "Why Grey's Seems So Bright." *Broadcasting and Cable*, May 30: 18–24.

Barnes, Sandra L. 2005. "Black Church Culture and Community Action." *Social Forces* 84: 967–994.

Bell Kaplan, Elaine, and Leslie Cole. 2003. "'I Want to Read Stuff on Boys': White, Latina, and Black Girls Reading Seventeen Magazine and Encountering Adolescence." *Adolescence* 38: 141–159.

Bogle, Donald. 2013. *Toms, Coons, Mulattoes, Mammies, and Bucks: An Interpretive History of Blacks in American Films*, 4th ed. New York, NY: Continuum.

Bonilla, Yarimar, and Jonathan Rosa. 2015. "#Ferguson: Digital Protest, Hashtag Ethnography, and the Racial Politics of Social Media in the United States." *American Ethnologist* 42: 4–17.

Chaney, Kathy. 2008. "Missing, Murdered Black Youth get Unequal National Media Coverage." *The Chicago Defender*, October 15. https://chicagodefender.com/2008/10/14/missing-murdered-black-youth-get-unequal-national-media-coverage (accessed April 4, 2017).

Chanick, Robert. 2016. "Johnson Publishing sells *Ebony, Jet* magazines to Texas firm." *Chicago Tribune*, June 15. http://www.chicagotribune.com/business/ct-ebony-sold-0615-biz-20160614-story.html (accessed April 4, 2017).

Clark, Naeemah, and Stephynie Chapman Perkins. 2007. "Parts of the Scenery, Leader of the Pack or One of the Gang: Diversity on Children's Television." Paper presented at the International Communications Association, May 23–24.

Costa Vargas, Joao H. 2004. "*The Los Angeles Times'* Coverage of the 1992 Rebellion." *Ethnicities* 4: 209–236.

Delaney, Yvonne. 1996. "Tyra Banks Calls Swimsuit Photo a Vote for International Unity." *New York Amsterdam News.*

Dixon, Travis L. 2005. "Schemas as Average Conceptions: Skin Tone, Television News Exposure, and Culpability Judgments." *Journalism and Mass Communication Quarterly* 83: 131–149.

Dixon, Travis L., and Juanita J. Covert. 2008. "A Changing View: Representation and Effects of the Portrayal of Women of Color in Mainstream Women's Magazines." *Communication Research* 35: 232–256.

Dixon, Travis L., and Keith B. Maddox. 2006. "Skin Tone, Crime News, and Social Reality Judgments: Priming the Stereotype of the Dark and Dangerous Black Criminal." *Journal of Applied Social Psychology* 35: 1555–1570.

Domke, David, Dhavan Shah, and Daniel Wackman. 1998. "Media Priming Effects: Accessibility, Association, and Activation." *International Journal of Public Opinion Research*: 51–74.

"Drawing on Diversity for Successful Marketing: African-American/Black Market Profile." Magazine Publishers of America. https://www.sec.gov/Archives/edgar/data/1131166/000101376208002707/ex992.pdf (accessed April 17, 2017).

Elliot, Stuart 2003. "Campaigns for Black Consumers." *New York Times*, June 13. http://ruby.fgcu.edu/courses/tdugas/IDS3301/acrobat/blackconsumers.pdf (accessed April 17, 2017).

Entman, Robert M. 1992. "Blacks in the News: Television, Modern Racism and Cultural Change." *Journalism Quarterly* 69: 341–361.

Entman, Robert, and Andrew Rojecki. 2001a. *From Bad to Worse: Black Images on "White" News*. Chicago, IL: University of Chicago Press.

Entman, Robert M., and Andrew Rojecki. 2001b. *The Black Image in the White Mind: Media and Race in America*. Chicago, IL: University of Chicago Press.

Enzensberger, Hans Magnus. 1974. *The Consciousness Industry*. New York, NY: Seabury Press.

Fisher, Celeste A. 2002. "America's Worst Nightmare: Reading the Ghetto in a Culturally Diverse Context." In *Say It Loud! African American Audiences, Media, and Identity*, edited by Robin Means Coleman, 229–248. New York, NY: Routledge.

Frazier, Mya, 2008. "The Catch-22 of Buying Black Media." *Advertising Age*, 79.

Friedman, Barbara G., and John D. Richardson. 2008. "A National Disgrace." *Journalism History* 33: 224–232.

Frisby, Cindy M. 2004. "Does Race Matter? Effects of Idealized Images on African American Women's Perception of Body Esteem." *Journal of Black Studies* 34: 323–347.

Gerson, Walter M. 1966. "Mass Media Socialization Behavior: Negro–White Differences." *Social Forces* 45: 40–50.

Gilliam, Jr., Franklin D., and Shanto Iyengar. 1998. "The Superpredator Script." *Nieman Reports* 52: 45–47.

Gilliam, Franklin, and Shanto Iyengar. 2000. "Prime Suspects: The Influence of Local Television News on the Viewing Public." *American Journal of Political Science* 44: 560–573.

Glenn, Cerise L., and Landra J. Cunningham. 2009. "The Power of Black Magic: The Magical Negro and White Salvation in Film." *Journal of Black Studies* 40: 135–152.

Gorn, Gerald J., Marvin E. Goldberg, and Rabinda N. Kanungo. 1976. "Role of Educational Television in Changing the Intergroup Attitudes of Children." *Child Development* 47: 277–280.

Grady, John. 2007. "Advertising Images as Social Indicators: Depiction of Blacks in Life Magazine, 1936–2000." *Visual Studies* 22: 211–239.

Grahn, Nancy Lee. 2015. Twitter. https://twitter.com/nancyleegrahn (accessed September 2015).

Greenberg, Bradley S., and Jeffery E. Brand. 1993. "Cultural Diversity on Saturday Morning Television." In *Children and Television: Images in a Changing Sociocultural World*, edited by Gordon L. Berry and Joy K. Asamen, 132–142. Newbury Park, CA: Sage.

Haider-Markel, Daniel, William Delehanty, and Matthew Beverlin. 2007. "Media Framing and Racial Attitudes in the Aftermath of Katrina." *Policy Studies Journal* 35: 587–605.

Hoovers. n.d. "Harpo, Inc." http://www.hoovers.com/company-information/cs/company-profile.harpo_productions_inc.61a5540d79d7cfdd.html (accessed April 17, 2017).

Jones-Webb, Rhonda, Susan Baranowski, and Alexander C. Wagenaar. 1997. "Content Analysis of Coverage of Alcohol Control Policy Issues in Black-Oriented and Mainstream Newspapers in the U.S." *Journal of Public Health Policy* 18: 49–66.

le Roux, Gordon Marc. 2005. "'Whistle While You Work': A Historical Account of Some Associations among Music, Work, and Health." *American Journal of Public Health* 95: 1106–1109.

McCombs, Maxwell E., and Donald L. Shaw. 1972. "The Agenda-Setting Function of Mass Media." *Public Opinion Quarterly* 36: 176–187.

National Advisory Commission on Civil Disorders. 1968. *Report of the National Advisory Commission on Civil Disorders* (Kerner Report). New York, NY: Bantam Books.

Pew Research Center. 2014. "African Americans and Technology Use: Demographic Portrait." Pew Research Center. http://www.pewinternet.org/2014/01/06/African-Americans-and-technology-use (accessed April 4, 2017).

Pickle, Kathryn, Sandra C. Quinn, and Jane D. Brown. 2002. "HIV/AIDS Coverage in Black Newspapers, 1991–1996: Implications for Health Communication and Health Education." *Journal of Health Communication* 7: 427–444.

Primm, Eric, Summer DuBois, and Robert M. Regoli. 2007. "Every Picture Tells a Story: Racial Representation on *Sports Illustrated* Covers." *Journal of American Culture* 30: 222–231.

Pritchard, David, and Sarah Stonbely. 2007. "Racial Profiling in the Newsroom." *Journalism and Mass Communication Quarterly* 84: 231–248.

Ramasubramanian, Srividya. 2007. "Media-Based Strategies to Reduce Racial Stereotypes Activated by News Stories." *Journalism and Mass Communication Quarterly* 84: 249–264.

Reed, Ishmael. 2010. "Fade to White." *New York Times*, February 5: 25.

Robichaux, Mark. 2006. "Rhimes' Anatomy." *Broadcasting and Cable*, February 27: 28.

Rothenberg, Randall. 1989. "Groups Plan to Protest Malt Liquor Campaigns." *New York Times*, August 23. http://www.nytimes.com/1989/08/23/business/the-media-business-advertising-groups-plan-to-protest-malt-liquor-campaigns.html?pagewanted=1 (accessed April 14, 2017).

Sengupta, Rhea. 2006. "Reading Representations of Black, East Asian, and White women in Magazines of Adolescent Girls." *Sex Roles* 54: 799–808.

Spratt, Margaret, Cathy F. Bullock, Gerald Baldasty, Fiona Clark, Alex Halavais, Michael McCluskey, and Susan Schrenk. 2007. "News, Race, and the Status Quo. The Case of Emmett Louis Till." *Howard Journal of Communications* 18: 169–192.

Squires, Catherine. 2009. *African Americans and the Media*. Malden, MA: Polity Press.

Stroman, Carolyn A. 1984. "The Socialization Influence of Television on Black Children." *Journal of Black Studies* 15: 79–100.

Stroman, Carolyn A. 1991. "Television's Role in the Socialization of African American Children and Adolescents." *The Journal of Negro Education* 60: 314–327.

Sullivan, Rachel. 2003. "Rap and Race: It's Got a Nice Beat, but What About the Message?" *Journal of Black Studies* 33: 605–622.

Taylor-Clark, Kalahn A., Felicia E. Mebane, Gillian K. Steel Fisher, and Robert J. Blendon. 2007. "News of Disparity: Content Analysis of News Coverage of African American Healthcare Inequalities in the USA, 1994–2004." *Social Science and Medicine* 65: 405–417.

TheWrap.com. 2015. "General Hospital Star Rips Viola Davis' Emmy Speech – and then Profusely Apologizes." http://www.thewrap.com/general-hospital-star-nancy-lee-grahn-viola-davis-emmys-speech-lead-actress-drama-htgawm (accessed April 4, 2017).

Tucker, Lauren R. 1997. "Was the Revolution Televised? Professional Criticism about '*The Cosby Show*' and the Essentialization of Black Cultural Expression." *Journal of Broadcasting and Electronic Media* 97: 90–108.

Vercolliti, Timothy, and Paul R. Brewer. 2006. "'To Plead our own Cause': Public Opinion toward Black and Mainstream News Media among African Americans." *Journal of Black Studies* 37: 231–250.

Watson, C.S. 2001. "A Nation of Millions: Hip Hop Culture and the Legacy of Black Nationalism." *The Communication Review* 4: 373–398.

5

Representations of Hispanics/Hispanic Americans

If you have your computer or phone handy, visit the Billboard Latin Airplay chart (Billboard.com/charts/latin-airplay). You'll likely see some names unfamiliar to you (Nicky Jam, Regularo Caro) mixed in with some extremely familiar names such as Ariana Grande, Christina Aguilera, and Enrique Iglesias. The chart is a representation of the state of Latino/as and Hispanics in the overall media world. Some musicians, actors, writers, and producers have found success in both mainstream and niche outlets. Others are extremely successful in the niche genre with little or no success in mainstream radio. For instance, traditional Latin music stations have been joined by formats such as La Preciosa (popular Spanish-language music from the 1970s, 1980s, and 1990s) and the wildly popular Hurban (Hispanic Urban) format and its signature sound of reggaeton. Daddy Yankee and Shakira are among the artists who have been able to appeal to wide US audiences by mixing the familiar beats of Latin music and hip-hop.

What has happened in the music industry with regard to its growing offerings of Latin music is indicative of what has been happening in other forms of mass media. Films and television programming that feature Hispanic characters and/or present plots that revolve around Hispanic culture are now more easily and prominently found. News outlets designed to serve the various Hispanic communities also have become widespread. As will be discussed in this chapter, much of this growth in Latin mass media is due to the growing Hispanic population in the United States.

The chapter begins by providing a historical background to how Hispanics have been represented in the US mass media. It then addresses how media depictions have evolved and how this group has defined itself through mass media. The case of Hispanic audiences is unique because any discussion of this group must contain issues associated with bilingualism and acculturation that occur as steady immigration makes the Hispanic population the largest minority group in the United States. These factors also affect how the media represent this large and diverse social group.

Historical Background to Hispanic/Hispanic American Representations

Before proceeding with a discussion of Hispanic representations, it is important to define the term "Hispanic" and examine its distinction from the other now widely used term, "Latino." Traditionally, "Hispanic" has been used to describe an ethnicity that encompasses different races and ancestries from areas once under Spanish rule (e.g., Central America, South America, Mexico). It is a term that was created by the United States government in the 1960s as part of the government's census efforts

Diversity in US Mass Media, Second Edition. Catherine A. Luther, Carolyn Ringer Lepre, and Naeemah Clark.
© 2018 John Wiley & Sons Inc. Published 2018 by John Wiley & Sons Inc.

(Valdivia 2010). "Latino" is also a US-originated term created to signify people living in the United States who are of Latin American origin or descent. In recent times, however, the two terms have been used interchangeably. In fact, some who are often categorized as Hispanic by the US government or by private institutions prefer to be called Latino. The authors of this book have chosen to more often use the term "Hispanic"; however, because of the fact that many studies use the term "Latino," while others use "Hispanic," usage of both terms will be found in this chapter.

Whether using the term "Hispanic" or "Latino," it is important to recognize that the terms do not describe a race but rather an ethnicity made up of distinct groups that have some common cultural traditions and similar languages. The United States accommodates cultures that have originated from people from such diverse areas as Mexico, Cuba, and Spain. In spite of such diversity, the tendency has been to depict Hispanics as a single, though broad, ethnic category, disregarding each group's distinctive cultural history, as will be made apparent in the following brief overview of the historical context of their mass media representations.

The Spanish settled in Florida nearly 50 years before the British settled Jamestown, Virginia. They also populated what is now Texas and California. Following the Mexican–American War, Mexico handed over to the United States lands which are now part of Utah, Arizona, Nevada, New Mexico, and Colorado. Under the Treaty of Guadalupe Hidalgo (1848), the United States pledged to recognize that certain portions of these lands belonged to Mexicans. However, what followed was a disregard of many land ownerships; much of the land was usurped and sold to white owners. In order to justify such actions, akin to what occurred with American Indians, images were conjured that were highly disparaging of Mexicans as being mentally inferior to Whites and criminal in nature (Mirande 1987). These images would carry over into the twentieth century and frequently be used in mass media portrayals.

Although an influx of Anglo settlers led to the displacement of Mexicans and other Hispanics, remnants of their cultures – such as food and architecture – remained. Thus, it could be considered that from 1513 when Spanish explorer Ponce de Leon searched for the Fountain of Youth in what is now Florida, Hispanics have played a major part in shaping the landscape of North America. In 2010, the estimated 50.5 million Hispanic population of the United States comprised in part those directly descended from these Spanish settlers and, in larger part, those who have legally and illegally migrated to the United States and their descendants. More than 30 million members of the Hispanic population were born in the United States and 18 million were foreign born (Humes, Jones, and Ramirez 2011) (see Table 5.1).

Table 5.1 Hispanic population, percentage of total US population by birth (2014).

	Foreign-Born Hispanics %	US-Born Hispanics %
1960	0.9	5.5
1970	1.8	7.8
1980	4.2	10.6
1990	7.8	14.0
2000	14.1	21.1
2010	18.8	31.9
2014	19.3	35.9

Source: Pew Research Center (2014).

As has been the experience of American Indians and African Americans in US history, Hispanics have faced the segregation, racism, and stereotyping that result from fear of ethnic minorities. Throughout this chapter, keep in mind that the issues related to the position of Hispanics in US media are made even more complicated since Hispanics in America live in two worlds. On the one hand, an Afro-Cuban man can be culturally Hispanic while embracing reggaeton music and his grandmother's favorite Spanish-language *telenovelas* (Spanish soap operas). On the other hand, that same man may be reliant on *USA Today* and the Fox News website to keep up with current events. Identifying with both groups in different situations is commonplace. One result of this straddling of cultures is that some Hispanics use English-language and Spanish-language media interchangeably. In 2014, close to 70 percent of Hispanics said they speak only English at home or reported that they spoke English "very well." In 1980, only 40 percent of Hispanics responded the same way. This difference is largely because there has been an increase of Hispanics born in the United States in the past 25 years.

It also should again be stressed that Hispanics are not one monolithic group in the United States. The media and related research tend to ignore the differences between the cultures or even languages of Dominicans, Mexicans, Nicaraguans, or El Salvadorans, and so on. Even though each of these groups has unique histories and communities in America, some researchers (for better or worse) have found it convenient and tidier to combine these groups into one mass group labeled "Hispanics." This chapter will, where possible, make these distinctions clear. However, because the chapter summarizes the work of others, these distinctions may not be known.

Hispanics/Hispanic Americans in Film

Some of the earliest images of Hispanics in the US cinema were found in the motion picture representations of violent Mexican revolutionaries, gypsies, violent half-breeds, Latin lovers (Don Juans), and exotic and sexualized *señoritas*. Darker skinned Mexicans were cast as *banditos*. Perhaps the best-known bandito is Mexican actor Alfonso Bedoya, who stole scenes from Humphrey Bogart in the classic film *The Treasure of the Sierra Madre* (1948). In the film, Bogart's character, Fred C. Dobbs, is on a manic search for gold in the Sierra Madre. While on his quest, he is confronted by an unkempt Gold Hat (Bedoya) who, with his rough group of banditos, tries to stop Dobbs by saying that they are the *federales* or police. Dobbs is skeptical:

> DOBBS: If you're the police, where are your badges?
> GOLD HAT: Badges? We ain't got no badges. We don't need no badges! I don't have to show you any stinkin' badges!

Even though this character and this scene have worked its way into popular culture, the subtext of the line is problematic. Here, a Mexican who is intent on stealing the gold of another prospector impersonates the police – the height of audacity. He has no regard for the law and is, in effect, enforcing lawlessness in his territory. This depiction has consistently been applied to Mexican characters.

Noted Chicano/Hispanic film historian Frank Javier Garcia Berumen suggests that decades of powerful and consistent stereotypes about Hispanics have influenced all moviegoers' understanding of the role of this social group. Not only is he concerned about the impact of what he deems the overwhelmingly negative and potentially destructive stereotypes on other social groups, but most importantly he sees the damaging effects on Hispanics' sense of self, their sense of historical context, and their understanding of their own future potential (Suro 2004). He notes that, starting with the earliest images of Hispanics in film, actors, writers, and directors brought their personal prejudices to work, which, as they were often based in general ignorance, yielded stereotypical results: "Sombreros and serape-draped Mexicans taking siestas on sidewalks; Mexicans consuming only the three diet staples of chile, tacos, and liquor; the Hispanic inevitably seeking political and social guidance, acceptance and 'enlightenment' of the Anglo" (Garcia Berumen 1995: 62).

Early Hollywood movie studios were not sensitive to the diverse nature of the various nationalities that make up the Latino/Hispanic social group. For example, in 1921 Rudolph Valentino earned the title "Latin lover" by playing a Frenchman who lived in Argentina in *The Four Horsemen of the Apocalypse.* In 1925, movie studio Metro-Goldwyn-Mayer cast Ramon Novarro, the son of a Mexican dentist, in the role of a Jewish prince in the silent film *Ben-Hur: A Tale of Christ* (1925). Spanish actor Antonio Moreno appeared as an Argentinian with eyes for other men's wives in two films – *My American Wife* (1922) and *The Temptress* (1926). The beautiful Mexican actress Delores del Rio played an exotic South Seas siren who swims naked and is ultimately sacrificed to a volcano god in *Bird of Paradise* (1932). Portuguese actress Carmen Miranda was erroneously nicknamed "the Brazilian bombshell" because of her ebullient performances and her appearance (e.g., wearing a hat piled with mountains of fruit, flowers, and feathers) in films such as *Down Argentine Way* (1940) and *That Night in Rio* (1941). These oversimplified casting decisions suggest that producers did not particularly care about the various cultural and ethnic differences between the social groups as long as the film's story could be told. Therefore, it should come as no surprise that the types of roles available to actors of Hispanic descent were stereotypic and one-dimensional.

Although the stereotypical roles in Hollywood persisted throughout the first six decades of the twentieth century (e.g., crazy violent banditos in *Butch Cassidy and the Sundance Kid* [1969]), Hollywood also celebrated the work of several actors of Hispanic descent playing Hispanic characters. In 1952, Anthony Quinn, who was born in Chihuahua, Mexico, earned an Academy Award for his work as the alcoholic brother of Mexican Revolutionary Emiliano Zapata (played by non-Mexican Marlon Brando) in *Viva Zapata!* In his role as Eufemio Zapata, Quinn helps his brother rebel against the Mexican president. After their successful revolution, Eufemio himself becomes a corrupt dictator. Even though the story was dramatized retelling of real-life events, it provided Americans a glimpse of some little-known aspects of Mexican history.

Another significant moment in the history of representations of Hispanics in film was the 1961 musical *West Side Story.* The film, a modern twist on the Shakespearean play *Romeo and Juliet,* centers on two teens from rival gang neighborhoods. As the Sharks (a Puerto Rican gang) and the Jets (a white gang) fight/dance, Maria, the sister of a Shark leader, falls in love with Tony, a Jet member. Even though the lead role of Maria was portrayed by Natalie Wood, the daughter of Russian immigrants, one of the film's breakout stars was Puerto Rican actress Rita Moreno. In one of the movie's most gripping scenes, Anita (played by Moreno) goes to the enemy camp to deliver news to the Jets and, while there, is verbally abused and almost raped by the white gang. Her rage at the boys is palpable and pivotal to the film. Moreover, this scene is illustrative of the racial strife that existed in urban neighborhoods in the country. The divide between races coexisting in common spaces caused tension and, at times, that tension exploded into violence, rioting, and crime. *West Side Story* won 10 Oscars including a Best Supporting Actress award for Moreno and the Best Picture award of 1961. Incidentally, Moreno is one of the few performers (of any ethnicity) to win Emmy, Grammy, Oscar, and Tony awards in the span of their careers.

The success of Moreno and Quinn generally allowed them to skirt the roles that pigeonholed actors of Hispanic descent. Still, stereotypic images remained, with roles of domestic workers, lazy gardeners, and ominous gang members becoming the primary roles for Hispanics in the 1970s, 1980s, and 1990s. A thoughtful analysis of films reveals that these stereotypes have not disappeared, though some have been altered slightly. For example, the domestic worker still appears in film, but these women now are given a voice. In *Spanglish* (2004), Paz Vega (a Spanish-born actress) plays Flor, a wise Mexican immigrant who struggles to maintain her and her daughter's heritage when she is hired as a live-in housekeeper for a wealthy white family in Los Angeles. Even though Flor falls in love with her employer (played by Adam Sandler), she knows that she must get away from the family so that her daughter will be proud of their ethnic origin. Actresses of Hispanic descent such as Jessica Alba (*Sin City*, 2005), Rosario Dawson (*Rent*, 2005), and Eva Mendes (*The Women*, 2008) have all been cast as sexually charged women, yet they use that sexuality for their own empowerment.

Although throughout film history there are some examples of Hispanic leads in movies, by and large, Hollywood has not fully utilized this group in its big-budget films. While African American stars such as Will Smith and Denzel Washington are known in the industry for bringing large audiences to theaters, Hollywood producers seem not to have the same confidence in Hispanic performers. Although some actors, such as Spanish actor Antonio Banderas, who has starred in box office hits such as *Philadelphia* (1993) and as the voice of Puss in Boots in three of the *Shrek* movies (2004, 2007, 2010), and Puerto Rican-Colombian actor John Leguizamo, who appears in Netflix's *Bloodlines* (2015 debut) and as the voice of Sid the Sloth in the *Ice Age* movies (2002, 2006, 2009, 2016), have become well known in films, there is a dearth of Hispanic actors in starring roles. To combat this lack of plum parts for these actors, some Hispanics have seized the reins of their own stories and their own careers to create work that is representative of their own experiences. The earliest efforts of Hispanic filmmaking were independent features made by artists who wanted to document the struggle of the ethnic group. One of these filmmakers, Luis Valdez, the father of Chicano theater, started his career by telling the stories of the civil rights struggle of Mexicans in the United States. In 1969, Valdez produced *I Am Joaquin* as a visual representation of an epic poem chronicling the fight for equal rights of Mexicans. As his acclaim grew, his budgets and audience widened. In 1981, he produced *Zoot Suit* (starring Edward James Olmos), which looked at the wrongful murder conviction of a group of Mexican Americans. The film was celebrated and was even nominated for a coveted Golden Globe Best Picture award. Valdez's most well-known film, *La Bamba* (1987), a Columbia Pictures biopic of 1950s rock star Ritchie Valens, not only propelled Valdez to national prominence as a mainstream filmmaker, but gave other Mexican American actors including Esai Morales (*My Family/Mi Familia* [1995]) and Rosanna DeSoto (*Star Trek VI: The Undiscovered Country* [1991]) nationwide success. The contribution of Valdez cannot be overestimated when considering the struggle to confront and replace limited and one-dimensional representations of Hispanics in film.

For the most part, however, when Hispanics have not been involved in producing films featuring Hispanic characters, the stereotypical representations established in the early years of film have tended to persist. An exception to this unfortunate rule was Adam Buncher's critically acclaimed *Hole in the Wall* (2014). This independent film tells the story of a Mexican American chef living in New York City who is doing his best to give his immigrant family the American Dream. The film has not been screened in many theaters, which means it has gone largely unnoticed by audiences. Sergio Castillo, who plays lead character Oscar Entrega in the film, penned an op-ed lauding the film's salience at a pivotal time for immigrants in the United States. Castillo (2016) wrote:

> The farcical election for the presidency of the United States has been an exhausting and brutal journey for anyone paying attention to it and the Latina/o/x community has been one of the primary targets of the unapologetic and wrathful rhetoric by the leading Republican presidential candidate and his dangerously devoted followers. But this sentiment didn't start with Donald Trump. He didn't create the racist attitudes toward Latina/o/x immigrants and Latina/os in general. He has merely made it politically acceptable to be open about the bigotry aimed at us. …
>
> President Obama has deported more immigrants than any other president in the history of the United States and almost more than all of the US presidents combined from the 20th century. He may exceed that goal by the time he leaves office. It is deeply tragic that so many immigrants have been forced back to their countries of origins. People like Oscar Entrega have proven themselves to be valuable assets to our nation, yet they remain largely invisible. When was the last time you had a serious conversation with the person who delivered your food?

The notion that the growing influence of Latinos in America would result in more of their stories being told is not new in US media. However, changes have been coming largely due to the efforts of Hispanic artists speaking up (Gruber and Thau 2003). Artists creating their own stories have impacted Hispanic representations in television – although with some uneven results.

Hispanics/Hispanic Americans in Entertainment Television

Perhaps the most well-known Hispanic character in television history appeared on the classic 1950s sitcom *I Love Lucy* (1951–1957). Desi Arnaz starred as Ricky Ricardo, a Cuban bandleader married to trouble-making redhead Lucy (played by Arnaz's real-life wife Lucille Ball) (Figure 5.1). In 1951, the idea of a white/Cuban couple on television may have been considered controversial, but the program humorously highlighted their differences by making Ricky's Spanish rants at Lucy a trademark of the show. Arnaz was not only a pioneer on television screens but also behind the scenes. He and Ball owned Desilu studios, which produced several shows in the 1950s and 1960s including *Star Trek* (1966–1969) and *Mission: Impossible* (1966–1973), until the company's sale in 1967.

Several television programs aired in the 1970s, 1980s, and 1990s that tried to address the changing ethnic landscape in America. For example, in *Chico and the Man* (1974–1978) Puerto Rican-Hungarian Freddie Prinze (father of actor Freddie Prinze, Jr.) played a young Mexican who worked and lived at a Los Angeles filling station. The owner of the garage, a cranky elderly white man named Ed (played by Jack Albertson), often struggled with Chico over their language and cultural differences. As the series progressed, the two came to forge a comfortable friendship that helped to make it a "top five" television program.

In the 1980s, ABC tried to introduce issues related to acculturation by showcasing Hispanic actors Paul Rodriguez and Elizabeth Pena in their own programs, *a.k.a. Pablo* (1984) and *I Married Dora* (1987–1988), respectively. Norman Lear, the groundbreaking producer of *All in the Family* (1971–1979) who was discussed in Chapter 4, produced *a.k.a. Pablo*, and tried to bring in the issues related

Figure 5.1 Ricky loves Lucy in the hit sitcom *I Love Lucy*, which ran from 1951 to 1957. Reproduced with kind permission of Getty images.

to a Hispanic character trying to find acceptance in the white world of entertainment, but ABC canceled the program after just six episodes. Mexican comedian Paul Rodriguez played Pablo, a struggling stand-up comedian. Part of the program's comedy came from Pablo's attempts to poke fun at his Mexican family and his family's disapproval of the jabs. *I Married Dora* only had 13 episodes, but the program was ahead of its time in that it featured issues related to immigration. Elizabeth Pena played Dora, the housekeeper for the middle-class Farrells. The widower father, Peter Farrell (played by Daniel Hugh Kelly), marries the housekeeper to keep her in the country. The series revolved around the family trying to keep the illegal marriage a secret from outsiders. Of course, it is no surprise that by the end of the 13 episodes Dora and Peter have fallen in love, but the subtext of the show was significant. Illegal immigration, although not new, was openly discussed in prime time because of this program. Dora's value to the family was worth a sham marriage as a way to avoid deportation. Although both of these programs were short-lived, they indicate that a concerted effort was being made to expand the ethnicities found on prime-time television.

At the December 2016 Golden Globe Awards, two raven-haired actresses walked up to the microphones at center stage:

"Hi, I'm Eva Longoria, not Eva Mendes," said Longoria.

"I'm America Ferrera. Not Gina Rodriguez," said *Ugly Betty*'s and *Superstore*'s Ferrera.

"And neither one of us are Rosario Dawson," Longoria added.

Figure 5.2 These Latinas in *Devious Maids* (2013–2016) are beautiful, strong, in control … and maids. Do they break or reinforce stereotypes?

This comic moment poked fun at the journalists and audience members who have confused Latina actresses for each other. Ironically, it is Longoria's success that has been credited with introducing other Hispanic actresses to the big and small screen. Longoria, a Mexican American actress, starred in the ABC hit *Desperate Housewives* (2004–2012) as Gabrielle Solis, a retired model and less than faithful wife. Her breakout stardom is credited with triggering the "Eva Effect," which told executives that Hispanics were bankable leads on network television (Deggans 2005). Her success demonstrates that audiences of all types will relate to Hispanic women on television.

After *Desperate Housewives* ended, Longoria channeled her success into executive-producing the Lifetime TV show *Devious Maids* (2013–2016). On this show five Latinas play maids that are savvy, sexy, and who often use their fiery looks and sexuality to get what they want (Figure 5.2). Does this portrayal play into the hands of the sexy señorita cultivated in Hollywood, or does she break this stereotype? Also, is the image negative if it's produced by a Latina?

Because of their groups' distinctive language(s) and cultural aspects, Hispanic audiences have a variety of content directed at them. What they choose to watch helps shape what media producers create for them and general audiences. Selective exposure theory suggests viewers usually choose to watch content that is in line with their beliefs and values, and to do otherwise causes viewers to become uncomfortable (Klapper 1960). Research indicates that Hispanic audiences choose different television programs than other racial or ethnic groups because that programming offers material that is, in some way, uniquely relevant to them. For example, viewers of Hispanic descent may have regularly tuned into *The George Lopez Show* (2002–2007) and *Ugly Betty* (2006–2010) because the programs frequently showcased Hispanic heritage and culture. *The George Lopez Show*'s executive producer, Sandra Bullock, recognizing the need for this connection, sent scouts to find a Hispanic comedian to star in a sitcom. Similarly, *Ugly Betty*'s producer, Salma Hayek, found that there was a paucity of positive Latinas on television, so she imported the Colombian television program *Yo Soy Betty la Fea* (1999–2001) and offered it to American audiences. While the success of both of these programs can be attributed to good writing and comedic acting, they also celebrate Hispanic culture – ranging from the use of the Spanish language to the food they eat – and both programs place great value on the characters' multigenerational families, a characteristic of many Hispanic homes. In a similar vein, CW's comedy-drama *Jane the Virgin* (2014 debut) weaves Hispanic culture into its telenovela-like storylines. Lauded for its strong writing and acting, the show is said to be the first network television show to feature as its main characters a cast of female Latinas. The show follows heroine Jane, played by Gina Rodriguez, as she navigates her love life, murderous intrigue, and the expectations of her multigenerational family. In the program, both English and Spanish are spoken, with subtitles provided during the Spanish.

Large media conglomerates are experimenting with the widespread appeal of Hispanic personalities. Comcast-owned *NBC Nightly News* has its first Hispanic television anchor, Jose Diaz-Balart, reading the news on weekends. Viacom's TV Land offers *Lopez* (2016 debut), a faux docu-series of the life of comedian George Lopez. Its content is similar to that found on HBO's *Curb Your Enthusiasm* (2000) or *Louie* (2010) on FX. Disney, perhaps the most well known of all media conglomerates, showcased its first Latina princess, Elena of Avalor, in her very own Disney Junior program in the summer of 2016. Princess Elena, a teenager inspired by the stories and culture of her Hispanic lineage, wears an apricot mallow in her hair, a flower native to California and Mexico (McDermott 2016) (see Box 5.1).

The multiplicity of channels found on cable or satellite television also serves Hispanic viewers. By 2009 there were several cable networks offering Spanish and/or bilingual programming; many had English language counterparts including Aztec America, ESPN Deportes, and MTV Tr3s. These entities were not only in competition with English-language networks but also were strong competition for the longstanding Univision and Telemundo (de Lafuente 2008). In an effort to study how Hispanics selected between the more diversified content of cable television, media scholars Alan Albarran and Don Umphrey surveyed 1,241 white, African American, and Hispanic residents of the Dallas television market (Albarran and Umphrey 1994). They found that Whites were the heaviest viewers of CNN, and Hispanics watched the Weather Channel more than the other racial groups. The researchers supposed the viewing difference might have been because Hispanics were more likely to be reliant on the weather for their work. The study also revealed that African Americans and Hispanics were more likely to watch home shopping channels than Whites. The researchers concluded that the minority groups turned to these channels as a ritualized experience much like going to a shopping mall. Understanding the rituals of these ever-growing minority groups enables television programmers and advertisers to reach this diverse audience efficiently. One custom of Hispanics that the entertainment industry has embraced is its bilingual nature: Spanish-language programming can be found in nearly every market in the United States.

Box 5.1 *Dora the Explorer:* **Breaking down barriers**

It is a commonly held belief that children, who are less media savvy than adults, are less able to interpret the messages that are presented to them. They are influenced, in a number of ways, by what they see. It stands to reason, then, that it is worth exploring some of the programming that children are exposed to that offers up representations of Hispanics today. Interestingly, at a time when there are relatively few representations of Hispanics in adult prime-time programming, there is a wide selection of children's programming that offers up cultural diversity, with Hispanic culture as a prominent element.

One such program is *Dora the Explorer* (2000 debut), a children's television program that airs on Nickelodeon and CBS, and features a 7-year-old bilingual Latina girl, who in each episode is sent on a quest of some sort, usually with one or more of her friends, some of whom speak only Spanish. Approximately one third of the episodes are culturally driven: for instance, she might explore a Puerto Rican folk tale or be tasked with bringing the special mambo shoes to her cousin Daisy's *quinceañera* (15th birthday party).

Nickelodeon created *Dora* as part of an initiative to expand the presence of Latino creators and actors on television. It has been reported that executives wanted to create a character that would resonate with children who grew up in bilingual households. Interestingly, *Dora*'s popularity has gone far beyond Latino children, who make up only 5 to 15 percent of *Dora*'s audience. Some researchers attribute the popularity of the program to the direct way in which Dora speaks to the audience. She often appears to be looking right at the viewer, requesting participation or for the viewer to repeat a Spanish "magic" word. She will pause, as if waiting for a response. Researchers suggest this type of interaction offers empowerment to Latinas, girls, and children alike, all groups that have historically struggled with feeling powerless (Ryan 2007).

Today, *Dora the Explorer* also airs for children in the United States on Univision, a Spanish-language television network.

Consider the children's programming you watched when you were young. Do you remember any Hispanic characters?

Have you seen *Dora the Explorer* or any other children's television show with Hispanic characters?

Examine the Nickjr.com website. How many of the programs listed appear to have minority characters? Compare these images to the characters you see during prime time.

Spanish-Language Programs in the United States

Audiences for Spanish-language television in the United States are relatively small, but the extremely loyal viewers spend a large amount of time exclusively watching Spanish-language channels (Barwise and Ehrenberg 1988). Univision and Telemundo are two television networks that have long served Hispanic audiences in America. Univision is the largest Spanish-language media outlet, claiming ownership of more than 50 television stations and 70 radio stations, record labels, and the website Univision.com, which attracts more than 1 billion visitors a year (Hoovers n.d.-a; n.d.-b). Univision commands some 80 percent of the market share of Hispanic viewers. In 2016, NBC Universal-owned Telemundo, the second-ranked network with Hispanic viewers, recruited former Univision superstar Don Francisco to appear on Telemundo (Figure 5.3). It has more than 50 affiliates and the cable channel NBC Universo (previously known as mun2) for English-speaking Hispanics.

Figure 5.3 For 53 years, Don Francisco was a staple for four hours every Saturday night on Univision with the zany variety show *Sabado Gigante* (1962–2015). Screenshot.

The content found on these networks is somewhat different from that found on general audience networks. For example, comparative studies completed by the Lear Center/Pew Hispanic Center during the 2004 presidential election determined that Univision averaged six and a half minutes of campaign news, two minutes more than its Spanish-language competitor Telemundo at three and a half minutes. Even so, both networks offered less than their English-language counterparts such as ABC, CBS, and NBC, which averaged eight minutes per half hour (Suro *et al.* 2011). The same study found that the Spanish-language networks aired scant amounts of news of the Iraq War, but because of the significance of immigration to this community, more news about world affairs, immigration, and trade than the major networks. A study of the 2012 US presidential election found that Spanish-language television was kinder to the sitting president than English-language television, except when it came to issues to immigration (Eshbaugh-Soha 2014).

The longstanding genre of Spanish-language media, the telenovela, also has been found to be a frequent source of bilingual information. These melodramatic soap operas are successful communicators because they provide some link between Latino roots and the lives of Hispanics in the United States. An in-depth analysis of Telemundo's *Ladron de Corazon* (2003 debut) found that the program's consultation with breast cancer experts and public service announcements that aired during the program made a difference to viewers. Calls to a cancer information line posted during the program increased during this storyline. Participants in phone surveys and focus groups revealed an increased awareness of breast cancer treatments and an increase in men's intentions to encourage the women in their lives to be screened for breast cancer (Wilken *et al.* 2007). A study of Televisa and TV Azteca found that some telenovelas use comic characters to teach tolerance of gays and lesbians (Tate 2011). Although some of the portrayals could be tropes (effeminate males wearing pink), the storylines demonstrate that familial and societal support are possible and desirable.

The large viewership of Univision and Telemundo does not mean that all Hispanics are satisfied with what Spanish-language programming has to offer. Even before the vast growth of the Hispanic population in the United States that occurred in the late 1990s and 2000s, critics thought that Spanish-language media were ignoring the cultural and linguistic differences of individual nationalities like Mexicans and Cubans. Focus groups conducted with Hispanics of different nationalities living in New York City found that the city's media had expanded in an effort to accommodate the growth in the Hispanic population. However, the participants acknowledged that the content producers were merging or "cross-fertilizing" popular culture between the groups to appeal to large numbers of consumers (Davila 2002). Although the content was growing, some participants were concerned that some messages, especially the telenovelas, were racially biased toward Mexicans, and that darker skinned Hispanics were not depicted as beautiful in these programs.

Hispanic women were asked about their relationship with Hispanic television and they, too, were conflicted. While they were pleased that Hispanics had some control over the airwaves, some educated, American-born Hispanics wanted to distance themselves from the content found on Univision or Telemundo. Some of these participants felt talk shows such as *Cristina* (1989–2010), a Miami-based program, were commercializing the poor (Rojas 2004). Cuban American Cristina Saralegui hosted a weekly Oprah-like talk show on Univision for more than 20 years. Also like Oprah Winfrey, Saralegui ended her talk show in 2010 to pursue other projects.

Where telenovelas are designed for adult viewers, television stations and networks have tried to serve the Spanish-speaking child as well. Hispanic children watch more than seven hours of television per day – over an hour more than their white counterparts (Henry J. Kaiser Family Foundation 1999). The US television market has made some effort to reap the economic and social benefits of Spanish-speaking children. An analysis of the US television landscape found that American companies had competency in entertaining and educating children via cable television; Disney En Español and DiscoveryKids en Español offered translated versions of English-language programs. Broadcast television was slower in adopting this stance. For example, in 2007, Spanish-language network Univision was fined a historic $24 million for violating the educational/informational standards spelled out in the Children's Television Act of 1990 (Labaton 2007). Other television outlets for Hispanic youth encourage some form of acculturation while celebrating heritage, including NUVOtv which is partially owned by Jennifer Lopez.

Hispanics/Hispanic Americans and Radio

The radio industry features niches designed to attract different audiences. Radio offers formats ranging from adult contemporary to country to hard rock to classical to hip-hop (Box 5.2). Undoubtedly, Hispanic listeners can be found listening to these stations, but the radio industry also offers Hispanic-targeted radio stations. Some are in English while others are Spanish or bilingual.

Box 5.2 Hispanic hip-hop

At the beginning of this chapter, the idea that Hispanic popular music is an amalgam of genres was introduced. One of the most successful musical culture clashes has emerged between artists who make "American" rap and the Latino artists who specialize in "tropical" rap. Although the genre has been almost entirely the province of African American rappers, Hispanic youth, especially those in large cities, have been raised on this music, the vernacular, and other aspects of this culture. As a result, Hispanic rap artists are creating their own style – using English and Spanish – of hip-hop music. Critics wonder if Latinidad music roots are being forsaken for more Americanized music, while others credit Hispanic hip-hop artists for expanding the genre and making it relevant for a younger generation.

One group that has had much success in getting attention from English- and Spanish-speaking listeners for this interweaving of sounds is Calle 13. This duo, much like rappers, has mixed politically charged lyrics and sexual overtones into its critically acclaimed music. One of their songs, "Los de

Atrás Vienen Conmigo," was a Top 100 song on the *Billboard* hottest 200 songs in the US, a Top 20 song on *Billboard*'s Top 20 chart, and a Top 5 song on *Billboard*'s Latin chart. Consider the lyrics:

Conmigo vienen, vienen los de atrás
conmigo vienen, vienen los de atrás
conmigo vienen, vienen los de atrás
los de atrás vienen conmigo, vienen los de atrás
yo vengo de atrás yo vengo de abajo
tengo las uñas sucias porque yo trabajo
me he pasado toda la vida mezclando cemento
para mantener a los gringos contentos
tu no sabes todo lo que yo cosecho
para dormir debajo de un techo
pero yo no soy blandito yo no me quito
tampoco me criaron con leche de polvito
soy la mezcla de todas las razas
batata, yuca, platano, yautia y calabaza
no me vendo ni que me paguen
a mi orgullo le puse un candado
y me trague la llave

With me come, those from behind
With me come, those from behind
Those from behind come with me, come those from behind
I come from behind I come from below
My nails are dirty because I work
I have spent all my life mixing cement
to make the gringos happy
You don't know all I sow
to have a roof over my head
but I am not soft and I don't get out of the way
because I was not raised on powdered milk
I am the mix of all races
sweet potato, cassava, plantain, yam, squash
I cannot be bought even if they paid me
I put a lock on my pride
and I swallowed the key.

These are just a few of the lyrics, but you can see the emotion in the storytelling. Elements of the mixture of Hispanic and American cultures create a powerful message.

Different Hispanic audiences select radio stations based on cultural proximity. This concept suggests that people are drawn to media from their own culture. Arbitron, Inc. data indicated that language plays a large role in the radio stations selected by Spanish-speaking Hispanics and English-speaking non-Hispanics. It comes as no surprise that Spanish-speaking Hispanics gravitate to Spanish-language media while English-speaking non-Hispanics listen to English-language stations.

However, English-speaking Hispanics have more "multicultural fluency," which makes them more apt to select media from a variety of cultures (Ksaizek and Webster 2008).

Of course, the radio dial offers more than just music. Talk radio adds another component to how Hispanics are represented on the airwaves. For example, *Latino USA*, a public affairs program, is able to thrive because of its purposeful decision to gain consensus by broadcasting in English and promoting the educational mission of the NPR station on which it airs (Tovares 2000). Host Maria Hinojosa offers audiences of all backgrounds stories such as the realities for Hispanic children brought to the United States via transnational adoptions and pieces about carving out unique identities in America. Furthermore, talk radio programs including Cristina Radio and Conservative Latino Talk Radio address issues important to Hispanics, giving the public an opportunity to discuss controversial issues such as immigration and health in a public square.

Representations of Hispanics/Hispanic Americans in the News

Several analyses of general audience newspapers find that people of Hispanic descent tend to be underrepresented. The news that did include Hispanics was frequently reported with institutionalized stereotypes that relegated the group to agricultural worker and/or victim status (Stein 2007). For example, McCauley, Minsky, and Viswanath (2013) conducted focus groups about the stigma, stress, and coping mechanisms related to the H1N1 virus, which was blamed on Mexican and other Latin pig farmers. Coverage of legal and illegal immigration also has been studied. For example, a 2012 study of cable news outlets finds that Fox News viewers (who selectively expose themselves to conservative political content) show higher support for strict immigration policies than those who watch CNN (de Zúñga, Correa, and Valenzuela 2012). Other studies indicate that much newspaper coverage perpetuates the notion that most of the Hispanics in America are undocumented immigrants (Calafell 2004).

As if the annihilation of this group were not already troubling, research also indicates that when there are appearances of Hispanics in the news, they are rarely used as authority figures. Often, newspapers will run stories *about* Hispanics, but the experts are demographically White (Carveth and Alverio 1996). These depictions turn "the voiceless" into weak and subordinate figures, an exercise that only serves to diminish Hispanics' power in American society. These characterizations (or lack thereof) are especially problematic when the representation of African Americans is considered. By repeatedly offering images of these groups as being violent, helpless, and hapless, the public receives a message that a large number of the people of color in this country are troubled, second-class citizens, or, even worse, nonexistent.

Discourse about the class status of Hispanics in America is especially salient because of the rapid growth of the group. The larger the group becomes, the more economically diverse it will be. Based on this trend, both the mainstream and African American press has discussed the shift in population in terms of the competition and tension generated between Hispanics and other minority ethnic groups. It is interesting to note that the Southern black press recognized and understood this change in positioning, but made little effort to cover significant issues regarding Hispanics in America (Weill and Castaneda 2004). Instead, their coverage concentrated on the concern that African Americans were being usurped as America's most prominent minority group.

Spanish-Language Newspapers in the United States

In 2015, Pew Research determined that 14 percent of Hispanics in the United States subscribed to a daily general audience newspaper whereas 31 percent of Whites and 28 percent of Blacks subscribed to a daily newspaper. These numbers do not mean that Hispanics do not read the newspaper; on the contrary, newspapers offer a significant role in the daily lives of members of this ethnic group. The Pew Hispanic Center found that nearly 80 percent of Latinos agreed that Spanish-language media, print and broadcast, were essential to the political and economic success of Hispanics in America (Suro 2004). Anna Crosslin, the president of the International Institute of St. Louis, said non-English-language newspapers serve as "an integration tool," teaching immigrants about American laws, community services, and culture, and that the newspapers, if bilingual, help the reader learn some English (Malone 2007). Newspapers also offer their readers a connection to their ethnic culture and traditions and enable specific groups to unify and create social power blocks in large cities, like, for instance, Cubans in Miami (Garcia 2000).

A study of two Spanish-language newspapers based in New York City finds another, perhaps more eye-opening result. These newspapers, *El Diario-La Prensa* and *Hoy*, were found to offer intercultural dialogue between different segments of the Latin community via features, news stories, and coverage of cultural events. At the same time, these papers also served as hosts to non-Hispanics, providing spaces for non-Hispanics to get information about these different ethnic groups (Coperías-Aguilar 2015).

Spanish-language or bilingual (Spanish/English) newspapers have a long presence in the United States. In the past two centuries, there have been about 500 newspapers providing a place to print news relevant to Hispanics, including Kansas City's *El Cosmopolita* (1914–1919), Los Angeles's *El Clamor Publico* (1855–1857), and Tampa's *Traduccion Prense* (1941–1956) (see Box 5.3). The circulation of Spanish-language newspapers has grown to more than 1.5 million readers, increasing as the circulation of English-language newspapers declined by 10 percent in the mid-2000s (Nealy 2008). This growth was cultivated in different ways and in markets with varying numbers of Hispanics. In 2001, the *Los Angeles Times* began a "Latino Initiative" to improve its targeting of the Hispanic audience, focusing on bilingual reporters and a shift in advertising markets. Although *Newsday's Hoy* and the *Chicago Tribune's Exito* are Spanish-language dailies, the *Los Angeles Times* printed the stories gained from the Latino Initiative in English because previous attempts at a Spanish-language *Los Angeles Times* were not profitable (Del Olmo 2011).

The coverage in Hispanic newspapers is intended to be different from that found in mainstream newspapers which are meant for the community at large. However, a study of mainstream, Black, and Hispanic newspapers found that there was not a great deal of difference in the coverage. However, the Hispanic newspapers were found to have more local health news stories and health stories with localized health information than those found in mainstream and majority Black newspapers (Wang and Rodgers 2013).

Pew Research Center found in a 2015 survey that there were 25 Hispanic newspapers with circulations of 100,000 or more. At the same time, the circulation figures for the three leading Hispanic newspapers – *El Diario La Prensa*, *El Nuevo Herald*, and *La Opinion* – have fallen in the past few years (Shearer 2016). There is evidence that these papers serve an important purpose for its readers as Hispanics have come to rely on newspapers as a frequent source of information about their communities. In 2004, the Pew Hispanic Center asked 1,316 Latinos which media they get any news from on an average weekday and 52 percent reported that they read newspapers – in both English

Box 5.3 Interview with Carlos Nicho, founder and editor of *Mundo Hispano*

Below are excerpts from an interview with Carlos Nicho, the founder and editor of *Mundo Hispano*, a Spanish/English bilingual newspaper based in East Tennessee. Mr. Nicho was born in Peru and raised in Venezuela. In 1999, shortly after moving to the United States, having learned about the publishing process while working at a printing shop, he established *Mundo Hispano*. Although the paper began as a strictly Spanish-language paper, he found that he was impacting on the lives of the Hispanic community and decided he wanted to also inspire them to learn English by making the paper bilingual. His paper is currently available in the Tennessee cities of Knoxville, Johnson City, Chattanooga, and Nashville. The paper also has a Twitter presence: @mundohispanotn.

Figure 5.4 Carlos Nicho, founder and editor of *Mundo Hispano*.

Q: What type of topics do you normally cover in your newspaper?

MR. NICHO: I mostly cover things that have to do with immigrant workers and their families, and I cover them from the perspective of an immigrant. There might be other things happening during the regular news day that I don't cover in *Mundo Hispano*. Those things might be important, but they might also be invisible for an immigrant who is thinking about other things. I concentrate on immigration topics or about the rights immigrant workers have and the services they can go for. My paper covers topics from the state down to the city level. In Nashville, there are five or six Hispanic newspapers. They are beautiful newspapers, but all of the information and news are from far away. There is no information about Tennessee or Nashville, so in my opinion, the people are not well served. That's why I stress the local things. For example, in my last issue, I had a story about how Volkswagen is offering employment in Chattanooga.

Q: Besides providing information to the Hispanic community, do you think you are serving any other purpose? In other words, what other role do you think you are playing with your Hispanic newspaper?

MR. NICHO: I've been trying to educate my community. They are not used to participation with the media. I try to tell them that, first of all, I am not someone who studied to be a journalist and that I'm like them, trying to do something good for the community. I open the doors for their opinion.

I'm shooting for them to get involved with what is happening in the cities. For example, when it's time to vote, I want them to vote and express their opinions. They are not used to that. Many of them did not vote in their own countries. I'm still on that trail of my mission to have space for them to write their own opinions. They don't do it too much. I wish they were more vocal, but I'm still open.

> Most of them watch things happening. They think someone else is managing it or doing it. They are only spectators. In the countries they came from, they didn't have a voice in what the government or the police were doing. For example, they couldn't say "The police abused me." They didn't have a voice. They think it is the same here and everywhere. My intention is to teach them – to educate them – through my paper. To say it is different here. It is not like your country. You can say things here.
>
> Q: What about the national media? How do you think they are doing in serving the Hispanic community?
>
> MR. NICHO: The national media just cover topics that might increase their ratings, like immigration stories that have to do with getting rid of the illegals. To really serve and be inclusive with this part of the community – I don't see it yet. Maybe when the numbers of Hispanic or Latino people voting increase, when they start being a weight in the voting moment, then things might change.

and Spanish. Bilingual residents of Miami have the choice of several English-language and Spanish-language newspapers. Arguably, the best-known newspapers in the city are *The Miami Herald* and Spanish-language *El Nuevo Herald*; the languages are different, but the approach each takes to social issues is really what differentiates these papers. For example, an analysis of coverage of the custody battle for Elian Gonzalez (a young boy who was found floating on a raft after his mother perished while fleeing Cuba) between his deceased mother's Miami family and his father in Cuba revealed that the Spanish-language paper offered distinct coverage of the issue (Guzman 2006). *El Nuevo Herald* tended to speak more to the members of the Cuban/Cuban American community; conversely, *The Miami Herald* used less emotive language to speak to the entire diverse community in Miami.

Spanish-Language Magazines in the United States

There is a wide variety of topics covered in Spanish-language magazines. For example, the growth in parenting magazines geared toward the exponential growth in American-born Hispanic babies has spurred several publications. These titles, including *Ser Padres* ("To be Parents"), joined the more than 350 magazines specifically designed to appeal to Hispanics – primarily women – in the United States (Wentz 2008). These magazines are accessible to Spanish speakers, share issues relevant to this audience, and acknowledge that people with brown skin are beautiful and viable consumers. Some of these magazines are produced for Hispanic readers, such as *Comida y Familia*, a monthly magazine about food and family published by Kraft Foods, while others have English-language general audience sister magazines and are operated by large media conglomerates. *People en Español* is published by Time Warner; Hearst publishes *Cosmo en Español*. And *Variety Latino* offers its legendary Hollywood news to Spanish readers. However, these magazines do not simply translate the English content into Spanish; new content is produced for these issues, and they sell and run separate advertising. These and other periodicals give readers an opportunity to read about Hispanic celebrities and culture in a style that has been successful targeting wide audiences.

Smaller companies, such as Latina Media Ventures, also find a market targeting Hispanic magazine readers. For example, Latina Media Venture's *Latina*, a women's lifestyle magazine with articles written in both Spanish and English in each issue, presents articles on fashion, beauty, and celebrity culture, but also covers more serious issues, such as media stereotyping, to a wide range of Hispanic readers. The magazine's breadth is a key to its strategy to sell to as many readers as possible. Recent circulation numbers show that it is a strategy that is working: in a time when many magazines are paring down or folding, *Latina*'s media kit reports to potential advertisers that it has an audience of 2.7 million, with 2 million monthly unique views on its web property Latina.com (*Latina* 2016).

Most of the research dealing with Hispanics and magazines looks at how women are depicted in their pages. These depictions raise questions about the portrayal of assimilation, beauty, and social status. A study of 1,600 editorial images of women in Hispanic women's magazines found that most of the women were light-skinned; only eight had dark brown skin. These images convey the idea that dark skin is not as desirable as light skin and that women with lighter skin have a social advantage. These images create an idea that there is a *panraza*/panethnic (or lack of ethnic differentiation) standard of beauty among all Hispanics (Johnson, Prabu, and Huey-Ohlsson 2003). In other words, the magazines are telling readers that Hispanics have blended into one indistinct group and that beauty standards are based on one type of woman. Aside from aesthetics, magazines targeted at Hispanic women – *Vanidades*, *Latina Style*, *Latina*, *Latina Bride* – are designed to showcase the lives and styles of the Latina. A case study of magazines of this type found that they did not take a revolutionary activist stand but did demonstrate some (albeit modest) level of empowerment in celebrating Hispanic heritage (Johnson 2000).

The magazine-style niched content directed at various Hispanic groups is like the content directed at all ethnicities, except some sites have a mix of English and Spanish content to expand their appeal. Latinsingles.com and Latinamericancupid.com are dating sites targeted at individuals of Hispanic descent. As with gossip blogs Perezhilton.com or Jezebel.com, Hissip.com offers "Latino gossip like you've never read it before." LatinPulseMusic.com gives musicians a chance to social network with fans. On the surface it may seem that these sites are just other ways to sell products to a growing population in the United States, but upon deeper reflection it is clear that they also provide users a chance to stay in touch with people who have similar linguistic and/or cultural backgrounds.

Hispanics/Hispanic Americans and Advertisements

It can be difficult to determine if a model in a photograph or on television is Hispanic based on skin or hair color because of the ethnic group's diverse heritage, but several studies have indicated that Hispanics have routinely been in the background or altogether absent in advertisements (Petty *et al.* 2003). When Hispanics do appear in marketing messages, stereotyping may occur because these messages are designed to tell a complete story on a single page or in 20 seconds. At times, the effort to create easily identifiable characteristics leads to stereotyping of intelligence, physical appearance, and social class. Advertising researchers Helena Czepiec and J. Steven Kelly's 1983 study of Hispanics in advertisements found that ads depicted this group as being uneducated (Czepiec and Kelly 1983). More than 10 years later, a content analysis of business publications found that Hispanics were rarely featured in professional, white-collar settings (Taylor, Lee, and Stern 1995). This type of representation leaves consumers with the impression that there are no Hispanics holding white-collar, professional jobs and, therefore, they are not educated or ambitious.

Further examinations of the representation of Hispanics in advertisements yielded contradictory results. Information sciences scholar Roberta Astroff's analysis of trade publications determined that advertisers had found much success or "Spanish gold" in the Latino market by reshaping stereotypes (Astroff 1988). For example, in a study of beer advertising on Spanish-language television, spots on Univision were found to include images of highly sexualized Latinas, macho Mexican men in low-rider Impalas, and some images of middle-class Hispanics drinking responsibly. The same study revealed that some of the ads' characters were Mexican, while other ads showed no discernable difference in appearance and/or accent between Hispanics from Puerto Rico, Cuba, Mexico, or any Spanish-speaking country. This move toward "panethnic marketing" targets the largest possible number of Hispanics while supporting the notion that there is no difference between nationalities or ethnicities. Again, this erasing of individual cultures sends a message to Hispanic viewers that their specific heritages are not valued (Perez 2003). Ironically, research shows that advertising messages directed to members of specific Hispanic communities have been found to work best. The messages that resonate most strongly with Hispanics feature family and close friendships and certain aspects of specific Hispanic cultures (Oetzel *et al.* 2007).

In a study of 272 Hispanics' feelings about English, Spanish, and hybrid commercials, results indicated that more viewers were swayed by the commercials that showed a mixture of English and Latin cultures. This preference for what Garcia Quintana and Nichols (2016) call "code switching" indicates that ads, like the Hispanic viewers, must live in two different worlds to be culturally relevant to the market.

Concluding Remarks

In many ways, Dominicans, Puerto Ricans, Mexicans, El Salvadorans, and others of Hispanic descent have adopted parts of the American media, but also still hold on to aspects of their culture that are familiar or comforting.

Interestingly, this trend of Hispanics wanting to hold on to language, culture, and tradition creates the assumption, and in some cases fear, among other ethnic groups that Hispanics do not or are not contributing to American society. At times, the media's depiction of Hispanics appears to reinforce this assumption. Stereotypic images of lazy gardeners, maintenance workers, violent gangsters, or the mere invisibility of this group in the media, are problematic, as these depictions solidify the concerns some have regarding Hispanics. As Hispanics become the dominant minority group in the United States, the role they play in society and how their societal contribution is considered will presumably change. The media will, undoubtedly, shape these feelings.

Superficially, it stands to reason that the more roots Hispanic families lay down in the United States, the more they will adapt to US culture. However, the growth in Spanish-language radio, websites, and magazines indicates that there will continue to be a divide between the Hispanic and American media. The media industry has acknowledged the buying power of the influx of Spanish-speaking immigrants in the United States. With this, the visibility of Hispanic media also has increased. In 2001, NBC paid $2.7 billion for Telemundo Television, demonstrating the industry-wide recognition of the Hispanic market as a lucrative and growing area (White 2001). Even more pronounced, one only has to follow the future success of Broadway writer, producer, and performer Lin-Manuel Miranda, who created the Tony Award winners *In the Heights* and *Hamilton*, to see how the public is ready to embrace Hispanic talent.

Reflection Questions and Thoughts to Consider

1. Are there any Spanish-language radio stations in your listening area? Why or why not? If you can hear such a station, who are the advertisers?
2. Pick up your town's Sunday newspaper. Are there stories about Hispanic members of your community? What type of stories are these? Are there photos of prominent Hispanic Americans in the society page, or the lifestyle section?
3. Watch two or three nights of prime-time network television. How many characters of Hispanic descent appear on these shows? What percentage of the characters you saw was Hispanic? How many were African American? How many were White? How are the Hispanic characters depicted? What themes do you see emerging in these depictions?
4. How does your family's background, traditions, rituals, or habits influence your media usage?

References

Albarran, Alan, and Don Umphrey. 1994. "Marketing Cable and Pay Cable Services: Impact of Ethnicity Viewing Motivations, and Program Types." *Journal of Media Economics* 7: 47–58.

Astroff, Roberta. 1988. "Spanish Gold: Stereotypes, Ideology, and the Construction of a US Latino Market." *Howard Journal of Communication* 1: 155–173.

Barwise, Patrick, and Andrew Ehrenberg. 1988. *Television and Its Audience.* Beverly Hills, CA: Sage.

Calafell, B. Marie. 2004. "Disrupting the Dichotomy: 'Yo soy Chicana/o?' in the New Latina/o South." *The Communication Review* 6: 175–204.

Carveth, Rod, and Diane Alverio. 1996. *Network Brownout: The Portrayal of Latinos in Network Television News.* Washington, DC: National Association of Hispanic Journalists and the National Council.

Castillo, Sergio. 2016. "We are Not Invisible: A Latino Actor in NYC Cinema." *Huffington Post*, April 18. http://www.huffingtonpost.com/sergio-castillo/we-are-not-invisible-a-la_b_9707654.html (accessed April 5, 2017).

Coperías-Aguilar, Maria Jose. 2015. "Double Intercultural Dialogue in the Hispanic Press in the United States: The Case of New York Newspapers." *Language and Intercultural Communication* 15: 376–390.

Czepiec, Helena, and J. Steven Kelly. 1983. "Analyzing Hispanic Roles in Advertising: A Portrait of an Emerging Subculture." *Current Issues and Research in Advertising* 6: 219–240.

Davila, Arlene. 2002. "Talking Back: Spanish Media and US Latinidad." In *Latino/a Popular Culture*, edited by Michelle Habell-Pallan and Mary Romero, 25–37. New York, NY: New York University Press.

de Lafuente, Della. 2008. "Social Networks." *Mediaweek*, May, 5: 18.

de Zúñiga, Homero Gil, Teresa Correa, and Sebastian Valenzuela. 2012. "Selective Exposure to Cable News and Immigration in the US: The Relationship Between FOX News, CNN, and Attitudes Toward Mexican Immigrants." *Journal of Broadcasting & Electronic Media* 56: 597–615.

Deggans, Eric. 2005. "The Story behind Television's Latin Star." *Hispanic* 18: 5–11.

Del Olmo, Frank. 2011. "The 'Latino Initiative' Reshapes the *Los Angeles Times's* Coverage." *Nieman Report.* http://www.nieman.harvard.edu/reportsitem.aspx?id=101665 (accessed April 5, 2017).

Eshbaugh-Soha, Matthew. 2014. "The Tone of Spanish-Language Presidential News Coverage." *Social Science Quarterly* 95: 1278–1295.

Garcia, J.E. 2000. "Life after Elian." *Mundo Hispanico*, June 8: 492.

Garcia Berumen, Frank Javier. 1995. *The Chicano/Hispanic Image in American Film.* New York, NY: Vantage Press.

Garcia Quintana, Ashley E., and Cynthia Nichols. 2016. "Code Switching and the Hispanic Consumer." *Hispanic Journal of Behavioral Sciences* 38: 222–242.

Gruber, Enid, and Helaine Thau. 2003. "Sexually Related Content on Television and Adolescents of Color: Media Theory, Physiological Development, and Psychological Impact." *The Journal of Negro Education* 72: 438–456.

Guzman, Isabella M. 2006. "Competing Discourses of Community: Ideological Tensions between Local General-Market and Latino News Media." *Journalism* 7: 281–298.

Henry J. Kaiser Family Foundation/Children Now. 1999. *Topline Report From: Talking with Kids about Tough Issues. A National Survey of Parents and Kids*. Menlo Park, CA: Kaiser Family Foundation.

Hoovers. n.d.-a. "Telemundo Communications Group, Inc." http://www.hoovers.com/company-information/cs/company-profile.telemundo_communications_group_inc.1e0c409492b1efa6.html (accessed April 5, 2017).

Hoovers. n.d.-b. "Univision Communications, Inc." http://www.hoovers.com/company-information/cs/company-profile.univision_communications_inc.a9ff6a528ba4bf61.html (accessed April 5, 2017).

Humes, Karen R., Nicholas A. Jones, and Roberto R. Ramirez. 2011. "Overview of Race and Hispanic Origin: 2010." http://www.census.gov/prod/cen2010/briefs/c2010br-02.pdf (accessed April 5, 2017).

Johnson, Melissa A. 2000. "How Ethnic are US Ethnic Media: The Case of Latina Magazines." *Mass Communication and Society* 3: 229–248.

Johnson, Melissa A., David Prabu, and Dawn Huey-Ohlsson. 2003. "Beauty in Brown: Skin Color in Latina Magazines." In *Brown and Black Communication: Latino and African American Conflict and Convergence in Mass Media*, edited by Diana I. Rios and A.N. Mohamed, 159. Westport, CT: Praeger.

Klapper, Joseph T. 1960. *The Effects of Mass Communication*. New York, NY: Free Press.

Ksaizek, Thomas, and James G. Webster. 2008. "Cultural Proximity and Audience Behavior: The Role of Language in Patterns of Polarization and Multicultural Fluency." *Journal of Broadcasting & Electronic Media* 52: 485–503.

Labaton, Stephen. 2007. "Record Fine Expected for Univision." *New York Times*, February 24. http://www.nytimes.com/2007/02/24/business/24fcc.html (accessed April 5, 2017).

Latina. 2016. "2016 Media Kit." http://www.latina.com/advertise (accessed April 5, 2017).

Malone, Roy. 2007. "Foreign-language Papers Serve Varied STL Communities." *St. Louis Journalism Review* 22: 27.

McCauley, Michael, Sara Minsky, and Kasisomayajula Viswanath. 2013. "The H1N1 Pandemic: Media Frames, Stigmatizaiton and Coping." *BMC Public Health* 13: 1116.

McDermott, Maeve. 2016. "Exclusive: How Disney Brought Elena of Alavor's Latin Heritage to Life." *USA Today*. http://www.usatoday.com/story/life/entertainthis/2016/07/12/meet-disney-channel-first-latina-princess-elena-of avalor/86982644/?hootPostID=3a84115ae85ba5f220637160b7b99042 (accessed April 5, 2017).

Mirande, Alfredo. 1987. *Gringo Justice*. Notre Dame, IN: University of Notre Dame Press.

Nealy, Michelle J. 2008. "The Spanish-Language Media Market in a Growth Phase." *Diverse Issues in Higher Education* 25: 18.

Oetzel, Juan, Felicia DeVargas, Tamar Ginossar, and Christina Sanchez. 2007. "Hispanic Women's Preferences for Breast Health Information: Subjective Cultural Influences on Source, Message, and Channel." *Health Communication* 2: 223–233.

Perez, Frank G. 2003. "Hispanics, Advertising, and Alcohol: Cultivation Theory and Panethnic Beer Commercials on the Univision Television Network." In *Brown and Black Communication: Latino and African American Conflict and Convergence in Mass Media*, edited by Diana I. Rios and A.N. Mohamed, 145. Westport, CT: Praeger.

Petty, Ross D., Anne-Marie G. Harris, Toni Broaddus, William M. Boyd, III. 2003. "Regulating Target Marketing and Other Raced-based Advertising Practices." *Michigan Journal of Race and Law* 8: 335–394.

Pew Research Center. 2014. "Statistical Portrait of Hispanics in the United States." http://www.pewhispanic.org/2016/04/19/statistical-portrait-of-hispanics-in-the-united-states-key-charts (accessed April 5, 2017).

Pew Research Center. 2015. "Newspapers: Daily Readership by Ethnic Group." http://www.journalism.org/media-indicators/newspapers-daily-readership-by-ethnic-group (accessed April 5, 2017).

Rojas, Viviana. 2004. "The Gender of Latinidad: Latinas Speak About Hispanic Television." *The Communication Review* 7: 125–153.

Ryan, Erin L. 2007. "*Dora the Explorer:* Giving Power to Preschoolers, Girls, and Latinas." Paper presented at the annual meeting of the Association for Educators in Journalism and Mass Communication, Washington, DC.

Shearer, Elisa. 2016. "'State of the News Media' Hispanic News Media Fact Sheet." Pew Center for Research. http://www.journalism.org/2016/06/15/hispanic-media-fact-sheet (accessed April 5, 2017).

Stein, M.L. 2007. "Racial Stereotyping and the Media." *Editor and Publisher*, August 6: 12–13.

Suro, Roberto. 2004. "Changing Channels and Crisscrossing Cultures: A Survey of Latinos in the News Media." http://www.pewhispanic.org/2004/04/19/changing-channels-and-crisscrossing-cultures (accessed April 5, 2017).

Suro, Roberto, Marty Kaplan, Ken Goldstein, and Matt Hale. 2011. "Univision Network Rivals ABC, CBS and NBC in Quantity and Focus of Campaign Coverage." The Norman Lear Center/Pew Hispanic Center. https://learcenter.org/wp-content/uploads/2004/10/LCLNASpanishRelease.pdf (accessed April 5, 2017).

Tate, Julee. 2011. "From Girly Men to Manly Men: The Evolving Representation of Male Homosexuality in Twenty-first Century Telenovelas." *Studies in Latin American Popular Culture* 29: 102–114.

Taylor, Charles R., Ju Yung Lee, and Barbara B. Stern. 1995. "Portrayals of African, Hispanic and Asian Americans in Magazine Advertising." *American Behavioral Scientist* 38: 608–621.

Tovares, Raul. 2000. "Latino USA: Construction of a News and Public Affairs Radio Program." *Journal of Broadcasting and Electronic Media* 44: 471–487.

Valdivia, Angharad N. 2010. *Latina/os and the Media.* Malden, MA: Polity Press.

Wang, Ye, and Shelly Rodgers. 2013. "Reporting on Health to Ethnic Populations: A Content Analysis of Local Health News in Ethnic Versus Mainstream Newspapers." *Howard Journal of Communications* 24: 257–274.

Weill, Susan, and Laura Castaneda. 2004. "'Empathetic Rejectionism' and Inter-ethnic Agenda Setting: Coverage of Latinos by the Black press in the American South." *Journalism Studies* 5: 537–550.

Wentz, Laura. 2008. "Hispanic Mags Post Double-digit Ad Gains, but Not All Are Thriving." *Advertising Age*, August 4: 20.

White, Elizabeth. 2001. "It's a Deal: NBC Buys Telemundo." *Media Life Magazine.* http://www.medialifemagazine.com/news2001/oct01/oct08/5_fri/news1friday.html (accessed March 17, 2011).

Wilken, Holley Thomas Valente, Sheila Murphy, Michael Cody, Grace Huang, and Vicki Beck. 2007. "Does Entertainment-Education Work with Latinos in the United States? Identification and the Effects of a Telenovela Breast Cancer Storyline." *Journal of Health Communication*, 12: 455–69.

6

Representations of Arabs/Arab Americans

Showtime's *Homeland* (2011 debut) is a spy drama about a Central Intelligence Agency officer who fights terrorism, while keeping an eye on a US Marine sergeant whom she suspects is secretly working for al-Qaeda, the terrorist organization that once held him captive. The Emmy award-winning series has been praised for its slick writing and riveting storylines. It has also, however, been criticized for reinforcing anti-Arab stereotypes and for insinuating that Muslims cannot be trusted.

In 2015, three graffiti artists employed by *Homeland*'s production company decided to protest against the program's use of stereotypes through subterfuge. Hired to paint graffiti in Arabic to heighten the authenticity of a set that was supposed to be a refugee camp, the artists did their job, but instead of painting common Arabic phrases, they painted subversive messages unbeknownst to the show's producers, director, and actors. Included among the messages was "Homeland is racist" (Izadi 2015). After the episode with the graffiti aired, the artists disseminated GIFs and screenshots of the graffiti scenes via social media and further took a stance against the show's use of stereotypes and its warped depictions of Muslims.

What further complicates troubling mass media portrayals of Arabs, such as those seen in *Homeland*, is that the impact extends beyond Arabs onto Arab Americans. Arab Americans are those Americans with ancestry from countries or regions, mainly in North Africa and the Middle East, in which Arabic is the official language (US Census Bureau 2005). Regardless of the fact that these individuals are Americans, in the minds of many viewers, mass media portrayals of Arabs living in other nations conceptually become portrayals of Arab Americans. In essence, Arab portrayals become transferred over to Arab Americans.

This chapter first explores the historical roots of Arab and Arab American representations. It then discusses the extent to which these portrayals have been maintained through the mass media, as well as how they have evolved.

Historical Background to Arab/Arab American Representations

In an article published in the late 1990s, communications professor Marouf Hasian, Jr. writes that Westerners throughout the centuries have been both "fascinated and repulsed" by Arabs

Diversity in US Mass Media, Second Edition. Catherine A. Luther, Carolyn Ringer Lepre, and Naeemah Clark.
© 2018 John Wiley & Sons Inc. Published 2018 by John Wiley & Sons Inc.

(Hasian 1998: 207). During the Crusades (1096–1291 CE) and Europe's later colonial expansion into the Middle and Far East, Arabs were depicted as an exotic race and one that hindered the progress of civilization. Western Europeans portrayed them as a people who represented all that stood against Christianity. These portrayals served as a means by which Westerners were able to justify to themselves and to others their resolve to colonize and dominate the Arab world.

Literary scholar and cultural critic Edward Said, in his influential book *Orientalism*, published in 1979, argues that the racial myths that were established during those years have persisted through the discourse of Orientalism. The term "Orientalism" was traditionally used to describe academic studies of the "Orient," now more commonly referred to as Asia. In its present usage, however, Orientalism can be understood as Western ideas regarding Middle Eastern people and cultures that emphasize difference and exoticism. No real correspondence may exist between these ideas and reality. Said describes Orientalism as a Western-formulated "dogma that not only degrades its subject matter but also blinds its practitioners (Said 1979: 105–106). He asserts that through the discourse of Orientalism, European and American traditions and values have been painted throughout the years as superior to those of Arabs, while the rich Arab histories and cultures have been essentially dismissed as valueless (see Box 6.1).

Said describes how Orientalism has threaded its way through various forms of Western culture from journalism and creative literature to academic publications. As an example, he quotes renowned Scottish scholar of the Middle East, H.A.R. Gibb, as having stated in one of his lectures back in 1945, "It is true that there have been great philosophers among the Muslim peoples and that some of them were Arabs, but they were rare exceptions" (1979: 106). Gibb then goes on to write of how among Arabs, there was an aversion toward rationalism, that there existed "the rejection of rationalist modes of thought and of the utilitarian ethic which is inseparable from them" (1979: 106).

As illustrated by Gibb's lecture, fundamental biases about Arabs that were originally created for political, economic, and military reasons have become "common sense," a part of our everyday understandings, and have clouded any efforts to truly understand Arab cultures and communities. According to Said, the cultural hegemony, or the pervasive cultural dominance (see Chapter 2), of the West has allowed Orientalism to powerfully persevere and obscure comprehension. All Arabs are lumped together and are presented as the "Other."

More recent analyses of cultural products have substantiated Said's claims regarding the strength of Orientalism and the ideological structure maintaining it. Mirroring Said's findings, anthropologist Greta Little found five patterns of "constructed realities" of Arabs present in books targeted at children and adults (Little 1998: 264–266). The five patterns are as follows:

- "Arabs are dirty and lazy."
- "Arabs are ignorant, superstitious, and silly."
- "Arabs are irrational, cruel, and violent."
- "Arabs mistreat women."
- "Arabs hate Christians and engage in the slave trade."

Although both Said and Little concentrated their analysis on Western literature, the constant images that they found have also been reflected in other forms of media, including films, television shows, and even news stories.

Box 6.1 Mass media representations of Arabs/Arab Americans and undergraduate student conceptions

---

In 2009 and then again in 2016, one of this book's authors asked her undergraduate students to take out a sheet of paper and write three words that came to mind when thinking about Arabs. After the students wrote their responses, the instructor collected the papers, shuffled them, and read aloud what was written on each one.

Table 6.1 below lists the descriptive words and the frequency of mention from the two time periods; 47 students participated in 2009 and 61 students in 2016. The table provides those descriptors that appeared more than twice in the student responses. It is interesting to see that while similarities in responses existed from both time periods, terms that have more neutral or positive connotations such as "culture" or "misunderstood" appeared in 2016. Students in 2016 also knew the term "hijab" (head scarf). Consider the impact subtle changes In film and entertainment television portrayals during the seven-year time span might have had on what words immediately came to the students' minds.

Table 6.1 Student thoughts about "Arabs" in 2009 and 2016.

Descriptive words	2009 (N = 75)	2016 (N = 101)
turbans	16%	9%
terrorists	15%	6%
religious	12%	2%
Muslim	12%	17%
Middle Eastern or Middle East	11%	27%
brown/dark-skinned	11%	8%
foreign	7%	6%
beards	5%	3%
strict	4%	0%
Islamic	4%	6%
family-oriented	4%	0%
hijab	0%	8%
culture	0%	3%
misunderstood	0%	3%
oil	0%	3%

Arabs/Arab Americans in Film

One of the more prolific researchers on the topic of mass media representations of Arabs is mass communication scholar Jack Shaheen. Shaheen maintains that Arabs are the most "maligned group in the history of Hollywood" and points out that since Hollywood's beginning, it has portrayed Muslims and Arabs as one and the same, although Arabs have long made up a minority of the Muslim population (Shaheen 2008). The end result has been a lack of recognition that religious diversity exists among Arabs and that the Islamic religion is present among other ethnicities.

Shaheen has examined depictions of Arabs in more than a thousand Hollywood films released from the early 1900s to the present. He has found that although the depictions have changed over time with a mixing of new stereotypes with the old, consistencies in images also exist. In particular, the linkage of violence and evil with Arabs has steadfastly continued. The film's time period and the scenarios shown might be different, but the characterization of Arabs as ruthless and villainous remains.

The earlier images of Arabs in Hollywood films typically consisted of camel-riding, desert-wandering nomads. Men were shown as dishonest and easily provoked to violence. Rich oil sheikhs with dancing exotic women surrounding them in their harems were set in stark contrast with poor and dirty street beggars. The two extremes were presented with no variation in between. Arab women were shown as exotic, subservient to men, and with no voice. Their only purpose was to serve men and satisfy their sexual desires. The 1921 silent film entitled *The Sheik* is one of the films that had such stereotypic depictions.

In *The Sheik*, an English lady, Diana (played by Agnes Ayres), is determined to experience adventure and travel through the Algiers desert. It is at the beginning of this journey that she encounters an Arab sheikh, Sheikh Ahmed Ben Hassan (played by Rudolph Valentino) (Figure 6.1). She immediately calls him "savage," but by the looks she gives him, it is easy to see that she is attracted to his handsome features. Ahmed makes advances toward her, but Diana rebuffs his attempts and continues on her journey.

The rest of the film follows Diana on her journey, during which she is attacked by vicious Arab bandits and almost defiled by an Arab rival of Ahmed. Ahmed eventually rescues Diana, but not before he is seriously injured.

Figure 6.1 1920s heart-throb Rudolph Valentino as *The Sheik* (1921). Screenshot.

Toward the end of the film, Diana is sitting next to Ahmed as he lies dying. She takes Ahmed's hand and says to the sheikh's English gentleman friend, who is also present, "His hand is so large for an Arab." With that, the sheikh's friend tells Diana that Ahmed is actually not Arab. He explains that Ahmed's father was an Englishman and his mother a Spaniard. Upon hearing this, Diana's feelings for Ahmed become fonder. After Diana pleads to God to take her life instead of his, Ahmed's eyes open and he smiles at Diana. Diana is overjoyed. The last scene of the film shows Ahmed saying to Diana, "Diana, my beloved! The darkness has passed and now the sun-shine," at which Diana places her head on his bare chest and they caress.

Although tenderness is shown between Diana and Ahmed, in the end, the audience finds that Ahmed is not Arab after all. If the film's creators had allowed Ahmed to remain as an Arab, it would have been a nice contrast to the negative images of Arabs that were shown in the film. In the film, Arab women are shown being auctioned off as sex slaves to be used in harems, while Arab men are portrayed as lecherous and violent. The decision by the creators of *The Sheik* to make Ahmed a non-Arab in the end most likely was due to the then existing Hollywood practice of not allowing white women to engage in relations with non-Whites in films. The Motion Picture Producers and Distributors of America, Inc. Production Code (1930–1934) later enforced this practice. Shaheen (1984) writes, "As some Code executives believed Arabs to be nonwhite persons, it became unthinkable for producers to show a white Western woman loving a dusky-skinned, swarthy Arab."

By the 1960s and 1970s, the theme of the threatening Arab was emphasized even further. With the Arab–Israeli conflict and the increasing wealth of the oil-producing Arab nations, feelings of animosity toward the Arab world grew in the United States (Semmerling 2006). These feelings were reflected in Hollywood films. In the films produced during this period, Arabs were often shown to be vicious and untrustworthy. For example, in the 1967 film *The Ambushers*, the hero of the movie (played by Dean Martin) scuttles the attempts of an Arab and his organization to secure a US flying saucer. The Arab gets close to attaining the aircraft through unscrupulous means and by strangling those whose trust he was able to gain. In the end, however, he receives his comeuppance by being scorched in a blazing fire in the aircraft.

From the 1980s to the present, the overarching Arab image has been that of "terrorist." Although still violent, the sleazy and rich sheikh has been for the most part replaced by the brutal and crazed Islamic extremist. As Soviet–US relations improved, the foreign policies of US Presidents Ronald Reagan and George Bush were increasingly focused on their Arab nemeses (Kellner 1995). This was then mirrored by Hollywood with such films as *The Delta Force* (1985) starring Chuck Norris, *Iron Eagle* (1986) featuring Lou Gossett, Jr., and *True Lies* (1994) starring Arnold Schwarzenegger that identified Arabs as the evil Other.

In *True Lies*, American spy Harry Tasker, played by Schwarzenegger, is faced with an enemy common in Hollywood scripts – the evil Arab terrorist. Scene after scene in the film, Arabs are depicted chanting prayers before detonating bombs, firing guns into the air, and slapping women around. On numerous occasions they are referred to as "raving psychotics." The Arab characters appearing in *True Lies* are not just villains, however; they are also portrayed as bumbling and inept, often played for comedic effect. In one particular scene, for example, as the terrorists videotape their threats to be sent to the media, the shaking Arab cameraman cravenly squeaks out in broken English that the batteries in the video camera are dead.

In the wake of the film's release, Arab American advocacy groups protested, arguing that the film's representations of Arabs as violent anti-American zealots are problematic. In defense of *True Lies*, a spokesman for the film's production company, 20th Century Fox, stated, "The film is a work of fiction and does not represent the actions or beliefs of a particular culture or religion" (*New York Times* 1994). A similar disclaimer appears at the end of the film's credits. For many, however, the film was not just insignificant fiction. It was offensive. After the film's release, long-time radio broadcaster and entertainer Casey Kasem, of Palestinian/Lebanese descent, called the disclaimer "an insult to anyone's intelligence" (Miller 1994: C2).

Arabs are also depicted as terrorists in the feature film *Rules of Engagement* (2000). In the film, American marines led by a colonel (played by Samuel L. Jackson) are sent on a mission to save the staff of the American embassy in Yemen. As the marines arrive at the embassy compound by helicopter, a mob of angry Yemeni women, men, and children are shown thrusting their fists in the air, yelling, and throwing firebombs at the embassy. Yemini snipers are also shown shooting at the embassy employees and marines. After three of the marines are killed, the other marines open fire at the crowd of Yeminis. In interpreting this scene, Tim Jon Semmerling writes:

> Since the Middle East is supposed to be a place where little makes sense, no explanation about Yemeni grievances is provided for the audience. Yemenis exhibit this behavior without reason or provocation, as if such behavior, and the hatred that inspires it, are innate traits of Arabs ... The Yemeni convergence on this American embassy relies on the American audience's ability to intertextually relate its cultural memory and fear of legendary Indian attacks on American outposts and the real-life siege of the American embassy in Tehran of 1979. (Semmerling 2006)

Negative stereotypes of Arabs have even appeared in animated films targeted at children. One animated film that has gained much attention for its stereotypes is Disney's *Aladdin*, released in 1992. American Studies professor Brian T. Edwards writes that traditional representations of the Arab world found in many of the earlier Hollywood films were revived in this animated work (Edwards 2001). Both exoticism and menace long associated with the Arab world are among the representations conveyed. The film is set in a mythical Arab land inhabited by rich sultans as well as poor peddlers. The film's hero, Aladdin, and heroine, Princess Jasmine, although dressed in traditional Arab attire, are given Anglo-Saxon characteristics, with Anglo-American accents and pale complexions. The peddlers and villains, however, are given thick accents, dark complexions, and stereotypic Arab features. The ruthlessness and deceitfulness of those characters are also played up.

The feature film shown in theaters had a song included in the opening segment that created much controversy; the song was later revised due to public pressure before the film was released on video. The original lyrics of the song were as follows:

> OH, I COME FROM A LAND,
> From a faraway place,
> Where the caravan camels roam,
> Where they cut off your ear,
> If they don't like your face,
> It's barbaric, but hey, it's home.

The portrayal taps into the long-held stereotypes of treachery and barbarism associated with the Arab world. Although the lyrics of the opening song were revised before video release, the other stereotypes included in the film remained. For example, in a scene in which the villain of the movie,

Jafar, is speaking to a thief who has stolen a magical scarab on his behalf, the following exchange takes place:

> JAFAR: You have it, then?
> POOR THIEF: I had to slit a few throats, but I got it.

(As Jafar attempts to take the scarab, the thief pulls the scarab back behind him.)

> POOR THIEF: Ah, ah, ah. The treasure.

(Although the thief expects to be presented with a treasure as his reward for getting the scarab, Jafar's parrot flies down and plucks the scarab from the thief's hand and presents it to Jafar.)

> JAFAR: Trust me my pungent friend. You'll get what is coming to you.

A few minutes after this scene, the poor thief ends up dying at Jafar's orders.

With both Jafar and the thief wearing traditional Arab clothing and having dark complexions, exaggerated features, and thick accents, connotations of treachery, violence, and filth, are associated with Arabs through these characters.

Even when featuring Arab Americans, Hollywood producers have persevered with these widely held stereotypes, and have transferred the nefarious images of Arabs over to Arab Americans as well. For example, in the 2001 urban action film *Two Degrees*, about a young African American couple trying to escape their run-down lives in South Central Los Angeles, two Arab American brothers, Faisel (played by Jihad Harik) and Reza (played by Elie Masara) are featured as owners of a liquor store. Prone to violence and crude in their behavior, the men are portrayed as self-indulgent, with their main interests being women and money. No positive aspects of these characters are shown. In the end, both brothers are killed due to their stupidity and abusive actions.

After the aircraft bombings of the World Trade Center in New York and the Pentagon in Washington, DC, on September 11, 2001, Hollywood's use of negative Arab images intensified. For example, the equating of Arabs with terrorists and the vilification of Arabs was made quite blatant in the 2004 action film, *Team America: World Police*, featuring puppets as characters. Although the film tries to make fun of the extreme measures taken by the United States in its war on terror, the film's end result is a reinforcement of the negative stereotypes of Arabs. Part of the film's plot involves a team of heroes who are out to stop terrorists from going forth with their objective of mass destruction. The terrorists are portrayed as turbaned Arabs who are systematically mowed down by the heroes.

In her doctoral dissertation Yasmeen Elayan (2005) extrapolated what these types of representations mean in the most practical sense. She found that pre-9/11 films rarely showed three-dimensional or positive Arabic or Muslim characters. She argues that these negative portrayals only served to strengthen the fear others had of Muslims in the United States, making easier for the public to condemn an entire race and religion for the actions of a few.

Another movie that pokes fun at the Arab as terrorist image is *Jackass Number Two* (2006). The movie, basically an extension of the MTV program *Jackass* (2000–2002) with Johnny Knoxville, features uncouth skits designed for cheap laughs. In one skit, one of the Jackass pranksters attempts to scare a taxi driver by entering a cab dressed in a manner fitting the Arab terrorist stereotype and holding a bomb. He instructs the taxi driver to drive him to the airport and suggests he is going to carry out a terror mission. In the end, the taxi driver turns against the prankster and threatens him with a gun. It turns out that the taxi driver is in on the prank and the tables are turned. The Jackass prankster is also informed that the fake beard that he is wearing is made out of the other pranksters' pubic hair. In his analysis of this film, Jack Shaheen notes, "Some Arabs and Muslims who grow beards in the tradition of the prophet Muhammad may find this to be a disturbing scene" (Edwards 2001: 14).

As more Americans, including policy makers, began questioning the actions taken by the United States under its "war on terror" banner, however, some positive or fair film images of Arabs and Arab Americans started to come to light. For example, the award-winning 2006 film *Babel* shows Arabs as multidimensional human beings. *Babel* follows three interconnected storylines that explore human behavior and relations. One of the storylines involves an Arab family, made up of two young boys, their sisters, baby brother, mother, and father, living in the mountainous areas of Morocco. They are goat herders. After the father, Abdullah (played by Mustapha Rachidi) receives a rifle from an acquaintance, he instructs the boys to take it with them to shoot jackals. The boys do so and during their playful competition of who can shoot the farthest, the younger boy shoots through the window of a passing tour bus. An American woman, Susan (played by Cate Blanchett), who is riding on the bus, is shot in the neck. What ensues is a desperate effort by her American husband, Richard (played by Brad Pitt) to save his wife's life, police searching for the shooter, and the guilt-ridden boys attempting to hide what they had done.

During the story, the Moroccan people are shown as real people with loving family interactions. When Richard tries to get medical help for his wife, the Moroccan tour guide, Anwar (played by Mohamed Akhzam), directs the tour bus to go to his nearby village and enlists the help of the village veterinarian, the best he can do under the circumstances. The Moroccans in the village are shown as compassionate and concerned about saving the life of the woman. In fact, it is an elderly Moroccan woman who comforts Susan in her pain by stroking her head and humming a song until Susan drifts off to sleep.

While the Moroccan villagers are portrayed positively, the Western tourists who had no choice but to go along on the bus are portrayed as uncaring and selfish. With their bigotry and suspicion of the Moroccan people, they are continuously asking Richard to let them go on their way. One of the tourists expresses his fear that the villagers were going to slit their throats. In the end, they do leave with the bus, leaving Richard, his critically injured wife, and the tour guide behind. When a medical helicopter finally arrives at the village to take the woman to a city hospital, Richard, in thanks, tries to give Anwar money for his help. Anwar refuses and, by his facial expression, you know that Anwar's only concern is to save Susan. At the hospital, a Moroccan doctor succeeds in saving Susan's life.

The 2006 psychological thriller *Sorry Haters* provides a positive portrayal of an Arab American. Set in New York City, the film's plot begins with the meeting of Phoebe (played by Robin Wright Penn), a hate-riddled, bitter woman, and Ashade (played by Abdellatif Kechiche), a benevolent Muslim cab driver of Syrian descent. After hearing that Ashade's brother was held in Guantanamo and deported to Syria after mistakenly being accused of terrorism, Phoebe takes it upon herself to exonerate Ashade's brother and uses violence to do so. In this movie, the white woman comes across as the crazed killer. It is the Arab American who is the rational and kind soul.

Another film that attempts to show an Arab American in a well-rounded manner is the 2007 film, *Rendition*. The film does so through its exploration of the controversial US practice of moving suspected foreign terrorists to an undisclosed non-US location where they are tortured for information. *Rendition* is about an Arab American chemical engineer, Anwar el-Ibrahimi (played by Omar Metwally), who is taken, while on a business trip to South Africa, by agents working for the US Central Intelligence Agency (CIA). Accused of being involved in a suicide bombing attack that killed a CIA agent, Anwar is transported to another unnamed country and is repeatedly humiliated and tortured. These disturbing scenes are juxtaposed with warm-hearted scenes of Anwar's pregnant wife and young son back in Anwar's home in Chicago. By the positioning of these scenes, the viewing audience comes to see Anwar as a family man who has found himself in dire circumstances because of the US government agents' bigotry and thirst for vengeance.

Even while certain positive images have become more noticeable in recent years, the parts that call for Arabs or Arab Americans to be featured in leading roles that are not tied to a plot that revolves around the critique of racism or ethnocentrism are still a rarity. Throughout Hollywood's years, Arab or Arab American characters have been shown only in cameo roles. Often they appear in order to make certain points in a quick manner. The characters are shown just long enough to create a scenario that producers believe audiences will be able to immediately comprehend due to the stereotypes associated with Arabs. An example of this is in the film *Back to the Future* (1985). The two key characters of the film, teenager Marty McFly (played by Michael J. Fox) and scientist Dr. Emmett Brown (played by Christopher Lloyd), are shown in a mall parking lot getting a time-machine vehicle run by plutonium ready for travel. Following Dr. Brown's brief statement that he was able to trick Libyans into giving him the plutonium, a van arrives with men carrying machine-guns and a bazooka. The men are shown wearing Arab headdress (*keffiyeh*) and appearing crazed. They succeed in killing Dr. Brown, but Marty is able to escape by traveling back in time with the vehicle. The entire segment lasts less than three minutes, but with the van, the traditional Arab clothing/headdress, and the weapons, no in-depth explanation is needed in terms of why the men are seeking the plutonium. The producers are able to tap into stereotypes to keep the story moving.

An award-winning documentary that sets out to counter such stereotypes is *A Thousand & One Journeys* (2015). Through interviews with prominent members of the Arab American community, including interviews with former Senator George Mitchell, former White House correspondent Helen Thomas, and comedian/actor Jamie Farr, the film presents an historical overview of the contributions that Arab immigrants and their descendants have made to American society. Executive producer of the film Abe Kasbo said he wanted to make the film to correct the "many misconceptions out there about what it means to be Arab-American" (La Gorce 2016). Of course, it is a sad commentary that such a documentary was felt to be needed.

The pattern of stereotype usage with regard to Arabs and Arab Americans is not confined to films alone; stereotypes are very much present in entertainment television programming as well. The same types of images of Arabs and Arab Americans found in films are also found in television. Jack Shaheen asserted in 1984: "Over the years, TV's Arab and Arab-American portraits have only become worse." Can the same statement be made today? Read the next section and decide for yourself.

Arabs/Arab Americans in Entertainment Television

In his book *The TV Arab*, Shaheen examined US television images of Arabs in the 1970s and 1980s (Shaheen 1984). The prevalent images he found, including the wealthy sheikh, the crazed villain, the barbaric anti-Western killer, and the hedonistic polygamist, mirrored those found in films. Many of those images were present in the earlier years of television as well. Even in old cartoons such as *Bugs Bunny*, *Popeye*, and *Batman*, the evil and conniving Arab was used for laughs and entertainment. Because of cable television and its need for large volumes of programming, these old television programs that depicted Arabs in stereotypical ways are still being viewed. Audiences are now watching these old images alongside the new stereotypes.

Following the events of September 11, 2001, 40 percent of the dramas that aired on television during the 2001–2002 season made reference to the 9/11 terrorist attacks (Cass 2007), and the theme of the Arab terrorist has since continued in television programming. In fact, it can be found in various episodes of highly rated prime-time television programs. For example, in one of the early episodes of the CBS television program *Criminal Minds* (2005 debut), an Egyptian, accused of being one of the masterminds of a plot to carry out a public terror attack in the United States, is incarcerated and continuously interrogated by FBI profiler Jason Gideon (played by Mandy Patinkin). Gideon attempts to find the location of the planned attack through nonconfrontational means. During the interrogation process, the Egyptian appears highly intelligent and articulate. At the same time, however, he comes across as violent and callous. When the FBI profiler describes the innocent people who would be killed in the attack, the accused terrorist contorts his face and angrily describes how those who would be killed are "infidels" and expresses no remorse for what needs to be done for the "jihad" (used to mean "holy war" in this context). In the end, the Egyptian is outwitted by the FBI profiler and inadvertently reveals the location of the planned attack. The attack is diverted and the terrorists are defeated. As this episode relates, many of the programs that feature Arabs tend to tie that ethnicity with Islam, which, in turn, is associated with violence or terrorism.

Another example of the usage of the evil Arab in entertainment television is in the Fox television program *24* (2001–2010). The program's central character is an individual named Jack Bauer (played by Kiefer Sutherland) who works for the US government to thwart domestic terror threats. The "evil Arab" image appeared in this series numerous times across different seasons. The show depicted both Arabs and Arab Americans as stealthily planning various acts of terrorism in a cold and methodical manner. Jack Bauer fearlessly thwarts these plans, using various, perhaps controversial, means. The idea that the torture and killing of individuals who plan terrorist activities is justified and even needed was repeatedly reinforced in the episodes.

Although the initial norm of *24* was to show Arabs in a negative light, toward the end of the series, positive images of Arabs and Arab Americans were shown. For example, in one storyline, the president of a fictitious Middle Eastern nation called the Islamic Republic of Kamistan, Omar Hassan (played by Anil Kapoor), comes to the United States to sign a peace agreement with the US President, Allison Taylor (played by Cherry Jones). President Hassan is shown as a rational and compassionate individual. He explains early in the storyline that he wants to sign the agreement with the United States in order to bring peace and economic stability to his country. When President Hassan finds out that if he proceeds with the signing, his life might be in danger, he states, "If the price for peace is my life, so be it." In fact, at the end of the storyline, President Hassan ends up sacrificing himself.

In this peace-agreement storyline, viewers are also introduced to President Hassan's wife, Dalia (played by Necar Zadegan), who contradicts the typical stereotypes associated with Arab women. Instead of the demure and understated Arab woman, President Hassan's wife comes across as a confident and strong woman who clearly expresses her opinion. A sense of independence seeps out of Dalia. In fact, the relationship between President Hassan and his wife is shown as an equal partnership.

The turn in imagery regarding Arabs in *24* might have been due to the producers' awareness of the criticisms that were continuously made against the show by various researchers and nonprofit organizations, such the Arab American Anti-Discrimination Committee (ADC). From its debut, *24* was criticized for perpetuating unfair stereotypes of Arabs and Arab Americans. In response to repeated calls to discontinue the negative images, the producers of the show might have decided to heed those calls to a certain extent by introducing positive portrayals to accompany the negative.

For it should be pointed out that negative images of Arabs still did persist in *24* even toward the end of the series. For example, in the storyline described above, Hassan's brother Farhad (played by Akbar Kurtha) is found to be a part of a plot to kill his brother. The viewers also find that his brother is involved with others in his home nation to buy nuclear material and to bring down Hassan's government. Nevertheless, by presenting contradicting images of people from the Middle East, the program attempted to veer away from the one-dimensional characterizations that had long predominated in the program. At the time of writing the second edition of this book, it was announced that a spin-off of *24* titled *24: Legacy* would premiere in 2017. It would be interesting to examine how characters of Arab descent are portrayed in the new show.

The television crime drama *Bones*, which premiered in 2005, is another example of a series that has attempted to convey the multidimensional aspects of those of Middle Eastern descent. *Bones* follows the work of forensic anthropologist Dr. Temperance Brennan (played by Emily Deschanel) and her group of lab interns, together with FBI special agent Seeley Booth (played by David Boreanaz). In its fifth season, a Muslim intern by the name of Arastoo Vaziri (played by Pej Vehdat) was added to the group of interns. Arastoo was first introduced into the program as a student of Iranian descent and spoke with an accent suggesting he was from the Middle East. In one of the episodes highlighting Arastoo, however, it is discovered that he was actually faking his accent. This discovery takes place when forensic specialist Dr. Camille Saroyan (played by Tamara Taylor) and Arastoo are sifting through human remains that are mixed with pig bones. Camille says to Arastoo that she is willing to excuse him from the job due to the fact that he is Muslim and that they are touching pig bones. Arastoo tries to explain to her that touching the pig bones would not go against his religion; Camille, however, is persistent in telling him that he may be excused. Exasperated, Arastoo finally fluently blurts out in an American accent, "I'm a scientist, okay, just like the rest of you, so back off and let me do my job like anyone else." After looking at Camille's stunned expression, he leaves, telling her that he has to do his prayers.

Cutting to another scene, the viewer sees Camille talking to Seeley and Temperance on speaker-phone. She asks them if they knew that Arastoo really does not have an accent. The viewer then sees Seeley and Temperance listening on the other end. At Camille's query, Seeley immediately responds by saying, "Yes, he does. Thicker than Akhmed, the rug merchant." He then turns to Temperance and states, "Is that racist? That sounds racist." Temperance gives him an annoyed look and replies to Camille, "I knew that despite the fact that he said he was Iranian, his accent was Jordanian." The viewer again sees Camille asking, "Don't you find it odd that he was faking an Arab accent of any kind?" Cutting to Temperance, the anthropologist responds by keenly stating, "Iranian isn't actually Arab."

The episode later cuts to a scene with psychologist Dr. Lance Sweets (played by John Francis Daley) asking Arastoo why he faked his accent when he is an American of Iranian descent who clearly speaks with an American accent. Arastoo explains that he thought speaking with an accent would help him complete the picture for others in terms of why he is a Muslim who prays five times a day. He says, "When I speak as though I just got off the boat, people accept my religious convictions ... plus fewer terrorist jokes. I don't know why." Lance gives his view on why there are fewer terrorist jokes by stating, "Because they are afraid of you."

This episode serves two positive purposes. It first points out how Americans tend to view individuals of Middle Eastern descent in black and white terms and how no distinction is made between Persians and Arabs. With the heavy accent and Muslim religion, colleagues of Arastoo at first think of him as an Arab. It is only when Temperance explains that those who are Iranian are not Arabs that they come to realize their error. The second aims to show how Americans look at individuals who are Muslim. Using the words of Lance, if a "rational, pragmatic, highly intelligent" person is Muslim and does not speak with a Middle Eastern accent, that person is viewed as a curiosity. *Bones*, and this episode in particular, illustrates how Hollywood creators are perhaps becoming more aware of the importance of questioning past portrayals of those of Middle Eastern descent and are exploring matters related to ethnicity in their programs.

Other exceptions to the negative portrayals of Arabs have been found in the television show *The West Wing*. Communication professor Philip Cass argues that *The West Wing*, which aired from 1999 to 2006, had portrayals that were not always limited to hostile stereotypes. He describes episodes in which the fictional US president and his staff encountered Arabs who were respectable and honest. Cass asserts that throughout the run of the series, positive portrayals appeared alongside negative ones.

The action drama television series *Lost* (2004–2010) also included positives with the negatives in its portrayal of one of its leading characters who was shown to be Iraqi. The Iraqi character, Sayid Jarrah, played by Naveen Andrews (actually of Indian descent), was among those passengers of Oceanic Air flight 815 who were stranded on a mysterious island after their airplane crashed. In several of the program's episodes, Sayid was frequently shown as caring and heroic, contradicting the "evil Arab" stereotype. When Sayid's background was revealed in the program in later episodes, however, it was discovered that Sayid was formerly an Iraqi soldier whose specialty was interrogation and torture. Even on the island, he exercised his skills in torturing when needed. When he was shown off the island, he engaged in systematic assassinations. Thus, the negative characteristics of Sayid were highlighted. It must be said, however, that the inclusion of an Arab character in a leading role was a definite step in the right direction on the part of the producers of *Lost*, and that when considering the series in total, it could be concluded that the positive and humane features of Sayid were demonstrated in the storylines more often than his negative aspects.

Even with the strides that have been made in the offering of more positive characteristics of Arabs and Arab Americans, for actors and actresses of Arab descent, typecasting still remains a problem. For example, not many can relay the stories of commercial success that actor Tony Shalhoub, who is of Lebanese ancestry, has had in his roles in the television sitcom *Wings* (1990–1997) and the crime drama series *Monk* (2002–2009), where his ancestry was either changed or not mentioned in his roles.

In 2014, FX created the US first family series centered around an Arab/Arab American Muslim family with *Tyrant*. In the series, Dr. Bassam "Barry" Al-Fayeed (played by Adam Raynor) takes his blonde American wife Molly (played by Jennifer Finnigan) and his two children to the fictional Middle Eastern nation of Abuddin to visit his family. Although he only intends for them to stay for a brief time, it isn't long before he finds himself immersed in the corruption of the dictatorial government by Barry's family. A drama centered around an Arab and Muslim family is rare and members of the Arab American viewing audience eagerly anticipated this glossy series. However, the public perception of the program was far from positive, with many taking to social media to express their angst. For example, one viewer tweeted after the program's premiere:

> #TyrantFX had a season's worth of racist stereotypes and Orientalist images in 1 episode. No need to watch any further.
> 11:32 PM - 24 Jun 2014

Another viewer tweeted:

> Angry Arab men, loud slaps, shooting and carnage, rape, domestic violence within first half of #TyrantFX.
> 11:15 PM - 24 Jun 2014
> (Huang 2014)

After the premiere, the national communications director of the activist group The Center for American–Islamic Relations, Ibrahim Hooper, issued a press release lamenting: "In the pilot of FX's *Tyrant*, Arab Muslim culture is devoid of any redeeming qualities and is represented by terrorists, murderous children, rapists, corrupt billionaires, and powerless female victims. ... In *Tyrant*, even the 'good' Arab Muslims are bad" (Hooper 2014). Even though *Tyrant*'s producers responded to feedback from the Muslim Public Affairs Council and Muslims on Screen and Television, the show's viewership steadily declined and FX decided to cancel the series in 2016.

A show that attempts to present multidimensional Arab American characters is the ABC network television show *Quantico* (2015 debut). In season 1, the show introduces to the audience a group of young FBI recruits who are being trained at the FBI Quantico training facilities. Two of the FBI recruits are Arab American Muslims, Nimah (played by Lebanese actress Yasmine Al Massri) and her twin sister Raina Amin (also played by Al Masssri). Both are being trained to switch identities with each other at a moment's notice once they are out in the field as FBI agents. As the program progresses, the audience comes to learn that Nimah and Raina are quite different in terms of beliefs and personalities. Nimah does not wear the hijab (head scarf), whereas her sister Raina does (Figure 6.2). Raina is conservative and more concerned about maintaining her parents' traditional values and expectations, whereas Nimah is more progressive and is self-driven. Both women, however, are strong and competitive.

Viewers, especially young Muslim American females, have applauded the program's efforts to present Muslims as diverse and not fitting into one stereotypic pigeonhole. Actress Al Massri is said

Figure 6.2 Actress Yasmine Al Massri in *Quantico* (2015–). Screenshot.

to have received a number of encouraging messages of support from her fans, many fervently hoping that the program does not decide to make the twin characters terrorists.

The nuanced Arab American roles presented in *Quantico*, however, are exceptions to the norm. Most actors of Arab descent have complained that the only roles available to them are the villain, the terrorist, the subservient female, or the belly dancer. Offerings of more diverse characters are short in number. Some have even gone as far as to change their names to Anglo-sounding names in order to attain more ordinary or complex roles. The problem might lie in the fact that not many shows are creating long-lasting characters that are of Arab descent. In analyzing the programs that have shown positive portrayals, the characters with positive attributes tend to be shown in more than one episode. When stories are created that involve an Arab or Arab American for only one episode, the tendency has been to fall back on stereotypes for those one-shot episodes. Reliance on widely held stereotypes becomes an easy solution for writers and producers. By relying on stereotypes, they can create scenarios without having to provide much background information. They are aware that if a character is presented as having an Arab background, they can tap into the stereotypes that exist about Arabs and move the story along in a succinct and simplistic manner.

The ease of storytelling that stereotypes offer unfortunately plays a part, not only in the entertainment media, but also in the mainstream press as well. Even where objectivity and fairness should be of utmost importance, in mainstream news stories, Arab stereotypes appear.

Representations of Arabs/Arab Americans in the News

The first sizeable group of Arab immigrants arrived in the United States in the late 1800s (Haddad 1983). A majority of them came from the Lebanese/Syrian region of the Middle East in search of a better livelihood. It was during this time that depictions of Arab Americans began to appear in mainstream periodicals in the United States. Much of the prose that appeared in these publications reflected the long-held stereotypes that were held of Arabs (Figure 6.3).

Religious scholar Theodore Pulcini writes that in a 1903 story printed in *Harper's Monthly*, the journalist covering a Syrian neighborhood in the city of New York tries to dispel some of the negative

Figure 6.3 Veiled Bedouin woman in *National Geographic* magazine (1995).

stereotypes in his article, but perhaps unconsciously confounds his attempt by also relying on those very same stereotypes. The journalist begins his story by writing:

> It was officer MacNamara, of dimlit beat, who first took me through the city street where these swarthy fellows, and their betters, have forgathered to live. The night was dark and gusty, and the rain had at last swept the swarm of hags and squalling children and silent glowering men from the pavements and shadowy doorways. (Pulcini 1993)

By beginning the article with a description conveying a neighborhood atmosphere of gloom and darkness, and a people of mystery and sullenness, the journalist provides a negative backdrop that places a shroud upon the positive notions he expresses about the neighborhood and people later in the article.

Those early images of Arabs in the news media have stood firm across time. In her examination of depictions of Arabs in *National Geographic* over a 100-year time period, women's studies professor Linda Steet found that images of the Arab world have not really changed over the years even though much political and economic change has indeed taken place in the Middle East. The colonialist rhetoric constructing Arabs as erotic, violent, and primitive continues even in the relatively more recent pages of *National Geographic*.

According to Steet's book, although the magazine presents its publication as upholding the highest standards of objectivity and as portraying people in their natural state, patriarchal and Orientalist discourses permeate the magazine (Steet 2000).

Mass communication professor Karen Gwinn Wilkins examined photographs of Middle Eastern women as presented in the *New York Times* from 1991 to 1993 (Wilkins 1995). She found that the portrayals defined women in the Middle East in the context of family or religion rather than any social or professional position. Furthermore, the women were frequently presented in passive positions or were cast in the role of victim. Wilkins concludes that the press images basically reflected the dominant Western ideologies regarding gender roles and Orientalism.

In examining the coverage of Arabs in *Time* magazine and *Newsweek* magazine from 1990 to 1993, communication professor Mahboub Hashem (1995) also found stereotypic images reflected in the content. Arabs were frequently depicted as living in a region of decline, unable to let go of the past, and treating guest workers in their countries as slaves. They were shown to be a people who could not have a democratic system and, instead, were increasingly moving toward autocratic and fundamentalist regimes. Hashem found that aspects of Arab cultures and values that could better inform the reader were not often contained within the news stories.

Negative portrayals of Arabs have not been limited to print news but have also appeared in broadcast news. Middle Eastern specialist Patricia Karl writes about a 1981 series in *TV Guide* that examined nightly newscasts during a 10-month period (1983). The series revealed an imbalance in coverage of the Israeli–Palestinian conflict. Israeli attacks on Palestinian regions were shown as military operations and none of the reports showed Palestinian victims. On the other hand, for the Palestinian raids on Israel, a majority of the reports showed Israeli victims. The author asserts that the end effect was a vilification of the Palestinians and not the Israelis.

Communication researchers Rebecca A. Lind and James A. Danowski examined transcripts of around 35,000 hours of broadcast content on ABC News, CNN News, PBS, and NPR from 1993 to 1996 (Lind and Danowski 1998). They found little coverage of Arabs and even less coverage of Arab culture in the news and public affairs programs. Moreover, in the limited coverage that they did find, many of the words that were associated with Arabs fit existing stereotypes. The more prominent associations involved words describing war, violence, and threats. Often, Arabs were covered within the context of their relations with Israel. What makes this particularly problematic is that while little was available in the press that provides a more rounded representation of Arabs, the public was being exposed to selected descriptions of Arabs in the news that fit the stereotypes and negative imagery of Arabs in the entertainment media.

The use of wording that invokes Arab stereotypes was especially prominent during the coverage of the first US–Iraq war in the early 1990s. Professor of political science and communications Gadi Wolfsfeld found that during the war, the US news media "faithfully followed the narrative offered by Bush [President George H.W. Bush], establishing Saddam Hussein as a genuine threat to the world order" (Wolfsfeld 1997). Wolfsfeld argues that by using Hitler as an analogy to describe Hussein and by painting Hussein and his followers as barbaric terrorists who were storing large quantities of nuclear and biological weapons, the news media were able to convince the public that Iraq's entry into Kuwait represented a major threat to the United States and the rest of the world. The US news media, in essence, were able to help establish a crisis situation in the minds of the public and convince the public of the need to engage in war with Iraq.

Also writing about the first US–Iraq war, communication professor Marouf Hasian, Jr. (1998) writes that little exploration was provided with regard to the Arab people and the various different communities and cultures that they represent. Instead, Arabs were separated into the categories of "good" Arab versus "bad" Arab. Arab countries that were considered as supporting the United States' entry into battle with Iraq were considered "good," while those who were critical of the US actions were labeled as "bad." While distinguishing the countries as such, however, all of the countries were characterized as in need of Western leadership and guidance. The long-held Western myth that the Middle East region was one that needed civilizing was brought forth in the war coverage.

Stereotypic treatment of the Arab people found in news media coverage during the first US–Iraq war appeared again in full force following the 9/11 attacks and during the second US–Iraq war that began in 2003. Rhetoric based on Arab stereotypes appeared even in US governmental edicts that were issued during this period. Media studies professor Deborah Merskin, in her analysis of President George W. Bush's speeches made shortly after 9/11, found that preexisting images of Arabs referenced in popular culture were also found in Bush's speeches. Images of darkness, evil, and threat were invoked, while the forthcoming battle with terrorists was referred to as a "crusade" (2004). Thus, the US government and the mainstream press tended to reinforce each other's rhetoric regarding Arabs and the "war on terror."

In examining the *New York Times* editorials regarding the Palestinian–Israeli conflict around the time of the 9/11 attacks, media law professor Susan Dente Ross found that the editorials did not show Palestine and Israel as equally responsible for the conflict. Palestinians were portrayed in highly negative terms, while Israelis were given more sympathetic portrayals. Palestinians were the aggressors; Israelis were the victims. Palestinians were described as racist and murderous. As Ross writes, "The image presented by the editorials is that the entire Palestinian population consists of suicide bombers. The typical Palestinian is a conflagration of hate, a plague of death, a suicide cult, and a puppet spouting venomous anti-American and anti-Israeli vitriol" (2003: 62).

CNN produced a 90-minute documentary titled *America Remembers*, made up of commentaries and news clips of the events on and following September 11. In his critical analysis of the documentary, Near Eastern languages and cultures specialist Tim Jon Semmerling (2006) characterizes the work as commercial entertainment. He argues that instead of providing an historical account of the events that unfolded on and following that fateful day, the documentary falls back on standard clichés and tropes. The author finds in the CNN documentary the same type of narratives found in Hollywood films about Arabs. The narratives were designed to invoke feelings of shock, horror, and hatred toward the Arab enemy and feelings of admiration for the American heroes. In describing the documentary, Semmerling writes, "One of the most notable of all tropes is the confrontation by Arab villains of American ideology and their threat to overturn American myth" (2006).

In considering Arabs and Arab Americans in the United States, representations about the role and place of women is a burgeoning area of scholarship as more and more negative rhetoric toward Arab states is tied to the treatment of women as merely following men. Even in stories about women as suicide bombers, the coverage is slightly differently than that for their male counterparts. Moran Yarchi (2011), a scholar of terror and media, finds that the media often will rationalize the violence committed by women as being a decision made for a specific reason. Female bombers are represented as having committed acts of terror out of love or for funds to support their families. As a result, this type of reporting leads to a further discussion of the religious faction the woman supported. In short, these perpetrators are more likely than men to be depicted as victims of their religion.

Negative images of Arabs have thus persisted, not only in the entertainment media but in the press as well. Following 9/11, several professional news organizations, such as the Society of Professional Journalists (SPJ) and Poynter Institute, did issue guidelines for journalists to follow so that they could report in a more neutral fashion when covering terror-related news and avoid racial profiling (see Box 6.2). Nonetheless, stereotypic images of Arabs still infiltrated mainstream news stories.

Box 6.2 The Society of Professional Journalists' "war" on terrorism coverage guidelines

The Society of Professional Journalists passed a resolution on October 6, 2001 urging journalists to avoid racial profiling in their coverage of the "war" on terrorism.
Below are excerpts from the guidelines established by SPJ:

Visual Images

Seek out people from a variety of ethnic and religious backgrounds when photographing rescue and other public service workers and military personnel.
Do not represent Arab Americans and Muslims as monolithic groups. Avoid conveying the impression that all Arab Americans and Muslims wear traditional clothing.
Use photos and features to demystify veils, turbans, and other cultural articles and customs.

Stories

Seek out and include Arabs and Arab Americans, Muslims, South Asians, and men and women of Middle Eastern descent in all stories about the war, not just those about Arab and Muslim communities or racial profiling.
Cover the victims of harassment, murder, and other hate crimes as thoroughly as you cover the victims of terrorist attacks.
Make an extra effort to include olive-complexioned and darker men and women, Sikhs, Muslims and devout religious people of all types in arts, business, society columns, and all other news and feature coverage, not just stories about the crisis.
When writing about terrorism, remember to include white supremacist, radical anti-abortionists, and other groups with a history of such activity.
Do not imply that kneeling on the floor praying, listening to Arabic music, or reciting from the Quran are peculiar activities.

Source: Society of Professional Journalists, *Diversity Guidelines:* http://www.spj.org/divguidelines.asp

Arab American studies scholar and political scientist Michael Suleiman argued in 1988 that reporters are not able to easily pull away from long-held stereotypes and report in an objective manner. Reporters might not be conscious of their biases or might refrain from reporting from a neutral standpoint because they are concerned about the reactions they might get from audiences who appear to not have favorable opinions of Arabs. With regard to those who might try to report objectively when covering Arabs, Suleiman writes, "If they present views or even information different from the 'accepted' ideas, they will have to fight or have conflicts with their bosses" (Suleiman 1988).

Concluding Remarks

The discourse of Orientalism and the negative imagery of Arabs have a long history in the Western world. Since the eleventh century and during the European colonial wars against people in the Middle East, Arabs have consistently been portrayed as barbaric, devious, belligerent, and even demonic. They have been depicted as a people who are religious zealots and who view women as objects existing only to satisfy the sexual appetites of men. Rather than these images attenuating over time, they have strengthened.

The central argument that has been provided as to why these images continue to persist is that they help to maintain Western dominance over the Arab world. The earlier images were nurtured in order to serve as justification for political and economic control over the regions of the Middle East. Since then, they have taken on a life of their own, continuing to provide reasons for why Westerners should impose their own ideology and lifestyles on the people of the Middle East, and why the Arab world should succumb to such impositions.

Several observers have written that, since the end of the Cold War between the United States and the Soviet Union, the new enemy has been the terrorist, often vaguely defined and simply associated with Arabs. In his influential work *Faces of the Enemy: Reflections of the Hostile Imagination* (1986), philosophy and religion scholar Sam Keen explores how demeaning or threatening images of those who are considered the "enemy" are created in order to set the stage for their degradation or extermination. The enemy cannot be represented as having any form of humanity. He cannot be portrayed as a loving father or husband, or else it becomes more difficult to vanquish him. A nefarious image must first be produced. Keen writes, "In the beginning we create the enemy. Before the weapon comes the image. We *think* others to death and then invent the battle-axe or the ballistic missiles with which to actually kill them" (Keen 1986).

With Arabs being equated with terrorists, the end effect has been an enemy image that impacts on all Arabs and those of Arab descent. The repercussions of this vilification must be seriously questioned and addressed (see Box 6.3). According to the American Arab Anti-Discrimination Committee, immediately following September 11, 2001, there was a surge in violent hate crimes against Arab Americans (American-Arab Anti-Discrimination Committee Research Institute 2011). Since then, there has been a steady increase in hate crimes in comparison to those years before 9/11. This has been the case not only with hate crimes, but also with discrimination in general. Law professor Susan Akram writes that US government legislation and policies targeting Arab and noncitizens have been on the rise since 9/11; they have been primarily designed for "selective interrogation, detention, harassment, presumption of terrorist involvement, and removal from this country [United States]" (Akram 2002). Thus, the negative imagery found in the media can also potentially impact on important policy decisions as well.

Box 6.3 News media coverage of building an Islamic community center at Ground Zero

In the summer of 2010, the print and electronic news media covered the Islamic faith more than it had since after September 11, 2001. Two stories in particular generated this attention. First, the media covered the tension between those who opposed and those who supported a plan to build an Islamic community center with a mosque near Ground Zero, the site where terrorist-flown planes flew into the World Trade Center's Twin Towers in New York City, killing more than 3,000 people. Those opposing the center considered it an affront to those killed by the radical Islamists who carried out the attacks. They judged that a mosque in the neighborhood would be a trophy of sorts for the terrorists responsible for the devastating attack.

Conversely, those who supported the religious center believed that protesting the site was a sign that some US citizens were unable to differentiate between the vast numbers of peaceful Muslims and the Muslim extremists who undertook the violent attack. Furthermore, many supporters asserted that it was fundamentally a US Constitution First Amendment issue, declaring that denying the building of the center and mosque would be akin to denying freedom of religion.

Related to this news story was the much-covered story of Pastor Terry Jones and his plan to hold a Qur'an burning rally. Even though Jones has a congregation of only a few dozen members on the outskirts of Gainesville, Florida, his intention to encourage people to burn copies of the holy book received worldwide media attention after the top US commander in Afghanistan, General David Patraeus, publicly worried that images of a burning Qur'an would fan the flames of hostility facing US soldiers serving in the Middle East.

While the above stories were widely covered on the news, some outlets took the story a step further and covered mosques around the country. For example, National Public Radio aired a feature story interviewing Arab Americans who were concerned for the future of their mosque in Fargo, North Dakota. CNN explored the controversy of a mosque being built in the small town of Murfreesboro, Tennessee, in a similar manner. *The Courier-Journal* spotlighted the construction of a new mosque in Louisville, Kentucky, and emphasized neighborhood support for the building and the noncontroversial nature of it. In these and other cases, news outlets that took the opportunity to shine a light on mosques did so using the words of Muslim worshipers, many of them Arab Americans, involved in the buildings. Unlike many of the news stories that focused on the controversial Islamic community center building near Ground Zero and Jones's plans to burn the Qur'an by simply interviewing the prominent players involved in these stories (e.g., Jones, non-Muslim protesters and supporters, General Patraeus, Imam Feisal Abdul Rauf who initiated the plans for the New York city Islamic religious center, etc.), these sidebar stories gave more of a voice to Muslim worshipers who were being directly impacted. Their words and the visual images accompanying them (e.g., women in brightly colored headscarves and children playing over calls for prayer) gave viewers an opportunity to see a side of this group not regularly seen in today's news media.

Reflection Questions and Thoughts to Consider

1. Reread the exercise in Box 6.1. If you were to have taken part in the exercise, what type of descriptive words would have come to your mind?
2. What films have you recently seen that featured Arabs or Arab Americans? How would you consider how these characters were featured? Were they positive or negative characterizations?

3. When actors of Arab descent are featured as positive characters in television shows, do you think the television producers should make a point of conveying to the audience that the characters are of Arab descent, or do you think that ethnicity should not be emphasized?

4. What steps do you think could be taken to improve the portrayals of Arabs or Arab Americans in the mass media?

References

Akram, Susan M. 2002. "The Aftermath of September 11, 2001: The Targeting of Arabs and Muslims in America." *Arab Studies Quarterly* 4 (Spring–Summer): 61.

American-Arab Anti-Discrimination Committee Research Institute. 2011. *Report on Hate Crimes and Discrimination Against Arab Americans* 2003–2007. http://www.issuelab.org/resource/2003_2007_report_on_hate_crimes_and_discrimination_against_arab_americans (accessed April 6, 2017).

Cass, Philip. 2007. "The Never-ending Story: Palestine, Israel, and *The West Wing*." *Journal of Arab and Media Research* 1: 32.

Edwards, Brian T. 2001."Yankee Pashas and Buried Women: Containing Abundance in 1950s Hollywood Orientalism." *Film and History* 31: 14–15.

Elayan, Yasmeen. 2005. "Stereotypes of Arab and Arab-Americans Presented in Hollywood Movies Released during 1994 to 2000." East Tennessee State University Electronic Theses and Dissertations. Paper 1003. http://dc.etsu.edu/etd/1003 (accessed April 6, 2017).

Haddad, Yvonne. 1983. "Arab Muslims and Islamic Institutions in America: Adaptation and Reform." In *Arabs in the New World: Studies on Arab American Communities*, edited by Sameer Y. Abraham and Nabeel Abraham, 64–81. Detroit, MI: Wayne State University.

Hashem, Mahboub. 1995. "Coverage of Arabs in Two Leading U.S. Newsmagazines: *Time* and *Newsweek*." In *The U.S. Media and the Middle East: Image and Perception*, edited by George Gerbner and Yahya R. Kamalipour, 151–162. London: Greenwood Press.

Hasian, Jr., Marouf. 1998. "Mass-mediated Realities and the Persian Gulf War: Inventing the Arab Enemy." In *Cultural Diversity and the U.S. Media*, edited by Yahya R. Kamalipour and Theresa Carilli, 207. Albany, NY: State University of New York Press.

Hooper, Ibrahim. 2014. "CAIR Asks Reviewers of FX's 'Tyrant' to Address Stereotypes of Muslim, Arab Culture." Council on American–Islamic Relations. http://www.cair.com/press-center/press-releases/12533-cair-asks-reviewers-of-fx-tyrant-to-address-stereotypes-of-muslim-arab-culture.html (accessed April 6, 2017).

Huang, Josie. 2014. "'Tyrant': Are there any Positive Media Portrayals of Arabs?" *Multi-American*. http://www.scpr.org/blogs/multiamerican/2014/06/25/16907/tyrant-fx-arab-muslim-portayr (accessed April 6, 2017).

Izadi, Elhade. 2015. "Artist got 'Homeland is Racist' Arabic Graffiti into Latest Episode of Homeland." *The Washington Post*, October 15. https://www.washingtonpost.com/news/worldviews/wp/2015/10/14/artists-got-homeland-is-racist-arabic-graffiti-into-the-latest-episode-of-homeland/?utm_term=.ed74fc4f3a7d (accessed April 17, 2017).

Karl, Patricia A. 1983. "In the Middle of the Middle East: The Media and U.S. Foreign Policy." In *Split Vision: The Portrayal of Arabs in the American Media*, edited by Edmund Ghareeb, 293. Washington, DC: American-Arab Affairs Council.

Keen, Sam. 1986. *Faces of the Enemy: Reflections of the Hostile Imagination*. San Francisco, CA: Harper & Row.

Kellner, Douglas. 1995. *Media Culture: Cultural Studies, Identity, and Politics between the Modern and Postmodern*. London: Routledge.

La Gorce, Tammy. 2016. "Two Projects Share a Goal: Challenge Stereotypes of Islam and Arabs." *New York Times*, April 19. http://www.nytimes.com/2016/04/10/nyregion/two-projects-share-a-goal-challenge-stereotypes-of-islam-and-arabs.html?_r=1 (accessed April 6, 2017).

Lind, Rebecca A., and James A. Danowski. 1998. "The Representations of Arabs in U.S. Electronic Media." In *Cultural Diversity and the U.S. Media*, edited by Yahya R. Kamalipour and Theresa Carilli, 207. Albany, NY: State University of New York Press.

Little, Greta D. 1998. "Representing Arabs: Reliance on the Past." In *Cultural Diversity and the U.S. Media*, edited by Yahya R. Kamalipour and Theresa Carilli, 264–266. Albany, NY: State University of New York Press.

Merskin, Deborah. 2004. "The Construction of Arabs as Enemies: Post-September 11 Discourse of George W. Bush." *Mass Communication and Society* 7: 165.

Miller, Aimee. 1994. "'True Lies' or Stereotype? Arab American Groups Blast Schwarzenegger Film." *Washington Post*, C2.

Pulcini, Theodore. 1993. "Trends in Research on Arab Americans." *Journal of American Ethnic History* 12: 27–60, 28.

New York Times. 1994. "Arab-Americans Protest 'True Lies.'" *New York Times*, July 16. http://www.nytimes.com/1994/07/16/movies/arab-americans-protest-true-lies.html (accessed April 6, 2017).

Ross, Susan Dente. 2003. "Unequal Combatants on an Uneven Media Battlefield: Palestine and Israel." In *Images that Injure: Pictorial Stereotypes in the Media*, edited by Paul M. Lester and Susan Dente Ross, 62. London: Praeger.

Said, Edward W. 1979. *Orientalism*. New York, NY: Vintage Books.

Semmerling, Tim Jon. 2006. *"Evil" Arabs in American Popular Film*. Austin, TX: University of Texas Press.

Shaheen, Jack, 1984. *The TV Arab*. Bowling Green, OH: Bowling Green State University Popular Press.

Shaheen, Jack. 2008. *Guilty: Hollywood's Verdict on Arabs after 9/11*. Northampton, MA: Olive Branch Press.

Steet, Linda. 2000. *Veils and Daggers: A Century of National Geographic's Representation of the Arab World*. Philadelphia, PA: Temple University Press.

Suleiman, Michael. 1988. *Arabs in the Mind of America*. Battleboro, VT: Amana Books.

US Census Bureau. 2005. *We the People of Arab Ancestry in the United States*. http://www.census.gov/prod/2005pubs/censr-21.pdf (accessed April 6, 2017).

Wilkins, Karen Gwinn. 1995. "Middle Eastern Women in Western eyes: A Study of U.S. Press Photographs of Middle Eastern Women." In *The U.S. Media and the Middle East: Image and Perception*, edited by George Gerbner and Yahya R. Kamalipour, 50–61. London: Greenwood Press.

Wolfsfeld, Gadi. 1997. *Media and Political Conflict: News from the Middle East*. Cambridge: Cambridge University Press.

Yarchi, Moran. 2011. "The Effect of Female Suicide Attacks on Foreign Media Framing of Conflicts: The Case of Palestinian-Israeli Conflict." *Studies in Conflict & Terrorism* 37: 674–688.

7

Representations of Asians/Asian Americans

In 2015, Cartoon Network debuted its new animated television series *We Bare Bears*, a cartoon about three anthropomorphic speaking bears living together among humans in San Francisco. The laid-back, funny – and some would even say cool – bears (Ice Bear, Grizzly, and Panda) immediately attracted a diverse audience, driving viewers to the network's video app and contributing to an increase in its website's video plays (Steinberg 2015). Created by Daniel Chong, the episodes have storylines that present or hint at Asian cultures. In fact, one of the cartoon's secondary characters is a 10-year-old Korean American girl named Chloe Park who becomes friends with the three bears. In the episode titled "The Clique," Chloe invites the bears to her home. As they approach the steps to Chloe's home, the door opens and Chloe's mom appears:

> Mrs. Park: "Oh. Hi."
> Chloe turns to her bear friends and says: "Hey guys. This is my mom."
> Ice Bear goes into a deep bow and with a perfect Korean accent says: "Anyonghaseyo" [Translation: "Hello"].
> Ice Bear's brothers look at him in bewilderment and try to follow suit. They clumsily bow while trying to mimic Ice Bear's greeting.
> Mrs. Park laughs and replies back to all three: "Anyonghaseyo."

Chloe and her mom then exchange words all in Korean, with no subtitles. After Chloe goes into her house, Mr. Park appears and speaks to his wife in Korean; again no subtitles appear.

The scene and the use of the Korean language in the scene evoked thousands of comments, likes, and shares via social media, especially among Asian, and more specifically, Korean Americans. You might ask, "Why such a strong reaction?" The fact that Koreans were included in the cartoon and that the Korean language was used without subtitles was viewed as novel and a huge plus for Asian Americans. On the Korean American Mommies Facebook page, the following was posted in reference to the scene: "Bears Are Speaking Korean!! … Fabulous!! This made my kids ears perk up and now they want to learn Korean even more! Keep it coming Cartoon Network!" Such enthusiastic responses, while positive, are also in some way a testament to the dearth of Asian or Asian American media representations that are not of the stereotypic type.

Asian and Asian American representations have been quite narrow and have been extreme in nature. While being depicted as docile, subservient, and intelligent, they have also been portrayed

Diversity in US Mass Media, Second Edition. Catherine A. Luther, Carolyn Ringer Lepre, and Naeemah Clark.
© 2018 John Wiley & Sons Inc. Published 2018 by John Wiley & Sons Inc.

as being evil, conniving, and criminal. From the "yellow peril" to the "brilliant geek," these Asian representations have consistently appeared in various forms of mass media throughout the years.

This chapter first looks at the historical origins of these images and examines how they are rooted in the power dynamics between the West and the East. It then discusses how these Asian and Asian American representations have been presented in film and television, as well as in the press. The chapter explores the consistencies in these representations across the differing forms of media and how signs of change have become noticeable in recent years.

Historical Background to Asian/Asian American Representations

Calls were made in the 1960s for use of the labels "Asians" and "Asian Americans" as a way in which to get rid of the derogatory term "Orientals." The term "Oriental" is derived from the Latin word for "east" and was used to identify people from Asian countries in terms of Asia's location relative to Europe. It came to be associated with the notion of Western domination over the East. Thus, getting rid of use of the term was seen as a form of empowerment. In recent years, the label "Asian American" has also been called into question. The fundamental problem is that, as with labels such as "African American," "Arab American," or "European American," the label "Asian American" lumps together cultures that are distinct. Its usage does not acknowledge the fact that Asian Americans are individuals from a broad range of linguistic and ethnic backgrounds. Nevertheless, in spite of the inherent problems associated with combining groups of people into one large category, for the sake of simplicity and to follow the general usage, the label "Asian Americans" is used here to represent those Americans whose ethnic origins can be traced to Pacific, Southeast, South, and East Asian areas of the world.

According to the 2010 US Census, 14.7 million individuals classified themselves as coming from an Asian heritage, making up close to 5 percent of the total US population. The Asian population is the fastest growing in the United States, with the 2010 Census data showing a 43 percent increase since 2000.

Asian Americans have experienced a turbulent history rooted in Western fears of Eastern cultures and peoples. The notion of "Orientalism" that scholar Edward Said (1979) identified as widely, and damagingly, applied to Middle Easterners can be applied to Asians as well. As is the case with the experiences of Arabs and Arab Americans, the racial myths and representations that were established about Asians during Western colonization of many of the Asian nations have persisted and found a new home in the form of modern media representations.

Western powers, from the mid-1700s and through the 1800s, in the interests of expanding their empires into Asian territories, represented the colonized as uncivilized and dangerous. By representing Asian people as debased, Western imperialists were effectively able to control the colonized native Asians and dissuade Whites from intermingling with them. According to communication researcher Yasmin Jiwani, the underlying thought was that allowing mixing between races "would make it increasingly difficult to legitimize foreign rule and further, the emergence of a mixed race could potentially result in a direct challenge to colonial powers" (Jiwani 2006: 163–164). Such a fear among Anglo-Europeans was similar to the fear that Anglo-Americans had regarding the mixing of Whites with Blacks, which led to anti-miscegenation laws as discussed in the introductory chapter. The potential encroachment of the Asian race on Westerners was later reflected in the Exclusion laws that were established in the United States.

Among the notable legal restrictions on immigration into the United States was the Chinese Exclusion Act of 1882. Up until that year, large numbers of Chinese immigrants had entered the

United States looking for employment. The impetus for this influx was the mining boom during the California Gold Rush and the subsequent building of the transcontinental railway system. As the US economy declined following the Civil War, however, and competition for available jobs grew fiercer, animosity toward Chinese immigrant laborers increased. With calls to restrict Chinese laborers intensifying, the US Congress passed an act that prohibited Chinese laborers from entering the United States for 10 years. The Chinese Exclusion Act was continuously renewed until its repeal in 1943, and thus effectively halted ethnic Chinese immigration into the United States (Pfaelzer 2007).

The Immigration Act of 1924 broadened the scope of restrictions on immigration by including nonlaborers and other Asian immigrants as well. The Act placed national origin immigration quotas that were essentially more restrictive toward those who were emigrating from Asian countries (Ngai 1999). Individuals from such Asian countries as Japan, Philippines, China, Korea, Vietnam, and India were targeted as undesirables. Such quotas remained in effect until the passage of the Immigration and Nationality Act of 1965.

The anti-immigration laws' particular harshness toward Asian populations illustrates the anti-Asian climate that engulfed the United States during the mid- to late 1800s and early 1900s. It is no surprise that many of the images and messages transmitted by the press during that period, and later sustained by other forms of mass media, reflected the essential disdain and phobia toward non-Whites of Asian origin.

Asians/Asian Americans in Film

From the early years of silent film to the present day, extreme images of individuals of Asian descent have often been presented in films. Men might be sexless and gentle in certain depictions, while in others they might be villainous and lascivious. Women might sometimes be demure and submissive, and in other instances sexually exotic and evil.

One of the early films to convey the notion that Asian men can be gentle as well as violent is the 1919 film called *Broken Blossoms* (Figure 7.1). This silent film was directed by pioneering American film director, D.W. Griffith, who also directed *The Birth of a Nation* and *The Battle at Elderbrush Gulch*, which were discussed in previous chapters.

Figure 7.1 A scene from D.W. Griffith's *Broken Blossoms* (1919). Screenshot.

The setting for *Broken Blossoms* is a run-down part of London, and the main characters are an Asian man referred to in the film as Yellow Man (played by non-Asian actor Richard Barthelmess) and a young white woman named Lucy Burrows (played by actress Lillian Gish). It should be noted that the casting of a non-Asian as Yellow Man was a consequence of the Hollywood practice of not allowing white actors to engage in relations with non-white actors in films, a practice that was later codified by the Motion Picture Producers and Distributors of America, Inc. in 1930 (the Hays Code), as discussed in previous chapters. The code remained in effect until 1934, but the practice lingered even into the 1960s.

In *Broken Blossoms*, Lucy is the poor daughter of a verbally and physically abusive father named Battling Burrows (played by actor Donald Crisp); Yellow Man is the owner of a small Chinese shop. One day, Lucy is beaten so badly by her father that she wanders the streets in confusion until she happens to stumble into Yellow Man's shop. Yellow Man finds Lucy and takes her up to his private quarters above the shop. There, he dresses Lucy in a beautiful Chinese robe and nurses her back to health. Lucy refers to Yellow Man as "Chinky" and they develop a friendship. Their happiness together, however, is short-lived. Lucy's father soon finds out where she is and retrieves her while Yellow Man is out on an errand. After they return home, the father beats his daughter to death. Yellow Man returns to find his home in disarray and Lucy missing. Emotionally distraught, he takes his gun to Battling Burrows' place. Finding Lucy dead, he fights and kills the father, then carries Lucy back to his home, prays before an altar, and kills himself as well.

In his actions toward Lucy, Yellow Man shows the gentility and lack of sexuality that is often associated in films with Asian men. In his reactions toward the father, he shows another side – the violent nature that is also frequently associated with Asian men. Although Lucy's father is the one who initiated the tragedy, Yellow Man is portrayed as not being able to contain his emotions, which results in him striking out in violence.

Broken Blossoms not only conveys stereotypes of Asian men, it relays the taboo of Asian men having relations with white women. Yellow Man looks upon Lucy with fondness and desire, but dares not overtly show affection toward her. At one point, he attempts to kiss her, but then kisses her robe instead. The maniacal outrage that Lucy's father demonstrates when he finds out that Yellow Man has been keeping Lucy in his private quarters reinforces the taboo of miscegenation. The message is that if relations between an Asian man and a white woman are pursued, it can only end in tragedy.

The representation of the violent Asian male that was shown at the end of *Broken Blossoms* was strongly reinforced from the late 1920s and into the 1940s, with the introduction of the Chinese character Dr. Fu Manchu. Dr. Fu Manchu, who first appeared in a novel and then was popularized in a series of Fu Manchu films, is a dark, villainous character who enjoys carrying out nontraditional means of torture and murder, such as using deadly creatures or natural poisons. He is shown in the films engaging in various illicit activities and masterminding plots to overthrow the "white man" with the help of his secret society of violent criminals. He becomes the epitome of the "yellow peril" stereotype. "Yellow peril" is said to have originated in the 1800s with the growth in Chinese laborers in the United States and the fear that the Chinese were taking jobs from white laborers, a fear that was reinforced by press editorials during that period (Pfaelzer 2007). Yellow-toned skin color was tied to the idea of terror in this phrase.

In the 1931 Fu Manchu film, *Daughter of the Dragon*, the audience is also introduced to the "dragon lady" stereotype. In this film, Dr. Fu Manchu (played by non-Asian actor Warner Oland) convinces his daughter, Ling Moy (played by Anna May Wong) to kill his nemesis. A dancer by profession,

Moy exudes sexuality, and the fact that she does not question her father about killing another human being suggests her female subservience to her father as a male authority figure. Moy's violent act also displays the inherent cruelty that resides within her. She is the female "yellow peril" version with an added twist of sexuality. Sexually enticing and deadly at the same time, she comes to personify the "dragon lady."

The "yellow peril" that Dr. Fu Manchu represented and the "dragon lady" that his daughter embodied were transferred over to the Japanese after Japan's attack on the United States in 1941. This transference illustrates how historical events, on both a domestic and international level, impact the shaping of ethnic images in the mass media. Although prior to World War II Japanese were generally depicted in US films as exotic yet unthreatening, the conflict between the United States and Japan inspired a large number of wartime films featuring the Japanese as the new "yellow peril." Among these war movies were *Blood on the Sun* (1942), *Black Dragons* (1942), *The Purple Heart* (1944), and *God is My Co-Pilot* (1945). Lasciviousness, treachery, and slyness were attributed to the Japanese in these films. For example, *Black Dragons* is about Japan's Black Dragon Society, a paramilitary right-wing group, plotting with the Nazis prior to World War II to transform, using cosmetic surgery, six Japanese society members to resemble American leaders. Their plan is to kill the actual American leaders, replace them with the Japanese, and take over the United States. In the film, the Japanese are shown as notoriously cruel and unethical, even going against the Nazis in order to further Japan's domination. The Americans in the film refer to the Japanese as "apes," "swine," and "japs."

During the 1930s and 1940s, film audiences were introduced to a gentler Asian in the persona of Charlie Chan. Chan, a Chinese detective, appeared as the leading character in countless films; in his first notable appearance he was played by non-Asian actor Warner Oland. The films followed Chan in his quest to solve crimes by using his wits in a nonthreatening manner. Although Chan is married with children, he is depicted in the films as lacking any sexual characteristics, and is portrayed as submissive to Whites. Originally a literary figure in the 1920s, Chan is presented as the ideal Chinese American male in these films. During a time when the Japanese posed a threat to America, this character was viewed as a welcome relief from the "yellow peril."

Charlie Chan can be considered one of the first characters to illustrate the "model minority" stereotype. Intercultural communication scholar Thomas Nakayama (1988: 65–73) describes the "model minority" as one that excels in both education and in employment. "Model minorities" are hardworking citizens who are law-abiding and frequently deferential to those in authority positions. It is a description that fits the Chan character and one which would resurface in other media forms. In addition to the resurfacing of this model minority in later years, the "yellow peril" image also resurfaced with strength in the 1970s and 1980s.

With the end of the US war with Vietnam, audiences began viewing depictions of the Vietnamese as the "yellow peril" in many of the films produced about the war. Hollywood focused on the returning Vietnam veteran who had flashbacks of the war or the Vietnam battlefields, and focused on the disillusionment of Americans about the war. Hit examples of such films were *Apocalypse Now* (1979) and *The Deer Hunter* (1978). In these films, the Vietnamese were shown as extremes. Vietnamese men were either depicted as docile and following orders or as sneaky and vicious, relying on guerrilla warfare. Vietnamese women, more specifically young adult women, were often portrayed as vixens or prostitutes who had to be kept an eye on by US soldiers because they could well be working for the Vietcong.

The Deer Hunter, which won an Academy Award for Best Picture, is about three friends, Michael (played by Robert De Niro), Steven (played by John Savage), and Nick (played by Christopher

Walken), from a small town in the United States, who are sent to Vietnam as soldiers. The three eventually meet in Vietnam and are taken as prisoners of war. In the prison, the North Vietnamese are shown as ruthless and sadistic. The friends suffer at the hands of their prison guards and are forced to put each other in harm's way. In the film's other scenes too, the North Vietnamese are portrayed as animalistic. For example, a North Vietnamese soldier is shown in one scene killing Vietnamese civilians, including women and young children. Throughout the film, young Vietnamese women were shown in the red-light district of Saigon, represented as oversexed and untrustworthy.

Although the films pertaining to the Vietnam War made in the 1970s did make social statements in terms of criticizing the US position in the war, they did not fully explore the complexity of the war, though it has been argued that with films like *The Deer Hunter*, that was not the point (see Box 7.1). Vietnamese perspectives were not presented, and standard images of the Vietnamese people were shown. The Asian seductress persona was assigned to young Vietnamese women, while the "yellow peril" image was transposed onto Vietnamese men.

Into the 1980s and through the early 1990s, when economic conflict with Japan was a major concern of US policy makers, Hollywood turned its attention to the Japanese and once again made

---

Box 7.1 *Tropic Thunder* – humorous or damaging?

Elements of Vietnamese stereotypes within the context of the Vietnam War continue even today. In 2008, Ben Stiller directed an action comedy, *Tropic Thunder*, about four American actors who believe they are acting in a film chronicling the Vietnam War. Instead, they find themselves in a real-life situation with a community of drug dealers in Vietnam. The drug dealers end up kidnapping one of the actors, Tugg Speedman (played by Stiller), and his remaining friends come to his rescue. It is during Tugg's time with the dealers and their family members that we see stereotypes of Vietnamese people. Although Tugg believes he can befriend his captors, he cannot, and they are ready to kill him. In fact, in one of the last scenes of the film, Tugg attempts to take with him a small Vietnamese boy as he escapes. He believes he is rescuing the boy and places the boy on his shoulders. As the boy sits on Tugg's shoulder, however, he begins to stab Tugg in the neck with a knife. Tugg ends up slinging the young boy off his shoulders and into a ravine.

The movie portrays the Vietnamese as depraved and murderous. Stereotypes actually abound in this film, in the name of comedy. One of Tugg's actor buddies is Kirk Lazarus (played by Robert Downey, Jr.). Kirk appears in "blackface," and instead of thinking he is playing an African American soldier, he actually believes he is African American. In doing so, he invokes the stereotype of the "jive-talking" tough black male who brutishly struts his stuff – reminiscent of the "bad buck" male stereotype discussed in this book's African American chapter. Interestingly, there was little outcry about this stereotype, perhaps because of the presence of a foil character in Alpa Chino, portrayed by African American actor Brandon T. Jackson, who regularly calls Kirk out for behaving in a stereotypical, and often ridiculous, way. The disability community objected to another one of Stiller's portrayals in the film – that of a mentally disabled man, Simple Jack. A coalition of disability groups called for a boycott of the movie on the grounds that they considered the film to be indulging in outright ridicule in its treatment of the intellectually disabled. Critics were particularly outspoken about the repeated use of the word "retard," and referred to it as hate speech.

Should viewers accept this film as simply a venue of satire or be concerned about the possible negative ramifications associated with the stereotypes?

them the "yellow peril." A film that epitomizes the reemergence of the Japanese "yellow peril" image is *Rising Sun* (1992). Based on Michael Crichton's novel of the same name, the film's central plot revolves around the murder of a young white woman at a Japanese corporate office in Los Angeles. Investigators of the murder, Web Smith (played by Wesley Snipes) and John Connor (played by Sean Connery), suspect a complicated conspiracy involving heads of the corporation. The film sparked controversy due to the fact that, as in the book, the film depicted the Japanese as being lascivious, ruthless, and corrupt. They were portrayed as willing to use any means to gain wealth and superiority. The central message was that the Japanese are inherently debased, violent, devious, and could not be trusted.

While the "yellow peril" image has persisted, the other extreme stereotype, the sexless Asian male, has also remained steadfast in films. It is rare to find an Asian male in a film's leading role. Most are relegated to secondary roles, often as sidekicks to white leading men, and are not shown expressing sexual interests. Hong Kong-born actor Jackie Chan has illustrated this in several of the films he has starred in, where he has combined his martial arts and comedic skills. For example in the 2004 film *Around the World in 80 Days*, Chan plays a Chinese valet named Passepartout who is sidekick to scientist and inventor Phileas Fogg (played by Steve Coogan). The two attempt to travel around the globe in 80 days. In their efforts, they are soon joined by a French artist named Monique (played by Cecile de France). Inevitably, it is Phileas and Monique who develop a romantic relationship, with Passepartout remaining as the sidekick. Throughout the film, he never shows signs of having sexual interests.

If an Asian man is involved in a romantic relationship, it is frequently portrayed in a comedic fashion. An example of this is the 1984 comedy film *Sixteen Candles*. The film follows a high school girl, Samantha "Sam" Baker (played by Molly Ringwald), who spends her birthday longing to be with heart-throb senior Jake Ryan (played by Michael Schoeffling). During her day, Sam is introduced to a Chinese foreign exchange student named Long Duk Dong (played by Gedde Watanabe) whom Sam is asked to take to her high school dance. Long is portrayed in a stereotypical manner. Sporting dark-rimmed, old-fashioned eye-glasses, he is shown to be socially inept and awkward. He is presented as a basic "intelligent geek" type. Long does end up meeting a large athletic white girl, nicknamed "Lumberjack," at the dance. The two develop an attraction, but with the mismatched body and personalities, they are a major comic relief in the movie. With a stilted accent, Long calls Lumberjack his "new-style American girlfriend."

Non-Asian actors have also played these comic relief Asian characters. Like the "scotch tape" Asian characters who were played by non-Asian actors in early film, these actors use tape to pull back their eyes and make them appear as slits. They often reinforce the stereotypic Asian figure by donning thick glasses, false protruding teeth, and speaking English with thick accents. A classic example of this is Mickey Rooney's portrayal of a Japanese photographer in the 1961 film *Breakfast at Tiffany's*. In the film, he wears dark-rimmed eyeglasses with thick lenses, his eyes are pulled back to the sides of his face, and he appears to be buck-toothed. He speaks English with a stereotypic accent and presents a surly personality toward his apartment neighbor Holly Golightly (played by Audrey Hepburn).

In the 1968 comedy film *The Party*, Peter Sellers plays a bumbling Indian actor, Hrundi V. Bakshi, who is accidentally invited to an elite Hollywood party after being fired from a film production. Sellers appears with tanned skin and speaks with a thick, purportedly Indian, accent. Because of Hrundi's presence at the party, a number of mishaps take place and at the end of the film the house in which the party took place is left in shambles.

Another Indian character played by a white actor appears in the 1986 adventure film *Short Circuit*. The film follows the story of a military robot that develops human traits after encountering a power surge because of a lightning strike. In it, Fisher Stevens plays an Indian scientist, Ben Jabituya, who speaks with a butchered Indian accent and makes grammatical mistakes when speaking English.

A more recent example of a "scotch tape" Asian character used for comic relief is the minister character appearing in the 2007 film *I Now Pronounce You Chuck and Larry*. The film centers on two male firefighters, Chuck Levine (played by Adam Sandler) and Larry Valentine (played by Kevin James), who go through the process of pretending to be gay and getting married in order for Larry to resolve life insurance issues. The couple get married in an outlandish chapel in Canada. The minister who officiates at the wedding is supposed to be a small-framed Japanese man. Played by Rob Schneider (who, granted, does have an element of Asian ethnicity given his maternal grand-mother was Filipina), the minister appears with his eyes pulled back and wearing eyeglasses with thick lenses. He also is buck-toothed and speaks English with an accent, unable to pronounce the *L* sound.

Another stereotype used in *I Now Pronounce You Chuck and Larry* is the hyper-sexual Asian woman. In contrast to the sexless Asian man, Asian women have been characterized as either the deferential Asian female (referred to as "China doll," "geisha girl" or "lotus blossom"; Larson 2006: 70) or the aggressive Asian female (called "dragon lady," as mentioned earlier), with both types being sexually provocative. For the most part, these sexualized Asian women are shown pleasing white men or choosing white men over Asian men.

In *I Now Pronounce You Chuck and Larry*, five well-endowed Asian women are presented to fit the role of the deferential Asian female with a ravenous sexual appetite. They appear in two scenes in the movie. In the first, the women come to pick up Chuck who has just come out of hospital. They are wearing skimpy shorts and tight tank tops. Tila "Tequila" Nguyen, who gained fame through her Myspace page by appearing in sexually suggestive poses, plays one of the women. The women run up to Chuck who is in a wheelchair and fawn over him; Chuck asks which of the ladies would like to be the first to "rub his a**." The five women again later appear in Chuck's apartment. As Larry and Chuck are having a conversation in the living room, the women run out of Chuck's bedroom to get a drink from the refrigerator. As they search the refrigerator, Chuck slyly suggests they bend down further to find the drinks. The camera cuts to a shot of the women's rear ends as they bend down. These scenes reinforce the eroticism and subservience associated with Asian women.

Negative imagery of Asian Americans represented through raunchy comedy also appears in *The Hangover* film series (2009, 2011, 2013). All three films follow the escapades of four, often inebriated, friends. In the first film in which the friends travel to Las Vegas for a bachelor's party, viewers are introduced to Leslie Chow (played by Korean American actor Kim Jeong), a Chinese international mobster who has a serious love of alcohol and drug-fueled partying. Chow's criminal activities, wild behavior, and evident joy in witnessing the sufferings of others reinforce the Asian stereotype of the "yellow peril." In that film and the sequels that followed, Chow continues to be cruel, sneaky, and criminal. The self-directed crude jokes he utters allude to the stereotype of the emasculated Asian male figure.

While extreme film images of men and women of Asian heritage tend to be the norm, exceptions do exist. An example is the 1993 film *The Joy Luck Club*, based on Amy Tan's novel of the same name. The film follows the mother–daughter relationships of four Chinese mothers and their Chinese American daughters. By showing various facets of the women's lives, the film breaks away from the commonly held stereotypes of Asian women. The film proved to be a huge success and helped to show that films with Asians as leading characters could become box office hits. Wayne Wang, a Chinese American, directed the film. Perhaps having a Chinese American director added to the strength of the film in terms of breaking away from accepted stereotypes of Chinese and Chinese Americans.

Another successful mainstream film directed by a person of the same ethnicity as the main character is the 1992 drama *Mississippi Masala*, starring Denzel Washington and Sarita Choudhury. Directed by Mira Nair, who was born in India and educated in the United States, the film explores the interracial love between an African American rug cleaner and the daughter of an Indian immigrant. The film was heralded as offering a fresh look at the barriers facing interracial couples and at Asian Indians. Nair also directed the commercially successful film *Monsoon Wedding* (2001), which follows the preparations for a traditional Punjabi wedding in Delhi and shows the intricate relationships between those involved in the wedding. In delving into these relationships, Nair is able to represent multiple Indian characteristics and personalities in an entertaining manner. The film was nominated for a Golden Globe Award and won the Golden Lion award at the Venice Film Festival.

More recently, in *Learning to Drive* (2015), Patricia Clarkson plays Wendy, a recent divorcée who takes driving lessons from Darwan (played by British-Indian Ben Kingsley), a Sikh Indian cabbie who chose his profession because he wouldn't have to "take off his turban, shave off his beard." The two talk about their respective marriages as Wendy learns to drive and become more independent. Although the film did not do well at the box office, movie critics provided positive reviews. For example, film reviewer Odie Henderson (2015) wrote, "Thankfully, 'Learning to Drive' doesn't treat Darwan as an Other whose sole purpose is to forward Wendy's plotline. Equal time is given to his life, forming a counterpoint to Wendy's experiences."

One of the few commercial films to present Asian Americans in leading roles that resonated with large teen and twenty-something audiences is the 2004 film *Harold and Kumar Go to White Castle*. The film features a Chinese American, Harold Lee (played by John Cho), and an Indian American, Kumar Patel (played by Kal Penn), in a story about two college students who encounter misadventures on their way to White Castle to eat hamburgers. The personalities of the two characters diverge from stereotypic notions regarding male Asians. Rather than filling the typical stereotypes of sexless, violent, awkward and/or nerdy, the two are portrayed in a more rounded manner with no real distinguishable characteristics. They are simply portrayed as two college students who are interested in having a good time.

Although not leading roles, Asian American characters that deviate from long-established stereotypes have also appeared in recent commercial blockbuster films. An example of this can be seen in the 2014 *The Maze Runner* and 2015 *Maze Runner: The Scorch Trials*. (Note: at the time of writing this book, the release date for the final *Maze Runner: The Death Cure* was set to be in 2018.) Based on James Dashner's science fiction thriller novels, the film series features the character of Minho (played by Ki Hong Lee), a physically fit teenager who exhibits smarts and leadership skills. He is among a group of teenagers, led by Thomas (Dylan O'Brien), who escape from a laboratory-like labyrinth only to find an external world made up of conflict and a deadly virus. It is a world that an organization, WCKD, is trying to control in order to find a cure for the virus at any cost. Although Thomas is the leader of the group and the focus of the film series, Minho plays a critical role in keeping the group alive. He is fast, strong, and level-headed even in the face of danger. With his boyish good looks, but also commanding stature, Minho does not sustain the stereotypes normally associated with Asians.

Another recent set of action thriller films that feature Asian Americans in positive roles is the *Divergent* series (2014, 2015, 2016). Based on the novels by Veronica Roth, the films' central characters are Beatrice "Tris" Prior (played by Shailene Woodley) and Tobias "Four" Eaton (played by Theo James), who lead an effort to escape and then change the futuristic city of Chicago that is divided into factions based on individual characteristics of strengths (Amity – peaceful; Candor – honest; Dauntless – brave; Abnegation – selfless; Erudite – intellectual) and separated from the outside world. Although not in one of the films' main character roles, Korean American actor Daniel Dae Kim appears in the secondary role of Jack Kang, the Candor faction leader. The character holds a powerful position, but also exudes fairness as well as compassion. Actress Maggie Q, of Vietnamese, Irish, and Polish descent, also appears in a secondary role in the *Divergent* series. She plays the character of Tori Wu who begins in the Erudite faction, but then switches to Dauntless. Tori is physically strong and bright. She helps Tris and Four escape the city just before being killed by a sniper.

As demonstrated by these recent films, subtle changes in the representations of Asians and Asian Americans are emerging. Nevertheless Asian stereotypes do still persist. This has also been the case with representations of Asians on television.

Asians/Asian Americans in Entertainment Television

The images of Asians and Asian Americans found in entertainment television have essentially paralleled their depictions in film. Throughout television history, most of the roles offered to Asian actors have been in supporting roles, especially as domestic help or action hero sidekicks. Examples are the "houseboy" character named Hop Sing (played by Victor Sen Yung) in the television series *Bonanza* (1959–1973), the female Japanese housekeeper, Mrs. Livingston (played by Miyoshi Umeki) in the television series *The Courtship of Eddie's Father* (1969–1972), and Kato (played by Bruce Lee), the Chinese sidekick in the 1960s television series *Green Hornet* (1966–1967). It is interesting to note that Lee, following his success as the hero sidekick in the *Green Hornet*, was hoping to play the lead role in the 1970s television series *Kung Fu* (1972–1975). Despite his hopes, network executives at NBC decided to give the role to David Carradine and made the character only half-Chinese. The executives were not willing to take a chance with an Asian male in the lead role (Chan 2001).

In the television series *Hawaii Five-0* (1968–1980), Asian characters were presented, but again, they were secondary to the leading white characters. Although the series was set in Hawaii, the plots mainly revolved around the two white detectives (played by Jack Lord and James MacArthur) and their efforts to solve crimes. As with the Charlie Chan character, the Asian detectives were portrayed as submissive and nonsexual. The tendency to depict Asian male sidekicks as nonsexual beings is also exemplified by the Lieutenant Sulu character (played by George Takei) in the popular 1960s space-travel television series, *Star Trek* (1966–1969). While most of the main characters were placed in romantic scenarios, this was not the case with Lieutenant Sulu. Instead, he was a sidekick who tended to strictly obey the orders of his captain (played by William Shatner).

One well-known female Asian character in a supporting role who was often criticized for reinforcing stereotypes of Asian females is Ling Woo (played by Lucy Liu) in the television series *Ally McBeal*. The show, which ran from 1997 to 2002, was about a single white female lawyer, Ally McBeal (played by Calista Flockhart), who constantly fantasized about her ideal world and allowed audience members to peer inside her psyche to see her interpretation of people and the events around her. Ling, a lawyer working at the same firm as Ally, was positioned as Ally's arch-nemesis. In line with this positioning, she was depicted as the stereotypic "dragon lady." Callous and egotistical, Ling used her sexuality in order to manipulate others. In her analysis of Ling's character, Tracy Owen Patton writes, "[Ling] embodies the Asian fantasy woman because she is the seductive temptress and expert in eroticism. [Ling] is the person who can turn on both women and men by uttering the word *sex*" (Patton 2001: 250). Sounds and visuals were used in the show to accentuate Ling's sexuality and evilness. For example, the music that was used in the film *Wizard of Oz* (1939) to indicate the presence of the wicked witch was used in *Ally McBeal* to mark the entrance of Ling Woo.

A more contemporary example of an Asian American character in a supporting role is the character Kimball Cho (played by Tim Kang) who appeared in the CBS television series *The Mentalist* (2008–2015). The show revolved around the crime-fighting efforts of a female law enforcement agent, Teresa Lisbon (played by Robin Tunney) and her mentalist consultant, and eventual romantic partner, Patrick Jane (played by Simon Baker). The character of Kimball, also an agent working under Teresa, tended to be detached and able to examine matters in a perfunctory and almost cold manner – although, with his wry sense of humor and interest in women, the character did show more of a personality than the Asian sidekick detectives of years past.

Recent comedy series have also featured Asian male characters in supporting roles. One such program is *Unbreakable Kimmy Schmidt*, introduced in Chapter 3. In season 1 of the comedy, Kimmy (played by Ellie Kemper) falls in love with one of her G.E.D. classmates, Dong (played by Ki Hong Lee), a recent immigrant from Vietnam. Kimmy and Dong's initial playful infatuation develops into an intimate relationship as the program progresses. While the mixing of races can be viewed as a positive (see Chapter 8 on mixed race individuals and couples), the depiction of Dong can be seen as problematic given that stereotypes of Asians are evoked by the character. He is intelligent with a knack for mathematics, speaks English with a thick accent, and works as a delivery person for a Chinese restaurant. Even his name elicits a crude joke from Kimmy when they first meet. Although the creators of *Unbreakable Kimmy Schmidt* are moving in the right direction by including an Asian whom a white woman finds attractive, they still rely on tiresome stereotypes for the sake of drawing laughs.

A recent comedy that includes a South Asian in a supporting role and that often relies on stereotypes in the interest of humor is CBS's *The Big Bang Theory* (2007 debut). The show is about four astrophysicist friends who struggle with their social skills, while striving to make a mark in the world of science. Among the group of friends is the shy and brilliant Rajesh "Raj" Koothrappali (played by Kunal Nayyar), who tends to be more in the background in comparison to the other friends. In the first few years of the program's airing, Raj is portrayed as awkward with women and only able to communicate with them when alcohol is in his system, reinforcing the smart, but somewhat asexual, stereotype of Asian men. By the sixth and seventh seasons, however, Raj does come out of his shell a bit and becomes involved in serious relationships with two women.

Community (NBC Television 2009–2014; Yahoo! Screen 2015) was a sitcom that featured an Indian American in a supporting role. The show was about a group of misfit students attending Greendale Community College. One of them was an Indian American character named Abed (played by Danny Pudi). Abed could be considered as almost a replica of the Raj character on *The Big Bang Theory*. He, too, was reserved, smart, and socially awkward.

An Asian Indian in a sitcom that broke away from such representation was the supporting character Tom Haverford (played by Aziz Ansari) on NBC's *Parks and Recreation* (2009–2015). The original premise of the show was a storyline about a group of quirky local government employees led by a mid-level career woman, Leslie Knope (played by Amy Poehler), in the Parks and Recreation

Department of Pawnee, Indiana. Tom played Leslie's assistant and through his actions often undermined the efforts of his boss. As the series developed, Tom's character also developed, with him leaving the bureaucratic job and setting up businesses of his own. Even with his occupational changes, however, the fundamental character of Tom did not change that much. Resembling the character of Kumar in the film *Harold and Kumar Go to White Castle*, Tom continued to be brash and smart. Always thinking of himself as a smooth "ladies' man," Tom exuded confidence that is not often found in representations of males of Asian Indian lineage.

A female Indian American television character who also bucked traditional stereotypes of Asians was the supporting character Kelly Kapoor (played by Mindy Kaling) in NBC's *The Office* (2005–2013). Rather than fitting any female Asian stereotype, such as being demure or sexual, Kelly was simply a well-rounded energetic and fun individual. She was obsessed with celebrities and, although a supporting character, was often shown as ready to express her opinion and be noticed. In one episode of note, the entire office staff attends the Kapoor family's annual Diwali celebration. This episode, written by Kaling, introduces the audience to Indian dancing and singing, a tradition rarely seen on television.

There has been some effort to feature Asian Americans in leading television roles. One of the earliest shows to do this was ABC's 1994 show, *All-American Girl*, starring female comic Margaret Cho as Margaret Kim. The show's weekly plots revolved around the exploits of a Korean American high school girl and her family. While the series was viewed as a breakthrough in terms of featuring Asians in prominent television roles, it was also criticized for falling back on certain stereotypes. In particular, although Margaret's character came across as a typical high school student, the Asian males introduced in the series tended to be studious and fitting the "nerd" image. The series lasted only a few episodes (Fong 2008).

Following *All-American Girl*'s demise, it was some time before an Asian character was again cast in the lead. A number of examples of such casting now exist, although many of the shows are ensembles. In the ABC television series *Lost* (2004–2010), a Korean couple, Sun-Hwa Kwon (played by Yunjin Kim) and Jin-Soo Kwon (played by Daniel Dae Kim), were included among the primary survivors of Oceanic 815's plane crash on a mysterious island. Not only were they two main characters in the show, but the couple was often seen and heard speaking Korean, with subtitles provided. Korean American actor Daniel Dae Kim also appears in the reincarnated *Hawaii Five-0* (2010 debut). In this CBS series, Kim plays Detective Chin Ho Kelly and is one of the four leads on the show. Although he is not the primary star, he is far from a sidekick. In the first episode of the show, mention is made that Chin was a star athlete in high school, and his athleticism clearly comes across. He is also shown as being smart, sexy, and charming. The character is native to Hawaii and, as a result, often enlightens one of the "mainland" Anglo detectives on the state's history and traditions. The show also features Korean American actress Grace Park as Chin's tough yet beguiling cousin, Kona Kalakaua. In the first 10 seasons of ABC's medical drama *Grey's Anatomy*, which debuted in 2005, the character Cristina Yang (played by Sandra Oh) was featured as one of the main group of doctors whose personal lives and work at Seattle Grace Hospital are followed. And in the NBC action drama *Heroes* (2006), two Japanese characters, Ando Masahashi (played by James Kyson Lee) and Hiro Nakamura (played by Masi Oka), were included among the superheroes who are trying to save the world with their superhuman capabilities.

The popular CBS crime drama *Elementary* (2012 debut) is a modern version of Sherlock Holmes and features actress Lucy Liu in the part of Dr. Joan Watson. Playing the part of a former surgeon and NYPD consultant who works with Holmes to solve crimes allows Liu to take on a character who is tough, intelligent, but also caring. Liu's character is nuanced, with many layers. It is a far cry from the role she played in *Ally McBeal*.

While the inclusion of Asian characters in leading roles is commendable, in certain storylines or scenarios, show writers often find themselves falling back on old Asian stereotypes. For example, in *Heroes*, Japanese company employee Hiro discovers he has the power to travel across space and time, and recruits Ando in his efforts to save the world with his newfound powers. In the midst of saving the world, Ando develops the ability to amplify the superhero abilities of the others. In their entanglement in the complicated plots that typify the show, different facets of Ando and Hiro's personalities are shown. At the same time, however, the stereotypic trait of treachery is highlighted through Ando, and the "intelligent geek" with a "samurai spirit" is depicted through Hiro.

Even in the ABC sitcom *Dr. Ken* (2015 debut), created and co-produced by Ken Jeong who also stars in the leading role, stereotypic jokes appear at the expense of Asian and Asian American characters. The comedy series focuses on the home and work life of Dr. Kendrick "Ken" Park, a self-absorbed, sharp-tongued Korean American general physician. Dr. Ken's family – wife Allison (played by Suzy Nakamura), teenage daughter Molly (played by Krista Marie Yu), and young son Dave (played by Albert Tsai) – comes across as a "typical" American family with run-of-the-mill issues. The problem with this is that when the family's ethnic background is highlighted, it tends to take place within the context of stereotypes told as jokes. For example, in an episode in which his parents and in-laws are invited for a Thanksgiving dinner, the audience is introduced to the fact that Dr. Ken's parents are Korean while Allison's parents are Japanese. While the episode does delve into the culture clashes that often arise in unions that involve differing ethnic backgrounds, the episode falls flat in terms of expressing any sort of substantive Asian American experience and relies on Asian stereotypes for humor, including Dr. Ken making fun of his father's broken English.

Fresh Off the Boat (2015 debut) is another ABC sitcom that also relies on ethnic stereotypes for humor, but does so in ways that provide opportunities to question the stereotypes. Based on a memoir, the show's premise centers around seventh grader Eddie Huang (played by Hudson Yang) whose Taiwanese parents, Jessica Huang (played by Constance Wu) and Louis Huang (played by Randall Park), move him and his two brothers from Washington, DC's Chinatown to the suburbs of Orlando, Florida. Some have criticized *Fresh Off the Boat* for its use of stereotypes, but others have hailed it as a show that is not afraid to raise difficult race-related issues and that accentuates the multidimensional experiences of Asians and Asian Americans living in the United States. For instance, culture writer Evette Brown (2015) writes in her commentary:

> *Fresh off the Boat* is subversive. Like *Jane the Virgin* and *Blackish*, *Fresh off the Boat* refuses to retreat from certain essentialist elements of Chinese-American culture. For example, Eddie loves hip-hop, but his mother still cooks traditional Chinese meals, regardless of her eldest son's complaints. For every Jessica who chooses to maintain tradition in her home, there are Chinese mothers who assimilate. Neither is wrong. *Fresh off the Boat* shows audiences that having multiple representations is more important than attempting to erase offensive ones.

Tangible positive developments in the portrayals of Asians and Asian Americans are evident in other recent shows as well. For example, in the first season of the immensely popular AMC drama series *The Walking Dead* (2010 debut), audiences are introduced to the character of Glenn Rhee (played by Steven Yeun). As he joins a group of survivors of a deadly virus and Zombie attacks, Glenn is shown as a clean-cut, intelligent, and somewhat socially awkward young Korean American

Figure 7.2 Actor Steven Yeun playing Glenn Rhee in an early episode and then in a later episode of *The Walking Dead* series (2010–). Screenshots.

adult, a character that could easily fall under the stereotype of the nerdy but bright Asian American. He follows orders without question and tends to take a back seat when confronted by interpersonal conflict. As the storyline of the program progresses, the audience sees a change in Glenn's character. He moves away from being the stereotype to becoming a strong and assertive member of the surviving group (see Figure 7.2). The turning point is when he meets and falls in love with farm girl Maggie (played by Lauren Cohan). As their relationship develops, Glenn becomes determined to protect Maggie at all costs.

The ABC drama series *Quantico* has also provided a multifaceted Asian American character through one of the show's leading roles of Alex Parrish (played by Bollywood actress Priyanka Chopra). The series' storyline begins with a group of highly competitive FBI recruits who are training at the FBI's academy in Quantico, Virginia. Through the use of flashbacks and flash forwards, the audience soon learns there is a terrorist among the new recruits and that Alex is accused of being that terrorist responsible for the bombing of New York's Grand Central Station. The first season of *Quantico* follows Alex as she attempts to clear her name and find the real terrorist. Through the various scenes, Alex was portrayed as intelligent, strong, independent, and not afraid to gratify her sexual appetite – all characteristics that have not traditionally been associated with females of South Asian lineage. Many of these characteristics came about thanks to Priyanka Chopra being insistent when signing on to the program that she be cast as a lead and not in a supporting role, and that her Indian heritage be recognized, but that her character should have multiple, stereotype-breaking identities (Deggans 2015).

Other recent programs are also not only breaking stereotypic notions of Asians and Asian Americans through character development, they are also directly challenging these notions in their script writing. One such program is the critically acclaimed Netflix series *Master of None* (2015 debut). Created by Aziz Ansari (from *Parks and Recreation*) and Alan Yang (who was a writer and producer for *Parks and Recreation*), the comedy is about a thirty-something Indian American named Dev Shah (played by Aziz Ansari) who is trying to make it as an actor in New York. With a majority of the episodes co-written by Ansari and Yang, each episode's script contains dialogue that serves as commentary on social stereotypes. For example, an episode called "Indians on T.V." from season 1 begins with a montage of scenes from movies and television shows portraying Indians in stereotypical ways. The episode opens with Dev at a casting call getting ready to read the part of an "unnamed cab driver." Dev says his lines, but then is asked by the director to say his lines with an accent. Dev responds, "You mean like an Indian accent? You know I'd rather not. I just feel kind of weird doing that voice. Is that okay?" The unhappy director dismisses Dev from the audition and he essentially is told he didn't get the part. Dev then meets up at a coffee shop with a fellow actor, Ravi (played by Ravi Patel), who is also Indian American and tried out for the same part. Dev asks him: "Isn't it frustrating so much of the stuff that we go out for are just stereotypes – cab driver, scientist, IT guy?" Ravi tells him that not all acting parts are like that and tries to give an example by reading a phone text his agent just sent him about an upcoming part: "Purdy – East Indian man with a spiritual air full of philosophical platitudes. He runs a convenience store, has a funny Indian accent." With his voice dropping in defeated tone, Ravi then says to Dev, "This is not a good example."

This episode from *Master of None* effectively hits home the present-day reality that although efforts have been made to include Asian or Asian American characters in either leading or supporting roles in television programs, mainstream producers and writers are still having trouble completely separating these characters from traditional Asian stereotypes. Such difficulties in breaking away from ingrained stereotypes are also evident in the press.

Representations of Asians/Asian Americans in the News

Many of the images exhibited in popular culture have also been present in the mainstream press. The images go back to the early years of Western colonization of Asian nations and efforts to curb Asian immigration into the United States during the 1800s and early 1900s. For example, in an issue of the *New York Daily Tribune*, dated September 29, 1854, the following excerpt can be found describing Chinese women and conjuring up the untamed and erotic images of Asian women: "[Chinese women] are uncivilized, unclean, filthy beyond all conception, without any of the higher domestic or social relations; lustful and sensual in their dispositions; every female is a prostitute, and of the basest order ..." (Jiwani 2006: 164).

The xenophobia expressed in newspapers on the subject of Chinese immigration to the United States is exemplified by the following 1863 editorial passage in the *New York Times*:

> if there were to be a flood-tide of Chinese population – a population befouled with all the social vices, with no knowledge or appreciation of free institutions or constitutional liberty, with heathenish modes of thought that are firmly fixed by the consolidating influence of ages upon ages – we should be prepared to bid farewell to republicanism and democracy. (Chan 2001: 30)

The image of the Japanese conjured up in the press throughout World War II was that of the "yellow peril." Not only through the words chosen in press accounts, but also in the visuals presented in editorial cartoons, Japanese were portrayed as bloodthirsty monsters who would not stop at any cost to conquer the world (Dower 1986). These attributes were conferred upon Japanese Americans as well, inciting suspicion of anyone with Japanese ancestry. Hostility and distrust grew to the point of individuals calling, through the American press, for the incarceration of everyone of Japanese descent. Even the famed columnist Walter Lippmann, in an essay of February 12, 1942, argued for the forced evacuation of all Japanese and Japanese Americans living on the West Coast, writing that "the Pacific Coast is in imminent danger of a combined attack from within and without" (quoted in Daniels 1975: 47).

The image-induced hysteria resulted in Executive Order 9066, issued on February 19, 1942, authorizing the internment of all individuals of Japanese ancestry living on the West Coast. Approximately 110,000 individuals of Japanese ancestry were forcibly uprooted from their homes, stripped of their rights, and transported to hastily erected internment camps; roughly 70,000 of those sent to these camps were US citizens (Taylor 1993).

On August 31, 1946, the *New Yorker* published a dynamic and persuasive image of Japanese people to the American public in an attempt to counterbalance the sentiments of the time regarding the use of the atomic bomb. "Hiroshima," written by John Hersey, was first published in a single issue of the magazine, the first time any article took over an entire issue of the *New Yorker*. In clinical detail, "Hiroshima" follows six Japanese survivors through the aftermath of the atomic blast, writing from the points of view of the victims. Hersey reconstructs scenes and explores survivors' thoughts and feelings on the strength of extensive interviews and reportage. He restricts the story only to the survivors' sphere of knowledge, choosing their points of view – omitting, for example, any information about the bomb itself or the decision to use it.

The magazine sold out in hours. The article was accompanied by a note that read:

> TO OUR READERS: The *New Yorker* this week devotes its entire editorial space to an article on the almost complete obliteration of a city by one atomic bomb, and what happened to the people of that city. It does so in the conviction that few of us have yet comprehended the all but incredible destructive power of this weapon, and that everyone might well take time to consider the terrible implications of its use. – The Editors. (Hersey 1946)

Hersey took great pains not to conjure images of the Japanese as the "yellow peril" nor to depict them as some "fanatical, militaristic Shinto horde" (Sharp 2000), a tendency so common in press accounts of the time. In fact, his very choice of the survivors was carefully chosen to counteract this stereotype: Christian clergymen, a widowed mother of three, a female office worker, and two doctors, whom the bulk of the article describes as dealing with the human cost of the bombing, including the extensive radiation sickness. Literature scholar Patrick B. Sharp argues that one of "Hiroshima's" greatest achievements is that it provided a powerful antidote to the pervasive message of the time, that heroes had conquered the evil "yellow peril" (Sharp 2000). Hersey presented the Japanese as sympathetic victims of the atomic bomb, not a faceless mob.

Although the "Hiroshima" article helped to humanize the Japanese and evoke sympathy regarding their postwar plight, there was no similar exposé that focused on the injustices and losses that Japanese Americans had endured during the war years. In fact, from the end of World War II, Asian Americans were virtually absent from US press coverage. On the rare occasions there was coverage, it tended to be inconsequential. From the 1960s onward, however, a renewed interest in Asian Americans was seen in the press. Much of this coverage was devoted to highlighting their success in the United States and stressing that they were the "model minority" group. An example of such articles is one published in *US News and World Report* in 1966. Titled "Success Story of One Minority Group," the story begins as follows:

> Visit Chinatown U.S.A. and you find an important racial minority group pulling itself up from hardship and discrimination to become a model of self-respect and achievement in today's America. At a time when it is being proposed that hundreds of billions be spent to uplift Negroes and other minorities, the nation's 300,000 Chinese-Americans are moving ahead on their own – with no help from anyone else. (Shim 1998: 349)

This passage affirms the proposition that anyone can make it in America if only they try hard enough. It reinforces the argument that scholars have made regarding the nefarious social undertones of the "model minority" stereotype: that it helps to set a standard for how minorities should and can behave (Nakayama 1988; Shim 1998). It can be, and often is, used to refute the notion that features of the social system in the United States hinder the social progress of those in the minority.

Asian Americans were said to have been conferred the title of "model minority" in the 1960s in order to rebut the arguments made by the African American community that there were systemic social injustices in the United States. By stressing how Asian American communities were able to succeed, it could be more easily argued that African Americans were failing not because of the system, but due to their own faults and weaknesses.

Several researchers have noted that press coverage of the "model minority" tended to rely on traditional Asian values to explain why Asian Americans were succeeding in society, thus having the effect of further placing boundaries around them as a unique "forever foreigner" group (Tuan 1998). This was the major finding in intercultural communication scholar Thomas Nakayama's discourse analysis of the model minority portrayals in US news magazines. In a *Newsweek* article, for example, he found the following statement: "The success of Asian-Americans is rooted in a traditional reverence for learning in Asian culture, the fierce support of family and, in some cases, a head start gained in no-nonsense schools back home" (Nakayama 1988: 68). Nakayama points out that the use of the phrase "back home" suggests that Asian Americans are fundamentally not true Americans.

The model minority stereotype became so steadfast in the decades following the 1960s that even advertisers began to use it. In their analysis of portrayals of Asian Americans in advertising, marketing professor Charles Taylor and colleagues (Taylor, Lee, and Stern 1995) found that Asian Americans tended to be portrayed as focused on their jobs, with little to no interest in leisure time.

In another study led by Taylor (Taylor and Stern 1997), he found that in television advertisements, Asian Americans were often situated in work settings, rather than in home or social settings. The researchers argue that by predominantly placing Asians in work environments, the advertisements reinforced the notion that Asians were all about work and no play. In yet another study directed by Taylor (Taylor, Landreth, and Bang 2005), the researchers examined whether portrayals of Asian Americans had become more diverse in recent years. What they found was that the images did not vary much over the years: Asian Americans were consistently depicted as technology-savvy, work-oriented, and intelligent (Figure 7.3).

Figure 7.3 Does this picture of an American of Indian descent talking on a cell phone and carrying a computer convey a stereotype? Reproduced with kind permission of Shutterstock.

With the characteristics associated with the model minority being generally positive, some might question the harm in such stereotyping. English professor Angela Reyes amply summarizes the harm when she points out that "the model minority myth upholds the American ideologies of meritocracy and individualism, diverts attention away from racial inequality, sustains Whites in the racial hierarchy, and pits minority groups against one another" (Reyes 2009: 44). Others have also written that the model minority stereotype has the effect of creating conflict between racial groups. Political science professor Stephanie Greco Larson (2006) argues that the stereotype helps to sustain white dominance over other groups by creating conflict between those in the minority and supporting the argument that the ideal situation is to have Whites remain at the top of the social hierarchy.

Aside from the broader social harm that might come of the model minority stereotype, it is not hard to imagine the potential harm at the individual level as well. Consider the Asian American who comes from an upper-middle-class, well-educated family background who does not fit the stereotype. What social repercussions might come about as a result? If an Asian American student is performing poorly in school, ostracism or teasing might result simply because of the existing model minority stereotype; there is good evidence that those who conform to stereotypes are generally looked upon more positively than those who do not (Perse 2001).

It is important to note that model minority status is conferred most often on individuals who are part of the middle or upper-middle class and come from an East Asian or South Asian background. For Southeast Asian Americans, the model minority is less often used (Bucholtz 2009). Instead they are portrayed as people dependent on governmental assistance and who contribute to social problems. This has been especially the case since the rise in Southeast Asian gang activities that began in the 1990s. Linguistics professor Mary Bucholtz writes, "While a racial status of 'honorary whiteness' is conferred – albeit ambivalently and partially – upon some middle-class Asian Americans, working-class East and Southeast Asian Americans are often subject to the same kind of racial profiling and problematizing as are working-class African Americans and Latinos" (Bucholtz 2009: 22).

Asian/Asian American Activism and New Media

As the preceding sections have illustrated, although strides have been made in the depictions of Asians and Asian Americans in US media content, further changes are needed. The ever-growing activism of the Asian American community, especially via social media, will no doubt lead to further progress.

Asian American activist groups have long been key in bringing about changes. One example of how an Asian American activist organization has made a difference involves the film *Rising Sun*, discussed earlier. While the film was in the making, representatives from the Media Action Network for Asian Americans (MANAA) were concerned that it might incite violence and resentment toward Asians and Asian Americans (see Box 7.2). They asked the producers if they might be allowed to view a rough cut of the film and provide feedback. MANAA also requested that a disclaimer be included at the beginning of the film stating that the film was "not meant to imply that all Japanese people are trying to take over America" (quoted in Fong 2008: 204). Although MANAA's request was rebuffed, the group apparently did have an impact. The script to the film was revised and the anti-Japanese sentiments that were strongly expressed in the book on which the film was based were toned down for the movie.

Another example of the impact protests from Asian American organizations can have concerns a statement uttered by Dallas Cowboys coach Bill Parcells in 2004. During a press conference at a

---

Box 7.2 MANAA vs. Paramount executives on *The Last Airbender*

On February 11, 2009, the Media Action Network for Asian-Americans (MANAA) sent a formal letter of complaint to Paramount studio producers regarding their making of the cartoon-based film, *The Last Airbender*. The cartoon is about a Chinese youngster who has the power to manipulate the elements of air, water, earth, and fire. MANAA objected to the fact that although the main characters are supposed to be Chinese, the studio producers chose to use white actors.

Below is a copy of the letter sent to the Paramount producers. Despite the efforts of MANAA to have individuals of Asian descent in the roles, the producers opted to go with the white actors, with Noah Ringer playing the main role of Aang.

The Last Airbender – Letter to the Producer
February 11, 2009

Dear Mr. Mercer:

I left two messages with you – one with your assistant Ricky on Monday and another with Lauren yesterday. I'm writing on behalf of the Media Action Network for Asian Americans (MANAA), which is dedicated to monitoring the media and advocating for balanced, sensitive, and positive depiction and coverage of Asian Americans. Since 1992, we have consulted with movie studios and met regularly with the top four television networks about ensuring diversity.

We would like *Avatar: The Last Airbender* to become a successful movie trilogy. However, given the recent outcry over the lack of Asian/Asian American actors in the lead roles, we fear bad word of mouth may doom the first film before it gets off the ground and stop the potential franchise dead in its tracks. Indeed, the outrage over its casting has been greater than anything we've witnessed in the last several years. On Entertainment Weekly's website alone, there are 78 pages of comments from people who feel a strong emotional connection with Avatar, and most of their responses are strongly negative with many threatening to boycott the film.

Surely you have already seen or at least heard some of these concerns. While the show Mike DiMartino and Bryan Konietzko created was a great success in creating a fantasy world inspired heavily by Asian and Inuit elements, M. Night Shyamalan chose Caucasian actors to play all four main characters. Recently, Prince Zuko's character went to an actor of Asian descent, but otherwise, the only Asian presence in the film is in the sets and background characters.

Compared to other shows, including many anime imports, *Avatar: The Last Airbender* was unique because it was created for an American audience yet used Asian faces for its main characters. We appreciated that the Nickelodeon series (with the help of Asian American consultants) was intelligent enough to avoid using many of the common Asian stereotypes – both positive and negative – often seen in the media, and that it even made strides in casting Asian American voice talent.

The Asian American community, and the movie-going public at large, is used to seeing Asian men depicted as villains and rarely get the opportunity to see Asian heroes they can get behind and cheer for. This is also an historic opportunity to give Asian American actors a chance to shine in a big-budget film franchise which would bolster their careers for future projects. You will get deserved credit for launching those careers and can break down barriers by understanding that the audience that loved the television series is ready (and expects) to see Asian Americans playing those characters on the big screen.

One of the reasons the Avatar television series was so well-received was that our former Vice President, Edwin Zane, served as its cultural consultant for the first two seasons and helped the producers avoid ethnic missteps. Likewise, please take advantage of us as a resource. We invite you to dialogue with us

(Continued)

Box 7.2   (Continued)

---

about the film so that it can really be something fans of the show (and potentially new future fans of the movie) can get excited about. I can be reached at [number removed] or [email removed].

Sincerely,
Guy Aoki
Founding President, MANAA

cc:
Mike DiMartino
Bryan Konietzko
Dan Martinsen, EVP corporate communications, Nickelodeon
Jenna Lutrell, executive in charge of production, Nickelodeon
Letter from http://manaa.blogspot.co.uk/2009/02/letter-to-producer-of-last-airbender.html. Reprinted with kind permission of MANAA.

---

football minicamp, Parcell made the following statement in reference to his quarterbacks coach Sean Payton and defensive coordinator Mike Zimmer always attempting to outdo each other:

> You've got to keep an eye on those two, because they're going to try to get the upper hand. Mike wants the defense to do well, and Sean, he's going to have a few … no disrespect for the Orientals, but what we call Jap plays. OK. Surprise things … No disrespect to anyone. (ESPN, June 7, 2004)

The head of the Japanese-American Citizens League (JACL), John Tateishi, stated the following in reaction to Parcells' statement:

> Bill Parcells is a brilliant coach. Unfortunately, he is ignorant about racial slurs. I take great offense by what he said. Parcells ought to know better. He sorely needs more education on what is offensive and non-offensive to Japanese Americans. I am shocked that he would say this. (ESPN, June 7, 2004)

Later, JACL offered to educate Parcells and the Dallas Cowboys organization concerning offensive language. Both Parcells and the Dallas Cowboys organization issued apologies.

The proliferation of social media has also helped with Asian American activism in terms of working to bring about change in US media practices. Asian American celebrities, in particular, have taken to social media in order to voice their concerns regarding Hollywood bias. The "whitewashing" – use of white actors to play characters envisioned to be Asian – has led to several Asian American actors posting messages of protest on various social media sites. The use of actress Emma Stone to play a half-Asian character in *Aloha* and the casting of white actors to play manga-originated Asian characters – such as Tilda Swinton as The Ancient One in Marvel's *Doctor Strange*; Scarlett Johansson as Major in *Ghost in the Shell*; Nat Wolff as Light Yagami in *Death Note* (producers changed the character's name to "Light" to match the ethnicity of the chosen actor) – all elicited strong criticism from not only actors but also Asian Americans working in the entertainment industry. *New York Times* writer Amanda Hess in an article in 2016 provides some of the social media posts of protests by actress Constance Wu (from *Fresh Off the Boat*):

> On Facebook, Ms. Wu ticked off a list of recent films guilty of the practice and said, "I could go on, and that's a crying shame, y'all." On Twitter, she bit back against Hollywood producers who believe their "lead must be white" and advised the creators of lily-white content to "CARE MORE." Another tip: "An easy way to avoid tokenism? Have more than one" character of color, she tweeted in March. "Not so hard."

Social media have also given rise to several Asian American groups that have allowed the exchange of information and act as conduits of support. For example, the Asian American Performers Alliance Facebook page provides information on acting roles and events involving Asian or Asian American performing artists. Online platforms have additionally given individuals a way to spread the word about any sort of Asian American accomplishments. For example, when CBS News' Elaine Quijano (who is of Filipino descent) was named as moderator of the Vice Presidential debate in October of 2016, and thus became the first Asian American to moderate a national debate, numerous posts expressing delight could be read on such platforms as Twitter and Facebook.

Concluding Remarks

Representations of Asians in US media are deeply rooted in the anti-Asian sentiments that ran strong in the United States during the late nineteenth and early twentieth century. It was during that period that the influx of immigrants into the United States was perceived as an economic and political threat to the stability of the white-dominated status quo. When labor was needed for gold mining and railroad building, Asians were welcomed. As the economy weakened, however, movements were organized to curtail further entry of Asians into the United States (Fong 2008). Those Asians who were already in the country were forced to seek haven in segregated communities. It was during this time that stereotypes of Asians gained prominence in the US press. Soon, these very same stereotypes were found in the entertainment media.

The repercussions of media-disseminated Asian stereotypes and the negative feelings they evoke need to be considered seriously, especially in light of the number of hate crimes toward Asian Americans that have been reported. According to the US Federal Bureau of Investigation, of the 4,724 racially motivated "single-bias" hate crimes that were reported in 2007, 217 were directed at Asian/Pacific Islander individuals (Fong 2008). Included are crimes against individuals as well as property. If incidents of hate that are not necessarily defined as crimes were to be included, the number would be much higher. Although political and economic circumstances can often spark crimes or incidents of hate, it is hard to refute the proposition that media representations of social groups can fuel the flames of such hatred.

Although great strides have been made in improving media representations of Asians and Asian Americans, insensitive comments and hurtful stereotypes of individuals of Asian descent continue to be circulated in the mass media. It should be kept in mind that even one program showing an Asian character in a stereotypic manner is problematic, especially considering that the overall number of Asian characters appearing on television is still quite low.

Reflection Questions and Thoughts to Consider

1. Go through commercial print magazines and take note of the advertisements that feature Asian models. In what roles are they shown? Would you consider them as fitting the "model minority" stereotype or do they break the stereotype?

2. US policy makers have recently engaged in much discussion concerning the rise in the economic powers of China and India. Do you believe such discussions will impact on the types of mass media representations we will see in regard to individuals from both nations?

3. Based on the material presented in this chapter, how do you believe non-Asians or non-Asian Americans in their sixties and seventies would discuss their impression of people from an Asian ethnic background? How do you think these impressions would compare to those of non-Asian or non-Asian American youngsters in their teens and pre-teens? Would they be similar or different?

4. Take a look at video games such as *Shinobi*, *Mirror's Edge*, or *League of Nations* that feature Asian characters. What sort of conclusions would you draw about Asians just based on the characters?

References

Brown, Evette. 2015. "One TV, One Character Can't Represent an Entire Culture." *bitchmedia*, November 25. https://bitchmedia.org/article/tv-one-character-cant-represent-whole-culture (accessed April 7, 2017).

Bucholtz, Mary. 2009. "Styles and Stereotypes: Laotian American Girls' Linguistic Negotiation of Identity." In *Beyond Yellow English: Toward a Linguistic Anthropology of Asian Pacific America*, edited by Angela Reyes and Adrienne Lo, 21–42. New York, NY: Oxford University Press.

Chan, Jachinson. 2001. *Chinese American Masculinities: From Fu Manchu to Bruce Lee*. New York, NY: Routledge.

Daniels, Roger. 1975. *The Decision to Relocate the Japanese Americans*. New York: J.B. Lippincott.

Deggans, Eric. 2015. "From Bollywood to Hollywood: Shattering Stereotypes on the Silver Screen." *NPR.org*, December 10. http://www.npr.org/sections/codeswitch/2015/12/10/459247595/from-bollywood-to-hollywood-shattering-stereotypes-on-the-silver-screen (accessed April 7, 2017).

Dower, John. 1986. *War Without Mercy*. New York, NY: Pantheon Books.

ESPN. 2004. "Parcells Apologized for Making Ethnic Remark." *Espn.com*, June 9. http://sports.espn.go.com/nfl/news/story?id=1817592 (accessed April 7, 2017).

Fong, Timothy P. 2008. *The Contemporary Asian American Experience: Beyond the Model Minority*, 3rd ed. Upper Saddle River, NJ: Pearson Education.

Henderson, Odie. 2015. "Learning to Drive." *RogerEbert.com*, August 21. http://www.rogerebert.com/reviews/learning-to-drive-2015 (accessed April 7, 2017).

Hersey, John. 1946. "Hiroshima." *The New Yorker*, August 31.

Hess, Amada. 2016. "Asian-American Actors are Fighting for Visibility. They Will Not Be Ignored." *The New York Times*, May 25. http://www.nytimes.com/2016/05/29/movies/asian-american-actors-are-fighting-for-visibility-they-will-not-be-ignored.html?_r=0 (accessed April 7, 2017).

Jiwani, Yasmin. 2006. "From Dragon Lady to Action Hero: Race and Gender in Popular Western Television." In *Asian Women: Interconnections*, edited by Tineke Hellwig and Sunera Thobani, 163–164. Toronto: Women's Press.

Larson, Stephanie G. 2006. *Media and Minorities: The Politics of Race in the News and Entertainment*. Oxford: Rowman & Littlefield.

Nakayama, Thomas C. 1988. "'Model Minority' and the Media: Discourse on Asian Americans." *Journal of Communication Inquiry* 12: 65–73.

Ngai, Mae M. 1999. "The Architecture of Race in American Immigration Law: A Reexamination of the Immigration Act of 1924." *The Journal of American History* 86: 69–70.

Patton, Tracey O. 2001. "Ally McBeal and Her Homies: The Reification of White Stereotypes of the Other." *Journal of Black Studies* 32(2): 250.

Perse, Elizabeth M. 2001. *Media Effects and Society*. Mahwah, NJ: Lawrence Erlbaum.

Pfaelzer, Jean. 2007. *Driven Out: The Forgotten War Against Chinese Americans*. New York, NY: Random House.

Reyes, Angela. 2009. "Asian American Stereotypes as Circulating Resource." In *Beyond Yellow English: Toward a Linguistic Anthropology of Asian Pacific America*, edited by Angela Reyes and Adrienne Lo, 43–62. New York, NY: Oxford University Press.

Said, Edward. 1979. *Orientalism*. New York, NY: Vintage Books.

Sharp, Patrick B. 2000. "From Yellow Peril to Japanese Wasteland: John Hersey's 'Hiroshima.'" *Twentieth Century Literature* 46(4): 434–452. http://tcl.dukejournals.org/content/46/4/434.full.pdf+html (accessed April 7, 2017).

Shim, Doobo. 1998. "From Yellow Peril through Model Minority to Renewed Yellow Peril." *Journal of Communication Inquiry* 22(4): 385–409.

Steinberg, Brian. 2015. "Cartoon Network Gives Second-Season Nod to 'We Bare Bears.'" *Variety*, August 12. http://variety.com/2015/tv/news/cartoon-network-we-bare-bears-1201568431 (accessed April 7, 2017).

Taylor, Charles R., Ju Yung Lee, and Barbara B. Stern. 1995. "Portrayals of African, Hispanic, and Asian Americans in Magazine Advertising." *American Behavioral Scientist* 38: 608–621.

Taylor, Charles R., and Barbara B. Stern. 1997. "Asian Americans: Television Advertising and the 'Model Minority' Stereotype." *Journal of Advertising* 26: 47–61.

Taylor, Charles R., Stacy Landreth, and Hae-Kyong Bang. 2005. "Asian Americans in Magazine Advertising: Portrayals of the Model Minority." *Journal of Macromarketing* 25: 163–174.

Taylor, Sandra C. 1993. *Jewel of the Desert*. Berkeley, CA: University of California Press.

Tuan, Mia. 1998. *Forever Foreigners or Honorary Whites?: The Asian Ethnic Experience Today*. New Brunswick, NJ: Rutgers University Press.

8

Representations of Mixed Race Individuals and Relationships

At the beginning of the 1967 classic film *Guess Who's Coming to Dinner*, Christina (Katharine Hepburn) and Matt Drayton (Spencer Tracy) are preparing a dinner party for their daughter Joanna (Katharine Houghton) and her new fiancé, Dr. John Wayde Prentice, Jr. (Sidney Poitier). Also invited are the fiancé's parents, Mary (Beah Richards) and John (Roy E. Glenn). Christina knows that her daughter's fiancé is black, but Matt does not. When the fiancé and his parents arrive for dinner, Matt is dismayed to find that the young man and his parents are black. The rest of the film delves into how both sets of parents struggle to come to terms with the couple's plans for marriage. Matt, always considering himself a progressive liberal, finds it especially difficult. By the end of the film, however, he comes to realize the love their daughter and her fiancé share. In the final moments of the film, Matt provides the following advice to the young couple:

> But you do know, I'm sure you know, what you're up against. There will be a hundred million people right here in this country who will be shocked and offended and appalled at the two of you. And the two of you will just have to ride that out, maybe everyday for the rest of your lives. You can try to ignore those people or you can feel sorry for them and for their prejudices and bigotry and their blind hatreds and stupid fears. But where necessary, you'll just have to cling tight to each other and say screw all those people. Anybody could make a case and a hell of a good case against you getting married. The arguments are so obvious that nobody has to make them. But you're two wonderful people who happen to fall in love and happen to have a pigmentation problem. But I think that now no matter what kind of case some b*stard could make against you getting married, there would be only one thing worse and that would be if knowing what you two are, knowing what you two have, and knowing what you two feel, you didn't get married.

Those words were uttered in a film that was made close to half a century ago. Do they still ring true today? Vast political and social changes have taken place since the 1960s and the number of interracial marriages has increased. According to a report from the Pew Research Center, in 1970, only 1.0 percent of all marriages were between individuals from different races; in 2013, that figure rose to 6.3 percent (Wang 2015). Among Whites, 7.0 percent reported having a spouse of a different race. For Blacks, the figure was 19.0 percent, for Asians, 28.0 percent, and for American Indians, it

Diversity in US Mass Media, Second Edition. Catherine A. Luther, Carolyn Ringer Lepre, and Naeemah Clark.
© 2018 John Wiley & Sons Inc. Published 2018 by John Wiley & Sons Inc.

was 58.0 percent. Changes in laws and increases in marriages, however, do not necessarily translate into changes in deep-rooted notions regarding race mixing.

This chapter will explore whether societal perceptions of mixed race coupling and mixed race individuals have changed over the years by considering their depictions in film, entertainment television, and the news media. To provide context, a brief historical overview of the origins of interracial mixing taboos and the laws that constrained mixed race unions are also presented. First, however, the reader should be reminded that, as discussed in Chapter 1, race is a social construct and should not be interpreted as biologically based. Nevertheless, given the fact that race is still institutionally used as a classification system to categorize individuals and provides an opportunity to interrogate beliefs and perceptions of racial mixing, the term is used in this chapter. As used in this book, "race mixing" refers to the coupling of individuals from different racial backgrounds. "Mixed race individuals" refers to those who are from multiracial or biracial backgrounds.

Historical Background to Representations of Race Mixing

Slavery in the United States during the eighteenth and nineteenth centuries provided an institutionally sanctioned demarcation between races. It unquestionably conferred power and control on Whites, while leaving Blacks powerless and condemned to servitude. The political and social system was predicated on the belief that the two races were inherently different and that one race was, by nature, superior to the other. Intimate interactions between Whites and Blacks were thought to be taboo, even though slave owners and overseers frequently viewed the women they owned as sexual possessions.

During the early colonial period, consensual sexual encounters did occur between African slaves and white indentured servants who worked and lived in close proximity (Gullickson 2006). When the number of biracial "mulatto" children, born as a result of interracial sexual relations, became noticeable, those in elite positions began to view the co-mingling of races and the racially "ambiguous" children as a threat to the institution of slavery. Their answer to the threat was the implementation of miscegenation statutes and strict separation of races. As slavery increased and the practice of indentured servitude waned, the segregation of Blacks from Whites became more pronounced. White male slave owners, however, continued to use their black female slaves in order to satiate their sexual desires.

Following emancipation, interracial sexual relations decreased with the passing of Jim Crow laws and the growth of racial segregation. Anti-miscegenation laws, designed to prohibit interracial marriage and even interracial sexual contact, proliferated in the United States and were not confined to Southern states. According to some legal scholars, arguments for anti-miscegenation laws were used as a political smokescreen in order to counter any measure to promote the rights of Blacks (Alvins 1966). The laws allowed the maintenance of a racial hierarchy that essentially privileged Whites and kept Blacks confined to a lower socioeconomic class. Many of the laws pertained not only to Black–White unions, but also to marriages between Whites and American Indians as well as Whites and Asians (Karthikevan and Chin 2002).

However, as historian Renee Romano has argued, "The black–white divide is the most tenacious of all American color lines, and in many ways the regulation of black–white relationships and the taboo against them are unique" (2003: 8). In the creation of anti-miscegenation laws and other related statutes, the narrative that was stressed was that the mixing of "black blood" with "white blood" would in some way contaminate "white blood." Tied to this was the "one drop rule" that emanated from the South and spread throughout the United States. The rule stipulated that if an individual had even a drop of "black blood," they were to be considered Black (Romano 2003: 47).

Also popular was the unfounded "scientific" theory that children of mixed race couples were inferior in every way in comparison to Whites and Blacks (Farber 2011). The beliefs that were disseminated were that mixed race children were morally deprived, physically challenged, and were more susceptible to communicable diseases. By the 1940s, however, a shift took place within the scientific community and ideas regarding the biological consequences of race mixing were debunked. A major driving force behind this shift was the information that had emerged regarding Nazi Germany's "Racial Hygiene" program designed to sustain the "racial purity" of the "Aryan race" and that led to the atrocities of the Holocaust (Farber 2011: 44–45).

Even after World War II, racism in the United States and opposition to interracial marriage remained steadfast. A 1958 Gallup Poll showed that only 5 percent of Whites who resided in non-Southern states and 1 percent of Whites in Southern states supported black–white marriages; the majority, irrespective of education and class, did not approve of interracial marriage (Romano 2003). To prevent civil unions between individuals of different races, mainly Blacks and Whites, even in states that did not have anti-miscegenation laws in place, the Mann Act of 1944 was often used. The act, which made it illegal for women to be transported across state lines for prostitution or sexual activity, was interpreted as making it a crime for mixed race couples to cross state lines in order to get married.

It was not until the 1960s with the rise of the civil rights movement that tangible results from efforts of those who were fighting anti-miscegenation legislation were seen. The fight to eradicate Jim Crow laws by black activists opened the door for all laws based on race to be critically reevaluated. Individual states, including Indiana, Arizona, and Nebraska, began to repeal their anti-miscegenation laws. The remaining, predominantly Southern states, however, remained unwavering in maintaining their anti-miscegenation laws – that is, until the 1967 landmark ruling by the Supreme Court in the *Loving vs. Virginia* case, involving the marriage of Richard Loving, a white man, and Mildred Jeter, a black woman.

Richard Loving and Mildred Jeter went to Washington, DC to marry in 1958, because their home state of Virginia banned interracial marriage. Upon returning to Virginia, both were arrested, charged with violating the state's anti-miscegenation law or its Racial Integrity Act of 1924. The two eventually pled guilty and were ordered to leave the state. The Lovings settled in Washington, DC, but as the civil rights movement began to gain momentum, and with their desire to return to Virginia, they decided to appeal their case to the Virginia Supreme Court. When that court upheld the lower court's decision, the case moved to the United States Supreme Court. On June 12, 1967, the Supreme Court struck down Virginia's anti-miscegenation law. In writing the opinion for the case, Chief Justice Earl Warren stated, "The Fourteenth Amendment requires that the freedom of choice to marry not be restricted by invidious racial discriminations. Under our Constitution, the freedom to marry, or not marry, a person of another race resides with the individual, and cannot be infringed by the State" (Wardle 1998: 304). After this decision, states that still had in place anti-miscegenation laws began to repeal them or at least stopped enforcing them. In 2000, Alabama became the last state to repeal its anti-miscegenation law (Farber 2011).

Since the Supreme Court's landmark ruling, the number of interracial unions has increased at a steady rate in the United States (Gullickson 2006). Yet while the number of marriages between people from differing racial backgrounds has seen a growth, barriers to full acceptance of mixed race couples have nevertheless remained persistent within the minds and hearts of people. As the next sections will show, mass media have reflected both the changes in attitudes as well as the tenacious aversions people have regarding race mixing.

Race Mixing in Film

One of the earliest films to focus on race mixing is the 1915 film *Birth of a Nation* that was introduced in Chapter 4 of this book. While the film has been heralded for its artistic cinematic presentations, the film's director, D.W. Griffith, unabashedly created a film supporting white supremacy and did so by tapping into audience fears of race mixing. As the three-hour film moves from its representation of the Civil War period to Reconstruction, it portrays the newly emancipated slaves as deprived, unable to enter civilization, and seeking only to prey on white women. The film's main villain is Silas Lynch (played by white actor George Siegmann in blackface), depicted as an evil licentious "mulatto" who is put in place as lieutenant governor of South Carolina by a powerful Northern abolitionist politician following the war.

Early in the film, Lynch organizes former slaves to take over South Carolina's House of Representatives and, once in office, the first bill they introduce is one that would allow marriage between Whites and Blacks. In the scene in which the bill is being passed into law, Griffith shows black congressmen leering lasciviously at two white young women who are observing the session in the viewing gallery. The director then cuts to a slate with the following ominous words, "Then. The grim reaping begins." What follows in the film is a series of scenes that reinforce the image of hypersexual black males set on making a conquest of white women.

In one of the film's more dramatic scenes, white heroine Flora Cameron (Mae Marsh) is shown frolicking in the forest before being spotted by her former black slave Gus (played by a white actor, Walter Long, in blackface) who is now a soldier. Gus approaches Flora and tells her that he wants to marry her. Flora frantically runs away, calling for help. Gus, appearing half-crazed, chases after her. Before Gus can reach her, Flora flings herself off the cliff. As she lies dying, her brother Ben (Henry B. Walthall) finds her and learns what has happened. Intent on gaining revenge, Ben forms the Ku Klux Klan. The film ends by showing the Ku Klux Klan as victorious and restoring order – preventing any further mixing of races to occur.

Birth of a Nation, in all of its visual glory and in its racist messages, is said to have been successful in stoking fears about race mixing and in strengthening racism. Membership in the Ku Klux Klan experienced a dramatic increase following the release of the film (NPR Staff 2015). It is interesting to note that Griffith did use black actors in the film to serve as extras, but for the two main roles, that of Silas Lynch and Gus, white actors in blackface were used. This was most likely due to the fact that the two roles called for the characters to come into physical contact with white female characters.

The decision Griffith had made in not using black male actors to play characters that called for them to touch white female characters was prescient of what was to come in the form of the Motion Picture Producers and Distributors of America (MPPDA) Production Code of 1930. The Code, which started to be enforced in the mid-1930s, explicitly banned suggestions of miscegenation, or sex between individuals of different races, from being included in Hollywood films (Friedman 2011). According to professor of English and film studies Ryan Jay Friedman, the Production Code Administration (PCA) that was established to enforce the code is said to have "used the 'miscegenation clause' to police the 'color line', steering studios away from any depictions of 'social equality' in the form of 'mixed' contacts not built around clearly marked, hierarchical distinctions" (2011: 105).

Films such as the 1931 film *Cimarron* and the 1932 film *Call Her Savage*, which both featured mixed race couples, managed to be released before the full enforcement of the MPPDA Production Code. In *Cimarron*, the leading married couple is a biracial Native American white male (played by white actor Richard Dix) and white female (Irene Dunne). In *Call Her Savage*, the leading character is a biracial American Indian white female (played by white actress Clara Bow), who is depicted as wild and having sexual relations with various white males. In these films, the mixed race individuals are portrayed as unstable and unable to attain happiness.

The 1936 film *Ramona*, based on a novel by writer and activist Helen Hunt Jackson, tells the story of a half American Indian and half white young woman named Ramona (played by white actress Loretta Young) who rejects the affections of the son of a wealthy ranch owner and instead falls in love with a poor sheepherder named Allesandro (played by white actor Don Ameche). Although the book's author had the goal of conveying the hardships and prejudice that the American Indian community faced in California, the film version makes the love interests of Ramona the focal point and falls short of making any kind of political or social statement. In his analysis of *Ramona*, historian J.E. Smyth writes: "Visually, Native American ancestry did not show in the white faces of actresses Clara Bow and Loretta Young. There was no physical visual marker to distinguish them from their white cohorts" (Romano 2003). In other words, whiteness was maintained in these films and "race was therefore something to be performed through costume" (Romano 2003).

As in the case of *Birth of a Nation*, all of the movies portraying a romantic relationship between individuals of different races that were produced and released during the decades in which the MPPDA code was reinforced only used white actors to play the part of the romantic partners. Such was the case with the 1949 film *Pinky*. Directed by Elia Kazan, the film's central premise involves a young woman coming to terms with her own racial identity and confronting racism in the South.

The film begins with the main biracial character Pinky Johnson (played by white actress Jeanne Crain) returning home to her black grandmother (Ethel Waters) in Mississippi after becoming a nurse in Boston (see Figure 8.1). The grandmother, who had raised Pinky, is still living in the small cabin that was once also home to Pinky. Upon returning home, the expressions of joy Pinky shares

Figure 8.1 Actresses Jeanne Crain and Ethel Waters appearing in *Pinky* (1949). Screenshot.

with her grandmother, who she calls "Granny," soon turn solemn. Before Pinky can confide in her grandmother that because of her light complexion she has been passing as white, going by the name of Pat, and has fallen in love with a white doctor named Tom Adams (William Lundigan), her astute grandmother confronts Pinky with the following words:

> Let me say something once and for all and never again. Why did you write me less and less as time go by? Why is it that after you go to the hospital I get no letters at all? No. You don't need to say nothing. You think I don't know. You think a poor, old, ignorant woman like me living in a shack like this don't know nothing. But you're wrong Pinky. I do know and I know what you done. And you know I never told you pretend what you is what you ain't.

In tears, Pinky tries to explain that she had not meant to pass for white; it just happened. Her grandmother, though, will not hear of any excuses and reprimands Pinky: "But that's a sin before God and you know it … Oh shame, shame be on you, Pinky. Denying yourself like Peter denied the good Lord Jesus." Before asking Pinky never again to mention what she had done, Pinky's grandmother forces her onto her knees and says, "That's where you belong. Now you tell the Lord what you done. Ask his forgiveness on your immortal soul."

That brief exchange between Pinky and her grandmother sets the stage for the rest of the film, which traces how Pinky comes to realize the bubble that she had been living in and discovers her true identity. Her journey toward self-discovery begins when she is convinced by her grandmother to stay in Mississippi to serve as the nurse of their ailing elderly white neighbor, Ms. Em (Ethel Barrymore). Ms. Em, who lives alone in her dilapidated plantation mansion, had once helped Granny during her time of sickness and Granny wants to return the favor. Although the relationship between Pinky and Ms. Em is at first antagonistic, it soon transforms into mutual fondness and Ms. Em ends up leaving her estate to Pinky before she passes away.

Following Ms. Em's death, Tom soon arrives in Mississippi and asks Pinky to marry him, but when Pinky realizes that he wants them to move to Denver to avoid people finding out about her race, she tells Tom: "I can't go with you. I'm sick of lying. We wouldn't be happy either of us." Tom reacts angrily, grabs Pinky and shakes her saying, "What do you expect to do? Crawl into a closet and live there the rest of your life. Close the door and lock it? Lock everything? Pat, look at me. Look at me. Would you come to your senses? You've got to make a break. Get away from it." Pinky frees herself from Tom and says, "I don't want to get away from anything. I'm a negro. I can't forget it and I can't deny it. I can't pretend to be anything else. I don't want to be anything else." In the end, Pinky does remain in the South and uses Ms. Em's home to establish a clinic and a nursery school for her black community. The film concludes by showing Pinky as strong and with purpose.

Pinky was able to tackle the injustices that Blacks faced in America due to the changing social and political climate following World War II. With the significant role that black soldiers played in fighting the war and with the growing realization of the atrocities committed in Nazi Germany against the Jewish people and other minority groups, film producers were willing to take on more substantive issues involving race relations by the end of the 1940s and into the 1950s (Jones 1981). The film, however, falls short of making a firm statement on the inequities faced by black Americans. Using a biracial or black actress to play the part of Pinky would have helped to provide a realistic and dramatic account of race relations in the South. The filmmakers, however, played it safe by choosing a well-known and well-liked white actress to play the role. Although the film depicted an interracial intimate relationship, including the showing of passionate kisses shared between Pinky and Tom, audience members knew that the kisses shared were between two white actors. Of course, the film was made and released during a time when the MPPDA censoring board was still intact, so the film would not have met the review board's approval had the filmmakers not opted for white actors. In the form that it ultimately took, the film proved to be a success with all three of the leading actresses in the film, Jeanne Crain, Ethel Waters, and Ethel Barrymore, being nominated for Academy Awards for their performances.

As enforcement of the MPPDA codes began to fade, and with the greater financial pressures on production companies to attract larger audiences following the introduction of television, other films exploring interracial relationships continued to be produced into the 1960s. Similar to the film *Pinky*, a central plotline of several of these films focused on the notion of "passing." The term "passing" can be traced to the days of slavery when those who were mixed race and light skinned would adopt a white identity in order to escape slavery. The term continued in its usage to signify individuals who were assuming a white identity in order to have access to the privileges offered to Whites.

The plotline norm in passing films involved a leading female character with light complexion passing for white in order to attain benefits usually reserved only for Whites. Adding a white male as the female character's love interest is said to have provided titillation for the primarily white viewing audience. The passing films had similar endings, with the passing-for-white character either meeting a tragic death or returning to her former non-white lifestyle.

As an example, in the 1960 film *I Passed for White*, the lead biracial (black–white) character (played by white actress Sonya Wilde) finds that she is having difficulty finding a job as a black woman and decides to take on a white identity. She leaves her black mother and biracial brother to begin a new life with a new name – Lila Brownell. As Lila, she finds success and marries a rich white man. She hides the fact that she is partially black from her new husband and lives a lie among his white family and friends. Upon getting pregnant, Lila fears that her child might be dark-skinned. She ends up going into premature labor and her child is stillborn. Under anesthesia, Lila asks if her baby is black. Her husband hears those words and suspects his wife has had an affair with a black man. With no child, her marriage ending in divorce, Lila decides to return to her family. The film reinforces the tragic "mulatto" stereotype that deprives mixed race individuals from finding any happiness.

The ill-fated ending that befalls mixed race couples in early films was not reserved for black–white couples. Other mixed race couples encountered similar fates. An example is the 1957 film *Sayonara*, based on a novel by James Michener. It tells the story of two US Air Force men who fall in love with Japanese women while stationed in Japan. One of the airmen (Red Buttons) weds his love interest (Miyoshi Umeki), but then faces discrimination and retribution by the US military. The forlorn couple ends up committing suicide together, fueling the other airman's (Marlon Brando) determination to marry his Japanese love (Miiki Taka) and fight the unjust system. Both Red Buttons and Miyoshi Umeki won Academy Awards for their performances.

The fact that Japanese actresses were selected to play the love interests of white men in *Sayonara* is interesting given that even as late 1960, a white actress was chosen to play the black–white biracial love interest of a white man in *I Passed for White*. The deep-seated taboo against black–white intimacy most likely played a part in that decision making. It was not until *Guess Who's Coming to Dinner*, introduced at the beginning of this chapter, that actors playing the part of black characters were actually black.

Commercial films that have since been produced have still tended to carry an underlying theme that sexual relations between Blacks and Whites should not take place. While scenes showing intimacy between black and white characters are now shown, the couple inevitably either are depicted as not able to sustain their relationship or end up encountering tragedy in their relationship. According to criminal law professors Barbara Perry and Michael Sutton, in consistently reinforcing this narrative, films as part of US popular culture are "reminding black and white people that 'thou shalt not' cross the boundaries of sexuality that have been built up since the first black slave was brought to North America's shores" (Perry and Sutton 2006: 887–904). Although African Americans have achieved socioeconomic gains, they are still viewed with suspicion and even with trepidation, especially in regard to sexuality. Philosophy professor and social activist Cornel West maintains that this fear is based on the perception of Blacks as having the power to control Whites either by their animalistic sexual prowess or through their demure sexual magnetism (West 1994). This perception continues to be manifested in the plotlines of films that focus on black–white intimacy.

A film that taps into the notion of the sexual allure of Blacks is the critically acclaimed 2001 film *Monster's Ball*. Set in the southern area of the United States, the film follows the relationship between a poor black woman, Leticia Musgrove (Halle Berry), and a white middle-income man, Hank Grotowksi (Billy Bob Thornton). The two become intimate after Leticia loses her son to a car accident and Hank, who had also tragically lost his son, helps her through her loss. Alongside the emotional connection, however, Hank has a powerful sexual attraction toward Leticia. In fact, the relationship begins with raw sex between the two characters. It occurs on the evening following the death of Leticia's son. Leticia invites Hank into her home after he drives her home from work. They both begin to drink small bottles of liquor and Leticia soon becomes intoxicated. She laughs and cries while reminiscing about her son. Hank rubs Leticia's back to comfort her and says, "I'm not sure what you want me to do." Leticia replies, "I just want you to make me feel good. Just make me feel good." Leticia's vocal tone becomes coarse and guttural. She continues, "Can you make me feel good? Can you make me feel good?" She lifts up her top and Hank helps her to pull it off. They kiss and begin to engage in sex. The sex is rough and lacking any sort of romantic subtlety.

Following this first encounter, the relationship between Hank and Leticia develops and viewers do see intimacy growing between the two with gentle embraces mixed in with sex. The relationship, however, appears to be based on sexual need gratification as well as financial need on the part of Leticia. Although Leticia holds some form of power due to Hank's desire for her, she is ultimately presented as a sexual object that exists to satiate a white man's appetite. In a scene in which Leticia encounters Hank's bigoted father, Leticia is crudely sexualized and demoralized. When the father realizes that Leticia is intimately involved with his son, he says to her: "In my prime, I had a thing for n*gger juice myself. Hank just like his daddy. He ain't a man until he split dark oak." The statement conjures up images of white male slaveholders raping their black female slaves.

Other films, such as *Jungle Fever* (1991), *O* (2001), *Rome & Jule* (2006), and *Lake View Terrace* (2008), that focus on the intimacy between white and black characters have also alluded to sexual exploitation and/or anti-miscegenation themes. They make as their primary focus the prejudices underlying the repulsion regarding the mixing of races. Even in the more innocuous films that tap into biases against white and black couples, such as *The Body Guard* (1992) and *Save the Last Dance* (2001), the relationships tend to dissolve toward the end of the film with suggestions that the characters will go their own separate ways.

Sociologist Angie Beeman maintains that warped representations of black–white couples in films are indicative of the institutionalized racism that she and other critical scholars assert exist in US society (Beeman 2007: 687–712). To help substantiate her claim, Beeman examined differences in depictions of black–white couples and same-race couples in a sample of blockbuster US films. She found that intimate physical contact and emotional connections were more often presented with white-only couples than with black-only couples or black–white mixed couples. Moreover, white-only couples were portrayed as having successful relationships more so than black-only couples or black–white mixed couples. Beeman concludes that in conveying such imagery to the public, the film industry was reinforcing racist attitudes toward Blacks and the taboo against mixed race relationships.

As Blacks and Whites strive toward parity of socioeconomic status, some films portray the interracial relationship in new ways, turning past notions of these couplings on their head. For example, *Guess Who* (2005) offers a modern twist on the aforementioned *Guess Who's Coming to Dinner*. In the film, Theresa (played by Afro-Hispanic actor Zoe Saldana) brings her longtime boyfriend Simon (played by white actor Ashton Kutcher) home to meet her father Percy (played by Bernie Mac). Simon is fearful that Percy will give him a hard time not only because he is white, but also because he's lost his job and Percy is very concerned about financial success. Theresa's family definitely is surprised. Percy even thinks Simon is the cab driver when they first meet, asking him to carry luggage into the house. Once Simon gets a job and teaches Percy how to dance, the couple receives his blessing.

As another example, in *Something New* (2006) Sanaa Lathan plays Kenya McQueen, a high-powered, uptight accountant who was born into an upper-middle-class black family. Kenya hires landscaper Brian Kelly (played by Simon Baker) to add some flair to her new yard, but Brian makes it his mission to add some flair to her life. Their inevitable romance adds a sense of authenticity to Kenya's life that she's never had before – including wearing her natural hair. Still, Kenya's brother Nelson (played by Donald Faison) refers to Simon as "the help" and introduces Kenya to a wealthy black lawyer to distract her from Brian. Again, the black family must deal with the trauma of adding a non-black member to its family where the white characters are open to becoming a part of the family.

With regard to movies that show mixed race coupling that does not involve a white character, because such films are few in number, it is difficult to assess the films' narratives and the degree of success these couples have in finding love. Examples do exist, however, of movies that end with the mixed race couple blissfully bonded together, for example, *Hitch* (2005), starring as a couple black actor Will Smith and Latina actress Eve Mendez, and *Our Family Wedding* (2010), starring Latina actress America Ferrera and black actor Lance Gross. When the couple does not include a white character, it appears the taboo against interracial mixing is weakened.

Movies involving intimacy between white characters and racially ambiguous characters have also had storylines with happy endings for the mixed race couple. Actors such as Vin Diesel, Dwayne Johnson, and Jessica Alba, who have all been described as racially ambiguous, have played characters that have had successful romantic relationships with characters played by white actors/actresses. Because of their mixed background and ambiguous appearance, these actors – as well as others such as Rosario Dawson and Jesse Williams – have been able to slip into various acting roles and appeal to broad audiences. In reference to actresses and actors from mixed Latino/a and European ancestry, critical and cultural studies scholar Mary Beltran maintains that because of Hollywood's privileging of fair skin, those actresses and actors have long enjoyed advantages (i.e., attaining leading roles) not offered to those not of European descent (Beltran 2008: 248–268). She highlights how Jessica Alba, of Mexican and European heritage, has found success by being cast in a variety of roles, including playing the part of super-heroine Sue Storm in *Fantastic Four* (2005, 2007) and an exotic dancer in *Sin City* (2005, 2014).

The questionable representations of race mixing in films appear to pertain chiefly to intimate relations between Blacks and Whites. Depictions of true romance between these two racial groups still appear to be constrained by deep-rooted and socially constructed beliefs about racial boundaries. As will be shown in the next section, progress in breaking these boundaries has been more noticeable within the medium of television.

Race Mixing in Entertainment Television

The 1950s popular sitcom *I Love Lucy* (1951–1957), briefly discussed in Chapter 5 of this book, is credited with being the first television show to feature an interracial couple (Bramlett-Solomon 2007). The show starred Latino Cuban-born actor and musician Desi Arnaz playing the part of a Cuban-born bandleader named Ricky Ricardo who was married to his lovable, but slightly ditzy wife Lucy (played by white actress Lucille Ball). Married in real life, Arnaz and Ball (who had star power at that time) are said to have had to talk CBS network executives into allowing them to play the parts of the married couple. Despite concerns, the program proved to be a major audience draw. However, the societal impact the show had in opening the door for other programs to feature mixed race couples is debatable. The program only allowed occasional hugs and kisses between the couple. In line with the television standards during that time period, both were shown sleeping in separate beds and even when Lucy became pregnant on the show, the writers were forced to write around the word "pregnant"; only subtle suggestions that Lucy was expecting were used in the script instead (Bramlett-Solomon 2007).

It would not be until quite some time later that another show presenting an interracial couple would be seen on prime-time television. With television networks coming under pressure to reflect diversity in their programming following gains made due to the civil rights movement, producers began to take chances on having programs with leading characters from diverse backgrounds. In terms of featuring interracial couples, one of the earliest programs to do so was the television sitcom *The Jeffersons* (1975–1985). As briefly introduced in this book's Chapter 4, the program was about a black family that lived in a high-priced apartment building in Manhattan. The family's patriarch was George Jefferson (Sherman Hensley), who managed to find something to be unhappy about on a daily basis, especially with regard to his neighbors – mixed race couple Tom (played by white actor Franklin Cover) and Helen Willis (played by black actress Roxy Roker). The inclusion of the mixed race couple in the program could be considered a positive advancement in television scripting, but it should be kept in mind that Tom and Helen were both secondary characters. Moreover, with practically every appearance, they had to endure the derogatory racial jokes lodged at them by their bigoted neighbor George.

The Jeffersons was aired for a full decade, but media observers and researchers have pointed out that when interracial couples are preeminently featured in programs, the shows often have a short broadcast run (e.g., *Kevin Hill*, 2004–2005; *LAX*, 2004–2005). If the show itself is not canceled, the interracial romance disappears. As sociologist Erica Chito Childs characterizes it, such romance tends to "fizzle" out before having "a chance to sizzle" (Childs 2009: 37). She provides as an example the show *Once and Again* (1999–2002) that had as its premise the romance between a divorced single mom and divorced single dad coming together to form a family. During its first season, the program introduced a romance between the mom's white teenage daughter and her black school classmate. The romance, however, ended abruptly and never witnessed development.

More recent examples can be provided of shows that ended the interracial coupling by either weaving in storylines of an ill-fated, conflict-based relationship or by simply killing off one of the characters. For example, in *Agents of S.H.I.E.L.D.* (2013–present), agent Grant Ward (played by white actor Brett Dalton) has intimate relations with both agent May (played by Chinese American actress Ming-Na Wen) and agent Skye (played by mixed race actress Chloe Bennet); both relationships, however, are based on deception. Grant turns out to be a villainous enemy infiltrator and the character is killed in season 3. In CBS's *Person of Interest* (2011–present), the friendship between detective Joss Carter (played by black actress Taraji P. Henson) and former CIA operative John Reese (played by white actor Jim Caviezel) grows stronger and they share an intimate kiss in a season 3 episode; during that same episode, however, Carter is shot and killed. In HBO's original *Game of Thrones* (2011–present), the marriage of Khal Drogo (played by actor Jason Momoa of Pacific Islander, Native American, and European ancestry) and Daenerys (Khaleesi) Targaryen (played by white actress Emilia Clarke) comes to a tragic end when Khal dies of a sword wound infection at the conclusion of season 1.

Nevertheless, whether or not the relationships are based on deception or end in tragedy, it needs to be stressed that the featuring of mixed race couples has become more noticeable on television over the last few years. Interracial families, which in the past were virtually invisible, are also making a presence. The company that has been at the forefront of featuring mixed race dating and racially/ethnically mixed characters is Walt Disney Television. One of the earlier Disney productions to have featured as its lead a mixed race character was the 1999 Disney television movie *Johnny Tsunami*. The movie tells the story of a young teenager, Johnny Kapahala, whose father is a Hawaii native of Asian ancestry and whose mother is white, having to face multicultural differences when his father relocates from Hawaii to Vermont. In Vermont, Johnny is sent to a prep school predominantly made up of very rich white kids and soon encounters racial and class prejudice. An excellent surfer, Johnny finds comfort in being able to snowboard and ends up developing close friendships with a more ethnically diverse group of students from a nearby public school. The movie ends with Johnny becoming a hero and bringing together the students from the prep school and public school. He is also successful in winning the heart of the popular white girl. *Johnny Tsunami*'s sequel, *Johnny Kapahala: Back on Board* was released in 2007. The sequel, however, did not explore racial struggles as the original movie had done and did not receive much audience attention.

In 2006, the Disney television movie *High School Musical* aired for the first time with great fanfare and featured a mixed race high school couple, Troy Bolton (played by white actor Zac Efron) and Gabriella Montez (played by actress Vanessa Hudgens – Asian and white racial background) as its leading characters (Figure 8.2). Troy is the star athlete of his high school and Gabrielle is a shy studious student. The movie follows the couple's efforts to be in their high school musical while falling in love. With its success, the film led to *High School Musical 2* (2007) and the theatrical release of *High School Musical: Senior Year* (2008). The first *High School Musical* film is still credited as the most successful Disney Channel Original Movie.

More recent Disney productions have often included mixed race individuals or have adopted storylines involving love interests between characters of different racial backgrounds. Examples are Disney Channel's *Good Luck Charlie* (2010–2014), with character Emmett (played by black actor Micah Stephen Williams) pursuing the affection of main character Teddy Duncan (played by white actress Bridgit Mendler); *Lab Rats* (2012–2016), with main character Leo Dooley (played by black actor Tyrel Jackson Williams) whose mother, Tasha Davenport (played by black actress Angel Parker) is married to a rich inventor Donald Davenport (played by white actor Hal Sparks); and *A.N.T. Farm*

Figure 8.2 Zac Efron as Troy Bolton and Vanessa Hudgens as Gabriella Montez in *High School Musical* (2006). Screenshot.

(2011–2014), with artistic tween genius Fletcher Quimby (played by white actor Jake Short) infatuated with main character Chyna Parks (played by black actress China Anne McClain).

Professor of media studies Angharad Valdiva makes the argument that Disney began featuring mixed race individuals and mixed race interactions on their programs because of monetary incentives. She writes, "Disney has gingerly begun to address issues of difference as it seeks to maintain ratings prominence and economic returns in the form of increasing revenues and profits for its shareholders" (Valdiva 2008: 269–289). Perhaps the innocent nature of the mixed race relationships between teenagers or tweens in the Disney programs also allowed the company to feel secure in taking a chance in featuring mixed race couples in its shows.

For television programs not targeted at a young age group, however, the storylines surrounding mixed race relationships have tended to be varied and not always positive. Situation comedies that have featured mixed race couples have taken a more upbeat tone regarding the relationships in comparison to television dramas. Even so, some shows still tap into negative stereotypes for the sake of humor.

While comedies have the potential to serve as a potential platform to explore racist attitudes toward mixed race couples, mainstream sitcoms have generally shied away from such social commentary and have instead attempted to present the couples as any other couple, with the usual relationship challenges. If race is mentioned, it tends to be brought up in a low-key manner and addressed through humor. As discussed in Chapter 7, an exception to this has been the Netflix original comedy series *Master of None* (2015 debut).

In the debut episode of *Master of None*, the audience is introduced to the lead character Dev Shah (played by Aziz Ansari of Indian ancestry) as he is waking up in his bed next to a woman he had just met the night before at a party. The woman, named Rachel (played by white actress Noel Wells), later becomes his girlfriend and, through that relationship, the viewer is witness to the program's social commentary on mixed race relations. For example, in one episode, when Rachel asks Dev if he wants to go with her to visit her grandmother, Dev responds: "Mmm. I don't know. Is she one of those racist grandmas who is going to be weird around someone with my skin tone?" Rachel then says: "I don't know. But it could be a fun gamble though."

As another example, in the last episode of the program's first season, Dev and Rachel are at a friend's wedding reception where Dev introduces Rachel to his friend's father, Arthur Ryan. Arthur looks at Dev and Rachel and says: "Aw. That's nice. I love seeing ethnically mixed couples. You two are beautiful together." Mr. Ryan then goes on to ask Rachel: "Had you ever dated an ethnic man before this, Rachel?" Rachel responds: "Oh. No. I was very nervous. I had been dating a lot of Whites, just so many Whites. And then one day I woke up and just thought 'Rachel, you have to go out there and try yourself an ethnic.' [*Rachel grabs Dev's arm and pulls him close to her*]. And here we are. It's going great." Missing the sarcasm in Rachel's voice, Ryan goes on to say, "Ah. Fantastic." After Ryan leaves the couple, Dev says to Rachel: "Wow. I mean. I think his heart's in the right place, but he really shouldn't be saying ethnic that much." Dev then asks Rachel: "What is the race breakdown of your previous dudes?" Rachel responds: "Uh, White, White, White, White, half Asian, and you." Dev says: "Whoa. So that half Asian guy, he was kind of a gateway drug to me?" Rachel responds: "I guess so. Who knows what'll be next?" At which Dev says: "I do. White guy." They then both laugh. It is through such exchanges that *Master of None* attempts to illustrate some of the mental schemas individuals have about the intermixing of races and the type of scenarios that those involved in mixed race relationships often encounter in society.

Some scholars, however, criticize such programs that use subtle humor to address racism as not going far enough. In her analysis of the married black–white couple Brad Williams (played by black actor Damon Wayans, Jr.) and Jane Williams (played by white actress Eliza Coupe) in the ABC sitcom *Happy Endings* (2011–2013), media studies researcher Jodi Rightler-McDaniels (2014) notes that the program provided only "glimpses" into the societal difficulties of being in an interracial relationship, but failed to offer any kind of dissection of the inequities. She provides an example from an episode in which Brad and Jane go out for dinner and end up waiting a long time for their food. When the people sitting at another table are served before them, Brad comments, "'Oh, come on. They got here like 20 minutes after us. This is totally because we're Black on blonde'" (Rightler-McDaniels 2014: 118). No follow-up is offered; it ends as a one-off punch line.

Other sitcoms have opted not to even bring up race as a factor in interracial relationships. Programs including NBC's *Parks & Recreation* (2009–2015), with the couple Tom Haverford (played by Aziz Ansari mentioned above) and Ann Perkins (played by Rashida Jones), and ABC's short-lived *Mr. Sunshine* (2011), with the couple Alice (played by white actress Andrea Anders) and Alonzo Pope (played by black actor James Lesure), simply paired individuals from differing racial/ethnic backgrounds without presenting any dialogue that touched on race. Even the popular CW sitcom *Jane the Virgin* (2014–present) starring Latina actress Gina Rodriguez as Jane Villanueva, an aspiring writer who has developed relationships with both hotel owner/manager Rafael Solano (played by Latino actor Justin Baldoni) and police officer Michael Cordero, Jr. (played by white actor Brett Dier), avoids touching on the racial difference between Jane and Michael. This approach of avoiding race as an issue in the depictions of interracial couples is also found in television dramas.

In dramas such as NBC's *Parenthood* (2010–2015), with married couple Crosby Braverman (played by white actor Dax Shepard) and Jasmine Trussell (played by black actress Joy Bryant), when problems are shown to exist in the interracial unions, the root of the problems are depicted as being due to diverging personalities, rather than anything associated with race. Children of the mixed race couple are also shown not to be struggling with racial identity issues, although in one episode of *Parenthood*, titled "The Talk," when Crosby and Jasmine's son Jabbar (played by mixed race actor Tyree Brown) hears a rapper using the "N word" in a song, the couple take time to help the young boy understand the history of racism and white privilege.

During its run, ABC's one-hour hospital drama *Grey's Anatomy* (2005–2016) incorporated several interracial relationships in its storylines including the following: Dr. Cristina Yang (played by Asian American Sandra Oh) and Dr. Preston Burke (played by black actor Isaiah Washington); Dr. Callie Torres (played by Latina actress Sara Ramirez) and Dr. Arizona Robbins (played by white actress Jessica Capshaw); Dr. Lexi Grey (played by white actress Chyler Leigh) and Dr. Jackson Avery (played by mixed race actor Jesse Williams). While the program occasionally explored the struggles of being in a mixed race relationship, for the most part its storylines were primarily focused on the idiosyncratic personalities of the characters.

A similar approach has been taken in the highly rated one-hour ABC television drama *Scandal* (2012 debut). One of the storylines involves the star character Olivia Pope (played by black actress Kerry Washington), a powerful DC political crisis manager, being pulled between two love interests, US President Fitzgerald Grant (played by white actor Tony Goldwyn) and former CIA operative Jake Ballard (played by white actor Scott Foley). Although Olivia was once engaged to a US Senator, Edison Davis (played by black actor Norm Lewis), she finds herself more attracted to Grant and Ballard, who are complicated and offer a tint of excitement and even pain. In all of these relationships, race is not made out to be a factor.

It should be noted that Shonda Rhimes, the creator and executive producer of both *Grey's Anatomy* and *Scandal*, in her various media interviews has stressed that when considering actors for her characters, she does not consider race. She bases her selection on who she thinks will play the character well. In an interview with *Elle* magazine, Rhimes noted, "For many showrunners, you have one black character or one Asian or one female, and then that character seems to represent everybody in your head – as opposed to making that character a person." Rhimes stresses that she has approached each character as being "its own organic thing" (Myers 2015).

However, Erica Childs (2009: 56) finds the lack of addressing race in the programs to be problematic. She argues that, "Just because race is not discussed does not mean it does not exist, rather in its deliberate denial it can be ever more present." She goes on to state, "The fantasy of interracial relationships can not be bogged down with the unpleasantness of racism, inequality, and discrimination, so it erases these structural and institutional realities that shape everyday social interaction" (2009: 57). (See Box 8.1.)

Such an assessment would resonate with the encounters that actress Diane Farr had when she tried to pitch an idea to Fox television for a series about an interracial couple, partially based on her experiences of being married to a Korean American man. Fox executives are said to have decided not to give her proposed program the green light because they had thought the script she wrote was too direct in dealing with interracial unions. In an interview with Montreal newspaper *The Gazette*, Farr expressed her frustration at seeing minorities written into scripts for the sake of having a minority. She is quoted as saying, "It's jarring, because rarely in American society do you see a mixed-race couple where there's never a comment about it. So welcoming as it seems to put in a black and white

Box 8.1 Scene from *How to Get Away with Murder*: How would you decode it?

Figure 8.3 Annalise Keating (played by Viola Davis) and Sam Keating (played by Tom Verica) in *How to Get Away with Murder* (2014–). Screenshot.

The ABC television hit drama series *How to Get Away with Murder* debuted in fall of 2014 and quickly attracted a mass following. Created by Peter Nowalk, who also serves as executive producer along with Shonda Rhimes (creator of *Grey's Anatomy* and *Scandal*) and others, the show stars black actress Viola Davis as Annalise Keating, a no-nonsense defense attorney and law professor at a prestigious university in Philadelphia. Annalise's courtroom approach is to win at any cost and she teaches this to the five law students she selected to intern at her private law firm. At the beginning of season 1, viewers are introduced to Annalise's husband, professor Sam Keating (played by white actor Tom Verica), who at first, by all appearances, appears to be a loving husband. It is soon revealed, though, that Annalise suspects Sam of having had an affair with and then murdering one of his students.

The scene in which Annalise confronts Sam with her knowledge is both provocative and gut-wrenching (Figure 8.3). In the scene, Annalise not only tells Sam about her suspicions, she also informs him that she too was having an affair. At the news Sam becomes enraged; he attempts to walk away from Annalise, but she follows and taunts him with descriptions of her affair. The following ensues:

ANNALISE: Which is how I could sleep with you all these months because I would think about him and I would be able to stand you on top of me.
Sam turns around, puts his hands around her throat and pushes Annalise against the wall.

SAM (*shouting*): And I'd think of Lila [*murdered student*] every time I tried to get off with you.

ANNALISE
(*in a hushed tone*): I bet you did. You killed her and I bet you enjoyed it. Strangling her. Letting her life go out of her body. You still think about it, don't you? Your hand around her neck, while you were still inside of her. It's exciting you right now, isn't it, remembering it. You want to do it to me now, don't you? Go ahead. Kill me. Kill me. (*now shouting*) Kill me!
Sam takes his hands away from Annalise's throat.

(Continued)

Box 8.1   (Continued)

SAM (*calmly speaking
     as if in shock*):   You're a monster.

ANNALISE: Monster, huh. Is that all you got? You can do better than that.

SAM: You want the truth? You're nothing but a piece of a*s. That's what I saw when I first talked to you in the office that day. Because I knew you'd put out. That's all you're really good for – dirty, rough sex that I'm too ashamed to tell anyone about it. That's how foul you are. You disgusting slut.

ANNALISE
(*in a hushed tone*):   Well. At least you were finally able to tell the truth.

In visualizing the above scene, what images come to mind? How might those images connect with embedded societal notions of what it means to be a black–white couple? Race is never brought up in the scene, but the scene may elicit certain race-related imagery. Sexuality paired with violence may produce images that harken back to the days of slavery when white male slave owners sexually abused their black female slaves.

---

couple or a Mexican and Asian couple, if everybody else on the series is white, it kind of begs for comment. And without comment, it kind of feels gratuitous" (quoted in Deggans 2011: C8).

It is within this trend of television shows presenting interracial couples without substantively touching on the societal struggles they face that the ABC one-hour drama series *The Fosters* (2013 debut), co-created by Peter Paige and Bradley Bredeweg and executive produced by Jennifer Lopez, comes across as especially unique. The program not only presents a diverse family – multiethnic children with lesbian parents, Stef (played by white actress Teri Polo) and Lena (played by biracial actress Sherri Saum) – which is rare in entertainment television, but it also deals with hard-hitting issues pertaining to societal experiences of mixed race individuals or those in mixed race relationships. Consider the following dialogue that takes place at the Quinceanera (fifteenth birthday party) thrown for Lena and Stef's adopted Latina daughter, Mariana (Cierra Alexa Ramirez). The conversation is between Lena, who is biracial and light-skinned, and her mother Dana (Lorraine Toussaint), who is a dark-skinned black woman:

DANA: This is a lot to spend on a birthday party.

LENA: Well, it's not just a birthday party. This is about Mariana embracing her cultural heritage, about being a part of a Latino community.

DANA: Which, of course, she isn't. I'm just saying that being Latina isn't just about the color of her skin.

LENA: But being Black is?

DANA: What?

LENA: For you, being Black has always been about the color of a person's skin.

DANA: That's not true.

LENA: Yes. It is.

DANA: All I ever said is that dark-skinned people have a different experience than light-skinned blacks.

LENA:	And by different you mean more authentic.
DANA:	I mean harder. Honey, dark-skinned people face more discrimination. That is just a fact of life.
LENA:	So maybe we are trying to make up for what we couldn't give Mariana, but I understand how she feels.
DANA:	Do you now? You were raised by a black mother.
LENA:	And by a white father. And I never felt accepted by either community, mom.
DANA:	Well, I'm so sorry you've had such a tough time being a beautiful, light-skinned woman.
LENA:	Oh, mom, come on.
DANA:	But like it or not, the color of your skin has afforded you more opportunities than anyone like me has ever had.
LENA:	You see. That is something you've always assumed. That being biracial has made my life easier.
DANA:	Because it has. Like it or not, you will never know what it is like to be a black woman in America.

Lena looks at her mother in disbelief and ends the conversation by walking away from her.

Although some may say inclusion of such dialogue is calling too much attention to race and taking away from the notion of just presenting a diverse group of characters in important roles, it and other scripting from *The Fosters* does raise important social issues that have the potential of spurring on further dialogue amongst viewers. In fact, when we move on to how the news media have covered mixed race individuals and unions, news stories for the most part have focused on the problems that such individuals or couples face in their everyday lives.

Representations of Mixed Race Individuals and Relationships in the News

The news media are often the locations where understandings can be gained on how and why certain discourses appear regarding race mixing. When the topic is covered, the focus tends to be on either the degree of societal acceptance of interracial couples or the identity struggles of multiracial/multiethnic individuals. As discussed in Chapter 2, however, the framing of messages within news stories often determines what take or assumptions consumers of those messages will take away from the stories. For example, in her analysis of news media coverage of the release of the 2000 Census data and its newly created "multiracial" category, communication studies professor Catherine Squires found variations in how the "white-dominant" press, the black press, and Asian American press covered the story (Squires 2007). Among the differences that she found was that the dominant press tended to highlight the idea that "race" as a system of classification would end with the growing emergence of multiracial individuals, while the black press was inclined to emphasize the impact that the new category would have on black political and economic power. The Asian American press tended to discuss the separation of multiracial Asians from Asian Americans and the political implications of undercounting Asian Americans.

Mass communication researchers Catherine Luther and Jodi-Rightler McDaniels (2013: 1–30) also found differences in how the mainstream press and the black press covered marriages between Blacks and Whites. The researchers examined news stories on the topic that appeared in the broad-reach magazines of *Time* and *Newsweek* and Black-targeted magazines of *JET* and *Ebony* over a

50-year time span beginning in 1960. They found consistent themes across the time period for both sets of magazines. The major theme, which all four of the news magazines shared, was that while marriages between Blacks and Whites were increasing in the United States, racist attitudes toward black–white couples still existed. The articles emphasized that individuals who were in interracial relationships and their children faced serious societal difficulties. The broad-reach magazines, however, presented children of mixed couples as beacons of hope for bringing about true racial unity because of their mixed ethnic background. On the other hand, the Black-targeted magazines tended to stress the importance of maintaining a black identity and encouraged biracial children to adopt that identity in order to survive psychologically. In both sets of magazines, long-ingrained notions of race and the social structures reinforcing such notions were not addressed. Instead, the theme that was connoted was that racism is fundamentally an individual-level phenomenon. The study's findings resonate with Catherine Squires's argument that "in most mainstream news media accounts, multiracial identity is yet another vehicle for denying the social import of race and reinforcing the dominant notion that race is a matter of individual tastes and psychology, not structural inequalities" (2007: 2).

A few documentaries or television news specials have been produced that have explored issues involving interracial unions and mixed race children. The 2014 documentary *Little White Lie* tells the story of Lacey Schwartz who comes to terms with her biracial background after finding out, while in college, that she is not white, but rather a mix of black and white. The film tells of how it was finally revealed to Lacey that her biological father was actually a black family friend. Although her physical appearance betrayed her racial background, her parents and her community had lived in denial, unwilling to face the truth. In 2012, Anderson Cooper had a special on CNN that examined the generational divide on acceptance of interracial dating. The program presented youngsters who were interested in dating an individual from a different race, but also were being either discouraged or forbidden from such dating by their parents/guardians.

If one goes on YouTube, several mini documentaries or video commentaries on the mixing of races can be found. Some are designed to make serious societal statements while others are for the purposes of proclaiming prejudicial messages. It is just one amongst a number of social media platforms that have been utilized by ordinary citizens to express opinions on the subject matter.

Mixed Race Individuals/Couples and New Media

Producers of films, television shows, and news media have increasingly utilized various forms of new media to reach out to consumers. Social media, in particular, have been used to better engage with their audiences and readers. Via microblogging and photo-sharing sites (e.g., Twitter, Instagram, Tumblr), entire online communities revolving around a particular film or show have emerged. Executive producer of hit dramatic television dramas Shonda Rhimes has been particularly active in using social media to promote her shows. In an interview with *Elle* magazine, Rhimes described how she enjoys interacting with fans through social media: "What I like about being online is that you can put your message out there immediately, and I can respond to something instantaneously. Fans get very intense" (Myers 2015). Using social media is a savvy way of getting audiences to discuss television shows and pull them in deeper to the ongoing storylines. Media studies researcher Naeemah Clark (2016: 179–193) examined *Scandal's* online community and found that members would often blur the line between fact and fiction. The members often experienced a real connection with the show's characters and expressed views as if they knew the characters on a personal level.

When examining general Twitter feeds regarding *Scandal* as well as other shows depicting interracial couples, however, one can also observe the darker side of social media. While social media have offered producers and consumers the opportunity to engage with each other and create online communities, social media have also made it much easier for individuals to spout out vitriol. For example, after the release of a General Mills Cheerios television/online commercial in the summer of 2013 that featured a black father, a white mother, and their mixed race daughter, hateful messages regarding the commercial appeared on social media. Although the ad had a heartfelt message about the daughter wanting her dad to remain healthy, it immediately provoked angry messages that were posted online on Facebook, Reddit, and YouTube among others. It got to the point where the comments were so ugly that Cheerios had to ask YouTube to shut down its posted commercial's "comments" function.

Mainstream news media picked up on the Cheerios story and the social media posts that then followed were positive and in support of the commercial. In 2014, Cheerios released another commercial featuring the same family – this time with the father announcing to his daughter that she was soon going to have a baby brother. The commercial debuted during the 2014 Superbowl broadcast. As it was Cheerios's first Superbowl commercial, observers speculated that the company, with the commercial's expensive placement, wanted to provide a firm affirmation of its support for the commercial's concept. Although the second ad did not receive the flurry of messages that the first ad received, hateful posts regarding the ad still appeared in number along with supportive posts.

Even though a commercial featuring a biracial couple elicited strong negative responses from viewers, it is interesting to note that similar phenomena have not been found with ads featuring individuals of mixed race. In fact, multiracial identity has become in vogue amongst advertisers. With the popularity of so-called racially ambiguous stars such as Nicole Scherzinger, Jessica Alba, Shannyn Sossamon, Zoe Kravitz, Vin Diesel, Mariah Carey, and Wentworth Miller, advertisers have sought models who are racially ambiguous to appear in their ads across all media platforms. The idea is that because consumers are uncertain of the racial/ethnic identity of the appearing model, the ads might be more successful in capturing a broader market.

Another idea that has been expressed by advertisers is the certain magnetism that they believe mixed race individuals bring to the table. President of IMG models Ivan Bart was once quoted as stating, in reference to a mixed race female model, that part of the model's allure was her racially ambiguous looks. He believed it made consumers "play a guessing game" and states, "The fact you can't be sure is part of her seductiveness" (Ferla 2003). From a critical standpoint, this trend for using models who are racially ambiguous because of their apparent seductive qualities does cause one to consider if exoticism or even eroticism that has long been ascribed to female persons of color is now being simply extended to multiracial/multiethnic individuals.

This notion of privileging mixed race individuals has also been discussed via social media. In fact, posts often quickly appear when celebrities make supportive comments about their own or their children's biracial or multiracial background. Actor Taye Diggs provoked social media chatter when during an interview he did while promoting his children's book *Mixed Me* he expressed his desire for his biracial son not to have to choose between being identified as black or white. While some applauded Diggs's stance via social media, others saw the comment as an affront to the black community and as a sign of Diggs's self-loathing due to his skin tone. In a similar vein, ABC's *The View* talk show co-host Raven-Symone caught a firestorm of criticism on Twitter when she shared with Oprah Winfrey during her appearance on OWN that she does not like to be labeled as African American. Although Raven-Symone attempted to clarify this by stating, "I don't label myself. What I really mean by that is I'm an American. I have darker skin. I have a nice, interesting grade of hair.

I connect with Caucasian. I connect with Asian. I connect with black," the statement led to viewers petitioning the ABC network to have her removed from *The View* (quoted in Hare 2014).

Partly to counteract negative messages on mixed race relationships/children and partially to build a support community, various related websites and Facebook pages have also appeared in recent years. Some are designed mainly to allow individuals to upload user-generated content related to interracial couples or mixed race individuals. For example, Ethnicouples.com allows couples to upload photo(s) and provide snippets of information about their union (e.g., how they met, length of relationship, public reactions to their union, etc.). The site organizes the photos by race/ethnicity of the couples so that visitors can do a search. After receiving inspiration from the mixed race family Cheerios ad, Wearethe15percent.com was created; it allows interracial families to post family photos as a form of celebrating mixed race unions. Other sites, such as Interracialmarriageandfamily.com, are intended to provide support and resources for interracial couples or families. MixTogether.org specifically offers users counsel on how individuals involved in an interracial relationship can deal with opposition from their family members or community.

Concluding Remarks

At the beginning of this chapter, a poignant quote was provided that conveys the uphill battles interracial couples often faced in the United States during the 1960s. The quote was from the 1967 film *Guess Who's Coming for Dinner*, and at the end of the quote, readers of this book were asked whether or not they believed the quote would still ring true today. So, after having read this chapter, and given your own personal insights, how would you respond? Our assessment is that although societal acceptance has shifted in a positive direction, further strides need to be made.

Mass media have indeed reflected society's ideas about the mixing of races. In the early years of film, indications of intimacy between races, especially between Blacks and Whites, were strictly restricted. As restrictions eased with the political and societal changes that took place to secure the civil rights of minority groups, films began to include plots designed to explore the injustices that mixed race couples or mixed race individuals faced.

In terms of television, following the gains made in the civil rights movement of the 1960s, television producers came under pressure to feature more characters who were people of color. Along with including characters from racial minority groups, a few television creators began to include, albeit in a minimal manner, mixed race couples in their programs' storylines. By the 2000s, the inclusion of interracial couples as well as mixed race individuals became more noticeable.

While these are signs of progress, the lack of longevity in the interracial unions and the almost doomsday scenarios attached to mixed race couples or individuals within films and television programs suggest that further work needs to be done in order to bring about true societal acceptance of racial border crossings. Even the news media still tend to highlight the problems that interracial couples and biracial/multiracial individuals encounter on a daily basis.

It appears that when steps are taken to move society forward in a positive direction by including storylines that feature mixed race individuals or couples, other forces appear that are designed to rein in the positive movement. For example, when the anxiously anticipated *Star Wars: The Force Awakens* opened in 2015, and the central plot and characters were revealed, some praised the inclusion of a black hero, Finn (John Boyega), and the white heroine, Rey (Daisy Ridley), and hints in the movie that the two might have affection for each other. At the same time, however, the casting sparked a degree of chatter on social media that frowned upon the possibility of Finn and Rey developing as a couple. It appears the acceptance of mixed race couples will only significantly diminish when racist views regarding differing minority racial groups are eradicated. The media have moved toward making this happen, but further advancements are required.

Reflection Questions and Thoughts to Consider

Some scholars maintain that the inclusion of biracial/multiracial characters or mixed race couples in media entertainment offers those in power the opportunity to argue that institutional racism no longer exists. They say that television shows (in particular) that present mixed race individuals or couples without addressing issues of racism are doing a disservice to society. What do you think? Should issues of race always be woven into the storylines of such shows or should such couples/individuals be simply placed into a show and treated as any other couple/individual?

1. In the summer of 2015, the racial identity of Spokane, Washington's NAACP chapter leader Rachel Dolezal came under question after her mother shared with the public that Dolezal was being dishonest about her race and that both of her parents were white. Up until that point, Dolezal had been representing herself as African American with also a mixture of Native American and White. The case elicited a number of comments on social media about "passing" and the idea that perhaps individuals could cross over to another racial identity ("transracial"). In fact, "transracial" became a trending hashtag on Twitter. What do you think? If race is a social construction, is it okay for individuals to adopt a racial category with which they have no connection?
2. Think about the depictions of mixed race relationships that you have seen on television. Do you think the type of treatment the couples receive depends on whether or not the characters making up the couple are both people of color versus if one of the characters is white?
3. Do you think that high-profile mixed race couples (e.g., reality star Kim Kardashian and hip-hop artist Kanye West; singer/actress Selena Gomez and singer Justin Bieber; singer/actress Ariana Grande and rapper Big Sean) have the power to shape general acceptance of mixed race couples?

References

Alvins, Alfred. 1966. "Anti-Miscegenation Laws and the Fourteenth Amendment: The Original Intent." *Virginia Law Review* 9(7): 1224–1255.

Beeman, Angela. 2007. "Emotional Segregation: A Content Analysis of Institutional Racism in USFilms, 1980–2001." *Ethnic and Racial Studies* 30(5): 687–712.

Beltran, Mary. 2008. "Mixed Race in Latinowood: Latino Stardom and Ethnic Ambiguity in the Era of Dark Angels." In *Mixed Race Hollywood*, edited by Mary Beltran and Camilla Fojas, 248–268. New York, NY: New York University Press.

Bramlett-Solomon, Sharon. 2007. "Interracial Love on Television: What's Taboo Still and What's Not." In *Critical Thinking about Sex, Love, and Romance in the Mass Media*, edited by Mary-LouGalican and Debra L. Merskin, 85–93. Mahwah, NJ: Lawrence Erlbaum.

Childs, Erica. 2009. *Fade to Black and White: Interracial Images in Popular Culture*. Plymouth, UK: Rowman & Littlefield.

Clark, Naeemah. 2016. "Connecting in the Scandalverse: The Power of Social Media and Parasocial Relationships." In *Digital Technology and the Future of Broadcasting: Global Perspectives*, edited by John V. Pavlik, 179–193. New York, NY: Routledge.

Deggans, Eric. 2011. "Is Television Colour-Blind to Interracial Couples?: TV's Mixed-Race Matchups Are Laudable, But Cultural Diversity Isn't Always Discussed." *The Gazette*, February 23, C8.

Farber, Paul Lawrence. 2011. *Mixing Races: From Scientific Racism to Modern Evolutionary Ideas*. Baltimore, MD: Johns Hopkins University Press.

Ferla, Ruth La. 2003. "Generation E.A.: Ethnically Ambiguous." *New York Times*, December 28. http://www.nytimes.com/2003/12/28/style/generation-ea-ethnically-ambiguous.html?pagewanted=all (accessed April 10, 2017).

Friedman, Ryan Jay. 2011. *Hollywood's African American Films: The Transition to Sound*. New Brunswick, NJ: Rutgers University Press.

Gullickson, Aaron. 2006. "Black/White Interracial Marriage Trends, 1850–2000." *Journal of Family History* 31(3): 289–312.

Hare, Breeanna. 2014. "Raven-Symone: I'm Not Gay, and I'm Not African-American." CNN. Accessed January 8, 2016. http://edition.cnn.com/2014/10/06/showbiz/raven-symone-gay-labels (accessed April 10, 2017).

Jones, Christopher John. 1981. "Image and Ideology in Kazan's Pinky." *Literature Film Quarterly* 9(2): 110–121.

Karthikevan, Hrishi, and Gabriel J. Chin. 2002. "Preserving Racial Identity: Population Patterns and the Application of Anti-Miscegenation Statures to Asian Americans, 1910–1950." *Asian American Law Journal* 9(1): 1–40.

Luther, Catherine A., and Jodi L. Rightler-McDaniels 2013. "'More Trouble Than the Good Lord Ever Intended': Representations of Interracial Marriage in U.S. News Magazines." *Journal of Magazine & New Media Research* 14(1): 1–30.

Myers, Robbie. 2015. "Shonda Rhimes on Power, Feminism, and Police Brutality." *Elle*. http://www.elle.com/culture/career-politics/q-and-a/a30186/shonda-rhimes-elle-interview (accessed April 10, 2017).

NPR Staff. 2015. "100 Years Later, What's the Legacy of 'Birth of a Nation'?" *NPR.org*. http://www.npr.org/sections/codeswitch/2015/02/08/383279630/100-years-later-whats-the-legacy-of-birth-of-a-nation (accessed April 10, 2017).

Perry, Barbara, and Michael Sutton. 2006. "Seeing Red Over Black and White: Popular and Media Representations of Inter-racial Relationships as Precursors to Racial Violence." *Canadian Journal of Criminology and Criminal Justice* 48(6): 887–904.

Rightler-McDaniels, Jodi Lynn. 2014. "Drawing the Primetime Color Line: A Critical Discourse Analysis of Interracial Marriages in Television Sitcoms." PhD dissertation, University of Tennessee.

Romano, Renee C. 2003. *Race Mixing: Black–White Marriage in Postwar America*. Cambridge, MA: Harvard University Press.

Squires, Catherine R. 2007. *Dispatches from the Color Line: The Press and Multiracial America*. Albany, NY: State University of New York Press.

Valdiva, Angharad. 2008. "Mixed Race on the Disney Channel: From *Johnnie Tsunami* through *Lizzie McGuire* and Ending with *The Cheetah Girls*." In *Mixed Race Hollywood*, edited by Mary Betran and Camilla Fojas, 269–289. New York, NY: New York University Press.

Wang, Wendy. 2015. "Interracial Marriage: Who is 'Marrying Out'?" Pew Research Center. http://www.pewresearch.org/fact-tank/2015/06/12/interracial-marriage-who-is-marrying-out (accessed April 10, 2017).

Wardle, Lynn D. 1998. "Loving v. Virginia and The Constitutional Right to Marry, 1790–1990." *Howard Journal of Law* 41(2): 289–347.

West, Cornel. 1994. *Race Matters*. New York, NY: Vintage Press.

9

Representations of Gender in Television, Film, and Music Videos

In *Entertainment Weekly*, on August 13, 2010, columnist Mark Harris suggested reintroducing a 25-year-old "rule" – the so-called Bechdel test, first made famous by Alison Bechdel, creator of the comic strip "Dykes to Watch Out For." The test was a simple one, designed to test whether or not a movie was worth seeing. The questions were:

1. Does the movie have at least two women in it?
2. Do they ever talk to each other?

and

3. Is that conversation about something besides a man?

A fourth question was added later:

4. Do the women have names?

If the answers to the questions were all "yes," the movie was deemed worth viewing.

Harris contends that though the Bechdel test standard is pitifully minimal, film studios today continue to fail the test, producing movies that marginalize women. He points out that females in movies deserve better names than "Female Junkie," "Mr. Anderson's Secretary," and "Topless Party Girl." While he astutely argues that not every movie needs to pass the Bechdel test, and some wonderful films would be made worse by having some artificial "rule of law" put down forcing quotas or types of women to be used in every movie, he questions why it seems so difficult to find, in many movies, gender balance and women treated like actual human beings instead of props.

Gender, like each of the racial/ethnic identities discussed in this book so far, is central in shaping a person's identity, determining not only how a person looks at the world, but also how the world looks at him or her. As mentioned in the introduction, gender is distinct from biological sex, though there is a relationship between the two. Sociologist and leading researcher on men and masculinity Michael Kimmel explains, "biological sex – by which we mean the chromosomal, chemical, anatomical apparatuses that make us either male or female – leads inevitably to 'gender,' by which we mean the cultural and social meanings, experiences, and institutional structures that are defined as appropriate for males and females. 'Sex' is male and female; 'gender' refers to cultural definitions of masculinity and femininity – the meanings of maleness and femaleness" (2000: 1–2).

Diversity in US Mass Media, Second Edition. Catherine A. Luther, Carolyn Ringer Lepre, and Naeemah Clark.
© 2018 John Wiley & Sons Inc. Published 2018 by John Wiley & Sons Inc.

Although gender identity and stereotyping of both sexes is certainly worthy of study, the bulk of this and the next chapter will focus on the framing and stereotyping of women, as this group has a longer history of marginalization in media and society. Today, men still dominate both the entertainment and news media environments. However, there are important issues of stereotyping that pertain to men. Those issues as well as a discussion of media representations of masculinity will be presented.

This chapter will first discuss gender theories, outline a brief history of women as a group and the women's movement in the United States, and then explore the history of gender representation in film, television, and music videos, along with specific examples within each medium.

Historical Background to Gender Representations in Film and Television

Numerous studies have been done on representations of gender in the media. Gender theorists, sociologists, and feminists critically analyze gender issues in television, film, and other media forms, offering much to consider. According to socialization theory, and other interpersonal theories that focus on the impact that relationships have on gender development, individuals learn about gender, and about what it means to be masculine or feminine, according to what they observe around them, including what they see in the mass media. From birth, people are socialized into gender roles, taught by parents and other people and elements in the cultural environment. How people come to understand themselves intersects with the way they see others like themselves constructed around them. Biology does not make women, for instance, more inherently qualified to care for an infant than a man, but certain cultures teach children that this is a gender norm. Anthropologist Margaret Mead (1935) found in her studies of primitive tribes in New Guinea that masculine and feminine gender roles had little to do with biologic sex. For instance, comparing two of the tribes she studied extensively, she found that in one tribe, women were the primary caregivers and the men were hunter-gatherers (much like US society), but in the other, the roles were reversed.

There have been times in history when gender has been the deciding factor in whether or not a person could hold a job, what kind of job a person could hold, if a person could inherit land or own a home, how a person was regarded by law, and how a person could acceptably dress. Though gender no longer so completely determines one's place in American society, there are unspoken rules for behaving as a man or a woman, and these "rules" are used to identify the gender of other people. When these "rules" are violated – for instance, if someone dresses and acts in a way that is gender ambiguous – it can be confusing and uncomfortable for those around them (Laflen 2010).

As discussed in Chapter 2, cultural theorists tend to look at gender through the lens of power and politics. In these theories, there are dominant groups, who control the majority of the power, wealth, and privileges, and there are targeted groups, who have less access to these resources (Holtzman 2000: 55–60). In the United States, historically men constitute the dominant social group, and women the targeted minority group. As media researcher Linda Holtzman (2000: 55–60) points out, this does not mean, however, that all men have tremendous power and wealth, nor that all women lack privileges and opportunities. Rather, the hegemonic domination of men over women creates a society in which masculinity is favored over femininity, and greater opportunities are provided to those men who possess masculine traits. In the end, this translates to greater economic and professional success for men.

Over the past 80 years, women, though comprising more than half of the population in virtually any given year, have had to fight for equal rights with men in terms of voting, pay, employment opportunity, leadership opportunity, and more. Like many of the other marginalized groups discussed in this book, women have found themselves forced to prove that, as a social group, they are deserving of the same rights and opportunities as men. Over this 80-year period, entertainment media have reflected and created the phases and changes that women as a group have experienced.

In the 1920s, first-wave feminists fought for the right to vote and basic rights for women. Forty years later, as generations of women were still being raised to believe that their place was best served in the home, the product of second-wave feminism was born: the 1960s career woman. She was single, working, and proud of it. While most women were still stay-at-home mothers or housewives, electronic media brought images of this new career woman into stronger focus, though a prominent image on television was still that of the "perfect nuclear family," with mom as the nurturer.

The 1970s continued the push by the second-wave feminists, who wished to address many de facto women's rights, including those related to reproduction, family, sexuality, and the workplace. Two groups of feminists became more prominent during this time (Steeves 1987). One group was the liberal feminists who stressed the principles of liberal political philosophy and called for an end to the economic and political inequities that they believed were holding women back in society. Their focus was on creating laws and institutions that would provide women with a broader range of employment opportunities and equal pay. The other group was the so-called radical feminists. These feminists stressed the innate biological differences between the sexes and called for radically alternative lifestyles that essentially entailed a separation between men and women. Radical feminists such as Mary Daly and Shulamith Firestone urged women to break free from the patriarchy that was dominating women. Daly went as far as to propose that women create their own language, arguing that the status quo language was helping to maintain patriarchy.

Both liberal and radical feminists have evolved since the 1970s. For example, many radical feminists today do not place as much stress on the biological source of domination, but rather put more emphasis on the patriarchal systems that they believe are political and cultural constructions. From this position, many radical feminists now share with liberal feminists the goal of educating women and helping them to rally against what many advocates viewed as cultural misrepresentations of women, and more specifically, the stereotypical images portrayed in the mass media, especially those in film and on television.

Although both liberal feminists and radical feminists have continued to fight for their causes, since the late 1990s they have been joined by a new group of feminists. Coming from different perspectives on feminism, these new feminists became part of the so-called third-wave feminism or post-feminism, which has been marked by both confusion and change. On the one hand, post-feminists, long taught that they can have it all (marriage, children, career, success, money), are taking a step back and realizing that though that may be true, they may not want it all. They are choosing the stay-at-home mother and wife route, acknowledging that they are not giving up their inherent rights, and that it is not merely acceptable, it is exemplary, to be the caregiver for one's family. They suggest that there is no shame, as feminists argued in earlier decades, in identifying with this traditional gender role. As long as women have a choice about the role they choose to fill, that is what is important. However, this very choice often leads to an identity crisis: "After all I have worked for, am I really going to give it all up just to stay at home?"

Others interpret this third-wave feminist movement as a declaration that women are equal and thus "done," needing no longer to fight as a collective group – a sisterhood fighting against "the man." Third-wave feminism encourages personal choices, empowerment, and individuality. Women should be strong, but do not need to – and should not – ignore their femininity: picture the powerful female executive with her pencil skirt and Manolo Blahniks.

One other theory worth noting that has added substantially to the way gender and gender roles are interpreted was presented by Judith Butler in her book *Gender Trouble: Feminism and the Subversion of Identity* (1999: 3–101). In this book, Butler discusses "queer theory," briefly introduced in Chapter 2 of this book. The theory fundamentally argues that gender is all about performance, and that there is no such thing as "gender identity." Basing her ideas on queer theory, Butler suggests that nothing within gender identity is fixed, and that a person has no "inner self." Everything having to do with gender is performed – often culturally constructed – and sometimes that performance is unconsciously chosen. These gender performances are reinforced through repetition.

Butler also argues, however, that because all of gender identity is performance, people can change. The socially constructed gender roles of masculinity and femininity are breakable, and should be challenged because gender is simply something a person does and not the essence of a person. Entertainment media, with its widespread public appeal, offers a perfect place to examine the portrayals of gender roles across the past century.

As a case in point, Patricia Arquette's seemingly courageous call for equity speaks to the complexity of gender dynamics. In a passionate plea to change the status of women in the film industry and in the country at large, Arquette used her time on the Oscar stage after winning the Best Actress award for her role of Mom in *Boyhood* (2014) to call on the world to respect the contributions of women. She said her thanks "to every woman who gave birth, to every taxpayer and citizen of this nation, we have fought for everybody else's equal rights. It's our time to have wage equality once and for all and equal rights for women in the United States of America."

However, once she got off the stage, she was asked to elaborate on her sentiments and she remarked, "It's time for all the women in America and all the men that love women, and all the gay people, and all the people of color that we've all fought for to fight for us now" (Hod 2015). To some, it sent a signal that feminism is generally only for white women. Intersectionality was not a part of her call to action. Moments such as this remind us that gender issues are multilayered and complex because womanhood comes in different shapes, sizes, colors, attitudes, and behaviors. It is necessary that media reflect all of these layers.

Gender in Film

In her book *Women and Media: Content, Careers, Criticism*, communication professor Cynthia M. Lont (1995: 265) writes that "in the 1920s, films stereotyped men and women. Women were flappers, working girls, virgins or vamps. Men were gallant and macho in such roles as pioneers, western heroes, thieves, pirates, and war heroes." The early 1930s brought a more liberated woman, who initiated sexual encounters, pursued men, and had power, such as the roles made famous by actresses Greta Garbo, Jean Harlow, and Marlene Dietrich. But this liberation would not last. Much of the reason for this limited range of roles was the Motion Picture Production Code, known as the Hays Code, also mentioned in other chapters of this book. In 1930, the Motion Picture Producers and Distributors of America, Inc. (1930) adopted a detailed list of rules (nicknamed for its creator, Will Hays) to set morality standards for moviemakers. Part of the code demanded that there be no scenes showing passion, sexual innuendo, and women of questionable character.

By the 1950s, the most popular films of the time, including *High Noon* (1952), *12 Angry Men* (1957), and *North by Northwest* (1959), almost always focused on male heroes. Men were sexually assertive, in charge, and powerful, while women were frightened, in need of protection, and there to provide love to support the male lead (Gauntlett 2002: 46–62). In *North by Northwest*, which follows the

Hitchcock formula of an ordinary man put into an extraordinary situation, advertising executive Roger O. Thornhill (played by Cary Grant) is pursued across the country after he is mistaken for a government agent. After sneaking onto a train headed toward Chicago, he meets a beautiful blonde woman named Eve Kendall (played by Eva Marie Saint). The two become close very quickly, and fall in love. As their sexual tension builds, Roger's masculinity, typical of movies of this time period, is apparent:

EVE: I want to know more about you.

ROGER: What more could you know?

EVE: You're an advertising man, that's all I know.

ROGER: That's right. The train's a little unsteady.

EVE: Who isn't?

ROGER: What else do you know?

EVE: You've got taste in clothes, taste in food …

ROGER: … and taste in women. I like your flavor.

EVE: You're very clever with words. You can probably make them do anything for you. Sell people things they don't need. Make women who don't know you fall in love with you.

ROGER: I'm beginning to think I'm underpaid.

At the end of the movie, Roger and Eve are chased to the top of Mount Rushmore. Though their lives are in the balance, Roger pauses for a moment and suggests that if they get out of this alive, they should go back on the train together for another romantic interlude. Even in the midst of danger, Roger still shows the audience his romantic chops. After scaling the face of the monument, Eve slips and falls, catching herself by her fingertips. Roger struggles to grab her wrist and just as he succeeds in pulling her up, the scene shifts to the train, and Roger is lifting Eve, his bride into the upper berth. The two embrace as the movie ends.

Although *North by Northwest* does feature a woman as a major character, in the end, it is the male hero who ultimately is responsible for doing the rescuing. Although Roger has moments of confusion, particularly at the beginning of the film when he does not understand what is going on, he still exudes charm, glamor, and sexual power.

In the 1960s and early 1970s, the trend of the strong male hero continued. Popular male heroes such as James Bond and the characters made famous by Clint Eastwood either ignored women altogether or treated them as disposable or as sex objects. Men were rugged individuals or self-made. There was a dearth of intelligent women on screen, and though there are exceptions, such as the characters made famous by actresses such as Barbra Streisand in *Funny Girl* (1968), Anne Bancroft in *The Miracle Worker* (1962), and Debbie Reynolds in *The Unsinkable Molly Brown* (1964), women generally were shown in a stereotypical way, as homemaker, wife, mother, assistant, secretary – and as submissive.

By the late 1970s, a new female character was on her way: one with a brain, power, and self-assurance. Princess Leia, from the major hit *Star Wars* (1977), could fight alongside the boys while often being the brains behind the operation. Lois Lane in *Superman* (1978) was a successful reporter. Though these women still needed to be rescued by the male heroes, they were not just window dressing. Other roles that showed a new, more powerful woman were seen in *Norma Rae* (1979), *Annie Hall* (1977), and *Julia* (1977).

In the 1980s, a vision of "ultra-masculinity" was the dominant male image, with most of the top-grossing films of the decade featuring the "reliable heroic male" or "likeable funny guy" as the prominent main character. The top-grossing films of the 1980s include *The Empire Strikes Back* (1980), *Return of the Jedi* (1983), the *Indiana Jones* series (1981, 1984, 1989), the *Rambo* series (1982, 1985, 1988), *Top Gun* (1986), *Platoon* (1986), *The Terminator* (1984), *Ghostbusters* (1984), *Back to the Future* (1984), *Beverly Hills Cop* (1984), *Three Men and a Baby* (1987), and *Batman* (1989). The underlying message in these films is that brawn or humor will allow you to conquer and get the girl. Anti-sexist male activist Jackson Katz, in his educational video on gender violence in the media (*Tough Guise*, 1999), argues that films such as *Rambo* reflect attempts by American males to regain their masculinity following the United States' loss in Vietnam and the gains in women's rights in the United States.

In examining representations of masculinity, it is also important to consider how race or ethnicity also comes into play. Film scholar Richard Dyer (1988) argues that mainstream cinema is primarily a reflection of white experience and society, and that representations of other races and images of racial differences can tend toward tokenization and thus be problematic. A review of films featuring African American males tends to support his argument.

Sidney Poitier's award-winning performance in *In the Heat of the Night* (1967) as Detective Virgil Tibbs perhaps marks the start of a long series of consistent roles for African American men: those of police officer and private detective. In detective films, researchers note that the black male is offered as heroic, though often the character is depicted as being isolated from a black community, or class, and as lacking sexuality (Gates 2004). There are, however, examples that diverge from this model, notably that of John Shaft, "the black private dick who's a sex machine to all the chicks," who appeared in the original *Shaft* film (1971).

Two movie series in particular – the *Beverly Hills Cop* series (1984, 1987, 1994) and the *Lethal Weapon* films (1987, 1989, 1992, 1998) – offer up black characters in central roles. *Beverly Hills Cop*, which starred Eddie Murphy as Axel Foley, a Detroit detective, opens with images that quickly contrast the racial and class differences between Axel's hometown and Beverly Hills, the city to which he is displaced. Detroit is shown as a city of boarded-up buildings, industry, and manufacturing, where lower class people of all ethnicities gather on the streets to hang out. When Axel arrives in Beverly Hills, the audience sees blue skies and palm trees, mansions and wealth. He has been transplanted from his almost all-black community to an almost completely white one. However, it can certainly be argued that most of the tension in this film comes not from race but from class. Axel is sexy, smart, and good at his job, but drives a junker of a car and dresses "like a hoodlum" (Gates 2004).

In the *Lethal Weapon* series, black actor Danny Glover portrays Detective Roger Murtaugh, starring with white actor Mel Gibson, who plays his partner, Martin Riggs. Film scholar Christopher Ames (1992) suggests that in this biracial buddy movie, when juxtaposed against a white counterpart, the emasculation and desexualization of the African American character becomes even more apparent. For instance, in the first film of the series, images of the two men are shown: Roger in a bathtub, body completely covered by bubbles, relaxing and contemplating his upcoming retirement, and Martin, stumbling out of bed, completely naked, searching for a cigarette and beer to begin his day. Martin is the "ultra-masculine" super cop, who is in total command of firearms and irresistible to just about any woman he encounters – including, in this movie, Roger's own daughter. Roger, on the other hand, uses a small gun (a point of humor in the movie), is a poor shot, and requires a girdle to fit into his uniform.

The tokenism that is apparent with regard to African American males as film characters is also apparent for African American females and other minority females. In fact, it could be argued that tokenism applies to virtually all female characters in mainstream movies of the early and mid-1980s. While movies with male heroes dominated at the box office during this decade, only three movies with primarily female main characters came even close in terms of revenue: the comedy *9 to 5* (1980), which starred Dolly Parton, Lily Tomlin, and Jane Fonda as working women who rebel against their harassing boss, and the tearjerkers *Terms of Endearment* (1983), which starred Shirley MacLaine and Debra Winger as a mother and daughter who struggle to find ways to get along, and *Steel Magnolias* (1989), which starred Dolly Parton, Shirley MacLaine, Julia Roberts, Sally Field, Darryl Hannah, and Olympia Dukakis, as a close-knit group of friends living in a small Louisiana parish.

By the end of the 1980s and the start of the 1990s, female roles continued to be in short supply, with studies showing that fewer than 30 percent of the major film roles went to women (Smith and Cook 2008). However, some strong roles did emerge, such as those played by Meryl Streep in *Postcards from the Edge* (1990), Diane Keaton in *Baby Boom* (1987), Jodie Foster in *Silence of the Lambs* (1991), Kathy Bates in *Misery* (1990), Jessica Tandy in *Driving Miss Daisy* (1989), and Julia Roberts in *Pretty Woman* (1990). Though meatier roles for leading ladies existed, writer Elayne Rapping lamented the majority of representations:

> Marriage, men, babies – to the exclusion of meaningful work – were being pushed down our throats in movie after movie … In each film, the nuclear family and old-fashioned love of the kind that leads to "happily ever after" were presented as more or less unproblematic ideals. Independent women, for their part, were portrayed as seriously in trouble, in one way or another, for reasons that ranged from garden-variety Freudian female neurosis to downright psychopathic evil. (Rapping 1994: 24)

In the early 1990s, women struggled for equal screen time, though they did not see as much of it as perhaps they would have liked. In a speech in 1991 addressing the Screen Actors' Guild, Meryl Streep said:

> Three years ago, women were down to performing only one-third of all the roles in feature films. In 1989, that number slipped to 29 percent. Of course, that was before the figures for [1990] were tabulated. Just wait till they factor in our contributions to *Total Recall, Robocop 2, Days of Thunder, Die Hard 2, The Hunt for Red October, The Abyss, Young Guns 2, Miami Blues, Last Exit to Brooklyn, Dick Tracy* and *The Adventures of Ford Fairlane*. We snagged a good six or seven major roles in those movies. If the trend continues, by the year 2000 women will represent 13 percent of all roles. And in 20 years, we will have been eliminated from movies entirely. (Screen Actors' Guild Women's Committee 1991)

While Streep's half-jesting predictions have been alarmingly accurate, as women do continue to be underrepresented in prestigious films, *Variety* reported that females represent only 12 percent of protagonists in the top-grossing films of 2014. While it may seem that actresses make up a larger portion, the study's author, Dr. Martha Lauzen, noted that it is because of a few high-profile cases, including blockbuster actresses like Melissa McCarthy, Shailene Woodley, and Jennifer Lawrence, our thinking gets skewed. Lauzen stated, "There is a growing disconnect or gap between what we might perceive as being the current status of women in film and their actual status" (quoted in Lang 2015). The study goes on to report that it isn't just primary roles where women have lost ground, but also in secondary roles. In 2014, females held only 29 percent of major characters and 30 percent of all speaking roles.

A study done in 2008 by Stacy Smith and a team of researchers at the University of Southern California found there has been no improvement in gender balance in Academy Award nominated films during the past 30 years in the Best Picture category (Smith *et al.* 2008). Their results show that there are almost three speaking males for every one female. Interestingly, Smith and her team also found that 84 percent of the characters were coded as "white," offering up the perspective that the common character profile of Best Picture nominated films selected by the academy is white and male.

Some research has been done to determine if the gender imbalance on screen is related to the gender representation of those working behind the scenes, as producers, directors, and the like (e.g., Smith *et al.* 2010). Smith and her team found that a total of 4 percent of films included in the Best Picture category featured one or more females as director, 26 percent as a writer, and 41 percent as executive producer or producer. In total, males behind the scenes outnumbered females in these occupations nearly 6.5 to 1. Smith also found that females are significantly more likely to be shown in films directed by women.

Another one of Smith's studies examined entertainment aimed at children to see if gender imbalance and stereotypical gender portrayals were evident (Smith and Cook 2008). Among the findings regarding children's entertainment films were that although females make up half of the population, they appear much less frequently than males, and are more likely to be depicted as hyper-attractive, hypersexual, and/or passive. Some of the other interesting findings included:

- Fewer than one out of three characters were female.
- After more than 4,000 characters were coded, the results showed that two types of females frequent films: the traditional and the hypersexual. *Hypersexuality* is defined as an overemphasis on attractiveness and sexuality by way of clothing and body proportions.
- Females are more likely than males to be depicted as parents and/or in a committed relationship in G- and PG-rated films.
- Across all ratings, females were more than five times as likely as males to be shown in sexually revealing clothing, and more than three times as likely as males to be shown as thin.
- Almost all the females were praised for their appearance or physical beauty.
- More than a third of the females in the films underwent some sort of physical metamorphosis of their outer shell in the film, taking the character from ugly (and thus implied, unacceptable) duckling to princess. For instance, in the film *The Princess Diaries* (2001), Mia must undergo a complete physical transformation before she can be presented to society as the heir to the throne (see Figures 9.1 and 9.2).
- Almost all the females in the films studied longed for love of some kind, generally a romantic relationship with a male. In some movies, finding romance is the primary focus of the plot (e.g., *The Little Mermaid*, 1989) or secondary (e.g., *Anastasia*, 1997). Love at first sight is a common theme, further reinforcing the importance of physical beauty, as is a romantic relationship being formed on deceptive foundations.

Social cognitive theory suggests that positive reinforcements delivered to media characters can increase the likelihood of a viewer learning or adopting the praised behavior (Bandura 2001). Therefore, a child watching these films may learn that being beautiful or attractive or thin is an intrinsic and desired part of being a female. As depictions of physical beauty are often extreme or distorted, the impact of the message could be detrimental or lead to a skewed view of beauty.

One positive result from this stream of research is that not all women are portrayed as the stereotypical damsel in distress; in many storylines targeted at children or young adults, the idea of rescue

Figure 9.1 Mia before her makeover in *The Princess Diaries* (2001). Screenshot.

Figure 9.2 Mia after her makeover in *The Princess Diaries* (2001). Note that she got the guy. Screenshot.

is reciprocal – the man rescues the woman, who in turn rescues him. Female protagonists are often physically active and healthy, and exhibit bravery in the face of danger. For instance, Ariel in *The Little Mermaid* (1989) saves Flounder, a boy fish, from being eaten by a shark, and Belle in *Beauty and the Beast* (1991) sacrifices her freedom for her father's release from captivity. In the Disney animation *The Princess and the Frog* (2009), the heroine is a young woman, Tiana, living in New Orleans, who works hard as a waitress, hoping to one day own her own restaurant. She is intelligent, fearless, and independent. Her focus is on her career, rather than on capturing the heart of any young man – although in the end, she does fall in love with a dashing prince, who joins her in building her dream restaurant. It should be noted here that Tiana was Disney's first African American princess. Similarly, in *Brave* (2012), Princess Merida defies the wishes of her parents by refusing to get married and pursuing her independence. Unlike princesses of the past, Merida does not have a svelte figure, has unkempt, long, wavy hair, and is a skilled archer. Her skills and bravery, in the end, save her kingdom from doom. The new princess character was praised for serving as a positive role model for young girls. It is no surprise, then, that when Disney came out with the Merida doll, there was public uproar about the look of the doll. Merida essentially received a makeover, with a thin figure, wider eyes, and flowing tamed hair. Nevertheless, the spunky character in the movie continued to attract young female fans who embraced Merida's looks and strengths.

Positive characterizations of women in adult-targeted films have also become more noticeable. The James Bond movies, featuring the British superspy 007, can serve to illustrate how female characters in movies have changed over time through their portrayals of the "Bond girl." Using a content analysis, a group of researchers examined the ways in which the 195 female characters in the 20 James Bond films released up to 2005 were depicted (Neuendorf *et al.* 2007). They found that, typically, there is at least one "Bond girl" who "is particularly striking – a woman with an adventurous nature, cunning attributes, strong potential for romantic entanglement with Bond, and sense of self-assurance" (Neuendorf *et al.* 2007). Other females appear in the films, as villains, as diversions, and in later films, as leaders (for instance, the character of M, who had long been played by a man, was taken over by Dame Judi Dench, a woman in her seventies, in the 1995 Bond movie *GoldenEye*; she played M in all the subsequent Bond movies through to *Skyfall* in 2012).

In this study, the researchers examined the female characters by looking for a number of characteristics, including sexual activity, physical characteristics, and aggressive predispositions. They found that, over time, female characters had an increased number of major roles; they also saw a trend toward more autonomous, actively participating females in the films. Extreme attractiveness, thinness, and youth are characteristics of women in Bond films that have not changed. Physical beauty is still of primary importance in the Bond world, and there are still strong and persistent allusions to violence and sex. However, it can be stated that although the archetype of the Bond girl has not completely changed, she has become more self-sufficient and more of an equal player. For instance, though *Casino Royale* (2006) and *Quantum of Solace* (2008) were not included in the study, the leading female characters presented in these later films support the notion that the new "Bond girl" is more capable and independent.

In *Casino Royale*, Eva Green plays Vesper Lynd, a beautiful, strong woman who Bond falls in love with. It is ultimately discovered that Vesper has been running her own deception in an effort to save a former lover. In the end, she sacrifices herself, and her strong personality and independence make her, in many ways, Bond's equal. In *Quantum of Solace*, the major "Bond girl" is Camille Montes, a Russian-Bolivian agent with her own vendetta against the story's villain. Camille and Bond are often working at odds, but come together to triumph in the end. And unlike the Bond girls of the past,

Camille and Bond never share a sexual relationship, though she is extremely attractive and certainly Bond's "type." It is interesting to note that although the female characters featured in the Bond movies have changed, the main male character of Agent 007 has not changed. He still epitomizes many of the strong male stereotypes that permeate film, stereotypes that can also be seen in the television landscape.

Gender in Entertainment Television

Over the past 60 years, viewers have seen television female character roles change and become more numerous. Many researchers would argue, however, that, like their film counterparts, women in entertainment television are still greatly underrepresented in major roles, and still commonly fall into gender role stereotypes. Broadcast historian Sydney Head found in a 1954 study that though there were fewer women than men on television in the early 1950s, they were not totally excluded. Most women were shown in situation comedies, perhaps best exemplified by Lucille Ball in *I Love Lucy* (1951–1961), who played a troublemaking screwball. Family sitcoms of the late 1950s and 1960s, such as *Father Knows Best* (1954–1963) and *Leave It to Beaver* (1957–1963), had women as main characters as well, but the typical female was a happy homemaker, competent and satisfied to spend her days cleaning the house and caring for her family. On *The Donna Reed Show* (1958–1966), which Reed herself produced, women were seen in the home, not working outside of it. Even family comedy shows that pushed the boundaries of realism in terms of topic or time period, such as *The Addams Family* (1964–1966) or *Bewitched* (1964–1972), continued this trend. Women were shown in the home, squarely positioned as homemakers serving the needs of husband and family.

The 1950s and 1960s tended to reflect social patriarchy and, to that end, male roles were more varied than female ones. In family sitcoms, men were depicted as the head of the household and the breadwinner. Men went out to work each day, and came home to their wives and families who would care for them. Men, specifically white, middle-class men, were depicted as decision makers, as highly rational, and, therefore, as highly masculine (Horvath 2008). Through the 1970s, as women's roles began to diversify, representations of men and masculinity remained relatively unchanged. Aleksandra Horvath (2008) writes: "though male characters became less overtly sexist, television shows continued to portray a divide between perceived women's and men's domains and tasks." For instance, men were rarely depicted taking care of traditionally feminine tasks like doing the laundry or doing the dishes. Over the course of the next several decades, as women began to become depicted as more autonomous and were placed in roles once reserved solely for men, men were still portrayed as dominant, financially successful, and aggressive.

The single, working woman began making an appearance on television in the late 1960s and 1970s. As the women's liberation movement began to gain ground, more producers were willing to take a chance on moving beyond the nuclear family model for sitcoms. With the successes of the civil rights movement, television producers even took a chance with the sitcom *Julia* (1968–1971), featuring a working African American single mom. In the show, the leading character (played by Diahann Carroll) was shown as a strong, smart, and independent woman who cared dearly about her son and her job as a nurse.

Of course, a show featuring an African American woman in the leading role was not the norm. Most of the shows with females as leading characters featured white females in those character roles. Notable was the hugely popular sitcom *The Mary Tyler Moore Show* (1970–1977). Unlike the single woman Ann Marie in the series *That Girl* (1966–1971), who remained watched over by her father and her fiancé for the run of the show, and by the end was off to get married, the main character in *The Mary Tyler Moore Show*, Mary Richards, was in her thirties, independent after having broken off her engagement. Show creators have been quoted as saying that they wanted the show to be a departure from the traditional depictions of women on television and to be both reflective of and to comment on the women's liberation movement. At the series' end, Richards, at the age of 37, was still romantically unattached, strong, and mature.

Other shows, such as *The Dick Van Dyke Show* (1961–1966), *Rhoda* (1974–1978), *Laverne and Shirley* (1976–1983), and *One Day at a Time* (1975–1984), portrayed single women as part of the workforce and sometimes taking care of a family single-handedly. However, a certain ditzy quality still lingered as a common trait among the female leads in many of the 1970s programs, and the common theme of searching for male companionship suggested that taking care of a family without a man around was not the ideal. In the popular series *Three's Company* (1977–1985), which revolved around two attractive women living together with a young man, the main female character, Chrissy, was depicted as a dumb, innocent blonde, who had no idea that her male roommate, Jack, was lusting after her. It was the kind of character that could have been easily found in the 1950s, and yet what made Chrissy different from her 1950s counterpart was that she had a job and was not entirely dependent on a male figure, although she was still very much interested in finding a male mate.

One 1980s television program is credited with changing the pattern of stereotypical "women in the workplace" portrayals: *Cagney and Lacey* (1981–1988). *Cagney and Lacey* was a police procedural drama starring Sharon Gless and Tyne Daly as New York City police detectives who led different lives: Christine Cagney was a single, career-minded woman, while Mary Beth Lacey was a married working mother. *Cagney and Lacey* is credited with being the first television program with two female leads. This program, and its popularity, paved the way for a new generation of women on television, the "superwomen," though arguably these depictions were as inaccurate as those in the 1950s and 1960s. Many of the women on television in the 1980s were able to work outside the home, raise a family, run the home with little or no difficulty, please their man, and look like they just stepped out of a beauty parlor. Women like this, such as those shown on *The Cosby Show* (1984–1994), *Family Ties* (1982–1989), and *Growing Pains* (1985–1992), never explored how much they had to do – they just carried it all off with aplomb. Single career women were still around, in shows like *Cheers* (1982–1993), *Flo* (1980–1981), *Kate and Allie* (1984–1989), and *Murphy Brown* (1988–1998), and they were portrayed as being in control of their work and home lives.

In the case of *Murphy Brown*, the title character, the successful anchorwoman of the newsmagazine *FYI*, finds herself unwed and pregnant in the 1991–1992 season. Then vice presidential candidate Dan Quayle questioned the morality of the sitcom's unwed mother storyline, which created a firestorm over the fictional character and the television program. In the end, the character Murphy Brown devotes an entire *FYI* episode to the changing makeup of families in the 1990s. What this fact-becoming-fiction situation revealed is that the personal choices women make were still up for public debate no matter how evolved the representations on television had become.

Though the 1990s showed a more diverse population of women, research shows that, overall, there were still fewer and younger women than men in prime-time programming (Lont 1995: 167–173). Women were shown in greater numbers in ensemble comedies and dramas, such as *ER* (1994–2009), *Friends* (1994–2004), *Seinfeld* (1989–1998), *Sex and the City* (1998–2004), and *Law and Order* (1990–2004). However, researchers still conclude that existing stereotypes were perpetuated.

In 1993, *Living Single*, a sitcom featuring African American friends living in a brownstone in Brooklyn, New York, debuted. African American producer Yvette Lee Bowser said she created the show in part to create positive images of four upwardly mobile black women. In an interview with *Essence* magazine, Bowser explained, "There used to be only two predominant images of black women on television – loud-talking sisters or 'Mommy' mother types" (Gregory 1994). The show, which aired for five seasons, followed the lives of magazine editor Khadijah James (portrayed by Queen Latifah), her cousin Synclaire James (portrayed by Kim Coles), boutique buyer Regine Hunter (portrayed by Kim Fields), and attorney Maxine Shaw (portrayed by Erika Alexander). The characters were each accomplished in their careers and remained rooted in their inner-city black community, which earned the series praise. However, others criticized the series for what was seen as a reliance on so-called blackvoice or what the characters call "ebonics" and the use of other ridicule in dealing with black women, such as Regine being teased for having "horse hair" (Means Coleman 2000: 111–119).

Researchers suggest that, in general, gender roles have changed a great deal since the 1970s, with more women moving out of the home and into the workforce; relationships between husbands and wives have become more equal, and men seem more willing to share in childcare and in work around the house (Glascock 2001). Therefore, it would seem fitting that television portrayals should reflect changing societal mores. However, as just shown in the overview of shows featuring female characters, although it is apparent that changes in female depictions have been made, with more women shown as independent and with careers, certain characteristics are still associated with the female figure in many television shows. Evidence also exists that male figures still tend to be privileged over female figures in these shows.

Content analyses of television programs and their characters show women as less likely than men to be serious or powerful, and less likely to work, particularly in jobs with status or power (Elasmar, Hasegawa, and Brian 1999). Fewer women in the 1990s than in previous decades were portrayed as being housewives, but they were still shown more often than men doing "homemaking" activities, like taking out the recyclables, doing laundry, and cooking. More than 44 percent of female characters had clearly defined employment outside the home, with the most commonly held jobs being blue-collar positions, including manual or assembly-line roles, and entertainment positions, including models, musicians, and actors. In addition, they were more likely to be cast in traditionally gender-specific occupations such as nurses and secretaries (see Table 9.1). Females were also found to be underrepresented based on population numbers, to be proportionally younger than their male counterparts, and to be more provocatively dressed. Distinct variations in speaking time of characters were also found (Table 9.2).

Since the days of Mary Tyler Moore and Rhoda, when audiences were just starting to see the image of a strong-minded, intelligent working woman, in contrast to the happy homemaker that had pervaded entertainment media, female characters have grown and changed with the times, though perhaps not as fast or as completely as some might like. Today, more women than ever appear and star in prime-time television shows and receive top billing in major films. Specialized cable television channels, including Lifetime, Oxygen, and WE, have thrived, reinforcing the idea that women are a large and important segment of the television viewing audience, and networks are recognizing the need for and desire on the part of the audience to see a cast of characters with a variety of ethnicities. Communication studies professor Amanda Lotz (2006: 1–35) argues that current shows have created roles for women that do not simply force women into preexisting categories or plug them into traditionally male roles, but that show women as complex, interesting, and dynamic. These characters often are still thin and attractive, but they are smart and complicated, thus offering the viewer a character that appeals to both men and women.

Table 9.1 Most frequent occupations for characters on prime-time network television.

Occupation	Number	%
Males		
Indeterminate	231	31.3
Police	89	12.1
Lawyer	36	4.9
Doctor	31	4.2
Criminal	26	3.5
Judge	17	2.3
Newscaster	13	1.8
Military Officer	11	1.5
Teacher	10	1.4
Guard	10	1.4
Total	738	
Females		
Indeterminate	183	44.3
Police	24	5.8
Nurse	18	4.4
Secretary	17	4.1
Lawyer	15	3.6
Journalist	14	3.4
Doctor	11	2.7
Teacher	10	2.4
Waitress	9	2.2
Actress	7	1.7
Total	413	

Source: Glascock (2001).

Table 9.2 Prime-time network television characters' speaking time by gender.

Variable	Total	Male	%	Female	%
Characters	1,269	803	63	466	37
Main characters	455	273	60	182	40
Speaking time (in seconds)*	1,284	813	63	471	37

*Average per show.
Source: Glascock (2001).

The macho male stereotypes in film are stronger than in entertainment television today, and any trip to the box office reinforces the message that muscled, powerful men with big guns equals manliness. For instance, the movie poster for the summer 2010 blockbuster *The Expendables*, starring Sylvester Stallone and Jason Statham, featured black and white images of nine heavily armed men, all dressed in black, standing with their legs apart in an attitude of defiance and power. The cast is a racially diverse one, but each man exudes toughness; there is no question that these are images of mainstream masculinity.

A wider variety of man is depicted on entertainment television (Box 9.1), ranging from a well-rounded male character, one more sensitive and nuanced, often seen in ensemble dramas, to an objectionable kind of stereotyped man, the bumbling buffoon. *Grey's Anatomy* (2005 debut) again provides a useful example of well-rounded male characters. Dr. Owen Hunt (portrayed by Kevin McKidd), for instance, began his time at Seattle Grace Hospital as a recently discharged army doctor, hard and nasty, and (as it turned out) suffering from post-traumatic stress disorder. Slowly Owen begins to let his guard down, falling in love with one of his fellow doctors, and his vulnerability shows. Though Owen is still a strong character, he is multidimensional, often breaking down in tears with regret, sadness, and fear as he deals with his army memories and medical experiences. Another character, Dr. Richard Webber (portrayed by James Pickens, Jr.), also offers viewers a more nuanced man. Richard, the chief of surgery, is a recovering alcoholic, and a workaholic, which causes continuous problems between him and his wife, Adele. Richard had an affair with another doctor, the mother of Meredith Grey, who now works at Seattle Grace, many years before, and that relationship continues

---

Box 9.1 Common male stereotypes

According to the 1999 report *Boys to Men: Media Messages about Masculinity*, the most common male character stereotypes are:

- **The Joker**, who uses humor and laughter as a "mask of masculinity." He is the life of the party. He is rarely serious or emotional, and always in search of a good time.
- **The Jock**, who regularly demonstrates his power and strength. He fights other men when necessary, is aggressive, and may compromise his long-term health. Women, and other men, admire and adore him for his physical prowess.
- **The Strong, Silent Type**, who contains his emotions at all costs, as losing control is a sign of weakness.
- **The Big Shot**, who is defined by his professional status. His success in the workplace is what makes him a valuable person, and what makes him attractive to those around him. The Big Shot is often nasty to subordinates, aggressive, and consumed by the pursuit of wealth and status.
- **The Action Hero** is strong, often angry, aggressive in the extreme, and – increasingly over the past few decades – violent.
- **The Buffoon** is usually well intentioned and light-hearted and ranges from being slightly incompetent to completely hopeless, often for comic effect, in domestic or workplace situations. (MediaSmarts n.d.)

Consider the entertainment television shows you watch and any recent films you have seen. Can you think of any examples of characters that fit the stereotypes listed above? Are the stereotypes the norm or the exception?

to create tremors in his life. Richard, more than anything, is shown as human: getting angry, making mistakes, doing things well, having a family and friends. It is a wonderful departure from the one-dimensional portrayals of years past.

This is not to say that everyone is perfectly satisfied with the current gender mix in entertainment media or with the ways in which genders are still stereotyped. Viewers may see a woman as president or secretary of state in such shows as *Commander in Chief* (2005–2006), *Prison Break* (2005–2009), *Madame Secretary* (2014), *House of Cards* (2013), and *24* (2001–2010), but researchers still point out that just "getting the job" is not enough. All too often, women portrayed in positions of power are either shown as the "good girl" or the "evil girl," with little nuance or depth. Other women may be shown as being at the top in their field, such as the television characters of Temperance Brennan, in *Bones* (2005 debut), and Olivia Dunham, in *Fringe* (2008 debut), or the film characters of Margaret Tate (portrayed by Sandra Bullock) in *The Proposal* (2009), or Amanda Woods (portrayed by Cameron Diaz) in *The Holiday* (2006), but often they lack a personal life or are almost completely socially inept. These women, interestingly enough, are still extremely attractive and often the object of the male lead's attention and affection, though the female character remains almost absurdly clueless about his interest.

Some of the strongest female characters in entertainment media arguably have come from the science fiction genre. Women, and men and women of color, are powerful, leaders, and dominant in shows like *Battlestar Galactica* (2004–2009), the *Star Trek* series, and *The X-Files* (1993–2002), or in films like *Star Wars: The Force Awakens* (2015) and *Wonder Woman* (2017). While viewers should applaud these multidimensional characters, perhaps they should also wonder why females and people of color as equals seem the stuff of futuristic legend and myth.

Two dimensions exist for male characters. They are either sex-crazed and "manly" or comical and inept. Common "manly" traits include bravery, adventurousness, being able to think rationally, and being strong. It is rare to see men or boys crying or showing vulnerability. The comical and inept male character is often a father figure who is forgetful and more like a child than a parent.

For instance, the character of Ray Barone in *Everybody Loves Raymond* (1996–2005) is a sports-writer, and married with three children (see Figure 9.3). The audience knows he is a successful journalist, because periodically the storyline of an episode involves him taking business trips,

Figure 9.3 Raymond talks to his daughter on the CBS hit *Everybody Loves Raymond* (1996–2005). Screenshot.

working on books, winning awards, and writing speeches. However, all of his abilities to care for himself, and more specifically for his children and his home, vanish the moment he steps through the door of his home. Of course, this is a comedy, and this ineptness is played for laughs; however, the message is relentless: a man cannot be trusted with the simplest of tasks or even with his own children. In one episode, Ray pleads with his wife in an attempt to avoid watching the children: "You're so great with the kids. You know what to do. If it were up to me, they'd be eating cereal for dinner and wearing the boxes." Perhaps even more damaging, argues communication researcher Marjorie Kibby, is that not only is the character of Ray an ineffective parent and a poor husband, but that the series continually shows the audience that it is "charmingly endearing" to be these things (Cameron 2005).

A number of prime-time shows have piqued the interest of feminist researchers in "beauty and the beast" situation comedy. In these programs, the main characters are mismatched couples: smart, witty, attractive women who are married to lazy, overweight, often sexist men, such as those shown in *The King of Queens* (1998–2007) and *According to Jim* (2001–2007). Communication researchers Kimberly Walsh, Elfriede Fursich, and Bonnie Jefferson (2008: 123–132) argue that these shows maintain a strong theme of patriarchy by consistently following two main storylines: (1) that the women are physically and intellectually superior to their husbands, regularly depicted through pointed jabs, nagging, and jokes, and (2) that despite this superiority, the woman regularly conforms to her inferior (yet dominant) husband's wishes and "accepts him as he is." The authors write:

> The beauty (e.g. Jane) commonly "liberates" the beast (e.g. Tarzan) by finally accepting him "as is." Attempts by the beauty to bring the beast into her environment fail. In an epic struggle between nature (essential maleness) and civilization (refined femininity), nature will prevail. It is up to the beauty (woman) to come around and accept the beast's (man's) true or authentic self. The sitcom version of this popular myth plays out the same storyline: In the resolution of the struggle between patriarchy and feminism, it remains the task of the female protagonists to acquiesce to the "natural" force of patriarchy. (Walsh, Fursich, and Jefferson 2008: 125)

The authors discuss a specific example in their article in order to illustrate their premise. In an episode of *King of Queens* called "Bun Dummy," Carrie, the wife (played by Leah Remini), appears at the beginning of a scene with her hair in a large bun. She is on her way to a spinning class, while Doug, the husband (played by Kevin James), lounges on a sofa in the garage drinking beer and eating chips with his friends. They jibe back and forth that she should work out twice as hard to make up for his lack of fitness, as his high school reunion is approaching. The implication is obvious that she will be his trophy wife at the event, and he states, as he trades a light beer for a regular one, "I am who I am." As the show progresses, Doug becomes increasingly irritated by her bun, which she is choosing to wear more often. He thinks it makes her look less attractive, so much so that when she tries to initiate lovemaking he is so distracted by her hair that he rejects her. They argue further and he says he does not want her to wear it to his reunion as it would embarrass him. He pays a friend to tell her it's ugly, and another of his friends tells her it is "ass ugly." Ultimately she wears her hair down to the reunion, and he parades her around the room like a show pony. While at the reunion, it comes out that she only wore her hair down because of his friend's comment, and they fight. She puts her bun back up, only to be confronted by a photo of a recently deceased librarian with a very similar bun. She quickly pulls her hair back down, appearing to admit her defeat and proving that Doug was right all along.

The authors point out that this plot narrative is a common one:

> Carrie is dominant: she orders Doug around, threatens him, corrects his mistakes, and makes fun of his obesity ... [but] Doug is in charge. Doug routinely goes against what Carrie asks of him, and then he lies or tricks her, not respecting her enough to tell her the truth. In the end, Carrie feels guilty, admits she is wrong or easily forgives Doug so he never has to feel bad about his behavior. (Walsh, Fursich, and Jefferson 2008: 127)

While these plotlines may amuse the audience, it can be argued that this double standard – the man is to be taken as he is, no matter how offensive or sexist, but not so the woman – presents a troubling example of what male/female relationships should be like.

Another interesting line of research concerns the character of Ally McBeal from the show of the same title (1997–2002). Communication researchers Elizabeth K. Busch (2009: 87–97) and Rachel Dubrofsky (2002: 265–284) contend that the character of Ally McBeal (portrayed by actress Calista Flockhart) is the ultimate example of the post-feminist heroine, in that she is an intelligent successful career woman who revels in and relies on her femininity and sex appeal yet yearns for the love, marriage, and babies she does not have. She is depicted as quirky, neurotic, indecisive, unhappy, and lonely. Her success in the courtroom leaves her unfulfilled, and she spends most of her time in a desperate search for storybook romantic love. She is torn between her talent and competence as a career woman and her desire for a husband and children.

Dubrofsky (2002: 269) defines post-feminism as "a reactionary movement ... [not so much to provide] an imperative to return women to the kitchen, to child-rearing, to nurturing and supportive roles, and to a reification of their roles as sex objects, so much as to claim that women have come so far that they now can reclaim these roles if they wish – it is, after all, their choice." Post-feminism represents a more introspective moment, as she describes it, not the traditional feminist outward-looking approach to societal or political impacts. Women now can stand back and decide for themselves what kind of life they want. Gender studies professor Suzanna Walters (1995: 116–125) proposes that certain feminists may have gone too far in rejecting all that is feminine, that women have lost a part of what makes them female. Walters writes:

> We thought we wanted liberation, but we found out that we really love too much. We thought we wanted equality, but realize instead that we cannot have it all. We thought we could finally be the prince in our own fantasies of power and pleasure, but discover our Cinderella complex weighs on us all too mightily. We envision cooperation, commitment, even community, but are told we are codependent after all. (1995: 121)

The character of Ally seems the manifestation of this school of thought, struggling each week to blend the two desires – career and a successful professional life – with her need for traditional, romantic love. She offered a change from feminist characters of years past, depicted as "frigid, masculine career woman" (Busch 2009: 92) and often the butt of jokes. Ally appears to offer an alternative. Women can be feminine and want a family, and still be a career success, and not be shown as a superwoman without any cracks in her facade. However, by the series end, what viewers are left with is the idea that these two desires are irreconcilable; in other words, Ally cannot have it all. She cannot have a career and a family. She must choose, which she does do in the season finale when she quits her job just as she is made partner, a tremendous career accomplishment, to move to New

York to be a full-time mother to the 10-year-old biological daughter she has just been introduced to, a product of an egg donation years earlier.

A quick examination of the most popular prime-time programming in recent years shows this post-feminist female character is alive and well. The women on shows such as *Grey's Anatomy* (2005 debut), although highly competitive and on their way to being accomplished surgeons, spend a vast proportion of their time thinking and talking about love, marriage, sex, children, and family, and debating the struggle to balance it all. The character of Meredith Grey is conflicted about what she wants and how to handle her competing life goals – is she a cut-throat surgeon, Mrs. Derek Shepherd, the wife of the head of surgery, or in later episodes, a widow raising her daughter as a single mom? The character of Miranda Bailey finds herself a single mother, having been divorced by her husband for spending too much time at work and not enough time at home. While she is fiercely proud of her accomplishments, her vulnerability surfaces time and again, as shown in episodes like the one in which her father appears and expresses how ashamed he is of her for letting down her family by working so much. The character of Cristina Yang is in many ways the most career-driven of the characters, perhaps best evidenced in a scene where, begging her mentor not to leave the hospital, she offers to give up her boyfriend, with whom her mentor is in love, if she will stay. However, Cristina is by no means immune to opposing life goals. One large story arc for this character concerned her engagement to another surgeon, who wanted her to be something she was not. He asked her to lie for him, to change herself for him, and she did. And in the end, he left her. The experience left her battered, untrusting, and even more cynical than she was before, though she came to realize that she had tried to turn herself into someone else for him, and that she could not compromise herself in that way in future. Her character now must deal with this realization that, in order to remain true to herself, she will need to find someone who understands that she is a surgeon first, and loves her because of it, not in spite of it.

Another example of the post-feminist woman on television is Rachel Bunch (played by Rebecca Bloom) in CW's *Crazy Ex-Girlfriend* (2015). In the musical comedy, Rachel is offered a partnership at her big city law firm during a meeting with her bosses, but freaks out and flees the meeting. While on the street she sees Josh Chan (played by Vincent Rodriguez II), the boy she loved in summer camp when she was 13. After chasing him down, he tells her that he's had enough of big city life; he's moving home to West Covina, California. Rachel ditches her law firm to follow him to the West Coast. The mere idea of moving away and pursuing a future with Josh Chan causes her to break into song and dance. When considered through a second-wave feminist lens, Rachel's choice to give up a prestigious career is jarring, but as a third-wave feminist, Rachel is perfectly content to opt for another choice. She opts for happiness because the life she had worked to build since she was 14 was no longer fulfilling. She starts her life over again in West Covina in an effort to find a time when she was excited about her day.

Television has also reflected a new type of woman in Max and Caroline (played by Kat Demmings and Beth Behr) on CBS's *2 Broke Girls* (2011 debut). The women represent the reality for many twenty-somethings trying to find their way in the world. They work as waitresses in a dingy diner, but their goal is to start a cupcake business with the profits they make from their pink-collar jobs. Again, the idea of women as waitresses on television is not the second-wave feminist ideal, but Max and Caroline are budding entrepreneurs with the mission of ultimately being in charge of their own destinies. Women designing a path that is right for them can also be seen in unconventional programs as well.

In 2013, Netflix premiered an original television series, *Orange Is the New Black* (OITNB), which focuses on the lives of inmates held in a fictional women's prison located in upstate New York. This show, created by Jenji Kohan and based on the book of the same name by Piper Kerman, has garnered widespread praise for its groundbreaking representation of women from all backgrounds. The series follows the story of Piper Chapman, who has been imprisoned for drug offenses, and the women she meets and interacts with during her incarceration. Notably, the show features a number of female characters that run counter to the stereotypical depictions on network programs. For example, television has historically represented the "socially accepted lesbian" as "gentle, sensitive, soft-hearted, soft-spoken, absolutely non-butch, and stereotypically feminine" (Harringon 2003: 2016). In OITNB, a wide range of lesbian characters appear, including butch lesbians and lesbians of color. Carrie Black (Big Boo) is one such character. Big Boo has been incarcerated for many years, and throughout her time she has had many "prison wives." She uses her size to intimidate other inmates, and has many tattoos, including the word "BUTCH" across her forearm. In the flashbacks characteristic of the series, the audience learns that Big Boo has spent her life trying to be accepted by her family and society for who she is. While at times she has attempted to dress or act differently to please people, including her mother, ultimately she stands up for herself and refuses to be anything other than what she is.

Another notable example of a female character depicted in a way that runs counter to stereotypes is that of Sophia Burset, a trans woman who is serving time for stealing credit card information to help pay for her transition. Burset, portrayed by transgender actress Laverne Cox, is continually dealing with transphobic treatment from other inmates and prison staff. During season 3, Burset is part of a hate crime storyline as she is sent to the SHU, or solitary confinement, "for her own protection" after she is harassed and attacked a number of times by various other inmates. While this hate crime should have been one that resulted in punishment for the bigoted perpetrators, it is Burset that is punished. One television critic noted:

> And the fact that she is sent into isolation following her violent attack is symbolic of so many struggles that trans people face on a regular basis. Rather than keeping this victim with the rest of the prison population, which might force others to get to know a trans person as a human being, she is erased from the community altogether and the entire topic of trans people is literally out of sight, out of mind. (Emswiler 2016)

In considering the representation of women on television, OITNB offers much food for thought (see Box 9.2). The *New York Post* proclaimed that the show has ignited "a TV revolution for women" (Rorke 2014). While other programs, such as those by Shonda Rhimes, have added female minority characters one by one, this show has dozens. Lorraine Toussaint, who plays the character of Vee, a drug den mother, stated:

> there are women of all different shapes. Many of the characters are over 40. There are short women, straight, gay, old; everyone is represented here. Our audience has fallen in love with these women in one way or another and totally identified with certain characters because women get to see themselves. It's so empowering to see yourself reflected in television shows. That's what this show is doing. It's a complete mythbuster. (Rorke 2014)

Rhimes added that this show has turned criminals into characters the audience cares about, and who have backgrounds that are three-dimensional, flawed, often unpleasant but always real. The characters are "a breathtaking riot of color and sexual orientation on screen" (Rorke 2014).

Box 9.2 *Orange Is the New Black* **and white privilege**

Orange Is the New Black is credited with being a conversation starter regarding gender, the representation of minority groups, and the prison system. During the show's first season, the show directly tackled the concept of white privilege, which is a term used to describe the societal privileges that benefit people with white skin, beyond those common to all others under the same social, political, or economic circumstances. White privilege can exist without white people consciously knowing it, and it helps to maintain the racial hierarchy (Avakian 2003). The concept of white privilege implies the right to assume the universality of one's own experiences, marking others as different or exceptional while perceiving oneself as "normal" (McIntosh 2003).

During the episode entitled "WAC Pack," several inmates form a committee tasked with putting forward suggestions to improve prison life. The discussion begins to divide along racial lines, with different groups of inmates (White, Black, Hispanic, "Golden Girl" inmates, etc.) electing a representative to tell the prison counselor's office their group's demands. At one point during the episode a group of black women are discussing specifically whether the Women's Advisory Council (WAC) can actually make a difference. When Sophia, played by Laverne Cox, starts talking about how they should be fighting for better healthcare and basic human rights, Poussey (played by Samira Denise Wiley) and Taystee (played by Danielle Brooks) respond by saying that is "white people politics." What follows is a funny yet pointed exchange with the two acting out a stereotyped display, complete with voice changes and mannerisms, to indicate imagined white privileged characters with names Mackenzie and Amanda:

TAYSTEE: Let's talk about healthcare, Mackenzie.
POUSSEY: Oh, Amanda, I'd rather not. It's not polite!
TAYSTEE: Well, did you see that wonderful new documentary about the best sushi in the world? Of course, now that I'm vegan, I didn't enjoy it as much as I might have before.
POUSSEY: You know, I just don't have the time. Chad and I have our yoga workshop, then wine-tasting class, and then we have to have really quiet sex every night at 9.
TAYSTEE: Did you hear that piece on NPR about hedge funds?
POUSSEY: Amanda, let me ask you – what do you think about my bangs these days? I mean, do you like them straight down, or should I be doing more of a sweep to the side?
TAYSTEE: Sweep to the side …

One suggested meaning a viewer can receive from this scene is that there are more nitty-gritty problems that the black inmates, and black people in general, face and that white people have no real idea how privileged they really are in their lives. Juxtaposed with this scene are conversations between several white inmates as they discuss racial stereotypes of "those" Hispanic and black people. Can you think of other depictions of white privilege in entertainment media? How do these portrayals work to change attitudes toward minority groups?

Gender in Music Videos

Up to this point in the chapter, portrayals of women and men have been discussed in the context of the audio/visual media of television and film. In the world represented by these media, men strive for power, aspire to highly prestigious occupations and careers, are aggressive, and remain unemotional while women are attractive, sensitive, sexual, and struggle between wanting a career and wanting to be married with a family (Box 9.3). Men outnumber women almost three to one.

Box 9.3 Have women come a long way?

In her article "Where Have You Gone, Mary Richards?" Aniko Bodroghkozy (2004) discusses the fourth episode of the then-new *Mary Tyler Moore Show* (1970–1977). In this episode, Mary and her friend Rhoda, who want cheap charter airline tickets to Europe, join the "Better Luck Next Time" club, a social group for divorcees. Bodroghkozy writes:

> Neither Mary nor Rhoda is the least bit interested in finding dates or mates among the club members, and the show portrays the divorcees as a rather pathetic and desperate bunch. Mary, in fact, is seldom shown to be particularly concerned about her romantic life. Mary, our representation of 70s new womanhood, is interested only in a cheap way to get to Europe with her pal Rhoda, and feels ethically torn about pretending to be a divorcee in order to do so.

Later in the article, Bodroghkozy contrasts this presentation of Mary and her friend, which aired during the burgeoning Women's Liberation Movement, with a more recent program. She continues:

> Fast forward to 2003 and ABC's third iteration of its hugely successful reality series *The Bachelor*. As in the previous two versions, 25 young women compete to "make a connection," "get a rose," and otherwise attempt to capture the heart (and presumably wallet) of protagonist Andrew Firestone, the heir to a vast fortune. Within the narrative world of *The Bachelor*, nothing about these women concerns us except their success or failure in being chosen by Mr. Firestone to be Mrs. Firestone.

Bodroghkozy concludes:

> The women of *The Bachelor*, our representation of new millennium womanhood, are interested only in marriage; none is portrayed feeling ethically torn in the least by their cat-fighting and backstabbing in order to win Mr. Firestone's affections.
> You've come a long way, baby …

The Bachelor (2002–current) is not unique. Dozens of similar reality shows litter the prime-time airways, each with women who flirt, flaunt their bodies, and primp their way to being chosen as the "winner" of a husband or other prize. Audiences cannot seem to get enough as these shows continue to get high ratings. For instance, many female players on the reality show *Survivor* (2000 debut) have, over the course of the more than 20 seasons, proudly used flirting, skimpy bathing suits, and so-called feminine wiles as their main strategy for winning the game – often with great success.

In other reality shows, like *The Swan* (2004–2005) and *Extreme Makeover* (2002–2007), women volunteer to undergo extreme plastic surgery procedures and other appearance "enhancing" activities in order to make their lives better and their families and husbands happier. The message of these programs is that outward appearances are of incredible importance, and that just by changing the way a person looks can make a life completely different and absolutely better.

Some would argue that the danger in programming like this is in the message it sends to viewers. On the one hand, the programs show the woman of today as a pretty princess, pushing out her chest and pouting her lips while waiting for the nearest man to save her. She stands to the side, either turning her back on the "I am woman, hear me roar" mentality so prominently featured in the shows of generations past or seemingly so dim-witted that she is unaware that the women's liberation movement ever existed at all. But is she really so clueless?

Perhaps the reality television woman of today is savvier than some would give her credit for. Perhaps all this eyelash batting is a calculated strategy to use any and all tools in order to win. If so, then should not the analysis of this reality female be more positive? This is a no-whining zone, one in which strong women make no apologies for the choices they make and are proud of all their qualities.

Consider your favorite reality television show, and the ways in which the women appearing on the show represent themselves. While it is important to acknowledge that though these shows are most certainly edited for dramatic purposes, and accusations of scripting have been leveled against some shows, in general, the ways in which women present themselves are based on their own choices. What impact might these portrayals have on audiences in contrast to the fictional character portrayals seen in other kinds of prime-time programming?

During the early 1980s, the music video became a new source of televised gender portrayals, bringing together the powerful medium of song with a visual story. Researchers and media critics immediately began investigating the music video, and discovered that while women may have been making strides toward a more multidimensional character in prime-time television and in the movies, in music videos, women were more stereotypical and hypersexed than ever. MTV, when first launched in 1981, was designed to be a "visual arena for rock music" (Lewis 1990: 38) and was targeted at young men. The videos themselves were solidly aimed at the teenage boy, and when it came to designing the sets from which the veejays would announce upcoming videos and music news, set designers attempted to recreate a teenage boy's bedroom: "stuff like stereo equipment, albums, wooden boxes, video games, and vaguely nifty doodads on the wall, including gold records donated from the likes of Men at Work, Loverboy and Journey" (Lewis 1990: 41).

"Male-address" videos were the norm in the early 1980s. Most videos implied the search by males for adventure, rebellion, sex, and dominance. When women were shown in these videos, it was common for them to be faceless bodies – long legs and provocative clothing – who were often objects of implied voyeurism and victims of violence. Women in these videos were there for men to "own" and to control, and the women not only allowed this type of behavior, they desired it. Videos including Jackson Browne's "Tender is the Night," ZZ Top's "Sharp Dressed Man," Stray Cats' "Sexy and 17," and Def Leppard's "Photograph" are prime examples of this male-address video. In an article published in 1985 in *Newsweek* magazine, writer Bill Barol writes of this trend:

> Music video sells fantasy. Fantasy, in turn, sells records ... For men, the damage hasn't been too great. They get to play a wide range of fantasy roles, from heroes to clowns. But women? All too often – especially as supporting characters in the videos of male singers – they're played as bimbos. Dressed in fishnet and leather, they drape themselves over car hoods, snarl like tigers, undress in silhouette behind window shades ... Most rock videos give free reign to the cheesiest imagery of women as playthings. (Barol 1985)

This line of thinking leads to a belief that music videos were all incredibly marginalizing to women, and contained few messages of empowerment. However, women's studies professor Lisa A. Lewis (1990: 38), in her book *Gender Politics and MTV: Voicing the Difference*, argues that such a blanket statement would be inaccurate. She agrees that there were images of women as objects and sex toys, but also offers up artists like Madonna, Cyndi Lauper, and Pat Benatar as female musicians who provided a vision of a more powerful woman, one who could play just like a man and stand up for herself (Box 9.4).

Box 9.4 Images of women in the music industry

In the world of music videos, women have not always been depicted as powerful figures. Bikini-clad women draped on sports cars or young girls in Daisy Dukes dancing for men have been often-used images in the videos of male artists. Conversely, female artists become powerful figures in their own music videos. One needs look no further than the videos that appeared in the early days of MTV for illustrations of powerful representations of women. Artists such as Madonna, Janet Jackson, Tina Turner, and Pat Benatar used their sexuality, honesty, and, in some cases, aggressive dance moves to assert their independence in an industry dominated by males. Although music videos are not as prevalent on television as they were two decades ago, there are still female artists who use them to tell stories where they are strong, independent, and in control of their own destinies. One such artist, Taylor Swift, has legions of devoted female fans who have responded to her unique display of power.

Swift is a perky young woman with wavy locks of blonde hair that frame her very nearly perfect face. She is a darling of country radio and has found crossover appeal with sweet melodies and lyrics she writes about her life. The message is clear: "I have control over my life and so should you."

The work of Swift resonates with many teens and girls because it is wholesome. She sends messages that are simple – good girls want to date good boys who ride horses and play guitars. Though this is the message she is sending, she makes it clear that she wants all of this on her terms. For example, in "Should've Said No," Swift confronts her cheating boyfriend with the admonition:

> You should've said no, you should've gone home
> You should've thought twice before you let it all go
> You should've know that word, 'bout what you did with her
> Would get back to me …
> And I should've been there, in the back of your mind
> I shouldn't be asking myself why
> You shouldn't be begging for forgiveness at my feet …
> You should've said no, baby and you might still have me

She has no intention of taking this boy back – no matter how much he begs. This storyline tells young girls that they do not need a boyfriend who disrespects them. As she tells him to get lost, she is found.

The song's accompanying music video is a live performance that put Swift on the map. The performance starts with her clothed in a hooded sweatshirt and jeans, but as the song continues, her dancers tear her clothes away to reveal a simple black dress. She moves effortlessly around the stage, draping an arm around her guitar player while he does a solo. In the end, in a sign of sheer defiance, Swift stands under an on-stage rainstorm while performing the last few lines of the song. As the audience members jump to their feet when the song ends, Swift looks out at the crowd with wide-eyed glee. Her expression also indicates that she knows she has wowed the crowd with her daring display and is eating up the ovation.

Another pop song that sends a strong message of "girl power" is "Fight Song," co-written and recorded by Rachel Platten. In this 2015 hit, Platten tells her own story about the struggle to break into the music business as a young, unknown female talent. She wanted to share how she dealt with the many rejections as she refused to give up on her dream:

> Losing friends and I'm chasing sleep
> Everybody's worried about me
> In too deep
> Say I'm in too deep (in too deep)
> And it's been two years I miss my home
> But there's a fire burning in my bones
> Still believe
> Yeah, I still believe
> And all those things I didn't say
> Wrecking balls inside my brain
> I will scream them loud tonight
> Can you hear my voice this time?
> This is my fight song
> Take back my life song
> Prove I'm alright song
> My power's turned on
> Starting right now I'll be strong
> I'll play my fight song
> And I don't really care if nobody else believes
> 'Cause I've still got a lot of fight left in me

Platten has stated she wants the song to empower people to keep going, and to keep fighting for what they believe in, no matter how tough the odds. As "Fight Song" flew up the pop charts, it also became an anthem of strength for people fighting life-threatening illness. In an interview, Platten said she is incredibly humbled and inspired by this turn. In fact, using the hashtag #MyFightSong, fans can post photos, videos, and messages about their struggles, and Platten herself curates them online (Jones 2016).

In 1989, MTV executives implemented a Program Standards Department, charged with rejecting videos that featured "explicit, graphic, or excessive depictions of sexual practices" (Goldberg 1990) as well as nudity, and violence against women. At first, there was evidence that these new regulations were being enforced: for instance, several videos were re-edited to remove questionable scenes, and some videos, including Madonna's "Justify my Love," were rejected entirely (Holden 1990). In one study of music videos shown on MTV from 1990 to 1992, the findings showed that instances of women as victims of violence were rare; women were still regularly depicted as sexual objects and often as no more than "legs in high heels" (Gow 1996).

In contrast to rock music videos, country music videos offer a different perspective on men and women. Communication professor Joli Jensen (1984) notes that, historically, "Women in country western songs are either angels (waiting at home, patient and loving), or fallen angels (sitting in honky-tonks with tinted hair and painted lips)." In more current country music, however, and specifically in more current country music videos, that simplistic and stereotypical characterization of women does not necessarily hold true. Sociologist Janelle Wilson (2000) notes that country music videos do not show the same kind of degrading or overtly sexual imagery of women that can be seen in other genres of music. Wilson conducted a content analysis of top country music videos that aired on the Country Music Channel from January to July of 1996. She found that the overwhelming theme of these videos was love, and that the content of most songs dealt with the idea of "you and me," with few references to the role and influence of social environments on behavior or attitudes. She noted several subsets of the overarching love theme: happy love, hurtin' love, and difficult/reconciliatory love, and that within these categories, music videos by female artists tended to portray women as active and assertive, less likely to self-blame, while male artist music videos tended to use more traditional imagery. These themes can be seen in current videos as well. For instance, in Carrie Underwood's video for "Before He Cheats" (Figure 9.4), Underwood smashes a car with a baseball bat, dances alone, and is basically instructing men that she is in control of her life and will be treated right. She first appears in the video wearing tight black leather jacket, torn jeans, and stilettos. She sings in a smoke-filled bar sneering at the camera the whole time. The lyrics of the song, which are often overtly aggressive in theme, instruct:

> I dug my key into the side
> Of his pretty little souped-up four-wheel drive
> Carved my name into his leather seats
> Took a Louisville Slugger to both headlights
> Slashed a hole in all four tires
> Maybe next time he'll think before he cheats

In contrast, country male artist Wade Hayes typifies the theme of hurtin' love and how the blame is all on him in the music video and song "What I Meant to Say." In this video, while Hayes sings about the mistakes he has made in his relationship, he appears to be walking forward, while all the activity around him runs in reverse. The viewer sees visions of happy families and couples – fathers playing on the playground with daughters, mothers walking with their babies in strollers, a newly married couple just emerging from a church, and an older couple walking hand in hand down the sidewalk – all around Hayes, as he mourns the bad choices he has made that ultimately led him to the present moment. He continues walking forward, as the viewer soon learns, back to the woman

Figure 9.4 Carrie Underwood getting revenge in her "Before He Cheats" video. Screenshot.

he has left behind, and at the close of the video, he appears to finally apologize, and race up the front stairs to take his woman in his arms. The lyrics tell how he accepts all blame:

What's been killing me is
I hurt you
What I didn't do was hold you
When I saw the teardrops fall
What I should have said was
I'm sorry
What I should have said was
Forgive me
What I meant to say was
What I didn't say at all.

Wilson (2000) notes that women are not just present in country music videos, they are strong, powerful, and often shown as being in charge. Female country music artists appear to be actively attempting to counteract an age-old stereotype, that of "old honky-tonk girl or country bumpkin" (2000: 301).

Several important things can be noted about these positive and more nuanced portrayals of women and men seen in country music videos. Music videos have been shown to be a powerful source of information about social roles and culture, and an "agent of socialization" (Christianson, DeBenedittis, and Lindlof 1985). The images seen in these and other country music videos offer up an alternative perspective for teens and adolescents, who make up the primary audience for music videos, showing them that behaving as strong women or as sensitive men is both acceptable and the norm. Given the tremendous popularity of country music in the United States, these music videos have the potential to reach enormous audiences: compared to every other genre of music other than jazz, country music album sales dipped the least in 2008, only 3.2 percent versus 12.7 percent for total album sales, and Taylor Swift, country–pop crossover singer, holds the title for the top-selling digital artist in music history (Vercher 2010).

Beyoncé's tour de force music video/short film *Lemonade* is a gripping discussion of womanhood and intersectional feminism. Her gender, class, and race all collide to create a powerful statement for all women, but African American women in particular. A *Huffington Post* piece by one of this book's authors explains the power of Beyoncé's visual story about adultery (Clark 2016):

It's a betrayal that chips away at Beyoncé's self-identity and, at points, sanity. Who is in the house when she's not there? What secret is he hiding that creates this bifurcated husband – one that's a good father and one that's destroying every fiber of the family in the middle of the night.

Blue Ivy's mother is surrounding her girl with a support system that all women need as they navigate becoming women. Tennis icon Serena Williams, intersectional feminists/actors Amandla Stenberg, Zendaya, and Somali poet Warsan Shire all have stories to tell of being broken by others and then rebirthing themselves stronger, better.

As images of contented Black women flicker across the screen, Malcom X's image reminds us that "(T)he most disrespected person in America is the Black woman. The most unprotected person in America is the Black woman. The most neglected person in America is the Black woman." Their smiles remind us that they, much like the city where they stand, are resilient in the face of nearly insurmountable odds.

Perhaps the betrayal can also be explained in *Lemonade*. The mothers of Trayvon Martin, Mike Brown, and Eric Garner (symbols of the Black Lives Matters movement) remind viewers that the black man has been literally broken and beaten. How would any man – even Jay Z – retain his psychological security in a world that cultivates his insecurity? Of course, it is from Becky with the good hair. What more does a man who has everything need? More validation of his masculinity.

Although music videos are considered to be marketing tools to sell songs, some artists have transformed them to address the thoughts and concerns of audiences who turn to music for answers to life's challenges.

Concluding Remarks

Without a doubt, defining gender and gender roles is confusing. There is no one singular experience, and no one universal mass opinion on how a particular social group should behave or should be depicted in entertainment media. Not only are there many dimensions to any gender identity, and how a person's gender identity is formed, but over time, and with societal and cultural changes, definitions of what constitutes femininity and masculinity change as well. When racial or ethnic identity is added to the mix – which of course it must be since it is impossible to separate one from the other – the gender role changes too.

Whether the argument is made that entertainment media reflect gender and society or whether society draws conclusions about gender as created in entertainment media, there has been a shift over the last half century toward a more complete depiction of women and men, though there is certainly still evidence that stereotypes of mainstream femininity and masculinity are alive and well in television, film, and music videos today. Moreover, as Box 9.5 explains, indicators exist that gender stereotypes that have long existed in traditional entertainment media can now be observed in video games. The growing popularity of video games opens up a new concern about the influence gender stereotypes in the virtual world might be having on young gamers, both female and male.

Box 9.5 Masculinity and video games

According to the Entertainment Software Association (ESA), 63 percent of American households have at least one person who plays video games regularly (at least 3 hours per week). The average gamer is 35 years old and has been playing for 13 years; 73 percent of all players are 18 or older, and 59 percent of gamers are males (ESA 2016). Video games are a $16 billion industry. The best-selling video games are in the shooter and action categories, and the top-selling video game of 2015 was *Call of Duty: Black Ops III*, a military science fiction first-person shooter game developed by Trayarch and published by Activision. *Call of Duty: Black Ops III* made more than $550 million in sales in the first three days of release (Grubb 2015).

Studies have consistently shown that most video game characters are white, heterosexual males (Trinh 2013). Domination, aggression, and hyper-masculine representations flood the video game market. An overwhelming number of shooter and action game male characters are violent and powerful. Blood, brutal weapons, and war are common and consistent throughout shooter and action games. While these elements are consistent, the types of roles and the settings for the video games vary widely: from the warlord in a future apocalyptic setting, to an assassin who fights for the greater good, to the Indiana Jones type of explorer trying to uncover history's biggest riddles, to a former soldier who survives a nuclear holocaust and works to rescue those he loves. In most cases, the male characters have a small emotional range, display no feelings, and lack any vulnerability. They feel no fear and show no guilt for the often many killings. The male bodies shown are incredibly muscular and out of proportion. It could be argued that while video game men are overdeveloped physically, they are underdeveloped mentally.

In addition, men are always expected to be the hero, no matter what. They suffer, and sometimes have strong backstories, like Joel from *The Last of Us*, but their brutality and ability to push on continues unabated. They are the leaders, the rescuers, and they are always in positions of strength, not weakness. For example, in the science fiction first-person shooter game series *Halo*, the main character is "Master Chief," an enormous, faceless biochemically and cybernetically enhanced super soldier. He has been raised to be a weapon since he was a child, is almost never seen without his helmet or armor, and speaks little. His duty is to protect and serve – including an artificial intelligence life form called Cortana – and his sole purpose is to come when he is called. This is true in the extreme: at the conclusion of *Halo 3*, his final words to Cortana are, "Wake me, when you need me."

We should think about the impact of the images of men presented in video games on men. Might these images affect men's attitudes toward their own bodies? Or toward their own emotional states and the ways they communicate with others? Would these images put more pressure on men to "man up," suffer in silence, and be a leader? Consider the video games you are familiar with. Do the representations of men promote male stereotypes or break them?

Reflection Questions and Thoughts to Consider

1. The "beauty and the beast" paradigm has sparked much debate by feminist scholars, who argue that the furthering of these types of storylines on television serve to encourage viewers to accept patriarchy as natural and to trivialize sexism as a laughing matter. In this chapter, the discussion of this paradigm focuses on sitcoms, and frames this argument in terms of the power of television and its ability to reinforce gender roles. There are connections, however, that can be drawn in film roles. Consider films like *Knocked Up* (2007), *The Hangover* (2009, 2011, 2013), and *Tommy Boy* (1995). What parallels do you see between the gender role representations in these types of films and those seen in the sitcoms discussed in the chapter? Can you think of other examples of the inferior yet dominant male character and superior yet submissive female character?

2. Stereotypical femininity is portrayed as natural, normal, and universal, but it is in fact a particular construction. It is largely a white, middle-class heterosexual femininity. Consider one evening of prime-time programming. How many main characters fall outside of this stereotype? How are these female characters constructed? Do you see other stereotypes emerging?

3. Male friendships on television are rarely intimate, and so-called buddy movies pair men as co-heroes, generally in action movies. Any intimate relationships between men are more likely to be found in sitcoms aimed at women and children. Why do you think this is so? Is this evidence of another kind of stereotype? Can you think of any examples to support your argument?

4. Consider the hugely popular Disney animation movie *Frozen* (2013) and the two sister characters, Anna and Elsa. Would you say that the two are post-feminist princesses? Why or why not? What kind of impact might these portrayals have on young girls' perceptions of gender roles?

5. Consider the presentation of white privilege in *Orange Is the New Black*. Across the story arc of several seasons, the audience sees examples of how Piper, the privileged white woman, is depicted as smarter, getting things she wants, while others from different racial backgrounds cry favoritism. Can you think of other examples where white privilege is depicted in entertainment media? What impact do you think these portrayals have on attitudes to inclusivity?

References

Ames, Christopher. 1992. "Restoring the Black Man's Lethal Weapon." *Journal of Popular Film and Television* 20(3): 52–61.

Avakian, Arlene. 2003. "What Is White Privilege?" May 10. https://www.mtholyoke.edu/org/wsar/intro.htm (accessed April 11, 2017).

Bandura, Albert. 2001. "Social Cognitive Theory: An Agentic Perspective." *Annual Review of Psychology* 52: 1–26.

Barol, Bill. 1985. "Women in a Video Cage." *Newsweek*, March 4: 54.

Bodroghkozy, Aniko. 2004. "Where Have You Gone, Mary Richards? Feminism's Rise and Fall in Primetime Television." *Iris: A Journal About Women*, September 22. http://www.accessmylibrary.com/article-1G1-127160507/have-you-gone-mary.html (accessed March 22, 2011).

Busch, Elizabeth Kaufer. 2009. "*Ally McBeal* to *Desperate Housewives*: A Brief History of the Postfeminist Heroine." *Perspectives on Political Science* 38(2): 87–98.

Butler, Judith. 1999. *Gender Trouble: Feminism and the Subversion of Identity*. New York, NY: Routledge.

Cameron, Alison. 2005. "Everybody Loves Lazy Stereotyping of Males Roles." *Sydney Morning Herald*, April 11. http://www.smh.com.au/news/Opinion/End-of-the-stereotype/2005/04/10/1113071851393.html (accessed April 11, 2017).

Christianson, Peter, Peter DeBenedittis, and Thomas Lindlof. 1985. "Children's Use of Audio Media." *Communication Research* 12(4): 282–301.

Clark, Naeemah. 2016. "From Generations of Infidelity and Pain, Beyoncé Makes 'Lemonade.'" *Huffington Post*, April 27. http://www.huffingtonpost.com/the-conversation-us/from-generations-of-infid_b_9787370.html (accessed April 11, 2017).

Dubrofsky, Rachel. 2002. "Ally McBeal as Postfeminist Icon: The Aestheticizing and Fetishizing of the Independent Working Woman." *The Communication Review* 5: 265–284.

Dyer, Richard. 1988. "White." *Screen* 29(4): 44–65.

Elasmar, Michael, Kazumi Hasegawa, and Mary Brian. 1999. "The Portrayal of Women in U.S. Prime Time Television." *Journal of Broadcasting and Electronic Media* 44(1): 20–34.

Emswiler, Kate. 2016. "OITNB: Read This If You've Been Wondering What Happens to Sophia on Season 3." *Popsugar*, June 24. http://www.popsugar.com/entertainment/What-Happens-Sophia-Orange-New-Black-Season-3-41708091 (accessed April 11, 2017).

Entertainment Software Association. 2016. "Essential Facts About the Computer and Video Game Industry." April. http://essentialfacts.theesa.com (accessed April 11, 2017).

Gates, Philippa. 2004. "Always a Partner in Crime." *Journal of Popular Film and Television* 32(1): 20–29.

Gauntlett, David. 2002. *Media, Gender and Identity: An Introduction*. London: Routledge.

Glascock, Jack. 2001. "Gender Roles on Prime-Time Network Television: Demographics and Behaviors." *Journal of Broadcasting and Electronic Media* 45(4): 656–669.

Goldberg, Michael. 1990. "MTV's Sharper Picture." *Rolling Stone*, February 8: 61–64.

Gow, Joe. 1996. "Reconsidering Gender Roles on MTV: Depictions in the Most Popular Music Videos of the Early 1990s." *Communication Reports* 9(2): 153.

Gregory, Deborah. 1994. "Yvette Lee Bowser: The Sister Who Took Living Single Straight to the Top!" *Essence*, December: 50.

Grubb, Jeff. 2015. "November 2015 NPD: Call of Duty Outsells Fallout 4 as PlayStation 4 Takes November." *Venture Beat*, December 10. https://web.archive.org/web/20151211044803/http://venturebeat.com/2015/12/10/november-npd-cod-beats-fallout (accessed April 11, 2017).

Harrington, C. Lee. 2003. "Lesbian(s) on Daytime Television: The Bianca Narrative on All My Children." *Feminist Media Studies* 3(2): 207.

Harris, Mark. 2010. "I Am Woman. Hear Me … Please!" *Entertainment Weekly*, August 13: 28.

Head, Sydney. 1954. "Content Analysis of Television Drama Programs." *Quarterly Journal of Film, Radio and Television* 9: 9–181.

Hod, Itay. 2015. "Patricia Arquette on Oscar Speech Fumble." *TheWrap*, March 3. http://www.thewrap.com/patricia-arquette-on-oscar-speech-fumble-i-would-have-chosen-my-words-a-little-more-carefully (accessed April 11, 2017).

Holden, Stephen. 1990. "Madonna Video Goes Too Far For MTV." *New York Times*, November 28: 18.

Holtzman, Linda. 2000. *Media Messages: What Film, Television, and Popular Music Teach Us about Race, Class, Gender, and Sexual Orientation*. Armonk, NY: M.E. Sharpe.

Horvath, Aleksandra. 2008. "Gender Roles on Television." In *Encyclopedia of Gender and Society, Volume 1*, edited by Jodi O'Brien, 374–378. Newbury Park, CA: Sage.

Jensen, Joli Kathleen. 1984. "Creating the Nashville Sound: A Case Study in Commercial Culture." PhD dissertation, University of Illinois at Urbana-Champaign.

Jones, Abigal. 2016. "Rachel Platten and the Story Behind 'Fight Song,' The Song You Can't Get Out of Your Head." *Newsweek.com*. http://www.newsweek.com/2016/03/25/rachel-platten-my-fight-song-436214.html (accessed April 11, 2017).

Kimmel, Michael. 2000. "Introduction." In *The Gendered Society Reader*, edited by Michael Kimmel, 1–2. Oxford: Oxford University Press.

Laflen, Angela. 2010. "Doing Gender." Lecture at Marist College, Poughkeepsie, NY, January 15, 2010.

Lang, Brent. 2015. "Study Finds Fewer Lead Roles for Women in Hollywood." *Variety.com*, February 9. http://variety.com/2015/film/news/women-lead-roles-in-movies-study-hunger-games-gone-girl-1201429016 (accessed April 16, 2017).

Lewis, Lisa A. 1990. *Gender Politics and MTV*. Philadelphia, PA: Temple University Press.

Lont, Cynthia M. 1995. *Women and Media: Content, Careers, Criticism*. Belmont, CA: Wadsworth.

Lotz, Amanda. 2006. *Redesigning Women: Television After the Network Era*. Urbana, IL: University of Illinois Press.

McIntosh, Peggy. 2003. "White Privilege: Unpacking the Invisible Knapsack." In *Understanding Prejudice and Discrimination*, edited by Scott Plous, 191–196. New York, NY: McGraw-Hill.

Mead, Margaret. 1935. *Sex and Temperament in Three Primitive Societies*. New York, NY: Dell.

MediaSmarts. n.d. "Common Stereotypes of Men in Media." http://mediasmarts.ca/gender-representation/men-and-masculinity/common-stereotypes-men-media (accessed April 11, 2017).

Means Coleman, Robin R. 2000. *American Viewers and the Black Situation Comedy: Situating Racial Humor*. New York, NY: Garland Publishing.

Motion Picture Producers and Distributors of America, Inc. 1930. "A Code to Govern the Making of Motion and Talking Pictures." http://productioncode.dhwritings.com/intro.php (accessed April 11, 2017).

Neuendorf, Kimberly, Thomas Gore, Amy Dalessandro, Patricie Janstova, and Sharon Snyder-Suhy. 2007. "Shaken and Stirred: A Content Analysis of Women's Portrayals in James Bond Films." Paper presented at the annual meeting of the NCA 93rd Annual Convention, Chicago, IL.

Rapping, Elayne. 1994. *Media-tions: Forays into the Culture and Gender Wars.* Boston, MA: South End Press.

Rorke, Robert. 2014. "'Orange Is the New Black' Ignites a TV Revolution for Women." *NYPost.com,* June 4. http://nypost.com/2014/06/04/orange-is-the-new-black-ignites-a-tv-revolution-for-women (accessed April 16, 2017).

Screen Actors' Guild Women's Committee. 1991. "Documents Gender Gap; Streep Speaks." *Media Report to Women* (January/February): 7.

Smith, Stacy L., Marc Choueiti, Amy Granados, and Sarah Erickson. 2008. "Asymmetrical Academy Awards? A Look at Gender Imbalance in Best Picture Nominated Films from 1977 to 2006." http://annenberg.usc .edu/sites/default/files/MDSCI_Gender_Representation_1977_2006.pdf (accessed July 1, 2017).

Smith, Stacy L., Marc Choueiti, Amy D. Granados, and Laurel Felt. 2010. "Gender Oppression in Cinematic Content? A Look at Females On-Screen and Behind-the-Camera in Top-Grossing 2007 Films." USC University of Southern California. http://annenberg.usc.edu/Faculty/Communicatio n%2520and%2520Journalism/~/media/C86F098063F54B75B272B58B875CEDAC.ashx (accessed March 22, 2011).

Smith, Stacy L., and Crystal Allene Cook. 2008. "Gender Stereotypes: An Analysis of Popular Films and TV." The Geena Davis Institute. https://seejane.org/wp-content/uploads/GDIGM_Gender_ Stereotypes.pdf (accessed April 11, 2017).

Steeves, H. Leslie. 1987. "Feminist Theories and Media Studies." *Critical Studies in Mass Communication* 4(2): 95–135.

Trinh, Long. 2013. "Masculinity in the Virtual World of Video Game: A Question of Agency." Honors Theses, Paper 7.

Vercher, Brody. 2010. "Country Music's Album Sales Could be Worse." *9513 Country Music,* January 11. http://www.the9513.com/country-musics-album-sales-could-be-worse-taylor-swift-is-the-top-selling-digital-music-artist-ever (accessed March 22, 2011).

Walsh, Kimberly R., Elfriede Fursich, and Bonnie S. Jefferson. 2008. "Beauty and the Patriarchal Beast: Gender Role Portrayals in Sitcoms Featuring Mismatched Couples." *Journal of Popular Film and Television* 36(3): 123–132.

Walters, Suzanne. 1995. *Material Girls: Making Sense of Feminist Cultural Theory.* Berkeley, CA: University of California Press.

Wilson, Janelle. 2000. "Women in Country Music Videos." *ETC: A Review of General Semantics* 57(3): 290.

10

Representations of Gender in Magazines, Newspapers, and Advertising

Redbook magazine's media kit appeals from the start. Beautiful fonts and bold shades of red and hot pink entice the reader in with words of encouragement. "Redbook is the only all-access pass to great style," it says, continuing, "we put the tools for a happy life into the hands of every American woman" (Redbook 2017). Empowerment seems to ooze from the web page, urging women to be their best selves, noting that "Redbook is [the reader's] trusted friend, the grown-up girl's guide to a happy, beautiful life" (Redbook 2017). It feels like the female empowerment poster child of magazines, finally providing women a change from the usual "how to please your man" or "drop 25 pounds in 6 weeks to fit into those size 00 jeans" that are the stock-in-trade of other popular women's magazines. While recent issues of *Redbook* have made efforts at inclusivity, including their September 2016 cover, which featured models of different ethnicities and sizes, like most women's magazines *Redbook* often disappoints, as mixed messages abound: while the taglines say one thing, cover images, which put forth idealized images of beauty, say another.

For example, in July 2007, the magazine featured country music singer Faith Hill beaming on its cover. Sort of, anyway. It turns out it was Faith Hill with a lot of Photoshop tweaking. Jezebel. com (2007), a pulls-no-punches website covering Hollywood, fashion, and politics for women, secured a copy of the original photograph taken of Hill and wrote a scathing article ripping *Redbook* for its Photoshop hatchet job, transforming an "already above-average 39-year-old" into "a female forgery." Among the things changed: trimming a "saggy" earlobe, thinning an arm so it looks fatless, boneless, and approximately one inch wide, removing all lines and wrinkles on face, lengthening the neck, adding hair to make it look fuller, and applying an overall slimming of the body. *Redbook* is not alone in idealized depictions, and some argue that this kind of airbrushing is common and just part of magazines today. Kelly Clarkson, the winner of the first season of *American Idol* (2002–2016), appeared on the September cover of *Self* magazine in 2009, and noted when asked about the final version of the cover: "It's very colorful, and they definitely have Photoshopped the crap out of me, but I don't care! Whoever she is, she looks great" (ETonline 2009) (see Figure 10.1).

Diversity in US Mass Media, Second Edition. Catherine A. Luther, Carolyn Ringer Lepre, and Naeemah Clark.
© 2018 John Wiley & Sons Inc. Published 2018 by John Wiley & Sons Inc.

Figure 10.1 Kelly Clarkson's computer-altered *Self* cover next to her real self. Reproduced courtesy of Jezebel.com.

But the writers at Jezebel.com argue that the alterations of women, which perpetuate what they call "The Cover Lie," has a damaging effect on the women who see these unrealistic and impossible-to-attain images day after day. They write:

> Magazine-retouching may not be a lie on par with [government lies] but in a world where girls as young as eight are going on the South Beach Diet, teenagers are getting breast implants as graduation gifts, professional women are almost required to fetishize handbags, and everyone is spending way too much goddamn time figuring out how to pose … it's [just] wrong. (2007)

This chapter will address how women and men have been represented in magazines, newspapers, and print advertising. Although this chapter is about issues regarding gender and the mass media, due to the preponderance of research on women and the press, its focus (as in the previous chapter) is mostly on female representations. First, a brief discussion about writer and activist Betty Friedan, magazines, and feminism may help explain why the representations of women are at times celebrated, problematic, and ultimately, evolving.

Historical Background to Women in Magazines

Women were the target audience for many of the first magazines published in the United States. Beginning with the short-lived *The Lady's Magazine and Repository of Entertaining Knowledge*, published in 1792, women's magazines have long been a large part of print media. Several of the most prominent women's magazines, commonly known as "The Seven Sisters," were launched in the late 1800s and early 1900s. These magazines were *Better Homes and Gardens, Family Circle, Good Housekeeping, Ladies' Home Journal, Redbook, Women's Day*, and the now-defunct *McCall's*. From the very beginning, women were urged to seek perfection. The magazines they read in the early 1900s included information on how to keep a better home, how to behave and look like a lady, how best to care for your husband and children, and how to cook to please your family. Magazine historian Frank Luther Mott (1968) notes that the constant stream of advice on how to be perfect was so prevalent he wondered if some might have grown weary of it. Considering that the popularity of these magazines continued into the 1960s, this was probably not the case.

Writer and activist Betty Friedan, in her 1963 book *The Feminine Mystique* ([1963] 2001: 79–123), threw much blame on women's magazines and their role in perpetuating the feminine stereotype of the "happy housewife heroine." Friedan was a former writer for many women's magazines, and she had become increasingly troubled by the image of the perfect woman she saw being formed within the pages of the popular magazines of the time: a woman in pursuit of blissful domesticity, which was characterized by home and husband – and that happiness was impossible without both. She writes:

> Experts told them how to catch a man and keep him, how to breastfeed children and handle their toilet training, how to cope with sibling rivalry and adolescent rebellion; how to buy a dishwasher, bake bread, cook gourmet snails, and build a swimming pool with their own hands; how to dress, look, and act more feminine and make marriage more exciting; how to keep their husbands from dying young and their sons from growing into delinquents. They were taught to pity the neurotic, unfeminine, unhappy women who wanted to be poets or physicists or presidents. They learned that truly feminine women do not want careers, higher education, political rights – the independence and the opportunities that the old-fashioned feminists fought for. (Friedan [1963] 2001: 58)

Friedan summarized what she called a typical issue of a popular magazine in the early 1960s: it included seven short stories about marriage, children, or the joy of being a housewife, a feature story on maternity fashion, patterns for home sewing and crafts, one article on dieting and another on how to prevent female baldness, an article called "An Encyclopedia Approach to Finding a Second Husband," and an article on overcoming an "inferiority complex." In commenting on such a typical issue, she writes:

> This was the image of the American woman in the year Castro led a revolution in Cuba and men were trained to travel into outer space; the year that the African continent brought forth new nations, and a plane whose speed is greater than the speed of sound broke up a Summit Conference; the year artists picketed a great museum in protest against the hegemony of abstract art; physicists explored the concept of antimatter; astronomers, because of new radio telescopes, had to alter their concepts of the expanding universe; biologists made a breakthrough in the fundamental chemistry of life; and Negro youth in Southern schools forced the United States, for the first time since the Civil War, to face a moment of democratic truth. But this magazine, published for over 5,000,000 American women, almost all of whom have been through high school and nearly half to college, contained

almost no mention of the world beyond the home. In the second half of the twentieth century in America, a woman's world was confined to her own body and beauty, the charming of man, the bearing of babies, and the physical care and serving of husband, children, and home. And this was no anomaly of a single issue of a single women's magazine. (Friedan [1963] 2001: 83)

Following, and perhaps because of, Friedan's groundbreaking book, women's magazines did begin to change, with an increased willingness to cover career women and issues beyond beauty and home, although many observers argue the change has been slow and not nearly as dramatic as one might suppose.

Gender in Magazines

"The Seven Sisters" reached the peak of their circulations in the mid-1970s, when they had an aggregate circulation of 46 million (Beasley and Gibbons 2003: 180–185). Increased competition from newer, more niche-oriented magazines slowly eroded this number. Many of these magazines reflected the social changes women were experiencing. For example, *Ms.* magazine, launched in 1972, offered a feminist alternative to the traditional women's magazines. The magazine was successful, covering topics such as politics and global current affairs, although circulation rates, even at its most popular, never came near those of the traditional women's magazines. But perhaps the best example of the break from the "happy homemaker heroine" occurred when author and businesswoman Helen Gurley Brown took over the reins at *Cosmopolitan* in 1964. When *Cosmopolitan* was originally launched in 1886, it was a family magazine, with sections for women that focused on fashion, household decorating, cooking, and childcare. Within a few years, as it grew in popularity, *Cosmopolitan's* focus changed and became a leading market for fiction, featuring major authors such as Edith Wharton, Rudyard Kipling, and Jack London. Its strength as a repository for fiction grew over the next 50 years, as did its reputation for investigative journalism. By the mid-1950s *Cosmopolitan's* circulation was declining, along with the circulations of many general interest magazines. This downward spiral continued for the next 10 years, until *Cosmopolitan* was redefined as a women's special interest magazine, but not in the mold of the women's magazines that came before, like *Ladies' Home Journal* or *Woman's Day*.

Gurley Brown, who authored the best-selling *Sex and the Single Girl*, was able to remake the magazine to assert that women should have a strong sexual identity, and emphasized the idea that independence and "living it up" were ultimate desires. *Cosmopolitan* now urges readers to believe that they have a right to enjoy sex, and that men are desirable but far from perfect. Being a "Cosmo Girl" means you are not afraid to be powerful, to dominate a man (especially in bed), and to be single. Critics would argue, though, that *Cosmopolitan's* message is fraught with contradictions: be single, but pursue a man; be yourself, but be beautiful and thin; be powerful, but do not work so hard as to not have lots of fun. And so the message to women remains confusing.

Nevertheless, women's magazines remain one of the most popular forms of media. The market today is flooded with women's titles, ranging from the more traditional offerings like *Glamour*, which focuses on a wide range of women's topics from beauty and fashion to health and politics, to *Bitch*, a feminist magazine focused on commentary of pop culture. Of the top 20 magazines by circulation at the end of 2015, 10 were women's titles including *Cosmopolitan, Redbook, Better Homes and Gardens, Good Housekeeping, Family Circle, Women's Day*, and *Ladies' Home Journal*

(Association of Magazine Media n.d.). Media researchers Maureen Beasley and Sheila Gibbons (2003: 180) note that celebrity culture has never been more popular in women's magazines than it is today, with women's lives routinely being explained through the experiences of well-known people. They also argue that the confusing message of years past continues: "the mixed messages many women's magazines send – empowerment and dependency, independence and entanglement, strength and seductiveness – can be confusing to women and girls and somewhat frustrating for them as they try and decode these messages for themselves" (Beasley and Gibbons 2003: 181).

Mainstream magazines, in general, have been found to present stereotypical portraits of women, and – although women's magazines today do cover issues related to politics or other world issues – the general formula is still beauty, fashion, weight loss, cooking, and sex. A 2003 study of the portrayal of working women in mainstream magazines by media researcher Juanita J. Covert found that if successful working women were presented in a positive way, they were likely to be described using stereotypically positive feminine qualities, such as having good beauty and fashion sense. Covert also found that though there were several articles about working women or the workplace in general in the magazines studied, the most common stories were about beauty and fashion. A strong emphasis was placed on "celebrities-as-working-women," and many of the magazines used this formula for the working-women stories.

Historically, images of women of color are distorted to fit the dominant group's ideals and cultural relevance (Johnson 2015). Unfortunately, this trend does not appear to have changed over time. In a 2015 study that examined the front covers of eight major consumer magazines in 2014, including *Cosmopolitan*, *Glamour*, *Vogue*, *Redbook*, and *Seventeen*, only 18 percent featured a woman of color. Approximately 5 percent of these covers featured black or African American women, 11 percent featured Latinas, 2 percent featured Asian American women. There were no Native American women. In addition, women of color were found to have been masked with whiteness, objectified, and portrayed with exoticism intensified.

While the women's magazine genre has flourished, magazines for men have had a slightly different history. Men's magazines first began to be published in the early nineteenth century, and covered news and information about crime, sport, adventure, hunting, and fishing. By the middle of the twentieth century, publications that focused on these topics continued and grew to not only include, but to be dominated by, those niche magazines that covered urban life and sex (Payne 1998). In 1933, *Esquire* was founded by journalist and businessman Arnold Gingrich as a magazine that combined fashion, humor, and high quality fiction and non-fiction from America's best writers. With the help of an article written by author Ernest Hemingway that was published in the first issue, *Esquire* was a huge success right out of the gate. During the 1940s, *Esquire* began running foldout "girlie art," which appealed to the male audience's more prurient interests (Sumner 2010: 82–83).

In 1953, businessman and self-proclaimed playboy Hugh Hefner, who had previously worked as a promotional copy writer for *Esquire*, adapted the *Esquire* formula and pushed the sex formula even further, publishing the first issue of *Playboy*, which included a nude centerfold photograph of actress and iconic sex symbol Marilyn Monroe. The magazine sparked many rival publications, including *Penthouse*, and plenty of controversy throughout its many years of publication. However, its circulation has dipped, especially since the advent of the Internet, which helped make pornography and nude content easily accessible and free. As a result, *Playboy* announced, in 2015, that it would eliminate nudity from its pages and become more of a competitor to, say, *Vanity Fair*. By freeing the magazine from images of nude women, the magazine would be permitted on social media platforms such as Twitter or Facebook and would be able to enter world markets that are considered conservative (Somaiya 2015).

Judith Levine (1994: 27–31), author of *My Enemy, My Love: Women, Men, and the Dilemmas of Gender*, argues that men's magazines fall into two basic categories: specialized magazines, such as those about squirrel hunting and CB radios, and those about sex. She writes, "My newsstand carries hundreds of both kinds. No fewer than forty publications displayed cater to automotive aficionados, almost as many to weaponry fanatics ... and I lost count at fifty skin magazines – past *Playboy* to *Juggs* and beyond." But she also notes a smaller category of general interest men's magazines that continue to thrive, though not nearly on par, circulation-wise, with the general interest women's magazines. *Esquire*, *GQ*, *Details*, *Maxim*, and *Men's Journal* are included in this category, and Levine suggests that these magazines are particularly good for analyzing messages of social transformation as related to masculinity. Magazines like *Details* and *GQ* offer up content that appeals to a heterosexual and homosexual audience, achieving the "ideal balance of 'fabness' and 'regular-guy attitude' – code for gay and straight – by assuming that whatever their sexual preference, men want to look good, feel good, read good writing, and have good relationships" (Levine 1994: 30), while *Esquire* and *Men's Journal* have maintained a "man's man" attitude toward content, focusing on rugged individualism, and a mainstream straight attitude to the audience.

Maxim, launched by Dennis Publishing in 1997, is targeted at young men and is part of the genre of men's magazines called "laddie magazines" or "lads' magazines." The magazine is aggressively heterosexual, filled with stories and advertisements focusing on sex, drinking, and sports. One communication scholar suggests the magazine, with its often lowbrow humor, connotes an "omnidirectional contempt and anger" toward women (particularly feminists), toward gays, toward "sensitive" men, and toward the readers themselves (Davis 2005). In the magazine, masculinity is defined and men are encouraged to look and perform in certain ways to regain their "manliness" and recapture the former male power that perhaps has slipped away from them. In characterizing lads' magazines, media professor Karen Ross (2010) writes, "Men are given nudge–nudge–wink–wink permission to be the worst example of their Neanderthal past, grunting, farting, and play fighting in the forest with their mates before going back to the cave at night to have rough sex with the women who have waited patiently and open-legged for their return." As a lads' magazine, *Maxim* is a step-by-step, how-to guide to being a "man," although some content seems so over the top that it is most likely being used either as parody or to get a quick laugh.

Men's and women's magazines are not the only magazine genres that appear to perpetuate gender role stereotyping (Box 10.1). Studies have also shown parenting magazines to depict men and women in stereotypic ways. Researchers of one 2008 study of the photographic images in four major parenting magazines found that men are drastically underrepresented, shown approximately one third as often as mothers or women. When men are portrayed they are more likely to be interacting with children in a playful or recreational way, such as participating in a sporting activity (Martinson, Hinnant, and Martinson 2008). Women are shown as nurturers, and, more often than men, are pictured expressing affection or caring for a child in a gentle way. However, in an encouraging result, the portrayals of boys and girls in photographs were not gender stereotyped, and the researchers argue that the repeated viewing of these gender-equal images might have the power to transform any existing stereotypes of how boys and girls should act.

Box 10.1 Should men care about gender stereotypes?

Consider the following excerpted article by Alex Gibson (2008) entitled, "Why Men Should Care About Gender Stereotypes." Do you believe that his points are valid? Can you think of examples of male gender role stereotypes that media perpetuate?

> Let's not kid ourselves: men as well as women are limited by gender stereotypes. The idea of men as stupid and sex-obsessed is an enduring generalization that is allowed to flourish in – dare I say it – a much more brazen way than the stereotypes about women, mainly because no man ever stands up and says: "Hey, that's sexist and it offends me!" The problem is, while women are encouraged to reject the ludicrous ideas that are held about them, men are supposed to embrace them.

> Christ, guys, have you seen what we're supposed to be like? Looking solely at stereotypes, men do not fare well. I would never dare to suggest that men have a harder time than women in general society, because that's just patently untrue, but in terms of stereotypes we fail utterly. Male perceptions of women are designed to make us feel smug in our superiority, but the way we've chosen to label ourselves should make any man feel thoroughly humiliated and ashamed of his gender.

> Men are often characterized as spoiled, helpless brats utterly unable to perform simple household tasks, too stupid to remember anniversaries and appointments and completely unable to understand these strange female creatures and their hysterical emotions. We're base brutes ruled by our overactive sex drives who simply can't help being crass and immature, because that is the way God made us. This is precisely the kind of ridiculous stereotype that, if applied to women, would be torn to shreds in intelligent debate. So why don't men object?

Gibson (2008) makes the argument that men have never had to think about gender:

> Here's the thing: men don't have anything remotely equivalent to feminism. From an early age, women are aware of their gender and what it means for their lives, far more than men are. Feminism encourages women to shed gender stereotypes and consider themselves as individuals. Men simply don't think about gender. Why would you, when it rarely impacts in a noticeable way on your life? Very rarely is your progress barred because you are a man and it is true that male culture generally does not promote frank and open discussion of such issues.

> So what can we, a group of individuals who clearly care about gender equality and despise gender stereotypes, do about this? A prevailing culture of stupidity just isn't good enough for men or women, even if the former often don't realize it. Men can be the attentive and understanding partners that women want, and it is a tragic shame that society has conditioned the male mind to reject this sensitivity as weak and inappropriate. The change that needs to be made is cultural, but that doesn't make it any less difficult.

Gender in Newspapers

Like the research done on many of the ethnic and social groups discussed in previous chapters, much of the research done on women has shown the representations, the stereotypes, and the overall frames used to depict women in newspapers to be problematic. For example, journalism professor Caryl Rivers (2007: 1–15), in her book *Selling Anxiety*, writes, "it's all bad news" for women. She argues that though the news media today do not relegate women to a "low-prestige 'women's page'" as in days past, there is a clear narrative frame that appears regularly, and though there are balanced, well-reported stories about women in the news media, there are innumerable "chain reaction" stories that jump from newspaper to television sound bite to magazine to the Internet and thus have thematic staying power. Women are not told they cannot achieve, but they are told that if they do, they will be miserable, as will their children (Figure 10.2). Their families and their sex lives will suffer. They will age badly. Day-care children become bullies, and nannies cannot be trusted. Women in power are scary, masculine, and lead personally unfulfilling lives. Rivers makes a strong case that these frames, coupled with the trend of women lagging behind men as sources in news stories, influence readers' perceptions of women and feminism in general (Box 10.2).

The way women and men have been portrayed in the news media, and the roles to which men and women have been assigned, have been the subject of research for several decades. Many of these studies have looked for basic counts on the numbers of men versus women who are present in news stories, including being used as sources or the focus. They have also looked at who are the reporters, presenters, and writers of news stories, and in what roles men and women are shown (i.e., in the home, in the workplace, as leaders, as victims, etc.). In most analyses, researchers find evidence of a general lack of representation of women.

In several studies done in the 1990s and 2000s, a distinct gender gap was reported in the use of men versus women as news sources. For example, in one of its studies, the Project for Excellence in Journalism (2005) examined 16,800 news stories across 45 news outlets over the course of nine months in 2004, and found that more than three quarters of the stories analyzed contained male sources, compared to only one third of stories that contained a female source (see Table 10.1). The only topic category in which women were used as a source more than 50 percent of the time were lifestyle stories, and the subjects in which women were least likely to be cited were foreign affairs and sports.

Figure 10.2 A harried working mom.
Reproduced with kind permission of iStock.

Box 10.2 Framing working women

Journalism professor Caryl Rivers, in her book *Selling Anxiety* (2007), suggests that the news media frame working women in two basic ways: as superwomen or as "twitching wrecks" (2007: 15). She writes, "The former are often profiled in business pages, lifestyle pages, and TV features. They are accomplished, incredibly organized, and never seem to sweat … On the other end of the media spectrum are the Twitching Wrecks. They seem to inhabit every 'working woman' trend story that rolls off the presses or onto videotape. Such women are endlessly miserable, eternally frazzled."

Consider the two following news story excerpts. Compare and contrast the "working woman" frames. What have your news media experiences shown you about these frames?

From the article "The Myth of Quality Time" by Kalb *et al.* (1997) in *Newsweek*:

> For the New York lawyer, it all hit home in the grocery store. She had stopped in with her 6-year-old to pick up a few things, but since the babysitter normally did the shopping, she was unprepared for what was about to happen. Suddenly there was her son, whooping and tearing around the store, skidding the length of the aisles on his knees. "This can't be my child," she thought in horror. Then the cashier gave a final twist to the knife. "Oh," she remarked. "So you're the mother."

The author continues:

> That was the moment when the lawyer was forced to admit that spending "quality time" with the kids didn't seem to be working. She and her husband, a journalist, had subscribed in good faith to the careerists' most treasured rule of parenting: it isn't how much time you spend with your kids, it's how you spend the time. But despite those carefully scheduled hours of parental attention between dinner and bed, their two kids were in danger of turning into little brats. Next month the family is moving to a suburb, and she'll go to work part-time.

Later in the article, the author argued:

> Not every family can, or wants to, make a life change on that scale. But many are starting to question whether time devoted to their children really can be efficiently penciled into the day's calendar, like a business appointment with a couple of short, excitable clients. No wonder a growing number of psychologists and educators who work with children would like to get rid of the whole idea of quality time. "I think quality time is just a way of deluding ourselves into shortchanging our children," says Ronald Levant, a psychologist at Harvard Medical School.

From the article "This Is How She Does It" by Riss (2009) in *Working Mother* magazine:

> She's among a handful of top advisors who sit down each morning with President Barack Obama. But before that meeting – or chief of staff, senior staff and legislative strategy meetings – Mona Sutphen has a sit-down of a different sort: at the family breakfast table. With husband Clyde Williams, she gets their kids ready for school. "I see Sydney and Davis amid the morning chaos and mayhem," Mona laughs. "Getting dressed, eating breakfast, finding art supplies …" Mona may have one of the most intense jobs in the country, but she takes time in the morning to make a really mean oatmeal.

The article continues:

> "She has an amazing ability to keep perspective about what's important and has a great sense of humor," says her friend Nina Hachigian. "She doesn't take herself too seriously, even though

(Continued)

Box 10.2 (Continued)

she's in a very serious position." As one of two deputy chiefs of staff, Mona helps coordinate the President's vast domestic policy agenda. Sure, there's inherent glamour in her high-ranking position – she works a few doors down from the Oval Office – but there's also constant stress and marathon days. Mona typically works from 7:00 a.m. to 9:00 p.m., five days a week, with half-days on Saturdays.

The author concludes:

The steady stream of serious and time-sensitive decisions that need to get made require Mona to offer recommendations and move things forward faster than she might like. More than a decade of experience in government, including traveling the world as a U.S. Foreign Service officer and serving in the White House during the Clinton administration, has primed her for the job, say colleagues. Mona realizes she's in the middle of an astonishing opportunity: "There are moments when I'm sitting in a cabinet meeting or in the Oval Office and I realize people will write about this conversation in history books."

Overwhelmingly, males dominated the front page of newspapers, being used as sources in stories 79 percent of the time, appearing in 69 percent of the photographs, and writing 66 percent of the stories (see Table 10.2). When stories were written about or by women, they were more likely to appear at the bottom of the page below the fold, a less prominent location. Photographs of women were also more likely to be below the fold. This study, compared with studies of females and males on the front page over the past three decades, shows that little has changed since the 1970s. Women

Table 10.1 Male and female sources in the news.

Number of times referenced per story	Males	Females
0	24%	67%
1	21%	20%
2 or more	55%	14%

Note: Totals may not equal 100 due to rounding.
Source: Project for Excellence in Journalism (2005).

Table 10.2 Male versus female representation on the front page of newspapers.

	Males	Females
Referenced in articles	79%	21%
Shown in photographs	69%	31%
Writers of articles	66%	34%

Source: Project for Excellence in Journalism (2005).

are as underrepresented now as they were then, although women now outnumber men in the general population (Lont and Bridge 2010).

One argument suggests that the common use of male sources stems from the fact that men are more likely to hold positions of power in our society and are therefore more accessible. Reporters on deadline have to seek out readily available sources and tend to use the same sources over and over again, when a source proves reliable and accessible. Diversity in reporting on deadline might not be a top priority. However, some researchers have attempted to debunk this perspective. Journalism professor Cory Armstrong (2004), in her study of the influence of reporter gender on source selection, found that women are more likely to seek out and use female sources in their stories, and that men are more likely to seek out and use male sources in their stories, regardless of story topic. If reporters seek out and use sources based on accessibility or on local prominence (for instance, approximately 60 percent of all privately held firms are owned and operated by men), a gender discrepancy might be expected. But if, as Armstrong's study found, women are more likely to use women as sources, then one might wonder – why are female reporters more likely to be able to locate female sources? Simple accessibility is no longer a valid argument. Armstrong suggests that it may come down to comfort level; women feel more comfortable contacting women, and men feel more comfortable contacting men.

Others have found that when women *are* used as sources, they most often are used in local news stories, and are represented as victims more often than leaders, heroes, or successful business people. In general, women are more often than men identified by personal information, such as physical description, clothing, marital or parental status, while men are more likely to be identified by occupation, experience, and background (Silver 1985). In her study on gender-role stereotyping in the news, media scholar Judy VanSlyke Turk (1987) found that there was no statistically significant difference between male and female reporters in the use of personal attributes as descriptors for sources; both were equally likely to use them.

Political stories, in particular, highlight gender-role stereotyping in news. Many researchers have analyzed female candidates in political races across the country. In general, these studies have found that male and female political candidates are presented in very different ways and along gender-role stereotypes (e.g., Benze and Declerq 1985). Female candidates tend to be presented as being compassionate and warm, and male candidates are presented as being tough and aggressive. Female candidates are more likely than male candidates to have substantive column inches devoted to appearance, emotionality, and personality. The use of sources in political stories, too, takes on added importance when it is considered that expert sources used in political stories have a substantial impact on voter attitude and understanding. Expert sources add value to a news story, and the use of a particular source by a journalist provides that source with a credibility and trust, which can build the level of authority attributed to that person. In other words, readers and viewers will trust in the credibility and authority of a particular source, in part because the journalist is telling them the person is an expert.

When thinking about how women are portrayed in print media, turning to studies on the coverage of how the press frames the most visible American woman, the First Lady, can offer an interesting perspective. The First Lady is the subject of much press scrutiny, and it has been widely held by researchers that societal norms about how women fit into the leadership realm and what the "appropriate role" for a woman should be complicates coverage of this powerful (and yet not powerful) woman. Over the past three decades, there have been changes in how women are viewed in our society, especially in terms of their political influence – and more specifically, the public perception of what role a First Lady should play is changing. Much study has been done on the First Lady and her office, with considerable attention paid in recent years to stereotyping and the use of frames (e.g., Scharrer and Bissell 2000; Stooksbury and Edgemon 2003; Watts 1997; Winfield and Friedman 2003). Jill Abraham (2004) suggests that as frames are often marked by controversy and social relevancy, and as First Ladies are often seen as symbols of American womanhood, the cultural controversy over gender roles provides a powerful frame through which the media cover these women.

First Lady scholar Betty Winfield (1997) defined four major frames used when a First Lady appeared in the news: as an escort, accompanying the President; as a style setter, serving as a social role model; as a "noblesse oblige," performing charitable good works; and in a policy advisor role. Another major frame used is one that emphasizes a stereotypical or traditionally expected gender role, such as that of the sacrificing, supportive spouse or the social function-performing lady of the house. Research has shown that the more politically active the First Lady, and the less of a behind-the-scenes wife stereotype she fulfills, the more negative the textual coverage (Scharrer and Bissell 2000).

Time writer Kurt Andersen (1985) writes that "the country expects its First Lady to represent some approximate ideal of American womanhood, and that perfectly modern superwoman is, in the 1980s, powerful but feminine, romantically alive, but socially engaged." Another *Time* article states:

> The person a pillow away from the presidency is held up to an undefined ideal: she bears all America's conflicting notions about women as wives, mothers, lovers, colleagues, and friends. A First Lady should be charming but not all fluff, gracious but not a doormat, substantive but not a co-President. She must defend her husband and smile bravely when he says stupid things. (Carlson 1989)

The article continues:

> She must look great, even fashionable, when a shower and clean clothes would suffice for anyone else; possess perfect children though such critters do not exist in nature; and traipse around the globe in a suit and sensible pumps when she would rather be home with a good book. She has both a day and a night job, but is not allowed a profession of her own. Hardest of all, she has to appear to love every minute of it. (Carlson 1989)

Hillary Clinton most often was framed as a feminist career woman. Interestingly, during the Monica Lewinsky sex scandal in 1998, when Clinton donned her "stand by your man" persona, a very traditional gender role, her favorability rating reached some of its highest levels during her term of office.

Laura Bush was framed as the "un-Hillary" (Brant 2001), a First Lady drawn from the traditional Barbara Bush cloth. Reports commented on her love of books and libraries, her composure under pressure, and as a "partner in her husband's life, but not his work" (Curtis, Roche, and Hylton 2001). According to one *U.S. News and World Report* article, Laura Bush is "more garden club than healthcare task force, more homebody than world traveler, more listener than stump speaker. And all, apparently by choice, ushering in her own era as perhaps the first post-feminist first lady" (Walsh and Cannon 2001: 20). She played a more traditionally feminine gender role and was as uncontroversial as any First Lady in the past two decades. Her approval ratings remained extremely high for her eight years in the White House, never falling below 80 percent.

Coverage of Michelle Obama, the Ivy League educated wife of Senator Barack Obama, has been interesting. Early on, she came under fire for being too outspoken and too aggressive, giving more ammunition to the overall discussion of gender role portrayal and societal expectations about women. She received some daggers for comments that were considered antipatriotic. She was a fist-bumping caricature, a stereotypical "angry black woman," and, to counter the negative attention, Obama changed her image. Obama showed "self-restraint and discipline by dialing back" (Samuels 2008) and worked to reassure voters that she was "just like you" (Gibbs and Scherer 2009). She made sure to demonstrate there was warmth between her and her candidate husband and show her children as the top priority. Feminists objected, but this more traditionally feminine woman played well in the press and with voters.

After the 2008 election, a neon-bright light was focused on the Obama family – especially Michelle Obama. *Time* invited its readers to "Meet the Obamas!" as if they were sitcom characters. In the article, Obama is not compared to any former First Lady, but to Laura Petrie, the *Dick Van Dyke Show's* "amiably needling supporter … asking him to take the girls to school the morning after the election" (Poniewozik 2008). Michelle Obama, being in a unique position to shatter black female stereotypes, was framed as the ideal mother, a fashion icon, a supportive wife, and a dignified First Lady (Butler 2013).

In 2015, a former First Lady began her second campaign for the presidency. Studies of the news media coverage of Hillary Clinton during both the Democratic primaries and her time as Secretary of State point to depictions that parallel findings from past studies on how women have been characterized in the media. Communication scholars Rebecca Curnalia and Dorian L. Mermer (2014) found that as a woman she was portrayed as being in a double bind (similar to a rock and hard place). As a female she had to demonstrate that she was feminine – warm and friendly, but not too feminine or emotional if she wanted to be taken seriously by voters. Coverage of Clinton assessed her when she, as Secretary of State, was facing scrutiny for her handling of the attack on the American embassy in Benghazi, Libya. Mass communications professors Dustin Harp, Jamie Loke, and Ingrid Bachmann (2016) studied the coverage through a feminine lens, finding that the news media questioned her competence as a leader if she displayed emotion. During a hearing where her decisions during the attack were questioned, Clinton's quick and curt responses were considered to be insincere and merely a way to escape culpability for the loss of American lives.

Gendered coverage of candidates does not just apply to Clinton. A study of media coverage of women running for political offices in 2008–2012 found that these candidates were framed as being novelties. Stories about candidates including Sarah Palin and Elizabeth Dole used words such as "unique" or "lone" in explaining the campaigns for their quest for high office (Meeks 2012). Words such as these only serve to emphasize that these women and other women were outliers and oddities in the history of leadership of the country. These aforementioned assessments of women as political leaders is illustrative of the contention that the media cements the images and expectations, rightly or wrongly, of what women should, can, and have to be.

Gender in Advertising

Generally speaking, advertising has been slower to change with societal norms, and nowhere is that more obvious than in the way women and men are presented in advertisements. In the 1950s, as with magazines, women were portrayed as housewives, caring for their families. They cooked, cleaned, did laundry, and made themselves look beautiful for their husbands. Men, on the other hand, were shown as business-oriented and pillars of the home. The message these advertisements sent was clearly that women belonged in the home, while men were the breadwinners. The 1960s brought some change, but men were still in dominant positions in comparison to women. Women were more often portrayed as sex objects, showing more skin, and when pictured with men, were beautiful, had hourglass figures, and were clearly "arm candy." Advertisers took advantage of the insecurities of women as pertaining to their looks. Writer and marketing consultant Michelle Miller (2005) describes one ad during that period: "Beauty cream was marketed with a magazine advertisement showing a distraught wife looking on as her husband talked with a beautiful young woman; the masthead read, 'Does Your Husband Look Younger Than You Do?'" As the ad demonstrates, sexism continued to rule in the 1960s.

Women were pictured more often in working roles in the 1970s, but these roles were more subservient than their male counterparts. Common occupations for women were secretary, hairdresser, and waitress. The message was still that women were not equal to men, were sexual objects to be used, and did not have any real power in society. In a large content analysis of general interest magazines, media researchers Alice Courtney and Sarah Lockeretz (1971) examined images of women and men in magazine advertisements. They found that:

- Women were rarely shown in out-of-home working roles.
- Few women were shown as professional or high-level business people.
- Women rarely ventured far from home by themselves or with other women.
- Women were shown as dependent on men's protection.
- Men were shown regarding women as sex objects or as domestic adjuncts.
- Females were most often shown in ads for cleaning products, food products, beauty products, drugs, clothing, and home appliances.
- Men were most often shown in ads for cars, travel, alcoholic beverages, cigarettes, banks, industrial products, entertainment media, and industrial companies.

The main message in these ads was that men were the protectors who carried out more important roles and had to make more significant decisions for themselves and for their families than did women.

A larger shift occurred in the 1980s. Women and men were still largely pictured in traditional gender roles, women in the home and men at work, but there was movement to a more modern depiction. Advertisements started showing men at home, helping out with the chores, and caring for children, and women began to be pictured with regularity in the workplace, and not always in a support role. Interestingly, though more women were shown in the workplace, stereotypes of the "working woman" were loud and clear. One study asked women their opinion about a 1985 American Express ad campaign, dubbed the Betty Briefcase campaign, which appeared in magazines and on television (Pieraccini and Schell 1995). In this ad, Betty, a career woman, always wore a tweed suit and carried a briefcase. She was never without the severe suit, and seemed to be clutching the briefcase with intensity. Lisanne Renner, writer for the *Spokane Chronicle*, notes:

> When Helen Homemaker frets about the waxy buildup on her kitchen floor and ring-around-the-collar on her husband's shirts, she's probably not making a good sales pitch to career women. To grab their attention, advertisers have created Betty Briefcase, who turns out to be another silly stereotype … She [wears] a tweed suit appropriate for the boardroom but she was sitting in the bleachers at a baseball game, cheering on the team with her two daughters … She's an exaggeration of the career woman, a blatant symbol in her dress-for-success suits, and she has become an advertising cliché. (Renner 1985)

More than 75 percent of women reported that they were insulted by this portrayal, and its implication that women who work outside the home must give up all hints of femininity to be successful. The superwoman image, in many of its forms, was openly derided, as Renner (1985) writes: "A perfume commercial a few years back featured a superwoman singing to a man: 'I bring home the bacon, fry it up in a pan … and never let you forget you're a man.' Cartoonist Nicole Hollander later ribbed the commercial with the remark: "That woman must be on drugs." By 1989, advertisers listened, and the images of harsh Betty were phased out in favor of a less stereotypical working woman, though the superwoman image lingered.

The 1990s brought more of the same. Women were still generally the ones cooking and cleaning, while men were depicted in suits, dominant at work, traveling for business, or working in the yard at home. What had grown much stronger, however, was the sexual objectification of women. Ann J. Simonton, a top model before becoming the founder and director of Media Watch, an educational nonprofit organization that has as one of its main focuses the exposing of the media's role in exploiting women, writes:

> The advertised woman is a conspicuous, two-dimensional artifice. Her lips are sensually parted. There is a finger in or over her mouth, as if to stop her from speaking. Sometimes her mouth is wide open, sucking and nibbling. She doesn't smile easily. If she does, her grin is her private secret. She appears to be teasing, angry, drugged, or scared. The advertised woman is made-identified; she often competes with other females for male attention. The advertised woman is the implied bonus that goes along with the trip to Hawaii, the sofa bed, that six-pack of beer. Her link to products is so common we fail to notice her, or question her purpose. (Simonton 1995)

For the past 40 years, Jean Kilbourne, award-winning documentarian, has done pioneering work on the images of women in advertising. In the *Killing Us Softly* films (1979, 1987, 2000, 2010), Kilbourne (2002) argues that advertising is everywhere, selling not only products, but values and concepts of love, sexuality, love, romance, success, and normalcy. Women in advertising are impossibly perfect, and the problem with these images is that they sell not only products to help create this impossible perfection but also an impossible standard of beauty and thinness. She suggests that implicit in these messages is that if women do not succeed in achieving this impossible standard, which of course they cannot, they simply are not trying hard enough, which seriously and permanently erodes women's self-esteem.

Other trends that Kilbourne notes include the practice of turning women's bodies into "things" or objects, like beer bottles or road signs. Women of color are often shown as animals, depicted in leopard skin or animal prints, with the implied message being that they are somehow "not fully human," further objectifying them. Advertising is, as Kilbourne puts it, "relentlessly heterosexual," with the often-repeated message that women need a man to be complete. Sex is everywhere, and used to sell everything from cars to watches to handbags.

Women take up less physical space in advertising than men do, and appear in stances of vulnerability, while men are depicted in stances of power and aggression. This is only reversed when race enters into the advertisement, and then the white model is depicted in the stance of power. Kilbourne acknowledges that in recent years, more advertising has appeared that objectifies men, with men appearing as body parts without heads, in lying-down positions of vulnerability, and nude, but she argues that these ads do not occur nearly as often as ads that objectify women, and are not as damaging. She argues that a far greater problem is that men are so often depicted as being the per-petrators of violence, and that this image of masculinity teaches young men that this is acceptable behavior and the norm. She notes,

> In general, human qualities are divided up, polarized, and labeled masculine and feminine. And then the feminine is consistently devalued ... which causes men to devalue not only women, but also all those qualities that get labeled as feminine by the culture. And by that I mean qualities like compassion, cooperation, nurturing, empathy, sensitivity. (Kilbourne 2002)

Today, studies have shown that there has been no fundamental change in the percentages of women portrayed in advertisements versus men, nor in the ways in which advertisements continue to stereotype both genders and to objectify women. Media scholar David Gauntlett (2002: 83–85) argues that the kind of women society expects to see is different – a more vibrant, busy, confident, attractive success – and while this is not always borne out, as the consumer changes, advertising changes too. For instance, consumers are likely to still see a woman peddling a cleaning product, and mopping the kitchen floor or scrubbing the range, but the message is that she wants to do it fast and easy, so she can get out the door and on to something else (though this something else is often another gender-typical task, like driving the carpool minivan).

"Freedom" and "liberation" are common themes in products marketed to women. Researchers point out that this speaks to the post-feminist superwoman: "Look at me, having it all, doing it all, smiling all the while ... thanks to this new, improved time-saving product." Glade tells a woman she can "fool her friends" into thinking she has baked and cleaned all day by lighting a candle. Crest Whitetrips tells women they can use their product while doing anything at all, even kissing, accord-ing to a recent advertising campaign. Sketchers and Reebok encourage women to wear their new muscle-toning athletic shoes that save them the time, money, and effort of going to the gym.

Even more literally, advertising tells women they can be freed and liberated from the biologic ele-ments of being female. Feminine health and beauty products tell women they can "fool Mother Nature," and any number of beauty products advise women they can "turn back the clock" and "fight the signs of aging" by using certain lotions and potions. Hair dye companies urge women literally to "fight" their grays because "why be gray when you can be yourself?" Drug companies lure women into asking their doctors for certain prescription drugs, from those that can help you grow longer, thicker lashes, to shots that purportedly keep bones strong, by appealing to the fear of growing old or unattractive. Today's beauty ideal stresses to women that "you can't be young enough, thin enough, or beautiful enough." Though advertising cannot alone be blamed for creating these ideas, researchers argue that consumers should hold advertisers accountable each and every time they promote them.

Gender Trends and the "Male Gaze"

Though this idea has been touched on in the previous section, it is worth exploring the concept of the "male gaze" on its own. The theory of the "male gaze" stems from feminist and film study research, and in simplistic terms implies that the image of a woman is created from the perspective of an implied male observer. In other words, females are shown offering up their femininity for the pleasure of an absent male spectator (Figure 10.3). From this male gaze perspective, women who view these ads may form ideas about what women are supposed to look like and how women are

Figure 10.3 This ad was used to promote Post-it Notes. What kind of message does this send? Screenshot.

supposed to act. For instance, women are shown as body parts, often without faces, as subservient and in lying down or crouched positions. Women are regularly depicted with their legs or mouth wide open, bending over, gazing at the camera (and thus the viewer of the advertisement) in either a sexually hungry way or in fear. Other ads show the concept of the male gaze even more directly with the women being directly ogled, appreciated, or dominated by one or more male viewers in the photograph. Researchers Amy Malkin, Kimberlie Wornian, and Joan Chrisler (1999) conducted a study of weight and body type of magazine cover models. They concluded that both men's and women's magazines communicate messages about weight, body type, and sexual attractiveness of women through their choice of cover models. Each type of magazine reflected the male gaze, "tend[ing] to portray what women should look like and what men should look for."

The idea of reading an advertising photograph for implied meaning is not a new one. Sociologist Erving Goffman, the author of a seminal study on women and advertising published in 1979, created a method for analyzing photographs of men and women in advertising which codes common poses in a number of ways, in an effort to draw assumptions about the portrayed masculinity and femininity of the people shown. Goffman's classification allows for a more nuanced evaluation of pictures that moves beyond a black and white typology (a picture is sexist or not) to a consideration of how a pose transmits messages about the appropriate roles, looks, or behaviors for women and men. For instance, Goffman's classification notes the use of the "feminine touch" in advertisements. Women most often are depicted lightly caressing an object, whereas men are more likely to be depicted as grasping or using an object. Women also are more likely to be touching themselves in a picture, such as resting their fingertips against their chin or neck. Body position is also considered. When a person is pictured reclining on the floor or lying on a bed, the impression is of sexual availability. If a person is pictured with the head, arm, or knee turned at an awkward or unnatural angle, this posture "can be read as one of an acceptance of subordination, an expression of ingratiation, submissiveness, and appeasement" (Goffman 1979: 46).

Goffman also describes a pattern, called *licensed withdrawal*, in which women more often than men are pictured as "removed psychologically from the social situation at large, leaving them disoriented in it, and presumably, therefore, dependent on the protectiveness and goodwill of others" (Goffman 1979: 57). Goffman, as well as other researchers, argue that the "other" that is providing protection is male. Examples of this licensed withdrawal could be found if the female in the ad was depicted as gazing in an undirected way into the middle distance, as preoccupied, perhaps by twisting a piece of clothing, as retreating behind objects, covering the face to conceal an emotional reaction and snuggling into, folding into another person, generally a male.

Many researchers have followed up on Goffman's work, and concluded that though some of his gender stereotypes have lessened over time, many still remain as commonplace. For instance, mass communication professor Mee-Eun Kang (1997) conducted a study of magazine advertisements that appeared in *Vogue, Mademoiselle,* and *McCall's,* using Goffman's categories and two categories she added: (1) body display, defined as the level of body display shown, either in the form of body-revealing clothing or in nudity; and (2) independence, designed to look at the "big picture" of the advertisement in terms of implied self-assurance. In this study, body-revealing clothes include, among others, miniskirts, tight shirts, evening gowns that expose cleavage, "see-through" clothes, or bathing suits. Nudity was defined as unclothed models, including models translucent under apparel and lingerie, models clothed in nothing except a towel, or models depicted with no clothing at all. She concluded that the images of women in 1991 advertisements did not significantly change from the images found in 1979 advertisements, except in two of the coding categories: licensed withdrawal and body display. In these two categories, advertisements in 1991 showed significantly higher levels of female licensed withdrawal, with women appearing to often appear "mentally lost" or "mentally drifting," and significantly higher levels of body display. She concludes that the advertising industry has not changed much at all in its depiction of women except, perhaps, to be even worse and certainly more sexually explicit.

Although much discussion focuses on the sexualization of women in advertisements, evidence exists that men are also increasingly being targets for sexualization. For example, social researchers Tom Reichert and his colleagues examined the portrayals of men and women in six US magazine advertisements from 1983 and 1993. They found that both men and women were more often sexualized in 1993 than in 1983. Furthermore, in that time span women were three times more likely to be dressed in a sexually explicit manner than men for both time frames (Reichert *et al.* 1999). Mass communication researchers Tiffany Shoop, Catherine Luther, and Carolynn McMahan (2008) examined images of sexuality in advertisements featured in US and Japanese fashion magazines. In their cross-cultural study, the authors found that all of the magazines they examined (US: *Cosmo, Glamour, Details, GQ;* Japanese: *Vivi, Cam Can, Men's Joker, Men's Non-No*) presented sexualized images of both men and women. Overall, however, the percentages of female models being shown in sexually provocative poses and dress were still higher than the percentages of male models.

Advertising narrows the definition of what it means to be a man (Nakayama 1989). Men are in charge, self-contained, and generally alone. When shown with other men, they appear aggressive. When shown with women, they dominate and overpower. The male body can be used to sell just about anything, but always present is a feeling of superiority and "barely controlled power." *Ad Age* coined the phrase "hunkvertising," for the increasing levels of objectification of men in ads (Gianatasio 2013). Though the use of good-looking men in advertising isn't new, a new slew of ads featuring men in various states of undress has caught the attention of some advertising professionals. Steve O'Connell, partner at Red Tettemer O'Connell + Partners, whose agency spearheaded a campaign in 2012 for Renuzit featuring tiny product shots of their latest air freshener next to various topless men, stated, "objectifying men doesn't really upset anybody. You really can't offend the white male" (Gianatasio 2013). The Renuzit ads featured taglines that almost poked fun at the ad's concept. For instance, one read, "Look at this gorgeous air freshener next to this gorgeous man," and another stated "Now *that* is gorgeous and the man is not so bad either."

In another print and television ad campaign, this time for Kraft's Zesty Italian Dressing, a barely clothed male model purrs sexual innuendos while cooking. In one print ad, Anderson Davis, the model, is stretched out on a picnic blanket with a corner barely covering his genitals and the tagline, "Let's Get Zesty." In a television ad, Davis plays chef, adding Kraft Zesty Italian to a hot skillet. As the flames shoot higher and higher, he asks the viewer, "How zesty do you want it? A little? A little more? How about a lot more?" Eventually his shirt catches fire and leaves his muscular chest exposed. Not everyone thought the ads were appropriate, notably the group One Million Moms, an offshoot of the conservative group the American Family Association, who called for a boycott of Kraft products until they cleaned up their advertising. However, both ad campaigns proved extremely successful, perhaps proving sex sells no matter the gender. It appears, therefore, that with strides being made toward gender equality, rather than portraying women in less sexualized ways, advertisers have opted to express equality by sexualizing both men and women in their ads. Perhaps it is hard for advertisers to veer away from the tenet that "sex sells."

Gender in New Media

The widespread use and popularity of the Internet has opened up opportunities for women's groups to advocate for equality and less stereotypical representation and to provide an outlet and a virtual gathering place for the exchange of ideas and friendship. Some interesting sites include the following:

- National Organization for Women (NOW) – http://www.now.org – founded in 1966, is the largest feminist organization in the United States and has as its goal to take action to bring equality for all women. The website offers news stories, calls to action, hot topics, chapter information, and blog links, among other resources.
- The Third Wave Fund – http://www.thirdwavefund.org – is a feminist, activist foundation that works nationally to support young women and transgendered youth through grant making, leadership development, and advocacy. The website offers links to leadership and job opportunities, as well as news stories and documentaries detailing Third Wave grant projects.
- BlogHer – http://www.blogher.com – is a blogging community for adult women and a part of SheKnows Media, the top women's lifestyle digital media company with 82 million unique visitors per month. It is a growing network that connects info-savvy bloggers, advertisers, and readers. BlogHer hosts a large social media conference for women each year. According to their mission statement, BlogHer's goal is to "facilitate and curate a community that empowers our members and creates value for all."

Concluding Remarks

It would be easy to deduce, based on the discussion in this and the previous chapter on gender and entertainment media, that men and women continue to fall victim to stereotypes. Men, however, tend to fare better in these stereotypes by being portrayed as the dominant and more important sex in our society. Although the mass media have increasingly started to objectify men as sex objects, women continue to be the ones who are marginalized and objectified in advertising. Even news portrayals often fail to show women as three-dimensional, productive, and intelligent human beings.

Nonetheless, positive changes are happening. Women's magazines, such as *O, The Oprah Magazine*, boast high circulation numbers and include a sense of today's more spiritual, empowered, multifaceted woman. More women are moving into the newsrooms of both print and broadcast outlets, and there is a trend for women to appear more often than in the past in news stories, both in focus and as sources.

Clearly, there is still work to be done. For instance, marginalizing and stereotypical images of women in advertising are not just the norm but are expected. A recent study of college women found that though they recognized the highly sexualized way that women were portrayed in advertising, they saw little wrong with it. It was just the status quo. Many reported that this was just "the way things were," and there was no reason to take offense. Perhaps this is the larger issue for consideration here – not just that these stereotypes exist, but that they are so prevalent that they are simply part of our cultural vocabulary. And in a world where harmful images are commonplace, and stereotypes are just part of the landscape, there is no impetus to change.

Reflection Questions and Thoughts to Consider

1. Compare and contrast the way women are presented in a variety of consumer magazines. Choose magazines targeted at a range of audiences: for instance, a teen magazine, a men's magazine, a Latina magazine, a traditional women's magazine. How do the portrayals vary? Do you see different manifestations or versions of stereotypes? What similarities do you see?
2. Perform the same exercise, only this time, consider how men are represented. How are men stereotyped? Do the stereotypes vary across magazines? As discussed in the previous chapter, common male stereotypes include the action hero, the buffoon, the big shot, the strong silent type, the jock, and the joker. Can you find examples of any of these in print media, as well as in entertainment media? Which are the most common? Are some more common than others in certain publications?
3. Consider the concept of the male gaze. Why do you believe it is such a pervasive form of vision in advertising and other forms of media? Can you locate any examples that show the male gaze?
4. The news media frame women in politics in a variety of ways. Examine several recent news stories written about Carly Fiorina, Mia Love, Nancy Pelosi, Olympia Snowe, or any other female politician you choose. Do you see certain themes repeated? Do you believe female politicians are treated the same as their male counterparts? How so or how not?

References

Abraham, Jill. 2004. "Media Frames, Public Opinion, and The First Lady." Paper presented at the meeting of the Midwest Political Science Association, Chicago, Illinois, April 15–18, 2004.

Andersen, Kurt. 1985. "Co-Starring at The White House." *Time*, January 14: 22–30.

Armstrong, Cory L. 2004. "The Influence of Reporter Gender on Source Selection in Newspaper Stories." *Journalism and Mass Communication Quarterly* 81(1): 139–154.

Association of Magazine Media (MPA). n.d. "Insights and Resources." http://www.magazine.org/insights-resources (accessed April 26, 2017).

Beasley, Maureen, and Shelia Gibbons. 2003. *Taking Their Place: A Documentary History of Women and Journalism*, 2nd ed. State College, PA: Strata Publishing.

Benze, James G., and Eugene R. Declercq. 1985. "Content of Television Political Spot Ads for Female Candidates." *Journalism Quarterly* 62: 278–288.

Brant, Martha. 2001. "The Steel Behind the Smile." *Newsweek*, January 29: 31.

Butler, Jazmyne E. 2013. "Professional First Ladies in the Media: Framing of Clinton Bush and Obama in the Washington Post." Honors thesis, The University of Southern Mississippi, Paper 148.

Carlson, Margaret. 1989. "The Silver Fox." *Time*, January 23: 22–30.

Courtney, Alice, and Sarah Lockeretz. 1971. "A Woman's Place: An Analysis of The Roles Portrayed by Women in Magazine Advertisements." *Journal of Marketing Research* 8: 92–95.

Covert, Juanita J. 2003. "Working Women in Mainstream Magazines: A Content Analysis." *Media Report to Women* 31(4): 5.

Curnalia, Rebecca, and Dorian L. Mermer. 2014. "The 'Ice Queen' Melted and It Won Her the Primary: Evidence of Gender Stereotypes and the Double Bind in News Frames of Hillary Clinton's 'Emotional Moment'." *Qualitative Research Reports in Communication* 15: 26–32.

Curtis, Gregory, Timothy Roche, and Hilary Hylton. 2001. "At Home with Laura." *Time*, January 8: 32–34.

Davis, James. 2005. "*Maxim* Magazine and the Management of Contempt." *Journal of Popular Culture* 6(38): 1011–1021.

ETonline. 2009. "Kelly Clarkson: Cover Controversy?" *Etonline.com*, August 6. http://www.wonderwall.com/entertainment/kelly-clarkson-cover-controversy-1519350.article (accessed April 12, 2017).

Friedan, Betty. (1963) 2001. *The Feminine Mystique*. New York, NY: Norton.

Gauntlett, David. 2002. *Media, Gender, and Identity: An Introduction*. London: Routledge.

Gianatasio, David. 2013. "Hunkvertising: The Objectification of Men in Advertising." *Adweek.com*, October 7. http://www.adweek.com/brand-marketing/hunkvertising-objectification-men-advertising-152925 (accessed April 16, 2017).

Gibbs, Nancy, and Michael Scherer. 2009. "Michelle Up Close." *Time*, June 1: 26.

Gibson, Alex. 2008. "Why Men Should Care About Gender Stereotypes." *The F Word: Contemporary UK Feminism*. http://www.thefword.org.uk/features/2008/02/men_stereotypes (accessed April 12, 2017).

Goffman, Erving. 1979. *Gender Advertisements*. New York, NY: Colophon.

Harp, Dustin, Jamie Loke, and Ingrid Bachmann. 2016. "Hillary Clinton's Benghazi Hearing Coverage: Political Competence, Authenticity, and the Persistence of the Double Bind." *Women's Studies in Communication* 39: 193–210.

Jezebel. 2007. "Faith Hill's Photoshop Chop: Why We're Pissed." http://jezebel.com/gossip/photoshop-of-horrors/faith-hills-redbook-photoshop-chop-why-were-pissed-279203.php (accessed April 12, 2017).

Johnson, Connie. 2015. "How Women of Color are Portrayed on the Cover of Magazines: A Content Analysis on the Images of Black/African, Latina, Asian and Native American (BALANA)." Paper 438, All Theses, Dissertations, and Other Capstone Projects, Minnesota State University, Mankato.

Kalb, Claudia, Pat Wingert, Robina Riccitiello, Patricia King, and Anne Underwood. 1997. "The Myth of Quality Time." *Newsweek*, May 12: 62.

Kang, Mee-Eun. 1997. "The Portrayal of Women's Images in Magazine Advertisements: Goffman's Gender Analysis Revisited." *Sex Roles* 37(11/12): 979.

Kilbourne, Jean. 2002. *Killing Us Softly 3: Advertising's Image of Women*. Media Education Foundation.

Levine, Judith. 1994. "The Man in the Mirror: What *Esquire*, *GQ*, *Men's Journal*, and *Details* Tell Us about the American Male." *Columbia Journalism Review* 6(32): 27–31.

Lont, Cynthia M., and M. Junior Bridge. 2010. "Confronting the Front Pages: A Content Analysis of U.S. Newspapers." In *Race/Gender/Media*, edited by Rebecca Ann Lind, 128–134. Boston, MA: Allyn & Bacon.

Malkin, Amy, Kimberlie Wornian, and Joan C. Chrisler. 1999. "Women and Weight: Gendered Messages on Magazine Covers." *Sex Roles* 40(7/8): 647–655.

Martinson, Melissa, Amanda Hinnant, and Barbara Martinson. 2008. "Visual Depictions of Gender in Parenting Magazines." *Media Report to Women* 36(4): 12–21.

Meeks, Lindsey. 2012. "Is She 'Man Enough'? Women Candidates, Executive Political Offices, and News Coverage." *Journal of Communications* 62: 175–193.

Miller, Michele. 2005. "Sexism in Advertising and Marketing to Women." *International Journal of Advertising* 24(1): 113–124.

Mott, Frank Luther. 1968. *A History of American Magazines, Volume 5: 1905–1930.* Cambridge, MA: Belnap Press.

Nakayama, Tom. 1989. "Images of Men in Advertising." Center for Media Literacy. Originally published Fall 1989 in *Media & Values*. http://www.medialit.org/reading-room/images-men-advertising (accessed April 12, 2017).

Payne, Darwin. 1998. "Magazines for Men." In *History of Mass Media in the United States: An Encyclopedia*, edited by Alan Day, 332. Chicago, IL: Fitzroy Dearborn.

Pieraccini, Tina, and Robert Schell. 1995. "You're Not Getting Older … You're Getting Better!" In *Women and Media: Content, Careers, Criticism*, edited by Cynthia Lont, 121–129. Belmont, CA: Wadsworth.

Poniewozik, James. 2008. "Meet the Obamas!" *Time*, December 1: 24.

Project for Excellence in Journalism. 2005. "The Gender Gap: Women are Still Missing as Sources for Journalists." Pew Research Center. http://www.journalism.org/node/141 (accessed April 12, 2017).

Redbook. 2017. "Redbook Media Kit." http://www.redbookmediakit.com (accessed April 12, 2017).

Reichert, Tom, Jacqueline Lambiase, Susan Morgan, Meta Carstarphen, and Susan Zavoina. 1999. "Cheesecake and Beefcake: No Matter How You Slice It, Sexual Explicitness in Advertising Continues to Increase." *Journalism and Mass Communication Quarterly* 76(1): 7–20.

Renner, Lisanne. 1985. "A 'Briefcase' Doesn't Help Cliché 'Betty." *Spokane Chronicle*, August 28: B1.

Riss, Suzanne. 2009. "This Is How She Does It." *Working Mother* 33(1).

Rivers, Caryl. 2007. *Selling Anxiety: How The News Media Scare Women.* Lebanon, NH: University Press of New England.

Ross, Karen. 2010. *Gendered Media: Women, Men, and Identity Politics.* Lanham, MD: Rowman & Littlefield.

Samuels, Allison. 2008. "What Michelle Means to Us." *Newsweek*, December 1: 28–32.

Scharrer, Erica, and Kim Bissell. 2000. "Overcoming Traditional Boundaries: The Role of Politics and Political Activity in Media Coverage of First Ladies." *Women and Politics* 21: 55–83.

Shoop, Tiffany, Catherine A. Luther, and Carolynn McMahan. 2008. "Advertisement Images of Men and Women in Culturally Diverging Societies: An Examination of Images in U.S. and Japanese Fashion Magazines." *Journal of International Business and Economics* 8(3): 188–199.

Silver, Diane. 1985. "A Comparison of Newspaper Coverage of Male and Female Officials in Michigan." *Journalism Quarterly* 59: 456–460.

Simonton, Ann J. 1995. "Women for Sale." In *Women and Media: Content, Careers, Criticism*, edited by Cynthia M. Lont, 148. Belmont, CA: Wadsworth.

Somaiya, Ravi. 2015. "Nudes are Old News at Playboy." *New York Times*, October 12. http://www.nytimes.com/2015/10/13/business/media/nudes-are-old-news-at-playboy.html?_r=0 (accessed April 12, 2017).

Stooksbury, Kara E., and Lou M. Edgemon. 2003. "The First Lady Scholarship Reconsidered: A Review Essay." *Women and Politics* 25(3): 97–111.

Sumner, David E. 2010. *The Magazine Century: American Magazines Since 1900*. New York, NY: Peter Lang.

VanSlyke Turk, Judy. 1987. "Sex-Role Stereotyping in Writing the News." *Journalism Quarterly* 64: 613–617.

Walsh, Kenneth T., and Angie Cannon. 2001. "Laura's Moment." *U.S. News and World Report*, April 30.

Watts, Liz. 1997. "Magazine Coverage of First Ladies from Hoover to Clinton: From Election Through the First 100 Days of Office." *American Journalism* 14(3–4): 495–519.

Winfield, Betty H. 1997. "The First Lady, Political Power, and the Media: Who Elected Her Anyway?" In *Women, Media and Politics*, edited by Pippa Norris, 166–179. Oxford: Oxford University Press.

Winfield, Betty H., and Barbara Friedman. 2003. "Gender Politics: News Coverage of the Candidates' Wives in Campaign 2000." *Journalism and Mass Communication Quarterly* 80(3): 548–566.

11

Representations of Lesbian, Gay, Bisexual, and Transgender People in the Media

First, consider the following. In a May 6, 2013 issue of *Sports Illustrated*, professional basketball player Jason Collins, after becoming a free agent, publicly announced to the world, "I'm a 34-year-old NBA center. I'm black. And I'm gay." Reaction to the revelation was swift and vocal. While some expressed dismay, others – including fellow basketball player Kobe Bryant, President Barack Obama, NBA Commissioner David Stern, and countless Hollywood celebrities – bestowed praise on Collins. Collins eventually went on to sign with the Brooklyn Nets in 2014, becoming the first openly gay athlete to play in a professional league in the United States.

Now, reflect on the following that occurred almost two decades ago. The April 4, 1997 issue of *Time* magazine featured a photo of comedienne Ellen DeGeneres and the headline "Yep, I'm Gay!" The cover story was DeGeneres's way of revealing her sexual identity to the world. At the same time, the character DeGeneres played in her sitcom *Ellen* (1994–1998) also disclosed in one of the show's episodes that she was a lesbian. After the disclosure, an advertiser of the program immediately pulled its sponsorship and the show's creators received death threats. DeGeneres also had to endure hurtful comments and an uncertain future career. Within the next year ABC canceled the four-year-old program. Some blamed the cancelation on the conservative standards of the Disney-owned television network.

Given the dramatically differing public reactions to the two announcements, one in 2013 and the other in 1997, do you think that societal views regarding gay individuals have shifted? If so, what role do you believe the media have played in possibly changing attitudes toward the gay community?

This chapter will address how this community has been portrayed in the mass media and how the LGBT (lesbian, gay, bisexual, and transgender) community has used the media to educate and advocate. In an effort to explain the representations of lesbians, gays, bisexuals, and transgender people in the media, the chapter will begin with a brief historical background to the experience of being gay in America.*

---

*Before discussing the historical background, it may be useful to define a handful of terms relevant to this chapter. These definitions are from the Stylebook (http://www.nlgja.org/stylebook/terminology) put out by the National Lesbian and Gay Journalists Association, which is an organization of journalists, educators, media professionals, and students who work within the news industry to foster fair coverage of lesbian, gay, bisexual, and transgender issues. This stylebook was created to be

(Continued)

Diversity in US Mass Media, Second Edition. Catherine A. Luther, Carolyn Ringer Lepre, and Naeemah Clark.
© 2018 John Wiley & Sons Inc. Published 2018 by John Wiley & Sons Inc.

Historical Background to LGBT Representations

The history of LGBT in the United States has been swathed in fear and oppression. The nation's early Judeo-Christian heritage is said to have laid a foundation for an anti-gay belief system that viewed homosexual acts as immoral and criminal (Eaklor 2008). Civil rights activist Suzanne Pharr (2002) has argued that US patriarchy also played a role in nurturing homophobia as a way to maintain male domination. She asserts that the strong patriarchal structures that were at the forefront in the nineteenth and early half of the twentieth century required that individuals abide by strict rules and social expectations related to biological sex. By sustaining notions of masculinity and femininity, the institutional system was able to keep men in places of power while relegating women to positions of subordination. Any behaviors or lifestyles that deviated from sex-related expectations were viewed as a threat to the status quo and social order.

It was during the early twentieth century, when US patriarchy was still in full force, that the notion of homosexual acts as immoral crimes shifted to the belief that homosexuality was an illness. The "medical model" of homosexuality was espoused. In describing that period, historian Vicki Eaklor (2008) writes, "American doctors considered sexual 'perversions' to be biological, and, typical in an era concerned with social reform and the progress of (American) civilization, they were as concerned with their effect on American society as well as on the specific individual" (2008: 36). The medical model and its use to explain homosexuality remained steadfast throughout much of the twentieth century. It was not until the LGBT community took a stand against their treatment in society that ideas regarding gay individuals began to truly change.

When considering representations of gay, lesbian, bisexual, and transgender people in US mass media, it is not hard to see how historically prevailing assessments and sentiments have shaped these media images. Before moving on to discussions of these representations, it is important to highlight relatively more recent and significant moments in LGBT history that have greatly impacted on media portrayals.

First, on the evening of June 28, 1969, at The Stonewall Inn in New York's Greenwich Village, a bar frequented by gays and lesbians, police arrived to make arrests. It was a form of harassment

---

(Continued)

used by journalists in conjunction with the Associated Press Stylebook and encourages the use of correct terminology and precise language.

Gay: Term used to describe men and women attracted to the same sex.

Lesbian: Commonly used term describing women sexually attracted to other women.

Bisexual: Term used to describe an individual who is attracted to both sexes.

Transgender: Term used to describe people whose physical and sexual characteristics may not match their gender identity. Cross-dressers, intersex individuals, and drag queens/kings may also identify as trans. The usage of "transgender" as a noun is considered offensive. Preferred usage is "transgendered people," "transgendered man," "transgendered woman," or "trans."

Cisgender: Term used to indicate a gender identity that is in concert with the sex and gender that were ascribed at birth. Also referred to as "cis."

LGBT: Acronym for "lesbian, gay, bisexual, and trans." Often referred to when referencing a community of people defined by their sexual orientation.

Note that the term "homosexual" should only be used in reference to a sexual activity or within a historical or medical/clinical context.

that the customers recurrently encountered. That night, however, the customers decided not to relent and fought against the police. When word got out of what was happening at the pub, others in the gay community also joined in, turning the incident into a major riot. The uprising was commemorated the following year with 5,000 protesters marching up Manhattan's Sixth Avenue. The rebellious act as well as the march garnered the attention of the national news media, shedding light on some of the negative treatment gay individuals were receiving at the time. The Stonewall riots now are regarded as the birth of the modern gay rights movement.

A second pivotal moment in the history of gay rights in the United Sates occurred in 1973 when the American Psychiatric Association declared that homosexuality was not a mental illness. Before that time, employers were able to discriminate against gays using their "mental disorder" as a sound rationale.

Another key historical moment that sheds light on the treatment of the LGBT community in the media occurred in the 1980s. The world saw an epidemic in gay men contracting immunodeficiency-related illnesses, or HIV/AIDS. Initially, the disease created or strengthened fear in and about the gay community. However, the onslaught of HIV/AIDS forced all Americans to consider safer, healthier sexual practices. Additionally, the disease encouraged the increased coverage of gay individuals and that coverage provided some sympathetic depictions that paved the way for a more open discourse about the LGBT community (Safe Zone 2011).

In more recent history, federal and state laws have been challenged to mandate equal treatment of gays and certain long-held restrictive laws have been overturned. President Obama, in the 2010 State of the Union address, initiated congressional hearings to overturn US Code: Title 10 §654, otherwise known as "Don't Ask, Don't Tell" (DADT). This policy had mandated that gay and lesbian members of the armed forces not disclose their sexual preference, marry/attempt to marry, or engage/attempt to engage in sexual behavior with someone of the same sex. DADT officially ended in 2011, after a federal appeals court ruled against the code, thus allowing openly gay individuals to serve in the military.

In 2013, the US Supreme Court ruled Section 3 of the Defense of Marriage Act or DOMA, which permitted the federal government to only recognize marriages between a man and a woman, unconstitutional. The court ruling allowed legally married same-sex couples to enjoy many federal rights that had not been available to them prior to the change in law. Those in same-sex unions were now able to file joint income taxes and receive many other partner benefits including social security benefits and hospital visitation rights. In 2015, the US Supreme Court also ruled that same-sex marriage bans that several states still had in place were unconstitutional. As a result of these changes, states have either eradicated or loosened their bans on same-sex child adoptions.

These historic events should be kept in mind when reading about the representations of lesbian, gay, bisexual, and transgender people in the media. How these events have played a role in the way LGBT stories are told and how members of this group tell their stories in the mass media should be considered. More than any other topic discussed in this book, identities related to sexual orientation and gender may be the most taboo in the media because of people's personal feelings, attitudes, and beliefs. Issues related to sexuality are often tied to morality, religion, family, and politics, making mediated representations and discussions of LGBT difficult. Not only do those who create media content have to be concerned with satisfying their advertisers, but they must also be sensitive to the general viewing public and the LGBT community.

LGBT in Film

Gay and lesbian subtexts have existed in film since the early days of Hollywood. Between 1930 and 1968, the strict Motion Picture Production Code, also known as the Hays Code, mentioned in previous chapters, established that films could not be distributed if they contained material thought to be objectionable, including sexual perversion (Denby 2016). Because it was considered a mental disorder, homosexuality could not appear in film. Of course, that does not mean some producers did not slip this type of content into films, but these storylines and scenes were quite subtle in their use of side glances, knowing smiles, touches, and veiled language. For example, Alfred Hitchcock's 1948 thriller *Rope* features longtime friends Brandon and Phillip, who murder a friend, David, and then host a dinner party using the dead man's makeshift coffin as a buffet table. The murderers have an undeniably close relationship. They seem to share an apartment and Phillip has a key to Brandon's vacation home. Early in the film, the two stand close together, simultaneously holding a bottle of champagne. Their discussion of the act of killing has some sexual undertones:

BRANDON: You're not frightened anymore, Phillip? Not even of me?
PHILLIP: No.
BRANDON: Good.
PHILLIP: You astound me ... as usual.
BRANDON: Well, that's even better. (Raises his glass) To David, of course.
PHILLIP: Brandon how did you feel ... during it?
BRANDON: I don't know. Really, I don't remember feeling much of anything. Until his body went limp and knew it was over. Then I felt tremendously exhilarated.

These men have committed murder for the first time, yet part of the discussion is similar to one they might have about their first sexual conquest. The nature of this conversation might not raise any suspicions about Phillip and Brandon's sexuality unless the viewer already assumed the characters were lovers.

Take 1959's Oscar-winning film *Ben-Hur* as another example of subtle gay character undertones during the Hays Code. The film's main character, Judah Ben-Hur (played by Charlton Heston), refuses to help his childhood friend Messala round up those who dissent from Caesar's rule. Messala, furious that Ben-Hur will not turn on his countrymen, throws him in jail. So where's the subtext of same-sex love? The film's director, William Wyler, told the actor who played Messala (Stephen Boyd) that the reason his character was so angry with Ben-Hur is because they were childhood lovers and Messala sees Ben-Hur's refusal as the ultimate rejection. Boyd played the role as if he were a scorned lover, not a disappointed friend, and Messala's outrage is palpable. Wyler, thinking Heston would disapprove of this direction, did not tell the film's star about this scenario (Epstein 1985).

Post-Hays Code, Hollywood explored gay identity in a much more overt way. In one of the most striking stories ever told on film, *Midnight Cowboy* (1969), country boy Joe Buck (played by Jon Voight) comes to New York City looking for a new life. He turns to male prostitution to make enough money to live in the city. The film is very graphic in its depictions of sexual situations, but its masterful storytelling is why it is still the only X-rated movie to have received an Oscar for Best Picture.

The free and open nature of sexual exploration of the 1960s and 1970s is a contrast to the sexually cautious culture of the 1980s when HIV/AIDS became an epidemic in the gay community. The public's fear about the disease may have been tempered by films such as *Longtime Companion* (1989) and *Philadelphia* (1993). The films not only shared the stories of men who were dying of AIDS, but also put a spotlight on the support system of these men. Instead of AIDS being branded a disease of deviance, those who were dying were depicted as real men with loving partners, friends, and parents who cared about them.

The aforementioned films, which because of their critical acclaim have been a part of the consciousness of many Americans for two decades, featured the stories of white men contracting and dying from the disease, but statistics from the Centers for Disease Control (2015) indicate that men of color are testing HIV-positive in greater numbers than their white counterparts. These results are, in large part, because of the scorn and secrecy of same-sex intimate relationships that continue to exist in Hispanic and African American communities. As a result, gay men are contracting the disease, and infecting women, often their wives, who do not know the men in their lives are gay. To tell this story, filmmaker Bill Duke tackled HIV/AIDS in the African American community in *Cover* (2008). The film was screened with much positive feedback at the American Black Film Festival in Los Angeles, and then premiered in a dozen black churches in hopes of getting the African American men and women to pay attention to a topic that is not handled in mainstream film productions (The Body, 2008).

Another more prominent theme that emerges in films dealing with LGBT characters revolves around the malleability of those engaged in same-sex love affairs. Some of these films have straight characters challenging the steadfastness of the gay character's decision to love someone of the same sex. Others involve gay and lesbians squashing their true feelings and drives for a myriad of reasons.

In 1997, Kevin Smith directed the romantic comedy *Chasing Amy*, which starred Ben Affleck as heterosexual comic book artist Holden McNeil, who falls for lesbian Alyssa Jones (played by Joey Lauren Adams). Holden, who is a conservative twenty-something, is immediately attracted to Alyssa, but quickly learns she is a lesbian and therefore is initially satisfied to just hang out and be her friend. The two become very close, and ultimately Holden confronts her with the truth: that he is in love with her.

In a pivotal scene, underlying issues surface between the two and questions are raised. Is sexual preference a choice? Is sexual preference something that can be "cured" or changed? After Holden expresses his love for her, Alyssa storms away, challenging Holden's (and perhaps the moviegoer's) presumptions of lesbianism:

ALYSSA: That was so unfair.

HOLDEN: It's unfair that I'm in love with you?

ALYSSA: No, it's unfortunate that you're in love with me. It's unfair that you felt the f***ing need to unburden your soul about it. Do you remember for a f***ing second who I am?

HOLDEN: So? People change.

ALYSSA: Oh, it's that simple? You fall in love with me and want a romantic relationship, nothing changes for you with the exception of feeling hunky-dory all the time. But what about me? It's not that simple, is it? I can't just get into a relationship with you without throwing my whole f***ing world into upheaval!

HOLDEN: But that's every relationship! There's always going to be a period of adjustment.

ALYSSA: Period of adjustment?!? There's no "period of adjustment" Holden! I'm f***ing gay! That's who I am! And you assume I can turn that around just because you've got a crush? Go home, Holden.

What follows after this, to some critics' dismay, is indeed a relationship between Holden and Alyssa, who some argue is really a bisexual choosing to identify herself as a lesbian, perhaps because she feels it would give her greater social acceptance. She notes in the movie that she has chosen to be with females because she went on a conscious search for her sexuality and that girls just "felt right," though it comes out later in the movie that Holden is not the first man with whom she has ever had sex. The issue that, for her, lesbianism was a choice, not a biological or genetic construction, was clearly stated in the film, and for some critics this is a point of contention, as many believe that being gay has nothing to do with choice or societal construction.

This notion of choice versus biological construction is also explored in the film *Kissing Jessica Stein* (2001). In this film, Jessica (played by Jennifer Westfeld, who also co-wrote and directed the film) is a successful, single, and straight Jewish woman living in New York City. After struggling to find a good heterosexual boyfriend, Jessica answers a classified ad looking for a woman to befriend. The ad leads her to an art gallery manager, Helen (played by Heather Juergensen, the film's other writer) who, after a series of disappointing relationships with men, begins to wonder if she is a lesbian. The two begin dating, much to the shock of Jessica's friends and family who only know her as being heterosexual. Still, the couple become close and move in together. In the end, Jessica realizes that she is not a lesbian, but appreciates the close bond she shares with Helen. Conversely, Helen realizes that she is a lesbian and no longer wants to remain in the relationship because it is clear that although Jessica loves her, she does not want to embrace the sexual intimacy required of the lesbian relationship.

It is significant that both of these films deal with women altering their sexual identities and behaviors in somewhat capricious ways. Two more recent films that broke away from this type of lesbian storyline are the films *Grandma* (2015) and *Carol* (2015). Both films became among the few mainstream films to feature lesbian characters in leading roles. A comedy drama, *Grandma*, starred Lily Tomlin as a lesbian grandmother, Elle, who after losing her life partner, goes on a road trip with her granddaughter who is dealing with an unwanted pregnancy. Through varying twists and turns during the road trip the audience sees Elle as a no-nonsense grandmother who is determined to live according to her own self-identity and sense of values. While critics hailed the performance of Tomlin and the film as progressive with its themes of women's rights, the movie failed to attract large audience numbers.

Set in New York City in the 1950s, *Carol* is a film drama about the friendship between two women, a young department store sales person Therese (played by Rooney Mara) and an older well-off married woman Carol (played by Cate Blanchett), that develops into a deep love. The movie was based on Patricia Highsmith's novel *The Price of Salt* (screenplay by Phyllis Nagy). While both actresses received Oscar nominations for their performances, the film, despite its high-level production value, failed to receive the same honor. In her article titled "Why *Carol* Failed to Become the Lesbian *Brokeback*" (2016), self-identified "Hollywood Queer" columnist Dorothy Snarker provides an explanation for why the film was snubbed in the prime categories of Best Film and Best Director: "*Carol* was just too gay and too female for the largely old white male voting base to consider. I mean, how could they possibly connect with a mid-century romance focused entirely on the unstoppable attraction between two women where neither has the decency to sleep with a man, suffer tragically or die at the end?"

The *Brokeback* that Starker refers to in her headline is the 2005 film *Brokeback Mountain* (2005). In an Oscar-winning film set in the 1960s, two male sheep herders, Ennis (played by Heath Ledger) and Jack (played by Jake Gyllenhaal) fall in love one winter. Although their romance is relatively brief, their love impacts them throughout their lifetimes. Ennis and Jack cannot be true to who they are. These men, who work in male-driven jobs in the 1960s, are forced to tamp down their desire to be together. They have relationships with women, but they are doomed to fail because they are always looking for the love they shared that winter. The film was a box office success and won three Academy Awards for Best Director, Best Adapted Screenplay, and Best Original Score. It also was nominated for Best Picture, but lost out to *Crash* (2004).

While some high-profile movies that feature LGBT characters have done well at the box office, such as *The Imitation Game* (2014), a biopic of gay mathematician Alan Turing, Hollywood seems hesitant to produce movies with LGBT characters. In a study conducted by the Media, Diversity and Social Change Initiative at the University of Southern California's Annenberg School for Communication (Smith, Choueiti, and Pieper 2015), results showed that of 4,610 speaking characters in the 100 top-grossing films of 2014, only 19 were lesbian, gay, or bisexual. None were trans. The study also showed the continuation of damaging stereotypes. For example, no gay or bisexual male characters were portrayed in a serious or committed relationship. Some suggest that this hesitancy to produce movies that feature LGBT characters stems from international box office predictions that fear the censors in markets like China or the Middle East (Robehmed 2015). In a follow-up study in 2015 (Smith, Choueiti, and Pieper 2016), numbers do not look much better. Of 4,370 speaking characters in the 100 top-grossing films of 2015, only 32 were LGBT, and these characters all appeared in 18 of the 100 movies. One character among these was a trans.

The depiction of transgender persons is an often-used convention in filmmaking, but it is usually framed as whimsical cross-dressing to get out of sticky situations. Several actors have played roles that required their characters to live life as the opposite sex to achieve some goal other than representing those struggling with their sexual identities. Some films, such as *Tootsie* (1982), *Yentl* (1983), *Mrs. Doubtfire* (1993), and *White Chicks* (2004), have actors dressed as the opposite sex as if it were an inconvenience, but oh so necessary solution. All of these trans characters were played by cisgendered actors.

Casting cis actors, actors who identify with the gender and sex they were assigned at birth, as trans characters has attracted some backlash. Examples are cis actor Eddie Redmayne playing a trans woman in *The Danish Girl* (2015) and cis actor Matt Bomer playing a trans sex worker in *Anything* (2017). Nick Adams, GLAAD's (Gay & Lesbian Alliance Against Defamation) director of programming for transgender media wrote in an opinion piece for industry magazine *The Hollywood Reporter* (2016) that "Hollywood needs to let go of the idea that putting a male actor in a dress, wig and makeup is an accurate portrayal of a transgender woman." He adds that the casting choice is troubling because it sends the erroneous messages: "1. that being transgender is an act, a performance, just a matter of playing dress-up; and 2. that underneath all that artifice, a transgender woman really is a man" (Adams 2016).

Ironically, the most controversial of these types of portrayals appears in a film made during the period of the Hays Code. In perhaps the most famous film with cross-dressing, *Some Like it Hot* (1959), two friends, Joe (played by Tony Curtis) and Jerry (played by Jack Lemmon) must dress like women so that they can join an all-girl band and hide from murdering mobsters (Figure 11.1). Joe falls in love with a young beautiful musician Sugar (played by Marilyn Monroe) while his female persona, Josephine, becomes her confidante. Meanwhile, Jerry, in his female persona of Daphne, is aggressively pursued by a wealthy older man, Osgood. Although Jerry is a heterosexual, he allows Osgood to fall in love with his alter ego Daphne so he can be a kept woman. At the end of the film, Osgood proposes marriage to Daphne while they take a romantic ride in a speedboat. At this point, Jerry realizes that he must come clean and reveal that Daphne is a man.

Figure 11.1 Tony Curtis and Jack Lemmon dressed as women in *Some Like it Hot* (1959). Screenshot.

JERRY AS DAPHNE:	Osgood, I'm going to level with you. We can't get married at all.
OSGOOD:	Why not?
JERRY AS DAPHNE:	Well, in the first place, I'm not a natural blonde.
OSGOOD:	Doesn't matter.
JERRY AS DAPHNE:	I smoke! I smoke all the time!
OSGOOD:	I don't care.
JERRY AS DAPHNE:	Well, I have a terrible past. For three years now, I've been living with a saxophone player [Joe].
OSGOOD:	I forgive you.
JERRY AS DAPHNE:	I can never have children!
OSGOOD:	We can adopt some.
JERRY:	But you don't understand, Osgood! (Jerry pulls off his wig.) I'm a man!
OSGOOD:	Well, nobody's perfect.

This is the last line of the film, leaving the audience to its own imagination. Jerry, who has been revealed to be a man, is still on a romantic boat-ride with his fiancé, Osgood. The 1959 audience is left to assume that the two men are *literally* riding into the sunset together.

Examples of two more contemporary comedic movies that were popular at the box office and that featured gay men and cross-dressing are *To Wong Foo, Thanks for Everything! Julie Newmar* (1995) and *The Birdcage* (1996). Movie reviewers noted that while it was certainly a positive that gay people were becoming more visible and accepted in our movie culture, and that both movies had themes of acceptance, they also criticized both movies for relying on "drag farces," with many unrealistic, stereotypical, and superficial (although also often sympathetic) scenes. *To Wong Foo, Thanks for Everything! Julie Newmar* starred Patrick Swayze, John Leguizamo, and Wesley Snipes as gay men who dress as glamorous women in their daily lives. Two of the characters, Noxeema (Snipes) and Vida (Swayze), have won a trip to Hollywood to take part in a national drag queen contest, and before they leave they decide to take an inexperienced "drag princess," Chi-Chi (Leguizamo), along with them as their protégé. They set out for a cross-country adventure, but when their Cadillac breaks down in a small town, they find themselves pursued by a homophobic and racist sheriff, and disrespected by the small-minded townspeople. Ultimately, the three win over the town with their positive attitudes and loving behaviors, and the townspeople are the better for their influence.

A similar moral can be found in *The Birdcage*. The lives of an uptight senator and his wife are comically turned upside down when their daughter becomes engaged to the son of Armand (played by Robin Williams), the owner of a gay cabaret, and his star entertainer/wife, Albert (played by Nathan Lane). Albert and Armand try to conceal their sexual orientation from the senator at a dinner to celebrate the engagement of the children, but ultimately cannot keep up the charade. The ultra-conservative senator, Kevin Keeley (played by Gene Hackman), who is the co-founder of the Coalition for Moral Order, becomes trapped in the apartment, which is located above the drag club, when paparazzi photographers are tipped off that the politician is inside. Fearing that the scandal will be the end of his political career, the movie reverts back to an old device: cross-dressing to get out of sticky situations. Albert dresses the senator, his wife, and daughter in drag and they are all able to leave the club as the night's show ends – and the audience is treated to an apparent change of attitude in Kevin as he comments not that he is worried about wearing the dress, but that it "makes him look fat."

The lives of transgender people are hidden, with tragic results, in *Boys Don't Cry* (1999), a film based on a true story. Hilary Swank's Academy Award-winning portrayal of the real Brandon Teena/Teena Brandon tells the true story of a transgender woman who lives as a man. She conceals her true sexuality even as she falls in love with Lana, the most beautiful girl in town. In the end, her gender is violently revealed.

Another attempt to show the life of a nearly sexually reassigned character can be found in *Transamerica* (2005). Felicity Huffman received acclaim as Bree, a man who has nearly completed his sexual reassignment surgeries and is already living as a woman. Bree must spend the money he has saved for the final procedure to bail his long-lost son out of jail. During their trip from New York to Los Angeles, they form an awkward and complicated friendship while Bree tries to hide his true identity from his son. Both *Boys Don't Cry* and *Transamerica* demonstrate the sad circumstances of those who must hide their true identities, in a society that may not be ready to accept them.

Film representations of LGBT lives have presented a wide variety of roles and characterizations. It should be clear from the movies referenced in this section that the depth of the portrayals has grown as a result of the relaxation of production codes in Hollywood. Additionally, independent filmmakers also have pushed the type of stories told. The substance of LGBT representations on television is due to networks' standards and practices departments and the tolerance of advertisers. The power of the advertiser can be just as instructive as a written code.

LGBT in Entertainment Television

In a 2008 episode of the PBS children's program *Postcards from Buster*, the program's star, an animated rabbit named Buster, visited real-life children whose parents make maple syrup in Vermont. Two of the families had lesbian mothers, leading Buster to decry, "Geez, that's a lot of moms!" The children's program quickly gained the attention of concerned citizen groups, leading PBS to not distribute it to its member stations. One side argued that children should not be exposed to this type of alternative lifestyle, while the other side contended that this type of family is a real part of life in modern America. The notion that images of same-sex relationships directed toward children engender controversy is not all that surprising given the relatively conservative stance the United States takes on mediated images of sexuality. Still, the increasing numbers of gays and lesbians on television programs indicate that objections to depictions of gay relationships are relaxing.

In the early days of television, LGBT people were almost invisible on the small screen. When they did appear, it was in very specific circumstances. In the 1970s, gay characters appeared on a few television programs. For example, the 1970s medical drama *Marcus Welby, M.D.* (1969–1976) featured a married man who had affairs with other men in one episode of the classic medical drama. *All in the Family* (1971–1979) briefly featured a trans, Beverly, who died after being attacked. A smaller number of programs even had regular characters who were gay, but these programs were short-lived. The first prominent gay character on a long-running prime-time television program was *Soap*'s (1977–1981) Jodie (played by Billy Crystal). Debuting in September of 1977, Crystal's character was regularly featured on the program and it garnered a good deal of attention. In the program's first episode, Jodie discussed having gender reassignment surgery so that he could live in the open with his closeted pro-football playing boyfriend. As a result, ABC was inundated with tens of thousands of letters of complaint. Still, the program – with Jodie – remained on air because of its critical success.

In the 1980s, appearances of LGBT characters became more frequent on prime-time dramas and comedies (Box 11.1 examines formula gay storylines). One of *Beverly Hills 90210*'s (1990–2000) main characters received the romantic attention of another high school girl; a *Thirtysomething* (1987–1991) episode contained a scene where two gay men were in bed together. But these characters were not regulars on the programs. Only at times were they principal characters – for example, *Dynasty*'s (1981–1989) Steven Carrington. Of note in the 1980s was *Love, Sydney*, an NBC sitcom that ran from 1981 to 1983, which featured an older gay man (played by Tony Randall) who takes in a friend

---

Box 11.1 Formulaic gay storylines

Television programming is very much reliant on following successful formulas. How many television programs feature competitions or challenges where the loser is kicked off in the end? How did the success of *One Tree Hill* (2003–2012) inspire television network CW to create other programs with gorgeous teens with scandalous lives?

In his often-cited book *The Prime Time Closet* (2002), Stephen Tropiano contends that storylines featuring gay characters also follow a formula that is repeated in situation comedies. There are four distinct plotlines that recur.

1. The "Coming Out" Episode: A former friend or boyfriend or girlfriend of a series regular appears on the program to announce a change in sexual orientation. In the end, the series regular accepts the friend's newfound lifestyle and a lesson is learned by all.
2. The "Mistaken Identity" Episode: A series regular is mistaken for being gay and the comedy ensues.
3. The "Pretend" Episode: A series regular pretends to be gay to receive a promotion, a new apartment, health insurance … only to be found out and forgiven for the deceit.
4. A "Very Special" Episode: In this plotline, the program takes the time to seriously handle a topic such as AIDS or discrimination.

These storylines are prevalent partly because a majority of them lend themselves to comedic situations. However, at the same time, some of these stories (i.e., "Mistaken Identity" and "Pretend" episodes) can intimate that being gay is something to shy away from or put on like an overcoat.

Can you think of any examples of Tropiano's storylines that you've seen recently?

and her young daughter. Although Sydney was gay, there was little discussion of his sexuality on the program. In April of 1997, ABC's *Ellen* (1994–1998) was the first program where the lead character came out of the closet during the run of the program. In the "Puppy Episode," Ellen Morgan (played by Ellen DeGeneres) reveals her intimate feelings for another woman, Susan (played by Laura Dern), to her therapist (played by Oprah Winfrey).

NBC's *Will and Grace* (1998–2006) was the first program built around the lives of two gay characters from its start. Will Truman (played by Eric McCormack) and Jack McFarland (played by Sean Hayes) were opposite sides of the gay male stereotype. Will meticulously managed his life, whereas Jack had a blithe attitude about everything – including his sexual partners. Unlike Ellen, these characters were comfortably living their lives as gay males, where Ellen (along with the network and the audience) struggled with her newfound sexual identity. *Will and Grace's* smartly comedic look at gay lifestyles, coupled with changing social mores, made it a successful part of NBC's Must See TV Thursday night umbrella for nearly a decade. The program continues to be seen nationwide via syndication.

Where *Will and Grace* humorously examines gay relationships with broad comedy, *Grey's Anatomy*, an ensemble drama that premiered on ABC in 2005, approaches the subject of lesbianism with a soberness rarely seen on television. In one of its earlier episodes, medical doctor Calliope (Callie) Torres (played by Sara Ramirez) tries to explain her lesbian life to her father who believes that his daughter can "pray away the gay." In one emotional exchange, the intermixing of religious teachings and sexual orientation collide:

MR. TORRES:
Leviticus – Thou shall not lie with a man as one lies with a female. It is an abomination.

CALLIE:
Oh, don't do that, Daddy! Don't quote the Bible at me!

MR. TORRES:
The outcry of Sodom and Gomorrah is great. And the sin is exceedingly grave.

CALLIE:
Jesus – A new commandment that I give unto you, that you love one another.

MR. TORRES:
Romans – But we know that laws ...

CALLIE:
Jesus – He who is without sin among you, let him cast the first stone ...

MR. TORRES:
So you admit it's a sin?

CALLIE:
Blessed are the merciful for they shall obtain mercy – Jesus. Blessed are the pure in heart for they shall see God – Jesus ... Jesus is my savior, Daddy, not you! And Jesus would be ashamed of you for judging me! He would be ashamed of you for turning your back on me. He would be ashamed!

Not only is the complexity of the exchange unique to prime-time television, but Callie's storyline is atypical because she had relationships with several male characters on the program prior to coming out. However, after meeting Dr. Erica Hahn (played by Brooke Smith) she realizes that she wants to pursue a romantic relationship with her. Even though the relationship was short-lived, it was significant in that it added another dimension to the program, and a new female character, Dr. Arizona Robbins (played by Jessica Capshaw), soon was introduced as a long-term love interest. Although this story progression is unique, its level of sophistication indicates that it is true to life. In fact, the writers of *Grey's* invited members of the Gay & Lesbian Alliance Against Defamation (GLAAD) to consult on the storyline to ensure the situation was a realistic representation.

Another realistic, albeit retro look at what it means to be gay in US society was depicted on AMC's Emmy winner *Mad Men* (2007–2015). Set in a large advertising agency in the 1960s, the program challenged many of the conventions from that period in time. In the show, actor Bryan Batt played the character of art director Sal, a closeted gay male who marries in order to divert attention from his hidden sexual orientation. Sal is flirtatious and often has clandestine sexual encounters with men. In one fateful episode, Sal rebuffs the advances of a male client. The client responds to the rejection by complaining about Sal's work. When Sal explains the pass, and subsequent rejection, his boss Don Draper (played by Jon Hamm) suggests that Sal should have done whatever the man asked in order to keep his lucrative account. Sal is fired. Although the program is definitely set in a more conservative time and corporate environment, Sal's firing is reminiscent of homophobic actions that occur in workplaces then and now.

Gay and lesbian representations are not the only ones that have been found on network television over the past few decades and today. Some programs have also touched on issues related to bisexuality. NBC's *Friends* (1994–2004) approached the subject through humor in one of its episodes, entitled "The One After the Super Bowl," that aired in January of 1996. The character of Phoebe Buffay (played by Lisa Kudrow), who is known for her offbeat songs, was invited to play at the public library for a group of children and wanted to sing songs that "told the truth." One such song went as follows:

Sometimes men love women,
Sometimes men love men,
Then there are bisexuals
Though some just say they're kidding themselves ...

Other programs, however, have handled bisexual and transgender people in a less humorous way. For instance, the Fox series *House* (2004–2012) featured a regular character, Thirteen (portrayed by Olivia Wilde), who is bisexual. Her sexuality had been the topic of conversation in several episodes, and certain storylines – ones involving one-night stands and drug use – at first led viewers to be highly critical of the portrayal, considering it yet another stereotypical portrayal of a promiscuous gay character. However, it turned out these reckless decisions had to do with a health crisis and not with her bisexuality. After the revelation, the series was praised for its quality portrayal.

The ABC series *Ugly Betty* (2006–2010) featured a regular transgender character, Alexis Meade (portrayed by Rebecca Romijn), until the end of season 3, when she became a recurring character. The long-running ABC's daytime soap *All My Children* (1970–2013) featured a regular transgender character for several months in late 2006 to early 2007. The character, known as Zoe, who was at the beginning of a male-to-female gender transition, was played by actor Jeffrey Carlson. Her transition process was part of her storyline, and she joined a transgender support group, discussed the decision with her mother, and worked at reconciliation with her father.

According to GLAAD, the number of regular LGBT characters on prime-time broadcast television has steadily increased in recent years. In its 2015 study, the organization found that the percentage of LGBT characters in recurring roles rose by 4 percent in comparison to 2014, although a majority of the characters were gay men and no transgender characters appeared. Together with this growth in LGBT television characters in general, the number of television programs presenting gay characters in leading roles has also seen an increase.

One of the first prime-time broadcast television programs to feature gay characters in leading roles is the ABC sitcom *Modern Family* (2009 debut). The inclusion of the couple, lawyer Mitchell or "Mitch" (played by Jesse Tyler Ferguson) and homemaker Cameron or "Cam" (played by Eric Stonestreet), as leading characters in the show was considered groundbreaking. Their storyline began

Figure 11.2 Eric Stonestreet and Jesse Tyler Ferguson as Cam and Mitch from ABC's *Modern Family* (2009–). Screenshot.

with the couple adopting a daughter from Vietnam (Figure 11.2). According to producer Steve Levitan:

> We wanted to do a family that was conventional ... We knew we wanted a gay couple raising a child. And we said from the very beginning, you know, this is going to mean that we probably won't be a giant hit, and we both said well you can't do a show about this, without this ... It can turn off a large portion of America, but it has to be. (Archive of American Television n.d.)

Levitan's instinct to go with a gay couple adopting a child was correct. Since its premiere, *Modern Family* has consistently been ABC's top-rated television program. In fact, in the series, Mitch and Cam go on to adopt an additional child.

Another program credited for bringing a diverse array of gay characters in leading roles to prime-time television is the show *Glee*, which aired on Fox television network from 2009 to 2015. The musical comedy drama followed the lives of young teenagers who are part of a glee club at a high school in Ohio and go on to find fame in New York City. Gay and lesbian students, a gay family, and transgender people were all included in various storylines of the show. Sensitive subject matters such as gender-neutral bathrooms and gender reassignments were topics that the program was willing to tackle, while bringing humor along the way.

Following in the steps of *Modern Family* and *Glee*, ABC debuted *The Real O'Neals* in 2016. The sitcom is about a five-person Catholic family that on the surface appears to be the perfect family – that is, until the audience is gradually introduced to the unique personal struggles of each of the family members. In the pilot episode, middle child, 16-year-old Kenny (played by Noah Galvin), comes out to his family, prompting other family members to also reveal their inner secrets. In one of the more talked about episodes that follow, Kenny goes to the prom with his dream date, another handsome teenager, and experiences his first kiss with another boy.

ABC network television perhaps would not even have included such a kiss scene between young-sters had it not been for the young kiss that came before it on the ABC Family cable show *The Fosters*. The show about a lesbian couple raising their biological and foster children, introduced in Chapter 8, elicited controversy when in one of its episodes 13-year-old foster child Jude (played by Hayden Byerly) shares a kiss with his classmate and first love, another 13-year-old boy. The kiss became the youngest kiss in television history. Public reaction, including on social media, was both positive and negative. In response to the negative comments regarding the kiss, show co-creator Bradley Bredeweg stated in an interview with *TheWrap*:

> When people question the scene my response has been: "Everyone has a first kiss and you remember it. How old were you?" Ninety percent of people who have an answer come back and say, "I was 12, 13 and 14 years old," and I say, "Exactly." It was time to see this, time to put this up for the world. (Sieczkowski 2015)

Cable television shows, in fact, have often been the first to take chances with frank and complicated portrayals of gay characters due to the nature of the niche or segmented audiences. While substantive discussions about sexual orientation can appear on CBS, NBC, ABC, and other broadcast television networks, cable audiences are looking for more in-depth discourse of topics that are relevant to them. Moreover, cable television networks do not run the risk of offending large, general audiences, because the cable audiences are smaller. The pressure to please the masses is not as prevalent in the world of cable television. MTV's long-running reality program *The Real World* (1992 debut) has shown the lives of many gay, lesbian, bisexual, and transgender youngsters, making them an essential part of the program every season. Most prominent of these was the life of Pedro Zamora, a gay man living with AIDS, in *The Real World San Francisco* (1994). Months before Zamora's death in 1994, the program showed his "marriage" to another man. In 2009, MTV made a movie about the life of Zamora to tell a more complete story than that seen on the reality program 15 years earlier.

Other cable networks, including HBO, Showtime, and Cinemax, have offered candid (and at times explicit) looks at same-sex romances on programs such as *Queer as Folk* (2000–2005), *Six Feet Under* (2001–2005), *The L Word* (2004–2009), *Boardwalk Empire* (2010–2014), and *True Blood* (2008–2014). All of these programs featured LGBT characters in prominent roles. The pay networks allowed these programs' producers to depict the real components of same-sex or bisexual relationships including nudity and graphic sexual encounters. This has also been the case with shows distributed on such streaming services as Amazon Prime, Netflix, and Hulu. Included among the programs that have attained large audiences and critical acclaim due to their effective storylines involving gay, lesbian, bisexual, and/or trans characters are *Orange Is the New Black* (2013 debut), *Red Oaks* (2015 debut), and *Mozart in the Jungle* (2014 debut).

Several researchers have studied the increase in images of LGBT in the media. Mass communications professor Ron Becker attributes the success of these gay-themed programs to the "SLUMPY" class. Television executives and psychographic research have determined that this group of Socially Liberal, Urban-Minded Professionals (SLUMPY) seeks edgier programs "as a convenient way to establish a hip identity" (Becker 2006). The mainstreaming of gay culture has also been credited with the approach taken on several programs. Programs that feature gays as helping straights improve their lives – ranging from clothes to their romantic lives – such as *Queer Eye for the Straight Guy* (2003–2007) encouraged viewers to see gays as contributing to the culture. Similarly, shows where the gay character is the helpful, counseling buddy of a hetero friend make gay individuals palatable to a wide range of audiences (not just the "SLUMPY"). Of course, this stereotype can be problematic in that it relegates these characters to one-dimensional roles, but in the past 50 years the depiction has made progress.

The increase may also be indicative of the changing mores of US society. Minority representation on television is said to sometimes evolve from non-representation (being ignored) to ridicule (being made fun of/scorned) to regulation (having limited, acceptable roles) and to some degree of respect (becoming woven into daily life) (Clark 1969). The representational evolution tends to mirror changes in a society's social structure, especially in terms of legal rights for minority groups, and shifts in social acceptance of the group members. There is some question as to whether or not images of gays, lesbians, bisexuals, and transgender people have reached the respect level.

There is no doubt that strides have been made in terms of the number of LGBT characters appearing on mainstream television. Nevertheless, some critics still question how those characters are being portrayed. They observe that a television trope that has found difficulty in being a thing of the past is the "tragic" gay, bisexual, or transgender person. Gay rights advocates have lamented that just when they are rejoicing at the introduction of LGBT characters on prominent programs, the characters are frequently killed off. Some of the characters that have met their demise on popular television programs have included Kira (played by Yaani King) on Syfy's *The Magicians* (2016 debut) and Denise (played by Merritt Wever) on AMC's *The Walking Dead* (2011 debut).

Advocates have also complained that racially diverse LGBT characters are needed. GLAAD, in their 2015 study, also found that the majority of the LGBT characters on television are white (69% on broadcast television; 71% on cable television; 73% on streaming services). The establishment of channels devoted to gay programming such as the Gay Television Network (GTN) and Logo TV has certainly helped with the lack of LGBT diversity by offering programs specifically focused on the lives of the LGBT community. For example, Logo's *RuPaul's Drag Race All Stars* (2014 debut) is a reality show that presents each season a competition hosted by RuPaul where 14 drag queen contestants vie for the title of "America's Next Drag Superstar." The contestants are often diverse, with several drag queens of color appearing, although some have criticized how race has been handled in the show's skits, with a reliance on old stereotypes.

It is difficult to determine if increases in the number and the diversity of LGBT characters on television actually impacts on individual attitudes about the community. However, there has been shown to be a link between viewers' parasocial interactions (one-sided interpersonal relationships; commonly those between a viewer and a celebrity or a fictional television character, with whom the viewer develops a bond of intimacy and a feeling of friendship – a feeling that the viewer really "knows" the celebrity or character) with television characters and their positive feelings about the mediated personas. For example, people who were frequent *Will and Grace* viewers and had frequent parasocial interactions, or friendships, with the characters tended to have less sexual prejudice regarding the gay characters on the show, Will and Jack. Even those who had little interaction with gays in their real lives had less prejudice against the characters if they had high parasocial interactions with the characters (Schiappa, Gregg, and Hewes 2006). Furthermore, media scholars Elizabeth Perse and Rebecca Rubin (1989) found that viewers can use television to familiarize themselves with people they don't know in real life. If a viewer does not have a lot of contact with gay men, the viewer can still form an impression about how they feel about gay people from the characters they see on television.

LGBT in Music and Radio

When it comes to the music industry, issues related to same-sex relationships are represented in a wide range of ways. The themes run from hip lesbian rock to rap lyrics that condone gay bashing.

In 2009, Katy Perry had a hit song with "I Kissed a Girl (and I Liked It)" that introduced pop radio listeners to bi-curious experimentation with a catchy tune and clever refrain ("I hope my boyfriend don't mind it"). The lyrics resonated with young listeners who have grown up in a culture where sexual experimentation is more prevalent in the media than ever before. In her lyrics, Perry explains:

> I kissed a girl
> And I liked it
> The taste of her cherry chapstick
> I kissed a girl just to try it
> I hope my boyfriend don't mind it
> It felt so wrong, it felt so right
> Don't mean I'm in love tonight.
> Us girls, we are so magical
> Soft skin, red lips, so kissable
> Hard to resist, so touchable
> Too good to deny it
> Ain't no big deal, it's innocent

Of course, there are times when being gay is referenced in popular songs and is not as lighthearted as Perry's. Rap and hip-hop music has been criticized for its anti-gay lyrics. Rapper Eminem's "Criminal" contained the line "Hate fags? The answer's yes." Another artist, DMX said, "I show no love for homo thugs" in his "Where the Hood At?" These lyrics are due, in part, to the genre's pervasive images of aggressive, macho men. These men's attempts to seem superior often come at the expense of gays and women in general.

Alternatively, some artists (Kanye West, for example) have spoken out against anti-gay lyrics. Openly gay musician Elton John's performance with Eminem at the 2001 Grammy awards signaled a change that the music world might be growing more tolerant. The two performed Eminem's controversial hit song "Stan," ending the duet with a hug and a bow during the crowd's standing ovation.

Gay males have also gained some ground in the rap music community. For example, artist Cushun speaks loudly about his status as a gay male. His frequently graphic lyrics contain suggestions that his sexual identity makes him stronger and better than any straight rapper. His boasting is noteworthy in a genre that frequently shuns the gay male as being weak. As a nod to the profitability found in embracing alternative lifestyles, Sony started its "Music with a Twist" label to recruit artists who are gay, lesbian, bisexual, or trans. The label, which started in January of 2006, was designed to bring artists that were already established with LGBT audiences to the mainstream (Hasty 2006). Also, while Frank Ocean eschews any labels on his sexuality, he has been open that he is sexually fluid. Further, his 2016 album *Blonde* is sprinkled with discussions about dynamic sexuality, with references to visiting gay bars; and included on one of the album's tracks is the voice of iconic trans-queen Crystal LeBeija. Similar to Ocean, hip-hop artist Young Thug does not label his sexual orientation but wears both men and women's clothing because he views gender as a false construct of society.

Reggae is another format that receives complaints from gay activists. However, some reggae artists, including prominent members of the reggae community (including artists who had previously promoted homophobia), have vowed to not produce songs that bashed gays. The Reggae Compassionate Act is a pledge between the industry and Stop Murder Music advocates that reads in part:

> It must be clear there's no space in the music community for hatred and prejudice, including no place for racism, violence, sexism or homophobia. We do not encourage nor minister to HATE but rather uphold a philosophy of LOVE, RESPECT and UNDERSTANDING towards all human beings as the cornerstone of reggae. (Queerty 2008)

The pact was the result of a three-year campaign where artists' shows were canceled if they did not rebuke sexism, violence, and homophobia.

Representations of LGBT in the News

Because of the controversies associated with being gay, coverage of the LGBT community rarely appeared in mainstream newspapers until the 1970s. It is not that there were no significant stories that could be told, but it was widely acknowledged that newspapers would not print stories or press releases sent by pro-gay organizations. It was rare that a newspaper would publish stories where someone who was gay was heroic or victorious. The mores at the time did not permit it. As a case in point, in 1965 the mother of *New York Times* publisher Arthur Ochs Sulzberger told her son that the *Times* was covering "homosexuality" too sympathetically. The editor of the paper assured Mrs. Ochs that the paper would take more care in the future and would cover issues related to sexual orientation with more discretion (Chomsky and Barclay 2005).

In more recent years, some newspapers have acknowledged aspects of the LGBT community. Coverage of HIV/AIDS and an increase in gay and lesbian journalists working for mainstream newspapers accounted for the increased numbers of stories about LGBT people in the 1980s. Much of that content dealt with tragedy in the gay community. An increase in AIDS-related deaths led to an examination of the language found in obituaries. For example, there was an increase in the number of young people appearing in the death announcements (Cameron and Cameron 2005).

In 1999, many of the 120 straight and gay newspaper readers who participated in the University of Southern California's Study of Sexual Orientation felt as though local newspapers were doing little to increase their knowledge of gay and lesbian current events (Aarons and Murphy 2000). A content analysis of these newspapers found that the newspapers covered issues of LGBT if the stories were related to crime, celebrity, or some sort of crisis. Similarly, journalism and media ethics scholar Rhonda Gibson's 2005 study of newspaper content over a 10-month period found that there were more than 400 articles dealing on some level with gays, lesbians, or bisexuals. However, most of the articles focused on the television programs *Ellen*, *Will and Grace*, and *Queer as Folk*. The second type of article found dealt with calendar events such as an announcement of a film festival featuring the work of gays and lesbians. Relatively little coverage was of LGBT lifestyle issues and, when there was, it was met with some consternation. In one example, in 2001, more than 350 subscribers to *The Roanoke Times* canceled their subscription when the paper published a four-part series about the city's burgeoning gay and lesbian population. One of the complaints of the series was that there was a photo of men kissing on the front page of the newspaper.

Although there are some who do not want to read about LGBT issues, newspapers cannot ignore them since they are closely tied to politics, health, and religion in the twenty-first century. For example, when politicians publicly debated overturning the controversial policy of "Don't Ask, Don't Tell" (which allowed gays to serve in the military only if they hid their sexuality identity), due to an escalating need for military personnel, newspapers had no choice but to cover the discussions. Other recent stories that have received national press attention include hate crimes committed against the gay community and the Supreme Court ruling against state bans on same-sex marriages.

Hundreds of newspapers, ranging from the *New York Times* to the *Grand Forks Herald*, have included civil union or marriage announcements of same-sex couples on their pages side by side with the wedding announcements of heterosexual couples. Increasingly, stories on celebrities who have married – and/or divorced – people of the same sex (Neil Patrick Harris/David Burtka, Ellen DeGeneres/Portia DeRossi, Lance Bass/Michal Turchin) appear in newspaper copies and online news sites across the country. Placing gays and lesbians in the lifestyle section of mainstream news outlets allows these couples to be a part of the norm. The practice has been met with both acceptance and opposition. Sociologist Kathleen Tiemann found that letters to a newspaper editor disagreeing with the published announcements were sent from those living in smaller towns near the more urban area where the newspaper was published (Tiemann 2006). Newspaper readers who were more tolerant of gays and lesbians tended to be more accepting of same-sex marriage and did not reconsider their attitudes even if a source in a newspaper held an opposing opinion (Hester and Gibson 2007).

LGBT and Magazines

The magazine industry seems to have been more responsive to the LGBT reader than newspapers, for two reasons. First, the narrative nature of magazines allows there to be coverage of more sensitive, involved, and personal topics than those that appear in newspapers. Second, most magazines are published to appeal to a specific type of audience; lesbians, gays, bisexuals, and transgender people are niche audiences willing to pay for specific content.

As was the case with newspapers, magazine coverage of issues related to sexuality has evolved over time. Initially, magazines catering to mainstream readers published stories about alternative lifestyles reluctantly. For example, between the years 1940 and 1959, collectively *Time* and *Newsweek* printed 23 stories about gays. When the articles were published, they frequently reinforced the notion of gays wanting to do harm to straight Americans since words such as "unnatural," "depraved," and "aberrant" appeared in them. Both *Time* and *Newsweek* contained articles painting gays as predators or "recruiters" for the young throughout the late 1990s (Bennett 2005). Furthermore, an analysis of *New Woman* and *Essence* magazines found these periodicals portrayed "crooked men" (gays and bisexuals) as being harmful to the health of both heterosexual women and couples (Gadsden 2002). However, the same study found that these magazines also featured editorial content that encouraged women to explore their sexual orientation as part of the normal human experience. Similarly, a study of *Seventeen* magazine articles between 1974 and 1994 found numerous stories about girls' sexuality, including topics focused on girls' empowerment over their own sexuality and a more positive perspective on being gay (Carpenter 1998). Reflecting a progressive trend in popular magazines, when Caitlyn Jenner decided to introduce her new look to the public after transitioning, she did so by appearing on the cover of *Vanity Fair* in a provocative bathing suit that revealed her cleavage. The reaction to the cover was mixed, similar to the reactions Caitlyn received when she appeared at the 2016 ESPY award ceremony to receive her Arthur Ashe Courage Award (see Box 11.2).

Box 11.2 Caitlyn Jenner: Deserving of Arthur Ashe Courage Award?

When it was announced that Caitlyn Jenner would be awarded the Arthur Ashe Courage Award at the 2016 ESPY (Excellence in Sports Performance Yearly) award ceremony, expressions of dissent circulated via traditional and social media. Critics argued that there were other candidates more deserving of the award. Even long-time sportscaster Bob Costas stated that the award going to Jenner was "a crass exploitation play, a tabloid play" (Braxton 2015). ESPY's organizing committee defended the choice, saying that Caitlyn's decision to invite the public to witness her transition from the 65-year-old Olympic Star Bruce Jenner was worthy of the special award that recognizes "individuals whose contributions transcend sports" (from the website). Gay rights advocacy groups also weighed in with their support, including one of the program directors at GLAAD, Nick Adams: "Caitlyn Jenner had to transition in the face of unimaginable public scrutiny, and in doing so has helped people around the world understand more about what it means to be transgender" (quoted in Braxton 2015).

Jenner did appear at the ceremony to accept the award, marking her first public appearance after her transition. She did receive praise for the moving speech she made, but observers still claimed it was a media stunt to raise ratings, especially with the entourage of Kardashians that showed up, walking the red carpet before the ceremony. Others also noted that it served as a perfect promo to Jenner's new E! Entertainment reality series called *I Am Cait*, which debuted a few months after the ESPY ceremony.

So now it is your turn. Reflect on the above and think about the positions each side has presented. In your mind, given what has been covered in this chapter, was Caitlyn Jenner deserving of the Arthur Ashe Courage Award?

Like any other group in America, the LGBT community has created its own publications as a way to speak to its specific concerns and interests. In the past, these publications were sponsored by civic organizations whose goal was to educate about homophobia and living life out of the closet. It was difficult for them to gain any nationwide readership because their literature was interpreted as obscene and was viewed as falling under restrictions put in place by the Comstock Act of 1873, which prohibited the sending of "obscene, lewd, and/or lascivious" materials through the US Postal Service. After the USPS along with law enforcement seized copies of its publication in 1954, *ONE Magazine*, an early magazine for the gay and lesbian audience, filed suit saying that the publication was educational, not titillating. The magazine lost its case and subsequent appeal; however, the Supreme Court looked more favorably on the rights of the magazine. On January 13, 1958, the Court held that *ONE Magazine* must have First Amendment protections extended to it, thereby making it possible for other gay and lesbian publications to be sent through the mail (Burroway 2008; Whitt 2001).

In more recent years, there has been a shift in the content found in these magazines. While there are some magazines that focus on community organization and politics, there are also glossy magazines that rival any other magazine on the newsstand. For example, *Out Traveler* offers gay-friendly travel ideas, *Genre* gives its readers fashion and lifestyle articles, *Echelon* is for LGBT business professionals, and *Cybersocket* is a gay web magazine. Fewer publications are specifically geared toward lesbians because these magazines generally have not had as large a readership, nor have they been as financially successful as those for gay males. The best-selling magazine for lesbians is *Curve*, which contains topics such as honeymoon destinations and celebrity features.

One of the most successful LGBT magazines is *The Advocate*. This news magazine founded in 1967, features current events with a slant toward issues related to LGBT such as worldwide gay rights and stories on transgender public officials. *The Advocate* offers its subscribers the choice to have the magazine delivered to their homes with or without a "privacy wrap" that hides the cover, spine, and back of the magazine. In other words, the publication is giving its readers the choice to not "out" themselves when the magazine is delivered to their homes or to be "out and proud" (Kirchick 2007).

LGBT and Advertisements

Any form of media is largely reliant on advertising for its survival. Therefore, it would seem that advertisers would tap any potential advertising venues to increase profits. However, there have been times when advertisers have backed away from controversy surrounding alternative lifestyles in an effort to satisfy one audience over another. In 2005, the American Family Association (AFA) led by Donald Wildmon threatened to boycott the Ford Motor Company if the company continued "supporting the homosexual agenda" (Peters 2005: 10). As a result Ford stopped running ads for Jaguar and Land Rover in gay and lesbian media. The AFA has not always been successful in these threats. The AFA demanded that Procter & Gamble stop advertising on *Will and Grace* and *Queer Eye for the Straight Guy*. The group claimed victory after an eight-month boycott of the company; however, it was revealed that Procter & Gamble did not stop these ads. In fact, they increased their ad buy by more than 30 percent during the boycott months.

Overall, however, images of LGBT in advertising are still few in number. In 1999, beer icon Anheuser-Busch created an advertisement for Bud Light featuring two men holding hands. The ad, which ran in a gay magazine with a small circulation in St. Louis, also featured a 1–800 number asking people to give their opinion of this new marketing campaign. Anheuser-Busch would not comment much on the campaign, but the public offered scores of pro and con comments. As might be expected, those who were tolerant of gays viewed the Bud Light ad more positively than those who were less tolerant of gays (Bhat, Leigh, and Wardlow 1998).

Research dealing with LGBT in advertising indicates that there is a range of depictions directed at different audiences. For instance, the image of the "hot lesbian" has been successful in selling products to heterosexuals. When lesbians appear in advertisements directed toward lesbians, they tend to be more androgynous and have a wider range of weights and ages than those in advertisements appearing in the mainstream press (Gill 2009; Milillo 2008).

The biggest advertising event of the year, across all platforms, is the Super Bowl. Besides the exciting competition on the field, one of the reasons to watch the football game is to enjoy the artistry, creativity, and downright silliness of the commercials that air during the game's commercial breaks. In past years, viewers have seen elegant Clydesdales, dancing supermodels, and talking babies placed in 30-second spots that cost up to $3 million to air. A commercial for Snickers that ran during the 2007 game caused a stir among viewers. In the ad, two men are standing in a garage with a hankering for the same Snickers bar. In their eagerness to eat the chocolate, they attack the bar from either end and quickly meet in the middle. They accidently touch lips. To stave off any thoughts that they are attracted to each other, they start beating each other with car parts. In another incarnation of the spot, the men kiss and then pull out their chest hairs to appear tough and *manly*. The ad and the related video content on the Internet were deleted after complaints from groups such as the Human Rights Campaign.

Three years later, more than 100 million viewers watched the New Orleans Saints defeat the Indianapolis Colts. One advertiser trying to reach this huge number of eyes was Mancrunch.com, an online dating site for gay men. The humorous commercial featured two young men on a sofa watching a sporting event – presumably the Super Bowl. While watching the game, the men simultaneously reach into a bowl of potato chips and their hands touch. This inadvertent contact sparks a flame between the two men and they begin to passionately kiss, while a wide-eyed third man watches them with a strange, almost puzzled expression. CBS opted to not run the ad, prompting the question whether the network was homophobic or was afraid to advertise an atypical type of spot. CBS countered that the network was neither. Instead, CBS maintained that they were working with Mancrunch to make a more acceptable advertisement.

A Mancrunch representative, Elissa Butcher, described CBS's decision not to air the ad as "straight-up discrimination." She said that although CBS told her that they also rejected the ad because they were not sure Mancrunch could pay for the $2.5 million 30-second slot, Mancrunch was willing to pay cash for the airtime. However, CBS spokeswoman Shannon Jacobs countered that there was no documentation that proved such an offer was made. The ad was posted to Mancrunch.com.

Ever since the US Supreme Court ruled, in 2013, against Section 3 of the Defense of Marriage Act (DOMA) that had supported state bans of gay marriages, however, major retailers such as Target, IKEA, JC Penney, Campbell's soup, and Kohl's have all produced ads featuring LGBT couples. While some of the ads have encountered harsh criticism, especially via social media, others have been applauded. For example, leading up to the holiday season in 2015, the large retailer Kohl's released an ad featuring a biracial gay couple that appeared to have just announced their engagement at a holiday family gathering (Figure 11.3). The ad ends with the family toasting the happy young couple. It was part of Kohl's #AllTogetherNow ad campaign and, with the ad's warm and positive feel, public response was overwhelmingly supportive.

Many observers have observed that the buying power of the LGBT community has gained the attention of businesses. Thus, the community has become not only socially visible, but economically visible as well.

Figure 11.3 Kohl's 2015 #AllTogetherNow ad featuring a biracial gay couple smiling and being toasted by family. Screenshot.

LGBT and New Media

A 2008 Harris Interactive study found that gay and lesbian adults read more blogs than heterosexuals. More than half of the gays and lesbians studied replied that they read at least one blog (Harris Interactive 2009). This result is not surprising, for two reasons. First, there is a relative lack of coverage of LGBT issues and media sources available in traditional media, so blogs fill that need. Second, the interactive nature of blogs allows for open, yet anonymous discussion of issues that are sensitive in some circles.

The Internet has become an outlet for open expressions of friendship, love, and grief for gay, lesbian, bisexual, and transgender individuals. For example, Facebook has more than a dozen groups for young people who have come out of the closet. TransFamilysos.org provides resources for individuals transitioning and their family members. "It Gets Better" is a YouTube channel that uses videos to tell LGBT teens that the confusion or bullying they are experiencing will not last forever. The Internet is a comfortable place for LGBT individuals to seek partners, because in a society that assumes people are straight, it gives those who are not straight a way of reaching out to those who are similar in sexual orientation. Additionally, the anonymity of the web can be appealing to those who are still uncomfortable being public with their sexuality. Furthermore, studies of LGBT dating websites find that the sites make it clear that many are looking for serious relationships and committed partnerships (Thorne and Coupland 1998).

Deep expressions of grief appear on the Internet because of the unfettered space it provides. More than 1,000 memorials devoted to those from the LGBT community who have died of AIDS can be found online. These sites are more than the traditional obituaries that appear in newspapers; these online memorials are remembrances of those who have died from a disease that some still associate with shame. The sites, which celebrate the lives of artists, doctors, teachers, and others, are written by parents, siblings, and partners. Finally, the family life of LGBT can also be found online. Because of lingering taboos associated with being gay, bisexual, or trans, the Internet has become an outlet for content catering to the LGBT community. For example, Mombian.com, with its subheading of "Sustenance for Lesbian Moms," is a lifestyle site designed to help lesbian moms by providing a variety of parenting tips and political and legal news that might affect them.

Concluding Remarks

It is clear that the representation and tolerance of lesbian, gay, bisexual, and transgender people in the media have changed over time. As the chapter demonstrated, there are varied opinions and levels of acceptance of the community. However, the images are evolving and growing. As images of sexuality appear in the media, being gay is becoming increasingly hip in some circles. In particular, the bisexuality implicit in iconic pop star Madonna's kissing of two other pop stars, Britney Spears and Christina Aguilera, on MTV, or actress Lindsey Lohan's relationship problems with her ex-girlfriend splashed on the cover of *People* magazine and on Perez Hilton's gossip blog normalize the behavior for young viewers. When Neil Patrick Harris receives replies such as "adorable family," "cutest family," after he tweets "Happy Halloween everyone!" and shows a picture of him and his husband appearing in a family photo dressed in Batman-themed costumes together with their young twin boys, the sense is that they are being received as any other celebrity couple would when appearing in such photos. The media, including social media, have made same-sex relationships more commonplace than at any other time.

Reflection Questions and Thoughts to Consider

1. The chapter lists several films depicting LGBT characters. How many of these films are available in your college or university's library? Does your library offer many feature films or documentaries dealing with LGBT lives? If you find that your library does not offer many of these types of films, how can you request a more comprehensive collection?
2. Select an ad out of your favorite magazine. Would this advertisement be the same in a magazine targeting lesbian or gay male readers? Why do you think this way? How would you change the ad you have chosen for a magazine that specifically targets lesbians, such as *Curve*, or gay men, such as *Instinct*?
3. Does your local newspaper present announcements of unions between gay couples? If not, check to see if there is any kind of policy against accepting such announcements. If so, dig into the online archives of the newspaper to determine when such announcements began appearing. Is there a pivotal event or state law that might have led to a marked shift?
4. As of the 2010 Census, one in five same-sex couples are raising children under 18, a number that is up substantially from 1990, when very few same-sex couples were raising kids. This chapter discussed the television programs *Modern Family* and *The Fosters* that feature a gay married couple raising children. Do you see these storylines as signs that same-sex families are gaining acceptance in society? Can you think of other media examples of LGBT parenting? Are they positive or negative portrayals?

References

Aarons, Leroy, and Sheila Murphy. 2000. *Lesbians and Gays in the Newsroom 10 Years Later*. Annenberg School of Communication, University of Southern California.
Adams, Nick. 2016. "Matt Bomer and Men Who Play Transgender Women Send a 'Toxic and Dangerous' Message (Guest Column)." *The Hollywood Reporter*, September 2. http://www.hollywoodreporter.com/news/matt-bomer-transgender-movie-anything-guest-column-925170 (accessed April 13, 2017).
Archive of American Television. n.d. "Steve Levitan Interview." http://www.emmytvlegends.org/interviews/people/steve-levitan (accessed April 13, 2017).
Becker, Ron. 2006. "Gay-themed Television and the Slumpy Class: The Affordable, Multicultural Politics of the Gay Nineties." *Television and New Media* 7: 184–215.
Bennett, Lisa. 2005. "Fifty Years of Prejudice in the News." *Gay and Lesbian Review* 7: 30–35.
Bhat, Subodh, Timothy W. Leigh, and Daniel L. Wardlow. 1998. "The Effect of Consumer Prejudices on Ad Processing: Heterosexual Consumers' Responses to Homosexual Imagery in Ads." *Journal of Advertising* 27(4): 9–28.
Braxton, G. 2015. "Is Caitlyn Jenner the Wrong Honoree for ESPY's Courage Award?" *Los Angeles Times*, July 15. http://www.latimes.com/entertainment/tv/la-et-st-caitlyn-jenner-courage-award-espys-20150715-story.html (accessed April 13, 2017).
Burroway, Jim. 2008. "Today in History: ONE Magazine versus the U.S. Post Office." *The Box Turtle Bulletin*. http://www.boxturtlebulletin.com/2008/01/13/1273 (accessed April 13, 2017).
Cameron, Paul, and Kirk Cameron. 2005. "Gay Obituaries Closely Track Officially Reported Deaths from AIDS." *Psychological Reports* 96: 693–697.
Carpenter, Laura M. 1998. "From Girls into Women: Scripts for Sexuality and Romance in *Seventeen* Magazine, 1974–1994." *Journal of Sex Research* 35(2): 158–168.

Centers for Disease Control. 2015. "HIV Surveillance Report: HIV Among Gay and Bisexual Men." https://www.cdc.gov/hiv/group/msm (accessed April 28, 2017).

Chomsky, Daniel, and Scott Barclay. 2005. "The Editor, the Publisher, and His Mother: The Representation of Gays in *The New York Times*." Paper presented at the American Political Science Association, Washington, DC, September 2005.

Clark, Cedric. 1969. "Television and Social Controls: Some Observations of the Portrayal of Ethnic Minorities." *Television Quarterly* 8: 18–22.

Denby, David. 2016. "Sex and Sexier: The Hays Code Wasn't All That Bad." *The New Yorker*, May 2. http://www.newyorker.com/magazine/2016/05/02/what-the-hays-code-did-for-women (accessed April 13, 2017).

Eaklor, Vicki L. 2008. *Queer America: A GLBT History of the 20th Century*. Westport, CT: Greenwood Press.

Epstein, Rob. 1985. *The Celluloid Closet*. DVD. Directed by Jeffery Friedman. Sony Pictures, USA.

Gadsden, Gloria Y. 2002. "Crooked Men and Straightened Women: Images of Homosexuality across Race in Two Women's Magazines, 1986–1995." *Journal of Homosexuality* 43(2): 59–75.

Gibson, Rhonda. 2005. "Coverage of Gay Males, Lesbians, in Newspaper Lifestyle Sections." *Newspaper Research Journal* 25(3): 90–95.

Gill, Rosalind. 2009. "Beyond the 'Sexualization of Culture' Thesis: An Intersection Analysis of 'Sixpacks', 'Midriffs' and 'Hot Lesbians' in Advertising." *Sexualities* 12(2): 137–160.

GLAAD. 2015. *2015–2016 Where We Are on TV. Glaad.org*. http://www.glaad.org/whereweareontv15 (accessed April 13, 2017).

Harris Interactive. 2009. "Gay and Lesbian Adults More Likely to Read Blogs and Use Social Networking Tools." *Businesswire.com*, June 9. http://www.b2i.us/profiles/investor/NewsPDF.asp?b=1963&ID=33672&m=rl (accessed April 13, 2017).

Hasty, Katy. 2006. "Gay, Lesbian Acts Find Sony Label Home 'With a Twist.'" *Billboard* 113(8): 12.

Hester, Joe Bob, and Rhonda Gibson. 2007. "Consumer Responses to Gay-Themed Imagery in Advertising." *Advertising and Society Review* 8(2). https://muse.jhu.edu/article/216980 (accessed April 13, 2017).

Kirchick, James. 2007. "A Magazine's 'Outing' Says Much about Gay Rights Today." *USA Today*. http://www.usatoday.com/printedition/news/20070822/opcomwednesday.art.htm (accessed April 13, 2017).

Milillo, Diana. 2008. "Sexuality Sells: A Content Analysis of Lesbian and Heterosexual Women's Bodies in Magazine Advertisements." *Journal of Lesbian Studies* 12(4): 381–392.

Perse, Elizabeth M., and Rebecca B. Rubin. 1989. "Attribution in Social and Parasocial Relationships." *Communication Research* 16: 59–77.

Peters, Jeremy W. 2005. "Under Pressure, Ford Will Cut Its Ads in Gay Publications." *New York Times*, December 6.

Pharr, Suzanne. 2002. *Homophobia: A Weapon of Sexism*. Berkeley, CA: Chardon Press.

Queerty. 2008. "Reggae Artists Have 'Straight' Pride." *Queerty.com*. http://www.queerty.com/reggae-artists-have-straight-pride-20080708 (accessed April 13, 2017).

Robehmed, Natalie. 2015. "Study Reports Too Few LGB Characters, No Transgender Roles In Movies." *Forbes.com*. http://www.forbes.com/sites/natalierobehmed/2015/08/06/study-reports-too-few-lgbt-characters-no-transgender-roles-in-movies/#2d3571ef74d1 (accessed April 13, 2017).

Safe Zone. 2011. "A Brief History of Homosexuality in America." Saint Louis University. http://www.slu.edu/organizations/safezone/downloads/reading.homosexuality%20in%20america.pdf (accessed April 13, 2017).

Schiappa, Edward, Peter B. Gregg, and Dean. E. Hewes. 2006. "Can One TV Show Make a Difference? *Will and Grace* and the Parasocial Contact Hypothesis." *Journal of Homosexuality* 51(4): 15–37.

Sieczkowski, Cavan. 2015. "There's Controversy Over that Gay Teen Kiss On 'The Fosters'." *Huffington Post*, March 5. http://www.huffingtonpost.com/2015/03/05/fosters-gay-teen-kiss_n_6809388.html (accessed April 13, 2017).

Smith, Stacy L., Marc Choueiti, and Katherine Pieper. 2015. "Inequality in 700 Popular Films: Examining Portrayals of Gender, Race/Ethnicity, LGBT, and Disability from 2007 to 2014." Media, Diversity and Social Change Initiative, USC Annenberg. http://annenberg.usc.edu/pages/~/media/MDSCI/Inequality%20in%20700%20Popular%20Films%208215%20Final%20for%20Posting.ashx (accessed April 13, 2017).

Smith, Stacy L., Marc Choueiti, and Katherine Pieper. 2016. "Inequality in 800 Popular Films: Examining Portrayals of Gender, Race/Ethnicity, LGBT, and Disability from 2007–2015." Media, Diversity and Social Change Initiative, USC Annenberg. http://annenberg.usc.edu/pages/~/media/MDSCI/Dr%20Stacy%20L%20Smith%20Inequality%20in%20800%20Films%20FINAL.ashx (accessed April 13, 2017).

Snarker, Dorothy. 2016. "Why *Carol* Failed to Become the Lesbian *Brokeback*." *IndieWire*, January 15. http://www.indiewire.com/2016/01/why-carol-failed-to-become-the-lesbian-brokeback-208759 (accessed April 13, 2017).

The Body. 2008. "Murder Mystery Film to Highlight HIV among African Americans." *TheBody.com*, January 4. http://www.thebody.com/content/art/art44635.html (accessed April 13, 2017).

Thorne, Adrian, and Justin Coupland. 1998. "Articulations of Same-sex Desire: Lesbian and Gay Male Dating Advertisements." *Journal of Sociolinguistics* 2(2): 233–257.

Tiemann, Kathleen A. 2006. "Why Is Their Picture on the Wedding Page: A Rural Community Responds to a Union Announcement." *Journal of Homosexuality* 51(4): 119–135.

Tropiano, Stephen. 2002. *The Prime Time Closet*. New York, NY: Applause Theatre and Cinema.

Whitt, Jann. 2001. "A Labor from the Heart: Lesbian Magazines from 1947–1994." *Journal of Lesbian Studies* 5(1): 229–251.

12

Representations of Age

Four women sit around a table, enjoying some food and drinks – and a candid conversation about sex:

DOROTHY:	Rose, is something wrong? Is it about Ernie?
BLANCHE:	He's lousy in bed, I knew it! I knew something had to be wrong with him!
ROSE:	No! He's not lousy! At least, I don't think he is …
BLANCHE:	Well, either he is or he isn't …
ROSE:	Well, I'm sure he's not. Although I have no proof that he's not, I'm sure he's not. I think.
BLANCHE:	I don't get it.
SOPHIA:	Neither does Rose!
BLANCHE:	Do you mean to tell me that you've been seeing Ernie for more than a month and you haven't done it yet? I mean, how long can you make conversation?
DOROTHY:	Blanche, there is more to conversation than just "Can I have a hanger for my pants, please."

Though this dialogue may seem pulled from an episode of *Girls* (2012–2017), and appear to be a conversation between girlfriends in their twenties, it is actually from an episode of *The Golden Girls* (1985–1992), and the ages of the characters speaking range from their mid-fifties to their mid-eighties.

The Golden Girls television series, with a cast of characters virtually all in their fifties, sixties and older, was a popular NBC show while on during prime time and remains a popular choice in reruns, often airing on cable television. In many ways, *The Golden Girls* is an anomaly, as research done over the past several decades shows that television and film characters with any "gray" factor tend to be portrayed stereotypically, commonly exhibiting characteristics of being sexless, being lonely, and rarely socializing with friends. Even this program, so often applauded for its positive representations of older people, still resorted to some stereotypical representations for comedic effect, particularly with regard to the character of Sophia (played by Estelle Getty), who was often played as the "cranky old woman."

Ageism, which is commonly defined as the discrimination, subordination, or stereotyping of a particular individual or group based on age, and the distorted representation of age, is not only

Diversity in US Mass Media, Second Edition. Catherine A. Luther, Carolyn Ringer Lepre, and Naeemah Clark.
© 2018 John Wiley & Sons Inc. Published 2018 by John Wiley & Sons Inc.

relegated to senior citizens and the elderly; stereotypical representations of teenagers also abound in American mass media. This chapter will discuss these two age groups and their representations in film, television, and print media; it will begin by exploring the myths of aging and ageist stereotypes, as well as definitions of these two age groups. It will look at how representations of these age groups either enforce stereotypes or attempt to debunk them by depicting characters and portrayals that show the elderly and teenagers as more complex. Finally, it will take a look at new media and see the influence of technology on these varied age groups.

Historical Background to Ageist Stereotypes and the Myths of Aging

The topic of aging is firmly cemented in many societal myths. Like most myths, the ones about aging include a confusing blend of truth, exaggeration, and falsity. Educational gerontology scholar James E. Thornton (e.g., 2002) has explored the topic of myths and aging. Traditional myths were folktales, mostly religious, and served to explain the universe to those who looked to understand it. Thornton writes that "early myths enshrined social values and validated social order, placing them in categories of accepted wisdom. They confirmed rather than questioned." Traditional myths explained phenomena when there was no knowledge in existence on a subject or idea, and often served as a means of maintaining the status quo of a society and a means to regulate social behavior. Today, myths often try to serve this same purpose; however, all too often, these myths are formed of stereotypes, exaggerated half-truths, or outright falsehoods about people who belong to certain social groups.

As these myths relate to aging, certain perceptions of and beliefs about growing old and the elderly not only continue to linger but are adamantly held to be true. Current aging myths serve to trivialize, marginalize, and debase the older person and the entire aging experience. Some of the commonly held myths and stereotypes regarding aging and the elderly include:

Myth #1: Older people are in poor health, often ill, often disabled, and lose control of their bodily functions, and will likely end up in a nursing home or other institution.

Myth #2: Older people lose interest in intimacy and sex.

Myth #3: Older people are unwilling to try anything new.

Myth #4: Older people lose their mental sharpness, become senile, and become childlike in their mental functions.

Myth #5: Older people have no social life, are sad, depressed, grouchy, and lonely.

Myth #6: Older people are poor, cannot function in the workplace, are heavily dependent on others, and cannot pull their own weight.

Myth #7: Older people do not understand technology and cannot use computers or the Internet.

Similarly, it can be said that myths regarding other generational labels, such as "GenXer," the generation of people born in the 1960s and 1970s, or "Millennials," the generation of people born between 1980 and the early 2000s, seek to pigeonhole an entire, multifaceted group of people in the same square box. Myths regarding these younger social groups are just as marginalizing as those about the older population, and most certainly can be seen to be as detrimental to the individuals who inhabit these groups when group stereotypes are applied in error. Some commonly held myths and stereotypes regarding teenagers include:

Myth #1: Teenagers are lazy.

Myth #2: Teenagers are disrespectful and irresponsible.

Myth #3: Teenagers are spoiled and self-serving.
Myth #4: Teenagers are obsessed with sex and pleasure seeking.
Myth #5: Teenagers, especially non-white males, are prone to violent behavior.
Myth #6: Teenagers abuse alcohol and drugs, and this abuse often leads to suicidal thoughts.
Myth #7: Parents are either irrelevant and often absent, or meddling to the point of detriment, in the lives of teenagers, and teens can get along just fine, if not better without them around. (Nichols and Good 2004)

Like all stereotypes, these myths of age would lose much of their power and potency without constant reinforcement within society and in our media. Much research has been done exploring how these stereotypes and myths continue to be fueled by media representations, and what some television programs, films, and press accounts are doing to combat these misrepresentations and create a more accurate and well-rounded view of the different age groups in our population.

Senior Citizens and Teenagers in the United States

The number of senior citizens in the United States is rapidly increasing. During the twentieth century, the US population under age 65 tripled, but those aged 65 and older increased by even more. The actual number of seniors grew from 3.1 million in 1900 to 36.7 million in 2008 (see Table 12.1). As of 2015, people who are 65 years of age or older (often labeled "older adults" or "the elderly") make up 14.9 percent of the total US population (US Census Bureau 2015), and their number is expected to grow to approximately 86.7 million people, which will be approximately 21 percent of the nation's population, by the year 2050. To put it in a more recent perspective, the United States has seen an increase in the senior citizen population of 78 percent since the mid-1970s. Americans aged 50 and older comprise more than 30 percent of the US population (US Census Bureau 2015; US Census Bureau n.d.).

In sharp contrast to some of the myths explored in the previous section, this older population, thanks in large part to the huge baby boomer population now moving into this age bracket, accounts for more than 80 percent of the personal wealth in US banks and financial institutions, and has 50 percent of the discretionary income (Snyder 2002). In 1965, approximately 29 percent of persons aged 65 or older were living below the poverty line; in 1998, only 10 percent were doing so. More than 17.5 percent of men aged 65 and older were still in the workforce, according to a US Bureau of Labor survey done in 2000, as were 9.4 percent of women aged 65 and older. In essence, there have been significant social and economic shifts in this older population, and experts expect it to continue as health and medical improvements continue to extend the human life span.

Table 12.1 Population of people in the United States over 65 (in millions) (US Census Bureau 2012).

	1990	2000	2005	2010
Total	29.6	32.6	35.2	38.6
Males	12.3	13.9	15.1	16.3
Females	17.2	18.7	20.0	21.5

According to the results of the 2012 US Census Bureau survey, 22 million teenagers (ages 15–19) live in the United States. Approximately 87.8 percent of teenagers are enrolled in a public or private school. Only 2.4 percent of teenagers are married, and 2.1 percent of female teenagers have reported a live birth within the past 12 months of the survey being completed. Approximately 37 percent of teenagers aged 16–19 are a part of the US labor force, and 5.2 percent are either not enrolled in school or are part of the labor force (US Census Bureau 2015; US Census Bureau n.d.).

Age in Film

Representations of Older and Elderly People

The depiction of aging in film and other visual media has, in general, not been positive. Many have argued that elderly populations suffer from almost complete negative stereotyping across media, and that many preconceived notions about growing old exist across society. Communication scholar Joshua Meyrowitz (1985) suggests that part of this is cultural. In American society, for example, older people are not appreciated as knowledgeable "elders," but as needy and failing. He writes, "Old people are respected to the extent that they can behave like young people, that is, to the extent that they remain capable of working, enjoying sex, exercising, and taking care of themselves."

In the film business, it can certainly be argued that there is a double standard in relation to aging. As Goldie Hawn's character in the 1996 film *The First Wives' Club* suggests, "there are only three ages for women in Hollywood: babe, district attorney, and 'driving Miss Daisy'." Women are judged and viewed more harshly for "looking old" (Harris 1994), just as some scholars have suggested that in general the social worth of women has been linked more closely with their physical appearance compared to men, and that aging only contributes to a sense of declining importance (Hatch 2005). Several researchers (e.g., Meehan 1983) have suggested that typical roles for older women, which are similar for film and television, include the good wife, the contented homemaker, the harpy, the matriarch, the feisty older woman, the loveable granny, and the bitch.

In 1997, a group of researchers examined 100 top-grossing motion pictures from the 1940s through the 1980s, 20 movies from each decade, to see how characters portrayed by older actors would be represented (Bazzini *et al.* 1997). In all, 829 significant characters were rated on attractiveness, character goodness/moral value, intelligence, friendliness, socioeconomic status, romantic activity/sexual activity, and the positivity of a character's outcome at the film's end (for instance, the character striking it rich and living happily ever after would be an extremely positive outcome). All older characters were judged to be less friendly, less attractive, and less likely to engage in romantic activity, but the negative correlation was particularly strong for the women. The researchers found that female characters over 35 were underrepresented in terms of actual population, and were more negatively portrayed than their male contemporaries. Older men were also underrepresented, but not by as large a margin. For the most part, this study also found that older females were perceived as less friendly, less intelligent, and less attractive than their male counterparts. The researchers in this study also found that there were significant age differences noted between the male and female leading characters. With the exception of the 1970s, each decade in the study showed that leading women were an average of six years younger than their leading men, and in many cases as many as 10 years younger. A more recent study found that the gap is getting worse. In an analysis of a trend that pairs older male actors with much younger female actresses, often as the main love interest, as the leading men grew older, their leading women grew younger (Buchanan 2013). For example, in

Denzel Washington's film *Flight* (2012), the actor was 57 years old. His love interest was played by 35-year-old Kelly Reilly. George Clooney was 49 when he filmed *The American* (2010); 34-year-old Violante Placido portrays the prostitute with whom he develops a relationship. Tom Cruise was 50 years old in *Oblivion* (2013), while Olga Kurylenko, who played his wife, was 33.

Time Labs sponsored a study in 2015 that charted how much more difficult it is for older women to find roles in Hollywood. Their results show that male actors see their careers peak at age 46, while female actors reach their peak at age 30. In addition, over time this trend has gotten even more pronounced, with fewer roles for women over 30 than ever before (Wilson 2015). According to a 2014 study by the Center for Study of Women in Television, men over 40 account for 53 percent of characters, while women that age represent only 30 percent. Dr. Martha Lauzen, the center's executive director, notes that this discrepancy does not just keep older women either invisible or stereotyped, it also keeps women powerless. "As we grow older, we gain personal as well as professional power," she said in an article published in *Variety* (Lang 2015). Women also speak less in films. A Polygraph study of more than 200 Hollywood screenplays reports that lines spoken by women over age 40 decrease substantially. For men, it is the opposite: more roles and more speaking lines (Anderson and Daniels 2016).

In a study looking at Academy Award nominees and winners for actors and actresses for the years 1927 through 1990, there was a striking bias in ages between men and women. In the 63 years of awards that were investigated in the study, only 27 percent of female award winners were over the age of 39, as compared to 67 percent of male winners (Markson and Taylor 1993). In another study of Academy Award nominees by the same researchers, films made between 1929 and 1995 were examined that featured actors and actresses aged 60 and older who had been nominated for an Oscar award some time in their lives to see if the characters portrayed differed in terms of gender roles. Throughout this period, men were more likely to be depicted as vigorous, employed, and involved in same-gender friendships and adventures (whether as hero or villain). Women were either peripheral characters or were portrayed as rich dowagers, wives/mothers, or lonely spinsters (Markson and Taylor 2000).

Take, for instance, the spinster stereotype. In the early nineteenth century, unmarried women, without a family of their own to care for, were often tasked with spinning the cloth and thread in their parents' homes, as a way of earning their keep, thus earning the spinster title. Over the years, the term has conjured up a mental image of a societal outcast – a frumpy, lonely, depressed, unmarried woman – trapped in her life, often serving as the carer for an elderly parent or other relative. She is often shown as longing to be "normal," like other women, and to have a family of her own. Spinsters often are shown as needing or wanting to be saved by others, through makeovers – the ugly duckling emerging – or being taught how to have fun. The spinster stereotype was commonplace for much of the twentieth century and can still be seen today.

An example of the spinster role is the character of Bessie (portrayed by Diane Keaton) in the 1996 film *Marvin's Room*. In this film, Bessie lives with her elderly father as the primary caregiver. Bessie is estranged from her only sister, Lee (played by Meryl Streep), who left home many years before after marrying to have a family of her own. Early in the movie, Bessie is diagnosed with leukemia, and her doctor tells her she needs a bone marrow transplant, which brings Lee back home. Bessie, who spends the bulk of the movie in prim and shapeless clothing, with limp, unattractive hair, is portrayed as the sacrificing and selfless caretaker. Though caring for her father and elderly aunt is both physically and emotionally draining, and she has moments of breakdown, she bears her responsibility almost as a badge of honor. Later in the movie, as the storyline develops, so does the spinster stereotype. Lee, who is in cosmetology school, gives Bessie a makeover and haircut, which is unveiled to much applause from the family.

While older men are not subject to the same type of stereotyping that women are in films, and roles for older men are in far greater supply, there are still some familiar roles regularly seen. The grumpy old man and the dirty old man are two of the most common stereotypes. In the aptly titled movie *Grumpy Old Men* (1993) Jack Lemmon and Walter Matthau bring to light virtually every facet of the older man stereotype – the two are set in their ways, are unfriendly, rude, bickering, and at times, lonely. When an attractive woman (played by Ann-Margret) moves onto their street, they become caricatures of lovesick schoolboys, lustily pursuing her, and dropping innuendos along the way. Though the movie is a comedy, and the over-the-top performances can be thought to be poking fun at these stereotypes, this is just one example of the many movies that utilize this formula.

It should be noted that more nuanced performances for older actors do exist. For example, Sally Field starred in the 2015 film *Hello, My Name Is Doris*. Field, 68 when the movie was filmed, portrays a single woman who falls for her much younger office colleague. Her personal life is in turmoil, as she has spent many years caring for an invalid mother in a home piled with clutter and trash. But it is a heartfelt comedy-drama, and the audience watches Field as Doris defy ageist stereotypes as she transforms herself, standing up to loved ones who attempt to bully her, and showing that old doesn't mean over. Another example is *Hope Springs* (2012), starring Meryl Streep, Tommy Lee Jones, and Steve Carrell. In this film, empty nesters (played by Streep and Jones) seek the help of a marriage counselor (Carrell) to reignite their spark. Jones's character refuses to see a problem in their marriage, and the counseling meets with limited success. However, once back at home, just as Streep's character contemplates leaving, Jones realizes how much he loves and needs her. Though a comedy with many bawdy moments, the movie was praised for showing real emotion and exposing the reality of a marital slump.

Representations of Teenagers

Films in the 1920s featured very few young and teenaged characters, and those that were shown were moral and straight-laced. In the movies made after the Great Depression, teen stars like Judy Garland and Mickey Rooney, who starred in the tremendously popular Andy Hardy series of movies, including *Love Finds Andy Hardy* (1938), portrayed optimistic and endearing characters. However, moviegoers saw a new kind of teen starting in the 1950s – the rebel without a cause, the juvenile delinquent as hero – most notably performed by James Dean. While there were still some "clean teen" performances, such as Elizabeth Taylor in *Little Women* (1949), "troubled youth" roles abounded. Soon movies like *Splendor in the Grass* (1961) and *Peyton Place* (1957) demonstrated the perils of teen sexuality. The 1960s saw a series of more carefree movies, designed to move away from the dilemmas of youth, including several beach films starring Frankie Avalon and Annette Funicello, and the popular *Gidget* (1959, 1961, 1963) movies, but counterculture movies continued to proliferate, including *Easy Rider* (1969) and *Wild in the Streets* (1968).

It would not be until the late 1970s and early 1980s that moviegoers would again be presented with a new generation of teens. The hit movies *Saturday Night Fever* (1977) and *Grease* (1978), both of which starred a young, sexy, and fit John Travolta, *Animal House* (1978), *Meatballs* (1979), and *Porky's* (1981) reintroduced teen characters in a big way, and paved the way for the main themes in films of the 1980s – music, sex, and style. The early 1980s, in particular, had a proliferation of teen "sex romp" or "sexploitation" films, with suggestive titles like *Goin' All the Way* (1982), *The Last American Virgin* (1982), and *The Sure Thing* (1985). An explosion of teen comedies and dramas followed, including the popular director John Hughes's movies including *Some Kind of Wonderful* (1987), *The Breakfast Club* (1985), and *Sixteen Candles* (1984), all starring actors who became known as the "Brat Pack." Between 1980 and 1989, there were six major approaches to teenage films, all of which followed in the footsteps of the movies of past decades: the horror film, e.g., *Halloween* (1983), *Slumber Party Massacre* (1982); the science film, e.g., *WarGames* (1983), *Weird Science* (1985), and *Real Genius* (1985); the sex comedy, e.g., *Risky Business* (1983); the romantic melodrama, e.g., *Pretty in Pink* (1986) and *Dirty Dancing* (1987); the juvenile delinquent comedy/drama, e.g., *Ferris Bueller's Day Off* (1986); and the school movie that had elements of the previous five, e.g., *Heathers* (1989), *Lucas* (1986), and *Can't Buy Me Love* (1987).

By the late 1980s, as the actors who comprised the so-called Brat Pack – including Emilio Estevez, Anthony Michael Hall, Rob Lowe, Andrew McCarthy, Demi Moore, Judd Nelson, Molly Ringwald, and Ally Sheedy – began to age and act in more adult-oriented dramas, the proliferation of teen movies began to wane, and teen-oriented films were in short supply until the next Hollywood cycle started up again in the mid-1990s. Popular and top-grossing movies including *Clueless* (1995), *Kids* (1995), *Scream* (1996), *Can't Hardly Wait* (1998), *She's All That* (1999), *American Beauty* (1999), and the extremely successful *Titanic* (1997) brought teenage characters back with force. This trend continues today. Teen movies in this decade have seen an interesting dichotomy: a return to a more innocent, "squeaky clean," and carefree teenager, as depicted in movies like the *High School Musical* series (2006–2008), *The Sisterhood of the Traveling Pants* (2005), *The Princess Diaries* (2001), *Ella Enchanted* (2004), and *Agent Cody Banks* (2003); and a more socially aggressive, sexually obsessed, self-absorbed teen, as depicted in films like *Mean Girls* (2004), *American Pie* (1999–2003), *Superbad* (2007), and *Bring It On* (2000).

Teen-targeted movie series such as the *Harry Potter* series (first film released in 2001), *Twilight* series (first film released in 2008), and *The Hunger Games* series (first film released in 2012) set box office records for sales (see Box 12.1). Each of these teen-targeted series is among the highest grossing film series of all time, earning billions worldwide (Box Office Mojo, 2016). Their popularity led to other film series targeting teenagers including the *Divergent* series (first film released in 2014) and the *Maze Runner* series (first film released in 2014), which also pulled in impressive figures at the box office.

In a report published in 1999, when asked what first comes to mind when thinking about today's teenagers, Americans used adjectives such as "rude," "irresponsible," and "wild," while younger children were characterized as "lacking discipline" and "spoiled" (Public Agenda 1999). A majority of parents, across all ethnic groups, said they believed that teens get into trouble because they have too much time on their hands, and are not learning values like honesty, respect, and responsibility. While most research about teenagers and the media has concentrated on the impact of media images on teenage attitudes and behaviors, in the past 10 years a few studies have been done analyzing the presentation of teen characters in film and the subsequent impact of those portrayals on adult attitudes toward teenagers.

Communication scholar Susannah R. Stern (2005) conducted a content analytic study of images of teenagers in popular films in 1999, 2000, and 2001. The author argues that some of the most salient images of teenagers appear in popular films, and that, despite their fictional nature, movies such as *American Pie* (1999), *Cruel Intentions* (1999), *Save the Last Dance* (2001), and *Traffic* (2000) cast images of contemporary teenage life into the public eye. The study's results indicate that modern Hollywood films promote an image of teenagers as self-absorbed, violent, disconnected from parents, and disengaged from civic life. The most common behaviors among all characters were hanging out

Box 12.1 Teen depictions in the *Twilight*, *Harry Potter*, and *Hunger Games* films

Figure 12.1 *Twilight*'s Bella dealing with teen angst and vampires. Screenshot.

Figure 12.2 *Harry Potter*'s teens in a harrowing scene. Screenshot.

Figure 12.3 In the *Hunger Games* movies, teens Katniss and Peeta fight to save society. Screenshot.

For the past 10 years, the most popular, highest grossing teen movies have been those in the *Harry Potter* series. Teens across the country were first captivated by the novels by J.K. Rowling, which follow Harry and his friends Ron and Hermione through their adventures at Hogwarts School of Witchcraft and Wizardry, and their battles against the evil Lord Voldemort. Teens were drawn in to the magical world, the powerful friendships, and the courageous battle of good versus evil in each story.

The movies just strengthened the love these teens felt for the *Harry Potter* series. It seemed nothing could supplant the young wizard in teen hearts – that is, until the vampire love story *Twilight* came along, followed closely by the dystopian *Hunger Games* series. The *Twilight* movies, also based on a series of books, written by Stephenie Meyer, trace the story of a human girl, Bella, who falls in love with a vampire, Edward. *The Hunger Games*, again, is based on a series of books, written by Suzanne Collins. They follow the trials of 16-year-old Katniss Everdeen, who lives in the post-apocalyptic nation of Panem, through an annual arena game in which girls and boys from all the different Districts are forced to fight to the death.

These three movie series offer some interesting points for discussion. For instance, though the *Twilight* and *The Hunger Games* stories are edgier, and feature young love more so than the good versus evil battle in the *Potter* books, all three series depict the main teen characters as honest "good guys," with strong morals, always working to protect the innocent; no drugs, and no alcohol. Though there is romance, and some kissing in each series, there is no sex in the *Harry Potter* series, Bella and Edward only have sex after they are married, and it is only implied that Katniss and Peeta have had sex by showing their children in the closing scene of the series' final film. This runs counter to the other strong trend in teen movies of this decade, that of the "mean girl" and the ever more explicit and raunchy themes prevalent in so many teen films popular today.

One writer wondered if perhaps the female teen audience, once so taken with Harry and his wizarding world, might be craving just a bit more of the "wild side." *Wall Street Journal* reporter Lauren E. Schuker wrote, in an article published in 2009 that while *Twilight* is not toppling *Harry Potter* just yet, the teens who formed the foundation of the *Harry Potter* fan base are growing up, and looking for books that offer a more mature storyline with more romance. Schuker, in the reporting of her story, spoke to one teen:

> Alicia Penner, a 13-year-old from Rocky Mountain House, Alberta, read the "Harry Potter" books 57 times. She watched the "Harry Potter" movies. The last fall, a friend lent her the teen vampire book series "Twilight" – and she was hooked. The "Harry Potter" poster that used to hang on her bedroom wall has been replaced by the "Twilight" poster she got for her 13th birthday … Ms. Penner says she has moved on from Harry.

While these movies run counter to the "reckless teen" stereotype, one common teenage myth that is perpetuated in all three film series is that parents either need the teens' help, or are absent, often irrelevant, and that teens can get along just fine, if not better, without them around. Teens are presented in the storylines as mature, strong, and independent. The main characters often are seen traveling alone, both domestically and internationally. Bella, for instance, at one point in the second movie in the *Twilight* series *New Moon* (2009), leaves Forks, Washington, on a moment's notice, without her father's permission – in fact without telling him at all – to travel to Italy to save Edward from the Volturi, a powerful coven of vampires. Though there is mention of her being grounded when she returns home, Bella is unconcerned about any punishment or consequence of her action; as far as she is concerned, she knows best and is doing what must be done.

If we examine these movies, what impact might the portrayals of these teen characters have both on teens as well as adult attitudes toward teens? Because these films take place in fantasy worlds, are they just too farfetched to be taken seriously, or do you believe these hugely popular movies have the potential to impact the existing cultural stereotype about teenagers?

(not at school), socializing at school, and making out. The teenagers who were depicted hanging out were frequently shown doing so at parties, nightclubs, at the beach, or at other unsupervised venues. The scenes showing socialization at school were rarely in the classroom – more often in the hallways or lunchroom. Hooking up and making out were full-time jobs, with characters engaging in a wide variety of sexual encounters.

A surprisingly high number of teens were depicted as either victims of violence (41 percent) or committing violent behaviors (40 percent). Rarely were behaviors shown that would cast teens in a more positive, realistic light. For instance, although almost half of US teenagers age 16 to 19 work, fewer than 5 percent of the film characters in this study were shown engaging in these behaviors, and although most US teens plan to go to college, fewer than 4 percent of the characters in this study were shown preparing for college in any way, and less than 25 percent were ever shown studying.

Some researchers have argued that teenagers enjoy films that show characters their own age, but ones that are living out social fantasies or rebelling in ways they never would in "real life." Movies provide an escape and a release from the regular, mundane lives they lead that are filled with chores, work, and other obligations. These images, however, may also reinforce adults' negative views of teens and serve as reasons to further distance themselves from the teenagers they meet in their own lives.

Another strong stereotype examined is that of the "mean girl." According to a 2005 *New York Times* article, "In recent years, girls have been increasingly portrayed in everything from serious journalistic studies to light comedies like 'Mean Girls' as tyrannical, bullying and devoted to a ruthless *caste system*" (Zinoman 2005). Communication researchers Elizabeth Behm-Morawitz and Dana E. Maestro (2008). The movie, which is semi-autobiographical and written by actress Nikki Reed, focuses on the relationship between two 13-year-old girls: Tracy (portrayed by Evan Rachel Wood) and Evie (portrayed by Reed). Tracy is an overachiever enrolled in a Los Angeles middle school, who after deciding she is tired of being in the nerdy group and of being her mother's "baby," sets out to befriend Evie, the hot, fearless rebel. Evie introduces Tracy to shoplifting, drugs, smoking, drinking, and boys. The author had anticipated the girls she was interviewing would find something in *Thirteen* to relate to, but discovered instead that they found the film to be overly dramatic, the sex and drugs to be unrealistic, and the characters to be disrespectful and annoying. In one exchange, the girls were very specific:

> KATE: Melodramatic representations of teenagers always bother me. It's not like you come home and you're like, "My life sucks!" And you throw down your bag and think about taking pills. It's not like when you reach adolescence you suddenly have nothing to live for.
>
> THANA: They make it seem like every 13-year-old is bipolar. And there are definitely those days where you come home and you want to be alone, but it's not like, I want to be alone and try to commit suicide.
>
> KATE: Yeah, it's like, yes, puberty affects you, but it doesn't make you go crazy. We're all fascinated with stories like this to some extent. But it's not like every 13-year-old's life is like the movie.

Although some teens do have tumultuous transitions into adulthood, the girls in this exchange disagreed with the heavy content in the film. Their lives did not reflect this filmed, dramatic reality.

Age in Entertainment Television

Representations of Older and Elderly People

In the 1950s and early 1960s, stars in their forties, fifties, and sixties like Jack Benny, Red Skelton, and Milton Berle were commonplace. Audiences were not just tolerant of their TV stars being older, they expected them to be. When the late 1960s and 1970s counterculture flourished, characters became younger, and audiences clamored for a more youthful representation of society. During this period, very few main characters were older, and the majority of images of the elderly were of poor, unhealthy, feeble, and pathetic people.

A landmark study done at the University of Pennsylvania's Annenberg School of Communication, which analyzed more than 17,000 television characters on network programs between 1969 and 1978, showed that people over 65 appeared on screen about one fifth of their actual proportion in the population and were treated disrespectfully most of the time (Gerbner *et al.* 1980). Old men were the villains or the victims. Old women were barely there. However, the 1980s brought a change and a disappearance of such extremely negative images of old age. New and popular television shows like *Murder, She Wrote* (1984–1996), *Dynasty* (1981–1989), *Falcon Crest* (1981–1990), *The Golden Girls* (1985–1992), *Matlock* (1986–1995), *Jake and the Fat Man* (1987–1992), and *In the Heat of the Night* (1988–1994) were prime-time shows that were extremely popular with both older and younger audiences. Characters like Jessica Fletcher (played by Angela Lansbury), the crime-solving lead in the hit series *Murder, She Wrote*, gave new life and a drastic change to the negative, feeble older woman stereotype that had persisted for more than 20 years. Her character was independent, intelligent, strong, and clever, and often outwitted younger villains. The four main characters in the show *The Golden Girls*, Joan Collins, who played Alexis Carrington on *Dynasty*, and Jane Wyman, a leading character on *Falcon Crest*, showed that women in their fifties, sixties, and beyond still had tremendous sex appeal and sex drive. Older male and female characters during this time were often portrayed as powerful, affluent, active, admired, and often quite physically attractive (Bell 1992).

However, the mid-1990s saw a swing back, and studies show that older and elderly people were still underrepresented, especially women, though images were less unflattering and stereotypical than they were in the late 1960s and 1970s. When race was added to the analysis, the percentages were quite skewed. For instance, in a study done in 1995, analyzing prime-time network fictional programming that aired in 1990, nearly 90 percent of older characters were white. The remaining 10 percent were African American. There were no depictions of Latino or Asian American adults over the age of 65.

In the past 20 years, several researchers have found evidence of a link between greater exposure to television and more negative views of aging (e.g., Donlon, Ashman, and Levy 2005). Many studies have been done by media researchers that have examined children's views of older people, young adults' views of older people, and even adults' and older adults' views of the stereotypes of growing old. A majority of these researchers conclude that individual attitudes toward older people are learned social responses that result both from media exposure and individual experience.

Two of the media theories that have been referenced earlier in this book offer some explanation for this phenomenon. Social cognitive theory suggests that viewers, especially children, will model the behaviors of television characters after observing them over time, just as they would by observing parents or other children (Bandura 2002). Proponents of this theory argue that after watching television shows, for instance, that depict elderly characters being treated as objects of scorn or mockery, or as a burden on society, children will begin to adopt these attitudes.

As referenced in other chapters, cultivation theory asserts that the more television a person watches, the more likely they are to adopt attitudes and beliefs based on television's stereotypical images (Gerbner *et al.* 1986). Heavy viewers, therefore, who are repeatedly exposed to skewed images of the elderly will also likely grow to believe the stereotypes to be reality. Children are thought to be particularly susceptible to these cultivation effects, especially if their real-life exposure to older people is limited or not any different to what they have seen on television. Much research has focused on children and their individual attitudes toward older people, and consistently these studies show that children have substantively negative views of the elderly. For example, in one study done in 1976, preschoolers were asked to describe the way older people look and act. The children used such phrases as "all wrinkled and short," "chew funny," "don't go out much," and "have heart attacks and die" (Jantz *et al.* 1976)

Several studies offer reasons why children may hold such stereotypical views. For instance, communication researchers Tom Robinson and Caitlin Anderson (2006) performed a content analysis of older characters in children's animated television programs, and note as part of their rationale for their study that children watch approximately three hours of television per day, according to recent surveys, and many of the programs they watch are cartoons. Therefore, there is the possibility that the kinds of images these animated programs present of the elderly might shape the way children view older people. In Robinson and Anderson's study, more than 45 hours of children's animated programming was coded, with the programs coming from Nickelodeon, Cartoon Network, ABC Kids, FOX Kids, and Kids' WB. The researchers found that older characters are not a dominant feature in these programs and that though a majority of these characters were described as having positive personality traits, a number of negative physical stereotypes were common. For instance, the older character might be ugly, toothless, overweight, slow moving, or use a physical aid. Just over 82 percent of these older characters had gray hair, 75 percent of the older characters were white, and 77 percent were male. These physical characteristics directly correlate to the responses given by children in studies like the 1976 study discussed in the previous paragraph (Figure 12.4).

Figure 12.4 Estelle Getty as Sophia on *The Golden Girls* (1985–1992). Screenshot.

As found in studies on older characters in film, older characters are underrepresented in television shows, and negative portrayals increase with the age of the individuals featured. Younger skewing shows have replaced the older skewing shows. For instance, crime dramas like *Murder, She Wrote* (1984–1996), *The Cosby Mysteries* (1994–1995), and *Diagnosis Murder* (1993–2001), which all had older main characters, have been replaced with shows like *Bones* (2005 debut), *CSI* (2000–2015), and *Criminal Minds* (2005 debut), all of which feature young, attractive thirty-somethings as crime-fighting whiz kids. Many of the same tired stereotypes (e.g., the dirty old man; the flaky, out-of-touch grandma; the sexless, often cantankerous, married couple; the rigid older boss) continue unabated. Neil Genzlinger, television critic for the *New York Times*, bemoaned the "immaturing" of older characters on network shows. He writes, "On television these days, if a character is yacking about flatulence, making randy remarks to a member of the opposite sex or being baffled by simple things, that character is likely to have gray hair. Somehow, it seems, the TV gods have decided that characters old enough to have adult children need to be vulgar, inappropriate or moronic. Or all three" (Genzlinger 2013). He points out several characters in particular as examples: Emmy-winner Margo Martindale, the mother of Will Arnett's character on CBS's *The Millers* (2013 debut), who spends most of her time talking about her stomach problems; Allison Janney, in the CBS series *Mom* (2013 debut), who spends most of her time talking about sex or drugs; and Madeleine Stowe, a vile and manipulative character on ABC's *Revenge* (2011–2015). He concludes that the days are gone when having a little gray hair was worthy of respect and the person looked up to for advice. In a particularly pointed barb, Genzlinger writes: "in the 1980s and early 1990s … Mr. [Bill] Cosby's character was often called upon to counsel his children as they grew to young adulthood:

THEO: Dad, I'm having trouble with math class.
CLIFF: Well, son, you need to prioritize. A little more time with your schoolbooks, a little less time hanging out with your friends.

It's hard to imagine that Mr. Cosby would want to be a part of such a scene the way it would be written today:

THEO: Dad, I'm having trouble with math class.
CLIFF: Yeah, and I'm having trouble with that bratwurst I ate last night, if you know what I mean.
THEO: Maybe you could look at these equations with me?
CLIFF: Is this the teacher with the cleavage? Hoo, boy, I'd like to look at her equations, if you know what I mean.

Streaming services such as Netflix, Hulu, and Amazon Prime have provided some alternative representations of aging. For example, during a time in which many aging actresses are finding difficulty in finding roles, Netflix debuted in 2015 its new sitcom starring Jane Fonda and Lily Tomlin in the lead roles. The show, *Grace and Frankie*, features Fonda (Grace) and Tomlin (Frankie) playing the parts of two women with vastly different personalities being drawn together after their husbands announce they are gay and in love with each other. The first season of the show follows the two women as they rediscover their own identities as newly divorced women in their seventies. The carefree, pot-smoking Frankie encourages her new friend, the uptight, beauty-obsessed Grace, to let go and even explore her own sexuality. Once Grace musters enough courage to date, she starts by finding a date through an online dating service and ends up dating more than one man, all of them much younger in age than herself. Grace and Frankie break the mold of older female television characters. If not for age, either of the characters could be interchangeable with any other thirty-something-year-old character that often appears on prime-time broadcast television. As will be seen in the next section, streaming services are offering different takes on teenagers as well.

Representations of Teenagers

As other chapters have demonstrated, television is, by and large, an unrealistic world inhabited by healthy, thin, attractive, middle-class, white people in their twenties and thirties. Much research has concluded that television has an impact on attitudes and behaviors, and teens and adolescents are estimated to spend more than three hours a day watching television. Based on the assumptions posited by cultivation and social learning theories, then, the images that are depicted of teen characters and their behaviors can be assumed to take on great importance. A trend of asymmetric gender representation has been occurring since the early 1970s, with many studies showing that male teen characters outnumber female teen characters three to two (Signorielli 1987). Research also has shown that stereotypical gender differences are common in entertainment television portrayals, with male teens being more likely to be depicted at work, active in sports, and aggressive, while female teens were more likely to be shown performing gender-specific chores like doing the dishes or laundry, grooming, crying or whining, and shopping (Signorielli 1997). Teenagers in general have been found to be depicted as violent or antisocial (or both), disconnected from their largely incompetent and frequently absent parents, and primarily interested in socializing and developing friendships (e.g., Signorielli 1987).

One of the most widely researched areas with regard to portrayals of teens on television deals with sexuality and the sexual behaviors of teen characters. These sexual images of teens in entertainment television have changed over time. Up until the late 1970s, teens on television were clean-cut, puritanical, and well behaved. Happy families and even happier teenagers abounded in shows such as *Leave it to Beaver* (1957–1963), *Green Acres* (1965–1971), *The Waltons* (1972–1981), *The Partridge Family* (1970–1974), *Eight Is Enough* (1977–1981), and *Happy Days* (1974–1984), though a glimmer of the 1950s charming but rebellious "bad boy" came through in *Happy Days* with the character of the Fonz.

The launch of the broadcast television network Fox, in 1986, brought with it new teen characters showing a more sexually aggressive teenager, perhaps best exemplified by Kelly Bundy, the promiscuous teenage daughter (portrayed by Christina Applegate) on the television show *Married, With Children* (1987–1997). This show seemed to herald a new generation of teen characters and acceptable depictions of teen behavior. Developmental psychology researcher L. Monique Ward (2003; Ward and Friedman 2006) conducted several content analyses of programs most watched by teens and adolescents in the early 1990s, which typically included at least one teen or adolescent character, such as Will Smith as *The Fresh Prince of Bel-Air* (1990–1996), the teenage daughters on the television show *Roseanne* (1998–1997), and the majority of the main characters on *Beverly Hills 90210* (1990–2000) and *Saved by the Bell* (1989–1993). Ward found that between 29 and 50 percent of the interactions between characters on these shows contained references to sexual issues.

Eventually, as more and more teenagers were allowed access to televisions in their bedrooms, often out of sight of their parents, more teen content was developed and soon entire channels, such as WB, which merged with UPN in 2006 to become the CW Network, existed for younger audiences. Teen-oriented shows have flourished over the past two decades, including such hits as *Dawson's Creek* (1998–2003), *My So-Called Life* (1994–1995), *One Tree Hill* (2003–2012), *The O.C.* (2003–2007),

Gossip Girl (2007–2012), *7th Heaven* (1996–2007), *The Hills* (2006–2010), *Veronica Mars* (2004–2007), *Party of Five* (1994–2000), *Pretty Little Liars* (2010 debut), *Friday Night Lights* (2006–2011), and *Gilmore Girls* (2000–2007). While some of these past programs featured teenagers who exhibited high levels of responsibility and who were more focused on academic work and family than sex, such as the character of Rory (portrayed by Alexis Bledel) on *Gilmore Girls*, this was the exception rather than the norm. A far more common character type is exemplified by the characters on the program *Gossip Girl*, including Serena (portrayed by Blake Lively), a party girl who has had many sexual relationships during her teen years, several of which are graphically depicted on the show, and Chuck (portrayed by Ed Westwick), who keeps a "little black book" filled with the names and numbers of girls he has "hooked up with" and who would make easy targets again in the future.

A smaller, but still popular subset of the teen-drama category includes science fiction or supernatural teen shows, including *Smallville* (2001–2011), which followed the adventures of Clark Kent (portrayed by Tom Welling), who resides in the fictional town of Smallville, Kansas, during the years before he becomes Superman, and *Buffy the Vampire Slayer* (1997–2003), a cult hit based on the movie of the same name, which focused on teenaged Buffy Summers (played by Sarah Michelle Gellar), the latest in a line of young women known as Slayers. Slayers are chosen by fate to battle against vampires, demons, and other forces of darkness. A supernatural teen drama, *The Vampire Diaries*, premiered on CW in September 2009, capitalizing on the popular vampire storyline of the time. Though these shows are clearly fictional, they do correlate with the findings of research that has been done on other types of teen dramas, including the stereotypical themes that teenagers are self-absorbed, disconnected from their parents, and primarily interested in socializing with the opposite sex. Similar themes are found in teen reality programs such as MTV's *16 and Pregnant* (2009 debut) and *My Super Sweet 16* (2005 debut) (see Box 12.2).

Box 12.2 Self-presentations in *My Super Sweet 16*

In 1959, sociologist Erving Goffman published *The Presentation of Self in Everyday Life*, an examination of how individuals negotiate the world around them (1959: 17–76). Goffman relies strongly on the use of a "life is a stage" metaphor, positing that each person is playing a role at all times when interacting with other people, and that how an individual acts largely depends on the situation and the other "players" involved. For instance, the way a student might interact in a classroom, when asked to speak in front of a professor and peers, might be quite different from the way that same student might present him- or herself later that night in a bar to an intimate group of friends. Each person may play many roles – some dictated by social order (how you behave at a formal event is prearranged and part of our societal norms) and some varying, based on the setting and the other individuals involved. Consider your own life: you likely behave differently in your own house, with your parents, sisters, and brothers, than you do with the principal of your high school or your roommate. Individuals create roles for themselves and consciously decide how they wish to present themselves.

Based on this sociological theory, consider this example:

In 2005, MTV debuted a new reality series titled *My Super Sweet 16*, with the program airing periodically for the next decade. In each show, a different teen was featured as her family and friends prepared to celebrate her 16th birthday by throwing her an over-the-top party. Episodes were marked, not with cheerfulness and appreciation, but with entitlement and rude behavior. Michelle

---

(Continued)

Box 12.2   (Continued)

Caruso, of the *Daily News*, published an article (2005) shortly after the second season began that sums it up well. She began:

> It sounds like a situation comedy: spoiled rich kids whose incredibly indulgent parents spend as much as $200,000 on a birthday party. And the kids are unhappy.
>
> But *My Super Sweet 16* is not a comedy. It's an MTV reality show that's more jaw dropper than knee-slapper.
>
> Unlike players on *Survivor* and *Fear Factor* who suffer on camera for a chance to win big bucks, the *Sweet 16* participants already have beaucoup Benjamins to host the lavish parties that land them on the show, which kicked off its second season last month.

Caruso continued, stating:

> But it's teens behaving badly – and parents who let them – that is the draw of the show.
>
> Take Ava, the Beverly Hills 15-year-old who wailed, shrieked, whined, manipulated and abused her divorced parents into throwing her the "Arabian Nights"-themed Sweet 16 bash of her dreams at the Four Seasons Hotel.
>
> Ava and her parents declined to be interviewed by the Daily News, but on the show, her dad Moussa said the tab for his daughter's big day was "close to $200,000, including the car" he gave her as a gift.

Caruso cited more examples of the spoiled teen behavior. She notes:

> When mom Mitra took her to Paris to shop for a gown, Ava complained that one $2,550 red creation looked like a "crayon." She scolded her mom: "You're so annoying. You kill everything."
>
> Ava groused while sitting in the $45,000-plus Mercedes-Benz sports car Daddy was buying her that it was "small and claustrophobic" and shrieked, "I soooo want a Range Rover."
>
> When the desired SUV didn't arrive on the morning of her 16th birthday, Ava threw a tantrum, even when her parents took her to dinner at the ultrachic Dolce. "They totally killed my birthday," she moaned.

But, Caruso notes, never fear:

> (Her party, and a ribbon-wrapped white Range Rover, came days later.)

Ava is just one of the many 16-year-olds that were featured on the show. Most presented themselves in a similar bratty, entitled, ungrateful way. Why do you think that these 16-year-olds chose to present themselves this way? What impact do these choices of presentation have on the perceptions the viewers, both teens and adults, have of teens in general? Are these examples simply so extreme as to not have any impact at all? What might mitigate any impact shows like *My Super Sweet 16* have on adult perceptions of teenagers and their behaviors?

Streaming service Netflix paid homage to all of the aforementioned notions found in the teen movies of the 1980s with its suspenseful sci-fi series *Stranger Things* (2016 debut). Although the show still features the preppy guy, a nerdy frump, the quiet guy, and good girl looking for love, the program uses these tropes in a new way as these teens help a group of young kids find one of their missing friends. The children in *Stranger Things* are not without parents, but they are the only ones that truly understand the other-worldly beings that have taken their friend. Ultimately, their immaturity – love of games, bikes, and pudding – help them become heroes.

Age in the News

Representations of Older and Elderly People

Most research concerning newspaper coverage of the elderly shows that the majority of stories published do not foster or create negative images. Rather, most studies show that stories published about older people are neutral in tone, which runs in accordance with basic journalistic and news-writing principles. In line with entertainment television and film portrayals, however, the elderly, especially elderly women, were underrepresented in newspaper coverage. One study that analyzed the news and feature articles that appeared in 11 Sunday papers in 1963 and 1983 found that less than 1 percent of the total space was devoted to any coverage of the elderly at all (Wass *et al.* 1985). Another study that content analyzed 2,217 magazine cartoons found that elderly characters rarely appeared, and when they did, they were most likely to appear in a negative light, generally either as extreme conservatives or as sexually dysfunctional (Smith 1979).

In February of 2000, *Palm Beach Post* columnist Frank Cerabino introduced a serialized novel entitled "Shady Palms: A Condo Caper." His stories about a fictionalized adult condominium residential community humorously poke fun at condo life and the retired. As of 2008, there were five "Shady Palms" novels, which sport titles such as "Shady Palms 4: Republicans in Love" and "Shady Palms 3: Viagra Falls," all of which feature a complete cast of older characters. *American Journalism Review* writer Jill Rosen (2002) calls the series "a geriatric '*Melrose Place*.'" In her article Rosen quotes the *Post*'s managing editor Tom O'Hara, editor during the serial's debut, as saying: "We knew it would play well in Palm Beach. It's about living in condos in Boynton Beach. Many, many, many of the *Palm Beach Post*'s readers are those people." As for the plot, Cerabino is quoted as saying he wanted it soap opera-esque, with mystery and suspense, but nothing too heavy. Readers were thrilled with the series and regularly emailed and called the paper to applaud the decision to offer this fun, wacky, positive portrayal of the life of the South Florida retiree. The series received so much feedback that the *Post* dedicated a phone line that readers could call daily to hear taped updates on the story.

Representations of Teenagers

Perhaps unsurprisingly, given the rampant stereotyping of teens previously explored in this chapter, the press tends to frame American teens as surly, oversexed, violent creatures. In fact, numerous studies have shown that in analyses of newspaper and magazine reports, researchers have consistently found that the most common type of news coverage of teens are stories about them as criminals or as victims of violence, and, more recently, as sexually promiscuous, often to the extreme. Though examples of positive imagery of teens in the news media certainly exist, such as teen athletes and scholars accomplishing goals and teens participating in volunteer projects, they tend to be overshadowed by the almost fearful tone many reports take on.

For instance, a 2009 headline on the ABC News website blared in large blue letters: "Teens: Oral Sex and Casual Prostitution No Biggie" (Shipman and Kazdin 2009). The accompanying story, which was a follow-up to a *Good Morning America* segment, discussed the shocking stories highlighted in a new documentary by Canadian filmmaker Sharlene Azam. Azam states in the segment that today's teens lead secret, extremely sexual lives, trading sexual favors and stripteases for handbags, money, and homework, and suggests that for teens today, "oral sex is the new goodnight kiss."

In another instance, following the 1999 Columbine shooting tragedy, *Newsweek* ran a cover story entitled "The Secret Life of Teens" along with cover art showing the face of a visibly troubled teen boy who looked angry and dangerous. The article makes the argument that teens today are harder to understand, and that unlike teens of the past who were easier to keep tabs on, with the advent of the Internet, violent video games like "Half Life," and "densely encrypted messages and camp nihilism" of music artists like Eminem and Marilyn Manson, teens are impossible to predict and hard to protect. The author of the article writes:

> With as many as 11 million teenagers now online, more and more of adolescent life is taking place in a landscape that is inaccessible to many parents. "That is apparent in the geography of households," says Marlene Mayhew, a clinical psychologist who runs an online mental-health newsletter. With the computer often in the teen's bedroom, Mayhew says, the power structure in the family is turned upside down. "Kids are unsupervised, looking at whatever they please." A parent who might eventually notice a stockpile of *Guns and Ammo* or pornographic magazines has fewer clues to a child's online activities. (Gordon *et al.* 1999)

US News and World Report published a story later that year entitled "Inside the Teen Brain" that portrays the typical teen as a moody lump who does not do chores or homework, but spends hours on the phone and can barely be roused for school. The lead of the story written by Shannon Brownlee (1999) reads:

> One day, your child is a beautiful, charming 12-year-old, a kid who pops out of bed full of good cheer, clears the table without being asked, and brings home good grades from school. The next day, your child bursts into tears when you ask for the salt and listens to electronic music at maximum volume for hours on end. Chores? Forget it. Homework? There's little time, after talking to friends on the phone for five hours every night. Mornings? Your bluebird of happiness is flown, replaced by a groaning lump that can scarcely be roused for school.

The author's conclusion? The article continues:

> Your home is now inhabited by a teenager.
> The shootings in Littleton, Colo., focused the nation's attention on aberrant adolescent behavior, but most teens never come close to committing violent acts. Still, even the most easygoing teenagers often confound their elders with behavior that seems odd by adult standards.

While the article goes on to discuss the chemical makeup and growth of the teen brain, offering scientific reasons for erratic behavior, the opening imagery presents a vivid stereotype of the teenager (Brownlee 1999).

Sociologist Stanley Cohen (1972: 1–58) suggests that the news media tend to take the view that if young people do not grow up to reproduce the patterns of life and the values of the previous generation, then they appear to represent a threat to the traditional order. Therefore, teens and adolescents will be portrayed as "folk devils," and subsequently will create what he called a "moral panic" about youth as threat. In other words, in an effort to make sense of a younger generation that reporters do not see as "just like them," they are cast as the "Other" and somehow at greater risk of not making an appropriate transition to becoming a contributing member of society.

In a *Huffington Post* blog, writer and social activist for teens Deborah Dunham decries the news media's tendencies to focus on negative stories involving teens. She points out that while positive stories may exist, they are often "overshadowed by the ones that paint our youth to be violent, drug-addicted, alcohol-drinking delinquents" (Dunham 2014). Dunham ends her piece by asserting, "We're not doing teenagers – *the future leaders of our word* – any favors by continuing to perpetuate this negative stereotype. Let's not give them any reason to further judge themselves. Because, in the end, that could very well backfire."

Age and New Media

Teens make up the largest plugged-in population in the United States, with current statistics showing 93 percent of teens online (Lenhart 2015). A 2015 Pew Survey report shows that 24 percent of teens go online "almost constantly," helped by the widespread use of mobile devices, and more than half go online several times a day. Smartphone adoption is driving much of these usage numbers, with nearly 75 percent of teens having access to a cell phone. African American teens are the most likely to have access to a smartphone (85 percent), compared with 71 percent of white and Hispanic teens. African American teens also report more frequent Internet use than white teens, with 34 percent going online "almost constantly." Teens spend the majority of their online time on social media sites such as Instagram, Twitter, Snapchat, Google+ and Facebook, Internet search sites such as Google and Yahoo!, and video sites such as YouTube. Texting plays an extremely important role in teen communication. According to this study, the average teen sends and receives 30 texts per day, through a variety of telephone company systems and messaging apps. They are not just content consumers either. Studies show that more than half of 12- to 17-year-olds are creating content – blogs, videos, or photos – and uploading them to be viewed either with restricted or unlimited access. Teens are thought to be super-communicators, updating friends and acquaintances with status updates multiple times a day, using a variety of communication tools.

Social networking sites offer an interesting case study opportunity to see how teens present themselves in a virtual environment. Social media researcher Danah Michele Boyd (2008) conducted a multi-year ethnographic study of teen use of Facebook and Myspace and learned that these social sites became surrogates for the same activities – flirting, joking around, sharing, hanging out – that took and still take place in reality. Social networking does not replace "the real thing," and teens still socialize and spend time in face-to-face interactions, but computer-mediated communication and relationships change, complicate, and influence relationships and the way teens deal with social situations, the way they present themselves to the public, and friendships. The way teens choose to present themselves online, with photographs, "about me" descriptions, quotes, and public groups tell much about themselves, just as locker decorations or fashion choices do in the bricks-and-mortar world. To make predictions regarding the future of these social networking sites and the long-term impact on teens is risky, as even since 2006 researchers have noted substantial changes in the way teens use these sites. In 12- to 17-year-olds, the volume of comments is down, as are blog posts and status updates. Approximately 71 percent of teens report using Facebook, 52 percent use Instagram, 41 percent use Snapchat, and 33 percent use Twitter (Lenhart 2015). Teens are starting to realize that things that are posted to the Internet are permanent and are thinking twice before allowing unlimited access, or are reporting that they have multiple Facebook profiles – one public under their real name and one or more under pseudonyms.

For the elderly population, using the Internet is not as common as it is with teens. According to the Pew Center, four in ten adults aged 65 and older do not use the Internet, and only 34 percent own smartphones. This percentage compounds when income and education are added into the equation. Those with less than a high school education are less likely to use the Internet, as are adults from households earning less than $30,000 per year (Anderson and Perrin 2016). Older Americans use the Internet to send email, participate in online dating, and to do business or make travel plans. One area that the Internet offers particular advantages and opportunities for older Americans is in the area of healthcare. Patients who are Internet savvy are not only able to search for information related to health conditions, diagnoses, and medications, and thus are able to take a more proactive role in their healthcare decisions, but are also able to band together with others of their age group to have their voices heard on issues that are important concerning healthcare plans and insurance options (Lenhart 2015).

While the Internet has contributed to societal change, and provided opportunities to revolutionize healthcare, especially with regard to patient empowerment, many researchers suggest that for the elderly population, it is more of an "evolution" than a "revolution" (e.g., Campbell and Wabby 2003 Lenhart *et al.* 2010). Nationally, research shows that currently older Americans are in danger of being cut off from this valuable source of information (Rainie 2016). However, more than 80 percent of the next generation of seniors (50- to 64-year-olds) now use the Internet. These findings suggest that though there is a digital divide among the oldest Americans, this gap will close in the next decade.

Recent studies show that anxiety about using computers, access to computers, lack of time, limited resources, and lack of certain cognitive skills (memory and organization) are significant barriers to the use of the Internet and computers in general (Campbell and Wabby 2003). Some studies suggest that training can help modify anxiety and skills, but access and money remain obstacles.

While many of the media representations of older people are negative, the Internet offers a variety of sites that present positive images of aging and insights into what it means to age well. For example:

- AARP Webplace – http://www.aarp.org – is a membership organization leading positive social change and delivering value to people age 50 and over through information, advocacy, and service.
- ThirdAge – http://thirdage.com – is a leading online life-stage media company focused on helping women navigate their health and their family life.
- The Beacon – http://thebeaconnewspapers.com – is a family-owned business dedicated to providing information and services to active seniors and their families living in – or moving to – the Greater Washington, DC and Greater Baltimore areas.

Concluding Remarks

Teenagers have stereotypes of the elderly and fear growing old. Older people have stereotypes of teenagers and fear for their safety. Ironically, both groups appear to be the victims of exaggerated depictions in entertainment media. The news media may be equally to blame for fostering these beliefs; journalists should be held to a standard that prevents rather than perpetrates erroneous images of age groups.

When it is remembered that every person who reaches middle age was once a teenager, and that, arguably, everyone aspires to live long enough to be considered part of the elderly age group, it is perhaps somewhat surprising that research has shown such stark overgeneralizations of age. Ageism does damage – one population fears another, one individual pushes away from another individual because of a group stereotype. Communication researcher Susannah Stern (2005) points out in her study of teens and film that the erroneous images could result in adults choosing to distance themselves from activities like volunteering with youth groups or coaching sports teams, shutting the metaphoric and physical door on opportunities to get to know a teen one-on-one. These failures to guide, and missed opportunities to understand, merely exacerbate the problem – which applies not only from adult to youth, but also from youth to elder.

Engaging in thoughtful conversation on the topic of ageism can help bridge the divide. Learning to see stereotypical portrayals of various age groups, and critically analyzing them, may even contribute to their eventual reduction, and open the door for a more realistic and complex depiction of the various age groups that make up the dynamic US population.

Reflection Questions and Thoughts to Consider

1. Which teenage character on television do you find to be most representative of the teenager you were? How so? Have you seen characters you found unrealistic? Why? What bothered you about the portrayals? Do you believe the unrealistic portrayals are doing harm?
2. Both men and women are susceptible to ageist stereotyping, but research has shown that women, especially in film and television, tend to be portrayed in a more one-dimensional manner. Does your experience with media correlate with this? Can you think of any examples that fit with ageist stereotypes? How about any that run counter to ageist stereotypes?
3. In the past few years, there have been a number of movie roles for older men and women that have broken through some strongly held stereotypes. Can you think of any examples? Discuss any you have seen recently.
4. Do you see a variance in the stereotypes between older and teenaged people of varying ethnic groups? For instance, how would you characterize the stereotypical older African American woman? The Asian American man? The Hispanic teen? Can you think of any specific entertainment portrayals that reinforce or debunk these stereotypes?

References

Anderson, Hanah, and Matt Daniels. 2016. "Film Dialogue from 2,000 Screenplays, Broken Down by Gender and Age." *The Pudding*, April. http://polygraph.cool/films (accessed April 14, 2017).

Anderson, Monica, and Andrew Perrin. 2016. "13% of Americans Don't Use the Internet. Who Are They?" Pew Research Center. http://www.pewresearch.org/fact-tank/2016/09/07/some-americans-dont-use-the-internet-who-are-they (accessed April 14, 2017).

Bandura, Albert. 2002. "Social Cognitive Theory of Mass Communication." In *Media Effects: Advances in Theory and Research*, edited by Jennings Bryant and Dolf Zillman, 121–153. Mahwah, NJ: Lawrence Erlbaum.

Bazzini, Doris G., William D. McIntosh, Stephen M. Smith, Sabrina Cook, and Caleigh Harris. 1997. "The Aging Woman in Popular Film: Underrepresented, Unattractive, Unfriendly, and Unintelligent." *Sex Roles* 36(7–8): 531–543.

Behm-Morawitz, Elizabeth, and Dana E. Maestro. 2008. "Mean Girls? The Influence of Gender Portrayals in Teen Movies on Emerging Adults' Gender-Based Attitudes and Beliefs." *Journalism and Mass Communication Quarterly* 85(1): 131–147.

Bell, John. 1992. "In Search of a Discourse on Aging: The Elderly on Television." *The Gerontologist* 32: 305–311.

Box Office Mojo. 2016. "All Time Box Office Worldwide Grosses." *Boxofficemojo.com*. http://www.boxofficemojo.com/alltime/world (accessed April 14, 2017).

Boyd, Danah Michele. 2008. "Taken Out of Context: American Teen Sociality in Networked Publics." PhD dissertation, University of California, Berkeley.

Brownlee, Shannon. 1999. "Inside the Teen Brain." *US News & Media Report* 127(6): 44–48, 50, 52–4.

Buchanan, Kyle. 2013. "Leading Men Age, but Their Love Interests Don't." *Vulture*, April 18. http://www.vulture.com/2013/04/leading-men-age-but-their-love-interests-dont.html (accessed April 14, 2017).

Campbell, Robert J., and James Wabby. 2003. "The Elderly and the Internet: A Case Study." *The Internet Journal of Health* 3(1).

Caruso, Michelle. 2005. "Sweet 16 Party Shocker: 'I So Want a Range Rover'." *The Daily News*, October 2: 17. http://www.nydailynews.com/archives/news/sweet-16-party-shocker-range-rover-article-1.586355 (accessed April 14, 2017).

Cohen, Stanley. 1972. *Folk Devils and Moral Panic*. London: MacGibbon and Kee.

Donlon, Margie, Ori Ashman, and Becca Levy. 2005. "Re-vision of Older Television Characters: A Stereotype-awareness Intervention." *Journal of Social Issues* 61(2): 307–319.

Dunham, Deborah. 2014. "Here's What the Media Is Doing to Teenagers Today." *Huffington Post*, August 30. http://www.huffingtonpost.com/deborah-s-dunham/heres-what-the-media-is-d_b_5541462.html (accessed April 14, 2017).

Genzlinger, Neil. 2013. "Kids These Days: They're All Older than 50: TV's Problematic Portrayal of Aging." *New York Times*, November 19. http://www.nytimes.com/2013/11/20/arts/television/tvs-problematic-portrayal-of-aging.html?_r=0 (accessed April 14, 2017).

Gerbner, George, Larry Gross, Michael Morgan, and Nancy Signorielli. 1986. "Living with Television: The Dynamics of the Cultivation Process." In *Perspectives on Media Effects*, edited by Jennings Bryant and Dolf Zillman, 17–40. Hillsdale, NJ: Lawrence Erlbaum.

Gerbner, George, Larry Gross, Nancy Signorielli, and Michael Morgan. 1980. "Aging with Television: Images on Television Drama and Conceptions of Social Reality." *Journal of Communication* 30(1): 37–47.

Goffman, Erving. 1959. *The Presentation of Self in Everyday Life*. New York: Overlook Press.

Gordon, Devin, Anne Underwood, Tara Weingarten, and Ava Figueroa. 1999. "The Secret Life of Teens." *Newsweek*, May 9. http://www.newsweek.com/id/88252 (accessed April 14, 2017).

Harris, Mary B. 1994. "Growing Old Gracefully: Age Concealment and Gender." *Journals of Gerontology: Psychological Sciences* 49(4): 149–158.

Hatch, Laurie Russell. 2005. "Gender and Ageism." *Ageism in the New Millennium* 3: 19–24.

Jantz, Richard, Carol Seefeldt, Amy Galper, and Kristin Serlock. 1976. *Children's Attitudes Toward the Elderly: Report to the American Association of Retired Persons and the National Retired Teachers Association*. College Park, MD: University of Maryland Press.

Joiner, Whitney. 2003. "Melodramatic Presentations of Teenagers Always Bother Me." *Salon.com*, September 6. www.salon.com/2003/09/05/thirteen_3 (accessed April 14, 2017).

Lang, Brent. 2015. "Study Finds Fewer Lead Roles for Women in Hollywood." *Variety*, February 9. http://variety.com/2015/film/news/women-lead-roles-in-movies-study-hunger-games-gone-girl-1201429016 (accessed April 14, 2017).

Lenhart, Amanda. 2015. "Teens, Social Media & Technology Overview 2015." Pew Research Center. http://www.pewinternet.org/2015/04/09/teens-social-media-technology-2015 (accessed April 14, 2017).

Lenhart, Amanda, Kristen Purcell, Aaron Smith, and Kathryn Zickuhr. 2010. "Social Media and Young Adults." *Pew Internet and American Life Project.* http://pewinternet.org/Reports/2010/Social-Media-and-Young-Adults.aspx?r (accessed April 14, 2017).

Markson, Elizabeth W., and Carol A. Taylor. 1993. "Real Versus Reel World: Older Women and the Academy Awards." *Women and Therapy* 14: 157–172.

Markson, Elizabeth W., and Carol A. Taylor. 2000 "The Mirror Has Two Faces." *Ageing and Society* 20: 137–160.

Meehan, Diana M. 1983. *Ladies of the Evening: Women Characters of Prime-time Television.* Metuchen, NJ: Scarecrow Press.

Meyrowitz, Joshua. 1985. *No Sense of Place: The Impact of Electronic Media on Social Behavior.* New York, NY: Oxford University Press.

Nichols, Sharon L., and Thomas L. Good, 2004. *America's Teenagers – Myths and Realities: Media Images, Schooling and the Social Costs of Careless Indifference.* Mahwah, NJ: Lawrence Erlbaum.

Public Agenda. 1999. "Kids These Days '99: What Americans Really Think About The Next Generation." https://www.publicagenda.org/files/kids_these_days_99.pdf (accessed April 14, 2017).

Rainie, Lee. 2016. "Digital Divides 2016." Pew Research Center. http://www.pewinternet.org/2016/07/14/digital-divides-2016 (accessed April 14, 2017).

Robinson, Tom, and Caitlin Anderson. 2006. "Older Characters in Children's Animated Television Programs: A Content Analysis of their Portrayal." *Journal of Broadcasting and Electronic Media* 50(2): 287–304.

Rosen, Jill. 2002. "The Old and the Restless." *American Journalism Review.* http://www.ajr.org/Article.asp?id=2500 (accessed April 14, 2017).

Schuker, Lauren E. 2009. "Harry Potter and the Rival Teen Franchise." *Wall Street Journal,* July 9. https://www.wsj.com/articles/SB10001424052970204261704574274276261288253316 (accessed April 14, 2017).

Shipman, Claire, and Cole Kazdin. 2009. "Teens: Oral Sex and Casual Prostitution No Biggie." ABC News, May 28. http://abcnews.go.com/GMA/Parenting/Story?id=7693121&page=1 (accessed April 14, 2017).

Signorielli, Nancy. 1987. "Children and Adolescents on Television: A Consistent Pattern of Devaluation." *The Journal of Early Adolescence* 7(3): 255–268.

Signorielli, Nancy. 1997. "Reflections of Girls in the Media: A Content Analysis Across Six Media and a National Survey of Children." March 30. Prepared for Children Now and the Kaiser Family Foundation. http://kff.org/hivaids/reflections-of-girls-in-the-media-a (accessed April 14, 2017).

Smith, M. Dwayne. 1979. "The Portrayal of Elders in Magazine Cartoons." *The Gerontologist* 19(4): 408–412.

Snyder, Robert. 2002. "The Age Wave Report." *The Journal on Active Aging* 16.

Stern, Susannah R. 2005. "Self-Absorbed, Dangerous and Disengaged: What Popular Films Tell Us About Teenagers." *Mass Communication and Society* 8(1): 23–38.

Thornton, James. E. 2002. "Myths of Aging or Ageist Stereotypes." *Educational Gerontology* 28: 301–312.

US Census Bureau. 2012. "Statistical Abstract of the United States: 2012." http://www.census.gov/library/publications/2011/compendia/statab/131ed.html (accessed April 14, 2017).

US Census Bureau. 2015. "USA People QuickFacts." https://www.census.gov/quickfacts/table/PST045215/00 (accessed April 14, 2017).

US Census Bureau. n.d. "Census Bureau Projects Tripling of Hispanic and Asian Populations in 50 Years; Non-Hispanic Whites May Drop To Half of Total Population." http://www.america.gov/st/washfile-english/2004/March/20040318124311CMretroP0.4814264.html (accessed March 24, 2011).

Ward, L. Monique. 2003. "Understanding the Role of Entertainment Media in the Sexual Socialization of American Youth: A Review of Empirical Research." *Developmental Review* 23: 347–388.

Ward, L. Monique, and Kimberly Friedman. 2006. "Using TV as a Guide: Associations Between Television Viewing and Adolescents' Sexual Attitudes and Behavior." *Journal of Research on Adolescence* 16: 133–156.

Wass, Hannelore, Lisa Hawkins, Evelyn Kelly, Cynthia Magners, and Ann McMorrow. 1985. "The Elderly in the Sunday Newspapers: 1963 and 1983." *Educational Gerontology* 11: 29–39.

Wilson, Chris. 2015. "This Chart Shows Hollywood's Glaring Gender Gap." *Time.com*, October 6. http://time.com/4062700/hollywood-gender-gap (accessed September 13, 2016).

Zinoman, Jason. 2005. "When Mean Girls Are Not Stopped." *New York Times*, January 26: 1.

13

Representations of People with Disabilities

In a 2009 appearance on NBC's *Tonight Show* with Jay Leno, President Barack Obama light-heartedly bantered with Leno about his bowling skills. Pointing out his low bowling score, the President made an off-the-cuff remark that his performance was "like Special Olympics or something." The remark received immediate attention from viewers, including those with disabilities. The President quickly called Special Olympics chairman Tim Shriver to apologize for his slip of the tongue. Although Shriver accepted the President's apology, he did stress that he hoped it was "a teachable moment" for the country and stated, "Words hurt and words do matter. Words can cause pain and result in stereotypes that are unfair and damaging to people with intellectual disabilities. And using 'Special Olympics' in a negative or derogatory context can be a humiliating put-down to people with special needs" (Special Olympics 2009).

When it comes to making jokes about human skills or aptitude by making references to people with disabilities or matters related to disabilities, many individuals accept these without thinking twice about the offensiveness of such jokes. People with disabilities are often placed in a category in which it seems okay to make fun of them. The most recent report on Americans with disabilities from the US Census Bureau estimates that 56.7 million people, approximately 19 percent of the total population, have a disability. More than 38 million of these disabilities are listed as "severe" (Brault 2012). Despite these statistics, many still consider them "the invisible minority" (Nelson 1996). Mass media images rarely show this population, and when people with disabilities are shown, stereotypes, "handicapping" portrayals, and images of this group as outsiders abound.

Perceptions of people with disabilities have tended to remain the same over the years, despite the continuing progress in technology and legal rights. People with physical disabilities are stigmatized because their bodies do not reflect the norm (Hardin *et al.* 2001). People with mental illness often are saddled with the stereotype of being violent or a burden on society. To some, equally harmful are the "feel good" stories, such as the "supercrip" storyline, which represents the person with disabilities as extraordinary, "overcoming" their handicap, and offering the reader or viewer an inspiring story. Disability advocates say these storylines, which news media tend to rely upon, do more damage than good – and in actuality are negative stories. They argue that any story that highlights a person with a disability doing something ordinary, but bills it as "gee-whiz isn't it amazing!," further marginalizes, isolates, and alienates people with disabilities as not being normal. These stories, while they may appear to be shedding a positive light on an inspiring person, actually are, once again, singling out a person with a disability as an oddity, further illustrating that a person's disability will always be what defines them. As explained by HolLynn D'Lil (1997: 14): "Being told that you're inspirational when you're doing something ordinary is an assault on your self-concept. Suddenly you're reminded once again of the traditional attitudes about disabilities, that no matter who you are, what you do, how you feel, to some people you'll always be a tragic figure."

By and large, the research shows that people with disabilities – a large group, who span ethnicities, genders, sexual orientations, and other social categories – are missing from US mainstream media. Though one in six Americans has some type of disability, and more than 120 million people are directly affected by the way this minority group fares – as a friend, or a medical or social worker, or a family member – journalists have resisted covering stories such as those on employment, housing, transportation, and discrimination that would be routinely reported on for other groups (Hardin and Preston 2001). This sparse coverage in the mainstream media, in combination with the small number of entertainment media portrayals in which disability is the centering theme, has allowed many of the worst stereotypes to persist.

This chapter will first provide an historical context to why certain images of people with disabilities have developed. It will then present examples of how people with disabilities have been portrayed in film, entertainment television, and in the press. The chapter ends by discussing how advertisers have included people with disabilities in their advertisements and the resulting reactions they have received.

Historical Background to Representations of People with Disabilities

Discussions of the number of people in the United States with disabilities often reveal discrepancies in the ways disabilities are defined. Just how broadly disability is defined is a key question, as that definition is critical in terms of law making, and in the ways that society perceives the psychological, social, economic, and political impacts of perpetuating stereotypes.

Disability activists protest against commonplace terminology used to describe the physically disabled, arguing that the use of such words as "crippled" marginalizes individuals. Many of these activists, as well as journalism groups like the Associated Press, have argued for the use of "person-first" terminology, such as "a person living with ADHD" or "a person with mental retardation," and avoiding the word "victim" when describing a person with a disability. Others argue that society and the media need to stop using descriptions like "wheelchair-bound" when describing a person who uses a wheelchair, because it perpetuates the idea that this person is, indeed, stuck in his or her wheelchair, which is inaccurate, and because it should be recognized as demeaning if the wheelchair is used to define someone first, as opposed to them being seen as a person first.

To better understand why the mainstream media have come to apply dehumanizing words to refer to people with disabilities, it is useful to look at the social construction of the category of disability. Over time, the construction has shifted in perspective, from a medical orientation to one with economic constraints to a sociopolitical one (Shultz and Germeroth 1998: 229–244). Historically, disability was a medical construct, focused on the idea that disability was a functional impairment. Society looked at disability issues from the perspective that medicine and technology were needed to "fix" the problem or to "cure" physical or mental issues that placed people outside the norm.

This view progressed into an economic perspective – how society was going to alleviate the cost burdens that people with disabilities faced as they sought medical treatment or solutions. The costs of treating disabilities were (and in many cases still are) exorbitant, and the economic hardship this expense placed on persons with disabilities compounded their difficulties.

From this economic perspective grew a sociopolitical one that seeks to ensure that persons with equal productivity are provided equal opportunities for wages and employment (Shultz and Germeroth 1998: 229–244). This is based on a civil rights/minority group model, and equates the experiences of persons with disabilities with those of African Americans and other minority groups. The aim of this model ultimately is to ensure that people with disabilities are included in mainstream society.

In 1990, a groundbreaking piece of legislation preventing discrimination and aimed directly at ensuring persons with disabilities were given equal opportunities was born: the Americans with Disabilities Act or ADA. Signed into law by President George H.W. Bush, Title I of ADA "prohibits private employers, state and local governments, employment agencies, and labor unions from discriminating against qualified individuals with disabilities in job applications procedures, hiring, firing, advancement, compensation, job training, and other terms, conditions, and privileges of employment" (US Equal Employment Opportunity Commission 2008). In addition to putting forth regulations regarding employment and the treatment of persons with disabilities, it also offered a definition, for legal purposes, of who is an individual with a disability. ADA states that an individual with a disability is a person who has a physical or mental impairment that substantially limits one or more major life activities. ADA requires employers to provide reasonable accommodation for an individual with a disability, to assist with essential job functions. For example, if a cashier has arthritis that makes standing for long periods of time difficult, she is within her rights to request a stool so that she may sit while doing her job.

ADA marked a radical change in the way our society views disability. Prior to the legislation, prejudice often played a major role: individuals with disabilities were often kept out of restaurants, not allowed onto buses and planes, and kept out of movie theaters; employers would often refuse to hire disabled workers, claiming they might be disturbing to able-bodied employees. ADA was important in shifting societal views that those with disabilities need to be rehabilitated, changed, or cured. While many argue that this legislation was just a starting point, it brought to the forefront of Americans' minds that, with accommodations, there was no reason why people with disabilities could not become better integrated into society. The fact that transportation, workplaces, schools, stores, homes, and churches were often inaccessible to those with physical disabilities meant that they were in danger of becoming social outcasts. ADA helped to address inaccessibility issues.

While ADA has made considerable strides in improving the treatment of persons with disabilities, for some it still is not enough. Activists advocate a radical transformation of societal attitudes toward disability and are attempting to eliminate the stigma attached to disability. Communication studies professors Kara Shultz and Darla Germeroth (1998: 232) argue that, "very much like the transition from civil rights in the early 1960s to Black power in the late 1960s, disability activists are shifting from the Americans with Disabilities Act of 1990 to a transformation of societal attitudes about disability wherein disabled people are seen as beautiful." Since the passage of ADA in 1990 the battle has only increased in intensity, and a growing number of people with disabilities are calling ADA merely a starting point and encouraging further changes.

Perhaps the clearest example of the outspoken disability rights advocate was Harriet McBryde Johnson. Johnson, who had a neuromuscular disease and died in her sleep at the age of 50 in 2008, spent most of her adult life as a lawyer and disability activist and advocate. In 2005, she wrote a memoir, *Too Late to Die Young*. In it she noted that it was the Jerry Lewis muscular dystrophy telethon that sent her the message, for the first time, that her disease would kill her. As a result, she began living her childhood in tiny increments, marking time with thoughts such as, "When I die, I might as well die a kindergartner" (Johnson 2005: 1–47).

Johnson was known for her outspoken criticisms of certain disability stereotypes and views on euthanasia. She drew national attention for her opposition to "the charity mentality" and "pity-based tactics" of the annual Lewis muscular dystrophy telethon. She protested the telethon for nearly 20 years. In another well-publicized debate, she sparred with Princeton University's famous and controversial bioethicist Peter Singer in a cover story for the *New York Times Magazine*. Singer argued that if a baby were born with physical or mental defects or disabilities, parents would be better off euthanizing the baby as he or she was not yet a person and that it was the kind, moral thing to do, as death would be preferable to the inevitable suffering to come. His argument was a highly controversial one, and it sparked a vigorous debate with Johnson, who was adamantly opposed to his views. In the end, her article was well received, and it achieved at least part of her intent: to shed light on the perception that persons with disabilities are in some way less human than those without.

It is the ways in which disabilities are thought of that is at the root of this hot issue, and this may be the hardest part in terms of societal change. On the one hand, there are regulations for accommodations for persons with disabilities, which intrinsically require the acknowledgment that there is a disability there to begin with, versus those who argue that physical, sensory, or mental impairments are not impairments at all – rather they are simply differences between people much like eye color or right- or left-handedness. As some activists explain, just because bodies or minds work differently does not make them "disabled," it makes them "differently abled."

On the other side of this issue are others who argue that ADA goes too far, and that attempting to pretend that disabilities do not make a person different from an able-bodied person makes no sense. They argue that unlike such characteristics as skin color or sexual preference, which do not affect physical ability or mental capacity, certain disabilities most certainly do affect a person's ability to function in certain situations. While this is not an argument against integration, it does raise an alternative point of view.

More than half of Americans admit that they feel embarrassed, and nearly half say they are fearful, around people with disabilities (Wolfe 1996). Anthropologist Robert Murphy (1995) noted that "the greatest impediment to a person's taking full part in his society is not his physical flaws, but rather the tissue of myths, fears and misunderstandings that society attaches to them." The media have, over the years, certainly been the "lifeblood" of this issue. Stereotypes of persons with disabilities abound in our news media, our entertainment media, and our advertising (Hardin *et al.* 2001). The embittered blind veteran in the film *Scent of a Woman* (1992), the charmingly eccentric, but troubled obsessive-compulsive detective on the television show *Monk* (2002–2009), and the resentful, angry doctors who walk with canes on the television dramas *ER* (1994–2009) and *House* (2004–2012) have become symbols of persons with disabilities.

The fostering of stereotypes about individuals with disabilities does not just influence interpersonal relationships and the way individuals view those with disabilities, it also has ramifications on issues of equal rights legislation and societal attitudes. Therefore, looking at our mass media with a critical eye and evaluating the potential impact of representations of persons with disabilities is vital.

People with Disabilities in Film

Scholars argue that perceptions of people with disabilities have remained stagnant, and that tired stereotypes still linger (Box 13.1). Media scholar Jack Nelson (1996) found six major stereotypes in film and television portrayals: the disabled person as victim (often seen in telethons); the disabled person as hero or "supercrip"; the disabled person as a threat (evil and warped); the disabled person

---

Box 13.1 *The Sessions* and explicit vs. implicit attitudes

The Sessions (2012) is a feature film that examines the intersection between disability and sexuality. In this drama, Mark O'Brien (portrayed by John Hawkes) is paralyzed from the neck down, is forced to live in an iron lung, and has never had sex. He believes he is near death, and so hires a professional sex surrogate, Cheryl Cohen-Greene (portrayed by Helen Hunt). She helps him with his intimacy issues over the course of several sessions, ultimately resulting in successful sexual experiences. The movie was considered a "breakout hit" at the 2012 Sundance film festival, in part for the overriding theme that people should "live a full life, whatever one's personal constraints" (McCarthy 2012).

This film shows a myth of disability not often talked about: that people with disabilities are uninterested in or not capable of expressing sexuality. But perhaps more than this, it is a film that expresses that a disability isn't always pretty, isn't always something to "overcome," and that people with disabilities can lead lives of great value and love. It allows for the demystification of a stigmatized concept.

Films like this are interesting to consider through the lens of the contact hypothesis. The contact hypothesis suggests that increased contact with "out-group members" can help improve implicit and explicit attitudes toward them (Allport 1954). Implicit attitudes are unconscious attitudes that occur outside awareness and control. An explicit attitude is one a person deliberately thinks about and expresses. It is under individual control. Explicit attitudes are frequently subject to social pressures and people are inclined to share opinions they believe are socially desirable. For example, a person might say she knows that men and women are both equally good at math in public, but she associates men with math without knowing it. In this case, this person would have an implicit men-math stereotype (Project Implicit 2011).

Study has been done on the implicit attitudes held by individuals toward disabled persons. Two researchers found that strong negative implicit attitudes and negative associations toward disabled people existed even though improvements have been witnessed in explicit attitudes. The more exposure to people with disabilities, the more positive the implicit attitudes became (Wilson and Scior 2014). This may not be surprising, but the authors' final conclusion is certainly troubling. They wrote, "research into explicit attitudes toward individuals with disabilities suggests that these have become less negative over time... It would appear however [from] the results of the studies included in this review that relatively strong negative implicit attitudes remain" (Wilson and Scior 2014: 319).

It can be argued that demystifying film and television representations of persons with disabilities is imperative to stigma reduction. With significant exposure, then, implicit attitudes might become more positive. Can you think of other examples like *The Sessions* that depict persons with disabilities and which could have a positive impact on implicit attitudes?

---

as unable to adjust (others around often telling him or her to "just buck up!"); the disabled person as one to be cared for and/or a burden; and the disabled person as one who should not have survived ("better off dead"). He also noted that disabled people were rarely shown as mothers, fathers, husbands, or wives, continuing the notion that those with disabilities either are or choose to be excluded from these important roles in our society.

Historically, one can look back and see that in books, drama, and early films, there were many negative, stigmatizing portrayals of people with disabilities. In literature, they were often associated with evil intentions. And the tradition persists in film, as exemplified by characters like James Bond movie villains Dr. No, with his metal hands (*Dr. No*, 1962), and Le Chiffre, with his bleeding, impaired eye and need for an inhaler (*Casino Royale*, 2006), Darth Vader, who requires a mechanical breathing device to live, in the *Star Wars* movies (first one released in 1977), Arliss Loveless, in the 1999 movie *Wild Wild West*, who is a double amputee and uses a wheelchair, or Captain Hook in *Peter Pan* (2003). Over the past 50 years, complex and realistic images of people with disabilities in entertainment media have been few and far between. As with the depictions of any minority, the way entertainment media depicts a social group can have a profound impact on the attitudes and beliefs society holds about them. Unless other information is available, such as first-hand knowledge, the stereotypical images shown in entertainment media can shape attitudes toward people with disabilities.

In the past, researchers have found that when a character with a disability (physical, sensory, or mental) appears in movies or on television, his or her life is shown as empty, narrowly defined, and completely centered on the disability in question (see Box 13.2 for discussion of the subject of euthanasia). However, some roles have provided a more in-depth depiction of characters with disabilities, allowing the viewer to gain more of an understanding that there is no one kind of

---

Box 13.2 *Million Dollar Baby* and disability

Controversy surrounded the 2004 drama *Million Dollar Baby* for its depiction of euthanasia, something many disability advocates feel perpetuates a message that "death is better than a disability." In the Academy Award-winning film, Maggie Fitzgerald (portrayed by Hilary Swank) is an amateur boxer with dreams of going pro. She approaches veteran boxing coach Frankie Dunn (portrayed by Clint Eastwood), asking him to train her. Though he originally refuses, he finally agrees to take her on, and the two grow close as her persistence and determination impress him. They become much like father and daughter, and she starts to win. In fact, Maggie becomes so good, she makes it all the way to the Women's Welterweight championship fight in Las Vegas, which has a million dollar prize.

As Maggie is on the verge of winning this fight, her career and life take a dramatic turn when she is the victim of a sucker punch after the bell, and she falls forward onto her stool, which Frankie has placed in the ring as the fight had ended. The fall breaks her neck and Maggie becomes permanently paralyzed from the neck down. She is now confined to a hospital bed and must breathe using a ventilator. She loses a leg to infection. Frankie is prepared to help her however he can, and begins to make plans to help her adapt to her situation; Maggie, however, wants none of it. She wants to die. Her reasoning is that she has been a champion, a victor, and she wants to die with this victory fresh in her mind, not after many years of suffering after what she calls her final defeat.

She cannot kill herself. She asks Frankie to help her, and as he did when she first asked him to coach her, he initially refuses. Maggie attempts, futilely, to kill herself by biting her tongue, in the hopes that she would bleed to death. Her determination and tenacity, once again, seem to wear Frankie down. Maggie is sedated so she cannot continue to hurt herself. Finally agreeing to her request, Frankie sneaks into her room one evening, disconnects her ventilator, and injects her with a lethal dose of adrenaline, which kills her. He then disappears into the night.

While disability advocates argue that this is mere pro-euthanasia propaganda, others suggest that the movie is too nuanced to dismiss it as such. Some argue that any time a Hollywood portrayal gets people talking about an issue, it is a good thing, and that simply having the subject introduced can only lead to positive and open discussions.

What are your thoughts on *Million Dollar Baby* and its handling of euthanasia?

disability, just as there is no one kind of man or woman. Arguably, however, as noted before, in many cases if a movie character has a disability and is central to the plot, they are in some respects defined by their disability. Some of the more notable portrayals in the movies include Eddie Redmayne as Stephen Hawking, in *The Theory of Everything* (2014), a portrayal noted for the in-depth look at the impact of a degenerative disease not just on the person but also on loved ones; Julianne Moore as Alice Howland, a college linguistics professor afflicted with younger-onset Alzheimer's disease in *Still Alice* (2014); two of the main characters in *Silver Linings Playbook* (2012), Pat (portrayed by Bradley Cooper), a man with bipolar disorder, and Tiffany (portrayed by Jennifer Lawrence), a woman suffering from depression; Daniel Day-Lewis as Christy Brown, a man with cerebral palsy in *My Left Foot* (1989); David Strathairn as Whistler, a main character in *Sneakers* (1992) who is blind; Marlee Matlin as Sarah Norman, a deaf woman, in *Children of a Lesser God* (1986); Russell Crowe as John Forbes Nash, a Nobel Prize-winning mathematician with schizophrenia, in *A Beautiful Mind* (2001); and two characters from the movie *Forrest Gump* (1994): the title character, played by Tom Hanks, a man with a developmental disability, and his commander in Vietnam, Lieutenant Dan Taylor (played by Gary Sinise), who has a spinal cord injury from the war.

People with Disabilities in Entertainment Television

Media researchers Timothy Elliott and Keith Byrd noted in their 1982 study that people with disabilities portrayed on prime-time television have been predominantly depicted as belonging to lower socioeconomic groups, and as unemployed, single, and victims of abuse. In more recent research, it has been found that while some stereotypes still hold, others have evolved. Scott Parrott and Caroline T. Parrott (2015) analyzed the depictions of mental illness in US crime dramas shows on basic cable television during the 2010–2013 seasons. They found that one in every two mentally ill characters committed a violent act, compared to one in five characters from the general population of the television world, reinforcing long-portrayed stereotypes. However, and perhaps more hopefully, their research showed that depictions of physical appearance were less stereotypical and exaggerated (wild hair, over-the-top mannerisms, straitjackets, etc.). Not only did mentally ill characters look like other characters (well-groomed, nice clothing), but they were also depicted as primarily being middle class and with loving families (Parrott and Parrott 2015).

GLAAD's "Where Are We On TV" initiative has been tracking the general diversity of television characters on broadcast programming and cable for more than a decade. The 2015–2016 report, which tracked broadcast, cable, and streaming television shows, showed upticks in black and Hispanic characters, in female characters, and in LGBT characters. The one group with no progress was people with disabilities. The report notes, "for the first time in two years, the percentage of regular characters depicted as living with a disability on [this type of] programming has dropped, down to 0.9% from 1.4% reported last year" (2015: 5). This decrease is especially significant given that their results show other minority groups getting increased representation in entertainment television shows. Additionally, given that people with disabilities represent the largest minority population in the United States – approximately 19 percent of Americans live with a disability – this is "grossly disproportionate under-representation" (Woodburn and Kopic 2016).

When disabled persons do appear on entertainment television, they have been found to be the butt of many jokes, and treated as outsiders, pitiable, angry, or powerless. One 1980 study of 85 half-hour prime-time television shows found that while sometimes a "handicapped character" held a major role, not one disabled character appeared as an incidental character, except in juxtaposition with other disabled characters. None were visible in groups of shoppers, spectators, jurors, customers, or workers, further reinforcing the "invisible minority" characterization (Donaldson 1981). Historically, these characters with disabilities were often shown in "extremely negative roles"; when shown as evil threats to society, the disabilities were incidental to the plot (eye patches, walking with canes, missing limbs), and when in seemingly positive portrayals – the disabled person as inspiration – the disability was central and dominant to the plotline and the character was defined by it.

In evaluating the presentations of disabled characters in entertainment media over the past several decades, disability scholar and activist Paul Longmore (2003) does note, however, that recent images of disability are more realistic than ever before, and that much of this is due to the impact of disability rights activism. Other researchers have also concurred with Longmore's assessment. Disabled characters, though still in short supply in comparison to population numbers, are more complex now than ever before. One author writes:

> they have relationships and careers; they move in various social and professional circles, and they can be alternately arrogant, mean, spiteful, jealous, understanding, kind, angry, and resentful, just like any nondisabled character. Their disability is not the defining feature about them … Were it not for the artifacts of their disabilities such as a cane, a crutch, or a wheelchair, the viewing audience would hardly know a character has a disability because the subject is rarely, if ever, discussed. (Kopuch 2009)

In addition to those portrayals in which the disability is peripheral, as with some movie roles, there have been disabled character roles distinctly created for television programs. Examples include: Geri Tyler, played by Geri Jewell, a comedian with cerebral palsy, on the series *The Facts of Life* (1979–1988); Tony Soprano as a sufferer of panic attacks and other disabling mental ailments on the HBO series *The Sopranos* (1999–2007); Tess Kauffman, played by deaf actress Marlee Matlin, a deaf district attorney on NBC's *Reasonable Doubts* (1991–1993); Corky Thatcher, played by a young male actor with Down syndrome, on the ABC series *Life Goes On* (1989–1993); Zach Addy, a forensic anthropologist with Asperger's syndrome on the Fox series *Bones* (2005 debut); and Gil Grissom, a crime scene investigator, who suffered from hearing loss for part of the series, on the CBS show *CSI* (2000 debut). In the teen drama *Switched at Birth* (debut 2011 on ABC Family), two high school girls discover they were switched at birth and grew up in very different environments: one in an affluent Kansas City suburb and the other in a low-income neighborhood. One of the girls is deaf (portrayed by hard of hearing actress Katie Leclerc), and the show regularly tackles challenges faced by deaf children in mainstream high schools. One entire episode, entitled "Uprising," which aired on the date marking the 25th anniversary of the "Deaf President Now" protests at Gallaudet University, was produced almost entirely in American Sign Language. Television critics hail *Switched at Birth* as "the most nuanced and complex depiction of deaf culture and individuals to ever air on television" (Lacob 2013).

In 2016, ABC debuted sitcom *Speechless* about a close-knit four-person family, the DiMeos, led by a strong and protective mother, Maya (played by Minnie Driver), who focuses much of her attention on her teenage son J.J. (played by Micah Fowler) who has cerebral palsy and communicates with the use of a laser pointer. Her focus, however, isn't pandering; rather, Maya is driven to make sure that her son is afforded the same types of opportunities offered to other teens of the same age. Television critics as well as viewers have praised the show for raising awareness regarding the disability while also entertaining audiences. *Rotten Tomatoes* rated the show as "Certified Fresh at 98%" and via Twitter such comments as "Love this show #speechless" and "Kind of revolutionary to see a disabled person using a toilet without making it super pity inducing #Speechless" appeared. Fowler who plays J.J. has a neurological disorder and, like his character, uses a wheelchair; in a press interview, Fowler expressed hope that audiences would "look past JJ's wheelchair and see his 'heart, humor, and big personality'" (Rovenstine 2016).

Perhaps one of the most vivid and controversial examples of a television show with several disabled characters, and minority characters in general, is the musical comedy-drama *Glee* (2009–2015). In this show, which had as its main focus a group of students and teachers who are involved with a high school show choir, also known as a glee club, one of the main characters and member of the glee club, Artie, uses a wheelchair. Another main character, Tina, speaks with a stutter (though she later admits that she has purposely given herself a disability to keep people from getting too close), and two characters have Down syndrome. While the show drew much critical praise both for its treatment of diversity issues and its humor, it also attracted a considerable amount of criticism from a variety of camps, including several disability activist groups.

Specifically, much of the controversy stemmed from an episode entitled "Wheels." In this episode, the team is planning its bus trip to sectionals. Unfortunately, the bus is not handicap-accessible, and the cost of renting one is prohibitive, and therefore, Artie would not be able to ride with the rest of the team. At first, the rest of the group suggests Artie just ride with his dad, like he always does, but Will, the glee coach, disappointed by their insensitive reactions, says they either travel as a team or they don't go at all. To further impress upon them the lesson, he purchases wheelchairs for the entire team and assigns them to use the chairs for the rest of the week, so that they can begin to understand what Artie deals with on a daily basis. Each member of the club is to spend three hours a day in their chair. The show is chock-full of scenes of the difficulties each encounters during their time spent in the wheelchairs, including not being able to reach things in their lockers, being hit in the face with backpacks as other students walk past, and struggling to maneuver the hallways. By the middle of the show, several of the able-bodied characters start using the wheelchairs to receive special treatment: one pretends to be the victim of a spinal cord injury to get marijuana at a lower price, and another pretends to be a wheelchair user in order to coerce an employer into giving him a job.

Meanwhile, Artie and Tina, who have been growing closer, share a kiss, after she shares that she has a whole new admiration for him after the experience of using the wheelchair. He replies that she must understand as she, too, has a disability – her stutter. They then have a heart-to-heart discussion, in which Tina admits that she has been faking her stutter for many years, to keep people from expecting too much from her, that she was shy and now she realizes that she has been missing out and doesn't want to do it anymore. She is sure that Artie understands. Artie replies with a stinging retort that he would never try to push people away. He tells her he thought they had something really important in common and that while he is glad that she "gets to be normal," he is at the same time angry: he explains, "I'm stuck in this chair for the rest of my life. It's not something I can fake" (Murphy and Barklay 2009). He rolls away from her then, leaving her alone in the hallway. At the end of the show, the glee team performs a rousing rendition of "Proud Mary" all in wheelchairs, rolling down ramps and rocking side-to-side in unison, and high fiving joyously (Figure 13.1).

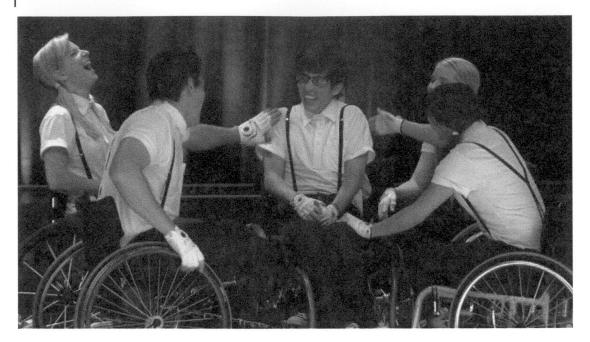

Figure 13.1 The cast of Fox's *Glee* did a rousing wheelchair dance to "Proud Mary." Is this an uplifting portrayal? Screenshot.

While some applauded *Glee* for taking on the disability discussion in an open and honest way, and in general Artie was treated no different from any other character and his being in a wheelchair was not made a central issue, others believed there was cause for outrage. For instance, S.E. Smith (2009), a staff writer for *Bitch Magazine*, wrote:

> The much anticipated Very Special Disability Episode of *Glee*, "Wheels" aired last night. And already the rave reviews are flooding in. It's "edgy," it's "a game changer," it's "controversial," it's "moving," it's "thought provoking." Twitter is aflutter with praise.
>
> Did everyone else watch the same episode I watched? Because what I got out of "Wheels" was tokenization and appropriation. I wrote three pages of notes while watching and they were filled with expressions of rage and horror, because this episode pretty much encapsulated, for me, everything that is wrong with the way *Glee* handles people living in marginalized bodies.

Smith continues:

> This show has been criticized from the start by activists decrying the use of [able-bodied actors in the role of Artie], and the tokenization of minorities. The mainstream media caught on this week, releasing a flood of articles expressing shock and surprise about how disability activists were angry about *Glee*. This episode was evidently supposed to put it all to rest: See, they are

actually sensitive to issues which people in marginalized bodies face and they aren't just using people with disabilities as props!

The author makes the argument further in the article that *Glee*'s method of handling minorities was to spend one episode focusing attention on a particular group, and then to move on – for instance, "the Very Special Gay Episode, The Very Special Black Episode, and now, the Very Special Disability Episode." She writes:

> [Now] we can go back to focusing on the white, conventionally attractive leads. Who are, of course, the draw, because the most common argument used to justify exclusion of minority groups from film and television is that no one wants to watch them.
>
> We got "disability is inspiring," "disability is a burden," "appropriation of disability for a Very Special Learning Experience," "faking disability," and "see my sister has a disability so I'm not a bigot."
>
> Here's the thing about tokenization, which is what this episode specialized in: It does nothing to advance the cause of people who live in marginalized bodies.

This is just one opinion, but it certainly raises an interesting argument. While one can argue that awareness leads to acceptance, there are varying ways to interpret this show.

Some actors have taken an activist role when playing a character with a disability. Tony Shalhoub, the actor who played the character of Adrian Monk who lives with obsessive-compulsive disorder, on the US series *Monk*, mentioned earlier in this chapter, teamed with the Anxiety Disorders Association of America to launch an OCD awareness campaign. In reference to the disorder, a condition that more than 2 million Americans live with, Shalhoub wrote in an article published on WebMD: "For a lot of people, there is a fear and embarrassment. But people who suffer with the disorder don't have to be outcasts. They can be and are contributing members of society" (Pearlman n.d.).

In 1978, one group began to exert quiet pressure on entertainment media groups on behalf of people with disabilities – the Media Access Office (MAO). Approximately 250 actors and actresses with varying disabilities advocate for the use of actors with disabilities to portray characters in a variety of roles, including minor or background roles as a part of "general society" as opposed to off in seclusion (Nelson 1996). They particularly encourage roles in which the disability is seen as incidental. Former MAO Chairman Alan Toy notes: "If only we could get that image of normality projected more, the more audiences would get used to seeing us as human beings, and the less aghast they'll be when they meet us in the street."

Another point of contention stems from the use of able-bodied and non-disabled actors to play disabled characters. A 2016 study done by the Ruderman Family Foundation found that 95 percent of disabled characters are portrayed by actors without a disability. The research examined the Nielsen top-rated scripted shows that aired during the 2015–2016 television season and shows listed as the "Best Online-Original TV Shows" (Amazon, Hulu, and Netflix) as noted by Tom's Guide (Woodburn and Kopic 2016). They note that a common argument for this fact is that there are few notable actors with a disability. However, according to Actors Access more than 4,000 registered professional actors identify themselves as having a disability. In an article for *Variety*, Jay Ruderman, president of the Ruderman Family Foundation, was quoted as saying, "The entertainment industry has a significant impact on how our society views various minority groups. Part of this is rooted in the fact that our population spends more time watching television than socializing with friends. Because of the widespread stigma in Hollywood against hiring actors with disabilities, we very rarely see people with real disabilities on screen" (Wagmeister 2016).

The influence of entertainment media portrayals of disability cannot be overestimated when considering the size of the audiences that flock to US theaters and the omnipresence of television in American homes. However, as the disabled community becomes more vocal and self-empowered, depictions and negative stereotypes will continue to change. The press, no doubt, will also play a role in bringing about such change.

People with Disabilities in the News

The press has the power to change perceptions, and it has the power to reinforce stereotypes. This is certainly true with regard to how the news media in the United States deal with disability issues. Study after study has shown that the mainstream media continue to do a fairly poor job of covering individuals with disabilities and, at its worst, perpetuate the stereotypes through poor word choice and stagnant, overused feature writing formulas (see Box 13.3).

In an article in *Quill* magazine, Leye Jeannette Chrzanowski (2000), a journalist who used a wheelchair (she died in 2016), attacked the media for what she characterized as downright biased coverage. She wrote:

> Many people with disabilities believe mainstream journalists are incapable of accurately covering stories about them. Generally, journalists either portray us as pitiful cripples, super achievers, or insane mental patients. These erroneous media stereotypes of people with disabilities are perpetuated because journalists consistently fail to understand or learn about people with disabilities and the issues that are important to us. (2000: 38)

Box 13.3 Language usage reinforcing stereotypes in the news

Consider the following article written by sports columnist Marc Narducci and published in the *Philadelphia Inquirer* on January 18, 2009. In this column, Narducci discusses the recent presentation of a humanitarian award to a college athlete who was injured during a football game damaging his spinal cord. How does the language the reporter chose to use reinforce stereotypes about disabilities?

> Adam Taliaferro has turned tragedy into triumph. He always remembered the help he received in time of need and is now spending the rest of his life giving back. Isn't that the definition of a humanitarian?
>
> Apparently the Philadelphia Sports Writers Association feels that way. During the 105th annual dinner, Taliaferro will receive the Humanitarian Award.
>
> Taliaferro's story is well known to many but inspirational no matter how many times it is recited.
>
> A former all-South Jersey running back from Eastern in 1999, Taliaferro has both an inspiring and uplifting message to spread every time he ventures out in public.

The article continues:

> He suffered a horrific spinal injury in September 2000, while playing football for Penn State against Ohio State. At the time of the injury, the prognosis was grim as to whether he would be able to walk again. His life appeared ***confined to a wheelchair***.
> We all know that Taliaferro defied the odds and has eagerly embarked on a new goal – to help others who have walked in his shoes.
> The Adam Taliaferro Foundation was started in 2001, and, according to director Tom Iacovone, this non-profit organization has raised nearly $300,000, helping others who have incurred spinal injuries.

The author discusses the foundation and Taliaferro's contributions in the paragraphs that follow:

> No, he was happy to be alive and to be able to contribute to society. And what a contribution it has been.
> "The day of the injury was horrible, but everything after that has been positive." Taliaferro said from the offices of Montgomery, McCracken, Walker & Rhoads, LLP in Philadelphia, where he works as a lawyer. "While on the road to recovery I didn't have a negative thing happen to me."
> What perspective.
> And in an odd way, he feels that the injury was a blessing of sorts.

The article concludes:

> "If I was still playing football, I would never have had this opportunity," he said. "I definitely believe things happen for a reason. So instead of playing football I can try to help people."
> And help them he has.

Disability scholars have found evidence that there may, indeed, be a discord in how persons with disabilities and disability issues are covered. Paul Higgins (1992) states that we as a society "make disability" through our language, our media, and other public ways. The news media actively construct and frame people with disabilities in their stories and images. Several studies have found that references to persons with disabilities tend to be in soft or feature stories rather than hard news stories, and to be about individuals with physical disabilities, mental retardation, or individuals identified by the generic labels "handicapped" and "disabled." There is evidence that people with disabilities themselves think that the media do not provide information that they deem important, and that the press's coverage of services, benefits, and programs that affect their lives is insufficient. Researchers report there is great dissatisfaction with the media's method of portraying people with disabilities, with Yolanda de Balcazar and her research team noting that "the media portray people with disabilities in a negative and unrealistic way, preferring the sensational or pitiful to the everyday and human side of disability" (de Balcazar, Bradford, and Fawcett 1998).

Content analysis studies of disability coverage in newspapers have found that the most common news reference is with regard to physical disabilities, which is a low prevalence disability category, followed by mental retardation, with very little reference to individuals with hearing or visual impairments, or other mental impairments. Reference to learning disabilities, which is a much higher prevalence disability category, is virtually nonexistent.

Newspapers have been found to write in emotionally laden ways about disabilities, and more than half of those accounts describe the negative impact a disability has on a person's life. Terminology such as "a victim of" or "suffers from" are common, as are phrases like "confined to a wheelchair," "wheelchair-bound," "felt like my life was over," and "trapped inside their bodies" (Keller *et al.* 1990).

Mental illness or mental impairment also has been found to be treated stereotypically in the press, and primarily placed under a stigmatizing light, when it is covered at all. Mental illness is rarely covered, though it impacts 1 in 10 Americans (Kessler *et al.* 2005). Communication scholar Carol Fletcher (2003) noted, in a study of young women's service magazines, that although a 17-year-old woman has a 1 in 100 chance of being diagnosed with bipolar disease and a 1 in 2,600 chance of being diagnosed with breast cancer, she is far more likely to come across articles on breast cancer in the service magazines she reads.

Fletcher also found that news magazines tend to blur the lines between mental impairments and illnesses, often treating them all as if they were the same. Furthermore, these news magazines often link mental illness with violence and suggest that "recovery is achievable and desirable," held back only by the failings of our country's mental health system. This is consistent with past studies, which show a history of media stigmatizing the mentally ill and assuming violence and crime to be correlates (Gerbner 1994).

Media researcher Beth Haller (1998) notes that the way the media frame disability has real implications for the lives of people with disabilities, as while an individual may not know a disabled person on an interpersonal level, he or she meets disabled people through the media on a regular basis. Haller continues, arguing that journalists may inadvertently assign "hero" or "villain" status to key players in a story, using longstanding cultural norms: (1) that society perceives disabled persons to be damaged, defective, and less socially marketable than non-disabled persons; (2) that society believes disabled persons must try harder to overcome obstacles in culture and should strive to achieve normality; and (3) that society attributes to disabled persons a preference to be with their own kind.

Disability scholars worry that the continued use of these negative and stereotypical portrayals will further cement the often-found public sentiment that individuals with disabilities should be feared or are outcasts of society. These depictions, it has been argued, may "immediately and lastingly affect our perceptions and constructs, and possibly our actions toward, persons with disabilities" (Keller *et al.* 1990).

An area that many researchers interested in news coverage of disability issues have focused on is euthanasia or physician-assisted death/suicide. Ever since a videotape was released depicting Dr. Jack Kevorkian injecting a lethal dose of drugs into the arm of a man with Lou Gehrig's disease, considerable research attention has been paid to the impact of a "better off dead" philosophy on individuals with disabilities. The main premise in this argument is that the news framing of disabled people in physician-assisted suicide stories presents an idea of disabled people being inferior to able-bodied people, being "defective," or as having a worthless status. As discussed in Chapter 2, framing is a system of organizing information, with specific choices being made about what is stressed and/or de-emphasized. Disability rights advocates argue that the news media continually set forth a frame of disability as "a fate worse than death," and that many journalists continue to represent disability as a medical problem or social deviance.

Several media researchers have looked at newspaper and media coverage of physician-assisted suicide to see what frames of people with disabilities might emerge and what impact these frames might have on readers and viewers. Disabilities and media scholars Kimberly Lauffer and Sarah Bembry (1999) found that believing that a disability is abnormal can influence public understanding of physician-assisted suicide. Philosophy scholar Leonard Fleck (1995) and former Surgeon General C. Everett Koop (1989) note that members of vulnerable groups, which include people with physical and cognitive disabilities, may be coerced or manipulated into "choosing" death, seeing it as their only viable option, or may be led to believe it is their duty to die. People with disabilities also may not have the power to choose or consent, being mentally or physically incapable of making an informed choice, thereby pushing the responsibility for deciding when those individuals become a "burden on society" and "better off dead" onto family members and other loved ones.

Journalism and mass media professors Beth Haller and Sue Ralph (2001) assert that this cultural narrative – that disabled people are "incurable" and "better off dead" – becomes even clearer when we contrast it with the treatment of people without disabilities who are suicidal. When a non-disabled person asks to die or shows suicidal behaviors, he or she is referred to a psychologist or psychiatrist for counseling. However, when a disabled person asks to die, society tends to say "of course." If the body or mind is damaged, some suggest that society decides that life is less precious and easier to let go.

Studies have shown a number of common frames in news articles about physician-assisted suicide, including (1) that it is more of an ambiguous legal and religious issue, rather than a human rights issue; (2) that disability issues are medicalized and treated as sickness; (3) that terminal illness and disability are synonymous; (4) and that the physician-assisted suicide of today is more humane and painless than years ago (Haller and Ralph 2001). Interestingly, these studies note that rarely is a disabled person used as a source or quoted commenting on the issue.

Other studies have also sought to examine the frames or portrayals of people with disabilities within another form of media – advertising.

People with Disabilities in Advertising

In 1984, the first television ad said to feature a disabled person aired across the United States. The Levi's commercial in which a wheelchair user popped a wheelie was evidence that people with disabilities were finally, albeit slowly, becoming a more visible and economically viable population in American advertising, after many years of being largely ignored or avoided. Advocates for disabled people in the United States note the importance of the "disabled consumer market," and cite statistics on buying power. For instance, in the United States, estimates show people with disabilities number 54 million, with an aggregate income of more than $1 trillion and $220 billion in discretionary spending power (Solutions Marketing Group n.d.).

Historically, most images of disability in advertising have been in relation to charity organizations, such as the Easter Seals, the Muscular Dystrophy Association (MDA), and the Multiple Sclerosis Society (MSS), and telethons and promotional advertisements. As the disability rights movement progressed in the 1970s and 1980s, more persons with disabilities began being included in print and television advertisements, and major companies such as Levi's and McDonald's opened the door to the recognition that non-disabled consumers would not be "offended" by seeing persons with disabilities in campaigns (Haller and Ralph 2003). Another factor that contributed to the increase of persons with disabilities appearing in advertising came in 1980 when closed captioning began on television, and the medium became more accessible to deaf people (Lipman 1989). There was greater evidence that those with disabilities were watching and that they were able to show their approval with their dollars. All of these factors meant the appearance of disabled persons in the media slowly was becoming less taboo.

According to the US Census Bureau, between 1990 and 2000, the number of Americans with disabilities increased 25 percent, outpacing any other subgroup of the US population, and was comprised of people of all ethnic backgrounds, cultures, and ages. The Bureau's 2013 American Community Survey found that 73.9 percent of people with disabilities live in a home with a computer and 62.5 percent have high-speed Internet connection (File and Ryan 2014), making it clear why Internet marketers are now taking notice of this often-overlooked population. According to research conducted by Solutions Marketing Group (n.d.), the popular notion that people with disabilities never leave their homes is untrue, as statistics show they spend billions in travel, and focus group data show that disabled participants eat out between two and 30 times a month.

In fact, many scholars note that advertising has been a catalyst for more positive images of disability across the media (Shapiro 1993). For instance, there were a number of televisions ads in the early 1990s that used characters in wheelchairs, showing them as "normal people doing things that normal people do" (Nelson 1996). Inclusive advertising has been demonstrated as effective with consumers, and mega-advertisers such as Coca-Cola, Kmart, McDonald's, IBM, Apple, Citibank, and others have included disabled characters, including deaf actors, persons in wheelchairs, and children with Down syndrome, in print and television ads (Shapiro 1993). One ad, in particular, is often cited as groundbreaking: department store chain Target used a photo of a girl with Down syndrome in a 1990 ad insert. The company received 2,000 thank-you letters from consumers, many of whom were parents of children with Down syndrome. One woman called a Target executive 30 minutes after the circular hit her doorstep. The executive said, "It was the mother of a girl with Down syndrome, thanking me for having a kid with Down syndrome in our ad. 'It's so important to my daughter's self-image,' she said" (Shapiro 1993).

Another ad, which aired during the 2001 Super Bowl, also garnered a great deal of positive attention and is credited with further reinforcing the idea that disabled individuals do not need to remain invisible in advertising. Cingular ran a commercial called "King Gimp" that featured a man named Dan Keplinger, an artist with cerebral palsy. The ad begins with Dan speaking, with subtitles over the image: "Yes, there is an intelligent person in this body." It then cuts to him painting, with subtitles stating, "I speak to the world in color and light. Art gives me a way to express myself. Most people think 'gimp' means a lame walk. Gimp also means a fighting spirit. I am an artist. I am unbelievably lucky." The tagline for the ad is, "There is no force more powerful or more beautiful than self-expression. What do you have to say?" (Keplinger 2007)

In 2016, one of the more memorable Olympic ads from Nike featured Kyle Maynard, the first quadruple amputee to climb Mount Kilimanjaro without prosthetics. The ad begins with a close-up of Maynard's face, breathing heavily (Figure 13.2). The voice-over intones, "Here is a man ... working hard, pushing his limits." Then the camera pulls back, showing Maynard's entire body. The voice-over asks, "You got this?" Maynard replies, "I got this!" Then, the voice-over continues, "Cool. He's got this. Wait, wha, you don't have arms. But you don't have legs either!" Maynard jokes in reply, "Ha. Oh, really? I must have left them at home." The commercial concludes with a long shot of Maynard

Figure 13.2 Nike featured Kyle Maynard, the first quadruple amputee to climb Mount Kilimanjaro, in a commercial aired during the 2016 Olympics. Screenshot.

climbing the picturesque mountain, and the voice-over noting, "You left them at … dude, that's not funny. You're on top of a mountain. That's dangerous …" in a joking tone. Some critics commented that this was just another example of the "supercrip" stereotype, and that the commercial wasn't the "right kind of inspiration or the best inclusion" presenting as it did "an oversimplified and one-dimensional representation of a person with a disability or any other minority" (Loebner 2016). For instance, what if the commercial featured a person of color or someone identifying with LGBTQ and the voice-over, instead of saying "you don't have arms," said in a shocked tone, "you're gay and on a mountain?" Viewer reaction would likely be very different. That said, raising the visibility of disabled people is a positive step and can lead to changing the mindset of people about this minority group.

Not everyone has been so enthusiastic about the advertising industry's use of people with disabilities in campaigns. It seems to be a "damned if you do, damned if you don't" discussion. Some experts claim that portraying people with disabilities in advertising is a political minefield, because of the way in which they are used. For instance, Nike's use of paraplegic marathon athletes in an ad campaign was criticized by some for implying that people with disabilities have to overcome their disabilities in superhuman ways (the "supercrip" syndrome) in order to be accepted (Bainbridge 1997).

Others have been criticized for their use of a token disabled person, the inference being that the use was exploitation. For example, in 1993, Dow Chemical Company released a television ad for Spray and Wash Stain Stick. The ad featured a little girl with Down syndrome and her mother, and the ad begins: "Halley has made my life very exciting. She's very affectionate, and she is very active. We use Stain Stick … because the last place we need another challenge is in the laundry room." The ad used a real mother and daughter, not actors. In response to the ad, a writer from *Advertising Age* called it exploitative and appalling, and "the most crassly contrived slice-of-life in advertising history" (Goldman 1993). However, Dow's toll-free comment line contradicted this opinion with more than 700 calls: all except for seven were positive (Haller and Ralph 2003).

Fashion marketing has been called out for its limited depiction of beauty. Psychologist and Ms. Wheelchair New York 2012 Danielle Sheypuk called for the fashion industry to pay attention to people with disabilities because this group of people also loved looking great and sexy in designer shoes and clothes. Sheypuk said, "we read the magazines, shop in stores, but nothing is ever pitched to us" (Woman eNews 2014). The fashion industry responded by having models in wheelchairs "stomp" the runway. Designer Carrie Hammer had Sheypuk in her New York Fashion Week runway show. Similarly, in 2015, FTL Moda had an array of women, including those in wheelchairs and with prosthetic limbs, in their runway show (Conelly 2015). The designer company worked with Fondazione Vertical, a foundation aimed at curing spinal cord injuries, and Models of Diversity, a model agency in London, to find models that more closely represented the real world.

These efforts are perhaps prescient in light of model/reality star Kendall Jenner's *Interview* photoshoot which features her in a leather bustier and choker, seated in a wheelchair. While the photographer Steven Klein intended the image to convey Jenner's power and control in the face of stifling scrutiny, critics viewed the image as offensive in its usage of the wheelchair as a prop. Model Gemma Flanagan, who was diagnosed with Guillain-Barré syndrome in 2011, countered that Jenner in a wheelchair was "not empowering. … (the wheelchair) is not a prop. It's our legs" (Unity Blott 2015).

Certainly, one issue that is raised through this discussion is the general state of advertising, and what sells products. There is a culture of beauty in the United States, and it shows up in the marketplace. Advertising today has a strong emphasis on what is considered as beauty and bodily perfection that may run contrary to the use of some people with disabilities. Disability activists argue that there needs to be more diversity in advertising, and that as companies and marketing executives realize the power of the "disability dollar," more positive images of disability in advertising campaigns will appear.

Looking toward the future of marketing and advertising and the impact of the growing population of disabled persons, it is worth noting the issue of aging, a topic covered in Chapter 12. With age comes a greater chance of disability, and current statistics confirm this: though the elderly are just 13 percent of the US population, they comprise 34 percent of those with a disability and 37 percent of those with a severe disability, according to the US Census Bureau (2012). In the next 10 years, the number of Americans over 50 will increase by 40 percent, so it follows that our disability numbers will increase as well. Considering that Americans aged 50 and over have more than $2.3 trillion in annual discretionary income, and billions more for necessities like housing and food, it is a group that advertisers cannot easily dismiss (The Dish 2016). It has yet to be seen whether they do so or not.

Concluding Remarks

Individuals with disabilities have made it clear that they do not want to be defined by their disabilities. They want equal rights in the classroom and in the workplace. They want to be treated as people first, who happen to have an inconvenience in their lives, and to be represented in the media with respect, dignity, and inclusion. Activists argue that this group, the largest minority group in the United States, deserves better treatment and representation from the media. While some argue that we are making strides in that direction, clearly there is still room for improvement. Recognizing perpetuated stereotypes and being a critical media consumer can point us in the right direction.

Reflection Questions and Thoughts to Consider

1. The word "disabled" implies an inability to do something and that something is not as it should be; being disabled means you deviate from the norm. In American society, the argument could be made that being "normal" is a primary goal of most citizens, and thus, a powerful force in the media, driving virtually every decision made by editors, producers, advertisers, and writers. Do you agree with this argument? Why or why not? Is it surprising, then, that the disabled population is not more present in our news and entertainment media?

2. Watch two hours of your favorite television channel. In a notebook, write down any commercials or shows that incorporate actors or actresses with a disability. How many did you find? If you found any, were the disabilities physical, sensory, or mental? How do your findings compare with those discussed in the chapter?
3. The "supercrip" story is an extremely popular one in newspapers and magazines. Many editors would argue that they are presenting an empowering image of a person with a disability, living life to the full. Why might these stories be doing more damage than good? Are these inspirational stories creating their own set of stereotypes? How so?
4. Interview a friend or roommate about commonly held beliefs about a person with a disability such as cerebral palsy or Down syndrome. Consider how stereotypical his or her attitudes are, and discuss from where these attitudes may have come (media, friends, parents). If you were working as a disability activist to raise awareness about cerebral palsy, what would you suggest doing?

References

Allport, George W. 1954. *The Nature of Prejudice.* Cambridge, MA: Perseus Books.

Bainbridge, Jane. 1997. "Overcoming Ad Disabilities." *Marketing*, August 7: 8.

Brault, Matthew W. 2012. "Americans with Disabilities: 2010." *Current Population Reports*, 70–131, Washington, DC: US Census Bureau.

Chrzanowski, Leye Jeannette. 2000. "Media Miss Importance of Disability Issues." *Quill* 88: 9.

Conelly, Catherine. 2015. "Models with Disabilities Just Took Over Fashion Week." *Sheknows.com*, February 17. http://www.sheknows.com/beauty-and-style/articles/1075655/fashion-week-models-with-disabilities (accessed April 14, 2017).

de Balcazar, Yolanda S., Barbara Bradford, and Stephen B. Fawcett. 1998. "Common Concerns of Disabled Americans: Issues and Options." *Social Policy* 19(2): 34.

D'Lil, HolLynn. 1997. "Being an 'Inspiration.'" *Mainstream* 22(3).

Donaldson, Joy. 1981. "The Visibility and Image of Handicapped People on Television." *Exceptional Children* 47(6): 413–416.

Elliott, Timothy, and Keith Byrd. 1982. "Media and Disability." *Rehabilitation Literature* 43(11–12): 348–355.

File, Thom, and Camille Ryan. 2014. "Computer and Internet Use in the United States: 2013." United States Census Bureau: American Community Survey Reports. https://www.census.gov/history/pdf/2013computeruse.pdf (accessed April 14, 2017).

Fleck, Leonard. 1995. "Just Caring: Assisted Suicide and Health Care Rationing." *University of Detroit Mercy Law Review* 72(4): 873–899.

Fletcher, Carol. 2003. "Criminal Injustice: Portrayal of Bipolar Disorder in Six American Newpapers." Media Ecology Conference proceedings, Hempstead, NY.

Gerbner, George. 1994. "Television Violence Profile No. 16." Annenberg School for Communication, University of Pennsylvania.

GLAAD. 2015. "2015–2016 Where Are We on Television." http://www.glaad.org/whereweareontv15 (accessed April 14, 2017).

Goldman, Kevin. 1993. "Dow Brands Criticized and Praised for Ad Featuring Disabled Child." *Wall Street Journal*, September 3: B8.

Haller, Beth. 1998. "Prizing in Disability in Journalism: Inspiration as Code." Paper presented at the Association for Education in Journalism and Mass Communication Annual Meeting, Baltimore, MD, August 1998.

Haller, Beth, and Sue Ralph. 2001. "Not Worth Keeping Alive? News Framing of Physician-Assisted Suicide in the United States and Great Britain." *Journalism Studies* 2(3): 407–421.

Haller, Beth, and Sue Ralph. 2003. "Current Perspectives on Advertising Images of Disability." In *Gender, Race, and Class In the Media: A Text-Reader*, edited by Gail Dines and Jean Humez, 293–301. Thousand Oaks, CA: Sage.

Hardin, Brent, Marie Hardin, S. Lynn, and K. Walsdorf. 2001. "Missing in Action? Images of Disability in Sports Illustrated for Kids." *Disability Studies Quarterly* 21: 21–32.

Hardin, Marie, and Ann Preston. 2001. "Inclusion of Disability Issues in News Reporting Textbooks." *Journalism and Mass Communication Educator* 56(2): 43–54.

Higgins, Paul C. 1992. *Making Disability: Exploring the Social Transformation of Human Variation.* Springfield, IL: Charles C. Thomas.

Johnson, Harriet McBryde. 2005. *Too Late to Die Young.* New York, NY: Picador.

Keller, Clayton, Daniel Hallahan, Edward McShane, E. Paula Crowley, and Barbara Blandford. 1990. "The Coverage of Persons with Disabilities in American Newspapers." *The Journal of Special Education* 24(3): 271–282.

Keplinger, Dan (appearance). 2007. Cingular advertisement. https://www.youtube.com/watch?v=_DIwQTFbn1g (accessed April 14, 2017).

Kessler, Ronald C., Wai Tat Chiu, Olga Demler, and Ellen E. Walters. 2005. "Prevalence, Severity, and Comorbidity of Twelve-month DSM-IV Disorders in the National Comorbidity Survey Replication (NCS-R)." *Archives of General Psychiatry* 62(6): 617–627.

Koop, C. Everett. 1989. "The Right to Die: The Moral Dilemma." In *Euthanasia: The Moral Issues*, edited by Robert M. Baird and Stuart E. Rosenbaum, 35–44. Buffalo, NY: Prometheus Books.

Kopuch, Viviane S. 2009. "Disabled Characters on American Primetime Television Programs." Master's thesis, Marist College, NY.

Lacob, Jace. 2013. "ABC Family's 'Switched at Birth' ASL Episode Recalls Gallaudet Protest." *The Daily Beast.* http://www.thedailybeast.com/articles/2013/02/28/abc-family-s-switched-at-birth-asl-episode-recalls-gallaudet-protest.html (accessed April 14, 2017).

Lauffer, Kimberly, and Sarah Bembry. 1999. "Investigating Media Influence on Attitudes Toward People with Disabilities and Euthanasia." Paper presented to the Association for Education in Journalism and Mass Communication Annual Meeting, New Orleans, LA, August 1999.

Lipman, Joanne.1989. "Disabled People Featured in More Ads." *Wall Street Journal*, September 7: 1.

Loebner, Josh. 2016. "Britain Wins Gold for Disability Adverts." *Advertising & Disability.* https://advertisinganddisability.com/2016/09/08/britain-wins-gold-for-disability-adverts (accessed April 14, 2017).

Longmore, Paul K. 2003. *Why I Burned My Book and Other Essays on Disability.* Philadelphia, PA: Temple University Press.

McCarthy, Todd. 2012. "The Surrogate: Sundance Film Review." *The Hollywood Reporter.* http://www.hollywoodreporter.com/review/sessions-film-review-284158 (accessed April 14, 2017).

Murphy, Robert. 1995. "Encounters: The Body Silent in America." In *Disability and Culture*, edited by Benedicte Ingstad and Susan Reynolds Whyte, 140. Berkley, CA: University of California Press.

Murphy, Ryan (writer), and Paris Barklay (director). 2009. "Wheels." *Glee*. New York, NY: Fox.

Narducci, Marc. 2009. "Taliaferro a Worthy Recipient of the Award." *Philadelphia Inquirer*, January 18: E7.

Nelson, Jack. 1996. "The Invisible Cultural Group: Images of Disability." In *Images That Injure, Pictorial Stereotypes in the Media*, edited by Paul Lester, 123. Westport, CT: Praeger.

Parrott, Scott, and Caroline T. Parrott. 2015. "Law and Order: The Portrayal of Mental Illness in U.S. Crime Dramas." *Journal of Broadcasting & Electronic Media* 59(4): 640–657.

Pearlman, Eve. n.d. "Actor Tony Shalhoub Takes on Obsessive Compulsive Disorder." http://www.webmd.com/anxiety-panic/features/actor-tony-shalhoub-takes-on-obsessive-compulsive-disorder (accessed April 14, 2017).

Project Implicit. 2011. "Frequently Asked Questions." https://implicit.harvard.edu/implicit/faqs.html (accessed April 14, 2017).

Rovenstine, Dalene. 2016. "Micah Fowler is the Breakout Star of *Speechless*." *Entertainment Weekly*, September 20. http://www.ew.com/article/2016/09/20/speechless-micah-fowler-breakout-star (accessed April 14, 2017).

Shapiro, Joseph. 1993. *No Pity: People with Disabilities Forging a New Civil Rights Movement*. New York, NY: Times Books/Random House.

Shultz, Kara, and Darla Germeroth. 1998. "Should We Laugh or Should We Cry? John Callahan's Humor as a Tool to Change Societal Attitudes Toward Disability." *The Howard Journal of Communication* 9: 229–244.

Smith, S.E. 2009. "The Transcontinental Disability Choir: Glee-ful Appropriation." http://bitchmagazine.org/post/glee-ful-appropriation (accessed April 14, 2017).

Solutions Marketing Group. n.d. http://disability-marketing.com (accessed March 25, 2011).

Special Olympics. 2009. "Official Statement from Special Olympics Chairman Timothy Shriver Regarding U.S. President Obama's Comment on the Tonight Show with Jay Leno." Special Olympics press release, March 20, 2009. http://resources.specialolympics.org/official_statement.aspx (accessed April 14, 2017).

The Dish. 2016. "Why Marketers Can't Ignore the Spending Power of the Boomers." *Fulltiltmarketing.net*, March 8. http://www.fulltiltmarketing.net/2016/08/03/why-marketers-cant-ignore-the-spending-power-of-the-boomers (accessed April 28, 2017).

Unity Blott. 2015. "'It's not a prop, it's our legs': Disabled Model Poses in a PVC Corset in Response to Kylie Jenner's 'Hypocritical' Wheelchair Shoot." *Daily Mail*, December 16. http://www.dailymail.co.uk/femail/article-3362220/Disabled-model-poses-PVC-corset-response-Kylie-Jenner-s-hypocritical-wheelchair-shoot.html (accessed April 14, 2017).

US Census Bureau. 2012. "Nearly 1 in 5 People have a Disability in the U.S." *Census Bureau Reports*, June 25. https://www.census.gov/newsroom/releases/archives/miscellaneous/cb12-134.html (accessed April 21, 2017).

US Equal Employment Opportunity Commission. 2008. "Titles I and V of the Americans with Disabilities Act of 1990." http://www.eeoc.gov/laws/statutes/ada.cfm (accessed April 14, 2017).

Wagmeister, Elizabeth. 2016. "Able-Bodied Actors Play 95% of Disabled Characters in Top 10 TV shows, Says New Study." *Variety*, July 13. http://variety.com/2016/tv/news/disabled-actors-television-study-1201813686 (accessed April 14, 2017).

Wilson, Michelle Clare, and Katrina Scior. 2014. "Attitudes Toward Individuals with Disabilities as Measured by the Implicit Association Test: A Literature Review." *Research in Developmental Disabilities* 35: 294–321.

Wolfe, Kathi. 1996. "Ordinary People: Why the Disabled Aren't So Different." *The Humanist* 56(6): 31–34.

Women eNews. 2014. "New York Fashion Week Features First-Ever Wheelchair-Using Model." *Media dis&dat*, February 13. http://media-dis-n-dat.blogspot.com/2014/02/new-york-fashion-week-features-first.html (accessed April 14, 2017).

Woodburn, Danny, and Kristina Kopic. 2016. "The Ruderman White Paper: Employment of Actors with Disabilities in Television." http://www.rudermanfoundation.org/blog/article/the-ruderman-white-paper-employment-of-actors-with-disabilities-in-television (accessed April 14, 2017).

14

Representations of Class

> Sometimes it seems like everyone is trying to get to the top, or struggling not to hit bottom, but we think Frankie and her family will find a lot of love, and a lot of laughs, somewhere in *The Middle*.

The above quote is the tagline from *The Middle* (2009 debut), an ABC sitcom starring Patricia Heaton. Here, "the middle" is referring to a family living in the middle of the country, at a middle-income level. Both parents work, the kids try hard in school, and they have frozen dinners just like millions of families across the country. The notion that a major television network would make a sitcom focused on the day-to-day activities of the average family should come as no surprise. Plenty of television hours are spent watching quirky characters living middle-class lives because these moments are relevant to a vast majority of viewers. On the surface, it may seem that showcasing the lives of the middle class would be simple, but, once they are examined, the factors that make up class distinctions are far more complex. One way to discuss class in America is to look at how it is constructed, reflected, and reinforced in our mass media. After all, it is a safe bet that many of the visions people daydream about come from media images.

Because the topic of class is so multifaceted, this chapter begins by examining how class structures have evolved over the course of time with economic changes in the United States, and the social construction of class. Then it looks at how film, entertainment, news, and advertising media discuss class and aspects related to class status. Finally, a glimpse into how the media shape individual desires to move up in class and materialism will be presented.

Historical Background to Class Representations

Before considering representations of class in the mass media, it is important to briefly reflect on the economic history of the United States, and how certain economic developments influenced class structure. In the United States, society is separated into distinct groups. The upper class is made up of people who are typically in the high-income bracket and who are powerful players in major social and political institutions. They control the production and flow of goods and services. The middle or middle-working class is in the mid-range income bracket, and supply their labor to support the economy. The poor is a class of individuals who are not part of the workforce or who are working at minimum wages that make them fall below the poverty line. Activist and author Bonnie Shoultz

Diversity in US Mass Media, Second Edition. Catherine A. Luther, Carolyn Ringer Lepre, and Naeemah Clark.
© 2018 John Wiley & Sons Inc. Published 2018 by John Wiley & Sons Inc.

(1992) writes that "this class is disproportionately filled with people with disabilities, single mothers, elderly people, and people of color."

In examining the historical development of class structure in the United States, many high school textbooks teach that early American history, especially the seventeenth and eighteenth centuries, was characterized by tremendous economic growth and opportunities for anyone to advance. However, many historians argue that this was not the case, especially for minority groups. Women, American Indians, and African Americans had little opportunities for advancement, and what chances there were for economic growth were open only to white men, and even they often struggled for advancement unless they were born into a family with money or power.

The mid-1880s to the early 1900s marked the Industrial Era, a time of big business. Railroad networks were built, and large corporations were developed. Demand for factory workers was tremendously high during this time period, as the growth of major industries was skyrocketing. In response to poor working conditions and concerns over pay, workers organized and resisted, ultimately forming labor unions. From a class perspective, though many have suggested this was a time reflective of the rags-to-riches mythology, which will be discussed later in this chapter, there is little evidence to support the idea that many laborers or factory workers ever moved from one class to another. In fact, data show that only 2 percent of American industrialists rose from the ranks of the working class.

In the post-World War I climate of the 1920s, the United States became the richest country in the world, with soaring land and real estate prices. It was an age of "conspicuous consumption" and Americans were encouraged to buy, especially with credit, in order to stimulate the economy. Technology played a big part in spurring economic growth. The first public radio station, the Model T Ford, and the first movie with sound were introduced. Not everyone, however, benefited from the 1920s prosperity. Some were denied privileges because of their own social identities. Racism and xenophobia (the fear or hatred of foreigners, and their customs and cultures) experienced an upswing in the aftermath of World War I, and membership in the Ku Klux Klan saw a rise, their primary targets being Roman Catholics, Jews, and African Americans (Holtzman 2000).

In 1929, the stock market crashed, ushering in the Great Depression. Unemployment rose from 3.2 percent in 1929 to 24.9 percent in 1933. The class divide became starker in the subsequent years, with jobs traditionally held by minority groups now being given to Whites. It was not until late 1941, when the United States entered into World War II, that the economic cycle changed once again. Jobs were created to produce war supplies, Americans were asked to sacrifice and ration for the cause, and the end result was massive economic stimulation.

The 1950s and 1960s continued with strong economic growth as the American workforce changed. The number of workers who provided services began to outnumber those who produced goods, and by the mid-1950s, a majority of US workers held white-collar rather than blue-collar jobs. This period is the one that represents the blurring of class distinctions. While some boundaries still existed, primarily because of race and gender, many Americans moved into the booming middle class. There was a migration from cities to single-family homes in the suburbs, as unemployment was low, business was growing, and initiatives like the GI Bill allowed for educational and home-buying opportunities(Friedman and Schwartz 1963). Government spending was high, mostly on social initiatives such as Medicare, as well as on the space program and the military.

However, although spending increased, which did increase prosperity in the short term, by the 1970s the government's failure to raise taxes or find another way to pay for these initiatives led to inflation, which caused federal budget deficits and the stock market to lag, leading to a deep recession that lasted until 1983. A change in economic policy by President Ronald Reagan, who was elected largely on his platform of supply-side economics, moved the United States out of the recession. Supply-side economics espouses the idea that if taxes are cut for the wealthy, who are investors and entrepreneurs, they will take the money that they do not have to pay to the government and either save it, spend it, invest it, and/or produce something with it, which ultimately will benefit the entire economy as it "trickles down" to the rest of the population. During this time period, Reagan also cut taxes and domestic spending programs that had previously been put in place to help lower-income families.

The Clinton administration of the 1990s saw low inflation, low unemployment, strong profits, and a soaring stock market. The housing market was booming. Technological innovations, especially in communication and computer hardware and software, revolutionized the way business and industry operated, and how people worked. This boom eventually led to the dot-com bubble. Ever since the terrorist attacks on the World Trade Center in New York and the US Pentagon in Washington, DC, on September 11, 2001, which many argue was the point in time that marked the onset of a series of economic disasters, the United States' economy has suffered. In 2008, the housing market collapsed, many of the largest banks in the world collapsed, and other companies, including insurance and mortgage giants, required government bailouts. President Barack Obama spent 2009 and 2010 pumping money into the economy in the form of government spending in the hope that it would stimulate the lagging economy and create jobs.

With the fluctuations the United States has experienced in its economy over the past century, changes have also occurred in class structures. While at the beginning of the twentieth century class separation tended to be between the rich and the poor, by the mid-century the middle class emerged as a distinct class. Even though the United States tends to tout its egalitarian ideal, where all individuals are provided with the opportunity to succeed, it appears the disconnect between those who are well off and those who are not continues to grow. Further, class is often discussed in conjunction with other demographic characteristics – for example, Asian Americans earn more than any ethnic group in the country. Also, taking into account age, gender, sexuality, and physical and mental ability as factors that contribute to class status and one's station in life makes sense (US Census Bureau 2014).

To illustrate this point, consider some of the following economic statistics:

- In 2014, 54.4 million men were year-round workers in the United States, whereas 44.4 million women were employed year round. On average men earned $49,149 a year and women earned 79.5 percent of that – $39,054 per year. As of May 2016, there were 158.5 million Americans over the age of 16 in the US labor force (US Bureau of Labor Statistics).
- By 1990, chief executive officers of US manufacturing corporations were paid 120 times higher than the average worker (Holtzman 2000).

Consider the following:

- Limitations due to health (including obesity, heart disease, and other physical impairments) are strongly related to socioeconomic status.
- Research firm Overlooked Opinions found that gay males make more money than their straight counterparts (Wilke 2002). Furthermore, because many gay men are childless, they have more disposable income than any segment in the population.
- Women who work full time earn 22 percent less than men who work full time.

- According to the US Census Bureau, in 1975, 71 percent of 30-year-olds were married, had a child, were not enrolled in school, and lived on their own. In 2016, just 25 percent can say the same.
- A 2008 study from the Urban Institute indicated that more than 30 percent of adults living below the poverty level say they have some disability such as arthritis, mental illness, or alcoholism that keeps them from working (Acs 2008).
- The US Bureau of Labor Statistics reports that in 2015 the unemployment rate of persons with a disability was 10.7 percent.
- Those who are LGBT (lesbian, gay, bisexual, transgender) report workplace discrimination ranging from lack of promotion to dismissal.

It will come as no surprise, then, that race, ethnicity, disability, gender, and sexuality all contribute to one's class status as racism, sexism, bigotry, discrimination, and affirmative action all affect income and earning potential and, as a result, class.

The problems related to the financial disparities between the classes are also compounded by the social connotations that are connected with each class. Although the word "class" is often simply associated with income level, it is actually a more complex concept. It envelops people's understanding of themselves, of others, and how they belong to the world. In describing the complexities of class, research scholar Donna Langston (1995) writes:

> Class is about money and it is about more than money. As a result of the class you are born into and raised in, class is your understanding of the world and where you fit in, it's composed of ideas, behavior, attitudes, values, and language; class is how you think, feel, act, look, dress, talk, move, walk; class is what stores you shop at, restaurants you eat in; class is the schools you attend, the education you attain; class is the very jobs you will work at throughout your adult life.

Critical scholars define class more in terms of ownership, power, and control. Using the term "classism," they view it as an institutionally imposed belief system privileging those who have money and power while oppressing those who do not (Holtzman 2000).

It is within this realm of understanding class as a social construction that we see the role of mass media. While someone of a different ethnicity or with a physical impairment may be seen at the mall or in school or college, interaction with people who are of a different socioeconomic status from one's own is rare. Neighborhoods, towns, and communities are generally organized (segregated) on a socioeconomic basis. Therefore, media representations of the poor, the wealthy, and those in between play a major role in forming opinions, showing viewers who these people are and, as a result, what to think about them. These representations help to paint mental pictures and also reinforce these images through entertainment, news, and advertising media. Essentially, the media can cultivate or promote impressions about members of each of the classes.

Class in Film

At the end of the holiday classic *It's a Wonderful Life* (1946), the film's hero, George Bailey (played by James Stewart), tearfully realizes that although he is in financial ruin, the love and support of his family and friends is the true measure of his value. The running theme throughout the film is that good, honest middle-class values will always win over the greed of the wealthy and powerful. Class status is a common story thread in films. A variety of representations emerge when considering how class appears on the silver screen. Whether it's a rags-to-riches tale, a weepy story of a poor family, or a story that shows the tragic downfall of a wealthy tycoon, Hollywood embraces stories of class.

The rags-to-riches archetype is one that is particularly common, and intrinsic to this storytelling form is the concept of the American Dream. American historian James Truslow Adams coined the phrase in 1931, and writes of it as being:

> that dream of a land in which life should be better and richer and fuller for everyone, with opportunity for each according to ability or achievement … It is not a dream of motor cars and high wages merely, but a dream of social order in which each man and each woman shall be able to attain to the fullest stature of which they are innately capable, and be recognized by others for what they are, regardless of the fortuitous circumstances of birth or position. (Adams 1931: 404)

This original theme was broader in scope than just the financial success story that most individuals now associate with the American Dream.

The rags-to-riches storyline teaches that individuals have limitless potential and endless possibilities for success as long as they believe in four main things:

- that everyone, regardless of race, gender, religion, or class, may always pursue their dream and can always start over;
- that one can reasonably expect success;
- that success is a result of individual traits and that actions are always under one's own control;
- that success is associated with virtue, merit, and strenuous effort. (Hochschild 1996)

Researchers argue that the problem with the American Dream is that, for many, it is simply a myth. Barriers to success exist, especially for certain minority groups or members of the lower classes that no amount of hard work or virtuous behavior can overcome. While there are times when individuals have succeeded, there are most certainly countless other times when class barriers have proved to be impermeable. For some, the danger of repeated portrayals of the rags-to-riches story and the American Dream theme in film is that they serve to perpetuate stereotypes about the lower classes. For instance, these types of movies might reinforce the idea that, but for a bit more hard work and a little more effort, the poor could take care of themselves, leading citizens to vote against social initiatives. The portrayals might also impact on the self-esteem of the working or lower class individuals viewing the films who find themselves trapped in a certain job or situation, unable to move.

Many movies have explored the theme of the American Dream, including *Gone with the Wind* (1939), *Rocky* (1976), *The Pursuit of Happyness* (2006), and *Joy* (2015). *Gone with the Wind* illustrates many of the main principles of success according to the American Dream, such as that hard work (and a bit of manipulating) will win out, starting over is always possible, and that individuals are in control of their own destiny. In one scene, the film's protagonist, Scarlett O'Hara (played by Vivien Leigh), after finding her estate, Tara, left barren by the Yankee army, proclaims her intent to start again, no matter what it takes. Standing in a field with her hands reaching up to the heavens, Scarlett swears: "As God is my witness, I will never be hungry again!" Several scenes later, she finds herself charming Rhett Butler and her sister's financially secure beau while wearing a reconfigured curtain for a dress. In the case of Scarlett, financial security comes with a bit of humility and a fair dose of charm. Hard work coupled with other talents were the ticket to success for Sylvester Stallone's famous boxer Rocky Balboa, Will Smith's hopeful stockbroker Chris Garber, and Jennifer Lawrence's Joy Mangano who started building a fortune selling mops on television.

Another common film storyline follows the lead character as he loses a fortune, survives with nothing, and then rebuilds class status. This also is seen as building character through hard work. Some films, including the classics *Baby Face* (1933) and *Citizen Kane* (1941), feature lead characters who started out poor but were willing to do anything, including sacrificing family and virtue, to become wildly successful.

This variation on the American Dream concept asks audiences to consider whether, for the main characters, trading their rags for riches was worth it. These rags-to-riches films were precursors to movies like *Wall Street* (1987) with its famous line "Greed is good." This film was made during a time in the mid-1980s when corporate raiding and hostile takeovers of companies to either liquidate or downsize them was commonplace. The main character, Bud Fox (played by Charlie Sheen), is a junior Wall Street stockbroker, raised by a blue-collar father who works as a maintenance chief for a small airline. Bud wants to get ahead as quickly as possible, and at the beginning of the film it is clear that, for Bud, success means making a lot of money and enjoying all the perks that come with it. He begins working with Gordon Gekko (played by Michael Douglas), a ruthless and greedy corporate raider. Initially, Bud is willing to do anything he can to try and impress Gordon, including passing on inside information about stocks. However, the more Bud works with Gordon, the more the latter's unscrupulous techniques cause problems for Bud, who ultimately finds that the values taught to him by his father about honesty and hard work are more important than financial success. In a film similar in tone, Leonardo DiCaprio played real-life stockbroker Jordan Belfort in 2013's *The Wolf of Wall Street*. Belfort was so consumed with the trappings of wealth – including drugs and women – that he defrauded his investors. His comeuppance for his avarice was a 22-month-long prison stay.

Another class status representation that occurs frequently in film is that of cross-class romance and/or a man saving the poor woman from a life of hardship (Box 14.1). Cross-class romance films have captivated audiences for many years. For instance, *Sabrina*, first released in 1954 and then remade in 1995, followed the love story of wealthy businessman Linus Larrabee and Sabrina Fairchild, the daughter of the Larrabee family chauffeur. In the 1997 blockbuster *Titanic*, the love story of the upper-class Rose DeWitt Bukater (played by Kate Winslet), engaged to a wealthy man whom she does not love but feels obligated to marry as her family is in need of money, and Jack Dawson (played by Leonardo DiCaprio), a poor artist who has won his steerage ticket on the doomed ship in a poker game, is a main focus. Other class issues were explored in the film, such as the fact that the few lifeboats on board the *Titanic* were used for the upper-class passengers, leaving the underprivileged passengers to perish.

In other films, such as *My Fair Lady* (1964), *Pretty Woman* (1990), *Maid in Manhattan* (2002), and *Dreamgirls* (2006), women are featured (in some cases, literally) on the streets in search of a lifestyle change. In these cases, the women were not only rescued by the males, but their ways of dressing, speech, and social graces were drastically retooled to be accepted by the upper class. In a reversal of the story, *Overboard* (1987) stars Goldie Hawn as Joanna Stayton, a wealthy amnesiac who is tricked by a lower class handyman, Dean Proffitt (played by Kurt Russell), into believing that she is his wife and mother of his brood of boys. After seeing her downtrodden living conditions and unending list of chores, Hawn's character, whom Dean dubs "Annie," is unsettled and says, "I don't belong here. I feel it. Don't you think I feel it? I can't do any of these

---

Box 14.1 Class crossing in the movies of John Hughes

If there has been one filmmaker who has taught Americans more about class stratification than any other, it is John Hughes. Hughes made movies in the 1980s full of teen angst, which told the stories of high school students struggling to find their place in the world. All the while, they are plagued with depression-causing hormones, families, and social statuses. Let us consider three of the films that introduced Generation X to class warfare.

Pretty in Pink (1986): Quirky teen girl Andi Walsh (played by Hughes muse Molly Ringwald) lives with her dad in a small house on the blue-collar side of town. Her best friend, Duckie (played by Jon Cryer), is a whimsical working-class kid who has fallen in love with her. Unfortunately, Andi does not return his affections as she is more interested in BMW-driving Blaine (played by Andrew McCarthy). Blaine is a rich, soft-hearted kid who asks Andi out even though his derisive friends caution him against the class differences, as Duckie does with Andi. In the end, the star-crossed lovers unite, despite all warnings, giving hope to every "wrong-side-of-the-tracks" girl who falls for a boy who drives a fancy car.

Some Kind of Wonderful (1987): This film has a similar tone to *Pretty in Pink*, but the roles are reversed. This time, Eric Stoltz plays Keith, a lower-middle-class boy who is in love with Amanda (played by Lea Thompson). Amanda's boyfriend treats her poorly, but is rich and buys her nice presents. Keith's best friend, Watts (played by Mary Stuart Masterson), is in love with him, but does all she can to help Keith have a perfect night with Amanda even though he has no money. In another twist from *Pretty in Pink*, Keith comes to realize that Watts is the perfect girl for him and, in this case, people from the same economic class find love.

The Breakfast Club (1985): Hughes's most famous film, *The Breakfast Club*, set the standard for teen films in the 1980s (Figure 14.1). Five students of different class standings must sit in the school's library

Figure 14.1 Teens trying to break out of Saturday detention in *The Breakfast Club* (1985). Screenshot.

(Continued)

Box 14.1   (Continued)

---

to serve weekend detention for offenses they committed earlier in the week, with the assignment being a 1,000-word essay on who they think they are. Claire Standish (played by Molly Ringwald), an upper-class redhead who eats sushi for lunch, received her detention for skipping school for an impromptu shopping trip. Middle-class Brian Johnson (played by Anthony Michael Hall) is dropped off for his detention in his mom's faded red Plymouth Reliant. His crime? He carried a gun to school with the intent of killing himself because his woodshop project was a failure. The failing grade was astronomical for a kid who has been raised to work hard and be a good boy. Additionally, the film features working-class bully John Bender (played by Judd Nelson), working-class wrestler Andrew Clark (played by Emilio Estevez), and upper-middle-class pathological liar Allison Reynolds (played by Ally Sheedy). By the end of the eight hours in the library, the kids have discovered things about each other and themselves, and viewers are reassured that class and stereotypes do not matter as much as friendship does. The film concludes with Brian's voice-over as he reads the essay he composed for the group that says: "You see us as you want to see us … in the simplest terms and the most convenient definitions. You see us as a brain, an athlete, a basket case, a princess, and a criminal … That's the way we saw each other at 7 o'clock this morning. We were brainwashed. But what we found out is that each one of us is a brain, and an athlete, and a basket case, a princess, and a criminal."

The 2010 Academy Awards ceremony honored John Hughes after his August 2009 death. The stars of his films spoke of his contributions to cinema and his creation of a genre where teenagers had strong voices and compelling stories that provided a glimpse into real life.

Are there films today that echo these themes for the Millennials and beyond?

---

vile things and I wouldn't want to. Oh, my life is like death." Although the scene is played for humor, it ultimately reflects the fact that being poor is never a goal, even though it is a fact of life for millions of families. Joanna ends up getting her memory back, and sympathizing with people she had previously written off as completely worthless. Her attitude has changed, and instead of wanting her old idle-rich life back, she is shown wishing for herself a more fulfilling life as a working-class wife and mother. Of course, that is not the Hollywood way, to leave the heroes stuck in poverty at a film's conclusion. Audiences are led to believe that she is about to give it all up for Dean at the movie's dramatic end. As she leaves her snobbish husband for the love of the poor man, however, Dean says to her, "I can't believe you gave all that up just for me." Joanna replies, "I didn't. The truth of the matter is it's all mine. The boat, the money, everything is all mine."

Images of the poor are not unheard of in film, but they are generally not "feel good" stories. The 2009 sleeper hit *Precious: Based on the Novel "Push" by Sapphire* was one film that focused on the harshest realities of being poor and uneducated. As already discussed, race and gender are frequently elements that influence class. In the case of Precious, an illiterate, African American teenage girl, her gender and race are strong determinants of her lot in life. The inconvenience of unwanted pregnancies, coupled with her living in environments that treat women of color as if they were invisible, serve to keep her without many options. By the end of the film, it is clear that while her life may improve, she will still remain poor. Despite this, she has some moments of joy at the end of the film and that creates her happy ending.

Straight Outta Compton (2015) uses the real-life struggles of the African American men that formed iconic rap group N.W.A. The celebrated biopic was lauded for its honest depiction of the positive and negative trappings that can come when money propels young men into a world that they had never known before. Where N.W.A members Dr. Dre and Ice Cube have become media moguls, member Eazy-E died of complications from AIDS, which he believed he contracted through promiscuous behaviors.

Stories of the poor can be extremely gripping, but careful storytelling can make the life of average middle-class people compelling as well. Filmic images of life in middle-class suburbia have entertained audiences for years. Frequently, these movies show life in the suburbs as ranging from mundane to insane. For example, *The Truman Show* (1995) creates a perfect middle-class community where the simple life of one of the residents is transmitted to the outside world, unbeknownst to him. His attempt to rebel and escape his cookie-cutter life fascinates the viewing audience – in the film and in the theaters. Similarly, *Edward Scissorhands* (1990), a film featuring a gardening oddity who fashions topiary using the blades he has for fingers, shakes up the otherwise uninspiring life of a middle-class neighborhood. Characters in both movies long to flee the banality of the pastel homes and manicured lawns in their neighborhoods by forcing a shift in their communities. Escape tends to be essential in the stories of suburbia because of the human desire to be an individual. The "sameness" that is encouraged by subdivisions is rejected in films – and often in real life.

An extreme form of flight in films that challenge the middle class has used abnormal sexuality and violence as deviant behaviors that soothe the characters' angst. In the Oscar-winning film *American Beauty* (1999), Lester Burnham (played by Kevin Spacey), who has become bored with his superficially ordered middle-class community, becomes so obsessed with his teenage daughter's friend that he dreams about her. John Waters' *Serial Mom* (1994) is about a suburban housewife who turns to a life of crime to add some zest to her days. This mom (played by Kathleen Turner) becomes a hero to the audiences. While it may appear that these films are poking fun at middle-class life, they are frequently satirical indictments of the homogeneity and static nature of suburban existence. Such indictments of middle-class life are also seen in television programs.

Class in Entertainment Television

When considering class and entertainment, there is an influential view that holds that there is high culture for those with power and taste (the upper class) and low culture for those who have none (the middle and lower class). If this notion, called *cultural capital*, were applied to television, it could be assumed that members of different classes are drawn to different types of programs (Bourdieu 1980). For example, wealthier audiences would be attracted to opera on the Ovation cable network, while lower class audiences would relish the reality television program *Married at First Sight* (2014 debut) on FYI. However, television may be an equalizer for the classes. PBS offers programs to those who may not be able to attend a ballet for geographic or economic reasons. Conversely, a wealthy person may enjoy the competitive nature of *Survivor* (2000 debut). So, as television portrayals of class are discussed, it is important to keep in mind that these programs appeal to people from all walks of life and may provide a glimpse (no matter how distorted) into how the other half lives.

History shows that entertainment television programs have tended to reflect trends in society and to have characters that viewers could identify with and others whom they could aspire to be. One of the best representations of the American Dream ideal on television can be found in *The Beverly Hillbillies* (1962–1971). This program introduces the Clampetts as a poor family living in the mountains who find oil on their land and become wealthy overnight. After striking it rich, they move – in a large jalopy of a pickup truck – to a luxurious mansion in Beverly Hills, California. The family interacts with the fancy and uptight Beverly Hills residents, making it obvious that there are vast differences between the poor Clampetts and their neighbors.

In the 1970s, blue-collar characters, as well as those in the middle class, were popular. Shows such as *Happy Days* (1974–1984), *Laverne and Shirley* (1976–1983), and *Taxi* (1978–1983) showed comfortable, modest homes, and characters who dreamed of wealth and success. In the 1980s, the number of working-class characters diminished, and the middle class was overshadowed by portrayals of the upper class and the wealthy. Millionaires were commonly depicted on daytime soaps and prime-time dramas. Programs such as *Miami Vice* (1984–1990) and *Moonlighting* (1985–1989) regularly depicted flashy cars, glamorous wardrobes, and mansions. Sitcoms such as *Family Ties* (1982–1989), *The Cosby Show* (1984–1992), and *Growing Pains* (1985–1992) depicted households in which both parents worked in white-collar jobs and discussions of economic issues or problems rarely surfaced. Some programs that did depict working-class characters did so as part of a plot that had the working class interacting with an upper-class or an upper-middle-class character, such as in *Who's the Boss?* (1984–1992), *Mr. Belvedere* (1985–1990), and *Diff'rent Strokes* (1978–1986). By the end of the 1980s, blue-collar characters were making a comeback, as some viewers seemed to desire programs that better reflected themselves. *Roseanne* (1988–1997), *Married … With Children* (1987–1997), and *The Simpsons* (1989 debut) showed characters who lived on budgets, struggled with bills, and worked hard to make ends meet. Other prime-time programs, such as *Frasier* (1993–2004) and *The Nanny* (1993–1999), continued to highlight the upper and upper middle class, who flourished and thrived, just as many did in society.

Generally, a perusal of current television listings illustrates that entertainment programs tend to feature the middle class and upper middle class in programs. The characters in *The Office* (2005–2013), *Reba* (2001–2007), *How I Met your Mother* (2005–2014), and *Fresh Off the Boat* (2015 debut) have lives that are considered to be more relatable to the average viewer. Even though the situations they find themselves in can be unbelievably heartrending or ridiculous, these characters have homes, clothes, and cars like the ones found in most neighborhoods. This image of the middle class can be mundane, but it is comfortable for viewers to see situations that could happen to them. The irony that wealthy Hollywood producers generate billions of dollars in profits a year trying to reflect the lives of the middle class or the poor for mass audiences should not be lost on the reader. Selling or the commodification of other cultures is commonplace in the world of media. When a culture is sold it is usually done in a stereotypical and one-dimensional way.

The small screen rarely celebrates the lives of the poor. Programs such as A&E's *Hoarders* (2009 debut) or ABC's *Extreme Makeover: Home Edition* (2003–2012) will frequently tell the real-life stories of those who have financial hardships, but the programs use their poverty as a point of fascination. For example, the 2010 season finale of *Hoarders* featured an elderly woman who, because of limited funds, chooses to live in a homeless shelter rather than pay to repair her home that has collapsed under the weight of the clutter she has been amassing for decades. For the audience it might be unfathomable that a person would choose to live this way, but the constraints of mental illness coupled with a lack of income created this barely credible story.

A problematic subcategory of lower class families that appears on television is that of "poor Whites" who have been humorously and pejoratively categorized as "white trash" in television programs. *Married with Children* (1987–1997), *Blue Collar TV* (2004–2006), *Mom* (2013 debut), and virtually every episode of the *Jerry Springer Show* (1991 debut) feature this lower class as a group to be made fun of and scorned. Studies of poor Whites tend to be cultural/critical assessments rather than empirical studies of images of people of European descent (Bérubé and Bérubé 1996). Often these studies find that the media depictions are rife with images of poor health and hygiene, criminal activity, and violence. The women are disheveled and the men are frequently useless and to blame for the plight of their families.

Throughout TV history, televised images of the lives of working-class white people (although members of the working class can be any race) have run the gamut between the pitiful and the proud. Fictional characters such as Jackie Gleason's iconic Ralph Kramden drove a bus on *The Honeymooners* (1955–1956); *The Simpsons'* (1989 debut) Homer is a laborer at a chemical plant; Dan Conner worked as a mechanic and construction worker while his wife was a waitress and factory worker over the run of *Roseanne* (1988–1997). The televised working-class female has been treated with some respect. Roseanne in the *Roseanne* show was the leader of her family. Programs such as *Ugly Betty* (2006–2010) showcase these downtrodden women as heroes. Conversely, working-class men are frequently written to be dimwitted. "Dimwitted" describes virtually any man on the Seth MacFarlane animated program *Family Guy* (1999 debut).

Reality television does provide the working-class male with some purpose. *American Chopper* (2003 debut), a program that focuses on the skilled laborer who reconstructs beloved motorcycles, glamorizes the craft and the lifestyle at a time when the status of the working-class male has been diminished. In this case, the program makes victorious artisans out of the blue-collar worker (Carroll 2008). Similarly, programs such as *Extreme Makeover: Home Edition* (2003–2012) depict carpenters and construction workers as life-changing miracle workers.

A more unique take on the working class is provided in the NBC sitcom *Superstore* (2015 debut). Unlike shows in the past that have relied on common working-class tropes and featured mainly white casts, *Superstore* presents individuals from diverse backgrounds and racial/ethnic makeups employed at a supersized retail megastore. Among the characters are Jonah (played by Ben Feldman), a young business school dropout who is convinced he really doesn't belong at the store; Garrett (played by Colton Dunn), paralyzed from the waist down, who works from his wheelchair as the store's PA announcer and often pulls pranks on his fellow employees out of boredom; Cheyenne (played by Nicole Bloom), a high school dropout who has a baby out of wedlock during the show's first season. Actress America Ferrera plays Amy, a single, working mom who had to give up college due to her pregnancy and who struggles to find childcare for her child on a tight budget. Amy, the central character of the show, is always leading efforts to rally the employees together to fight workplace injustices. In one of the show's episodes, which serves as commentary on big business, Cheyenne goes into labor but refuses to leave the store; she continues to work because the superstore does not provide paid maternity leave.

Television frequently displays wealth and the upper-middle-class lifestyle as something to seek, display, and flaunt. For example, NBC's *The Apprentice* (2004 debut), MTV's *My Super Sweet 16* (2005 debut), and Bravo's *Real Housewives* (2006 debut) series all feature Americans who strive for or have extreme wealth. The media's emphasis on financial success is nothing new. Sociologist Diana Kendall conducted a framing analysis of all genres of media from the 1850s until modern times and found that the media have long created a "hedonistic" fever for material goods and wealth (Kendall 2005) (Box 14.2). In her study, television's portrayal of upper-class Americans shows them as being altruistic and charitable, whereas the poor are often faceless statistics. Although poor children are treated with sympathy by the media, their parents are depicted as violating the tenets of the American Dream.

Box 14.2 Materialism and the media

What is unique to this chapter of the book is that, unlike race/ethnicity, gender, and other topics in this text, class is widely considered an area in one's life that can be changed. In 2005, a *New York Times* poll found that 75 percent of respondents thought they had a greater chance of moving to a higher social class than had been the case in 1975 (Correspondents of *The New York Times* 2005). In other words, Americans believe that their opportunities for success are steadily increasing. After all, the United States is based on meritocracy; if you are bright and work hard, it is possible to improve one's class standing. Right? Aspiring to the trappings and niceties of higher classes is a part of the American Dream. The media certainly play a role in creating that dream. The ease with which one can become a world-famous recording artist, model, or chef, complete with a six-figure salary and new car (made possible by the sponsor of a television program), adds to the notion that rising above your class status is possible – and relatively fast and easy.

A desire to attain a higher status is, in part, tied to the materialism created through media consumption. While other factors certainly play a role in cultivating materialism, commercial media are designed to create some level of materialism because the industry is reliant on the success of advertising to pay the bills. Television networks, newspapers, magazines, and cable outlets sell audiences to advertisers who are free to lay out their wares to these consumers. The purpose of advertising is to make a product or service desirable to the viewer – whether or not they can afford it. Thus, consumer materialism is the ultimate goal of commercial media. Although the research has been somewhat conflicting, there is an indication that heavier viewers of television (see cultivation theory in Chapter 2) tend to be more materialistic than light viewers (Shrum, Burroughs, and Rindfleisch 2005).

Communication scholars Kara Chan and Gerard Prendergast (2007) define materialism as "a set of attitudes which regard possessions as symbols of success where possessions occupy a central part of life and which include holding the belief that more possessions lead to more happiness."

Does this definition apply to you in any way? Think about the programs you watch and the publications you read. How do they contribute to your visions of the future? Of course, different people view the trappings of the higher classes differently. If you are a regular reader of *Vogue* you may think having the ability to buy a pair of Jimmy Choo shoes whenever you would like as a sign of being upper class. A recent immigrant may aspire to own a home like the ones on the average sitcom; a teenage boy who is a fan of hip-hop may see owning a car like one from a music video as a symbol of success.

The American Dream of having a beautifully appointed home is emphasized daily through cable television channels such as Home and Garden Television and Fine Living. One of HGTV's most popular programs, *House Hunters International* (2006 debut), frequently will showcase a couple buying their "home away from home" abroad. In one episode, a couple under the age of 40 seeks a second home in Greece. Their $350,000 budget can buy them a hilltop home with a breathtaking view of the Greek isles and a crystal blue swimming pool. This type of fare gives viewers the impression that lives with freshly laundered linens and manicured lawns are within grasp. Nowhere is this impression more profound than in the content from Martha Stewart's Omnimedia. Stewart has built an empire on entertaining and homemaking designed to impress friends and neighbors. Female fans of the domestic maven find that the programs generated fantasies of a celebrated upper-class existence where domesticity could create the appearance of upward mobility (Mason and Meyers 2001). In a February 2010 episode of her syndicated daytime television program, Stewart taught her audience how to make lobster ravioli and purchase one-of-a-kind modern furniture. Surely, these helpful hints are not realistic for those who are struggling to pay for their weekly prescriptions or rent. The fantasy is propelled further by Stewart making her products available at discount stores such as Kmart. Other celebrities promoting lifestyle brands that are, for most, difficult to attain are movie star Gwyneth Paltrow (GOOP), Reese Witherspoon (Draper James), and *Suits* actor Megan Markle (The Tig). The lifestyles they spotlight feature beaches, bike rides, and recipes with expensive ingredients. Still, *anyone* can live a refined life … right?

Representations of Class in the News

In 1936, Dorothea Lange's iconic image "Migrant Mother" was published in the newspaper the *San Francisco News* (Figure 14.2). The black and white photograph of 32-year-old Florence Owens Thompson with her children starving in a frozen pea field alerted readers to the plight of the migrant worker during the Depression.

Figure 14.2 Dorothea Lange's iconic photo "Migrant Mother," taken of Florence Owens Thompson and her children in 1936. Thompson, 32, was looking for work picking peas when the photo was taken.

A person living in a comfortable suburb may only have access to those living in poverty through the news stories and photographs published in newspapers or magazines. News photographs are particularly powerful because these images are what linger in the mind of the audience (Entman 1990). The people in the pictures become the images associated with a circumstance. Whether these photos are images of vulnerable people waiting for their lives to change or of proud, hardworking Americans, they are frequently one-dimensional figures. Printed images also are problematic in that these images are not accompanied by information about the context or back-story that led to the poverty or hardship.

In her research of how the poor are depicted, sociologist Diana Kendall (2005) has found that newspapers repeatedly use frames to tell the stories of the poor and homeless. The poor are often statistics and not real people. They are also often framed as deviant, needy members of society. Newspaper stories of the homeless sleeping on park benches are often used when discussing a story dealing with this population. Also, if a homeless person commits a crime, the designation "homeless" comes before the name of the perpetrator. By announcing the perpetrator's homeless status, the newspaper is generating fear of all of those who are homeless, not just the few who commit crime.

Large media corporations have been accused of stereotyping the poor while telling their stories. Single women who struggle financially and receive government assistance have been depicted as "welfare queens." These women are depicted as ignorant, lazy, and sexually promiscuous with many children (Bullock, Wyche, and Williams 2001). African Americans have been disproportionately depicted as being poor in the news media (Clawson and Trice 2000). Again, stereotypes of laziness and a lack of ambition and motivation persist. The coverage of poor African Americans was illuminated in the days after Hurricane Katrina. In a study of images in four newspapers (*New York Times*, *Wall Street Journal*, *USA Today*, and *Washington Post*), white individuals were portrayed in active roles such as residents preparing for the storm, soldiers, or relief workers (Kahle, Yu, and Whiteside 2007). African Americans were rarely shown as preparing for the storm or protecting their positions; instead, they were depicted as being more passive than their white counterparts (i.e., receivers of assistance, evacuees).

Perhaps more representative of the depiction of class, Whites were shown returning to their homes and starting over. In these cases, the images reinforced the perception of African Americans as being poor, hapless, and incapable of taking care of themselves. The editorial copy that accompanied many of these images referred to those fleeing New Orleans as "refugees," a term frequently applied to people who are exiled, migrants, or immigrants. To refer to the African American residents of New Orleans wading through the waters of their own city as refugees relegates them to the status of an unwanted "Other" that is fleeing one land in hopes of being accepted by another. In this case, the word had the power to act as a second displacement for the survivors of Hurricane Katrina (Edgerly 2007).

Newspapers are uniquely positioned to discuss matters relating to class, and often have "local" sections that are tailored for specific neighborhoods or sides of town. Ultimately, these special sections are designed to cover and speak to residents of those areas as a means to address what is most relevant to those communities. Of course, journalists are not always products of the communities or members of the classes that they cover. Many reporters with bylines and those who sit behind news desks often do not have much in common with most Americans who struggle to pay bills. Although they can be out of touch with certain communities, some newspapers conduct civic journalism activities such as health screenings and town hall meetings designed to help members of the communities.

In the past 20 years, some newspapers have taken on an advocacy role in an effort to assist the poor in other civic journalistic activities. In these cases, the newspaper serves a dual purpose: a source for disseminating information and an active, contributing member of a community. Although this approach has been condemned for taking newspapers away from their role as objective reporters of society, civic journalism has shed a light on societal ills. For example, ethnic newspapers have reported on environmental racism where harmful factories or landfills were placed in areas where the poor lived (Heinz 2005). In these cases, the poor (who are often racial and ethnic minorities) are given access to the media in a new way – more friend than foe. As another case in point, on March 15, 2010, *African-American News and Issues*, an online newspaper, featured a story focusing on a protest march where African Americans demanded that the federal government create more jobs in the tough economic times of the early twenty-first century. The paper was positioned as a voice for groups that are frequently ignored – the poor and people of color:

> On Aug. 28, 1963, Dr. Martin Luther King, Jr. delivered the famous, "I Have a Dream" speech at the National Mall of Washington, D.C. to over 200,000 fed up African Americans. ... Almost 50 years later, African Americans find themselves in as economically disparate [*sic*] a situation as ever ... Yet, politicians, including the nation's first Black president, have consistently failed to address the disparity, or it is dismissed as the Black man's inability to get a job due to lack of education or criminal history. ("Enough is Enough" 2010)

The frank nature of the reporting may be startling to some, but, again, these types of newspapers reflect the stark feelings of those who are struggling financially.

Those suffering extreme poverty across the country also use the print media as a way of reclaiming some of their economic and social power. The North American Street Newspapers Association is dedicated to printing stories related to poverty and homelessness. These newspapers are distributed by members of the homeless population in large cities in the United States and Canada. Not only do these newspapers give homeless citizens an opportunity to work and earn money, but the papers also provide a space for the most invisible members of our country to publish their writing and artwork. These newspapers, including Puget Sound's *Real Change* and Boston's *Spare Change*, distribute some 300,000 newspapers each month. Issues of these papers may be tough to come by for those not from these areas, but *Spare Change* has a blog featuring stories about social justice, the arts, and health.

In an effort to reach their typical audience or the "average American," newspapers cover middle-class issues in each edition. Stories about school board meetings, grocery store openings, and everyday topics related to the average person's life are common. There are times, however, when these publications highlight the needs of this community. Often the coverage depicts the middle class as being the norm and the other classes as the extremes that the middle is fighting against. For example, a *Seattle Times* article of February 21, 2008 warned that "America's middle class is losing ground" to an ever more distant wealthy class and a lower class that is plucking families from the ranks of the middle class (Ervin 2008). The word "crisis" appears frequently in these stories to accentuate the nature of the situations. For example: "The middle class feels the insurance crisis," "The middle-class cocaine crisis is now official," and "Government must stop middle-class debt crisis" are some eye-catching headlines seen recently. They also indicate that the newspapers acknowledge that their readership considers itself middle class and, as such, will be engaged by such important information.

In 2008, the US economy started to show signs of trouble as banks began losing money, mortgages became hard to come by, and the stock market plunged, which wreaked havoc on people's retirement funds. In newspaper accounts related to this recession, the middle class was painted as "David" to the upper-class "Goliath." The wealthy were often depicted as preying on the middle class or the poor for profit. Headlines about "Main Street versus Wall Street" were plentiful. Although many wealthy people lost significant funds, every story needs a villain. In this case, it was frequently wealthy stockbrokers and CEOs. In one case, Bernie Madoff, a financier who bilked people from all walks of life and charitable organizations out of billions of dollars, became the public face of the rich taking advantage of others. Stories exposing his Ponzi scheme, his trial, imprisonment, and sale of his lavish homes and belongings seem to be run-of-the-mill investigative journalism. These stories, however, are cathartic for the middle- and lower class Americans struggling to make ends meet. In other words, seeing Madoff's ill-gotten gains taken away gave onlookers a sigh of relief and a sense of justice being done.

Television news has been especially criticized for treating the poor as a nameless group without explaining the root causes of poverty when telling their stories (Bullock, Wyche, and Williams 2001). Incomplete and uneven news media coverage of those who are suffering can influence the help that group receives. America's homeless population is one such group. In a study of 13 years of coverage of the homeless on network news programming, political scientist Todd Shields concluded that the networks rarely discussed what *causes* homelessness. Instead, they virtually ignored the homeless problem until an effort such as a charity event (i.e., 1984's Hands Across America) or winter came around, enabling them to broadcast a celebration of the people who "helped" the homeless. When the homeless were depicted, they were seen as nameless deviants, thus reinforcing the divide between "us" and "them" (Shields 2001).

The news media tend to depict members of the working class as a bit more multidimensional than the poor. For example, an examination of print and electronic news coverage of the 2002 Sago mine disaster found that the mythic themes of patriotism and family were tied to the coal miners. The miners were depicted as loving, hardworking fathers and their wives as doting and traditional. The miners worked in the dangerous underground conditions to provide America's energy in a sign of patriotism (Kitch 2007).

On the flip side of the noble blue-collar worker depiction is the television news long shot of a handcuffed former CEO walking from a courthouse escorted by a uniformed officer. In recent years, the millionaire "perp walk" has become a staple of the cable news networks. Disgraced executives such as Enron's Ken Lay and the aforementioned Madoff were trailed by camera crews once news of their financial misdeeds became public. When Madoff's $7 million luxury apartment went on the market, television morning news programs took viewers on a room-by-room tour of the home and the expensive décor and furniture that filled those rooms. Again, these televised images allow those who have not been so financially fortunate to delight in everything the rich guy has lost.

Concluding Remarks

Cable channels, magazines, and sections in the newspaper are devoted to the wealthy, Wall Street, and big business; there are few counterparts for poor or working-class America. Open discussion about class disparities in a society that emphasizes wealth and success is tricky because covering the poor and failing parts of America is uncomfortable. Reporter Mary Ellen Schoonmaker considered this dilemma, saying that reporters are responsible for "calling attention to serious public problems that have been ignored" and should talk about those who are providing solutions for those who are poor (Schoonmaker 2008).

Although the distance between those with access to relatively pricey technology (a digital divide) and those without persists, federal money has been put into purchasing computers, providing Internet access, and training teachers in schools to bridge the distance.

As people become more tech-savvy, the Internet, because of its low cost of production, can become a viable venue for the poor. Members of a particular group or audience can play an active role in collecting, analyzing, and disseminating news and information, and therefore can actively work to represent a particular perspective. This practice is called "citizen journalism"; it encourages media consumers to contribute to the public discourse in ways never known before the Internet. For example, in February of 2009, ABC network news anchor Diane Sawyer reported on Appalachian families living in poverty. The *20/20* documentary found that these communities faced problems such as poor health, lack of higher education, and drug use. Among the sites that invited viewer comments about the program was Huffingtonpost.com. One user wrote, "I'm one of these people from Kentucky … I hate it when people who don't really know the mountain people judge them. (There's) nothing wrong with hard work and honesty." Another user noted, "I, too, have once known that kind of poor. There is a stark difference between mountain poor and city poor. First, mountain poor is, or was until now, hidden poor." Clearly, in this case, these television viewers turned to the Internet as a means of expressing their personal opinions about the depiction of this community.

Reflection Questions and Thoughts to Consider

1. Is there any difference in the way the media treat the poor of different races? For example, are poor Hispanic fathers depicted differently than poor white fathers on television? Do you see a difference in the way working-class fathers of different races are treated?

2. Are the ethical standards different when publishing images of the poor in tragic situations versus images of the wealthy in similar situations?

3. Consider how often you see images of members of different classes interacting in film or entertainment television. How do these interactions usually take place? Now consider images of members of different classes interacting in the press. What kinds of examples can you find?

4. On the reality television program *The Voice* (2011 debut), at the beginning of each season tryouts for the show air. During these tryouts, certain contestants are singled out for profile features to highlight particularly dramatic stories. A number of these profiles feature those of lower classes and those who are poor, and the stories focus on the theme that if only they can get a chance to be on the show, they could rise up out of their terrible situations. Do you think that singling these people out is a violation of their privacy and dignity or do you think there is nothing wrong with it?

References

Acs, Gregory. 2008. "Poverty in the United States, 2008." Urban Institute, September 10. http://www.urban.org/research/publication/poverty-united-states-2008 (accessed April 20, 2017).

Adams, James Truslow. 1931. *The Epic of America*. Boston, MA: Little, Brown.

Bérubé, Allen, and Florence Bérubé. 1996. "Sunset Trailer Park." In *White Trash*, edited by Matt Wray and Annalee Newitz, 15–39. New York, NY: Routledge.

Bourdieu, Pierre. 1980. "The Aristocracy of Culture." *Media, Culture and Society* 2: 225–254.

Bullock, Heather E., Karen F. Wyche, and Wendy R. Williams. 2001. "Media Images of the Poor." *Journal of Social Issues* 57: 229–246.

Carroll, Hamilton. 2008. "Men's Soap Operas." *Television and New Media* 9: 263–283.

Chan, Kara, and Gerard Prendergast, 2007. "Materialism and Social Comparison among Adolescents." *Social Behavior and Personality* 35: 213–228.

Clawson, Rosalee, and Rayuka Trice. 2000. "Poverty as We Know it: Media Portrayals of the Poor." *Public Opinion Quarterly* 64: 53–64.

Correspondents of *The New York Times*. 2005. *Class Matters*. New York, NY: Times Books.

Edgerly, Louisa. 2007. "The Politics of Naming: Hurricane Katrina and the Metadiscursive Construction of 'Refugees'." Paper presented at the annual meeting of the International Communication Association, San Francisco, CA.

"Enough is Enough: Minority Groups March on Washington for Jobs." 2010. *African-American News and Issues*. http://www.aframnews.com (accessed March 2011).

Entman, Robert. 1990. "Modern Racism and the Images of Blacks in Local Television News." *Critical Studies in Mass Communication* 7: 332–345.

Ervin, Keith. 2008. "Area's Middle Class is Losing Ground." *Seattle Times*, February 21. http://www.seattletimes.com/seattle-news/areas-middle-class-is-losing-ground (accessed April 28, 2017).

Friedman, Milton, and Anna J. Schwartz. 1963. *A Monetary History of the United States, 1867–1960*. Princeton, NJ: Princeton University Press.

Heinz, Teresa L. 2005. "From Civil Rights to Environmental Rights: Constructions of Race, Community, and Identity in Three African American Newspapers' Coverage of the Environmental Justice Movement." *Journal of Communication Inquiry* 20: 47–65.

Hochschild, Jennifer. 1996. *Facing up to the American Dream: Race, Class, and the Soul of the Nation*. Princeton, NJ: Princeton University Press.

Holtzman Linda. 2000. *Media Messages: What Film, Television, and Popular Music Teach Us About Race, Class, Gender, and Sexual Orientation*. Armonk, NY: M.E. Sharpe.

Kahle, Shannon, Nan Yu, and Erin Whiteside. 2007. "Another Disaster: An Examination of Portrayals of Race in Hurricane Katrina Coverage." *Visual Communication Quarterly* 14: 75–89.

Kendall, Diana. 2005. *Framing Class: Media Representations of Wealth and Poverty in America*. New York, NY: Rowman & Littlefield.

Kitch, Carolyn. 2007. "Mourning 'Men Joined in Peril and Purpose': Working-Class Heroism in News Repair of the Sago Miners' Story." *Critical Studies in Media Communication* 24: 115–131.

Langston, Donna. 1995. "Tired of Playing Monopoly?" In *Race, Class and Gender*, edited by Margaret L. Andersen and Patricia Hill Collins, 96–100. Belmont, CA: Wadsworth.

Mason, Ann, and Marian Meyers. 2001. "Living with Martha Stewart Media: Chosen Domesticity in the Experience of Fans." *Journal of Communication* 51: 801–823.

Schoonmaker, Mary Ellen. 2008. "Keeping Poverty on the Page: Covering an Old Problem in New Ways." *Columbia Journalism Review*. http://www.cjr.org/q_and_a/keeping_poverty_on_the_page.php (accessed April 17, 2017).

Shields, Todd G. 2001. "Network News Construction of Homelessness." *The Communication Review* 4: 193–218.

Shoultz, Bonnie. 1992. "Social Class and Disability." The Center on Human Policy. http://thechp.syr.edu/resources/bulletins/disability-and-family-policy (accessed April 28, 2017).

Shrum, L.J., James E. Burroughs, and Aric Rindfleisch. 2005. "Television's Cultivation of Material Values." *Journal of Consumer Research* 32: 473–479.

US Bureau of Labor Statistics. 2015. "Persons with a Disability: Labor Force Characteristics." http://www.bls.gov/news.release/disabl.nr0.htm (accessed April 17, 2017).

US Bureau of Labor Statistics. 2016. "Who Are We Celebrating?" https://www.census.gov/newsroom/facts-for-features/2016/cb16-ff14.html (accessed April 17, 2017).

US Census Bureau. 2014. "Full-Time, Year-Round Workers and Median Earnings in the Past 12 Months by Sex and Detailed. Occupation, 2014." http://www.census.gov/people/io/publications/table_packages.html (accessed April 17, 2017).

Wilke, Michael. 2002. "Are Gays All Rich?" *I Have an Idea*, October 24. http://ihaveanidea.org/articles/2002/10/24/are-gays-all-rich (accessed April 20, 2017).

15

Representations of Religion and Faith in the Media

Patriarch of the *Duck Dynasty* (2012 debut) family Phil Robertson was quoted in a 2013 *GQ* magazine article defining sin as starting with "homosexual behavior and just morph[ing] out from there. Bestiality, sleeping around with this woman and that woman and that woman and those men." Then, to bolster his point, the star of A&E's hit docu-series cited passages from the biblical epistle Corinthians: "Don't be deceived. Neither the adulterers, the idolaters, the male prostitutes, the homosexual offenders, the greedy, the drunkards, the slanderers, the swindlers – they won't inherit the kingdom of God. Don't deceive yourself. It's not right." At the same time, he insisted that he, as a Christian, does not judge. "We never, ever judge someone on who's going to heaven, hell … That's the Almighty's job. We just love 'em, give 'em the good news about Jesus – whether they're homosexuals, drunks, terrorists" (Magary 2013).

Many members of the public judged Robertson's statements as being close minded, hurtful, and bigoted. The complaints became so loud that Robertson's words earned him a month-long "hiatus" from his ultra-successful cable network television program. However, his comments also earned him the public support of many who appreciated his paraphrasing of the Bible. In fact, some called Robertson's suspension an attack on his strongly held Christian beliefs. One blogger accused the liberal media of trying to make Christianity "a hate crime" (Mr. Conservative 2015).

The controversy was a reminder that many who live in the United States have strong feelings about the role faith and religion plays in their lives and those feelings extend to the media they choose. To that end, this chapter looks at how faith and religion are represented in the media – from derision to advocacy. Perhaps more than any other chapter in this book, the discussion of how faith is represented in US media is reliant on historical facts as well as the intersection of race, class, and gender in the country. As a result, there is no end to what could be examined. Therefore, it is necessary to acknowledge that not every dogma will find its way into the chapter, but their absence is not intended to be a slight on any particular faith. Instead, this chapter will offer a broad overview of how faith and religion have been represented in groundbreaking, controversial, and evolutionary ways in the media. To begin this discussion, it is important to address how religion was paramount in the founding of the United States.

Diversity in US Mass Media, Second Edition. Catherine A. Luther, Carolyn Ringer Lepre, and Naeemah Clark.
© 2018 John Wiley & Sons Inc. Published 2018 by John Wiley & Sons Inc.

Historical Background to Religion and Faith Representations

The history of religion, media, and the United States are undeniably linked. In 1620, the Pilgrims (a group of English Protestants dissatisfied with the Church of England) boarded the *Mayflower* from Plymouth, a port in the south of England. A faithful 120 paying passengers set sail on an arduous two-month journey across the Atlantic with the hope of finding a home where they could freely practice their religion. This group settled in what is now Massachusetts (Johnson 2006). Less than 20 years later, the Puritans, a stringent group of English Protestants that also settled in Massachusetts, ejected Roger Williams, a former leader of their church, for being too progressive in his religious views. He and his followers who were not hard and fast adherents to the Puritans' beliefs established a settlement in Rhode Island.

In the seventeenth century, other US colonies became the home to others who practiced Christian faiths. For example, Anglicans seeking fortunes settled in Jamestown, Virginia; English Catholics came to Maryland; British Quakers, under the leadership of William Penn, settled in Pennsylvania where they conducted a "holy experiment" to welcome those of all faiths (Quakers in the World 2015).

The Protestant faith that had dominated the 13 colonies underwent a significant shift as settlers moved west across the frontier between 1790 and 1840. During this period known as the Second Great Awakening, revivals, evangelism, and charismatic preachers were introduced as ways to gain followers and share the word of the Lord. The energy of these church services and camp meetings brought religion to those that did not conform to the more austere sermons found in Catholic or Anglican houses of worship. Baptist and Methodist churches began to dot the new frontier as clergy/ cowboys rode their horses across the Midwest (Posey 1966).

Thirty years before the Pilgrims came ashore in Cape Cod, Catholic Spaniards charted their way throughout the West beginning in New Mexico. The Franciscan friars built missions all over the West to spread their faith amongst the native people, but the Spanish were ultimately run out of the territories after the Pueblos revolted against the strict demands of the Franciscans and the desecration of their tribe's religious artifacts (PBS 2015). In the late 1760s, the Franciscans expanded their missions across the territory between San Diego and San Francisco, California. Again, the Spaniards hoped to "tame" the Native people with the teaching of Catholicism, but the experiment was met with a tepid response. The Catholic missions were secularized by the early 1800s. Alternatively, Catholicism thrived in the American South and upper New England as many French Catholics settled in New Orleans, Louisiana, and US territories bordering Canada (New Advent 2015).

While the Christian faiths were prominent in the United States, Judaism was another of the earliest faiths practiced in the New World. In the 1650s, Jewish settlers arrived in New Amsterdam, today known as New York City, from Dutch Brazil. Similar to the Pilgrims that arrived 34 years earlier, this group of 23 came to America hoping to practice their religion free of persecution. While these were the first documented practicing Jews in the United States, this group of Spanish and Portuguese descent was just the first wave. Between 1790 and 1880, Jewish immigration grew from 1,000 to 250,000, with the majority being from Germany and Austria. For Jews that were facing anti-Semitism in Europe, the American settlements were considered as being more religiously tolerant to minority groups (Diner 2004).

It is worth noting here that (as will probably be remembered from elementary school days) all of the aforementioned colonies and territories were inhabited by indigenous people who had their own faith and religious beliefs but were frequently viewed as primitive by the European interlopers. Still, many of these Native faiths are still practiced in the United States today. In other cases, these Native faiths have been interwoven with the Catholic and Protestant teachings of those who came to America seeking religious freedom. Similarly, many enslaved Africans combined elements of their Islamic religious practices from their homelands and spirituality developed from hardship with the teaching imposed by their slave owners.

As these various religious groups were finding homes, churches, and clergy across America, the country was battling to gain independence. Once that independence was gained, the Founding Fathers of the United States worked to unify a nation built on difference and tolerance of others' beliefs. The United States Constitution, which came into effect in 1789, was intended to be that powerful document. Inspired by the thoughts and writings of James Madison, the First Amendment to the Constitution reads: "Congress shall make no law respecting an establishment of religion, or prohibiting the free exercise thereof; or abridging the freedom of speech, or of the press; or the right of the people peaceably to assemble, and to petition the Government for redress of grievances." The expressed freedoms related to press, speech, and religion further solidified the country's resounding support for each of these.

Churches and religious organizations published newspapers, periodicals, and pamphlets that spread information about their religion and stories of their congregations. These publications were used to announce births, marriages, and deaths, and publish obituaries, ultimately becoming genea-logical and historical records for state governments. The fact that states sanctioned the distribution of these non-secular documents is further evidence that the United States was a robust supporter of religious freedoms. Furthermore, it served as an invitation for others to worship as they chose, leading to a nation with a rich variety of religious and spiritual doctrines.

Today, the US population has many religions and faiths, with Christianity (including Protestants, Catholics, and Mormons) being the largest with 71 percent declaring this affiliation. Judaism is the second largest affiliation. Approximately 1 percent of the population identifies with the Islamic faith. Segments of US citizens also practice faiths such as Buddhism, Humanism, Scientology, or paganism. Moreover, some say they are unaffiliated (spiritual, but not adhering to any specific religion) or atheist (having no religion). Over time, research has shown societal shifts in faith and a belief in God. A 2012 study from the Pew Research Center found 68 percent never doubted the existence of God, while a 2007 study found that more than 80 percent never doubted that there was a God (Pew Research Center 2015a).

As the historical background of faith and religion indicates, the intersection of religion and race and ethnicity is deeply rooted in this country. As the United States becomes more integrated and multiracial, churches are becoming less segregated. Figure 15.1 charts the intersection between religion and race. However, many churches are still full of people from the same race or ethnicity. As a result, the way films or television shows depict faith is often linked with a character's race or ethnicity. This chapter will review such depictions and also address how the media have represented the intersections of class, gender, sexual orientation, and religion since the thread of faith intrinsi-cally links many components of the American fabric.

Religion and Faith in Film

French Catholic film critic André Bazin likened the art of filmmaking to the biblical creation of the world. He believed that a camera shot was a religious incarnation of life and the audience could witness the miracle in a darkened theater, the only light being on the silver screen (Fam People 2015). Bazin, one of the most prominent film critics in cinematic history, found images of the divine in

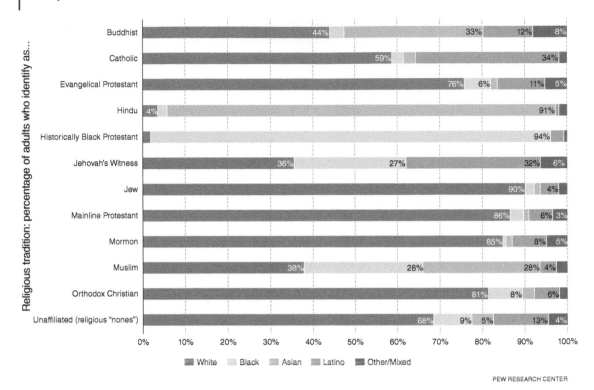

Figure 15.1 Graph showing racial and ethnic composition by religious group.
Source: Pew Research Center (2015b).

film compelling and always present. In his essay "Cinema and Theology" he categorized the religious themes in three ways. Although he sketched out these categories in 1951, the patterns still hold true for contemporary films. The first category is made up of stories taken from the Bible and religious texts. The second category consists of films that tell the lives of martyrs or of those working to achieve sainthood. The third category features characters, often members of the clergy, that are struggling with their faith or are doubters (Blake 2015).

Using Bazin's categories is a tidy way to begin thinking about the representations of religion and faith at the movies. From the beginning of the film industry, stories from preexisting religious texts made their way to theaters. Biblically based stories such as *The King of Kings* (1927), *Samson and Delilah* (1949), *The Ten Commandments* (1956), and *Ben-Hur* (1959) were large-scale stories that depicted the drama found in the Bible with artistic cinematography, ornate costuming, and picturesque scenery. More recent biblical tales have been told in the grand films *Exodus: Gods and Kings* (2014), where Welsh actor Christian Bale played Moses, and in *Noah* (2014), starring New Zealander Russell Crowe as the shipbuilder.

In a comedic twist, Steve Carell plays Evan Baxter, a politician turned Noah-figure in *Evan Almighty* (2007). Evan, even in the face of losing his family and friends, builds an ark on God's (played by Morgan Freeman) orders to save Washington, DC from an impending flood. Initially, Evan resists God's wishes to build the ark, but Evan's life becomes life increasingly difficult each time he disobeys God's commands. While this version of God is persistent, it is also wise and loving. In a key scene in the film, Evan's wife Rita (played by Lauren Graham) asks God, who is disguised as a waiter (complete with name tag reading Al Mighty), why her husband believes that God has asked him to build an ark. God replies that it's not a punishment, but an opportunity:

> Let me ask you something. If someone prays for patience, you think God gives them patience? Or does he give them the opportunity to be patient? If he prayed for courage, does God give him courage, or does he give him opportunities to be courageous? If someone prayed for the family to be closer, do you think God zaps them with warm fuzzy feelings, or does he give them opportunities to love each other?

Rita is calmed by the old man's wisdom and sees Evan's ark as a blessing for her family (Figure 15.2).

Filmmakers have taken some liberties in all of these films. For example, Jesus is a blue-eyed blond in 1988's *The Last Temptation of Christ*, contrary to the Bible's description. The overriding theme in each is that the supreme deity is paramount. He is all seeing, all knowing, and (much like a film's director) omnipotent. The sheer scale of the floods, wars, and vast landscapes in these films was designed to illustrate the fear and respect for the power of the Father, Son, and the Holy Spirit. At the same time, the power of God is ultimately benevolent and rewards those that are dutiful.

Films based on the Muslim holy book, the Qur'an, frequently share themes and even characters from stories said to be based on the Bible or the Jewish holy books of the Talmud or Torah. For example, the 1998 DreamWorks film *The Prince of Egypt* used the story of Moses, sprinkling some elements from the Qur'an into the film, including a passage from the book. Still, some devout Muslims asserted the film deviated from the true teachings of the Qur'an. Some followers of the Jewish faith also condemned the film for making changes to religious texts while taking creative

Figure 15.2 Morgan Freeman as God in *Evan Almighty* (2007). Screenshot.

license to tell a better story. For example, Jews are taught that Moses had a strained relationship with the Egyptians, including Ramses; yet, in the film they are friends (Rationalist Judaism 2013).

Martyrdom in Film

It is difficult to name a film where one of the characters does not try to make the life of another character better through perseverance, selflessness, or sacrifice. However, when discussing representations of faith and religion, the term "martyr" – defined as "a person who is killed or who suffers greatly for a religion or cause" – often comes to mind. Religious martyrdom has been depicted in a variety of faiths and manners.

The crucifixion and martyrdom of Jesus has been frequently documented in film. Jesus' life has been told in films such as *The Greatest Story Ever Told* (1965) and *Jesus of Nazareth* (1977), but its depiction in *The Passion of the Christ* (2004) caused a controversy. The film's director Mel Gibson took great pains to show the raw violence and brutality that would occur in the final 12 hours of Christ's life. Gibson's Christ (played by Jim Caviezel) has his skin torn off in sheets and blood flows down his face from gashes made by the crown of thorns that sits upon his blood-soaked hair. Gibson wanted the audience to see the abject torture Christ suffered, but some viewers thought the violence was too graphic. *Newsweek* critic David Ansen wrote, "The relentless gore is self-defeating … I felt abused by a filmmaker intent on punishing an audience, for who knows what sins" (Ansen 2004: 60).

While Jesus is the most well-known religious martyr in the world, Anne Frank may be considered among the most poignant. *The Diary of Anne Frank* (1959) is a cinematic retelling of the actual journal entries by a 13-year-old Jewish girl (played by a 21-year-old Millie Perkins) hiding from Nazis in occupied Amsterdam. When the film begins, we learn that Anne's father has returned to the attic where they hid for two years, but that Anne has died in a concentration camp. The Anne in the film is sweet, innocent, and bright; she has dreams and loves movie stars. The viewers fall in love with Anne and she becomes the embodiment of the horrors associated with the Holocaust (Figure 15.3). Furthermore, *The Diary of Anne Frank* serves as evidence to Holocaust deniers (Mitgang 1989).

Although *The Passion of the Christ* and *The Diary of Anne Frank* are worlds apart in their depictions of martyrdom, the end result is the same. Mel Gibson used the graphic crucifixion sequences to remind viewers of the torment of religious persecution; legendary director George Stevens used Millie Perkins's wide-eyed charm and lilting voice to make the audience mourn the loss of potential and hope of Anne and all Jews who perished during the Holocaust.

Another film that immortalizes a real-life martyr is *Malcolm X* (1992). X (played by Denzel Washington) is a gang member turned follower of Elijah Mohammed and the Nation of Islam, a religion that celebrates Black Muslims. Using the pro-Black sentiments of the Nation of Islam, X uses powerful and charismatic speeches to call for the separation of Whites and Blacks – even if that separation was achieved through violence. Toward the end of the film (and his life), X travels to Mecca, learns about Sunni Muslims and sees the diversity of the Muslim faith. His previous intolerance toward Whites wanes and he begins deviating from the powerful Elijah Mohammed. Three Black Muslims killed X in February 1965. As is the case with many of the aforementioned films, this film was met with controversy: similar to the critiques of actors that portrayed Jesus, disciples of Malcolm X lamented that the walnut skin tones of Denzel Washington did not resemble the reddish hues of Malcolm X (Williams 1992).

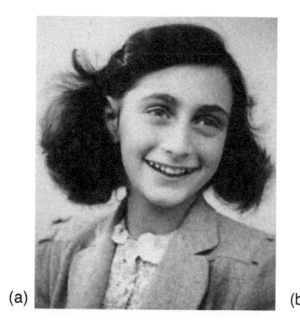 

(a)   (b)

Figure 15.3 (a) Anne Frank as a young teen. Reproduced with kind permission of Alamy. (b) Millie Perkins, who played her in *The Diary of Anne Frank* (1959). Reproduced with kind permission of Millie Perkins.

Films about Those Struggling with Faith

The human struggle with faith and religion are the most used tropes in films about religion and faith. For example, the film struggles of spiritual leaders range from substance abuse (*Mass Appeal*, 1984; *Dogma*, 1999; *Constantine*, 2005), abuse of power (*Elmer Gantry*, 1960; *Doubt*, 2008), to curiosity about sexuality (*Priest*, 1994; *Agnes of God*, 1995; *V for Vendetta*, 2006), and to seeking retribution from vampires (*Priest*, 2004). Stories using this dichotomy of good versus evil are common and familiar. What is rarer for a film about religion and faith is to show the emotional attempts of a character trying to navigate the acceptance of a faith that doesn't want him or has, in effect, pushed him away. The films *Witness* (1985), *The Jazz Singer* (1927), and *Yentl* (1983) each tell stories about a similar struggle.

Harrison Ford submerges himself in an Amish community in the 1985 film *Witness*. Ford plays John Book, a big-city police officer who moves to Pennsylvania Dutch Country to protect an Amish boy who witnessed a murder. The boy's mother (Kelly McGillis) and others in her community do not want the boy to be a part of the "English" world and they try to push Book away. However, after Book is injured, he has no choice but to stay with the Amish. He learns the traditions of these plain people, falls in love with the boy's mother, and ultimately relies on the Amish community to save him when bad guys come looking for him. The film shows the Amish traditions through the eyes of an outsider, which allows the viewers to see how austere, yet lovely a faith built on simplicity can be. Not surprisingly, the Amish of Pennsylvania Dutch Country were concerned that the mere idea of a film focusing on their lives was counter to the quiet lives they cherished. Additionally, the Amish asked the public to boycott the film because the attention the film would receive would also increase the number of tourists that visit the Pennsylvania Dutch. Although some of the Amish use tourism as a way to sell their homemade goods, others find the tourism unseemly as it makes their religion a subject for gawkers ("Amish Ask Boycott" 1985).

The solemnity of Jewish faith and the outside world has been featured in several films released in the United States. For example, in *The Jazz Singer* (1927), young Jakie Robinowitz (played by Al Jolson) is beaten and leaves home when he opts to sing secular jazz music as opposed to becoming a rabbi's cantor like his father. His father vehemently opposes his son singing to audiences in a bar, saying, "I'll teach him better than to debase the voice God gave him!" In the end, Jakie, now performing under the name of Jack Robin, becomes a successful jazz singer and his mother realizes that performing this style of music *is* his way of singing for God and that "he belongs to the whole world now." At the end of the film, Robin sings a loving song to his mother who understood how he could still be faithful and sing jazz music.

A parent's hold over a child's commitment to faith is also at the heart of *Yentl* (1983), in a vastly different way. Yentl tells the story of a young woman (played by Barbra Streisand) who loves studying the Talmud, but cannot continue her education because women in the early 1900s were forbidden from attending yeshiva school. She poses as a man so that she can attend the school. While at school she secretly falls in love with one of her male classmates (Avigdor, played by Mandy Patinkin), but must marry a woman (Hadass, played by Amy Irving) in order to keep up her ruse. It is in this plotline that the lines between religion and sexuality become intertwined. Hadass, thinking Yentl's a gentle boy, falls in love with Yentl who is trying her best to be an attentive, yet non-sexual husband. In the end, Hadass and Avigdor fall in love. Yentl, flying in the face of the conventions of most romantic films, leaves Poland in the hope of studying in America where she can be free to study as a woman. Incidentally, the final scene of the film has Yentl on a ship's deck singing to her late papa, hoping he would be proud of her decision to follow her path in America. This scene harkens back to Jack Robin singing to his proud mother at the end of *The Jazz Singer.*

Clearly, these three films have different plots, but the interaction of faith (or lack thereof) and family, community, and acceptance of change in the face of these traditions helps the audience understand multifaceted aspects of faith. In these cases, religion is essential, but weighed with the demands of flawed lives. The representation of religion and faith in films can provide wider ways of thinking about self.

Films as Windows into Faith Traditions

While Bazin's three categories of films cover most types of religious-based films, another should be added. Because Christianity is overwhelmingly predominant in US homes, entertainment films have become sources of religious enlightenment. For example, films such *Monsoon Wedding* (2001), *Bend It Like Beckham* (2003), and *The Best Exotic Marigold Hotel* (2011) introduce elements of Hindu faith traditions found in wedding parties and funeral services. Similarly, elements of Buddhism have come to American audiences in films such as the Tina Turner biopic *What's Love Got to Do with It* (1993). In *Seven Years in Tibet* (1997) a hiker (Brad Pitt) befriends a teenaged Dalai Lama. Also in 1997, Martin Scorsese's *Kundun* provided another story of an even younger Dalai Lama in a screenplay written by Melissa Mathison, who also wrote the screenplay for *E.T.: The Extraterrestrial* (1982). Other films including *The Matrix* (1999) and *Donnie Darko* (2001) have themes that reflect the spiritual and meditation tenets of Buddhism. In these cases, these films have helped build awareness of and support for faiths not seen in most US homes (Whalen-Bridge 2014).

Representations of Religion and Faith on Television

Entertainment Television

Religion has been on entertainment television in some of its earliest, most prevalent genres: soap operas. Daytime dramas had long used religion as the voice of morality in towns such as Springfield, Pine Valley, and Salem. Even some of their titles and opening sequences alluded to an all-knowing being. *The Guiding Light* (1952–2009) used a searching lighthouse as a metaphor for some higher power leading the way, and *As the World Turns* (1956–2010) gave viewers a heavenly view of a spinning globe as if there were an omnipotent power watching over us all. Other daytime dramas including *Dark Shadows* (1966–1971) and *Passions* (1999–2008) used pagan beliefs such as vampirism and witchcraft in their story arcs. As audience tastes and habits changed, soap operas became less about these morality plays and more about romance. Today, very few daytime dramas remain on the air, but religious content has frequently been used for entertainment in prime-time comedy and drama.

Television writer and producer Norman Lear challenged the mores of viewers by allowing his working-class anti-hero Archie Bunker to use racial and religious slurs in *All in the Family* (1971–1978). Although Archie was bigoted in almost every way, he had a soft heart, as seen in an episode where his friend Stretch Cunningham, a Jew (unbeknownst to Archie), dies and Archie is asked to speak at his funeral. He says: "I wouldn't have believed Stretch was Jewish because he wasn't a doctor or a lawyer or in the dress business or nothing like that ... And you could never tell by looking at his face and ... I ain't seen nothing else" (Archie Bunker Quotes 2015). Archie then tearfully pats Stretch's casket and whispers "Shalom" as he walks past.

Other programs tried to infuse discussions of religion and faith with varied success. In 1997, ABC tried a drama-comedy starring Kevin Anderson as Father Ray, a charming, liberal priest in *Nothing Sacred.* The program lasted less than one season, in part because of poor scheduling, but primarily due to a large-scale boycott of Disney (ABC's parent company) from the Catholic League (Armbrust 1997). The League was concerned with Father Ray being depicted as a conflicted priest who often flirted with a former girlfriend and supported condom use among teens contrary to church teachings. Former presidential candidate and Catholic League advisory board member Alan Keyes lamented that the show was little more than "propaganda dressed up as entertainment, the way the Nazis used to make movies. The entertainment elite's belief that there are no moral absolutes deeply contradicts the religious view of Christianity" (quoted in Dowd 1997).

Programs where religion was used to save the day have been received far more favorably. Series such as *Highway to Heaven* (1984–1989), *Father Dowling Mysteries* (1989–1991), and *Touched by an Angel* (1994–2003) featured an angel, a priest, a nun, and another angel, respectively, roaming the country providing holy help to the distressed, and delivering a message of God's salvation as they leave. The shows weren't terribly sophisticated or complex, but they were wholesome fare that kept families tuned in for years. These shows were far more common than programming showing that other religions could be "problem solvers" or something to that effect. The dominance of Christianity in the United States was reflected in this type of formulaic storytelling as well.

In the past few years, some networks have tried to take more chances (Box 15.1). The smarties on the *Big Bang Theory* (2007 debut) challenged the audience to think in new ways, and religious symbolism has been brought into several episodes. In season 1, episode 5, Sheldon, Leonard, Howard,

---

Box 15.1 Portrayals of Rumspringa

Figure 15.4 Young adults participating in a Rumspringa-type experience on TLC's reality program *Breaking Amish* (2012–). Screenshot.

TLC's *Breaking Amish* (Figure 15.4) is an unscripted program showing young Amish men and women adjusting to big city life in Los Angeles or New York. Although this program has been revealed as being a sham (some of those featured had already lived in large cities and two of the participants were actually married to each other), there is a nugget of truth. Amish youth are encouraged to participate in Rumspringa where they leave the confines of their community to determine if the conservative Amish life is right for them.

Watch a bit of *The Devil's Playground* (2002), a documentary about young people and Rumspringa. Draw parallels to leaving for college. Include thoughts of how your fears, inhibitions, communication styles, clothing, and social habits changed in the new college environment. In what ways were changes inevitable? In what ways do you think others adapted to you?

---

and Raj are sitting in the Cheesecake Factory, using condiment dispensers and salt shakers to reenact the Battle of Gettysburg:

SHELDON:	Alright, I'm moving my infantry division, augmented by a battalion of Orcs from *Lord of the Rings*, we flank the Tennessee Volunteers, and the North once again wins the Battle of Gettysburg.
HOWARD:	Not so fast, remember the South still has two infantry divisions, plus Superman and Godzilla.
LEONARD:	No, no, no, no, Orcs are magic, Superman is vulnerable to magic, not to mention, you already lost Godzilla to the Illinois Cavalry and Hulk.
RAJ:	Why don't you just have Robert E. Lee charge the line with Shiva and Ganesh?
PENNY (waitress):	Hi, you guys ready to order?
HOWARD:	Hang on, honey (to Penny). Shiva and Ganesh? The Hindu Gods against the entire Union army?
LEONARD:	And Orcs!

PENNY: I'll be back.

RAJ: Excuse me, Ganesh is the remover of obstacles, and Shiva is the destroyer. When the smoke clears, Abraham Lincoln will be speaking Hindi and drinking mint juleps.

In this scene it is clear that these guys frequently play a game where they intermix the powers of actual Civil War figures, Hindu icons, and comic book characters. Upon first viewing, the scene is absurd, but when considered with the thought processes of these GenXers, it makes complete sense. Their generation is one where faith and popular culture collide with real life all of the time. To play a game combining all three is not only funny, but a testament to their genius.

The Learning Channel (TLC), in an effort to reach out to the growing interest in Muslims in America, offered *All American Muslim* (2011–2012). This reality show followed the lives of five Lebanese-American/Shia Muslim families from Michigan. The program aired for one season. One reason for the cancelation of the critically acclaimed show was a controversy surrounding sponsorship of the series. The one-man staffed advocacy organization Florida Family Association (FFA) sent emails to TLC's sponsors (among them Kayak.com, Campbell's Soup, Sears) questioning their loyalty to American values. For example, home repair store Lowe's pulled its ads, justifying its decision in the following letter:

> As you know, the TLC program "All-American Muslim" has become a lightning rod for people to voice complaints from a variety of perspectives – political, social and otherwise. Following this development, dozens of companies removed their advertising from the program beginning in late November. Lowe's made the decision to discontinue our advertising on Dec. 5. As we shared yesterday, we have a strong commitment to diversity and inclusion, and we're proud of that longstanding commitment. If we have made anyone question that commitment, we apologize. (Potts 2015)

Although some big names, including a representative from the Obama administration, urged advertisers to ignore the FFA's complaints, their voices were not enough to convince Lowe's to reconsider.

Fear of offending audience members with strong religious beliefs is one reason that broadcast networks are hesitant to tell controversial stories about religion. Further, broadcast networks cannot afford to turn off large swaths of viewers because networks are reliant on audiences to deliver advertisers that pay for the programs. As a result, substantive religious conversations are often found on channels and outlets that don't have commercials such as premium cable (HBO, Cinemax) or over-the-top outlets (Netflix, Amazon Prime).

HBO's *True Detective* (2014 debut) and *Boardwalk Empire* (2010–2014) both used religion as discussion points for main characters. *Boardwalk Empire*'s crime boss, Nucky (played by Steve Buscemi), grapples with his wife Margaret (played by Kelly MacDonald) over how his life's work is in conflict with her Catholic faith. At one point, Margaret is so frustrated by his violent behavior that she gives some of his land to the Catholic Church. Buscemi said that it's not that his character is against religion, it's just that he doesn't understand how people can "fall for it" (HBO 2015). *Daily Beast* blogger Andrew Romano questioned if *True Detective* is anti-Christian. One of *True Detective*'s lead characters, Rustin Cohle (played by Matthew McConaughey), argues that having a blind faith in the "fairytale" that is Christianity "dulls critical thinking" and that organized religion appeals to those that suffer from "fear and self-loathing." This indictment of religion is paralleled with the importance of using evidence and truth when solving crimes (Romano 2014).

HBO also tackled a faith in the 2015 documentary *Going Clear: Scientology and the Prison of Belief*, based on the book of the same name. Director Alex Gibney explores the history of the church, which has its origins in the science fiction novels of church founder L. Ron Hubbard. The film also examines former church members who have gone to the media with claims that the church is a scam or a cult and have faced retribution from the church. The network ran the film only after its lawyers scrutinized Gibney's claims against Scientology (Stelter 2015). For their part, the leadership of the Church of Scientology ran full-page ads decrying the film as a piece of fiction based on lies and faulty journalism (Labrecque 2015).

Subscription services Amazon Prime and Netflix can also take on tough topics without concern for fretting advertisers. *Transparent*, Amazon Prime's acclaimed show about a middle-aged father (played by Jeffrey Tambor) who undergoes a transgender transition also realistically weaves Jewish life into the complicated Pfefferman family. The Pfeffermans aren't terribly religious, but they are active in a Los Angeles Jewish community center and use Yiddish in daily conversations. Executive producer and creator Jill Solloway prides herself on the authenticity of the show, yet laments the anti-Semitism of some viewers: "It is so Jewy. We got away with that much Jewiness? I can't believe it … it's more controversial to be Jewy than trans … There are more people saying horrible things [in online comments] about Jews than about trans people. It's crazy" (Cohen 2014).

Netflix's *Orange Is the New Black* dug into Judaism when one of its characters embraced the faith. Initially, several of the inmates at Litchfield Correctional Facility for Women say they are Jewish in order to get the tastier kosher meal from the prison cafeteria. When a rabbi comes in to verify that they are in fact Jewish, their jig is up. However, one of the women, "Black Cindy" (played by Adrienne C. Moore), opts to learn about Judaism so that she can continue receiving the kosher meals. In this process, Cindy finds that the Jewish faith gives her a peace she's never had before. In the season finale, Cindy's conversion is completed with a *mikvah* (submersion in water) when she bathes herself in a lake behind the prison. In turn, the other women of the prison also undergo a spiritual rejuvenation from their literal and figurative chains as they all bathe in the lake with Cindy.

Where the Pfeffermans and Cindy embrace elements of their faith, Kimmy in *Unbreakable Kimmy Schmidt* (2015 debut) tries to distance herself from her religious upbringing. In this Netflix comedy created and produced by Tina Fey, Kimmy (Ellie Kemper) is freed from an underground bunker where she and other cult members were waiting out the apocalypse. Cult leader Richard Wayne Gary Wayne (played by Jon Hamm) had kidnapped the women 15 years earlier, convincing them that he was the messiah who could save them from annihilation. Kimmy moves to New York City to rebuild her life and figure out her true identity. As the theme song reminds viewers, "females are strong as hell," and Kimmy's can-do attitude and resilient spirit drives this point home for the binge-viewing audience.

While the premise seems far-fetched, writer and former cult member Boze Herrington says there are elements of Kimmy's life that resonate. Herrington was not concealed in an underground bunker, but he did live in a closely cloistered community that was controlled by a charismatic leader. He said he shared Kimmy's sense of confused wonder and social awkwardness when he emerged and entered society after leaving his religious group and leader. He applauded *Unbreakable Kimmy Schmidt*'s delicateness and warmth in handling the unique situation of being released from an insulated religious group (Herrington 2015).

Televangelism

In the early days of radio, religious services were broadcast as a way for church leaders to spread their teachings far and wide. Today, this same practice occurs on television. To some viewers, these religious, largely Christian, services are another way to connect with God on a regular basis. For others, televangelism is a scam designed to get homebound believers to send money to fast-talking "holy rollers."

Billy Graham is probably the best known television minister. Graham was a trusted figure around the world, was a personal consultant to many US presidents, and had several television specials airing throughout the 1960s and 1970s that garnered large audiences. While he is thought of as a Protestant of the people, other televangelists have not maintained the same reputation. Jimmy Swaggart and Jim and Tammy Faye Bakker were television preachers who triggered scandals. Swaggart, a Pentecostal minister, has a weekly program, *The Jimmy Swaggart Telecast* (1977 debut). In 1988, after Swaggart was found in the company of a prostitute, he tearfully and famously told his congregants, "I have sinned against You, my Lord, and I would ask that Your Precious Blood would wash and cleanse every stain until it is in the seas of God's forgetfulness, not to be remembered against me anymore" (Swaggart 2015). Three years later, he committed the same sin, this time telling his church that the Lord told him that his sins were none of the church's business.

Jim and Tammy Faye Bakker hosted a few television programs on The Christian Broadcasting Network in the 1960s and 1970s. They started Trinity Broadcasting, a television network devoted to their ministry. Their signature program, *Praise the Lord* or *PTL Club* (1974–1987), constantly asked audience members to donate funds for prayers. Although some of the money went to founding their Heritage USA theme park, in 1987 Jim Bakker was indicted for financial fraud, including giving close to $300,000 to silence a former church secretary's claims of Jim's sexual misconduct against him. After serving nearly five years in prison, Bakker now hosts an eponymous television program (2003 debut) with his new wife, Lori.

One of the longest running religious programs, *The 700 Club* (1966 debut), is currently running on the Christian Broadcasting Network. This daily show features new celebrity interviews, and prayer. The program's long-time host Pat Robertson's opinions about the role of Godlessness in America has received quite a bit of news coverage. He has blamed the September 11 attack on paganism and homosexuality, Hurricane Katrina on legalized abortion, and the 2010 Haitian earthquake on devil worship (NBC News 2010).

Although they have their roots in the tele-ministries of the past, the new generation of TV preachers is trying to reach a broader audience by delivering messages about fiscal and personal success. This type of prosperity ministry attracts millions of viewers a week. TV preachers such as Joel Osteen, Creflo Dollar, and Joyce Myers have mega-churches with television cameras pointed to their informally dressed parishioners smiling, nodding, and taking notes of the words of wisdom. The modern televangelists still ask for money. In 2015, Creflo Dollar received much criticism for asking his followers to donate money so he could buy a $65 million private jet; they used the web for the bulk of their fundraising (Ohlheiser 2015).

Songs and music are important components of religious telecasts. It is therefore perhaps no surprise that faith music in general has also experienced growing popularity (see Box 15.2). Music with religious themes typically is heard on stations targeting faith. Interestingly though, the amount of non-secular music being heard on secular radio stations is growing.

Representations of Religion and Faith in the News

Practically every day newspapers have stories where religion and faith play a role. In general, stories discussing religion found in US newspapers are connected to domestic or international politics, not explorations of the specific faiths. In 2014, members of the Religion News

---

Box 15.2 Faith in popular music

In the summer of 2015, longtime gospel singer Erica Campbell took a break from her Grammy award-winning duo Mary Mary to release the solo album *Help*. The standout hit was "I luh God." The song was a hip-hop/gospel hit where Campbell sings of her love of God with an energetic, danceable beat. The song's similarities to secular songs – a rap break, hip-hop vernacular, flashy video – garnered some controversy, but the song's lyrics are in line with other gospel songs:

> I luh God
> You don't luh God?
> What's wrong wit chu?
> I don't think I could live no other way
> Truth be told, I'm living how I wanna, aye
> Nah, this ain't no blessings in the modern day
> The Lord I serve, He gives them to me everyday

"I luh God" topped Billboard's Hot Gospel chart and found some crossover success on R&B radio stations. The message in the song resonated with listeners of different genres, resulting in tens of thousands of downloads and records sold and one million YouTube views. That said, the absoluteness of the song is striking. In clear language, Campbell is saying that if listeners don't love God, there must be something wrong with them ("What's wrong wit chu?"). This type of evangelical sentiment is unheard of on popular radio. Although Christian singers such as Michael W. Smith ("Place in This World") or Bob Carlisle ("Butterfly Kisses") have had hits on secular and nonsecular music charts, these songs are more inspirational and less proselytizing.

Anthropologist John Lindenbaum (2012) wrote that black gospel singers find more multiethnic, crossover success in the music industry than white Christian singers. Black gospel singers such as BeBe and CeCe Winans and Kirk Franklin and God's Property have been heard on pop stations and as judges on network singing competitions. Most music about devout Christianity has been confined to Contemporary Christian Music stations (Schaefer 2012). This popular music form is one of the most used forms of entertainment for some 70 million white American Christians, with groups such as Lifehouse and Kings of Leon having pop hits. A more burgeoning format is Jewish Rock. Ross Levy ("Fall to Pieces") and Hagad Nahash ("Ma Sheba Ba") are top artists in this rhythmically diverse and bilingual format. The best known artist in his genre is Matisyahu, born Matthew Paul Miller, who emerged onto the music scene as a Chassidic ska/hip-hop/reggae artist, but now focuses on acoustic folk songs.

Association voted that the top religion story was the extreme violence in Syria and Iraq perpetrated by the so-called Islamic State (IS) group ("Islamic State of Iraq and Syria"). A close second was coverage of the religious concerns companies such as Hobby Lobby had regarding contraceptive mandates tied to the Affordable Care Act, also called "Obamacare" (Religion News Association 2014). Stories about faith-based initiatives to help those with Ebola, controversies associated with clergy officiating same-sex marriages, and the abundance of Bible-based films also appeared on the list.

Throughout his campaign and presidency, some news sources discussed Barack Obama's faith. While he frequently proclaimed his Christianity, some reports questioned whether his international upbringing led to a belief in Islam (Meadows 2014). Media researcher Laura Meadows studied the role the media played in maintaining, clarifying, and explaining Obama's religious background. Meadows found several themes in the way the media discussed this controversy including its coverage of the President and his family's visits to church, the marginalization of the President's identity, and his connections to the Muslim faith. In some cases, the media failed to clarify the President's faith and, as a result, corroborated the incorrect information which only served to authenticate the falsehoods.

Ironically, while news stories related to some religions do appear on a daily basis, the overall amount of journalism directly dedicated to covering religion has dwindled. In March 2007, ChristianityToday.com reported that newspapers were foregoing their religion sections and reporters in an effort to save money. As a result, First Amendment proponent and head of the Freedom Forum Charles Overby criticized the fact that newspapers tended to cover the peculiarities of faith. The newspaper industry's lack of attention to the day-to-day coverage of religion has resulted in diminished discussion of faith in mainstream stories (Pullium 2007). This shift also has led to poor reporting of religion including incomplete analyses and biased reporting.

Although journalists may pride themselves on objectivity, religion scholar Mark Silk argues that members of the news media have difficulty separating their own religious views from how they cover minority religions. In *Unsecular Media* (1995), Silk finds that journalists use what they have learned through their largely Judeo-Christian upbringing as a lens through which they see minority religions. As a result, mainstream religions are privileged in and by the press. Although some scholars have found that newspapers have been objective in their coverage of minority religions (see Rick Clifton Moore's research of the Dalai Lama's 2005 visit in the *Idaho Statesman*), time constraints and lack of expertise have also led to slanted reporting (Moore 2008; Wright 1997). To that end, coverage of faith must be done with care. For example, new religious movements tend to be marginalized and categorized as cults. Followers of new religions find the characterization of their faiths as cults to be offensive. In a study of media coverage of religious groups in which members have killed themselves or others (e.g., Heaven's Gate; Aum Shinrikyo, etc.), the researchers found that journalists tended to be more pejorative when making statements about the religious movements (Hill, Hickman, and McLendon 2001). Conversely, individual followers received more judicious treatment (Buddenbaum 1998).

To determine how to best represent religion in the press, journalists and other media content creators should turn to the Associated Press Guide and to the professional organizations that represent various religious groups. Members of the media that follow a particular faith frequently have ethical codes that guide their work. Not only do they have their workplace standards enumerated by their professions (e.g., Society of Professional Journalists, Public Relations Society of America), but their religions offer ethical standards as well. For example, the Catholic Press Association provides Catholic journalists a list of fair practices they can use when making workplace decisions. In part, the code reads:

> The ethics we Catholic publishers and journalists practice are on public display in our publications and in our conduct with news sources, contributors, advertisers, co-workers and others. Our ethics significantly affect our readers and their understanding of the Catholic Church, as well as society at large and ourselves.
>
> This code applies principles derived from the Catholic faith and its guidelines mirror those followed by secular professional journalists' organizations.

This code follows certain moral principles. Truth must be the cornerstone of all our work. Pursuit of the truth will lead to the Truth that is God. So telling the truth must be our first priority, whether in a story, a photo, a quote, the presentation of an offer in an advertisement or the publication's dealings with its various publics. Any breach of this prime directive hurts ourselves and other people, sullies reputations and damages the credibility of our publishing institution and the Church. (Catholic Press Association n.d.)

In this case, the Catholic Press Association is telling its members that their behaviors as Catholic journalists shape the way the public perceives the tenets of Catholicism. The code expects media professionals who are Catholic to serve as representatives of the Church in all of the work they do – whether they work for secular or non-secular publications.

In the same vein, the Evangelical Press Association expects its members to be representatives for Christianity. However, the Evangelical Press Association expects its members to be not only representatives of their faiths, but also teachers and proselytizers. The organization's website states that its core purpose is to "strengthen evangelical periodicals through inspiration, instruction, and networking." It also expects media professionals who are evangelicals to uphold the core values of:

- **Faith** – We are committed to advancing the work and witness of Jesus Christ through biblical truth, which informs and permeates everything we do.
- **Excellence** – We aspire to the highest standards of professionalism, accountability, and authenticity in our viewpoint.
- **Credibility** – We strive for accuracy, context, and credibility in our publications to earn the trust of our readers and the approval of God.
- **Community** – We express our collegiality by encouraging each other through competition, recognition, and networking.
- **Education** – We will provide the very best resources to enhance our competency and effectiveness. (Evangelical Press Association 2015)

Denominational Magazines

Journalism professor Ken Waters, in a comprehensive study of religious magazines (2015), found that these periodicals tend to focus on social justice activities such as advocacy for the downtrodden and analysis of political issues through the lens of particular faiths. Although these religious publications have relatively small, denominationally homogeneous circulations, the content can be rich and thought provoking. Waters found that, in the past, the readers of these magazines could read about "national debates about slavery, prohibition, personal piety, doctrine and theology, science, abortion, gay marriage and a variety of other human and civil rights issues" (Waters 2015). The needs of the readers were paramount: in the 1850s in the *Christian Recorder*, publishers spoke to its largely African Methodist Episcopal members about racial uplift and the importance of understanding black history; conservative Protestants could turn to the pages of *Christian Century* when looking for voices to eschew the pro-evolution and scientific lessons that undergirded the Scopes Monkey Trial of 1923.

Online shopping powerhouse Amazon.com's list of the top-selling religious and spiritual magazines illustrates the diversity of faiths represented in the United States. The top-selling religious magazine is *Guideposts*, which features political and celebrity stories with an inspirational bent. The second most popular periodical, *Tricycle: Buddhist Review*, shares Buddhist teaching for a largely Western audience. In some of its more recent editions, the publication has offered stories about forgiveness, celebrations of celibacy, and reflections on atheism, modernity, and death. Third on Amazon's list is *Light of Consciousness: Journal of Spiritual Awakening*, which focuses on meditation and living consciously. The rest of the list contains titles such as *Paranormal Review, Angels on Earth, Reiki*, and *The Catholic Digest*.

One religious publication that has been known to be in homes of the religious, agnostic, or atheist is the *Watchtower Announcing Jehovah's Kingdom*. Jehovah's Witnesses spread their faith through field service where they ring doorbells and spread the word. When they leave, they gift the home's residents with *The Watchtower*. The publication, printed in 247 languages, boasts an international circulation of more than 50 million readers a month. The issues are often built around a theme where biblical stories are examined and society's big questions, such as war, are pondered using the teachings of Jehovah's Kingdom.

Although these magazines and similarly minded publications have survived for decades, denominational magazines struggle to survive. As Lutheran and journalist Daniel J. Lehman wrote in *The Lutheran Magazine*, his and other religious publications are doing battle with shifting technologies, social mores, and the economic model where many religious publications are distributed to congregants for free (Lehman 2015). The Associated Church Press, an interdenominational Christian press organization that represents print and online media, crafted a statement urging churches and religious magazine publishers to maintain their missions in the face of financial pressures and "stop the erosion of religious journalism" (ACP 2015).

Concluding Remarks

In the first edition of this textbook, we did not consider adding a chapter about media representations of religion and faith. However, when thinking about what would add even more depth to the text, images of religion and faith instantly surfaced. In the past few years, discussions of how the understanding of religion affects families and politics have become woven into the fabric of our society and, as a result, our media systems.

One area that needs to be further elaborated – perhaps in the third edition – is the onslaught of celebrity worship as a guide for life. While they are not necessarily religions, some find these celebrity-based philosophies to be life changing, while others judge followers as being eccentric. For example, a small group of devoted fans have created a religion based on the teachings of Kanye West, called Yeezianity. The group's website touts that it follows the belief "that the one who calls himself Yeezus is a divine being who has been sent by God to usher in a New Age of humanity." Its five pillars are:

1. All things created must be for the good of all.
2. No human being's right to express themselves must ever be repressed.
3. Money is unnecessary except as a means of exchange.
4. Man possesses the power to create everything he wants and needs.
5. All human suffering exists to stimulate the creative powers of Man. (Grossman 2014)

While Kanye West hasn't officially ordained the group of anonymous followers, Oprah Winfrey has created a cable network for her devotees. Winfrey's content teaches people to live with positive thinking, self-analysis, and manifesting abundance. She invites New Age thinkers that she follows – Eckhart

Tolle, Brené Brown, Marianne Williamson – to share their teachings on her programs including *Super Soul Sunday* (2011) and *Iyanla: Fix My Life* (2012) (Mohler 2015).

Whether ancient or newly derived, the influence of religion and faith are interwoven into American neighborhoods and media. In all cases, a lack of understanding about the teachings leads people to judge how others live their lives. As a result, the representation of faith can be overly simplistic, focused on extremism, and biased. Ignorance breeds fear and, in some cases, violence. So, in the end, the key to successful media representations is fairness and accuracy in the depictions.

Reflection Questions and Thoughts to Consider

1. The *Washington Times* declared 2014 as the "Year of the Faith Film" because of the onslaught of faith-based films in mainstream theaters. Do you agree with this contention or have faith-based films been a mainstay in Hollywood for decades? To what do you attribute this increase in films about religion – particularly Christian teachings?
2. Can journalists be objective in covering religions other than their own when faith is such an intrinsic part of one's identity? Is reporting the tenets of another's faith being disloyal to one's own religious upbringing?
3. In March 2011, *South Park* (1997) writers Trey Parker and Matt Stone produced *The Book of Mormon*, a Broadway musical about two young men's mission in an African village. The controversially raunchy (and yes, hilarious) play won critical acclaim, including a Tony Award. How does this entertainment piece potentially hurt the Church of Jesus Christ and Latter Day Saints (LDS)? Could it be beneficial to the LDS Church? How so?
4. Consider the Twitter feeds or Snapchats that you might be viewing. How often is religion brought up? Do you feel comfortable expressing your own religious (or lack of) beliefs via social media? Why or why not?

References

ACP. 2015. "ACP Affirmation of Religious Journalism." Associated Church Press. http:// www.theacp.org/acp-affirmation-of-religious-journalism (accessed April 18, 2017).

"Amish Ask Boycott of movie 'Witness.'" 1985. *Pittsburgh Press*, February 16.

Ansen, David. 2004. "So What's the Good News?" *Newsweek* 143: 60.

Archie Bunker Quotes. 2015. *Religion!* http://archiebunkerquotes.com/2.html (accessed April 18, 2017).

Armbrust, Roger. 1997. "Catholic League Boycotts ABC's 'Nothing Sacred.'" https://www.backstage.com/ news/catholic-league-boycotts-abcs-nothing-sacred (accessed April 30, 2017).

Blake, S.J., Richard A. 2015. "Finding God at the Movies … And Why Catholic Churches Produce Catholic Filmmakers." http://www.georgetown.edu/centers/woodstock/report/r-fea79a.htm (accessed May 12, 2015).

Buddenbaum, Judith M. 1998. *Reporting News about Religion: An Introduction for Journalists*. Ames, IA: Iowa State University Press.

Catholic Press Association. n.d. "Fair Publishing Practices Code." http://c.ymcdn.com/sites/catholicpress .site-ym.com/resource/resmgr/files/fair_practices_code-_english.pdf (accessed April 18, 2017).

Cohen, Debra Nussbaum. 2014. "How Jill Solloway Created 'Transparent' – the Jewiest Show Ever." *Forward.com*, October 21. http://forward.com/culture/207407/how-jill-soloway-created-transparent-the-jewiest (accessed April 18, 2017).

Diner, Hasia. 2004. *The Jews of the United States*. Oakland, CA: University of California Press.

Dowd, Maureen. 1997. "Liberties; The Devil in Prime Time." *New York Times*, September 24. http://www.nytimes.com/1997/09/24/opinion/liberties-the-devil-in-prime-time.html?ref=maureendowd (accessed April 18, 2017).

Evangelical Press Association. 2015. "Core Values." http://www.evangelicalpress.com/about-epa (accessed April 18, 2017).

Fam People. 2015. "André Bazin: Biography." *FamPeople.com*. http://www.fampeople.com/cat-andr%C3%A9-bazin (accessed April 18, 2017).

Grossman, Samantha. 2014. "We're Gonna Let You Finish, Christianity, But Yeezianity Is the Best Religion OF ALL TIME." *Time*, January 14. http://newsfeed.time.com/2014/01/14/were-gonna-let-you-finish-christianity-but-yeezianity-is-the-best-religion-of-all-time (accessed April 18, 2017).

HBO. 2015. "Steve Buscemi on Religion, Staying Clueless and Nucky's Decision-Making Skills." http://www.hbo.com/boardwalk-empire/episodes/02/24-to-the-lost/interview/steve-buscemi-on-religion-staying-clueless-and-nuckys-decision-making-skills.html (accessed April 18, 2017).

Herrington, Boze. 2015. "'Unbreakable Kimmy Schmidt' Is a Tender Portrayal of Cult Survivors Like Me." *The Guardian*, March 12.

Hill, Harvey, John Hickman, and Joel McLendon. 2001. "Cults and Sects and Doomsday Groups, Oh My: Media Treatment of Religion on the Eve of the Millennium." *Review Of Religious Research* 43: 24–38.

Johnson, Caleb H. 2006. *The Mayflower and Her Passengers*. Indiana: Xlibris.

Labrecque, Jeff. 2015. "Church of Scientology Sets Up Online Response to 'Going Clear' Doc." *Entertainment Weekly*, January 28. http://ew.com/article/2015/01/28/scientology-going-clear-response (accessed April 18, 2017).

Lehman, Daniel J. 2015. "Magazines Face Unclear Future." *The Lutheran Magazine*. http://content.yudu.com/htmlReader/A2gu61/LutheranNov2013/4.html?page=4 (accessed April 28, 2017).

Lindenbaum, John. 2012. "The Pastoral Role of Contemporary Christian Music: The Spiritualization of Everyday Life in a Suburban Evangelical Megachurch." *Social & Cultural Geography* 13: 69–88.

Magary, Drew. 2013. "What the Duck?" *GQ*, December 17. http://www.GQ.com/story/duck-dynasty-phil-robertson (accessed April 18, 2017).

Meadows, Laura. 2014. "Creating, Sustaining, or Dispelling Misconceptions: Discourse Analysis of Mainstream Print Media's Coverage of Obama's Religious Identity." *Journal of Media & Religion* 13: 138–152.

Mitgang, Herbert. 1989. "An Authenticated Edition of Anne Frank's Diary." *New York Times*, June 8.

Mohler, Jr., R. Albert. 2015. "The Church of Oprah Winfrey – A New American Religion?" *Christian Post*. http://www.albertmohler.com/2005/11/29/the-church-of-oprah-winfrey-a-new-american-religion-2 (accessed April 18, 2017).

Moore, Rick Clifton. 2008. "Secular Spirituality/Mundane Media: One Newspaper's In-depth Coverage of Buddhism." *Journal of Media and Religion* 7: 231–255.

Mr. Conservative. 2015. "Duck Dynasty Stars Decry War against Christianity". http://mrconservative.com/2013/12/29478-duck-dynasty-stars-attack-on-them-is-a-war-against-christianity (accessed April 18, 2017).

NBC News. 2010. "Robertson on Haiti: 'Pact to the Devil.'" *First Read*, January 13. http://firstread.nbcnews.com/_news/2010/01/13/4436174-robertson-on-haiti-pact-to-the-devil?lite (accessed April 18, 2017).

New Advent. 2015. "French Catholics in the United States." *Newadvent.org*. http://www.newadvent.org/cathen/06271c.htm (accessed April 18, 2017).

Ohlheiser, Abby. 2015. "Pastor Creflo Dollar Might Get His $65 Million Private Jet after All." *Washington Post*, June 3.

PBS. 2015. "Timeline: Faith in America." *Pbs.org*. http://www.pbs.org/godinamerica/timeline (accessed April 18, 2017).

Pew Research Center. 2015a. "Nones" on the Rise. *Pew Research Center: Religion & Public Life*. http://www.pewforum.org/2012/10/09/nones-on-the-rise (accessed April 18, 2017).

Pew Research Center. 2015b. "America's Changing Religious Landscape." *The Pew Forum*. http://www.pewforum.org/2015/05/12/americas-changing-religious-landscape (accessed April 18, 2017).

Posey, Walter Brownlow. 1966. *Frontier Mission: A History of Religion West of the Southern Appalachians to 1861*. Lexington, KY: University of Kentucky Press.

Potts, Kimberly. 2015. "Mia Farrow, Russell Simmons Urge Lowe's Boycott After Muslim Ad Drama." *TheWrap.com*. http://www.thewrap.com/mia-farrow-russell-simmons-urge-lowes-boycott-after-all-american-muslim-ad-drama-33526 (accessed April 18, 2017).

Pullium, Sarah. 2007. "Religion Sections Deleted." *Christianity Today*. March 7. http://www.christianitytoday.com/41380 (accessed April 24, 2017).

Quakers in the World. 2015. "The Holy Experiment, in Pennsylvania." http://www.quakersintheworld.org/quakers-in-action/8 (accessed April 18, 2017).

Rationalist Judaism. 2013. "The Prince of Egypt." *RationalistJudaism.com*. http://www.rationalistjudaism.com/2010/12/prince-of-egypt.html (accessed April 18, 2017).

Religion News Association. 2014. "News & Press: Top 10 Religion Stories." http://www.rna.org/news/206740/Actions-by-Islamic-State-extremists-top-Religion-Newswriters-2014-Religion-Stories-of-the-Year.htm (accessed April 18, 2017).

Romano, Andrew. 2014. "'True Detective's' Godless Universe: Is the HBO Show Anti-Christian?" *TheDailyBeast.com*, March 6. http://www.thedailybeast.com/articles/2014/03/06/true-detective-s-godless-universe-is-the-hbo-show-anti-christian.html (accessed April 18, 2017).

Schaefer, Nancy. 2012. "'Oh, You Didn't Think Just the Devil Writes Songs, Do Ya?' Music in American Evangelical Culture Today." *Popular Music & Society* 3.

Silk, Mark. 1995. *Unsecular Media*. Chicago, IL: University of Illinois.

Stelter, Brian. 2015. "Scientology Mounts Media Offensive against Upcoming HBO Documentary." *Money.CNN.com*, March 17. http://money.cnn.com/2015/03/15/media/scientology-documentary-alex-gibney (accessed April 18, 2017).

Swaggart, Jimmy. 2015. "Apology Sermon." *AmericanRhetoric.com*. http://www.americanrhetoric.com/speeches/jswaggartapologysermon.html (accessed April 18, 2017).

Waters, Ken. 2015. "Religious Magazines: Keeping the Faith." In *The Routledge Handbook of Magazine Research: The Future of the Magazine Form*, edited by David Abrahamson and Marcia R. Prior-Miller. New York, NY: Taylor & Francis.

Whalen-Bridge, John. 2014. Introduction to *Buddhism and American Cinema*, edited by John Whalen-Bridge and Gary Storhoff. Albany, NY: State University of New York Press.

Williams, Lena. 1992. "Playing With Fire." *The New York Times*, October 25.

Wright, Stuart. 1997. "Media Coverage of Unconventional Religion: Any 'Good News' for Minority Faiths?" *Review of Religious Research* 39: 101–115.

16

Mass Media Industries Addressing Diversity

The previous chapters have explored mass media representations of various social groups. The overarching conclusion reached in these chapters is that although there is evidence of improvements in these representations in recent years, many of the recurring and prominent images that have been associated with so-called minority groups still remain. This chapter examines the steps that have been taken by the mass media industry to address perceived problems involving minority group representations. It describes the initiatives that media companies have developed and the degrees of success these initiatives have attained.

The chapter begins with a discussion of what news organizations have done to increase their female and ethnic minority workforce. This is followed by a similar discussion regarding efforts by the entertainment media industry. The chapter concludes with interviews with media professionals that provide insight into their views on diversity issues and the extent to which media companies have attempted to create a more diverse workplace environment as well as more equitable representations.

Broadcast News and Newspaper Industries and Diversity

Beginning in the late 1960s with the women's movement and the establishment of affirmative action laws, many news organizations were required to reconsider their hiring practices and put in place strategies to recruit members of minority groups. The National Advisory Commission on Civil Disorders report in 1968 (informally known as the Kerner Report), which heavily criticized television stations and newspapers for failing to adequately employ and represent African Americans, galvanized serious discussion within news organizations to address diversity issues (Byerly and Wilson 2009). Following the report, one of the influential pieces of regulation to be established was the Federal Communications Commission's 1969 Equal Employment Opportunity (EEO) rule. It required broadcast stations to document their efforts at recruiting ethnic minorities. In 1971, this rule was broadened to include women as well. The newspaper industry followed suit and also adopted objectives to increase women and minority representation in its workforce.

News organizations began to implement practices designed to increase minority employment, including targeted recruitment and mentoring programs. Minority professional journalists also organized associations for themselves. In 1975, the National Association of Black Journalists was founded.

Diversity in US Mass Media, Second Edition. Catherine A. Luther, Carolyn Ringer Lepre, and Naeemah Clark.
© 2018 John Wiley & Sons Inc. Published 2018 by John Wiley & Sons Inc.

This organization was followed by the Asian American Journalists Association (1981), the Native American Journalists Association (1983), and the National Association of Hispanic Journalists (1984).

By the 1990s, positive results from these initiatives became visible. There was an increase in the number of women and minorities working in news organizations. To strengthen the voice of these four minority journalists' national associations, and in their quest to further increase opportunities for minority journalists and improve coverage of minority groups, they merged in 1994, and created a new organization titled UNITY: Journalists of Color, Inc. Despite the organization's advocacy efforts, however, the deregulatory environment in the 1990s and a major court ruling that eliminated the FCC's EEO rules placed a damper on the increase of minority employment within the news industry. From the early 1990s until the present day, minority employment growth rates for the news industry have remained relatively flat (Nicholson 2007). In fact, the last few years actually have seen a slight drop in overall ethnic minority representation, although there has been an increase in female representation.

In broadcast news, a survey conducted by the Radio Television News Directors Association (RTNDA) in conjunction with Hofstra University found that, in 2015, a record high number of women were working in television news (Papper 2015). The figure was 42.3 percent, which was more than two percentage points higher than it was in 2010. In radio news, women made up 39.2 percent of the workforce, up over 10 percentage points from 2010.

Along with the increase in female representation, the overall minority representation in television news has also risen over the past five years. Minority representation in radio news is up from 2010, but saw a sharp decline between 2014 and 2015. As shown in Table 16.1, which compares television news workforce figures from 2010, 2011, 2012, 2013, 2014, and 2015, while decreases of almost one percentage point occurred in the employment of African Americans from 2010 to 2015, the percentages of Hispanics grew by almost 2.5 percent. Asian Americans working in television news grew slightly during that same time frame. The figure has remained the same over the past five years for Native peoples.

In radio news, the percentages of white employees decreased, while the percentages of African Americans, Hispanics, and Asian Americans increased (see Table 16.2). While some of these percentages of minorities in broadcast news show positive gains, when considering the increase in the percentage of minorities in the United States, they seem less of a victory. Over the last 15 years, the minority population in the United States has risen by 11.5 percent. During the same time period, the minority television news workforce increased by only 4.4 percent; in radio news, the minority workforce actually dropped to one percentage point of what it was in 1990.

Table 16.1 Minority workforce in television news.

	2010 %	2011 %	2012 %	2013 %	2014 %	2015 %
Caucasian	79.8	79.5	78.5	78.6	77.6	77.8
African American	11.5	9.3	10.2	9.9	10.4	10.8
Hispanic	5.8	7.3	7.8	7.8	9.1	8.2
Asian American	2.3	3.5	2.9	3.2	2.5	2.9
Native American	0.5	0.4	0.5	0.4	0.4	0.3

Source: Papper (2015). Reprinted with the kind permission of the author and RTDNA.

Table 16.2 Minority workforce in radio news.

	2010 %	2011 %	2012 %	2013 %	2014 %	2015 %
Caucasian	95.0	92.9	88.3	89.1	87.0	90.2
African American	2.9	3.9	5.2	2.3	4.8	4.4
Hispanic	0.7	2.6	4.6	5.7	6.2	2.7
Asian American	0.4	0.0	0.8	1.3	0.3	1.7
Native American	1.1	0.6	1.1	1.6	1.7	1.0

Source: Papper (2015). Reprinted with the kind permission of the author and RTDNA.

In the newspaper industry as well, the numbers of minorities in the newsrooms have not mirrored the growth of minority populations. In 1978 the American Society of News Editors (ASNE) challenged newspapers to achieve a minority workforce percentage that would be similar to the percentage of the overall minority population in the United States by the year 2000 (Dates 2007). By the mid-1990s, however, it became quite apparent that the newspaper industry would not be able to achieve the stated goal. In 1998, ASNE renewed its goal and set 2004 as its new deadline. Even with the association's earnest concern to increase diversity within the news industry, the deadline passed and equivalence between the overall minority population and minority representation in newspapers had not yet been achieved.

In their 2009 annual report, ASNE stated that the economic strains newspapers had been experiencing had resulted in the situation becoming even more dire (American Society of News Editors 2009). In newsrooms alone, 5,900 jobs were lost and 854 of those positions were staffed by minorities. Of the 931 daily newspapers that responded to ASNE's survey, over 50 percent (458 newspapers) reported having no minorities on staff. According to ASNE's 2016 survey of daily newspapers in the United States, the situation has improved. In 2016, minorities comprised about 17 percent of employees at daily newspapers and 23 percent at online-only sites. At newspapers with daily circulations of 500,000 and above, nearly 25 percent of the average workforce was made up of minorities. Women make up approximately one third of newsroom employees overall. At online-only sites women make up nearly half of news organization employees.

It has been difficult for the news industry not only to increase its minority workforce, but also to achieve representation of women and ethnic minorities in high-level managerial and executive positions. Although they do exist, only a small percentage of minorities are CEOs, publishers, editors, or managers. For example, ASNE reports that 13 percent of newsroom supervisors are minorities and 37 percent are women. In 2015, 87.8 percent of television general managers were white and 81.8 percent were men (Papper 2015). Even digital newsrooms are manifesting the same gender imbalance found in traditional newsrooms, with men making up the majority of the top management positions (Griffin 2014).

Several reasons have been cited for the lack of advancement among women and ethnic minorities. Retention has been the main issue. Because of deficiencies in mentoring and development training opportunities, many minorities have opted to move on to other, non-news-related careers. In addition, a negative perception regarding the importance of addressing diversity within the newsroom has also been a hindrance. Some have viewed initiatives to increase diversity within news organizations as a form of social engineering (Swanston 1995). The *Washington Post* experienced this dilemma when, in 1995, another publication, The *New Republic*, published a story saying that white staff members working for the *Post* believed that special accommodations had been made to black staff members and that standards had been lowered. Although the *Post* denied any race-related problems among its staff members, the story illustrated the sentiment of social engineering that existed in media companies.

To move away from such negative viewpoints regarding diversity initiatives, corporate diversity consultants have recommended that news organizations stress the benefits of a diverse workforce in terms of good business. As a consultant in diversity issues, Walterene Swanston (1995), writes with regard to the newspaper industry: "The cause of diversity is helped enormously when managers and employees understand the business advantage it can bring. They include helping newspapers reach new readers and advertisers, attracting talented employees who can bring new perspectives to reporting and editing the news, and increasing productivity throughout the paper."

According to research conducted by the media companies, it behooves news organizations to increase the diversity of their employees as studies have shown that increasing numbers of women and ethnic minorities in the newsrooms often translates into increasing profits. One study in particular found that those newspapers that had greater diversity tended also to have larger circulation figures (Nicholson 2007). With regulation to promote diversity appearing no longer to be a realistic option, it is primarily now up to newspaper and television news organizations to further their efforts to increase minority representations in their workforces and particularly in their executive positions. The same could be said of the magazine industry. Because of niche marketing, magazines on the surface appear to offer more in terms of diversity, yet research shows that even magazines do not reflect diversity in their workforce.

The Magazine Industry and Diversity

Magazines with diverse audiences as their targets are showing relatively strong circulation numbers in an environment that is in economic decline. For example, *Out* looks at celebrities and fashion with the gay reader in mind; *Aubrey* is a lifestyle magazine that speaks to Asian American women from varied ethnicities including Chinese, Japanese, Filipino, Indian, Pakistani, and Nepalese; African American titles such as *Vibe*, *Ebony*, and *Essence* offer advertising and editorial content that appeals specifically to the interests of their readers.

Hispanic readership has been shown to be growing faster than the African American audience. The titles that have targeted the Hispanic market in the past decade and a half, including *Latina*, *Disney en Familia*, *Automundo*, *Siempre Mujer*, *Vanidades*, and the most successful Hispanic magazine, *People en Español*, have resulted in more than $378 million in ad spending in Spanish-language magazines (Advertising Age 2016).

There are several reasons for the growth in this audience. Superficially, the increase could be due to the increase in the Hispanic population in the United States. Sonya Suarez-Hammond, vice president of Multicultural Marketing Insights for the research firm Yankelovich, found that Hispanics were drawn to magazines because these periodicals offer content that is culture-specific. Suarez-Hammond's research indicated that Hispanics were committed to family, food, history, and tradition, and that magazines were one way to preserve these interests (Ayala 2007).

The Internet is also offering a means by which to spur on the growth of web-based magazines targeted at niche groups. The user-friendly, individualized nature of the Internet makes it ideal for catering to distinct audiences. For example, Advocate.com and *Gay Parent* magazine are two online publications that speak to wide-ranging issues for members of the LGBT community. *Hispanic Network* magazine (Hnmagazine.com) targets Latino professionals and offers articles focusing on careers, education, and lifestyles. In another example, the *Washington Post*, recognizing the lack of news focused directly at the African American audience, started *The Root* in 2008. Created by *Post* Chairman Donald Graham and Harvard University professor Henry Louis Gates Jr., *The Root* offers commentary from African American columnists and scholars that is not regularly seen in mainstream web magazines. Its popular Facebook page (www.facebook.com/theRoot) characterizes the magazine as providing an "unflinching examination of political and cultural news through insightful debate and commentary from both established and emerging black thought-leaders."

Even with such signs of diversity in titles and content, however, the profiles of those working for the magazine industry, as a whole, do not live up to the diversity that is exhibited externally in titles and content. Although female workers are commonplace, the magazine industry lags behind in hiring members of African American, Hispanic American, Asian American, and American Indian groups. The *New York Observer's* Lizzy Ratner (2006) termed this paucity the "glossy ceiling" because writers of color have historically had difficulties finding work at large audience, mainstream titles. Instead, these writers find themselves pigeonholed at magazines targeted to smaller minority audiences. As a result, these writers do not earn the same amount or advance as far in the industry as writers at mainstream publications.

A 2005 assessment of magazine mastheads found that only a handful of people of color staffed editorial positions at mainstream publications. For example, at the time only 3 percent of the names appearing on the *Vanity Fair* masthead belonged to people of color; four of the 73 members of *Rolling Stone's* editorial staff were members of ethnic minorities (Ratner 2006). The leadership at magazines has also been largely white. As a testament to this, when Condé Nast announced in May of 2016 that Elaine Welteroth, an African American woman, would be *Teen Vogue's* new editor-in-chief and the company's new editor-in-chief at large, the announcement garnered much media attention. The *Observer* had as its headline, "Condé Nast Taps Second African American EIC in 100+ Year History" (Street 2016). *Essence* magazine hailed her in its headline: "Elaine Welteroth Named new Editor-in-Chief of *Teen Vogue*, and we all Rejoice" (Wilson 2016). The magazine also spread word of the choice via social media with the hashtag #BlackGirlMagic.

Other publications have also recently employed people of color for their top executive positions: Betty Wong Ortiz, an Asian American woman, was the editor-in-chief at *Fitness* and now serves as the Director of Editorial Strategy and Operations for *Bon Appetit & Epicurious* (Condé Nast); Wyatt Mitchell, an African American man, was the creative director at the *New Yorker* until his recent move to Apple; Scherri Roberts, an African American woman, is Senior Vice President/Director of Human Resources at Hearst Publications. Still, minority managers in the industry tend to lead publications targeting minority readers.

The lack of diversity in the magazine industry workforce can also be found in the television and film entertainment industries. As discussed in the previous chapters, problems also exist in the content that is offered.

The Entertainment Industry and Diversity

After the fall 1999–2000 line-up of broadcast network programs failed to feature minority actors in leading roles, the Asian American, Hispanic, and American Indian civil rights groups, along with the National Association for the Advancement of Colored People (NAACP), formed a coalition to lobby the networks to put substantial efforts into increasing the number of members of minority groups in their programs (Elber 2008). The lobbying proved to be fruitful in that the broadcast networks agreed to create programs designed to stimulate the hiring of minority actors, directors, writers, and executives as well as help with minority recruitment and training. The NAACP, along with other outreach groups including the National Latino Media Council, the Asian-Pacific American Media Coalition, and American Indians in Film and TV, worked with the broadcast networks to increase their focus on diversity. NBC, CBS, and Fox created vice president-level positions dedicated to increasing minority hiring.

In recent years, however, the NAACP has been vocal in stating that although the broadcast networks created various programs to increase minority representation in the workplace and in programming, they have not resulted in a huge increase in minority characters on broadcast television. Since the 1999–2000 television season the NAACP has tracked the number of minority actors on broadcast television and they have found that the figures have been steadily level over the years. Although the phrase "virtual whiteout" cannot be used now to characterize television programming, as it was used in 1999 by then NAACP head Kweisi Mfume, the number of minorities represented in television programming has not changed to a large extent over this past decade.

In a report released at the end of 2008, the NAACP was particularly critical of the change in programming that the CW broadcast network took after being established by the merger between UPN and WB networks. Both UPN and WB networks had featured a number of programs starring black actors; after they were merged into CW, many of these shows were dropped and replaced by programs featuring white actors. What took place was the replacement of shows such as *The Steve Harvey Show* (1996–2002) and *Eve* (2003–2006) with *Gossip Girl* (2007–2012) and *One Tree Hill* (2003–2012). Since that time, though most of the CW programming has featured white leads, it has introduced the popular and critically acclaimed show *Jane the Virgin*, a loose adaptation of the Venezuelan telenovela *Juana la Virgen*, also referred to in this book's chapters on representations of Hispanics and mixed race couples. The show stars a number of Hispanic actors and actresses. The executive director of NAACP's Hollywood bureau has attributed the lack of change in minority representation to the lack of minorities in top executive positions. The thinking is that if the individuals with the power to make the ultimate decisions in programming are not minorities, the chances of minorities being fully represented in programming are slim.

In her analysis of prime-time broadcast network programming from 2000 to 2008, communication professor Nancy Signorielli (2009) paints a bleaker picture. She found that there was actually a downward linear trend in the presence of black characters, while there was an upward trend in the number of white characters. She also found that other minority groups, including Hispanics, rarely appeared. What her findings show is that prime-time programs on broadcast networks have not reflected the growth in the United States' minority populations.

Members directly working for the television and film entertainment industries have also compiled data that point to problems in minority and gender representations. For example, Hollywood producers have an agreement with the Screen Actors Guild (SAG) (2009) that stipulates that they would ensure diversity and non-discrimination, and would realistically portray the "American Scene." In order to measure whether or not producers are upholding this agreement, SAG gathers diversity-related casting information (i.e., performer's gender, age, race/ethnicity, etc.) from big budget, low budget, and independent films, and television episodic and non-episodic television programs. They then provide a summary of which groups are under-cast and underrepresented in television and films based on their collected data. The main points of the most recent survey findings (2009) are as follows:

- Overall, representation of people who were non-white was in supporting and not leading roles.
- Although 56 million Americans report having a disability, virtually no television characters exhibited one.
- For every female role in film and television there are two male roles.
- More than 40 percent of the roles for males went to actors over 40; only 28 percent of the roles for women went to women aged 40 or older.
- An overwhelming majority of acting roles went to white performers (see Table 16.3).

Women and racial/ethnic minorities do not fare much better behind the scenes. The lack of female writers was highlighted in 2009 when, after a scandal involving talk show host David Letterman's revelation that he had had affairs with several of his female staffers, there was much chatter about the lack of women in this field. Entertainment website Jezebel.com reported that the evening television talk shows – including *The Daily Show* (1996 debut), *The Tonight Show* (1962 debut), and *The Late Show with David Letterman* (1993–2015) – only had a sprinkling of female writers, all of whom were white. Even though at least half of these shows' audiences are made up of women, the writers do not mirror this audience (Carmon 2010). According to the Writer's Guild of America, women make up 29 percent of television writing staffs (Mitchell 2016). While women and minorities have made minor advances in share of writing employment, they are still drastically underrepresented. The lack of women writing in television is stark, but there are even fewer women writing for film; only 17 percent of the writers in feature films are women.

Racial/ethnic minorities are also missing from most writers' rooms. Racial/ethnic minorities made up 13 percent of writing staffs in 2015. Moreover, a majority of the African American television writers work for shows with predominantly African American casts. Of course, work is work, but these data raise the question of whether or not talent from diverse backgrounds is considered hirable in a variety of genres and for a variety of people/characters.

A 2016 report, which is based on 2014 data, by the Writers Guild of America, West, shows an income gap between men and women, with male writers making more than women, though the gap is closing. Women, on average, make 89 cents for every dollar earned by men. Median pay for male writers is $133,500 versus $118,293 for female writers. The WGA report also indicates that there was a large gap in salaries between racial/ethnic minorities and white males. Median earnings for minority writers is just $100,649 compared to the $133,500 of white male counterparts.

Table 16.3 Racial/ethnic performers on film and television, 2008.

Caucasian	72.5%
African American	13.3%
Hispanic	3.4%
Asian/Pacific	3.8%
Native American	0.3%

Source: Screen Actors Guild (2009).

In television both men and women made more money in 2014 than they did in 2012, and the increase was a larger percentage for women. In the film industry, the earnings for both men and women decreased. Across all racial lines, TV writer earnings increased except for Asian Americans, who are the highest paid of all the races/ethnic groups. All film writers saw a decrease in their earnings, except those who identify as multiracial (Hunt 2016). (See Tables 16.4 through 16.7.)

Table 16.4 Median earnings for television writers, by gender.

	2012 $	**2014 $**
Men	124,905	127,768
Women	113,350	118,910

Source: Hunt (2016), reprinted with kind permission.

Table 16.5 Median earnings for film writers, by gender.

	2012 $	**2014 $**
Men	80,000	75,000
Women	62,138	50,938

Source: Hunt (2016), reprinted with kind permission.

Table 16.6 Median earnings for television writers, by race.

	2008 $	**2012 $**	**2014 $**
African American	75,300	87,728	99,199
Latino	80,633	90,907	92,400
Asian	105,000	124,860	122,336
Native American	51,826	97,738	n/a
Multiracial	n/a	110,890	117,418
White/Other	99,103	119,176	126,253

Source: Hunt (2016), reprinted with kind permission.

Table 16.7 Median earnings for film writers, by race.

	2008 $	**2012 $**	**2014 $**
African American	49,500	40,636	29,739
Latino	33,209	58,500	42,889
Asian	62,500	126,250	52,415
Native American	n/a	38,637	n/a
Multiracial	n/a	3,700	61,116
White/Other	75,000	76,825	71,358

Source: Hunt (2016), reprinted with kind permission.

Age seems to be an equalizer in the writing business. Writers between the ages of 41 and 60 had 54.5 percent of the writing jobs in 2014. Writers who were 31–40 had 32 percent of the writing jobs. The entertainment industry embraces older writers – 55.1 percent were between the ages of 41 and 60.

In spite of the apparent imbalance in minority representations within the mass media industry workforces, many media companies have made strides to increase the hiring of underrepresented populations.

The Mass Media Industry and Diversity Statements/Initiatives

At the rudimentary level, the law mandates diversity in the media workforce. In order to be in compliance with Equal Employment Opportunity Commission laws, employers are supposed to look beyond race, gender, physical impairment, and other characteristics that may marginalize the employee. Additionally, the federal Office of Personnel Management has rules regarding discrimination on the basis of marital status and, de facto, sexual orientation in their hiring and employment practices. This standard is set by federal law and will often appear on employment websites and job applications. Once hired, employees generally have legal recourse if they find they are victims of harassment or unequal pay, or other matters of systematic prejudice.

Aside from these legal provisions, many media companies make statements about their philosophies regarding diversity and how they will treat employees, content, and their communities to demonstrate their commitment to diverse groups. Whether these proclamations are altruistic and/or done for financial gain, they provide guidelines for the companies' content and employment practices. A sample of these diversity policies and/or statements reveals that some companies make a far-reaching effort to be inclusive of diverse populations. Of some note are the diversity strategies and initiatives of Time Warner, Viacom, and 21st Century Fox (see Box 16.1).

Time Warner is the behemoth corporation that owns several media companies including CNN, *Time* magazine, TNT, TBS, the CW, and Warner Brothers movie studio. This company has taken a fairly aggressive approach to its diversity efforts. It has a leadership staff charged with finding diverse program content and training employees to be open to a more inclusive workplace. A glance at Time Warner's television programming reveals that the company has made some efforts to bring diversity content to its audience. For example, *Tyler Perry's House of Payne* (2006 debut) and *Meet the Browns* (2009–2012), two programs with all African American lead characters, can be found on Time Warner's TBS channels. In 2016, CNN's Anderson Cooper won the Gay and Lesbian Alliance against Defamation (GLAAD) Media Excellence award for best television journalist.

Viacom is one of the world's largest media conglomerates. It is the parent company of Paramount Pictures, DreamWorks Pictures, Marvel Studios, MTV Films as well as other film-related entertainment entities. Viacom's cable networks include BET, Nickelodeon, TV Land, Comedy Central, CMT, VH1, MTV, Spike TV, and Logo TV. Introduced earlier in this book, Logo TV provides programming targeted at the LGBT community, whereas BET presents news and entertainment primarily targeted at African American audiences. As of the writing of this book, talks were under way to merge CBS with Viacom, thus creating a media conglomerate that would have an even stronger business clout and audience reach.

Box 16.1 Diversity/inclusion statements from Time Warner, Viacom, and 21st Century Fox

---

Time Warner

At Time Warner, we believe that in an increasingly multicultural world, we must expand our efforts to reach and understand the diverse people and cultures we serve. A key to our success is hiring and retaining a staff that is as diverse as our audiences. What's more, when we think about diversity, we must go beyond race, ethnicity and gender to include all the things that make us unique, including life experiences, geographic backgrounds, sexual orientation, skills and talents.

Diversity from Top Down

In order to ensure that Time Warner's diversity initiative is a central and integrated priority for senior management on an enterprise-wide and divisional level, diversity is incorporated into every senior executive's goals. As such, corporate senior executives and division CEOs will set strategic direction and establish accountability for diversity across the company.

Diversity in Hiring

At Time Warner, diversity is the essence of our ability to create the richest range of products and services that engage and inspire the broadest audiences around the world. We are committed to preserving a culture of opportunity, inclusion and respect, both as a point of ethical conduct and as a driver of competitive advantage.

Many divisions across Time Warner encourage and support employee networks that foster networking, teambuilding, professional development and contribute to the fulfillment of the competitive edge that Time Warner strives for every day.

Business Resource Groups

The richest range of products and services that engage and inspire the broadest audiences around the world. We are committed to preserving a culture of opportunity, inclusion and respect, both as a point of ethical conduct and as a driver of competitive advantage.

Many divisions across Time Warner encourage and support employee networks that foster networking, teambuilding, professional development and contribute to the fulfillment of the competitive edge that Time Warner strives for every day.

The groups include, but are not limited to, the following:

- **HBO:** Alianza, EMERGE, MOSAIC, HBO Out
- **Time Warner Corporate:** Asian & Pacific Employee Exchange at TW (APEX), Black Employees at Time Warner (BE@TW), Emerging Professionals at Time Warner (EP@TW), OUT at Time Warner, Time Warner Women's Network (TWWN)
- **Turner:** Black Professionals at Turner, Turner Asia, Turner LEADS, Turner NextGen, Turner Parents, Turner Seasoned Professionals, Turner Women Today, TurnerUNO, TurnOUT
- **Warner Bros. Entertainment Group:** Black Employees at Warner Bros. Studios, Emerging Professionals at Warner Bros. Studios (EP), NAPA @ Warner Bros., OUT @ Warner Bros. Studios, UNIFDOS @ Warner Bros. Studios, Women of Warner (WOW)

Content Diversity

As a leading media and entertainment company, we believe that important stories should be told across all of our media platforms to a global audience. In Film and Television and the Internet,

Time Warner provides millions of people with a broad range of products and services that reflect the diverse backgrounds, interests and cultures of our customers. In addition, the company's networks provide multiethnic and foreign language programming from producers throughout the world.

(Time Warner Diversity Statement n.d.)

Viacom

At Viacom, the spirit of inclusion feeds into everything we do, on-screen and off. From the programming and movies we create to employee benefits/programs and Viacommunity outreach initiatives, we believe that opportunity, access, resources and rewards should be available to and for the benefit of all. For us, it's more than an idea, it's part of our business. Being open to all voices and viewpoints behind the screen helps us connect with audiences and retain the best talent, who know that they can bring their full selves to work.

(Viacom Global Inclusion Statement n.d.)

21st Century Fox

Twenty-First Century Fox, Inc. (the "Company") appreciates the importance of valuing and servicing a diverse marketplace. Different backgrounds and characteristics, such as race, ethnicity, gender, disability, culture and sexual orientation, bring innovative viewpoints and merit to the creation of our content and products.

Integrating diversity and inclusion initiatives across the Company is essential to our business strategy and long-term success. Therefore the Company has established resources to focus on:

- expanding and embracing diversity across our Company;
- strengthening our partnerships with diverse national and local community organizations;
- increasing our procurement spend with minority- and women-owned business; and
- entertaining and informing our audiences in a way that fairly reflects and respects the world's diversity.

The diversity and inclusion objectives, and progress toward achieving them, will be assessed periodically in light of the needs of the Company's businesses.

(Twenty-First Century Fox Diversity Statement n.d.)

21st Century Fox, formerly part of News Corp, is one of the world's largest media entertainment and news corporations. Its holdings include Fox Television, FX television, Fox Sports, National Geographic Channel, 21st Century Fox films, Fox Searchlight Pictures, and Fox News Latino. Fox News Latino is targeted at the Latino community living in the United States. Via its online site, it provides news on politics, money, sports, and entertainment.

One of the top media companies, Omnicom, owner of the BBDO and DDB Needham advertising agencies, has taken overt action to bring diversity to the advertising industry, which has frequently been criticized for its absence of racial diversity. In 2006, Omnicom committed $1.25 million over five years to support its Diversity Development Advisory Committee and its minority hiring efforts. This effort is significant, but it raises the question whether this sum will make any difference in combating the longstanding and systemic lack of people of color working in advertising.

Media companies also take on projects to maintain a solid relationship with their diverse publics. Companies offer diversity-related activities as a way to be inclusive to their diverse employees. For example, Google has different outreach groups for its employees including Gaygler (LGBT employees), Greygler (employees aged 40 and older), the Asian American Good Network, and the Google Capability Council (employees with disabilities). Moreover, these companies recognize that they are financially and socially responsible to a wide range of consumers. As such, these companies offer community outreach programs such as Viacom's Black Entertainment Television's programs to improve the health of African Americans and Time Warner's project giving college scholarships to underserved populations.

In 2016, media companies that relied on subscriptions and not advertisers seemed to sweep awards based on sexual identities. For example, GLAAD awarded Netflix's *Orange Is the New Black*'s (2013 debut) Ruby Rose the Stephen F. Kolzak award, which is given to an LGBT media professional who has made a difference in promoting equality and acceptance. Netflix's *Sense8* (2015 debut) won Best Drama Series and Amazon's *Transparent* (2014 debut) won for Best Comedy.

Aside from the large corporations, several mass media associations have also implemented schemes to bolster diversity. The Screen Actors Guild, Writers Guild, Directors Guild, and Producers Guild of America each offer programs to encourage diverse talent. For example, SAG has its own "Diversity Month" celebration in October that kick-starts its year-long initiatives. SAG's past events have included a National Coming Out Day and a town hall meeting discussing issues related to SAG's American Indian members. The Directors Guild of America provides awards for African American, Asian American, Latino, and women student filmmakers. As a final example, the Producers Guild of America hosts a master class for racial/ethnic minorities who are interested in becoming a TV show runner or executive producer.

When the Oscar nominations were announced in 2015 and 2016, the 20 best actors and actresses in lead and supporting categories were all white. Furthermore, in 2016, when there were nominations for films about people of color, Whites received the nod – *Straight out of Compton* (2015) screenwriters Andrea Berloff and Jonathan Herman and *Creed*'s (2015) supporting actor Sylvester Stallone got the coveted nominations. Social media responded with the hashtag "OscarsSoWhite." Shortly after the nominations, prominent African American moviemakers such as Spike Lee, Jada Pinkett, and Will Smith called for a boycott of the awards ceremony, saying that the Academy should revisit its voting rules to create a more diverse celebration.

In answer to the pressure from the industry, on January 18, 2016, Academy President Cheryl Boone Isaacs – the first African American in that role – announced changes to the voting process designed to make the voting membership more inclusive when it comes to gender and race. In part, members of the Academy will have to be employed in the film industry at least once every 10 years in a 30-year period to vote for nominees and winners. This policy is designed to filter out older, less diverse voters over time. Critics of the changes said they were merely an ageist remedy for racism, but the change will bring new voters to the prestigious process.

Thus, as this chapter has shown, although the number of minorities currently working in the news and entertainment media industries suggests ample room for improvement, select media organizations have made concerted efforts to recruit and nurture minority employees. As the presence of minority groups working within these media organizations increases, significant minority representations in media content will more likely result. To provide further perspectives on diversity and the mass media, this chapter ends with a section that provides excerpts from interviews conducted with six media professionals.

Interviews with Mass Media Professionals

Brent Merrill

Mr. Merrill (Figure 16.1) is an author, photographer, filmmaker, and movie producer, who is currently self-employed as a public relations consultant. He is an enrolled member of the Confederate Tribes of Grand Ronde, and he is of Kalapuya and Northern Paiute descent.

How did you get started in your career?

Working on my high school newspaper, then my college newspaper, then the local weekly newspapers in my area and then working for the Tribes on Tribal newspapers and all publications and media relations.

What was your first job in the media industry?

I first worked as a reporter and photographer.

Figure 16.1 Brent Merrill. Reproduced with kind permission of Brent Merrill.

Did you ever receive a scholarship or an internship opportunity designed to help a minority group? Did it make a big difference in your life?

I was the first Grand Ronde Tribal member ever to be honored with the Eula Petite Scholarship. It was the first big scholarship given by our Tribe back then so I was extremely honored and I loved Eula. She was an amazing lady.

Can you share an example of a time when race impacted your job?

When I first came to work for my Tribe I thought it would be a good idea to gather the stories of Elders for Elders' feature for the Tribal newspaper. I tried and tried to get an Elder gentleman to talk to me about his life and each time I went to his house he offered me a cigarette. Each time I turned him down. Each time I got nothing from him. Finally, I learned that (because of my family experiences on the Reservation) if I accepted the smoke, I could get his story. He laughed as I turned green and rolled around in sickness on his front porch, but he told me his life. It was one of the best experiences of my career and it has been the subject of many presentations throughout my career.

Does your current employer have a diversity policy in terms of hiring?

Tribal hiring preference.

It has been said that the press should fulfill the role of "the great public educator." Do you believe it is doing so? In your opinion, are the images we see in the media accurate and representative of the diverse population in this country?

That might be our "big picture" role in society, but it is doubtful in my mind if we are or have ever fulfilled this objective correctly and accurately. We still get it wrong consistently when we cover minority neighborhoods and issues in dominant culture publications. We want to put people into square pegs even when they don't fit. Media wants to categorize everyone – I teach my clients to allow that type of categorization if it is to your advantage. If not, we fight it.

What advice would you give a minority student who was interested in a career in your area?

Be the best you can be regardless of what your ethnic background is. Just try to be the best at what you can do. Have integrity. Learn what journalistic ethics are and then live it. If you can't do it, it's okay, just find another job. It's a burden, but it's a burden that comes with the job. If you are not willing to protect your source, then find another occupation that doesn't have longstanding, traditional ethical responsibilities attached to it.

Rebecca Traister

Ms. Traister (Figure 16.2) is a writer-at-large for *New York Magazine* and *The Cut*. She also serves as a contributing editor for *ELLE*. She has written two books about women and politics, both published by Simon & Schuester: *Big Girls Don't Cry: The Election That Changed Everything for American Women*, published in 2010, and *All the Single Ladies: Unmarried Women and the Rise of an Independent Nation*, published in 2016.

How did you get started in your career?

I worked as an editorial assistant at the now-defunct magazine *Talk*, which was published by Hearst and Miramax. I just got coffee and made copies, but I met a number of young editors who thought I would make a good reporter, and who eventually helped me find work as a fact-checker/reporter at the *New York Observer*, a weekly Manhattan newspaper.

Has your gender ever impacted how you were treated on the job? Can you give me an example?

Figure 16.2 Rebecca Traister. Reproduced with kind permission of Rebecca Traister.

My gender has helped me develop my beat, which is (broadly speaking) feminism, so it's had a very positive impact.

Can you share an example of a time when your gender hindered your ability to perform your job? Were you ever kept from an opportunity because of your race or gender?

Can't think of an instance in which it hindered my ability to perform the job. I certainly have been passed over for particular reporting assignments that were given to men. But I'm often assigned to profile and write about women, which again helped me eventually to home in on and develop a beat.

Can you share an example of a time when your gender helped you perform your job? Were you ever given an opportunity because of your gender?

My whole career was born out of the opportunity to tell stories from a female/feminist perspective, an opportunity that was ironically born of the limited number of women doing just that.

It has been said that the press should fulfill the role of "the great public educator." Do you believe it is doing so? In your opinion, are the images we see in the media accurate and representative of the diverse population in this country?

Media narratives tend to reflect small slivers of the population – slivers that are often white, often privileged, and slightly less often male. In part because (certainly not in every case; I'm speaking in generalizations) the media tends to offer a reflection of itself, and the media remains very white and predominantly male. But that changes. This is anecdotal, but in my view, there are loads more young women reporters today than there were even 10 years ago. Then again, there are many fewer publications. As the print/online media shrinks, so do fresh possibilities for diversifying it.

What advice would you give a minority student who was interested in a career in your area?

In addition to basics like learning to get facts correct and tell stories responsibly, remember and insist – to yourself, to your teachers, and to your future employers – that your perspective is valuable and too infrequently heard.

Kent Takano

Mr. Takano (Figure 16.3) is the owner of Kent Takano Media and the previous Executive Producer/Vice President of Branded Entertainment for HGTV in Knoxville, Tennessee. As a Japanese American working in the South, he has found that his race makes him a sounding board for issues related to race and ethnicity on many occasions.

How did you get started in your career?

I started as an intern at the CBS affiliate in San Francisco. I'd graduated from UC Berkeley a year prior, and before committing to four years of law school wanted to try an acting course. Turns out my acting partner was a producer at KPIX who was looking for an intern. So I re-enrolled in school for one unit and – *voilà*! – "qualified" as an unpaid intern in the eyes of the TV station.

Figure 16.3 Kent Takano. Reproduced with kind permission of Kent Takano.

What was your first job in the media industry?

My first unpaid job was as an intern. My first paying job was part-time as a researcher for *PM/ Evening Magazine*. The national office was located in San Francisco, so I pitched and researched stories. I worked 40 hours but got paid for 20!

Is there an example of how your race ever impacted how you were treated on the job?

With race – and living in the South – it's a larger part of your identity than it was living in the Bay Area. You become a lightning rod for those who are looking for information about working and living in the South, as well as internally, where Asians are not very well represented as creators of content. So I've been asked on numerous occasions as to my opinion on content as it pertains to race. Or, if needed, I will speak up and address issues on-screen that may or may not be accurate or appropriate. One example was when a host "stood up" her chopsticks in a bowl of rice. Seems innocuous, right? Well, in the Japanese culture, this is a sign of death and, obviously, is not acceptable table manners. There was also an issue in an episode of a very famous chef – non-Asian – wearing a silk, Mandarin-style coat while he prepared food for the Chinese New Year. I got a note from a viewer who said this was unacceptable, that he was making a mockery of the Chinese culture. I watched the episode three times and, having noted nothing offensive, responded to this viewer with my opinion. I was extremely deferential and responded with a long note of explanation from the networks' perspective. And, most importantly, since Chinese is not my culture, I asked her to point out specific example(s) of what she deemed offensive. I made a promise that if she and I agreed that there was something that was culturally degrading or offensive, I would have the episode removed. In the end, the woman never responded back. But again, it was an example of being a sounding board, both externally and internally.

It has been said that the press should fulfill the role of "the great public educator." Do you believe it is doing so? In your opinion, are the images we see in the media accurate and representative of the diverse population in this country?

I think the press does have an obligation to be the "great public educator," but with the caveat that it's not wholly responsible for educating, but providing as many sides of an issue being debated or reviewed. What the viewer or reader gleans from this information is not the press's responsibility, as long as the information on both sides is fairly presented. As for accuracy, that's a more difficult question to answer, mainly because we have our own personal biases that may perceive certain issues to be skewed.

Press is a great asset as we, the public, need a "face" that has access to people most do not; it is the default checks-and-balance that our system relies on to keep those in the news, those who run our government, first and foremost, honest. (Readers are voters.) I believe the term "accuracy" often gets a bad name when misguided journalists believe the "truth," no matter how sensational, is also a right for everyone to know. Here, the matter becomes fuzzy, depending on where you stand on the topic.

What advice would you give a minority student who was interested in a career in your area?

(1) Be diligent. Learn how to write a sentence. Learn how to express your thoughts. And as much as we think we're "not different," we certainly are. But use this difference to your advantage

by never using race as a platform. Too many in the majority expect minorities to "fall back" on their race, play the race card. When this is "played" for the benefit of one and not the group, it's the worst thing anyone can do. (2) Also, remember that when someone hires you, they're hiring you for your knowledge, your potential for knowledge, and your ability to make the hiring manager look good. Do not do anything to jeopardize that. Too many times I've seen minority students with chips on their shoulder, believing they're entitled to something, somewhere, somehow. Nothing could be further from the truth. We are all hired for our perspective, but ours is one of many and won't always be heard. (3) Lastly, exit every job you have the same way you came in – confident and humble. It will serve you well in this very "small world" business.

Aminda Marques Gonzalez

Ms. Marques (Figure 16.4) is the Executive Editor and Vice President of the *Miami Herald*. She is of Hispanic descent. She is responsible for the strategic leadership of all *Miami Herald* news operations in print, online, and in a variety of digital media, including mobile apps for smartphones.

How did you get started in your career?

I first became interested in journalism thanks to a middle school teacher. She assigned the class to read *The Diary of Anne Frank*. I was about the same age as Anne Frank and reading her daily chronicles – the average teen boy crush woven into the day-to-day fear of living in hiding from the Nazis – touched me in profound ways. When the teacher returned my graded paper, she told me I should consider a career as a writer. She suggested I join the school newspaper, which I did. And that was my first

Figure 16.4 Aminda Marques Gonzales. Reproduced with kind permission of Aminda Marques Gonzales.

job in journalism. I continued to work on the school newspaper in high school. Growing up in Miami, I became obsessed with the idea of working for the *Miami Herald*. I went to the University of Florida – and it was a big deal for my Cuban parents to let me leave home to attend college. I also did some freelance work for the then *Independent Alligator*, a respected off-campus college newspaper. An older student told me I needed to try to get an internship as soon as possible – and he told me about an internship at the *Lakeland Ledger* in Central Florida. (I can't recall if it was a minority program or not.) I applied and got the internship during the summer between my sophomore and junior year. I believe to this day it made a huge difference in my career. It helped me secure a second internship the following year at the *New York Times* (that program was slated for journalists of color). I later discovered that I had been an alternate for the internship, but when someone else dropped out of the program, I was selected to fill the slot. That summer, I had only applied to two places: the *New York Times* and the *Miami Herald*. The *Miami Herald* called to offer me an internship after I had already accepted the slot at the *New York Times*.

What was your first job in the media industry?

When I graduated from the University of Florida in 1986, I had a job offer from the *Orlando Sentinel* and an internship offer from the *Miami Herald*. I took a gamble and accepted the summer internship rather than the full-time job in Orlando because I wanted to end up at the *Miami Herald*. I worked that summer in the paper's twice-a-week community publications called *Neighbors*, where I covered religion and features. At the end of the summer internship, I was offered a full-time job in *Neighbors*. This was a time of expansion at the *Miami Herald* and, at its peak, the paper had more than 45 reporters working in these hyper-local sections. Even then, the *Miami Herald* hired seasoned reporters for the community section but they did occasionally hire from the intern pool. Given the mission to cover South Florida's diverse neighborhoods, many of the *Neighbors* reporters were "minorities" – black, Hispanic, Asian. In the first office where I was hired (which covered several large majority–minority cities) the majority of the reporters were of color. This group of reporters turned out to be a great talent pool, almost like a journalism farm team. Many of those *Neighbors* hires have gone on to top jobs in the industry. Just off the top of my head, I can think of Manny Garcia, recently named the east region executive editor for the USA Today Network, and Ronnie Ramos, who was just named editor of the *Indianapolis Star*.

Did you ever receive a scholarship or an internship opportunity designed to help a minority group? Did it make a big difference in your life?

I grew up in the city of Hialeah, a working-class city that was (and still is) predominantly Hispanic. My parents were both born in Cuba, but they came to the United States in the mid-1950s (BC – Before Fidel Castro). All four of us siblings were born in New York City, but we moved to Florida when I was just in the first grade. I say all this for context. Fast forward to my senior year in high school, where I was a co-editor of the student newspaper. I was sitting in journalism class and had already been accepted into the University of Florida. Mrs. Bonnie Sipe – the journalism teacher – came by my desk and handed me a scholarship application. I thanked her – I needed all the help I could get to pay for college – then started to read the requirements. Within a few minutes, I was back at her desk, returning the paper. "I can't apply for this," I told her. "Why not," she asked. "Because it's for minorities." She looked at me and said: "You are a minority." That is when I realized I was a minority. (Moving to Gainesville, Florida, certainly cured me of any notions that I wasn't a minority, but that's a different story.) But that application opened a huge door for me. I went and bought a thick book that listed every scholarship available – and I applied for anything that I thought I could qualify for to help me pay for college. (My mother worked in a factory and my father was a carpenter.) Over my four years, I ended up applying for over 30 scholarships of varying amounts and probably received about half of those – mostly small $250 to $500 awards that covered books and some living expenses. I vividly recall receiving a scholarship from Women in Communication and from the National Association of Hispanic Journalists. I graduated from college debt-free thanks to Pell grants and those scholarships.

Clearly, the internship at the *New York Times* – the only one I recall was slated for minorities – was a huge help in my career. At the time, the concept for the internships was for us to "observe and learn through osmosis," but you could hustle and get published, even if you didn't get a byline. (It was their policy at the time that only staffers got bylines, with few exceptions.) One exception was a real estate feature called "If you're thinking of living in ..." and I pitched Elmhurst, where I was staying with my aunt and uncle. The editor accepted and the story was published *and* I got a byline. It also helped connect me to key editors at the *Miami Herald* since one of the editors at the *NYT* knew an editor at the *Miami Herald* and gave me an introduction.

Can you share an example of a time when race impacted your job?

The one instance that stands out for me was a classroom reporting assignment while I was attending the University of Florida. There was a local election and we were told to go to the polls and interview voters. I approached one woman and asked a question. "You ain't from these parts, are you?," was her response. It was a sharp contrast to a year earlier, when I was surrounded by so many people who looked like me that I didn't even think I was different.

Does your current employer have a diversity policy in terms of hiring?

I do not believe we have a corporate diversity policy (beyond being an Equal Employment Opportunity employer). However, the *Miami Herald* has a long record of having one of the most diverse newsrooms in the business if you look at ASNE's annual survey. Much of that goes back to the hiring practices I outlined earlier when the newspaper established its community news operations. Also, South Florida has been at the forefront of this country's seismic demographic changes for 20 years so we are today where the rest of the country will be in another decade or so. For us, having a diverse workforce makes smart business sense. We simply couldn't cover this community if we didn't have reporters, editors, photographers and videographers who reflect the community and understand the different cultures. We have reporters who speak Spanish and Creole, we have Hispanics from many different countries, we have African Americans and Haitians. We emphasize a diverse pool of candidates for every hire, which is more important now than ever as hires are more precious and rare. From a company-wide standpoint, we have four top female leaders of color: myself; the editor of the Spanish-language newspaper, who is Hispanic; the editor of the editorial page, who is African American; and the publisher, a Hispanic female.

How are you working to change the landscape of journalism to better represent minorities?

I believe in extending a hand, the way that so many did for me during my career. As stated above, we actively seek diversity when we are hiring for an opening. We have a strong internship program, where we also seek out diverse candidates. (They often become the candidates for job openings not just at the *Miami Herald* but at our sister publications.) And we have a specific program with our local university, Florida International University, which is majority minority. Those four-to-six students work part-time year round in our newsroom.

What advice would you give a minority student who was interested in a career in your area?

First and foremost, learn to be a great journalist. In this digital age, we need a lot of new skill sets that we didn't even contemplate a decade ago – social media, SEO [search engine optimization], video, data. But none of that matters if the important tenets of great journalism are missing. This is a craft, so get experience as early as possible. Having an internship during my sophomore year in college gave me a tremendous advantage. I had professional clips before I was even in the college of journalism. And be as persistent in seeking out these opportunities. Be flexible and learn everything – from writing and reporting a great story to shooting video. The convergence in media means the distinctions we used to make between print and broadcast are quickly fading.

Traditional news sites are aggressively producing video. TV websites are writing stories. Also, start to create a network that can help guide your career. Make sure the college professors and advisors know you and your professional goals and what you want to do. Go to job fairs, write for college publications or local media. Then mine the professionals at those organizations. Be as relentless in your professional pursuits as you would be chasing a good story. This is still one of the few professions where you get to wake up every morning and make a real difference, from a brief on a hit and run that ends up in an arrest to the investigative project that changes state laws.

Richard Prince

Mr. Prince (Figure 16.5) writes "Richard Prince's Journal-isms," a three-times-a-week column on diversity issues in the news media for the website of the Maynard Institute for Journalism Education. He is also a part-time copy editor at the *Washington Post* and was a founding member of the William Monroe Trotter Group, an association of African American newspaper columnists.

How did you get started in your career?

I majored in journalism at New York University.

What was your first job in the media industry?

In college, I worked part-time as an ad checker at the *New York Times*, then as a reporter on weekends and summers at the *Star-Ledger* in Newark, New Jersey.

Figure 16.5 Richard Prince. Reproduced with kind permission of Richard Prince.

Has your race ever impacted how you were treated on the job? Can you give me an example?

Of course. It influences what I write about and has led to discussions about coverage, story selection, and the like. In 1972, six colleagues and I filed a discrimination complaint against the *Washington Post* with the Equal Employment Opportunity Commission.

Can you share an example of a time when your race helped you perform your job?

Since I write about diversity issues in the news business, my identity as an African American is integral to my work. I am sure that when news organizations have been conscious of the need for diversity, my identity has played a role.

Does your current employer have a diversity policy in terms of hiring? If so, what?

The *Washington Post* has articulated its commitment to diversity in hiring.

It has been said that the press should fulfill the role of "the great public educator." Do you believe it is doing so?

I believe the press is fulfilling that role. However, it is up to the public to be discerning about the media it chooses to consume.

What advice would you give a minority student who was interested in a career in your area?

Go in with your eyes open, do what you love doing, network and learn all you can.

Huma Razvi

Ms. Razvi (Figure 16.6) is an Emmy-award winning producer for the weekend edition of the Today show. She started with NBC after graduating from college and has been there for 10 years. Ms. Razvi is of Pakistani descent. She is part of the first generation of her family to be born and raised in the United States. As of the date of this book's publication, Ms. Razvi is taking a break from broadcast news to focus on her family.

How did you get started in your career? What was your first job in the industry?

After graduating from college, I was working a temp job while I tried to find the right "first job." I had always wanted to work in news and loved my local NBC station. So, I called the newsroom one day and asked if they were hiring. I somehow got to the right person and had an interview two days later. I got the job and spent the next three years

Figure 16.6 Huma Razvi. Reproduced with kind permission of Huma Razvi.

learning the ropes as a production assistant on the weekends. I was responsible for distributing the show's rundown, printing and running scripts, helping the assignment desk, and ordering lunch and dinner for my team!

What do you like best about your job?

I am a firm believer that freedom of the press is one of the most essential elements of a democracy. I love that I'm able to be a part of making democracy work. In addition, the challenge of learning something new every day – whether it's researching a new topic or meeting people who have amazing stories to tell – is rewarding.

How are you working to change the landscape of journalism to better represent minorities?

NBC News is very committed to diversity. We have a Diversity Council as well as affinity groups for various ethnicities and genders. The purpose of these groups is to have an ongoing dialogue about how we can improve our outreach to people from all backgrounds and to provide them with news and information that meets their needs. Currently, I sit on a committee focused on supporting the needs of Asian Americans – those who watch our network and those who work at NBC. Our goal is to make sure that we are telling the stories that are important to this community.

In your opinion, are the images we see in the media accurate and representative of the diverse population in this country?

Unfortunately, the face of the media will never be – in my opinion – an equally balanced picture of the diverse population in this country. And, that's simply because nothing is ever perfect. But, as time passes, I think (read: hope) more will change for the better. There are more women and minorities on television than when I was growing up. And, I hope that by the time I have children old enough to read a textbook like this one, even more will have changed for the better. But, you should also remember that the faces you see on TV are not always a true representation of the media industry and its makeup. There are thousands of people who work behind the scenes – whose faces never get on air, whose names never get a byline – that are helping to shape the stories you see every day. And, they are a more diverse bunch than the faces you see on air.

What advice would you give a minority student who was interested in a career in your area?

I have two important pieces of advice, minority or not. The first sounds trite and the second sounds counterintuitive. But, in my experience, both are true.

First of all, trust your gut. It's a saying you've probably heard more times than you can count. And, well, that's because it's true. You'll get a lot of advice from well-intentioned people. But, in the end, only you know what's best for you.

Second, throw out any career roadmap you have in your head. Having that so-called 5- or 10-year plan can keep you from exploring all the wonderful, unexpected experiences and opportunities you never would have dreamed of for yourself. Have goals, but making a roadmap for yourself that stipulates where you want to be at a certain age or time frame will only haunt you on your journey.

Finally, remember that, as a journalist, part of your responsibility is to make sure that all sides are heard. And, being a minority makes you more in tune with the voices that are left out sometimes – not always a result of malice or bad intentions – but simply because of ignorance. Remember that it's your responsibility not just as a journalist but as a human being to speak up for those whose voices are not being heard.

Reflection Questions and Thoughts to Consider

1. To what extent do you think legislators should become involved in further increasing diversity within the mass media industry? Do you think diversity should be industry driven on a voluntary basis or be legally driven and enforced?
2. If you were a television station manager who wanted to increase minority representation within the station's workforce, what types of strategies do you think you might implement?

3. Studies show that women get fewer acting roles as they age, but films starring Meryl Streep, Cate Blanchett, Helena Bonham Carter, and Judi Dench, actresses whose ages range from late 40s to over 80, are commercially successful. Why do you think Hollywood shies away from scripts that star older women?

4. What is the diversity landscape in your student media organizations? How many women work on editing or run cameras? How many students with visual or hearing impairments pull an air shift at the campus radio station? How many students of color work on your newspaper or magazine?

5. Keith Woods, vice president of diversity in news and operations at NPR, was recently quoted as saying, "The mere presence of people you are trying to represent does not guarantee success. Just because you have an organization with leadership as women, or with its leadership as people of color doesn't ensure that the goal you're trying to reach in content and in voices gets met. That only comes with vigilance and perseverance no matter who's in charge." Do you agree with his premise? Or do you believe that hiring more minority reporters will, if not ensure, than certainly go a long way toward ensuring, that news is presented in a more complete and diverse way?

References

Advertising Age. 2016. "Hispanic Fact Pack 2016." *Advertising Age.* http://adage.com/trend-reports/view.php?whitepaper_id=109&cNum=1997645 (accessed April 18, 2017).

American Society of News Editors (ASNE). 2009. "U.S. Newsroom Employment Declines." American Society of News Editors, March 6. http://asne.org/content.asp?contentid=151 (accessed April 25, 2017).

American Society of News Editors (ASNE). 2016. "ASNE Releases 2016 Diversity Survey Results." American Society of News Editors. http://asne.org/content.asp?contentid=447 (accessed April 18, 2017).

Ayala, Nancy. 2007. "Rethinking Multiculturalism: Beyond 'Cultural Relevancy.'" *Adweek*, September 17. http://www.adweek.com/brand-marketing/rethinking-multiculturalism-beyond-cultural-relevancy-90298 (accessed July 6, 2017).

Byerly, Carolyn M., and Clint C. Wilson II. 2009. "Journalism and Kerner Turns 40: Its Multicultural Problems and Possibilities." *Howard Journal of Communications* 20(3): 209–221.

Carmon, Irin. 2010. "The Only Women in the Late Night Writers' Rooms." *Jezebel.com*, May 14. http://jezebel.com/5539213/the-only-women-in-the-late-night-writers-rooms (accessed April 18, 2017).

Dates, Jannette L. 2007. "Women and Minorities in Commercial and Public Television News, 1994–2004." *Women in Mass Communication*, 3rd ed., edited by Pamela J. Creedon and Janet Cramer, 73–83. Thousand Oaks, CA: Sage.

Elber, Lynn. 2008. "Diversity in Media Stories: Diversity on Television Stalled, Says NAACP." *The Associated Press*, December 20, 2008.

Griffin, Anna. 2014. "Where Are the Women? Why We Need More Female Newsroom Leaders." *Nieman Reports*. http://niemanreports.org/articles/where-are-the-women (accessed April 18, 2017).

Hunt, Darnell M. 2016. "2016 Hollywood Writers Report." *Writer's Guild of America, West.* http://www.wga.org/the-guild/advocacy/diversity/hollywood-writers-report (accessed April 18, 2017).

Mitchell, Gregg. 2016. "WGAW Releases 2016 Hollywood Writers Report." Writers Guild of America West, March 24. http://www.wga.org/news-events/news/press/2016/wgaw-releases-hollywood-writers-report (accessed April 25, 2017).

Nicholson, June O. 2007. "Women in Newspaper Journalism (since the 1990s)." In *Women in Mass Communication*, 3rd ed., edited by Pamela J. Creedon and Janet Cramer, 35–46. Thousand Oaks, CA: Sage.

Papper, Bob. 2015 "Minority Numbers Slide, Women Make Gains." *RTNDA/Hofstra University 2015 Survey*. http://www.rtdna.org/article/research_minority_numbers_slide_women_make_gains (accessed April 18, 2017).

Ratner, Lizzy. 2006. "Vanilla Ceiling: Magazines Still Shades of White." *New York Observer*. http://observer.com/2006/01/vanilla-ceiling-magazines-still-shades-of-white-2 (accessed April 18, 2017).

Screen Actors Guild. 2009. "Latest Casting Data Follows Historical Trends and Continues to Exclude People with Disabilities." http://www.sag.org/press-releases/october-23-2009/latest-casting-data-follows-historical-trends-and-continues-exclude-p (accessed April 18, 2017).

Signorielli, Nancy. 2009. "Minorities Representation in Prime Time: 2000 to 2008." *Communication Research Reports* 26(4): 323–336.

Street, Mikelle. 2016. "Condé Nast Taps Second African American EIC in 100+ Year History." *Observer*, May 19. http://observer.com/2016/05/conde-nast-taps-second-african-american-eic-in-100-year-history (accessed April 18, 2017).

Swanston, Walterene. 1995. "The *Post* and Diversity." *American Journalism Review* 17(9): 16.

Time Warner Diversity Statement. n.d. http://www.timewarner.com/careers/working-with-us/diversity (accessed April 18, 2017).

Twenty-First Century Fox Diversity Statement. n.d. https://www.21cf.com/corporate-governance/diversity-statement (accessed April 18, 2017).

Viacom Global Inclusion Statement. n.d. http://www.viacommunityreport.com/report/inclusion (accessed April 18, 2017).

Wilson, Julie. 2016. "Elaine Welteroth Named New Editor-in-Chief of *Teen Vogue*, and We all Rejoice." *Essence*, May 19. http://www.essence.com/2016/05/19/elaine-welteroth-teen-vogue-editor-in-chief (accessed April 18, 2017).

17

Conclusion

Now that you have read through this entire book and have probably reached the end of the semester, the authors have a challenge for you. Consider what you know now that you did not know before. For example, are you more aware of how history plays a role in the way the media treat people today? Maybe you now better understand how and why television programs and films have relied on stereotypic racism, sexism, and homophobia as a comedic story device? Perhaps you have come up with some ways to improve the representations of social groups once you enter into the workforce.

The authors would like to use these concluding pages to help you connect the dots that hopefully have already started to surface for you. This chapter draws together the chapters that have preceded it by showing the underlying common threads that exist in the ways that the minority social groups discussed in the chapters have been represented in the mass media. It summarizes the extent of progress that has been made in furthering equitable representations of social groups and the factors that have helped in such progress, and discusses the challenges that still exist.

Common Threads in Mass Media Representations

Scholars have long argued that social groups do not naturally exist, but rather are products of social processes that are intertwined with power relations in societies.

When examining the images that have been associated with minority social groups, it becomes quite apparent that their primary common feature is that minority groups are portrayed in such ways as to suggest that they are below, or not as important as, the dominant groups in society. A hierarchy appears to exist in mass media representations, in which white, able-bodied, heterosexual males are placed at the top.

Conflicting arguments can be made as to which groups follow the top position of the mass-mediated social group hierarchy. Some argue that black, able-bodied males now are seated at the second-top position. Feminists argue that women are inevitably always left at the bottom of the hierarchy. No clear-cut argument comes to the fore as being the strongest. What can be stated without much contention, however, is that, in most situations, those who do not fit the profile of a white, able-bodied cis-gendered male are portrayed as lacking any real power, existing merely to serve or sustain those in the dominant societal position.

At any point in your reading or class discussions, did you or one of your classmates ask: "If women don't want to be portrayed as property, they should just stop posing for those pictures?" Or "If Arab

Diversity in US Mass Media, Second Edition. Catherine A. Luther, Carolyn Ringer Lepre, and Naeemah Clark.
© 2018 John Wiley & Sons Inc. Published 2018 by John Wiley & Sons Inc.

men do not want to be seen as being terrorists, then they shouldn't audition for those parts?" Or "We're a country born out of the Christian faith. Why can't minority religions just adapt to what the norm is in this country?" While these are valid questions, the answers all lie in the power structure of media industries. If a Hispanic actor living in New York wants to find work, he may have to take a role as a murderer on *Law and Order: SVU.* That may not be his preference, but those are the roles made available by those who control the media industries. As scholars such as Edward Said have observed, political and economic objectives often underlie the creation of negative and disparaging images of certain social groups (Said 1979). The images provide justification for one group to wield power over another. When Great Britain sought to expand its power in parts of Asia and the Middle East, the inhabitants of those nations were portrayed in popular writings as being uncivilized and unfit to govern on their own. They were associated with all that went against Christianity and were depicted as debased. Such portrayals were also present when the European Americans encroached on the lands of American Indians. Native peoples were either depicted as immoral, ruthless, and not to be trusted, or as gentle creatures of nature incapable of leading the way toward social progress. No amount of agency or power was conferred upon the American Indians.

History has also shown that when a social group without power shows signs of rising up and rebelling against unjust social and political conditions, those in the dominant group, out of a need to squash or curtail the rising power of a particular group, will often fortify its portrayals of that group as the "Other" or as belonging to the out-group, rather than the in-group. The degree of rhetoric that characterizes the group as being a serious threat to the status quo is heightened. For example, it was in the nineteenth century when anti-slavery activism was gaining momentum that the number of pro-slavery publications increased. Literary characterizations of Blacks became even more nefarious (Fredrickson 2001). A binary was created, with Blacks equated with savagery and Whites with civilization. Arguments were made that Blacks were essentially happy under the control and direction of Whites because it helped them to become civilized.

As discussed in the previous chapters, throughout history the mass media, in various forms, have tended to support the power of the dominant group by presenting to the general public highly negative, emotion-evoking images of minority groups. Mass media have also taken the other extreme route of utterly ignoring the existence of certain minority groups. This was the case with gay individuals in the 1960s and 1970s. They were either portrayed as having a mental illness or they were disregarded and not recognized in the mass media. It was also the case with people with disabilities. They were either treated as broken individuals in need of repair or as nonexistent. In essence, these social groups were annihilated by the mass media.

To test this assertion, browse through the magazine aisles at your favorite mega-bookstore or take a glimpse at the prime-time television schedule. It appears as though much of the content is geared toward women. But, dig a bit deeper. What messages are these magazines, television commercials, and sitcoms delivering? Further, consider if these messages are directed at poor, lesbian, Hispanic, Asian American, or Muslim women. In most cases, they are not. Most magazines, television programs, films, and advertising is geared toward white women or women of European descent. Advertisers consider the middle- or upper-class cis-gendered, heterosexual white woman as "all" women and, therefore, symbolically annihilate women of color, those who are multiracial, people of lower economic status, and other minorities.

In addition to negative images of minority groups serving the purpose of maintaining the power structure of society, the images are said to also serve the purpose of comforting, at a psychological level, those who belong to the dominant group. For example, it is argued that by having the mass media depict people with disabilities as "objects of pity" who are in need of medical help, it eases the anxiety of those who do not have a disability by stressing the message that they are okay and the "others" are not (Haller 1998). In other words, as with cases involving other minority groups, the mass media serve to remind the dominant group that all is well with them and that it is in the natural order of things to have them take leading positions in society and enjoy the privileges that come with those positions. Studies have shown that such messages impact not only on the psyche of the dominant group, but also on those within the minority group who are being portrayed.

Psychological Impact of Mass Media Representations

A number of studies show how distorted and negative images of social groups can psychologically impact on those belonging to the group. The impact of mass media images of unrealistically thin bodies on women is one area that has received much research attention. Several studies have found that exposure to media presentations of the thin ideal has led to women craving this ideal, as well as experiencing less body satisfaction and a tendency toward eating-disorder behavior (Botta 1999; Harrison 2001). The negative impact of media presentations of thin ideal female figures has even been shown among females coming from cultures that are normally accepting of larger female figures. For example, one study found that although Hispanics have traditionally been accepting of large female sizes, the ideal body for both the younger and older generation of Hispanic women living in the United States was thin and toned (Pompper and Koenig 2004). Although the older women were more likely to acknowledge that this media-driven ideal was unrealistic, they still shared with their younger counterparts a desire for what they considered as the ideal body.

Signs of the negative impact of ideal images on males have also come to light in recent years. For example, in one of the earliest experimental studies to examine the impact of mass media disseminated images of ideal male bodies on young men, a group of researchers found that for men who were exposed to advertisements featuring muscular men, significant differences were found in how these men perceived their own bodies and their ideal body image. These men expressed feelings of inadequacy regarding their own bodies due to their exposure to the muscular male model image (Leit, Gray, and Pope 2002).

The mass media are able to influence not only people's perceptions of their external appearances, but who they are, internally, as individuals as well. Professor of communication Richard Allen, for example, found that mainstream mass media are able to have deleterious effects on the self-consciousness and self-esteem of African Americans (Allen 2001). In particular, he found that those African Americans who had high levels of exposure to mainstream television programs were more likely to report low levels of self-esteem. They were also less likely to have a sense of group autonomy and a belief that African Americans should create their own organizations and institutions based on their cultural values and interests.

Minority Media as Counteracting Agents

Partly to counteract negative mass media portrayals and their damaging impact, members of various social groups have established their own minority media. Their mission has been to not only help the groups they represent fight against unjust treatment and attain social as well as political parity with the dominant groups in society, but also to bring about a sense of empowerment and cultural awareness for their groups. Similarly, periodicals based in religion and/or faith provide readers with edifying and informative content, while reaffirming their spiritual beliefs.

One of the early ethnic/racial minority media to be established in the United States was the black press. Two African Americans, Samuel Cornish and John B. Russwurm, founded the first, entitled *Freedom's Journal*, in New York City in 1827. With its front-page banner reading, "We will plead our own cause. Too long have others spoken for us," the publication was clearly created to give a voice to African Americans and provide a platform to oppose acts of injustice committed against them. It served to raise the racial consciousness of African Americans as well as to promote social change (Allen, Thornton, and Watkins 1993). Since then, countless other publications together with television programming produced by and targeted at African Americans have entered into the media market. National magazines *Essence* and *Ebony* are thought of as cultural milestones in the exploration of African American experiences. The cable network Black Entertainment Television (BET), although owned by media giant Viacom, has provided opportunities for African American producers, directors, and actors to present their own unique take on television programming.

Media products created by other minority social groups have also found a way to serve their targeted social group. Examples of those representing Hispanics living in the United States are magazines such as *Latina Style*, *Latin Business Today*, *ALMA*, and *Vanidades*. Representing South Asian Americans are magazines such as *Little India* and *Rivaaj*. Examples of news media serving East Asians are the Japanese American newspapers *Nichi Bei Weekly* and *Rafu Shimpo*, and the Korean American newspaper *Korea Daily*. *Able* newspaper is marketed as "The Newspaper *Positively* For, By, & About the Disabled" (see www.ablenews.com). Some of these have found crossover success in terms of attracting a broad audience, while others remain a niche product.

Although mainstream newspapers have suffered a severe decline in circulation numbers, the ethnic press is still seeing growth. New America Media, a non-profit organization headquartered in California that advocates for ethnic news organizations, characterizes ethnic media as "the fastest growing sector of American journalism" (www.newamericamedia.org/about). The growth can be attributed not only to the increase in the immigrant population, but also to its perceived value. Observers have noted the high quality of the stories that are often produced in the ethnic press. Mainstream news media have taken notice and have even patterned their coverage after some of the ethnic press coverage. For example, following New York's Pakistani press coverage of the closure of immigrant-owned businesses on Coney Island, the *New York Times* picked up on the story and ran a similar article (Conner 2004).

Collaborations between ethnic press and mainstream press have increased in recent years. The nature of collaboration can vary. It can range from reporters simply working together to more formal partnerships. For example, the southern California Vietnamese newspaper *Nguoi Vet Daily News* has a weekly English-language publication targeted at young Vietnamese Americans called Nguoi Vet 2; that publication shares content with the *Orange County Register*. All three publications are said to have benefited in improved coverage as well as in marketing.

It should be pointed out, however, that alliances between the ethnic and mainstream press do make certain mainstream journalists nervous. They assert that the central purpose of ethnic media is to serve as advocates of their particular ethnic group and, therefore, they question the form of coverage that is being offered by the ethnic media. Those who conduct research in the area of ethnic media also pose the possibility that the ethnic press might be co-opted and lose their importance in terms of providing alternative or unique perspectives and cultural flavors. A fear also exists that the political and social significance of the ethnic press might also be weakened. For example, in discussing the minority press, political science professor Stephanie Greco Larson writes: "The black press is less vast and vital than in the past. As the Spanish-language press has grown, it has become less political and independent. Some Native American newspapers are instruments of local elites. Asian-language papers are prevalent, but the degree to which they promote a political agenda varies" (Larson 2005: 275).

Nevertheless, in spite of the expressed concern regarding the direction of the ethnic press, the increase in numbers and the better recognition of minority media, in general, can be thought of as positive, especially given the finding that minority media can provide psychological benefits for minority group members. Studies have shown that minority media can have a positive impact on individuals in terms of self-perception and social identity. For example, communication professor Richard Allen's work has shown that the images from black media can act as a buffer against the negative images that are presented in the mainstream media (Allen 2001). They are able to increase among African Americans an awareness of the positive attributes of their racial/ethnic group and thereby raise self-worth. By having their self-worth raised, they are, in turn, able to reject the negative stereotypes regarding their group that are being presented to them via the mainstream mass media.

The importance of minority media continuing to have a substantive political and social voice cannot be overstated. After all, it is the minority media and the minority groups that support them that have, throughout history, pushed to make significant societal changes. These groups have also been responsible for pushing the mainstream media to make changes and address minority issues. Thanks to the efforts of these groups, as presented in Chapter 16, mainstream media industries have attempted to increase minority representation not only in the mass media workforce, but in content as well. Without minority media and the minority organizations that act as watchdogs of the mainstream media, the momentum that has been gained in taking positive steps forward might very well be entirely lost.

Time has shown that the move toward diversity in mainstream mass media has tended to be incremental, shifting forward, then backward, and then forward again. It appears that as progress is made, a step backward often ensues. For example, when television programs show signs of giving voice to an underrepresented group, if controversy or decreased ratings are outcomes, the signs suddenly disappear and only resurface years later. This was the case with representations of lesbians in broadcast television. With the well-known "coming out" of Ellen Morgan (played by Ellen DeGeneres) on the *Ellen* show in 1997, the LGBT community believed that a significant step had been taken in furthering representation of an alternative lifestyle on television. As the ratings for *Ellen* dropped, however, the show was canceled, and it would be some years before another broadcast television show took a chance in featuring lesbian relationships that were not based on stereotypes. When considering that DeGeneres now has a daytime talk show where her wife Portia de Rossi frequently appears and talks about their relationship to audiences across America, it is easy to imagine the degree of representational progress that has been made over the past couple of decades.

Given the tendency for mainstream media to be inconsistent in addressing diversity issues, it is critical that minority groups, through their own organizations as well as their own publications and programming, continue to voice concern on egalitarian issues and drive the mainstream media toward diversity initiatives. New media will certainly help in this realm. With the costs of creating and maintaining websites decreasing, more minority groups will have further opportunities to have their voices heard by a broader audience by creating their own media websites. Considering that extremist groups have found homes on the Internet to voice their vitriolic opinions about various social groups in society, it is important for minority groups to counter the hateful messages directed at them with their own positive messages. Further, the possibility exists that with an increased minority group presence on the Internet, mainstream media, especially the news media – that are increasingly reliant on information provided on the Internet in order to feed their vast media outlets and public appetite – might also begin to increase their reliance on minority group perspectives.

The need for minority groups to have their voices heard more widely is also accentuated by calls from critics that mainstream media, even with their recent efforts, need to go even further. Media scholars Theodore Glasser, Isabel Awad, and John Kim (2009), for example, remain skeptical about the diversity-related steps that have been made by mainstream news organizations. In reference to what newsrooms have done to tackle diversity issues, the authors assert that by focusing on "improving coverage of minority communities by in large part hiring, training, and retaining minorities," those working in news have neglected to address the core basic problems that lie at the heart of social inequality and the lack of representation (2009: 59). That is, they do not deal with the problems that emanate from the social, political, and economic power relations that exist.

Such a critique is also expressed by scholars who take the position that the diversity initiatives that have been taken up by media companies, as well as other businesses and governmental entities, actually hide the underlying problems still existing which act to sustain social inequities (Littlefield 2008).

Thus, although progress has been made in increasing reflections of diversity within the mass media, further efforts are needed to not only increase such reflections, but also to analyze and tackle the core political and social problems that are at the root of unequal treatments of social groups. Many of those who have fought for increased varied voices in the mass media have tied the importance of diversity to the notion of democracy (Glasser, Awad, and Kim 2009). They argue that in order to achieve a true democracy in which, borrowing the phrase from sociologist and philosopher Jürgen Habermas, "participatory parity" exists, all social groups should have their interests, perspectives, and cultures reflected in the mass media. Some of those perspectives might be unpalatable to certain individuals; however, the importance lies in having them expressed and disseminated. It is the hope of the authors of this book that through a better understanding of how minority social groups have been represented or even neglected in the mass media, further steps can be made to make changes not only within the media but also in the underlying notions and mechanisms that have sustained social inequity.

Reflection Questions and Thoughts to Consider

1. Given the notion that inequities in media representations are rooted in power relation imbalances between social groups, do you think that it is even possible to have fair and equal social group representations in the mass media?
2. Do you think that as the traditional forms of media, such as broadcast television and radio, become things of the past, and we all become reliant on information and entertainment conveyed through other digital platforms, our thinking of what diversity means will change?
3. Twenty years from now, which social groups do you think will be considered minority groups and will media representations of these groups still matter?
4. After having read this book, what future challenges do you think lie ahead in terms of diversity in the media?

References

Allen, Richard L. 2001. *The Concept of Self: A Study of Black Identity and Self-esteem*. Detroit, MI: Wayne State University Press.

Allen, Richard L., M. C. Thornton, and S. Watkins. 1993. "An African American Racial Belief System and Social Structural Relationships: A Test of Variances." *National Journal of Sociology* 6: 156–186.

Botta, Renee A. 1999. "Television Images and Adolescent Girls' Body Image Disturbance." *Journal of Communication* 49: 22–41.

Conner, Dierdre. 2004. "Media Outlets Serving Ethnic Groups Continue to Grow, Break News." *Quill Magazine*, October/November: 16–17.

Fredrickson, George. 2001. *The Black Image in the White Mind: The Debate on Afro-American Character and Destiny, 1817–1914*. New York, NY: Harper & Row.

Glasser, Theodore L., Isabel Awad, and John W. Kim. 2009. "The Claims of Multiculturalism and Journalism's Promise of Diversity." *Journal of Communication* 59: 57–78.

Haller, Beth. 1998. "Crawling Toward Civil Rights: News Media Coverage of Disability Activism." In *Cultural Diversity and the U.S. Media*, edited by Yahya R. Kamalipour and Theresa Carilli, 89–98. Albany, NY: State University of New York Press.

Harrison, Kristen. 2001. "Our Selves, Our Bodies: Thin Ideal Media, Self Discrepancies, and Eating Disorder Symptomatology in Adolescents." *Journal of Social and Clinical Psychology* 20: 289–323.

Larson, Stephanie Greco. 2005. *Media and Minorities: The Politics of Race in News and Entertainment*. Lanham, MD: Rowman & Littlefield.

Leit, Richard S., James J. Gray, and Harrison G. Pope, Jr. 2002. "The Media's Representation of the Ideal Male Body: A Cause for Muscle Dysmorphia?" *International Journal of Eating Disorders* 31: 334–338.

Littlefield, Marci Bounds. 2008. "The Media as a System of Racialization: Exploring Images of African American Women and the New Racism." *American Behavioral Scientist* 51: 657–685.

Pompper, Donnalyn, and Jessica Koenig. 2004. "Cross-cultural-generational Perceptions of Ideal Body Image: Hispanic Women and Magazine Standards." *Journalism and Mass Communication Quarterly* 81: 89–107.

Said, Edward W. 1979. *Orientalism*. New York, NY: Vintage Books.

Digging Deeper

Over the next few pages, we will review some of the overarching themes that have emerged and intersected over the course of this textbook, and offer suggestions for areas to explore for research papers and term projects.

One Representation Replaces Another

Though times may change, and certain representations and media tropes may fall out of use, either because of complaints from minority advocacy groups or because of evolving cultural norms, it is disheartening to observe that oftentimes just as one marginalizing image dies off, another one appears to take its place.

Take, for example, the representation of the "magical Negro" discussed in Chapter 4, which emerged in films during the early 1990s to join the images of the mammy, the bad buck, and the tap-dancing butler. In this representation, the African American character has mystical powers, relies on folk wisdom instead of intelligence, and often sacrifices him- or herself and his or her interests to save the white main character. This magical minority representation is not reserved solely for African Americans, however. Mystical or mysterious representations have also been associated with American Indians and Asian Americans, as we have discussed in Chapters 3 and 7, respectively.

Suggestions for Further Exploration

- Conduct a content analysis of one week of prime-time television programming. How many social group stereotypes do you see in the programs?
- Consider the representations discussed in this textbook and the mass media images of social groups you have recently encountered. What other examples can you find that you believe simply have evolved from old representations?

Sexuality and Power

For many social groups, images are presented that either desexualize or hypersexualize the group as a means of weakening or removing their power. For instance, Asian American men, people with disabilities, and certain African American women, especially those cast in "mammy" roles, are desexualized. Young African American women ("jezebels"), Asian American women, gays, and

Diversity in US Mass Media, Second Edition. Catherine A. Luther, Carolyn Ringer Lepre, and Naeemah Clark.
© 2018 John Wiley & Sons Inc. Published 2018 by John Wiley & Sons Inc.

Arab American men have all been depicted as overly sexual and provocative. By defining certain individuals with a heightened central characteristic, those individuals become one-dimensional and thus subordinate. In a similar vein, taking away a central human characteristic effectively neuters a group of people; the individuals become weaker, because they are less whole. As discussed in the chapters of this book, the need to represent minorities as less powerful largely stems from a dominant social group's fear of the minority members. Scholars argue that, in the United States, it is middle-class to upper-middle-class white men who see minorities as potential threats to their power.

Suggestions for Further Exploration

- Some issues of sexuality are more complicated than others. For instance, in some cases, African American men are hypersexualized, such as when they are the main characters in blaxploitation-type films, and in other cases they are desexualized, such as when they are portrayed in "buddy" roles. Explore these contradictions and what they might mean.
- Some films over the past 20 years or so have featured men of color dressed as women. Try to find and review some of those films. Consider how those men are being represented. Also consider what the filmmakers might be saying about the position of women in this country.

Rules and Regulations Impact Representations

Several places in this text discuss laws or self-regulatory practices that have influenced the representations of groups in the media. For example, Chapter 4 references Jim Crow laws, which, in effect, legalized the segregation of African Americans in the South, increasing the marginalization of the group. Chapter 7 details Executive Order 9066, which mandated the removal of those with Japanese ancestry from society and their subsequent placement into internment camps. Again, this legalized physical separation only contributed to the "Othering" of the group and encouraged hurtful representations in the media.

The media industries also mandated harmful representations. For example, as Chapters 7, 8, 9, and 11 illustrate, the Hays Code encouraged casting decisions and film storylines that were limiting to Asian Americans, women, gays, and other groups. Although the industry set these standards as a way to enforce morality in the movies, the impact led to racial and ethnic minorities being distant and untouchable, women in films being powerless, and gays being invisible.

Suggestions for Further Exploration

- Based on what you have read, what rules or laws have been put in place to correct some of the stereotyping or hurtful representations in the media?
- Should the various media industries set standards for themselves about how the groups discussed in this text are represented in film, television, or in other media platforms?

The Symbolic Annihilation of a Social Group

In her often-cited, classic work, media scholar Gaye Tuchman (1978) suggests that the mass media symbolically annihilate minority groups by ignoring them, either through a lack of press coverage or by invisibility in entertainment roles, trivialization, and condemnation. Examples of this annihilation run throughout this text, especially as it relates to people with disabilities, the old, American

Indians, and the poor. Chapter 13 discusses how images of the disabled are virtually nonexistent in entertainment media and advertising, and how those few that did exist were negative and stigmatizing. Chapter 14 discusses similar findings regarding the poor. In Chapter 11, however, research shows that while representations of LGBT people were few and far between prior to 1970, in the decades since then, changes have been occurring and this group has seen wider screen and press time.

Another form of annihilation that has long existed is the casting of white actors in roles that were initially designed for people of color. In more recent times, the same phenomenon can be seen with transgender characters being played by cis-gendered actors or people with physical disabilities being played by able-bodied actors. Directors and producers explain these casting choices in pure economic terms. They argue that they need to have big names in these roles in order to draw in audiences.

Suggestions for Further Exploration

- Compare the box office profits for films that have people of color in casts and the profits for films that have replaced characters of color with white actors. Is there something to be said about the argument that Hollywood needs white actors to draw audiences or do you think the argument has no foundation? Do the same for cis-gendered actors being cast as trans characters and able-bodied actors appearing in roles that call for individuals with physical disabilities.
- Try to think of other social groups that have seen advancement away from symbolic annihilation. Consider the underlying reasons for the advancement.
- Consider whether you believe invisibility is worse, better, or just as problematic as a negative stereotype.

Minorities as the "Other"

Several chapters, while discussing the historical representations of the chapter's social group, outlined the extensive history of the "Other." The "Other" often translates into someone who is violent, evil, and not totally human. Over the course of the last century, there have been many examples of various ethnic groups being depicted as the "Other," and many continue today. For instance, in Chapter 3, you read about American Indians being shown as savages, uncivilized, and as one with nature. In Chapters 6 and 7, examples of images of Arab Americans and Asian Americans as villainous and not to be trusted were discussed. In Chapter 10, you read about how women were carved into body parts and made into objects in advertisements, and how African American women, in particular, were regularly depicted as animalistic. These are just a few of the examples across this textbook that illustrate this theme; others also exist in the discussions on people with disabilities, the LGBT community, and Hispanics.

Suggestions for Further Exploration

- Gather several recent issues of popular fashion magazines, such as *Vogue, Harper's Bazaar,* or *Glamour,* and several recent issues of men's fashion magazines, such as *GQ, Details,* or *Esquire.* Review each advertisement in these magazines. Compare and contrast how women and any people of color are presented. Are they made into objects? Do they appear as the "Other"?
- Consider how history has contributed to the systematic "Othering" of the poor, women, or ethnic minorities.

Reliance of the News on White "Expert" Sources

In Chapters 4 and 5, a discussion was presented suggesting there is an overreliance on using white "expert" sources in stories about African Americans and Hispanics, and it was argued that these depictions reinforce the idea that African Americans and Hispanics, and minority groups in general, are voiceless and weak. This, in turn, diminishes the power that African Americans and Hispanics and other minority groups hold in society. Chapter 10 also offers evidence that men are used as expert sources more than women.

Suggestions for Further Exploration

- Conduct a content analysis of the op-eds that appear in your local newspaper. Whose stories are being told? These stories often provide context for complex current events, so the stories that are published are important to the readers.
- Conduct an analysis of the experts who appear on television news programs during Internal Revenue Service tax season in April. How many of these experts are women and/or people of color?
- Conduct an analysis of pundits appearing during prime time on the cable news networks (CNN, Fox News, MSNBC, etc.). Who are the talking heads offering their take on politics?

"False" Framing and Misrepresentation

Another common theme across this book concerns how the press continues to frame minority groups in ways that further marginalize or stereotype them, and how the press, through its choices of what to cover with regard to minority groups, misrepresents certain group characteristics and issues. This "false" framing and misrepresentation creates the environment for audiences to have attitudes toward and beliefs about social groups that are both incorrect and damaging. For instance, in Chapter 14, we looked at how framing the poor as a smaller group than it is might lead the audience to not believe that poverty is a problem in America and to vote against social programs to help those in need. In Chapter 4, an example of the misrepresentation of African Americans as violent criminals was shown, which could lead to increased levels of fear and prejudice toward African Americans.

Suggestions for Further Exploration

- Compare and contrast how Martin Luther King, Jr.'s march on Washington, DC, on August 28, 1963, was covered by the *New York Times*, the *Chicago Defender*, and the *Atlanta Journal*. Are there differences? Why or why not?
- Select one issue (same-sex marriage in American states, for example) and consider how media ownership might shift the way that the story is covered on cable television news.

Online = New Opportunities

Just as minority media offer new opportunities for minority voices to be heard, so does the Internet. Each chapter in this book offers examples of how social groups are utilizing online sources to make their voices heard, to join together, and to promote positive images about themselves. The Internet offers a chance for advocacy as well as interconnection and relationship building within a social group.

Suggestions for Further Exploration

- Examine several podcasts that focus on minority issues or discuss minority representations. Determine who created and maintains the podcasts. Compare and contrast the content of each site based on which are created by and for minority group members and which are not.
- Choose a particular social group and try to examine how they are being portrayed in Vine videos. Now think about how those portrayals compare to the images you see in traditional entertainment media.

Changes, Contradictions, and an Ever-Moving Continuum

Perhaps the most important connection that could be drawn at the end of this book is to note that there are no solid answers and no definite conclusions. Every day, cultural norms change, and media representations move along with them. While some might move in one direction, others might slide backward. It is a messy, ever-moving continuum, and there is no one standard to be set for what is the "right thing to do," though certainly there are libraries full of books arguing for one thing over another. There are plenty of contradictions as well – for instance, there is no one single message about what constitutes the ideal feminine or masculine identity.

This book has worked to present you with background, examples, and things to consider, not hard and fast rules, and certainly not written-in-cement predictions for the future. As you think about the chapters you have read, and the social groups that have been discussed, consider the connections you see. What intersections do you see in how the various groups have been represented in media? Consider the changes you see having been made over time. And then make up your mind about where you see things going and how you interpret the media world around you.

Suggestions for Further Exploration

- Explore the notion that inequities in media representations are rooted in power relation imbalances between social groups and examine your thoughts on whether it is even possible to have fair and equal social group representations in mass media.
- After having read this book, what future challenges do you think lie ahead in terms of diversity in the media? Examine some of these challenges, or other changes, contradictions, and connections.

Reference

Tuchman, Gaye. 1978. "Introduction: The Symbolic Annihilation of Women by the Mass Media." In *Hearth and Home: Images of Women in the Mass Media*, edited by Gaye Tuchman, Arlene Kaplan Daniels, and James Benét, 3–38. New York, NY: Oxford University Press.

Glossary of Key Terms/Concepts

A

ageism: A term referring to the discrimination, subordination, or stereotyping of a particular individual or group based on age, and the distorted representation of age.

agenda setting: The news media influences what the audience thinks about, depending on whether a topic is covered in the news. The agenda also is set by where the story is placed on the page or in a newscast.

American Indian Movement (AIM): A Native American activist group that was formed in 1968 by members of an American Indian community in Minnesota. Its mission was, and continues to be, addressing important issues involving Native Americans, including treaty issues, poverty, and community rights. The group broke into two factions in 1993 because of organizational grievances.

Americans with Disabilities Act (ADA): Signed into effect by President George H.W. Bush. Title I of ADA "prohibits private employers, state and local governments, employment agencies, and labor unions from discriminating against qualified individuals with disabilities in job applications procedures, hiring, firing, advancement, compensation, job training, and other terms, conditions, and privileges of employment."

Arab Americans: Americans with ancestry from countries or regions, mainly in North Africa and the Middle East, in which Arabic is the official language.

Arab American Anti-Discrimination Committee (ADC): A nonprofit civil rights organization that strives to empower Arab Americans and bring about understanding of the Arab world.

Asian Americans: Label used to represent those Americans whose ethnic origins can be traced to Pacific, Southeast, South, and East Asian areas of the world.

B

bisexual: Term used to describe a person who is physically and sexually attracted to both sexes.

blaxploitation films: Movies, generally made in the 1970s, starring African American actors as brash and empowered men and women. Black characters were exploited as pimps and criminals; white characters were oppressors.

Brown v. Board of Education: (347 U.S. 483 [1954]). The US Supreme Court determined that laws that allowed for separate public schools for black and white children were not equal. Separate schools denied black children an equal opportunity to the same education that their white counterparts had.

Diversity in US Mass Media, Second Edition. Catherine A. Luther, Carolyn Ringer Lepre, and Naeemah Clark.
© 2018 John Wiley & Sons Inc. Published 2018 by John Wiley & Sons Inc.

C

caste system: A term that refers to a rigid system of social structure, used by some researchers to define how teenagers, and teenage girls in particular, are often represented in film and entertainment television.

Chicano: Someone of Mexican heritage or descent.

Chinese Exclusion Act of 1882: US Act that prohibited Chinese laborers from entering the United States for 10 years beginning in 1882. The Act was continuously renewed until its repeal in 1943.

cisgender: Term used to indicate a gender identity that is in concert with the sex and gender that was ascribed at birth. Also referred to as cis.

citizen journalism: The practice of members of a particular group or audience playing an active role in collecting, analyzing, and disseminating news and information.

civic journalism: The practice of news media outlets reaching out to the public and listening to the audience, making the news outlet a forum for discussion of community issues. The tenets of civic journalism include favoring issues, events, and problems important to ordinary people, and situating professional journalists as active participants in community life, rather than as detached spectators.

civil rights movement: A reform effort in the United States (roughly between 1955 and 1968) where citizens asked that racial discrimination be outlawed. During this time Congress passed several laws (the Civil Rights Act of 1964 and the Voting Rights Act of 1965) designed to give African Americans equal rights.

class: A group sharing the same social and economic status. Often class hierarchy is related to one's occupation, familial wealth, and the level of education achieved.

cognitive schemas: Interrelated conceptual units of information that assist individuals to coherently organize information.

cognitive script theory: A theoretical proposition stating that individuals form cognitive templates or scripts of behaviors that help them to then quickly assess and react to future behaviors.

commodification: Mass production for the purposes of sale.

commodification of culture: The packaging of elements of diverse groups to produce a media story. For the purposes of our book, media producers create (package) some part of an ethnic/racial culture such as an ethnic music genre and sell it to mass media audiences. The packaging can lead to stereotypes and limited representations.

conglomerate: A company with a grouping of business. In the media industry, a conglomerate may produce and/or distribute content for audiences.

constructionist approach to representation: Asserts language does not reproduce things or convey the intentions of the language producer; rather, it is a part of the systems of knowledge production through which meanings are created.

content analysis: Studying the communication of an organization (newspaper, television program, film, etc.) to determine meaning.

cultivation theory: This theory asserts that the more television a person watches, the more likely they are to adopt attitudes and beliefs based on television's stereotypical images.

cultural capital: The notion that social power is achieved through the attainment of intangible social properties such as education. It also refers to the proposition that there is high culture for those with power and taste (the upper class) and low culture for those who have none (the middle and lower class).

D

Dawes Act: Established in 1887, the act was designed to sanction the breakup of tribal lands into parcels to allow individual Indians to farm or ranch their own land. It had the damaging effect of allowing speculators to grab lands that had belonged to the Indian tribes, and often left many American Indians landless and in poverty. The Act remained in effect until 1934.

digital divide: The space between those who have computers and access to the Internet and those who have not. Often this divide means people with money have access to more information (and opportunity) than those without money.

diversity: State of being composed of different characteristics or traits.

"dragon lady": A phrase used to describe an Asian female character who exudes sexuality but is cruel and deadly at the same time.

E

ebonics: A term coined for "Black English," which is a mixture of slang, African, and Afro-Caribbean vernacular. The term was particularly controversial in the 1990s when some school boards considered allowing the dialect to be taught in the classroom along with or in preference to standard American English.

Equal Employment Opportunity (EEO) rule, 1969: The Federal Communications Commission's rule that required broadcast stations to document their efforts at recruiting ethnic minorities. In 1971, this rule was broadened to include women as well.

ethnicity: A more fluid concept than race. Ethnicity encompasses an individual's heredity, national origin, and culture.

euthanasia/physician-assisted suicide: The act of ending the life of someone who has a terminal illness or an incurable condition. In the United States, physician-assisted suicide is legal in Oregon, Washington, Montana, and to a limited extent, in Texas (as of the printing of this book).

"evil savage": A derogatory label used to represent an American Indian as a subhuman and vicious figure that was opposed to civilization.

Executive Order 9066: A US governmental order that was issued on February 19, 1942, authorizing the removal of approximately 110,000 individuals of Japanese ancestry from their homes into hastily erected US internment camps.

F

The Feminine Mystique: A groundbreaking book written in 1963 by Betty Friedan that is considered to have ignited the women's movement of the 1960s. It was called one of the most influential books of the twentieth century by the *New York Times*.

feminist theory: Interpretations under this theory vary depending on perspective (i.e., radical feminist, liberal feminist, etc.). What all perspectives share is an acknowledgment that female points of view and input are needed in understanding the political and social world.

first-wave feminism: Refers to the first concerted movement working toward reforming women's social and legal rights in the early nineteenth century. Key concerns of first-wave feminists were education, employment, and the right to vote.

framing: A process in which a perceived reality is organized in such a way that certain aspects of the reality are stressed, while others are de-emphasized, leading to a particular definition or understanding the social world.

G

gay: Term used to describe men and women attracted to the same sex; preferred over "homosexual" except in clinical contexts or references to sexual activity.

gender: A social construction that is distinct from biological sex.

GenXer: A term used to represent the generation of people born in the 1960s and 1970s.

glossy ceiling: Phrase making reference to the lack of ethnic minorities working for large, mainstream magazines.

Great Depression: A period of economic decline in the United States that lasted from 1929 to 1939.

H

hate crime: A crime that is committed by an individual against another individual due to the group (based on ethnicity, gender, sexual orientation, religion) to which the victim belongs.

Hays Code: A self-regulatory list of rules that the Motion Picture Producers and Distributors of America, Inc. implemented. This list of "dos" and "don'ts" set standards for morality on the silver screen between 1930 and 1968.

hegemony: The dominance of political and social elites over those with less power. The dominance is not through force or coercion, but rather through use of culture or public consent.

high culture: The attitudes, values, goals, and practices of the upper-class part of society that enjoys what is considered to be literary and artistic sophistication.

Hispanic: Those individuals who have origins in Mexico, Puerto Rico, Central America, and South America.

hypersexuality: An overemphasis on attractiveness and sexuality by way of clothing and body proportions.

I

Immigration Act of 1924: US act that broadened the Chinese Exclusion Act of 1882 by placing restrictions on other Asian immigrants. The act placed national origin immigration quotas and remained in effect until 1965.

intentional approach to representation: Assumes meanings that exist are conscious creations of the authors, and that pictures or words are conveying what the source of those words or pictures intended to convey.

J

Jazz Age: The period between 1920 and the Great Depression that saw free thought in music and the arts.

Jim Crow laws: State and local laws in place between 1876 and1965 in the United States that provided for separate facilities including hotels, restaurants, drinking fountains, and restrooms for Blacks and Whites. The separate facilities were maintained differently, and, as a result, were unequal.

K

Kerner Report: A 1968 report issued by the National Advisory Commission on Civil Disorders, which heavily criticized television stations and newspapers for failing to adequately employ and represent African Americans.

L

lesbian: Commonly used term for women who are sexually attracted to other women.

LGBT: Lesbian, Gay, Bisexual, and Transgender; often referred to when referencing a community of people defined by their sexual orientation. Also abbreviated LGBT.

licensed withdrawal: A pattern, often seen in advertising images, in which women more often than men are pictured as removed psychologically from the social situation at large, leaving them disoriented in it, and presumably, therefore, dependent on the protectiveness and good will of others.

liminality: Scientifically, the term refers to existing between two different states. In reference to diversity, the term means changing or evolving social status.

low culture: The attitudes, values, goals, and practices of the part of society that enjoys more popular expressions of art and literature. People who enjoy low culture are considered to be less educated and not as financially well off as those who enjoy high culture.

M

male gaze: Phrase that emerged from feminist and film study research. It implies that the image of a woman is created from the perspective of an implied male observer.

materialism: A set of attitudes that regard possessions as symbols of success, where possessions occupy a central part of life. Includes holding the belief that more possessions lead to more happiness.

Millennials: A term used to represent the generation of people born between 1980 and the early 2000s.

miscegenation: A mixing of races through cohabitation, marriage, or sexual intercourse. Comes from the Latin words *miscere* ("to mix") and *genus* ("a kind or category of things that share common characteristics").

model minority: An individual of Asian descent who is law-abiding, bright, and deferential to authority figures.

mulatto: Label ascribed to an individual of mixed black and white ancestry. Now considered a derogatory term, it should only be used within an historical context.

N

National Association for the Advancement of Colored People (NAACP): US civil rights organization. Its mission is to ensure the political, educational, social, and economic equality of rights of all persons and to eliminate racial hatred and racial discrimination.

Native Americans: Label used to represent those Americans who have at least one quarter of tribal blood. A large percentage of American Indians now reject the usage of this label, calling it a generic term created by the US government.

news framing: The process of filtering and transmitting information through an angle or "frame" in order to favor a particular perspective.

niche: Content that is designed to have a specific appeal. For example, the television channel ESPN appeals to a sports niche.

"noble savage": A derogatory label used to signify an American Indian as a child-like, innocent creature who was in touch with nature and did not pose a threat.

O

Oriental: Formerly used to identify people from Asian countries. Was dropped from usage when the term became associated with the notion of Western domination over the East.

Orientalism: Traditionally used to describe academic studies of "the Orient," now more commonly referred to as Asia. Today, it is understood to mean Western ideas regarding Near Eastern people and cultures that emphasize difference and exoticism.

the "Other": The social group that is considered to be a part of the out-group, rather than the in-group. The group that is considered to be a serious threat to the status quo.

P

panethnic: Encompassing many groups, each having its own common culture, language, and/or religion.

parasocial interactions/relationship: Phenomenon where audience members create friendships with the figures they see in the media. Also related to the perceived interactions between the audience member and the media figure.

participatory parity in media: The state in which all social groups have their interests, perspectives, and cultures represented in the media.

passing: Term used to signify individuals who assume a white identity in order to have access to the privileges offered to Whites. In the days of slavery, it referred to light-skinned individuals of mixed race who adopted a white identity to escape slavery.

post-feminism: See *third-wave feminism*.

priming: The process by which activated mental constructs can influence how individuals evaluate other concepts and ideas.

Q

queer theory: A theory of social action that rejects human categorizations set up by societal power structures. It promotes social justice-related activism by challenging heteronormative narratives including those presented in mass media.

R

race: A classification of individual genetics originally based on geographic origin.

reflective approach to representation: Assumes language can stand in for or replicate the likeness of what exists in reality.

reggaeton: Dance music with Caribbean roots. This music has a mix of hip-hop and rap elements.

representation: The forms of language (e.g., words, images, musical notes, etc.) that are used to convey ideas that are generated in society for purposes of communication and the production of meaning.

S

"scotch tape" Asian characters: A phrase used to describe characters played by non-Asian actors in early film who used tape to pull back their eyes and make them appear as slits.

second-wave feminism: Refers to the increase in feminist activity in the late 1960s and 1970s. This movement was primarily concerned with de facto women's rights, including those related to reproduction, family, sexuality, and the workplace.

selective exposure theory: Phenomenon that holds that audience members prefer arguments in line with their preexisting beliefs.

"the Seven Sisters": A group of the oldest, most prominent women's magazines, launched in the late 1800s and early 1900s: *Better Homes and Gardens, Family Circle, Good Housekeeping, Ladies' Home Journal, Redbook, Women's Day,* and the now-defunct *McCall's.*

social cognitive theory: Posited by Albert Bandura, this theory suggests that positive reinforcements delivered to media characters can increase the likelihood of learning or adopting praised behavior.

social comparison theory: A theoretical proposition that individuals have a natural drive to compare themselves with others for self-evaluation purposes and to understand the social standards that exist.

social identity: Self-concept that is based on group membership and the emotional attachments associated with that membership.

social learning theory: This theory suggests that viewers, especially children, will model the behaviors of television characters after observing them over time, just as they would by observing parents or other children.

socialization: Processes through which individuals, beginning at an early age and continuing throughout their lives, learn about societal norms, values, and beliefs.

socioeconomic class: Stratification based on social background and income level of individuals.

stereotype: Beliefs about characteristics or attributes of a social group.

"supercrip": A derogatory term referring to individuals with disabilities portrayed in the mass media as having heroic and extraordinary abilities.

T

telenovela: Latin American melodramatic television series. Often aired daily like a US soap opera.

third-wave feminism/post-feminism: Refers to the feminist activity of the 1990s and the 2000s, and is marked by social activism, though in a less directed way. Third-wave feminism encourages personal choices, empowerment, inclusivity, and individuality.

transgender: People who have acquired the physical characteristics of the opposite sex or present themselves in a way that does not correspond with their sex at birth.

Y

"yellow peril": A phrase that is said to have originated in the 1800s with the increase of Chinese laborers in the United States. It refers to the fear that the Chinese were taking jobs from white laborers. Yellow-toned skin color was tied to the idea of terror in this phrase.

Index

Page numbers in *italics* refer to figures and tables; those in **bold** indicate boxes.

Diversity in US Mass Media, Second Edition. Catherine A. Luther, Carolyn Ringer Lepre, and Naeemah Clark.
© 2018 John Wiley & Sons Inc. Published 2018 by John Wiley & Sons Inc.